PUBLIC ADMINISTRATION

PUBLIC ADMINISTRATION

HERBERT A. SIMON

Carnegie Institute of Technology

DONALD W. SMITHBURG

Illinois Institute of Technology

VICTOR A. THOMPSON

Illinois Institute of Technology

ALFRED A. KNOPF: *NEW YORK*

1964

JF
1351
.S5

THIS IS A BORZOI BOOK,
PUBLISHED BY ALFRED A. KNOPF, INC.

Published 1950
Reprinted six times
Eighth printing 1964

Foreword

THIS book represents an approach to the subject of public administration that evolved first in the practice of administration and then in the classrooms of the authors and some of their friends. Our teaching, following upon some years of participation in governmental organizations, has made us acutely aware of two major instructional problems. The first problem is to make sure that what we teach about public administration accurately reflects what goes on in the real world of government—that it makes sense when applied to the actual experiences of administrators. The second problem is to convey these experiences to the student in such a way as to give him concrete pictures of how people behave in governmental organizations, to enable him to visualize situations he has experienced only in a very limited way, if at all, and to prevent him from forming elaborate abstract verbalizations that he cannot translate into concrete patterns of behavior.

The reader can judge for himself how far we have solved these problems. We should like to indicate, however, the principal guides we followed in attempting to give the book realism and intelligibility.

1. *Emphasis.* There appear to be three major areas of interest in public administration today. First, there is the question of how the major governmental structures—Federal, state, and local— should be organized or reorganized. Interest in this question is at a high level as a result of the reports of the Hoover Commission, and several state reorganization studies currently under way. Second, there is a growing awareness that there is a "human aspect" to administration, that administration is concerned with the behaviors of human beings. A considerable body of current research in administration is concerned with the psychology of administra-

v

tive behavior. Third, there is a renewed interest in reexamining the traditional theory of the relationship between politics and administration, and in reevaluating the role of the administrator in the formation of policy.

A textbook in public administration must deal with all three sets of issues. To acquaint the reader with the important issues of reorganization, it must treat the major problems of top-level organization. To avoid sterile formalism and dogmatism, it must be grounded thoroughly on the psychology of human relations in organizations. To secure a true relevance to practical problems, it must analyse administration in its broader political and governmental setting. The authors of this book believe that no one of these sets of questions can be treated apart from the others. In particular, we believe that a clear understanding of the problems of top-level organization and of the relation of administration to politics can be reached only through an analysis of the basic psychological processes involved in administration. Hence we have tried to obtain a synthesis of all three problems through a realistic, behavioral description of the processes of administration.

In most colleges, courses in public administration are given to large groups of students with diverse backgrounds and with a multiplicity of educational objectives. Some will take the course as part of their preparation for intelligent citizenship; others as a stepping-stone toward careers in the public service. Of the latter, some hope to become specialists in administration; others will be accountants, engineers, economists, or health officers who wish to supplement a subject-matter specialization with some knowledge of the techniques of administration. Some students will have had previous courses in American government, others will not; some will be undergraduates, others graduates. Most will have had little or no work experience; but some will bring to the course rich experience obtained as employees or administrators in government agencies or private businesses.

In facing the problem of communication with readers, we have attempted to keep always in the forefront that an administrative organization is a group of people—of flesh-and-blood human beings—who behave in certain ways, partly because of the ideas, prejudices, personalities, and abilities they bring to the organization, and partly because of the influence upon them of the other members of the administrative group and the society about it.

There is great danger, particularly for the reader who has not had much practical experience, that he will learn the lessons of public administration at a purely verbal level. It is probably important that a college graduate entering the public service have in his vocabulary such terms as "line and staff," "span of control," "independent regulatory agency." It may be fatal to him if he has acquired this vocabulary without being able to recognize or deal with the phenomena to which it refers when he finds these phenomena in an actual organization. And he will certainly feel cheated if he has been taught to discuss sagely the problems of the Presidency but has not been given the practical insights that will enable him to understand a particular small organizational unit from the worm's-eye view of his first job. The principal safeguard against this danger is to make sure that all abstractions are tied down to observable realities—that they refer to the trials and tribulations of real human beings in real organizations.

For this reason, the text places at least as much emphasis upon the problems of organization units of moderate sizes as upon the grand issues of executive organization. The reader who has acquired an insight into the workings of a section of a government agency—with all its relations with the larger organization and the political scene—may at the same time have gained some understanding of the problems of the presidency or the governorship. The events he is asked to visualize are on a scale and of a kind that is not entirely beyond the limits of his experience, even if that experience has been slight. Once he has grasped these simpler situations, he may be at least partly prepared for the vastly more difficult ones that occur in large-scale organization. To proceed the other way round appears an almost hopeless instructional task.

2. *Arrangement.* For the reasons just stated, we begin our analysis in terms of individual human beings and small groups, and try to show how the complexities of behavior in organizations can be unravelled and interpreted through the application of a few basic, almost common-sense, notions of psychology and sociology. We do this on the basis of a rather strong conviction that this will represent a progression for most of our readers from what they know to what they do not know. It gives the reader a chance to transfer to administration what he already knows about people and about society, instead of treating this field as some-

thing new, different, and unrelated to the other aspects of life. Hence, while the arrangement of materials may appear novel to some instructors who are accustomed to approach the subject from the other end, we are convinced that the arrangement will appear entirely natural to most readers.

We take definitions seriously. We urge the reader to do likewise. In proceeding from the concrete to the abstract, we attempt to explain each new word in the technical vocabulary of administration in terms of the simpler behavioral concepts that have preceded it. We have tried to use technical terms clearly and precisely in order to avoid the cloudiness that surrounds discussions of administration when terms like "managerial staff," "functional organization," "coordination," and the like are tossed about with abandon.

The reader who is impatient to judge the utility of our arrangement of the material may wish to examine the chapters on "Large-Scale Organization" where we apply our concepts to reorganization problems, including the problems faced by the Hoover Commission; or the chapters on "The Struggle for Existence" and "Responsibility," which are chiefly concerned with the relations between politics and administration.

3. *Evidence.* We encourage in the reader a critical attitude toward evidence. In stating generalizations about administration, we have tried to present the evidence on which these generalizations are based, where such evidence exists. Where evidence is inadequate, we have sometimes tried to indicate what empirical studies are needed to test our propositions. We hope the reader will apply the same standards of rigour to our unproved generalizations that we have applied to the generalizations of others. We hope that some of our readers may be inspired to join in the great task of substituting fact for fancy in the theory of administration —of replacing ambiguity and proverb-like wisdom with valid propositions that meet the tests of reason and experience. No doubt we face the risk, as administrative theory progresses, that much we have said in this book will be shown to be nonsense. We take this risk gladly.

We have tried to illustrate, wherever possible, the generalizations that we make. Most of our illustrations are drawn from actual experience, many (particularly those concerned with top-level organization) from events the reader may already have encountered in the newspapers or in history books. In using such examples from life, our purpose is to *illustrate*, not to *describe*. Nowhere have we attempted a systematic description of the formal structures of Federal, state, or local organizations. Descriptive material, telling the reader in detail how particular processes are handled in particular organizations (or how the regulations say they are handled), will generally be out of date and forgotten by the time the reader needs it. Hence, while we have tried to expose the reader to a wealth of illustrative material, the basic framework is analytic rather than descriptive. We feel that there is no point in trying to incorporate in the book the whole content of the U. S. Government Manual or the compiled statutes of the forty-eight states.

4. *Training in Administration.* We are under no illusion that an administrator can be trained in a college. Beyond a very definite point, the development of his skills must take place through their actual practice. All that academic training can give him—but of course it is a very vital "all"—is a kit of fundamental tools that he will later learn to apply to practical problems. Among these tools, a realistic knowledge of how administration actually *is* carried on, will be at least as important as a knowledge of how it *ought* to be carried on. Excessive preoccupation with "ideal" or "desirable" administrative arrangements may be seriously misleading (since final truths are still a long way off in this field) and may leave the student unprepared for the realities of administration as he later finds them. In training students to advise the President, universities have not always trained them to discharge the first modest responsibilities that are placed upon them in government employment. The disillusioning shock that students of public administration have so often experienced in the past should warn us against this danger.

Here too, the remedy would seem to lie in a more realistic analysis of how people behave in organizations, why they behave in these ways, and how their behaviors are to be taken into account in prescribing for the ills of organization. Administrative actualities must be given the same emphasis in the course on administration that political actualities have gradually achieved in the course on American government and political parties.

We believe that a study of administration constructed on this framework will be as useful to the student who wishes citizenship training as to the student who wishes preparation for an administrative career. We believe that this, or a similar, approach must guide the teacher if he is to reach effectively the student who has had little administrative experience, and if he is to relate theory meaningfully to practice for the student who has had such experience.

* * *

In writing this book we have incurred numerous and heavy debts—to our administrative and academic colleagues and to our students. Most of what we have learned through the informal communication channels of our profession must remain unacknowledged, except as our footnotes indicate a few of the sources of our ideas. We are particularly indebted to Messrs. Pendleton Herring, Harold Stein, and William R. Divine for providing us with and directing us to valuable case materials that we have drawn upon for illustration. We owe special acknowledgement to Professor V. O. Key, Jr. of Yale University, for his valuable contributions to the manuscript; to Messrs. Eugene Jacobson, Daniel Katz, Nathan Maccoby, and Ben Willerman, of the Survey Research Center, University of Michigan, for their careful criticism of some of the psychological portions of the text; and to Miss Ruth Bouril for her thorough searches of the literature and for her comments on early drafts. The Macmillan Company has kindly permitted us to draw upon some passages from a work of one of the authors— *Administrative Behavior.*

The law of conspiracy, wiser in this respect than the traditional theory of administration, accepts the proposition that three men may be responsible for one and the same act. If anything in this book is deserving of criticism, all three of us will have to share the blame. The writing of the book has been for the authors a most enjoyable and instructive experience in collaboration. We will be satisfied if our readers get from reading these pages a small part of the instruction we received in planning and writing them.

H. A. S.
D. W. S.
V. A. T.

CONTENTS

�

Contents

PUBLIC ADMINISTRATION

CHAPTER ONE

🔰

What Is Public Administration?

WHEN two men cooperate to roll a stone that neither could have moved alone, the rudiments of administration have appeared. This simple act has the two basic characteristics of what has come to be called administration. There is a *purpose*—moving the stone—and there is *cooperative action*—several persons using combined strength to accomplish something that could not have been done without such a combination. In its broadest sense, *administration* can be defined as the activities of groups cooperating to accomplish common goals.

The scope of this book will of course be much narrower than the scope of administration defined in this very broad sense. The following pages of this chapter are designed to give the reader a view of the subject matter that we propose to treat and of our general approach to it. After exploring further the nature of administration, we shall delimit the specific field of public administration and point out some of the similarities and differences between public and business administration.

Next, we will survey briefly the growth of governmental organizations and the resulting demand for expert and efficient governmental service. We will see how this led, in turn, to programs of research and training in public administration.

The final section of the chapter will set forth some fundamental distinctions between the "scientific" and the "practical" (i.e., "advice-giving") approaches to administrative theory. It will explain why this book emphasizes the underlying sociological and psychological phenomena involved in administrative behavior rather than specific rules and "know-how" for manipulating human beings in organizational situations.

The Nature of Administration

We have defined administration as cooperative group behavior. The term administration is also used in a narrower sense to refer to those patterns of behavior that are common to many kinds of co-operating groups and that do not depend upon either the specific goals toward which they are cooperating or the specific technological methods used to reach these goals. For example, the two men rolling the stone could have used various techniques in accomplishing their purpose. They might have merely pulled and shoved the stone in some manner. Or they could have used a pole or a steel bar as a lever. They might have fastened a rope to it, with a pulley attached to the nearest tree. They might have broken the stone with sledge hammers and then carried away the fragments. The methods of moving the stone are legion.

However, administration in the more restricted sense is not basically concerned with the technological methods selected. It is concerned with such questions as *how* the method was chosen, how the two men moving the stone were selected and induced to co-operate in carrying out such a task, how the task was divided between them, how each one learned what his particular job was in the total pattern, how he learned to perform it, how his efforts are coordinated with the efforts of the other.

With respect to selecting the method for moving the stone and communicating it to the two men, for example, the coordination of the two stone-movers could have been achieved in many ways. There might have been a simple, perhaps even unspoken, common recognition that the stone had to be moved and a recognition of the type of activity necessary to move it. Or the problem might have been talked over and a common agreement reached as to the best method. There might have been an employer-employee relationship between the men, so that one of them decided on the technique and then ordered the other to assist in a given way. These alternative methods might be considered in organizing almost any other kind of cooperative task—fighting a fire, paving streets, processing claims for unemployment compensation, or sorting letters in the post office. Hence, they are a part of administration in the narrower sense. It is this narrower area of administration—the patterns of behavior that are common to human cooperation in organizations —that will form the subject matter of this book.

THE NATURE OF FORMAL ORGANIZATION

Any activity involving the conscious cooperation of two or more persons can be called organized activity. However, in modern society cooperative activity is carried on within a much more formal structure than the one just described. Participants have tasks assigned to them; the relationships between participants are ordered in such ways as to achieve the final product with a minimum expenditure of human effort and material resources. Thus, by *formal organization* we mean a planned system of cooperative effort in which each participant has a recognized role to play and duties or tasks to perform. These duties are assigned in order to achieve the organization purpose rather than to satisfy individual preferences, although the two often coincide.

Although the illustration of the two men and the stone expresses the basic characteristics of administration, the complexity of modern life requires organized activity much more involved and specialized. To build and market an automobile, for example, calls for a complex system of interrelationships. Specialists of a bewildering variety must bring their competences to bear on the problem at exactly the right time and the right place. Raw materials must be bought, processed, and transported to the place of assembly. The factory must be planned and built. Thousands of men with exactly the right tools and skills must be on hand at an appropriate time. Thousands of independent parts must be put together in a certain sequence. After the automobile is completed it must be transported and sold—a task requiring the aid of still another group of persons. In all of this activity, every step is essential to the completion of the next step and any failure to cooperate at any one point may disrupt the whole pattern and make the accomplishment of the goal impossible. If the steel makers fail to provide the steel; if the wheel maker fails to produce the wheels; if the dealers fail to sell the cars; the factory will close. The key to the whole process is effective cooperation among the persons engaged in the operation.

Since the problems are complex, the work has to be carefully planned. Estimates must be made as to what materials and persons will be needed at a given place and at a given time. The participants must be induced to cooperate. And because resources are limited, the amount of materials and the amount of human energy used to accomplish the task must be held to a minimum. The employment of ten clerks to accomplish a task that one clerk could do is inefficient—it brings more energy to bear on a task than is necessary for its accomplishment.

THE UNIVERSALITY OF ADMINISTRATION

Since administration is concerned with all patterns of cooperative behavior, it is obvious that any person engaged in an activity in cooperation with other persons is engaged in administration. Further, since everyone has cooperated with others throughout his life, he has some basic familiarity with administration and some of its problems. The boys' club, the fraternity, the church, the political party, the school, and even the family require administration to achieve their goals.

Much of this administration is unconscious—that is, not deliberately or formally planned—but it is administration nevertheless. The father is often considered the head of the household, but he is not consciously selected as such by a formal vote. Unless he is completely henpecked, he certainly performs administrative functions, making decisions for the family and assigning tasks to its members.

Most persons, while they are engaged in administration every day of their lives, seldom think formally about the process. That is, they seldom deliberately set out to consider the ways in which the cooperative activities of groups are actually arranged; how the cooperation could be made more effective or satisfying; what the requirements are for the continuance of the cooperative activity. In most of the simpler organizational situations in life—the family, for example—there are traditional and accepted ways of behaving that are gradually acquired during childhood and that are seldom the objects of conscious attention or planning. Like Molière's hero who had talked prose all his life without knowing it, most persons administer all their lives without knowing it.

The governmental organizations whose administration is the

subject of this book are more complex than these everyday administrative situations we are all familiar with. The difficulties of securing effective cooperative action in performing large and intricate tasks become so great that they force themselves upon the attention. Traditional, customary ways of behaving no longer suffice, and cooperation becomes conscious and requires planning. The "rules of the road" that govern family life and the relations among family members are informal, carried around in the heads of parents and children. The rules of the road that govern the relations among the employees of a government agency may fill ten volumes of a looseleaf "Administrative Manual."

If large-scale organizations are to accomplish their purposes; if the extremely complex interrelationships of an industrial era are not to break down, organizational life—its anatomy and its pathology—needs to be understood. Those who participate in and operate the formal organizations through which so much of our society's activity is channeled must know what makes cooperation effective and what hampers it. Either through experience or through formal education, or both, they must study administration. Our concern is with the formal study of *public* administration.

Public Administration

For purposes of study, administration can be divided into certain problem areas. The problem area to be studied in this book is that of *public administration*. By public administration is meant, in common usage, the activities of the executive branches of national, state, and local governments; independent boards and commissions set up by Congress and state legislatures; government corporations; and certain other agencies of a specialized character. Specifically excluded are judicial and legislative agencies within the government and non-governmental administration.

The selection of the problem area is an arbitrary one, made partly because of a traditional academic breakdown of specialties; partly because of the necessity of limiting our attention to an area that can be mastered within a relatively limited period of time; and partly because there are certain problems and practices in government agencies that differ from those in other organizations.

EXCLUSION OF LEGISLATIVE AND JUDICIAL ADMINISTRATION

Legislative and judicial agencies are excluded from books on public administration, but not because they do not have administrative problems. They do. Handling a bill in Congress often requires administration of a very delicate character; the proper presentation and consideration of a case in court requires administration of a high order. But because legislative and judicial bodies have problems peculiar to their structures, and because those problems require extensive treatment, legislative and judicial administration are not included in this book.

Legislatures and courts are, however, a part of the environment within which public administration must be carried on. The activities, attitudes, and methods of these agencies will often powerfully influence the process of administration in the organizations with which we are concerned. And so, while the operations of legislatures and courts will not be examined here directly or systematically, their effect upon public administration will have to be considered as the discussion progresses.

GOVERNMENTAL AND NON-GOVERNMENTAL ADMINISTRATION

It has been customary in this country to make a sharp distinction between governmental and non-governmental administration. In the popular imagination, governmental administration is "bureaucratic"; private administration is "business-like"; governmental administration is political; private administration is non-political; governmental administration is characterized by "red-tape"; private administration is not. Actually, the distinction is much too sharp to fit the facts. As we shall see in the course of this book, large-scale public and private organizations have many more similarities than they have differences. It is possible, therefore, in examining the activities of public administration to use the results of research carried on in private business. In actual administration there is often a greater difference between small and large organizations than there is between public and private ones. For example, the differences in organization and in administrative problems be-

tween a hospital with 1000 beds and one with 50 beds will be far
greater than the differences that result from the fact that one hospital is privately owned and the other publicly owned.[1]

Similarities Between Public and Private Administration. The
similarities between the problems of administration in public and
private organizations can be readily observed when a private
organization is taken over by the government. Not long ago the
elevated railways and the surface lines in Chicago were transferred
to public ownership. To the observer, the difference is imper-
ceptible. The same tracks are there; the same cars are used; the
same fare is charged (or was, until inflation caused an increase);
the same time schedule is followed; the same employees do the
same tasks and work for the same immediate bosses. Only in the
financial organization of the company and in the replacement of a
few top-level persons is there a change. The change in the financial
organization changed the identity of the persons to whom interest
on bonds is paid. It also allowed the company to raise capital for
the installation of new equipment. The influence of the changes in
top personnel is not yet observable. Both changes, however, could
have been accomplished without a change in ownership. If the city
of Chicago had sufficiently desired that the lines be left in the
hands of private owners, provision could have been made for a
subsidy to make new equipment possible. The private owners
might have made the identical changes in personnel. Owned by
LaSalle Street or City Hall, the transit system's major administrative problems remain the same.

Many of the same skills are required in public and private administration. A statistician might transfer from a large insurance
company to the Bureau of Labor Statistics in Washington and
find his tasks almost identical. He possesses skills that can be used
by a great many organizations, public or private. Similarly, a doctor performing an appendectomy will use the same technique
whether he is employed in an Army hospital or in private practice.
General Dwight Eisenhower left the Army to become President of
Columbia University. Two more different organizations would be
hard to imagine. Yet it is likely that the administrative problems
of the two organizations are sufficiently similar so that he had little
difficulty in making an adjustment to this new position.

[1] Cf., M. T. MacEachern, *Hospital Organization and Management* (2nd ed.,
Chicago: Physicians' Record Co., 1946).

Differences Between Public and Private Administration. While the similarities between governmental and non-governmental organizations are greater than is generally supposed, some differences nevertheless exist. Most often these are differences in degree rather than in kind.

For example, both governmental and non-governmental organizations are usually based on law. Activities of a government agency are usually authorized by statute or executive order based on statutory or constitutional authority. All corporations and a good many other non-governmental organizations operate under a legal charter. The officers of both types of organizations are legally required to carry out their activities within the law. However, the duties and responsibilities of the public administrator will usually be described by law in much greater detail than those of his private counterpart, and there will usually be greater possibilities for holding him accountable in the courts for the discharge of these duties in a lawful manner. For example, a corporation can ordinarily authorize its officers and employees to make purchases for it under any procedure the board of directors sees fit to approve. A public purchase, however, must usually satisfy numerous legal requirements with respect to advertising for bids, letting the contract to the lowest responsible bidder, authorizing the expenditure, and so forth. A contract to purchase equipment for a government agency may be invalidated by the courts for failure to follow these statutory procedures.

The public administrator may be the subject of Congressional criticism or investigation. For political and other reasons the legislative body frequently wishes to determine "who killed Cock Robin?" The extensive Congressional hearings to establish responsibility for the Pearl Harbor disaster are a good example. The private administrator may also be the subject of investigation, but he is much less likely to be, and then usually only in cases where he has business transactions with a government agency or in areas where his business is subject to public regulation. With the increasing scope of governmental regulation of business, however, his chances of being the object of public investigation are growing rapidly.

The private administrator is often given much more latitude in interpreting the relationship between his organization and the general welfare than is the public administrator. It is accepted that the former is in business primarily to further his private ends; the latter is expected to serve the public interest, and it is considered unethical for him to use the advantages of his position for personal gain. In 1947, governmental employees who speculated in the grain market were objects of public censure, even in cases where they possessed no "inside" information that gave them special advantage. Of course, the price and production policies of business may also be scrutinized when it is felt that they impinge upon the public welfare.

Differences in Public Attitudes Toward Public and Private Administration. During World War II, the government found it necessary to "seize" the coal mines to insure continued production in the face of strikes by the miners. Such seizures consisted in hoisting an American flag over the mines, appointing an Army officer to run the mines—and nothing else. Yet the miners returned to work for the same bosses, doing the same work, under the same conditions. The only factors that had been added were the presence of a uniformed officer and a flag. The miners, however, apparently held a different attitude when the government was "running" the mines. They felt that it was somehow wrong or dangerous to strike against the government. This psychological factor led to a change in worker attitudes that, in turn, changed the administrative problem.

On the other hand, there is a widespread conviction that what governments do is inefficient and often corrupt. A common stereotype of the bureaucrat is an overbearing, lazy, tax-eater. Stemming from the *laisser-faire* doctrine and the frontier tradition, this attitude is one that must constantly be taken into account by public administrators working with public problems. It poses problems not generally shared by private administrators.

There are certain, but largely undefined, limits in the extent to which the public administrator is allowed to influence (or to attempt to influence) public attitudes toward his agency's product. It is accepted that the businessman will advertise his particular brand of breakfast cereal in almost any way he finds profitable. Congress, on the other hand, has exhibited strong hostility toward "public relations" expenditures by government agencies that could be interpreted as attempts to obtain public approval for agency programs. Appropriations for such purposes are almost always among the first casualties of an economy drive.[2]

The foregoing examples are merely illustrative, not an exhaustive listing or analysis of the possible differences between public and private administration. Apart from these differences, however, whether one is studying the administration of a church, a labor union, a corporation, or a government agency, many of the basic problems will be the same. To the extent that this is so, it is possible to work out a general theory of administration that will encompass all kinds of organizations.

The Growth of Administration

When the fifty-five men met in Philadelphia to write the Constitution, the United States consisted of about four million people living on the eastern seaboard, most of them east of the Allegheny Mountains. The great proportion of the population were farmers and most of them were relatively self-subsistent. They made their own shoes and clothes, grew their own food, built their own houses, distilled their own whiskey. The need for government was slight, and what cooperative activity was necessary could be accomplished with a minimum of organization. To build a road, the neighbors turned out and, with only rudimentary organization, managed to grade the surface and erect needed bridges. A county poorhouse provided for the few aged persons who had no families to take care of them. To control transgressors, an amateur constable aided by volunteers raised the "hue and cry" and captured the culprit or chased him from the community.

Modern foibles like running water, paved roads, labor unions, large corporations, sewage systems, telephones, electric lights, airplanes, automobiles, movie theatres, and atom bombs, all of which require some public supervision of their use, were unheard of. In that earlier kind of simple social structure government was limited in cost, specialization, and number of employees.

[2] An interesting exception is government advertising to assist private business in a particular state or city. State governments, in particular, spend substantial sums to advertise products manufactured in the state—Wisconsin cheese and California oranges—or to attract industry.

The growth of population, the very growth in size of the United States, and, particularly, advances in technology have changed the picture. Many things that could have been handled in Revolutionary times without public authority must now be handled by governments. Many problems that could then be solved by the spontaneous cooperation of neighbors now require the highly organized cooperation of professional specialists.

REASONS FOR THE GROWTH

Critics of government often try to explain the extent of modern government as a conspiracy between un-American individuals and politicians of the opposing political party. Special interest groups continually warn that more governmental interference will lead to socialism or worse. Such warnings are often coupled with an idyllic portrait of life in earlier and more sensible periods in our history when the activities of governments were held to a minimum. While citing the ills of modern civilization, the orators fail to mention the difficulties attendant on primitive life. The expense of maintaining a public health service is bemoaned, the agonies of yellow fever and diphtheria forgotten. The regulation of the telephone is berated, the advantages of phone service at reasonable rates ignored. The gasoline tax is taken as an abhorrent example of the burden of government, the advantages of paved highways taken for granted.

There is room for debate, of course, as to the desirable scope and magnitude of the services of government. But the fact is that even those who advocate the greatest restriction of governmental activities do not seriously believe that they can bring about more than a moderate reduction in the scale of public expenditures. The actual political battles about governmental expenditures are concerned with whether the Federal government should spend 25, 35, or 45 billions of dollars a year. Almost no one thinks these expenditures could be reduced to a billion or even five billion dollars. For better or for worse, then, modern civilization has brought with it demands for governmental services and activities that make of modern government a very large-scale enterprise.

Sociologists have compared the growth of governmental activities to the rate of industrial invention and traced the demands for governmental action to the impact of various technological advances.[3] An obvious example of this process is the invention of the automobile. The automobile has required a great many governmental innovations. We now have a Federal Roads Administration; in every state there are highway commissions; at the local level there are both county and city road and street departments. A system of Federal grants-in-aid to states and state grants to localities for road administration has appeared—with the consequent employment of new administrative personnel. New techniques of regulating traffic have been devised with an army of policemen to enforce them. Licenses have had to be issued—both for the vehicles and the drivers. Fast transport has increased the scope of interstate commerce and the problems of handling it. New problems of balancing the interests of the automobile and the railroad have appeared and have required increases and adjustments in governmental activities. The general problem of law enforcement is changing, with increasing emphasis on state and federal law enforcement officers because of the ability of criminals to cover long distances in a short time. Roadhouses and autocamps have sprung up, throwing increased demands on enforcement officials. The automobiles are costly, and the common practice of financing them by borrowing has necessitated new regulations covering installment selling. Almost no phase of American life has escaped the impact of this technological innovation, and in a great many phases the impact has led to an increase in governmental personnel.

In addition to technological change as such, the tremendous diversity and specialization of modern life has also led to increased governmental activity. People are no longer self-subsistent. A period of depression or a period of inflation dramatizes the degree to which the man in Portland, Maine, and the man in Portland, Oregon, are dependent on each other for their collective well-being. Increasingly, the government is the agency that must cope with this problem of interdependence. Nor do voluntary aid societies organized by a single community, no matter how well meaning, aid materially in solving problems that are nation-wide. The experiences of local communities in their unsuccessful efforts to meet the depression of the 1930's and the inflation and housing shortage of the 1940's illustrate the futility of this approach to solving

[3] Cf., William F. Ogburn, *Social Change* (New York: The Viking Press, 1922); National Resources Planning Board, *Technological Trends and National Policy* (Washington: Government Printing Office, 1937).

community problems. An economy organized on a nation-wide basis requires nation-wide governmental activity.

THE GROWTH IN NUMBERS AND COSTS

At the present time about one out of every ten employed persons works for government—national, state, or local. Of the readers of this volume, since they are most likely to engage in a "white collar" occupation, it would not be an exaggeration to guess that one in every five will ultimately be employed at some level of government. Government in its various ramifications is by far the largest employer in the country. In expenditures, government dwarfs completely any corporation. About 23 per cent of the national income went to government in 1948.

While the expansion of the Federal and city government has been the greatest, the states and the counties have also increased the numbers of their personnel as the scope of their activities has widened. As the number of persons employed by government has zoomed upward, the cost of government has also increased at a very rapid rate. The rate of the increase is hard to imagine even with the aid of figures. In the fiscal year 1947 President Truman recommended a budget totalling approximately 37 billion dollars. In 1840 the annual budget for the national government was a little over 24 million. The 1947 budget is more than fifteen hundred times as great as that of 107 years ago. At the same time the population is now only a little more than eight times what it was in 1840.

THE GROWTH IN DIVERSITY OF TASKS

It was the opinion of Andrew Jackson that the tasks of government were sufficiently simple so that any person of intelligence could perform them without preparation or training. He advocated a system of rotation in office so that the government might be held closer to the people. Governing could and should, in his opinion, be done by amateurs, rather than by persons prepared or trained for the job.

The situation is vastly different today. The government has on its roster representatives of nearly every known profession and trade—hemotologists and welders, theoretical physicists and professional safecrackers, electrical engineers and locomotive engineers, economists and home economists, mathematicians and mechanics. All are needed to carry out the tasks of government. In addition, the governmental services employ hundreds of professional and skilled people whose opportunities are almost totally limited to government itself. Forestry schools, for example, train their students almost exclusively for the public service. Criminologists, fingerprint experts, and military and naval personnel are other examples of persons trained primarily or exclusively for governmental agencies. The list of occupations represented by the government worker reads like the occupational index of the United States.

The Study of Administration

With large-scale government engaged in an ever growing number of tasks and absorbing an ever larger proportion of the national income, there has been an increasing demand that the functions be performed in an efficient manner—that the maximum attainment of goals be obtained with a minimum of effort. In answer to this demand, specialized courses in colleges and universities, as well as systematized investigation within the government itself, have attempted to increase the understanding of the problems involved in administration. When interest in the study of public administration first developed, attention was directed to the elimination of graft and inefficiency associated with the "spoils" system.

SLAYING THE DRAGON OF PATRONAGE

There has always been, in the American mind, a deep suspicion of politics and politicians. At the same time, the reluctance of the majority of able youths to enter politics as a career has left the pursuit of politics to professionals who have used public jobs as rewards for political activity. As long as the tasks of government were simple and limited, the change in officials with a change in party fortunes was relatively unimportant. As the need for highly trained specialists increased, so did the public annoyance with patronage. Early advocates of more efficient government tended to concentrate their efforts in getting civil service systems under which employees would be selected on a merit basis.

In the national government, the assassination of President Garfield by a disappointed office-seeker provided impetus toward establishing a Federal civil service under the Pendleton Act in 1883. Widespread disclosure of corruption in the states and municipalities led to an increasing adoption of civil service in state and municipal governments. Gradually, over the years, the practice of selecting civil servants on the basis of examination rather than on political preferences or political activities has been extended. At the present time, while the use of patronage is by no means dead, civil service systems in national, state, and municipal governments cover a very large proportion of persons publicly employed.

EFFICIENCY AS A GOAL

Advocacy of efficiency in the performance of governmental tasks was, in good part, a taxpayers' movement. Governmental inefficiency was expensive; it tended to raise taxes. Therefore, even those who violently opposed the extention of governmental activities to new areas were insistent on having efficiency in those activities that were deemed necessary.

Intellectually, both the efficiency and the anti-patronage movements were made possible by assuming an almost air-tight distinction between "policy" and "administration." It was assumed that the legislatures and the elected officials would lay out the policies, and the administrative officials would merely carry them out.[4] In the first place, on this assumption, only the elected officials need be politically responsible. Administration could, without loss of democracy, be entrusted to "neutral" civil servants selected under civil service procedures. In the second place, these civil servants would not then be responsible for formulating policies but only for carrying them out without waste of public funds—that is, as efficiently as possible.

Most theorizing about public administration, and most of the administrative principles proposed by writers on the subject, have accepted this assumption that efficiency is the criterion by which the administration of government agencies is to be judged. In the

---

[4] See Chapter 15 below for an analysis of this distinction and the problems it raises.

course of this study some of these principles will be examined in terms of a broader conception of the administrative process.[5]

PUBLIC ADMINISTRATION TRAINING

Formal courses in public administration are quite recent in this country. The first comprehensive textbook was published in 1925, and gradually courses, mostly offered within departments of political science, began to appear in the major universities.

The training has had two basic emphases. First, students could "major" in public administration, looking forward to careers in government via civil service examinations. The Institute of Public Administration affiliated with Columbia University and the Maxwell School of Citizenship and Public Affairs at Syracuse University were among the institutions that pioneered in graduate public administration training. Most of the persons so trained tended to go into "staff" positions in local, state, and Federal governments— that is, into positions as personnel or budget technicians, administrative assistants, or employees of government research agencies. Civil service procedures were gradually adapted to provide employment opportunities for college graduates in administration. Under the influence of Leonard D. White, the United States Civil Service Commission held examinations for the position of Junior Civil Service Examiner for the first time in 1934, and a number of government agencies drew upon this list. This examination, later broadened into a number of social science options of the Junior Professional Assistant examination, has been a significant means of recruiting persons with training in administration into the federal government.

A far greater number of students than the number specializing in public administration have studied this subject as an adjunct to some other professional specialization. More and more, some instruction in public administration is considered an essential part of the training of persons, whatever their profession, who plan to make a career in government. A number of engineering schools recommend or require such courses for civil engineers interested

[5] For a critical analysis of some of the currently accepted principles of public administration, see Herbert A. Simon, *Administrative Behavior* (New York: The Macmillan Co., 1947), chap. 2, and Dwight Waldo, *The Administrative State* (New York: The Ronald Press, 1948).

in the public works field, and several law schools are beginning to make special provision for students planning government careers.

Because of this increasing demand for formal public administration training, the schools have had to try to define the field—to distinguish it from other subjects such as public law or political science. This task has not been easy, and it is probably fair to say that the schools and writers are, for the most part, still uncertain of the precise course that training in administration should take.

Goals of Public Administration Theory

The study of public administration may have two goals, which can be separated in conception but which in practice are often interlocking. It may be concerned (1) with understanding how people in organizations behave and how organizations operate, or (2) with practical recommendations as to how agencies can be most effectively organized. Of course, just as the practice of medicine can advance only as rapidly as does scientific knowledge of human biology, so the techniques of effective organization and administration must rest upon a sound theory of human behavior in organization.

THE STUDY OF ORGANIZATION BEHAVIOR

The study of the behavior of persons in organizations can be non-normative—that is, it can be freed from the desires, values, and prejudices of the person making the investigation and can be made to rest upon an objective analysis of human interaction. To use the medical analogy again, the values of the biologist conducting research on cancer—his desire to find a means of protecting human beings from a painful disease—provide a motive for his work, but they have nothing to do with the content of his discoveries. He would seek the same knowledge of the human organism if he desired to produce cancer as he does in striving to cure it. As a matter of fact, one of the important advances in cancer research was the discovery of ways in which cancer could be experimentally produced in animals.[6]

[6] Bacteriology provides an even more striking example of this proposition, for here we actually find some scientists applying the basic knowledge of the field to the eradication or cure of disease, while others are adapting the same knowledge to the development of more effective methods of bacteriological warfare.

Although the same kind of objectivity is necessary and attainable in the social sciences as in the natural sciences, it has proved in practice much more difficult to reach. The attitudes and wishes of the investigators are not easy to remove from the scene. In most writing on the subject of public administration, administrative "biology" and "medicine" have been confusingly intermixed, and the values of the writers have been mingled with the propositions they have set forth.

There has been considerable discussion as to whether public administration is concerned with analyzing organization problems or with giving advice to administrators. Historically speaking, it has in fact been concerned with both. This is perfectly proper, provided that the objective and scientific aspects of the subject are distinguished from the value elements, and provided that the advice as to how to attain these values is based on an objective science of organization behavior.

This book will largely be concerned with administration as a science—not science in the sense of the exactness that the physical sciences have achieved, but science in the sense of an objective understanding of the phenomena without confusion between facts and values. This emphasis on the factual does not mean that we discount the importance of values. It simply reflects our belief that the competent practitioner reaches his desired ends—whatever they may be—through a mastery of the phenomena he is dealing with and a clear, objective understanding of their behavior.

RECOMMENDATIONS OF "GOOD PRACTICE"

There are several reasons why a study of administration should begin with the objective analysis of organization behavior rather than with rules on "how to be a successful executive" or "how to organize a government agency." The first reason is that practical rules simply do not exist which can be applied in an automatic or mechanical fashion to actual organization problems. Practical administrators find that formal principles of administration are of far less importance to them than an ability to size up an administrative situation—to understand the psychological processes at work—and then to apply common sense once the situation is thoroughly understood. At the present stage of knowledge, administrative theory is of far more practical use in diagnosing situations than in prescribing suitable courses of action.

A second reason is that the practice of administration involves skills—skills that have become thoroughly incorporated in the administrator's personality—rather than mere intellectual knowledge. Rules as to how one ought to behave are of no use unless the actual *ability* to behave according to the rules has been learned and practiced. Formal training will be of greater help in developing the skills of administration if it concentrates upon an understanding of the reasons behind the rules than if it emphasizes the learning of specific rules that cannot possibly cover the whole wide range of situations that will be encountered in practice.

A third reason for avoiding a "how-to" approach in the study of administration has already been mentioned. Practical recommendations for organization action always depend upon the values of the person making the recommendation. For example, a person primarily interested in doing a job *efficiently* may make a recommendation different from that of a person interested in doing the job so as to preserve *democratic responsibility*, and different again from a person interested in doing it in a manner that will interfere as little as possible with the property or other *rights of individuals.*[7]

The problems of enforcing the Prohibition Amendment, for example, were largely problems of values rather than technical questions of selecting effective administrative methods. Those methods of enforcement that would have been technically effective in achieving the goal violated important values—such as freedom from arbitrary search and seizure—that were widely held and that were considered by many to be more important than temperance.[8]

[7] Waldo, *op. cit.*, has shown conclusively that the most fundamental differences among the various propounders of administrative "principles" stem principally from the varying weights they attach to values such as those mentioned here. The most serious criticisms, for example, of the recommendations of the President's Committee on Administrative Management have been on grounds of the excessive preoccupation of that committee with the value of efficiency. Disputes among the members of the Hoover Commission also tended to result from differences of opinion as to the values being promoted.

[8] The current political scene provides another highly important example of this: the Federal loyalty program. The methods being used to eliminate Communists from Federal employment are probably very effective for that purpose. Persons who would subscribe to propositions such as "freedom of speech and conscience must be maintained" and "a man is innocent until proved guilty" might decide, however, that the dangers to such values resulting from present enforcement methods far outweigh the possible danger to the government from failing to weed out all Communists.

To make practical recommendations for organization action one must assume either that he possesses values that are generally shared or that his values are "right" in some absolute sense. Plato, in his *Republic*, tried to realize the second alternative: to devise a society in which "philosopher kings," because of training and wisdom, would establish the correct value system for the community. In the constitutional governments of the Western world, we have tended to operate on the contrary theory: the community should decide—by the political processes we call democracy—what values are to be sought, and the administrator should be bound by those values.[9]

For these reasons, this book is concerned chiefly with how people behave in organizations rather than with specific recommendations for "better" organization of the American governmental structure. Its propositions will generally be stated in a descriptive or in an "if-then" form: "If you do this, that will result." Propositions so stated may be adapted to any set of values that the persons using the information may hold.

ADMINISTRATION AS MANIPULATION

The position has been taken in these pages that knowledge of administration, like all knowledge, is amoral. It becomes "good" or "bad" only in terms of the value assumptions added to it by the person who uses it—in terms of his attitudes towards goals and methods. Knowledge gives man power—but power to do either good or evil. An exploding atom bomb is a product of the same physical knowledge that may soon produce atom-generated electricity.

Knowledge of administration is amoral in an even deeper sense, for it is knowledge of how to manipulate other human beings—how to get them to do the things you want done. The study of administration discloses techniques for influencing human behavior. To carry out a program of action, the administrator is constantly trying to predict what the consequences will be of a particular course of action and to act in ways that will produce the behaviors

[9] This democratic belief is itself a value assumption which provides the ethical basis for the distinction between "policy" and "administration" that was mentioned earlier. For a discussion of the philosophical underpinnings of this problem see Hans Kelsen, "Absolutism and Relativism in Philosophy and Politics," *American Political Science Review*, 42: 906–14 (October, 1948).

he desires and inhibit those he does not want. Only this distinguishes a realistic plan from a vague wish.

One of the most fundamental values in Western civilization has been the dignity of the individual human being. It is not easy to express the whole meaning of this value, but certainly it means, among other things, that human beings are not to be manipulated as marionettes attached to strings. In an administrative organization where only the manipulator stands to gain by the achievement of the organization goal and where the other participants all lose, effectiveness in reaching the goal unavoidably infringes on the dignity of the individual.

Hence, the dignity of the individual can be respected only in an administrative situation in which all participants will gain, in one way or another, from the accomplishment of the organization goal. In such a situation, administration can be "cooperative" in the broadest sense. It can be a constant process of behavioral interaction, with the plan being influenced by the reactions of the clientele and of all participants in the organization as often as by the conscious manipulative design of a "boss."

Nevertheless, we must not make the reassuring—but fallacious—assumption that this kind of cooperation will always be the most effective means of reaching the organization goal, unless this goal is defined broadly enough to include the values of all participants. This belief in some preordained harmony between administration that respects the individual and administration that is efficient in the usual sense mars the otherwise perceptive writings of Elton Mayo and others of the "Hawthorne Group." [10]

To be sure, there is a kernel of truth in the idea that "democratic" administration, allowing broad employee participation in decisions, is more efficient than "autocratic" or "paternalistic" administration. In our own society, at least, "democratic" administrative techniques are important in securing a high level of employee morale and participation. Much evidence has been gathered on this point in the last twenty years, almost all of it pointing in the same direction. However, there is little reason to believe that the harmony is complete. On the contrary, every administrator encounters situations where effective action dictates

[10] Cf., Elton Mayo, *Social Problems of an Industrial Civilization* (Cambridge: Harvard University Press, 1945); Fritz Roethlisberger, *Management and Morale* (Cambridge: Harvard University Press, 1941).

some infringement upon the desire of the individual not to be manipulated as a mere tool. He encounters many situations where there is conflict as well as community of goals—higher salaries to employees versus more economical service to taxpayers, for example.

No knowledge of administrative techniques, then, can relieve the administrator from the task of moral choice—choice as to organization goals and methods and choice as to his treatment of the other human beings in his organization. His code of ethics is as significant a part of his equipment as an administrator as is his knowledge of administrative behavior, and no amount of study of the "science" of administration will provide him with this code.

☙

CHAPTER TWO

How Governmental Organizations Originate

GOVERNMENTAL organizations, like all formal organizations in the community, arise because some persons feel that a new organization is needed to attain some desired goal. The nature of the organization that is created, its structure, and the degree to which it is actually adapted to the solution of the problem that called it into existence will vary, depending on the conceptions of its advocates and the environment—physical and social—in which it originates.

Much can be learned about organizations from a study of their origins. Many peculiar facts about existing operations—structure, program emphasis, and even staffing—become understandable only when their history and the forces that presided at the organization's birth are known. Further, information about the groups and forces that urged or opposed the creation of a new governmental organization is often somewhat more accessible than information about its struggle for continued existence. The major crises in an organization's life, including its birth, generally bring it to legislative and public attention, and these crises are duly recorded in documents and by the press. The day-to-day adjustment of an organization to its environment—the steps it takes to anticipate possible attacks from enemies, its efforts to win quietly important friends—are more often carried on in conversations and conferences that are hard to piece together, even when known, into a complete picture. Hence, this chapter will provide an introduction to a broader topic, the study of organizations as social systems in equilibrium, a topic that will provide the central theme for many later chapters of this book.

The material of the chapter will be limited in several respects.

In the first place, it will concentrate particularly on situations in which a government undertakes a new activity rather than upon those in which a new organization unit is created by a regrouping of existing activities. As we shall see, there is no hard and fast line between these two situations, but an example of the first would be the creation in 1862 of the U. S. Department of Agriculture; an example of the second would be the establishment of a city Department of Public Safety by combination of the police, fire, and health departments.

In the second place, attention will be directed primarily to organization units of sufficient importance to be the subject of legislative attention—a city recreation department, or the U. S. Bureau of Standards, for example. This emphasis should not obscure the fact that organizations often start more humbly as sections or branches of larger units, and that these later sometimes achieve the status of bureaus and departments. (As a matter of fact, we shall see that this is what happened in the case of the Department of Agriculture.)

How Problems Give Rise to Organizations

The first condition of organization is a problem. Someone wants to accomplish something he cannot accomplish alone. Problems giving rise to organizations are as varied as the whole spectrum of human needs, but to explain how they give rise to organizations we must understand:

(1) why it is felt that the problem must be solved by organized rather than individual action;

(2) why a governmental organization rather than an organized effort outside the governmental structure (a corporation or a voluntary association) is selected as the means for meeting the problem.

We will also be interested in two more specific questions:

(3) the location of the organization in the governmental structure—whether it is established as a local, state, or Federal agency; and

(4) the particular form it is given—whether it is incorporated in an existing department, given departmental status, or established as an "independent" agency partially insulated from executive control.

The first question need not detain us, since it has already been discussed in Chapter 1. The second—why governmental organization is preferred to private association—requires some examination. The answer to this question depends upon two sets of considerations: the powers of government and the attitudes of the community toward government.

POWERS OF GOVERNMENT

The common reason for entrusting a particular task to government is that government agencies may be vested with certain powers not possessed by private associations—in particular, the power to raise revenues by taxation and the power to regulate the behavior of persons who are not members of the organization. Most governmental activities were undertaken in order to gain the benefit of one or both of these powers. Public health activities provide a good example of both. Private individuals are not permitted to decide for themselves what protection they want from communicable diseases, because those who refuse to pay for the service would benefit along with those who finance it, and because those who refuse the service might endanger the health of those who accept it. Thus, taxes are levied to force the community as a whole to support sanitation services of benefit to all, and regulations are imposed—for example, compulsory vaccination or quarantine rules—to prevent individuals from spreading communicable diseases.

There are a few examples of governmental activities that could be carried on by private organizations without taxing or regulatory powers. Many cities own and operate water, gas, and electric utilities. In this case, the choice is between government operation and operation by a private company which, because of the essential nature of its service and its monopolistic character, would have to be closely regulated. In the United States, however, most governmental activities are of a kind that could not readily be carried on by private organizations without the power to regulate or to tax for revenue.

COMMUNITY ATTITUDES TOWARD GOVERNMENT

In a community where there is a tradition of self-reliance there may be a great reluctance to call upon government as a mode of solving community problems. Where there is a suspicion that government officials will abuse, in their own interests, the power that comes from official position, the desire will generally be to solve whatever problems exist outside the framework of government if such solutions are at all possible.

On the other hand, persons who are accustomed to using the machinery of government, who look to and trust government officials, or who are accustomed to seek governmental approval for every action, are likely to think first of government when a problem looms on the horizon.

From the time of the establishment of the United States as a republic, attitudes favoring the use of government in dealing with community problems have existed side by side with a strong individualistic tradition. On the pro-governmental side, we have had the Federalist program, sponsored by Alexander Hamilton, for the encouragement of manufactures; Clay's "American System" of internal improvements; Theodore Roosevelt's Progressivism; the New Freedom of Woodrow Wilson; and the New Deal of Franklin Delano Roosevelt. Anti-governmentalism has been an important ingredient in the political philosophies of Thomas Jefferson, Calhoun, the conservative group that formed a majority of the Supreme Court from about 1880 to 1937, and most recent leaders of the Republican party.

Even more important than the existence of these two competing attitudes has been the common agreement that the American political system must somehow provide room for both of them. Hence, the American tradition provides numerous precedents both for and against any specific proposal that may be advanced for a governmental activity, and the ghosts of Washington, Jefferson, Jackson, and Lincoln often are invoked by orators on both sides.

The post-war debate about the housing problem illustrates the way in which general attitudes toward government affect policy. On the one hand, there was general agreement as to the existence of a serious housing shortage. On the other, there was violent disagreement as to the scope and form of governmental intervention to alleviate the shortage. Some persons, taking an extreme *laisser faire* position, argued that the private economy operating through the normal price mechanism would solve the problem without intervention. Others accepted the idea of governmental assistance, provided it did not extend to actual public construction and management of housing. Still others insisted that this was an area where the private economy could not operate effectively, and that at least for low income groups only public housing could solve the problem.

It is sometimes said that political arguments appealing to American governmental traditions are only a cloak for the advancement of private interests—that real estate groups opposing public housing stand to lose by it, and that low income groups who favor it would gain economically by it. Still, the fact that appeal is made to accepted political traditions in arguing the case indicates a belief that such appeals have some political effectiveness and that not all attitudes toward political measures are determined by the calculation of the immediate effects of those measures on the pocketbook.

Laisser Faire. The anti-governmental philosophy rests in part upon an economic argument—upon the idea that government should not interfere with the operation of a free competitive market. Thus, when Federal wages and hours legislation was being debated, Nelson Gaskill, formerly chairman of the Federal Trade Commission, said in a statement to the press that "the proposed minimum-wage measure would lay violent hands upon the economic law proved through the experience of many generations. This law has been that the prices of commodities and the price of labor, under conditions of free competition, will move up and down freely in response to conditions of supply and demand, and under these conditions the price of service or commodities constantly tends to equalize cost. . . ." [1]

On the other hand, those advocating government economic regulation have generally attempted to meet the *laisser faire* argument not by general denial but by showing that a particular regulation is consistent with its underlying philosophy. Woodrow Wilson's New Freedom, for example, emphasized the restoration of competition, threatened by monopolies, and the protection of the bargaining power of the small business and the workingman.

Protection of Individual Rights. Another part of the anti-governmental tradition has emphasized political problems—the dan-

[1] *New York Times*, June 6, 1937. III:7:1.

gers to individual liberty stemming from too great a concentration of governmental powers. The cry of "bureaucracy" and "dictatorship" can often arouse distrust and opposition to legislation even on the part of persons who would benefit from it economically. It is not necessary to outline here in detail the political theory that underlies this distrust—a theory that had already found clear expression in the seventeenth century in the writings of John Locke. It is a theory that views government as a necessary evil to be restrained within the narrowest possible bounds. It was to this theory that Senator Vandenberg was appealing when, in a radio speech opposing the Wages and Hours legislation, he criticized the measure as "making for a centralized authoritarian state with its tyranny of government blessed monopolies." [2]

Humanitarianism. Equally a part of the American tradition is the humanitarian argument—that government should be employed to protect the poor and the weak, to advance economic and social democracy. This point of view is seldom attacked head-on by opponents of governmental intervention. Rather, opposition is generally based on the argument that the proposed activity will not have the desired result. Arthur Besse, representing the National Association of Wool Manufacturers, justified his opposition to the Wages and Hours Bill saying: "We have a sincere reluctance to oppose a bill of this nature realizing that to those who do not understand the real nature of the bill we appear opposed to the principle of minimum wages and maximum hours, and reluctant to support the abolition of child labor. That is not true. There is no child labor in the wool textile industry." [3] He then proceeded to attack the specific measures proposed in the bill.

We have perhaps indicated in sufficient detail some of the typical attitudes that influence the choice between governmental and non-governmental instruments for solving problems. At a later point in the chapter we shall see that, even in cases where it is decided that governmental activity is needed, attitudes will affect the particular form of governmental structure that is chosen.

[2] *New York Times*, June 6, 1937. III:9:3. Friedrick A. Hayek, *The Road to Serfdom* (Chicago: University of Chicago Press, 1944), is the best known recent exposition of this point of view. Although written by an economist, the central argument of the book is concerned with the danger of governmental power rather than the economic theory of *laisser faire*.

[3] Joint Hearings on S. 2475 and H. R. 7200, pp. 556–71, June 9, 1937.

Dynamics of Organization Origin

There is nothing automatic in the way that the community meets new problems as they arise. Before a governmental activity is undertaken, a problem must exist not merely in fact, but in peoples' minds as well. Millions of persons died of typhoid fever before impure drinking water was identified as an important cause of the disease. The problem of purifying drinking water did not exist until medical science had discovered the relationship between water and disease and this discovery was generally accepted.

Furthermore, the idea of using government to solve a problem depends on the invention of possible solutions. Smallpox was recognized as very much of a problem, but the possibility of preventive measures, governmental or otherwise, had to await the discovery of vaccination. In a certain sense, of course, necessity really is the mother of invention, for if a problem is recognized as sufficiently serious, the search for solutions will be stimulated. Indeed, a governmental unit may be selected as the agency to conduct the research—as in the important early research of the U. S. Department of Agriculture into pleuro-pneumonia of cattle, hog cholera, and other animal diseases.[4]

A number of typical stages can generally be recognized in the prenatal development of a government agency: recognition of the problem, advancement of proposals for its solution, legislative action on the proposals, and establishment of the agency.

First, a few persons recognize the problem in its early stages and begin to write and talk about it. Their efforts may be fruitless over a considerable period of years, but if the problem persists, and particularly if it becomes intensified, a larger and larger segment of the public becomes aware of it.

Meanwhile, tentative suggestions will begin to be made for possible solutions. Some of these may include programs of governmental service or regulation. Organized groups will begin to interest themselves in the issue. As the demands for some remedy grow louder, advocacy will begin to center around a few solutions,

---

[4] John M. Gaus and Leon O. Wolcott, *Public Administration and the United States Department of Agriculture* (Chicago: Public Administration Service, 1940), p. 10.

particularly about those that appear to have some likelihood of political acceptability. Sooner or later, specific proposals will be made in the form of legislative bills or requests for governmental appropriations.

At this point the whole complex legislative process will begin. If the problem is a sufficiently vital one, it may involve the machinery of elections, pressure groups and lobbying, public newspaper discussion, party leadership, and the like. If it is a problem of narrower interest, discussion may be confined to trade journals, to a few interested groups, to the relevant legislative committees, and to a few administrators in related fields of activity.

In either case, advocacy may finally be terminated—sometimes only after many defeats have been suffered—with the creation of a new piece of legislation, a new governmental unit, or a new appropriation. Throughout all these stages, as the support of wider groups is enlisted and new sources of opposition appear, the proposal undergoes numerous alterations and transformations as its advocates seek the needed support.

THE RECOGNITION OF NEED

The early stages of problem recognition and of the formulation of proposals may take place either outside or inside the governmental structure. Where the problem falls outside the area of any existing governmental program, it may first be recognized by private citizens, and solutions may be proposed by private groups. For example, until the last quarter of the nineteenth century when a unit first called "Forestry Investigations" was established in the U. S. Department of Agriculture, the forest conservation movement was initiated largely outside the government.[5]

The problem may first become evident to persons in some profession or industry that is closest to it. Members of the social work profession have been a source of initiation of many new governmental programs in the public welfare field. Members of the medical profession have initiated ideas for new public health measures.

In other cases, an accident of personal experience may lead a private individual to concern himself with a problem and to crusade for many years to establish a government agency for dealing with

[5] Gaus and Wolcott, *op. cit.*, p. 25. See also Herbert A. Smith, "The Early Forestry Movement in the United States," *Agricultural History*, October, 1938, p. 326.

it. Helen Keller's work for the blind is an example of this. So is the contribution of Clifford Beers (who was for a time confined in a mental institution) to the introduction of modern institutions for the treatment of the mentally ill. Such individuals, particularly if they do not find a ready response in the organized social groups or if they encounter the organized resistance of established groups, may work without any visible success for a long time. But if the situation is favorable and the problem attracts increasing public attention, a larger and larger group of persons may come in time to support actively the proposal.

On the other hand, where a government agency is responsible for a broad area of activity, problems lying within that area may first be pointed out by the personnel of the agency. The U. S. Department of Agriculture played a major role in the recognition of the problem of agricultural overproduction and in devising the parity principle as a solution.[6] Most often, both governmental and non-governmental groups are involved. Building inspection as a means of fire prevention was sponsored both by municipal fire departments and by the National Board of Fire Underwriters and the National Fire Protection Association.

In some cases, a problem will be met first by a voluntary association and the activity later transferred to a government agency. The volunteer fire department of the small town, financed by an annual Fireman's Ball, becomes first an official volunteer fire company and then a department with paid employees as the town grows to be a city. Charitable foundations have frequently financed health services and free libraries as demonstration projects which were later taken over by government as tax-financed services. Important projects of this kind, which gave great impetus to the city planning movement, were the Regional Plan Association of New York, assisted by the Russell Sage Foundation, and the Wacker Plan for Chicago, sponsored by the Commercial Club.[7]

SECURING ORGANIZED SUPPORT

In almost all cases before a problem receives serious legislative consideration there intervenes an intermediate period during which

[6] Gaus and Wolcott, *op. cit.*, pp. 163–5.

[7] Initiation by private groups and gradual transfer of responsibility to government was also characteristic of the early municipal recreation movement. See *Municipal Recreation Administration* (2nd ed., Chicago: International City Managers' Association, 1945), p. 36.

interest in the problem spreads from the person or persons who first initiate discussion to organized groups in the community. An individual, for example, who during a visit is impressed by the city planning work in another city may conceive the idea of establishing a city planning agency in his own community. If he is a member of the Chamber of Commerce, the Rotary Club, or other group, he will probably launch the idea with his associates, and it may be taken up by the organization and become a part of its program.[8]

What determines, at this stage, whether an idea will catch on, will capture the support of ever-widening groups, and will ultimately attain success; or whether, on the other hand, the initiators will fail to gain interest and attention, and the proposal will die stillborn? To answer this question, we must look more closely at the motives of the persons who initiate and conduct campaigns for the establishment of new programs and organizations. These motives are as diverse as the situations to which they relate, but certain rough generalizations can be stated. First, for one reason or another, the initiators generally have a strong interest in the program goal. The reason may be economic—they stand to gain from the activities of the new organization. It may be professional —the new organization would realize goals important to their profession. It may be philanthropic. This interest must be sufficiently strong to induce the initiators to devote a considerable time and effort to the campaign. It must be particularly strong if the cause is a difficult one and the fight is long.

However, human beings sometimes evince a remarkable capacity to support causes in which they have no direct economic or personal interest and which appear to be practically hopeless of success. Examples of this kind of behavior are the movement to establish Esperanto as an international language, the thirteen-month calendar movement, and possibly the movement for simplified spelling (although the latter has some possibilities of eventual success). Such movements raise two puzzling psychological questions. First, what is the source of the monomania that induces individuals to spend their whole efforts in working for such seemingly esoteric objectives? Second, how is optimism sustained without visible prospects of success? Whatever may be the answers to these

---

[8] Nationally federated local organizations are often a source of initiation in a slightly different way. The national headquarters of such federations assist in the rapid transmission of ideas for organizations from one part of the country to another by their recommendations of action programs for the local affiliates.

questions, it is certainly a fact that there are in the community, at any given time, a vast number of potential "causes" each advocated by an individual, or a small group of individuals, and each capable at any moment of being fanned into live public issues should circumstances favor them.

When a proposal begins to receive organized support on a larger scale, this wider circle of supporters must also have its motives for devoting time and effort to the cause. In most communities there are organizations of persons who obtain satisfaction from advancing proposals for public projects. The so-called "service" organizations and the League of Women Voters are examples. These organizations are continually casting about for projects to support, and it is to these that the initiator, as already noted, may make his appeal. Alternatively, his cause may be taken up by existing special interest groups who see some advantages to be gained from it.

If the problem appears to some people to be a sufficiently important one, they may even form a new organization to sponsor their proposals for its solution, as did the sponsors of civil service reform in the United States.

> The progressive degradation and degeneration of public life under the spoils methods called forth a movement in the late sixties which demanded a reform of the civil service. . . . This movement was inaugurated and carried on by a small group of high-minded and public-spirited men, most of whom belonged to the class known as "intellectuals" or "idealists." . . . Indeed, for a short time the professional politicians refused to take them seriously. . . .
>
> Throughout the seventies and eighties the movement for civil service reform gained momentum, until it culminated in the passage of the Civil Service Act of 1883. . . . The real father of the movement was George William Curtis, who, with a small band of like-minded idealists, pressed the problem and the proposed solution on the public in season and out. . . .
>
> The New York Civil Service Reform Association, the first in the country, was organized in 1877. By 1881 there were at least thirteen similar associations scattered from Massachusetts to Missouri when the time seemed propitious for affiliating them with a national organization. The National Civil Service Reform League was accordingly formed and has continued in existence to the present day. . . .[9]

[9] William E. Mosher and J. Donald Kingsley, *Public Personnel Administration* (Rev. ed., New York: Harper & Bros., 1941), pp. 20–4.

More important than the question of actual initiation, then—
one can almost say that every conceivable sort of organization and
proposal is being initiated by someone—is the question of which
of this myriad of prospective causes will be taken up by service
organizations, by special interest groups, or by single-purpose reform groups. The competition will be severe, since such groups are
limited in size and number and can effectively prosecute only a few
causes at a time. Some proposals go through a long period of
incubation during which interest grows gradually to the point
where it leads to action. In other cases, dramatic events may focus
attention on a proposal that has previously gained little support.
(In the case of civil service reform the assassination of President
Garfield in 1881 served this purpose.) In still other cases, a proposal
remains peripheral and never attracts enough interest but what it
is repeatedly crowded off the agenda by other questions that seem
more vital. The proposal never gets beyond the initiation stage.

In the stage where a problem has come to be the subject of organized discussion and action, a number of concrete proposals may
evolve for its solution. The definite proposals will, in turn, focus
the discussion more sharply and bring it to the stage where legislative consideration is feasible. The evolution of concrete proposals
will also usually reveal that the various groups interested in the
problem and agreed that action is needed are not agreed as to the
precise form of action. Hence, an intricate process of compromise
will generally follow, designed to discover a proposal that will
retain the interest of diverse groups and that will receive the support of enough of them to give it a chance of legislative success.
Sometimes the final measure will bear little resemblance either in
terms of purpose or structure to the original idea of its sponsors.

It is important for the initiators to recognize in advance the
areas from which opposition is likely to arise and to develop means
for coping with such opposition. It is also necessary to have clear
objectives so that compromises can be accepted gracefully when
they do not endanger the major objectives envisaged. It is often
possible after an agency has become established to strengthen by
amendment provisions in its basic legislation that had to be compromised when it was first set up, as was done with price control
legislation during the war. There, the President signed the original
measure despite serious defects, and when the need became ap-

parent, he was able to have some of the limitations in the original act removed.

One common difficulty in the creation of new organizations is that, in their enthusiasm for the organization goals, the advocates and workers tend to develop a certain rigidity in their approach to the political process. Revisions of a minor nature are often regarded as a threat to the achievement of the goal. Since the project is evolved with a logical completeness in the minds of the initiators, they often fail to concede that minor violations of logic are quite characteristic of all organizations.

PERIODS OF EXPANSION

It is not surprising that new government organizations, particularly in the economic field, mostly originate in definite periods of governmental expansion. Wars, depressions, and similar crises create new problems requiring governmental solution and temporarily weaken the forces opposing broader governmental programs. Although some of the programs undertaken in crisis are temporary —the Works Progress Administration of the great depression, or the Office of Price Administration of the last war—each crisis seems to leave behind it a residue of new agencies. The Agricultural Adjustment Administration and the Federal Public Housing Administration are two examples of depression agencies that became permanent. Selective Service is an example of a war-time agency that became permanent.

In the case of cities, the stimulus for new programs is partly given by the growth of the city itself. As population increases, the sheriff's protection is augmented by a police department, the fire company is made an official department, private water supplies are supplanted by a municipal system, and privies are replaced by a sewer system. As growth continues, children need public play spaces, parks are developed, a library is established, and so forth. The lag between the growth of the city and the growth of its services and the role of city departments in protecting programs and budgets, once these have been established, have been investigated by William F. Ogburn. He has demonstrated that per capita budgets for various city services are generally substantially larger in cities whose populations are stable or declining than in cities that are growing rapidly.[10]

Invention and initiation also play an important role in determining the time of birth of new agencies. Once a solution to a particular problem has been invented, it will probably first be adopted in one governmental jurisdiction and then spread rapidly to a number of others. So-called "urban redevelopment" laws were first devised as a partial solution to the city slum problem about 1940. Three states adopted such laws in 1941—Illinois, Michigan, and New York; one state in 1942; four in 1943; one in 1944; eleven in 1945; three in 1946; and eleven in the two following years. In a similar manner, states like New York, Wisconsin, and Massachusetts pioneered in the adoption of certain types of social legislation at the turn of the century, setting an example that was gradually followed by other states.[11]

The Post-Natal Period

It should not be concluded from the preceding pages that the important events in the evolution of governmental programs all take place prior to the time when the birth of a new agency is legitimatized by legislative enactment. On the contrary, existing agencies are undergoing a continual process of adaptation and change that may so transform them over a span of years as to make them into almost new organizations.

The Department of Agriculture, for example, has exhibited fundamental changes in program and philosophy during a century of existence. Its first orientation was toward research: improvement of plant and animal breeds and the treatment of plant and animal diseases. In a second stage of its activity, regulatory enforcement—disease quarantines and enforcement of pure food and drug legislation—claimed more and more of its attention. Then, interest began to focus on the economic aspects of agriculture: first, the economics of farm management; then, farm marketing problems; and, finally, broad economic policies to solve the problem of de-

    [10] William F. Ogburn, *Social Characteristics of Cities* (Chicago: International City Managers' Association, 1937), pp. 66–8.
    [11] See, for example, Walter F. Dodd, *Administration of Workmen's Compensation* (New York: Commonwealth Fund, 1936), pp. 11–29.

clining markets and overproduction.[12] No one with a photograph of the infant that was christened "The Department of Agriculture" in 1862 would be prepared to recognize in this infant the full-grown giant of the same name in 1950.

DIFFERENCE BETWEEN THE PRE- AND POST-NATAL PERIODS

In a sense, the distinction between the period before and after the legislative creation of a government agency is an artificial one. The census was recognized as a Federal activity from the time of the adoption of the Constitution (since it was necessary to conduct a census in order to apportion the House of Representatives). Gradually, it was realized that the census could provide important economic and sociological data, and its scope was accordingly broadened. In 1910 a permanent organization was established to carry on the activity. Once established, the Census Bureau itself became a principal source of initiation and pressure for proposals to broaden further the census and to supplement the decennial census with more frequent surveys of manufactures and agriculture.

The principal significance of the assignment of a governmental activity to a definite, recognized organizational unit is that this step creates a group of employees who are professionally concerned with the activity on a full-time basis. This group then becomes an important point of initiation for the further development of the program. In large part, this organizational activity is tied up with the organization's struggle for survival and growth—a topic that will be treated at length in Chapters 18 and 19. Without entering at this point into the details of this process, we shall want to see what implications it has for the development and transformation of governmental programs and of the agencies that administer these programs.

DEVELOPMENTAL INFLUENCES

The evolution of agency programs is a response to influences of several different kinds. It results in part from efforts of the organization to secure the support of outside groups, in part from the

[12] Gaus and Wolcott, op. cit., chap. 1.

interpretation that employees and their professional groups give to the organization goals and programs, and in part from the changing conditions and problems of the society in which the organization operates.

Response to Outside Groups. Through constant contact, and through a recognition of political realities, an organization often undertakes active steps to secure the support of important client groups affected by its program. These client groups may have a very different set of values and conceptions of the organization program than the groups responsible for its establishment. As the price for their sympathy and support, they may insist on a voice in determining policies, and their participation in policy formation may result in major changes in the program.

The TVA provides a striking illustration of this process. Founded as an experiment in regional development, the TVA was committed from the outset to a philosophy of grass-roots participation by the inhabitants of the Tennessee Valley in policy formation. But the politically important groups in the Valley had a very different idea of regional development from the original conception of TVA. As a result, local support and participation was secured only by sacrificing important elements in the New Deal philosophy and even, in some cases, by refusal to cooperate with New Deal agencies like the Farm Credit Administration.[13] Many of the more controversial of its goals have had to be dropped or negated.

Response to Employees. Employees, particularly at the professional level, may play an important role in redirecting agency objectives. This is particularly likely when the employees form a coherent professional group that is active in defining professional goals and objectives. A city that establishes a city planning agency and employs one or more professional city planners on its staff immediately exposes itself to the conceptions of city planning that are current in the profession. These conceptions may be considerably broader than the motives that led to the establishment of the agency—perhaps the existence of a serious traffic or parking problem, or the desire to erect a civic center—and the agency's program may be correspondingly broadened.

---

[13] A penetrating analysis of the impact of "grass-roots democracy" upon the TVA program has been made by Philip M. Selznick, *TVA and the Grass Roots* (Berkeley: University of California Press, 1949).

The same sort of thing may result from the appointment to an organization of even a single administrator with strong convictions. John Studebaker, former Commissioner of the U. S. Office of Education, was strongly convinced of the value of locally-sponsored public forums as a citizenship education device. As a result, the stimulation of public forums became a much more central part of the Office of Education's program than would have been the case had someone else been commissioner.

The arrival of new members with differing ideas concerning goals can, and very often does, change the orientation of an existing organization. Making new appointments is one way in which a new political regime makes its impact on the permanent civil service. New persons with new views do not always assure the acceptance of new goals and new means to reach them, but they may do so. The gradual shift in emphasis which characterized the Federal Trade Commission in the period of Republican rule in the 1920's was largely due to the replacement of key personnel by persons with ideas concerning its functions different from those of persons who had staffed the agency at its inception. It is often through the constant replacement of personnel that new ideas and new techniques taught in the colleges are brought into the practices of the existing agencies.

Response to Changing Conditions. This third category of influences is not entirely independent of the ones already discussed. The initiation of change always takes place through *people,* and the changes that take place in society can only have their impact upon organizations through the people who are influential in those organizations.

The processes whereby problems are brought to public attention and become stimuli for changes in organization programs are virtually identical with the processes described in the earlier part of this chapter whereby problems lead to the creation of new organizations. Only two further points need to be noted. First, the fact that one or more organizations already is operating in a particular field of activity probably hastens the recognition of, and adjustment to, new problems. When the depression of 1929 created vast new problems of unemployment and destitution, existing social welfare agencies (in the area of unemployment relief), and the U. S. Department of Agriculture (in the area of agricultural relief), were major centers of initiation of new action programs.

Second, when an important new problem begins to capture public attention, existing agencies are immediately stimulated to discover aspects of their programs which can obtain additional budgetary support by being related to the burning issue of the day. When President Truman's Point Four (assistance to backward areas) was picked up by headline writers, numerous Washington agencies began to explore possibilities for capturing a part of the Point Four activity (and budget). The offices of Public Affairs and International Information, and the Office of Financial and Developmental Policy in the State Department, the Technical Assistance Division in ECA, the Office of International Trade in the Department of Commerce, and many others began to stake out their respective claims in this area.

A similar process could be seen at the beginning of the last war, when the civilian agencies of government had to justify their relevance to the war effort, and when, consequently, they began to emphasize those activities that were most easily justified on that basis. Low cost housing became housing for war workers; recreation departments set up facilities for soldiers in nearby camps; the public employment services were nationalized and turned to manpower utilization problems, and so forth.

FACTORS MAKING FOR INERTIA

Balanced against the forces that cause the gradual development and modification of organizational programs are other important forces that tend to produce resistance to change and that reduce the adaptability and flexibility of existing organizations. Most of these inertial forces are fairly obvious. They include the formation of personal and institutional habits, sunk investments of equipment and training in going programs, the use of precedent in making decisions, the human costs of dealing with the novel and the unfamiliar, and the tendency of organizations to recruit and retain persons sympathetic with their programs.

Institutions, like persons, develop habits to which values become attached. Precedent, as a justification for particular actions, is not confined to judicial agencies. Precedent conveys a certain sanctity in all administration, and there is often considerable pressure to continue to solve problems in the manner that has been tried rather than to venture out into the treacherous channels of the unknown. Siepman cites such a case in the Federal Communications Commission.[14] The agency made a particularly bad decision, admitted that it was bad, but justified it on the ground that to have done otherwise would have meant the reversal of a precedent of seventeen years standing.

These inertial tendencies are often reinforced in the recruitment and retention of personnel. Critics of the "striped pants" character of the Foreign Service point out that the Service tends to recruit college graduates in its own image—i.e., those who will "fit in"— and that the occasional maverick who sees the need for fundamental changes is gradually induced, after running against a number of blank walls, either to conform or to resign. Whether true of the Foreign Service or not, such processes certainly can be found in many organizations, and certainly are an important reason for inertia.

SUBSIDENCE OF PUBLIC INTEREST

The date of actual creation of an agency is also of importance in redirecting public discussion and controversy over the program. Once the agency has actually been set up, it usually becomes a more or less accepted part of the governmental structure, at least for a time, and the public interest that was generated by the process of its creation begins to subside. Hostility toward it on the part of its opponents will tend to be redirected toward restriction of its budget and the scope of its activities rather than outright destruction. The decision having been reached to establish it, the inertia that made its creation a difficult process will now operate to protect it against termination.

Determinants of Form and Structure

We come now to the second set of questions posed at the beginning of the chapter: what determines whether a new agency is to be placed at the Federal, the state, or the local level; and what de-

[14] Charles Siepman, *Radio's Second Chance* (Boston: Little, Brown & Co., 1945), p. 154.

termines whether it is to be incorporated in an existing department, given departmental status, or established as an "independent" agency?

At the outset, we must recognize that many arguments about form and structure are really rationalizations or concealments of arguments about substance. An effective method for opposing almost any proposal for new organization is to agree with it "in principle," but to object to the particular organizational form embodied in the measure. Thus a proposed Federal program may be attacked on the grounds that the program should be at the state level, or that the Federal government has no constitutional power to enter into the particular field in question, or that instead of assigning the program to a department under a head appointed by and removable by the President it should be headed by some kind of board or commission.

The effect of an unwanted governmental program can also sometimes be nullified by its opponents if they are able to entrust it to an organization that will be unsympathetic to it. Proposals for independent agencies headed by boards or commissions are often advanced by groups who are anti-governmental in their attitudes or who are opposed to the particular administration in power and believe that the independent agency will be less responsive to executive control than the single-headed department.[15]

Even if we grant that persons who oppose programs on organizational grounds are often rationalizing their opposition to the programs themselves, we cannot dismiss debates about form and structure as unimportant. The only reason why opposition on organizational grounds is often effective is that the groups to which such arguments are directed (although not necessarily the groups advancing the arguments) have attitudes and beliefs about the relative desirability of various organizational arrangements. Unless there were a genuine and fairly widespread states-rights sentiment in the general public, opposition to Federal programs on the ground that they invaded the proper sphere of action of the states would be simply ineffective. Hence, in examining issues of form and structure, we shall be more concerned with attitudes widely held by the American public than with the attitudes and motives of those who argue such issues in legislative debate.

[15] Whether independent agencies will *in fact* be less responsive is another question. The important point here is that they are commonly believed to be.

STATES' RIGHTS

An important argument that is a heritage from the American tradition is that of localism. American government should be held close to the people, and that can be accomplished only if various functions, particularly those offering service, are handled by states and the localities. The argument is often a smoke screen for those who well recognize that (due to the expansion of the economy, competition between states, and for other reasons) state regulation means no effective regulation at all. But the drive for state control can still evoke a strong response. For example, on the wages and hours legislation, George B. Chandler, speaking for the Ohio Chamber of Commerce against the legislation said, "What we resent is the brazen and, as we believe, illegal entry of the Federal Government within our own borders to tell us how to run our own affairs. . . . We deny the moral right and question the legal right of the United States Government to regiment our business life, to prescribe our wages, designate our hours of work, refuse us the privilege of commerce with our sister states, and fine and imprison our citizens for exercising the rights permitted by our laws and our own courts." [16] It should be pointed out that this testimony is almost identical with that of many of the leading figures during the Constitutional debates who argued against the acceptance of the Constitution in the first place. It has deep roots in American doctrine.

The growth of a complex and integrated American economy has gradually weakened the appeal of the states' rights argument. The failure of state regulation of monopolies toward the end of the nineteenth century, the need for effective national action in two world wars, and the fiscal inability of the states to meet the problems of the Great Depression have all contributed to a more favorable public attitude toward the use of national powers. Nevertheless, the broadening of national powers has been accepted more as a necessary evil than as a negation of the principle of localism, and the states' rights argument must still be reckoned with as an impressive opponent to any further extension of national functions.

Parallel to the issue of Federal versus state administration of programs is the issue of state versus county or city administration. One form in which the issue is posed is in the demand of cities for

[16] Joint Hearings on S. 2475 and H. R. 7200, pp. 866–87, June 14, 1937.

greater freedom to determine their own local governmental programs without undue restriction by the states. Here the root of the political trouble generally lies in the lack of confidence of the cities in state legislatures dominated by rural representatives.

In the past fifteen years, there has also been extensive controversy as to the allocation of public welfare functions among state, county, and city agencies. In 1939, a survey of the organization of general relief programs showed that in 14 states the programs were conducted by local agencies with substantially no state supervision; in 15 states there was very limited state supervision; in 11 states there was extensive state supervision; while in 8 states a state agency had primary responsibility for relief administration.[17]

Complex political processes, varying in their pattern from state to state, have produced this result. The political forces supporting and opposing local administration of relief programs in California were succinctly summarized as follows:

> Welfare administrators appearing before the Section agree that all welfare service should be integrated either at the state or at the county level.
>
> However, for the last seven years the Governor and the Legislature have been unable to agree upon these steps to establish a properly organized, non-political centralized system covering all the public assistance services. Whatever the theoretical advantages of state centralization, it is now outside the range of political feasibility. . . .
>
> "Home rule" is a chief argument for complete county control. . . .
>
> Desire for power enters into any argument for control. Ambitious local officials dislike "dictation" from above whether state or federal, regardless of benefits to local citizens.
>
> Protection of vested interests is another factor. Employer groups can more easily control small independent units of a public welfare agency than they can a strong state-wide organization, especially as to the amount of assistance to be paid and who shall qualify for it.
>
> Liberal or radical groups, however, seem to have found it easier to influence a centralized state welfare administration than local units.[18]

[17] Illinois Legislative Council, *The Administration of Relief in Illinois* (Springfield: The Council, 1940), p. 9.

[18] "Report of Municipal and County Government Section of the Commonwealth Club of California," *The Commonwealth* 17:394 (February 18, 1941). In further explanation of these comments, which substantiate several of the hypotheses set forth here, it should be pointed out that at the time of this report the Governor of California was a Democrat while the State Senate and most of the rural county governments were under Republican control.

GOVERNMENT OF LAWS

Another attitude that strongly influences the form of governmental organization is the American reverence for "the law" and for particular legal forms in carrying out governmental action. There is a deep-seated feeling that the court system successfully prevents tyranny and that anything which smacks of "arbitrariness" or personal power is bad. Everything should be reduced to the written word, and where discretion is necessary it should be limited by definite criteria and standards and subject to court review.

Thus, in the debate over wages and hours legislation, an early proposal that the minimum wages be set by a board after a hearing to determine the facts affecting each particular industry met with bitter opposition as an excessive delegation of power to administrators. Arthur Besse, representing the National Association of Wool Manufacturers, stated that his association "can see nothing but disaster resulting from the attempt to endow a board with power to set any and all standards of labor remuneration based on criteria of which the board itself is sole judge. . . . I want to add our voice to the others raised in protest against this delegation and surrender of power on the part of Congress. . . ." [19]

At least in part because of this criticism, the bill was changed to provide a flat minimum wage stated in the bill itself and to place enforcement of the law in the hands of a single administrator.

INDEPENDENCE VERSUS EXECUTIVE RESPONSIBILITY

The question almost always arises as to whether a new organization is to be headed by a single official reporting to the chief executive, by an appointive board or commission, or by an elective executive or board. At the present time there is seldom any strong support for the creation of new elective offices. However, both the single executive and the appointive board have their strong advocates, and attitudes favoring both of these arrangements are prevalent.

The single executive directly responsible to the chief executive has been a form generally favored by those advocating governmental reorganization as a means of improving governmental

[19] Hearings, op. cit., pp. 556–71, June 9, 1937.

efficiency. At the beginning of the century the short-ballot movement sought to reduce the number of city and state department
heads that were directly elected and hence independent of the
chief executive. During the nineteen-twenties the state reorganization movement aimed at the same objective. The council-manager form of city government, providing for a single appointive
professional manager to whom the department heads report, represents the same general philosophy. This viewpoint can also be
found in the 1937 reorganization proposals of the President's Committee on Administrative Management, which recommended the
abolition of the U. S. Civil Service Commission and a number of
other Federal independent agencies and their replacement by
single-headed departments.[20]

The proponents of this type of organization structure have generally stressed two arguments. First, such organizations would
conform to the general principles of efficient administrative organization that had been developed by students of business organization. Second, integration under the chief executive would
create clear lines of administrative responsibility extending back
from the executive to the legislative body and ultimately to the
voting public.

There are also strong arguments against integration and in
favor of independent boards. The independent board has been
extolled as taking particular governmental programs "out of
politics." That is, it is argued that such boards will be less subject
to partisan pressures and machine influence than will single executives. In particular, this argument is widely accepted by groups
interested in promoting specific governmental functions. Planning
officials generally believe that city planning agencies should adopt
the board form; recreation officials believe the same of recreation
agencies; educators of school systems; and so forth. In these cases,
support for the independent board is largely a reflection of the desire for autonomy and freedom from control by the chief executive
and the city council.[21]

---

[20] For a discussion of this whole movement, and references to the voluminous
literature, see Waldo, *The Administrative State*.

[21] What little objective evidence exists does not substantiate the hypothesis
that the independent board is actually an effective means for taking an activity
"out of politics." The two best studies are Robert A. Walker, *The Planning Function
in Urban Government* (Chicago: University of Chicago Press, 1941), and Jerome J.
Kerwin and Nelson B. Henry, *Schools and City Government* (Chicago: University of

The board form has also been proposed for agencies carrying on regulatory programs and performing functions of a "quasi-judicial" character. In this case, the argument for an independent board becomes an argument for impartiality—for a "government of laws and not of men."

Legal Limitations and Organization Form

All governmental organizations have some ultimate legal basis in either a Constitution (national or state) or in laws passed by Congress or a state legislature. To be sure, some Federal organizations are originated by an Executive Order of the President, or even more informally, but such actions always occur within the framework of some more general legal authorization. Securing the proper legal basis raises problems of a particular nature for those who would originate a governmental organization. It also may have important effects upon the form that the organization will take.

THE LEGISLATURE AND ORGANIZATION FORM

Legislative bodies have the legal power to determine the structure of new administrative organizations to any extent they desire and likewise to change the structure of existing organizations. The legislation launching a new governmental organization may carry a very extended description of the new organization's structure, or may leave such questions to the people who will run the new organization. Consequently, conditions surrounding the legislative birth may be crucial in determining whether the new organization is to be a monster, so to speak, or a normal, healthy child.

Amateur "organization experts" among the legislators may trot out their favorite "principles of organization." Representatives of hostile interest groups may try to thwart the new organization and its program from the beginning by getting crippling structural arrangements written into the basic act. Lawyers in the legislative body (and there will always be many) may try to force the new organization into the mold of the organization with which

Chicago Press, 1938). In neither case are the authors, by virtue of previous training and association, entirely free from suspicion of holding an "integrationist" bias.

they are usually most familiar—a court of law. Well-meaning friends may try to forestall the tactics of the enemy by freezing certain aspects of structure in the basic legislation as a future protection against hostile pressure groups.

Because of the many points of view and conflicts concerning regulatory activities, a new regulatory organization is much more likely to suffer birth scars (and scars from post-natal operations) than is a service organization. A municipal fire department may find its basic authorization in a sentence or phrase in the city charter or state statutes, while the structure of the city zoning agency may be the subject of several pages of legislative act.

To avoid these difficulties attendant on birth, proponents of new governmental activities very often try to make use of the existing body of law (insofar as a liberal interpretation of the law will allow) rather than go through the process of enacting new law. Also, there is every temptation on the part of those who administer government organizations already in existence to keep the structure intact rather than to risk the perils of proposing changes to the legislature.

In 1938, the experience of a year had shown the administrators of the Wages and Hours Act that it was deficient in many respects. Accordingly, amendments to the Act were proposed. But the amendments could not be confined to the procedural improvements desired by the agency. Instead, opponents of wages and hours legislation were offered an opportunity to propose substantive amendments to the Act that would, if adopted, have crippled the operations of the agency. Consequently, the administration's proposed amendments were withdrawn.

THE PROBLEM OF JUDICIAL REVIEW

Not only do governmental organizations have to be in a form that will satisfy the legislature; they must also be set up in such a way that they can meet with the approval of the courts. This means that they must meet what the United States and state Supreme Courts have considered to be the standards of constitutionality. Thus, in framing the basic legislation, the originators must attempt to predict what the courts will do when they review the activities of the new organization.

The review of constitutionality extends, of course, to the substance of each governmental activity as well as to the form of the organization set up to administer it. A particular program may be illegal in any form because it is considered by the courts to deprive private individuals of their life, liberty, or property without due process of law. The test of "due process" was an extremely difficult hurdle for both state and federal legislation during the period from about 1880 down to 1937, when the United States Supreme Court was generally dominated by a majority of justices to whom "due process" meant something akin to *laisser faire.*

Through this judicial test, the anti-governmental attitudes embodied in conservative American opinion became, for a time, a part of the constitutional law. Since 1937, when a liberal majority gained control of the court, the test of substantive due process has proved to be a relatively simple one to meet. In general, the state courts have followed the United States Supreme Court in liberalizing the concept of due process, but the due process clauses of some state constitutions are still applied to limit the permissible sphere of governmental activity.

During this same period of conservative control of the United States Supreme Court, constitutional requirements also had a great deal of influence upon the placing of programs at the state rather than the national level. For example, a narrow interpretation of the powers of the national government prevented Congress from legislating against child labor under either its commerce or its taxing powers.[22] There can be little doubt that, with a more liberal interpretation of national powers, the Federal government would have undertaken some activities that instead were located at the state level. The Supreme Court became during this period an important source of influence not only for the *laisser faire* philosophy but for the doctrine of states' rights as well.

This situation has also been changed by the liberal majority on the Court since 1937, and the Constitution does not, at the moment at least, present a serious barrier to the location of governmental agencies at the national level. Nevertheless, the Court's earlier position has had its continuing effect, both upon organizations already in existence when the change in position took place and also

[22] *Hammer v. Dagenhart* 247 U. S. 251 (1918); *Bailey v. Drexel Furniture Company* 259 U. S. 20 (1922).

upon the minds of those who draft new Federal legislation. It no doubt partly accounts for the continued extensive use of grants-in-aid rather than direct national administration of programs.

On the side of organization structure and procedure, constitutional requirements are still of considerable practical importance. Among the important rules are: (1) the requirement of separation of powers; (2) the limitation upon the delegation of legislative powers; and (3) the requirement of proper procedures in regulation of private persons (procedural due process). These rules are of principal importance in relation to regulatory agencies.

Under the doctrine of separation of powers, administrative agencies must not be permitted to exercise legislative or judicial functions. At the time when the early state regulatory agencies were established, this doctrine gave the courts considerable trouble. When state utility commissions issued rules for the conduct of utility companies were they not legislating? And when they found a particular utility to be in violation of the rules and issued a corrective order were they not adjudicating? The courts, impressed by the usefulness of the independent regulatory agency as a governmental device, solved the problem by inventing the terms "quasi-legislative" and "quasi-judicial" to distinguish the things that administrative agencies were doing from the activities that legislatures and courts had always carried on. Whether or not such distinctions can be justified on logical grounds, they have served to remove the limits that the doctrine of separation of powers would otherwise have placed upon the forms of government regulation.

The doctrine that the legislative power, being a delegated power, cannot be re-delegated is closely allied to the doctrine of separation of powers. Its main practical effect has been to require a more detailed legislative specification of the powers and procedures of administrative agencies than would otherwise have been necessary or desirable. Thus, when the power to make rules is delegated to an administrative agency, the act of delegation must set standards to govern the rule-making power and safeguards to assure that the standards will be applied.

At the present time, the constitutional requirement of greatest significance is that one which requires due process to be observed in government regulation. In the first place, the requirement has some rather specific influences on the structure of regulatory agencies. Although the courts have never insisted upon it as a constitutional requirement, there is a general attitude that a board or commission is the appropriate organ for the exercise of rule-making and judicial powers.[23] In the second place, there has been a general belief that within the regulatory agency there should be some separation between the prosecuting and the judging functions. Whether it would actually be unconstitutional in the eyes of the courts for the same persons to exercise both functions is a debatable point of constitutional law.

An even more important consequence of the requirement of due process is a procedural one. To meet the due process requirements the rules and regulations governing the activities of administrative bodies must meet traditional legal standards which may or may not suit the needs of the agency. Since court opinion cannot be predicted with any certainty, accepted patterns will usually be followed in drafting legislation to avoid the risk that the procedures will later be found illegal. Another consequence is that the lawyer as a lawyer comes to occupy a key position in American administration. Most action must be screened by attorneys, and the process of planning new activities very often falls to persons trained in the legal profession. Quite naturally, attorneys will tend to draft legislation not only to meet the legal limits of the courts but to satisfy their own professional standards as attorneys. Their views on administrative arrangements are often not acceptable to persons trained in professional disciplines other than the law.[24]

Conclusion

In this chapter we have presented an over-all picture of the process whereby a new government organization comes into existence. As we have seen, the process begins with the recognition of a problem by some person or small group and a belief that the problem can be handled only through governmental activity. The problem, like a

[23] The only actual point of constitutional law depending directly on the character of these functions was the limitation upon the removal power of the President over members of independent regulatory commissions imposed in the decision in *Rathbun v. U. S.* 295 U. S. 602 (1935).

[24] See Jerome Frank, *If Men Were Angels* (New York: Harper & Bros., 1942); also, F. M. Blachly and M. Oatman, "Sabotage of the Administrative Process," *Public Administration Review*, 6:213-227 (Summer, 1947).

stone cast into a pond, creates an ever-widening circle of ripples as it comes to the attention of new groups and individuals.

Each new group that is exposed to the influence of a group of initiators will respond in terms of its particular beliefs, interests, awarenesses, and motivations. If a proposal is appropriate in time and place, it may receive a ready response and soon be embodied in a concrete organizational form. If it lies outside of the experiences and interests of those to whom appeal is made, response will be lacking and the efforts of the initiating group will very likely soon be dissipated.

The rest of this book will be devoted largely to the study of organizations already in existence. But the central concept of this chapter—the idea that the growth and decline of organizations is determined by an interplay between the organization goals and the motives and interests of the individuals participating in them—will provide a central theme for our whole study of administration.

CHAPTER THREE

Human Behavior and Organization

THE present chapter will focus attention upon the individual employee of governmental organizations, upon the forces that account for his behavior, and upon the influences that the organization brings to bear on him in order to secure his contribution to the organization's tasks. At first sight there hardly seems to be a problem here. If we employ a man to direct activities at a playground, *of course* he will spend his time each day from nine to five at the playground; *of course* he will organize and direct play activities there; *of course* he will carry out the policies formulated by the directors of the organization who are responsible for planning its program. Only the many instances of organization failure—instances where an organization does not carry out its task or where it succeeds at an excessive economic and human cost—warn us that there is really nothing automatic about the process.

Organizational behavior is such an obvious part of everyday experience that we are seldom conscious of the psychological reasons for its successes and failures. We sometimes forget that an organization is a group of *people* behaving. These people are not tools or machines. They have feelings, hopes, and fears. They get sick, hungry, angry, frustrated, happy, sad. Their behavior is subject to a whole range of influences extending back to their births (and before, many psychologists believe) and impinging upon them from all directions at every moment. Their behavior in organizations is a resultant of all these influences. Some of the more important of the influences will be described in this chapter.

Characteristics of Behavior in Organizations

A person can do but a limited number of things at any particular time. However, there are a nearly unlimited number of things he might be doing at that time. To explain a person's behavior, we must understand why he is doing what he is doing in a particular way rather than something else or in another way.

Joe Smith, armed with a heavy axe, is cutting a hole in the roof of a building. Why? When we are told that Joe Smith is a city fireman and that the building is on fire, his behavior becomes comprehensible to us. We can picture a whole series of steps leading up to his behavior at this moment. At some time in the past Joe Smith made up his mind to be a fireman and took steps to get a job in the city fire department. In so doing he ruled out a whole range of possible occupations in favor of the one he actually took up. When he joined the department he was instructed in fire-fighting techniques—appropriate ways to behave at fires if one is trying to put them out. Then he was assigned to a particular fire company out of the dozen or so in his city. This assignment determined which fires he would fight and which he would not and whose instructions he would follow at the scene of a fire. An hour ago an alarm sent him to this fire (he might otherwise be pitching horseshoes at the station house), and the company captain sent him to the roof with the axe where his former training instructed him where a hole should be cut.

This explanation of Joe Smith's behavior is, of course, very incomplete. If he is working slowly and carelessly, we may find that he dislikes the company captain and is resentful of his instructions; or he may not be feeling well on this particular day; or he may have been poorly instructed; or he may be afraid of falling through the weakened roof, and his fear may cause him to forget his training. All of these things and undoubtedly many others are influencing his behavior. Some of the influences are conscious, many unconscious; some are rational, some irrational; some are consistent with the goal of the organization, some inconsistent.

Those aspects of human behavior that involve conscious choice are the easiest to study. The selection of a profession and the acceptance of a particular job are important examples of such choices, but so are all the multitude of decisions that any individual makes every hour of his life.

For example, the playground director says to himself: "It looks like rain today. I will have to organize some indoor activities. I wonder if I could start a basketball game among these boys here." Or perhaps he is confronted with a discipline problem and says to himself: "John doesn't seem to be having much fun, and he is always bothering the smaller children. Shall I send him home, or can I find some activity he would enjoy that will keep him out of trouble?" Or he sees that one of the tennis nets is worn and wonders whether he should requisition another from the equipment storehouse or whether he should leave it for a few days. The activity of a recreation department is simply the sum total of all these behaviors of the playground directors and other employees. The success of the department in carrying on a recreation program is determined by the appropriateness of these behaviors.

There are equally important behaviors that are unconscious, determined by previously developed habits and skills. A competent typist "decides" several times a second which keys of the typewriter to strike and which fingers to use in striking them. If she has been thoroughly trained, the choices are made by her fingers rather than her head. Yet just such behaviors as these—built into employees' habits and conditioned reactions—will determine the efficiency of an administrative organization.

BEHAVIOR PREMISES

Important in the explanation of organization behavior are the *premises* upon which employees behave—that is, the criteria or guides they use in narrowing down the multitude of possibilities to the single actuality. Before the recreation director decides to requisition a new tennis net, he probably considers such points as: (a) how worn is the old one—will it likely go to pieces at any moment?; (b) how much are the tennis courts used—could we get along for a few days with one out of use?; (c) has the head of the department laid down any rules as to when equipment should be replaced? Whether or not the director decides to request a new net will depend on his answers to these and other questions.

In explaining behavior in terms of the "premises" of the actor, we are concerned primarily with behavior that is conscious and rational. As already noted, much human behavior is neither conscious nor rational. In many cases the actor cannot explain why he behaves in a particular way—or if he does explain, the explanation is simply a rationalization of the real unconscious motivations. Since organizations are set up to accomplish purposes, the study of administration must necessarily be concerned with the rational aspects of human behavior. But if we are to explain the failures of organizations as well as their successes, we must also understand non-rational behavior. In a later section of this chapter some of the non-rational aspects of behavior will be discussed; for the present, the emphasis will be upon those behaviors that can be analyzed as deliberate and purposive choices.

Close examination of the premises that underlie any administrative choice will show that they involve two distinct kinds of elements: *value elements* and *factual elements*. Speaking very roughly, the distinction between value elements and factual elements corresponds to the distinction between *ends* and *means*, respectively. Before an individual can rationally choose between several courses of action, he must ask himself: (1) "What is my objective—my goal?" and (2) "Which of these courses of action is best suited to that goal?"

Examples of values that the playground director would have to consider in dealing with a disciplinary problem would be: "Is it the aim of the recreation department to provide wholesome recreational activities only for normal, adjusted children, or does the department also assume some responsibility for remedial work with problem children? If both aims are to be considered, what relative weights should be given them?" An example of factual considerations would be: "What will happen to John if I send him home? If I permit him to stay, is his unruly behavior apt to be contagious with the other children?" The former set of questions involves values and is presumably to be settled by reference to the organization objectives. The latter set of questions is purely factual, although the answers to them may not be precisely known and may require considerable judgment and "common sense."

It would be very useful and convenient if the premises of administrative choices could always be divided sharply into factual premises and value premises. Unfortunately, a clear separation of these two types of premises is not usually possible. Almost every value premise has some factual element imbedded in it—an element that cannot be completely removed—because most ends or goals are at least partly means to more final ends rather than ends in themselves. For example, when asking for its budget appropriation the recreation department may argue that play for children is not merely an end in itself but also an essential means for preparing these children for useful adulthood. The budget decision then hinges on the *values* to be realized, but it also raises the factual question of how much effect *in fact* the play activity of a child has upon his subsequent behavior as an adult.

This difficult problem of separating the value elements in choice from the factual elements cannot be examined in detail in this book. It will suffice for our purposes if the reader understands that the justification of any choice depends, first, on the ends to be achieved and, second, on the appropriateness of the particular course of action chosen for the realization of these ends. The stated ends or goals of an administrative choice can usually be further analyzed as means to some more final goals.[1]

SOME IMPORTANT VALUE PREMISES

There are certain types of value premises that we will encounter repeatedly in organization decisions. Perhaps the most important of these are (1) the organization objectives, (2) the criterion of efficiency, (3) standards of fair play, and (4) the personal values of the individual making the decision.

The Organization Objective. We have seen in the example of the recreation department that the *organization objective* is one of the important value premises that enters into almost every administrative choice. A basic test of any proposed course of action is whether it will contribute to the organization objective. Determining the objective of an organization usually involves not only questions of what values the activity is to be directed toward, but also what groups of people it is to serve and what level or quality of service it is to provide. Thus, the recreation department will have to decide to what extent it is interested in character-building or in health-building programs; it will have to decide whether it will provide activities for the whole community or whether it will con-

---

[1] The reader who wishes to pursue this question further will find a more complete analysis in Simon, *Administrative Behavior*, chaps. 3 and 4.

centrate on low-income areas where families are least able to provide their own recreation facilities; it will have to decide whether to operate its playgrounds on a year-round basis or only in the summers.

In the previous chapter, the intimate connection between the organization objective and the process by which a new organization comes into existence was pointed out. In later chapters (particularly Chapter 18) it will become equally clear that the organization objective is of vital significance in the survival and continued existence of the organization. The organization will receive support from groups that approve its objective; it will be attacked by those that oppose it. Particular groups may seek to capture the organization and put it to work for their own purposes.

Consider, for example, the attitude of the agricultural bloc in Congress toward program planning activities in the Bureau of Agricultural Economics. This agency was attacked by Congressman Tarver in the 1945 hearings of the Appropriations Committee because he felt that it was paying some attention to the interests of consumers instead of planning solely in the interests of agriculture! Said the Congressman: "While the information it furnishes should, of course, be accurate, (the Bureau of Agricultural Economics) is supposed primarily to be working for the benefit of agriculture and of the farmer and . . . too much of its effort has been devoted to an attempt to prove that the condition of the farmer is satisfactory, and that he is being accorded a fair deal in comparison with other classes." [2]

Efficiency. A second value premise involved in most administrative choices is the *criterion of efficiency.* This may be stated: "If two courses of action will give the same results in terms of the organization objective, that one should be preferred which involves the smaller cost"; [3] or, alternatively, "If two courses of action involve the same cost, that one should be preferred which will give the greater results." This premise underlies almost all acts of rational

[2] Quoted by Charles M. Hardin, "The Bureau of Agricultural Economics Under Fire," *Journal of Farm Economics* 28 (August, 1946), p. 650, from 90 Congressional Record 2941, March 22, 1941.

[3] The term "cost" here refers to the entire social cost, of which the money cost may be only a small part. Unpleasant or unhealthy work conditions for employees, for example, would represent a cost, even if this were not reflected in the wages paid. For more exact definitions of "efficiency" and "cost" see Chapter 23, below, where the relation of the efficiency criterion to organized activity will be examined at length.

choice. In fact, some writers have argued that the whole science and art of administration is concerned with the efficient use of resources by administrative organizations.[4]

Fair Play. A third set of value premises, of particular importance when an agency regulates the activities of private persons, are *standards of "fair play."* It has always been a fundamental principle in our governmental system that when government regulates it must do so with proper regard for the rights of individuals. The methods of regulation and enforcement must not be arbitrary; they must satisfy certain standards of "due process." Even the confessed criminal must have his day in court. Hence, in the selection of regulatory methods, consideration is given not only to their effectiveness from the standpoint of enforcement, but also to whether the procedures properly safeguard rights of person and property. In the same way, the rules and regulations that apply to employees themselves are expected to be fair and equitable and not show favoritism. A clerk in the Department of the Interior, for example, should not receive higher pay than a clerk doing the same kind of work in the Department of Commerce.

Personal Values. The values mentioned thus far are all "organizational" in the sense that they refer to the achievement of the organization's goals. The personal values of the employee himself also enter into his decisions. For example, how rapidly or slowly he works may depend quite as much upon his personal comfort or his drive for recognition as upon the requirements of the organization. Employees constantly evaluate decisions, consciously and unconsciously, in terms of their own personal goals: possible salary increases or promotions, relations with superiors and subordinates, status in the organization, physical comfort, and the like.

The survival and success of any organization depend upon its ability to get employees and other participants to behave in terms of organization values to a sufficient extent. Personal values interfere with the operation of the organization when they lead to behavior that conflicts with the requirements of the organization values. For example, a supervisor may keep an incompetent person in a strategic position because that person is a personal friend. As another example, employees frequently restrict output—in con-

---

[4] See for example, Luther Gulick, "Science, Values and Public Administration," in L. Gulick and L. Urwick, eds., *Papers on the Science of Administration* (New York: Institute of Public Administration, 1937), pp. 191–5.

flict with the value of efficiency—because they fear the intentions of management to force a speed-up, or because they fear some of them will be discharged as superfluous if average production rises.

On the positive side, the organization appeals to personal values as inducements to the employees to behave in terms of the organizational values. That is, it offers inducements or rewards for behavior that contributes to the organizational values and imposes penalties on behavior that conflicts with those values. Salary increases for meritorious work and wage incentive plans that reward high production are among the most obvious examples of material incentives that the organization offers to employees. In the federal government, for example, (and in many other governmental jurisdictions) employees are rated periodically by their supervisors, and those who receive sufficiently high ratings are given salary increases.

Incentives, then, are the appeals that the organization makes to the personal values of the employee in order to induce him to accept the organization's values in making his choices and decisions. Chester I. Barnard has set forth a rather comprehensive list of such incentives that may be summarized briefly here.[5]

1. Material inducements—money or goods;
2. Opportunities for distinction, prestige, and personal power;
3. Desirable physical conditions of work—clean, quiet surroundings, for example, or a private office;
4. Pride of workmanship, service for family or others, patriotism, or religious feeling (what Barnard calls "ideal benefactions");
5. Personal comfort and satisfaction in the social relationships of the organization;
6. Conformity to habitual practices and attitudes—familiarity with, and acceptance of, the customs and behavior patterns of the organization;
7. Feeling of participation in large and important events.[6]

[5] Chester I. Barnard, *The Functions of the Executive* (Cambridge: Harvard University Press, 1938), pp. 142–8.

[6] It is interesting to compare Mr. Barnard's list with the list of personal goals proposed by E. Wight Bakke: (1) respect of fellows; (2) creature sufficiency; (3) increasing control over one's own affairs; (4) "knowing the score"; (5) full utilization of one's capacities; (6) the desire to experience consistency within one's self, among the parts of one's world, and a significant relationship to that world. Cited in Neil W. Chamberlain, *The Union Challenge to Management Control* (New York: Harper & Bros., 1948), p. 247.

The reader can probably supply examples from his own experience of the ways in which each of these types of inducement enhances his personal willingness to contribute to organizational goals and values.

One point about Mr. Barnard's list deserves special comment. Like virtually all modern writers on this subject, Mr. Barnard emphasizes that material incentives—salaries, wages, or bonuses—are probably not the most important influences that induce an employee to give his active and enthusiastic support to an organization. Employees may "go along" with an organization and do a routine job for an employer because of the salary they receive, but few will produce at a high level or exercise much initiative unless they receive non-material satisfactions as well and unless the mores of the work group—the attitudes of their fellow-workers—encourage high production.[7]

Interplay of Values. The interplay of organizational and personal values can be studied to good advantage in conference situations.[8] If we watch a group of administrators engaged in a conference—say a meeting of division heads with their bureau chief discussing a proposed reorganization of the bureau—we see their behavior influenced by a wide range of values.

At the verbal level, the proposal will probably be discussed in terms of organizational values. That is, if we examine what is actually *said* in the conference, almost all of the discussion will be concerned with the supposed consequences of the proposed reorganization for the organization's goals and values. Division Head Jones recommends the proposal on the grounds that it will enable the bureau to do its job with a smaller staff—that is, more efficiently. Smith opposes it, arguing that clients of the agency will be

[7] The first careful demonstrations of this point were the "Hawthorne" studies. See Fritz J. Roethlisberger and William J. Dickson, *Management and the Worker* (Cambridge: Harvard University Press, 1939). A more recent study by Dalton shows clearly that "rate-busters"—workers who make high production records in defiance of informal limits imposed by the work group—are persons who are unusually interested in financial incentives and unusually insensitive to the opinions of their fellows.

[8] The late Kurt Lewin and his associates made important pioneering studies, now being continued at the University of Michigan and elsewhere, of behavior in conferences. The discussion here is based upon the work of this group of investigators and the largely independent work on the social organization of factories by the "Hawthorne Group." See Roethlisberger and Dickson, op. cit., and the bibliography at the end of this book.

inconvenienced by having to deal with three separate divisions instead of only one, as previously.

But in order to understand what is going on in the minds of Jones, Smith, and the other conference members and why they are taking particular positions, we must pay attention also to their personal values—largely unexpressed and partly unconscious. Although Smith may refuse to admit it even to himself, his opposition may be based on the fact that under the reorganization his division will have a smaller, less important job—perhaps will suffer an actual reduction in staff. Robinson may side with Smith because he is a rival of Jones for promotion.

Even more deeply buried in the subconscious mind will be motivations based upon satisfactions or dissatisfactions arising out of the conference process itself. Trimble, a fourth division head, is an insecure individual who desperately needs a feeling of solidarity with the group. If he senses that the group has reached a nearly unanimous position for or against the proposal, he will probably make a little speech expressing his agreement with the views of the others. If strong disagreement persists, he will most likely remain silent—and vaguely uncomfortable. The division chief, Wilson, who supports the reorganization, is a strong-willed individual and tries to influence the conference by talking a great deal in favor of the proposal. The feeling that he is being "pressured" by Wilson and Jones brings Ambly, who always wants to have a "say" in matters, into the ranks of the opposition.

The more evenly balanced the advantages and disadvantages of the proposal in terms of organization values and calculated personal advantage, the more likely is it that these partially unconscious and non-rational personal motives will largely determine the positions of the conference members. The outcome of a conference may depend heavily upon the personal satisfactions and dissatisfactions arising out of the conference process itself.

SOME IMPORTANT TYPES OF FACTUAL PREMISES

It is not easy to catalogue in a significant way the wide range of factual considerations that enter into administrative choices. The variety of factual knowledge required in administration is as broad as the variety of activities that government carries on and the variety of technologies it uses.

It is useful to distinguish *skills and knowledge* that enable employees to deal with a wide variety of situations from *information* about current situations that is needed to apply these basic skills to the specific problems at hand. A forest ranger is trained in techniques (skills and knowledge) for dealing with forest fires. Before he can cope with an actual fire, he must be informed where it is, how large it is, what the wind and weather conditions are, and so forth.

The distinction just made is significant because these two types of factual premises are acquired by the organization employee in different ways. In the one case, it is a matter of training and experience to develop permanent skills and abilities. In the other case, it is a matter of on-the-spot information that must be obtained by direct observation or by prompt communication.

Many government agencies have specialized units whose function it is to see that employees possess the correct factual premises for dealing with their jobs: *training* units for transmitting to employees skills and knowledge; *intelligence* units for collecting and communicating current information. Specialized training and intelligence functions are highly developed in military organizations, but they can be found in most large civilian organizations as well. An example of the first is the recruit training school of a fire department, of the second, the communications division in a police department.

Among the facts that influence employees' behavior are knowledge and information about what other members of the organization are doing or will do. If the playground director knows that the tennis net will not be replaced unless he reports its condition, he will act differently than if he knows that equipment is periodically inspected and maintained by a special group of employees. The whole process of "coordination" is largely concerned with giving each member of the organization an understanding of what his particular tasks are in relation to those of other employees.

Influences Upon the Premises of Behavior

The differences between the behavior of an employee of an organization and the behavior we would expect from him if he were not in the organization are due largely to the influences of other members of the organization upon him. In fact, in all but the very smallest organizations we have many employees (the "executives" and "supervisors") whose main contribution to the organization is made through their influence upon the behavior of other ("operative") employees. Thus, the head of the recreation department does not himself conduct children's games, but through the influences he is able to exert upon playground directors he may have a great deal to do with what games are played and how they are conducted. Similarly, the fire chief puts out fires only through his indirect influence upon the behavior of the firemen who handle the hoses, ladders, and axes.

Hence, if we are to understand what goes on in an administrative organization, we must understand how the organization influences its members in their decisions. It is to this task that we turn next.

THE CUMULATIVE EFFECT OF INFLUENCES

The choice an individual will make in any situation is compounded from (1) his skills, knowledge, character, and personality, as these have been formed by the whole of his life's previous experiences and (2) the specific influences that act upon him at the time of decision. In most situations, the former will be vastly more important than the latter in determining his behavior. When the playground director changes his program of activities for the day because the weather looks bad, he is reacting to an immediate stimulus, but this stimulus will not have any effect on his decisions tomorrow or the day after. It does not in any way alter his skills or his personality.

On the other hand, if the director handles his disciplinary problem by shaming John for annoying the smaller children, he may simply be repeating a pattern of behavior that was impressed upon him many years earlier, when he himself was disciplined by his parents. This earlier influence has been "internalized"—has become a permanent part of the director's personality or attitudes. Another director whose childhood experiences have molded him differently might have handled the situation in quite another way —say, by warning John that he would call a policeman. A third director influenced by college training in child psychology might have approached the same situation by first seeking the causes of

John's aggressive behavior. In each case, the director's solution would reflect the cumulative effect of a whole mass of his earlier experiences—experiences that had been significant enough or often enough repeated to become an integral part of his habits of behavior.

The overwhelming weight of these long-range "internalized" reactions is of great importance for the processes of administration. It accounts for the tremendous inertia that is found in any organization—not inertia in the sense of laziness but of unwillingness and inability to alter patterns of behavior that have become habitual and fixed. Every police chief who has tried to impress on his men the futility of "bawling out" traffic offenders has felt the force of this inertia. A policeman's wrathful exhibition of authority to an erring motorist is probably not the result of a carefully reasoned decision that this course of action will discourage a repetition of the offense; it is more likely an expression of inmost forces in the policeman's personality—forces of which he may be largely unaware.

It follows that the most important influences the organization can exercise on its employees are those long-range, cumulative influences that are internalized and become part of their outlooks and personalities. For example, the recreation department might conduct a thorough training program for new playground directors, including training in the handling of discipline problems. Or the department might employ as playground directors only persons who have had college training in child psychology.

THE RANGE OF INFLUENCES

Postponing for the moment a discussion of the specific ways in which an organization influences the behavior of its employees, it will be useful to survey first the range of influences—those outside as well as those inside the organization—that determine the employees' behavior. It is convenient to group these influences in four classes:

(1) Conditioning that the individual received before he became a member of the organization. Included here would be his previous education and work experience as well as the whole mass of experiences that were formative of his personality and character.

(2) Influences upon the employee while a member of the organization but from sources outside the organization. The organization

occupies his time and attention only a certain number of hours each week. He may be affiliated with a union or a professional association. He may be happily or unhappily married. Any number of such outside influences are at work on him.

(3) Influences upon the employee through formal organizational processes. The distinction between "formal" and "informal" aspects of organization will be developed at a later point. For the present, we may cite as examples of formal influences the assignment to him of particular duties or responsibilities, direct orders, training programs, statistical reports, and the like.

(4) Influences upon the employee through the informal social structure that develops in the organization. Friendships grow up between particular organization members. Certain employees eat lunch together regularly. Loyalties, rivalries, and jealousies develop. All of these and similar phenomena may exercise a powerful influence upon choice and behavior.

Influences From Outside the Organization

It would be impossible to treat here all the influences from outside the organization (the first two of the four categories just listed) that affect the behaviors of employees. A thorough examination of these influences would have to include the whole subject-matter of psychology and would carry us far afield from the problems of public administration.

For our purposes, we can be satisfied with something less than a survey of the whole field of human behavior. We will look specifically at those prior influences and experiences that are of greatest significance for an understanding of administration. The most important of these are: (1) generalized community attitudes and behavior patterns, forming a part of society's folkways and *mores*, that tell the individual how it is appropriate for him to behave in administrative situations; (2) elements of personality that are of particular importance in administrative activity; (3) conditioning from experiences in "outside" organizations—the family, church, labor union, political club; and (4) formal education, training, and previous work experience.

In the case of the recreation director, an example of the influence of community mores would be his feeling that he should be loyal to any organization in which he participates. An example of an important personality trait would be his shyness in dealing with other people. An example of the influence of an "outside" organization might be his interest in the problem of juvenile delinquency developed through participation in a Rotary Club committee on delinquency. An example of the influence of formal training would be the skills he has developed in a college course on group leadership.

INFLUENCE OF COMMUNITY MORES

The *mores* of a society are those established patterns of behavior that are enforced on all members of the society by the attitudes of social approval or disapproval of their fellows. In our society, for example, a woman would soon be ostracized if she appeared at afternoon bridge parties in a bathing suit. Likewise, social disapproval is generally visited upon a man in our society who permits his wife to support him.

A large part of the training of every child consists in inculcating upon him the mores of the society in which he has been born. By the time he has reached adulthood, most of the mores—the proper way to dress, eat, greet strangers or friends, or to behave in the most varied circumstances—have become so habitual with him that they appear perfectly natural. In general, he will be aware of them only in those exceptional cases when he violates them (his conscience will bother him), and he will only rarely be conscious of the social attitudes that enforce them.

Many of the mores of a society specify the proper behavior in organizational situations. For example, certain kinds of clothing are considered appropriate to certain occupations; the boss is to be spoken to in one way, a co-worker in another; it is proper for an employee to stay home when he is ill but not simply because he has a hang-over.

A government agency does not exist in isolation; it is always imbedded in the customs and practices of the society that surrounds it. A government agency in China (and, for that matter, under some situations in the United States) would have to adapt itself to the widespread acceptance of graft ("squeeze") as an inevitable part of administration. Administrators in Japan must make allowance for a general unwillingness of subordinate employees to initiate action without direct orders from above. In Germany, at least under the Weimar Republic, much more literal obedience to authority could be expected than under most conditions in the United States.[9]

Authority. This textbook is concerned with public administration in the United States in our own generation. What mores are prevalent in our own culture that have an important bearing on the way governmental agencies operate? Of first significance are attitudes toward *authority*. Although our society is perhaps more anarchistic than most—tolerating to a remarkable degree individual resistance to authority and even, under many circumstances, making a virtue of disobedience—still there are many situations where a person is expected to, and expects to, accept the authority of others.

Most discussions of the use of authority in organizations stress the importance of sanctions—potential rewards and punishments—in enforcing this authority. If the employee does not obey orders, he can be fired or refused a raise. In reality, sanctions of this kind are probably of no more importance in maintaining authority relations than are the reactions of disapproval that a person receives from his fellows when he refuses to accept "the rules of the game." No other explanation is possible of the acceptance of the decisions of the group in a sand-lot baseball game, for example, where disapproval and ostracism are almost the only sanctions available.

Authority patterns are widely prevalent in our society. It is generally taken for granted that if an individual accepts a job in an organization he is obligated to accept the commands, within reasonable limits, of those who control the organization. Insubordination becomes particularly unattractive for an individual when the other participants accept the prevailing authority relations and when the individual in question values their opinions of him. For this reason, the really important cases of insubordination usually involve the resistance of an entire group of participants to the authority of others who are somewhat distant from them.

While most persons in our society are prepared to accept authority as a condition of employment, there are almost equally

[9] See Robert A. Dahl, "The Science of Public Administration: Three Problems," *Public Administration Review* 7:1–11 (Winter, 1947); and Milton J. Esman, "Japanese Administration—A Comparative View," *Public Administration Review* 7:100–12 (Spring, 1947).

strong attitudes that oppose the use of authority in an arbitrary manner. Few persons like to have their subordinate status rubbed in by a boss whose curt manner of giving orders constantly reminds them of his authority. The days when a foreman or supervisor could "cuss out" his subordinates and get away with it are very nearly past.

Status. Closely akin to mores concerning authority are mores that specify status relationships. Although status rankings are less sharp and rigid in our society than in many others, they are still of great importance, particularly in organizations. In our relations with other people, we tend to rank them as higher, equal, or lower than ourselves and to behave differently toward them according to their status. Failure (by either a subordinate or a superior) to observe the status system accepted in the organization will be greeted by disapproval. Moreover, employees will not usually be given tasks that are inappropriate to their status—a division chief will not be asked to move furniture.

Efficiency. Another attitude that prevails widely in our society is the acceptance of the criterion of *efficiency*. Behavior that deliberately wastes resources or makes less use of them than would be possible is generally thought irrational, if not immoral. After fifteen years the American people still remember with disapproval the little pigs that were killed and the wheat that was plowed under in order to raise agricultural prices during the depression of the 1930's. This disapproval does not stem from an economic analysis of the policy followed, however wise or foolish it may have been, but from generalized attitudes toward "waste." Organizations usually try to give rewards for efficiency (incentive pay plans, for example) and to impose sanctions for inefficiency, but it is probable that most people would try to be efficient under most circumstances even were such sanctions not applied. This attitude has deep roots in the economic, and even the religious, institutions of our society.[10]

It is accepted in an organization that the members will be loyal to their own groups in the competition among administrative units

---

[10] In fact, Max Weber, in *The Protestant Ethic and the Spirit of Capitalism* (London: Allen & Unwin, 1930), argues that the religious attitude of Protestantism toward thrift and waste was the most important factor in the development of our modern society. For an interesting partial confirmation of Weber's hypothesis see M. Dalton, "The Industrial 'Rate-Buster': a Characterization," *Applied Anthropology* 7:5–18 (1948).

for funds, for jurisdiction over a particular activity, or for other forms of power. The administrator who does not "go to bat" for his unit, who does not fight for advancement of his men, or who is not an ardent advocate for the unit's objective finds it difficult to maintain the morale of his group. This fact stems not so much from a reasoned attitude as from a group loyalty spirit that is prevalent in our society.

Other Mores. Many other beliefs in our society could be mentioned that help to mold the behavior of employees in public agencies. All of these, together with the ones that have been treated above, point to the tremendous capacity of human beings for role playing. The great variety of institutions the world over shows that, while "human nature" may be the same everywhere, human behavior patterns are capable of almost infinite variety.

To be sure, there are also wide personal differences among the many individuals who go to make up a single society like our own, but a comparison of the range of variation *within* a society with the range of variation *between* societies would show that most variation is social rather than individual. Most of us are conformists most of the time, and the most fundamental explanation of a great deal of human behavior is that it is the behavior which is socially expected under the circumstances—that it is demanded by the mores.

To a considerable extent, a large organization can create its own social climate, particularly if employees stay with it for reasonably long periods. The officers' corps of military organizations are perhaps the best examples of this. Even so, the mores of an army in democratic America are noticeably different from the mores of an army under a dictatorship, and there is continual social pressure to modify the military mores when these are in conflict with the general practices of the society.[11] Administrative practices of any organization cannot depart too widely from the practices and beliefs of the society in which it operates.[12]

When an organization appoints new employees, one of its im-

[11] Criticism of the preferred treatment of commissioned officers in the American army and demands for a democratization of the court-martial procedure are good examples.

[12] The lack of a single, generally accepted set of mores governing race relationships in the United States creates very difficult administrative problems for the national government—as seen in the periodic debates about segregation in the armed forces. Whatever the letter of the law regarding racial equality in federal employment, it is well known that federal field agencies adapt their employment policies quite considerably to the racial mores in the areas where they are located.

portant training tasks is to indoctrinate them in the particular behavior patterns that are accepted in that organization. In almost all organizations, the newcomer is expected not to be too "forward" until he has learned his place in the scheme of things. This informal probationary period—during which the new employee will generally have very little influence—may last for several years, particularly in established organizations with little personnel turnover.

PERSONALITY DIFFERENCES

As pointed out earlier, much human behavior has its roots very deep in the subconscious and non-rational parts of the mind. Hence, an explanation of behavior must not be satisfied with an individual's own reasons or rationalizations for what he has done. It must examine the whole structure of his personality, many parts of which may be understood only after deep probing by psychoanalytic and similar methods.

The process of growing up in our society is difficult and often painful, leaving deep scars in the personality. The drives and wishes of the individual often conflict with the demands society makes upon him. In part, this conflict is internalized as the attitudes of society become a part of the individual's own conscience (or what the psychoanalysts prefer to call his superego). The conscience can apply a powerful sanction to the individual by punishing him with guilt feelings. It can apparently also suppress from his conscious mind many of the forbidden drives and divert their energies into other channels.[13]

Many of the behaviors that appear to an observer irrational and inexplicable are simply reflections of the struggle going on within the human personality. When the boss "blows up" over some seemingly trivial incident, he may only be discharging the anger over his failure to receive a promotion the previous week. He may or may not be conscious of the real reason for the violence of his reaction, depending on how thoroughly he has rationalized his failure to himself.

[13] The concepts set forth in this paragraph are derived from Freudian psychology. In one or another modification, they have gained quite wide acceptance among psychologists, even those not belonging to the Freudian school, and there is a considerable mass of evidence to support the Freudian theories of guilt and repression.

For our present purposes it is more important to recognize the symptoms of personality—the way it shows up in administrative behavior—than it is to search out the underlying causes. Among the variables here are the *objectivity* of the individual, his *ascendance*, his *ambitiousness*, his *impulsiveness*, and his *sociability*. These are only a few of the items that might be listed, but they will serve to illustrate the role of personality in administrative behavior.

By *objectivity* is meant the degree to which behavior is controlled by the requirements of the real situation rather than by the desire of the individual for self-expression. When a superior relieves his feelings by bawling out a clerk, the behavior is more correctly understood as an expression of the psychological needs of the supervisor than as an intelligent method for improving the clerk's performance. The behavior that the psychologist would call neurotic or psychotic is behavior that is ill-adapted to the situation in which the employee finds himself. Hence, the "objective" person is one who can deal with situations rationally because he is relatively free from neurotic or psychotic drives.

Non-adaptive or non-objective behavior often results from frustration. Human beings react quite differently to a choice between two very unpleasant alternatives than they do to a choice between two desirable goals or one in which desirable and undesirable consequences must be weighed against each other. Persons who are frustrated by being thwarted or by being confronted with a dilemma may react in any one of several irrational ways. They may become aggressive—even to the point of physical violence. They may regress to childish responses—name-calling and the like. They may become fixated on accustomed ways of doing things and unresponsive to suggested changes of even the most reasonable kind. Or they may become resigned, losing all semblance of initiative and morale. Any of these responses unfits them for effective participation in organization.

The symptoms of frustration can often be seen clearly in a government agency that is tainted by spoils or graft. Those employees who are not part of the spoils system, if they are unable or unwilling to find other jobs, become outwardly submissive but lose their enthusiasm for their work. Back-biting and rumor-mongering are common in such organizations. From time to time some employees may break out in open defiance and revolt, even when they realize that resistance is hopeless.[14]

By *ascendance* is meant the tendency to take initiative or exercise control in interpersonal relations. There are wide differences among administrators with regard to this quality—from those who are constantly straining for increases in their budgets or for new activities and undertakings to those who are content to carry along routine administrative programs. Ascendance may vary with the situation as well as with the man. An administrator may be ascendant in his dealings with subordinates but submissive in the presence of superiors—or even vice versa. Extremes of ascendance or submissiveness are usually indications of frustration or other underlying disturbances of the personality.

The *ambitious* man is continually interested in status and in his personal advancement in the organization. In his actual behavior he may or may not be ascendant, but he is highly sensitive to changes in his rank, his salary, or other marks of his status. Burleigh Gardner has used the term "mobile" for the highly ambitious individual, pointing out that the presence of such individuals creates special problems of personnel management.[15]

As a matter of fact, the methods that organizations usually use to encourage the efforts of their employees are much better adapted to stimulating the man who is highly ambitious than the man who is not. In recent years there has been growing realization that there are many persons in any organization who have a definite, and rather low, ceiling on their aims and ambitions. A good example is provided by the numerous young women in clerical positions who are interested merely in holding a pleasant job until they are married and who often are reluctant to accept work that requires them to assume serious responsibilities or involves less pleasant social relations.

Individuals differ widely in *impulsiveness* and *firmness*—the tendency to reach decisions quickly and to stand by decisions once reached. The correct timing of decisions is, of course, important; but many, if not most, administrators are handicapped to some degree by forces in their personal makeups that drive them to pre-

[14] For a more complete analysis of the effects of frustration, see Norman R. F. Maier, *Psychology in Industry* (New York: Houghton Mifflin Co., 1946), chap. 4.

[15] Burleigh Gardner, *Human Relations in Industry* (Chicago: Richard D. Irwin, Inc., 1946).

mature, ill-advised decisions, or that prevent them from reaching decisions promptly enough. The tendency to stall when an unpleasant decision must be made is familiar to almost every administrator.

By *sociability* is meant the sensitivity of the individual to the attitudes and desires of those with whom he has face-to-face contact. As already noted, this sensitivity is one of the principal means for securing conformity to the mores of the group. A synonym for sociability, as the term is used here, would be "tendency to conform." For employees of low sociability, incentives that appeal to one as an individual are likely to be effective.[16] Such employees may work hard to earn a bonus or to secure rapid advancement even in the face of the disapproval of their co-workers.

For employees with a high degree of sociability, such inducements are likely to be relatively ineffective unless the appeal can be made to the whole work group. For such employees, congeniality of their work environment or the group-shared feeling that there is an important job to be done may be the key to motivation.

INFLUENCES FROM "OUTSIDE" ORGANIZATIONS

In attempting to fit its employees into the desired pattern of behavior, the organization is constantly meeting opposing (or reinforcing) influences from the numerous social contacts these employees have outside the organization. These influences are clearly visible in far-flung field organizations where individual employees or small groups are geographically separated from their headquarters office and are constantly subject to the pressures of the communities in which they operate. Such employees may find that the line of least resistance is to satisfy their neighbors even at the cost of disregarding instructions from the distant headquarters.

This fact was recognized by the gasoline rationing branch of the Office of Price Administration when it authorized the issuance by local rationing boards of "hardship" rations to satisfy strong local demands for gasoline for purposes not recognized in the national regulations. The hardship rations acted as a safety valve, permitting the local boards to yield to particularly insistent local pressures without endangering the authority of the Washington headquarters.

[16] See Dalton, op. cit.

The labor union is an important example of an "outside" organization whose claim for the loyalty of its members may conflict with the organization's control over its employees.[17] Many cities have refused to permit their policemen to join labor unions on the grounds that such affiliation would lessen their reliability if they were called upon to handle a strike. A government agency that is controlled by a political machine may find it difficult to influence employees who know that they owe their jobs and their loyalty not to their nominal superiors in the organization but to the machine.

On the other hand, external ties may reinforce organizational allegiance and discipline rather than compete with them. An employee may be stimulated to work hard for promotion because of the prestige that a higher position will give him with his wife or with friends who play poker with him. A labor union may assist an agency to discipline employees who have gone out on an unauthorized strike. A political machine may force employees who are opposed to a promised reform to carry it out.

INFLUENCE OF PRIOR TRAINING

There is no need to discuss at length how the previous education, training, and work experience of an employee give him knowledge and skills that he needs in meeting new situations. One very common and largely unintended by-product of education does deserve mention, however—the attitude of *professionalism* that it frequently produces. The lawyer, the doctor, the accountant, the forester are set apart by their strong loyalties to their professions as well as by their special skills.

The strength of professionalism as an influence upon behavior is due to the fact that the professional attitudes the employee brings to the job—produced by his prior training—are continually reinforced by his associations with other members of his professional group. Professionalism results, then, from the combined influence of prior training and association with an outside group—the profession.

In an organization made up entirely or primarily of one profession—for example the professional staff of the United States Public Health Service or the employees of a city police department

[17] See Neil W. Chamberlain, op. cit., particularly p. 111.

—the professional loyalty reinforces the organization loyalty and makes for a closely knit group. Many organizational tasks require, however, the cooperation of several professions, and here the professional loyalties may compete with organizational loyalties. The Controller of a government agency, sensitive to his professional responsibilities, may refuse to approve an expenditure that is strongly desired to further the organization's goals, because he believes the expenditure illegal.

SELECTION OF EMPLOYEES

It is clear from the foregoing discussion that a new employee is not a blank sheet of paper on which the organization can write what it wills. He is usually a fully formed personality, thoroughly steeped in the community's mores, possessing his own individual personality traits, holding membership in a number of outside social groups, and educated in specific vocational or professional skills. There are definite limits on the ability of the organization to direct or influence his behavior. For this reason one of the most important influences the organization can use is its freedom to select its employees. If the organization will meet resistance in modifying personality traits and behavior patterns, at least it can select employees who will be most likely, because of the traits they bring to the organization, to cooperate in carrying out its tasks. A public housing agency, for example, would be inclined to reject as employees persons strongly opposed to the idea of public housing.

In part—and particularly at the professional level—employees are self-selected. They desire employment in a particular agency because they like the kind of work they will be required to do or because they believe in the significance of the agency's activities. A man will not usually seek a job as playground director unless he thinks that a recreation program for children is important and unless he thinks he would enjoy directing children's play activities. The self-selection of employment actually begins with the individual's selection of professional or vocational training.

Of course, an agency cannot rely to any great extent upon self-selection in its recruitment policies. Certain types of jobs and agencies attract would-be employees because of the supposed "glamor" of their work or because the pay is good. It cannot be assumed that the person for whom these attractions are greatest will make the best employee. In other situations self-selection would actually lead to serious problems. Every mental hospital has to be constantly on guard against persons with sadistic tendencies who would like jobs as attendants because of the power they would have over the inmates.

The selection process then is one of the most important and powerful of administrative tools. It will receive a more complete analysis in Chapter 15.

Influence of the Formal and Informal Organization

We have now examined at some length the influences on the employee's behavior that lie outside the organization. We have seen that what he does and what decisions he makes are to a very considerable extent determined by the personality, character structure, knowledge, and attitudes that have been impressed upon him before he comes into the organization and by influences that operate upon him outside the sphere of his organizational life. If this were all that could be said about human behavior, we would not need special books about administration. If these outside influences completely determined behavior, people would behave in organizations just as they did everywhere.

But in fact, individuals placed in organizational situations—employed as stenographers, or laborers, or recreation directors, or foresters, or department heads—do behave differently than they would if they were outside organization, or if they were in different organizational situations. The organizational system itself brings to bear upon them strong influences that modify and redirect their behavior tendencies. The final pages of this chapter and most of the remaining chapters of this book will be concerned chiefly with these organizational influences upon behavior—with the fact that the organization in which he finds himself is an important determinant of what the individual does and decides.

CHARACTERISTICS OF BEHAVIOR IN ORGANIZATION

To the extent that a person's participation in an organization subjects him to psychological influences, we find that his behavior tends to take on the following characteristics: [18]

[18] We are describing here what the sociologist would call the assumption of an organizational *role*—an organizationally and socially defined standardized pattern

Value Premises. The value premises (goals, objectives) upon which the employee bases his decisions tend to be the objectives of the organization or organizational unit in which he works. When the forest ranger is advised that a fire has started in his district he immediately makes decisions and takes actions that are directed toward the objective of putting out the fire. If he were merely a camper in the woods his main concern about a fire would probably lie in not being trapped and burned. Even if he possessed social attitudes that led him to try to do something about the fire, he certainly would not feel the same responsibility, the same single-minded purpose to extinguish it, that would be felt by the ranger.

To be more accurate, the value premises that the individual employee incorporates into his behavior are not usually the goals of the organization as a whole, but intermediate goals—means to the larger organization ends—that define his particular job in the organization. The forest ranger acts not in terms of extinguishing fires in general, but of extinguishing those in his fire district. Hence, behavior in organization is characterized by the division of the complete task of the organization into partial tasks that serve as goals for particular employees or groups of employees.

Acceptance of Influence. The employee tends to accept influences that are "legitimately" imposed upon him by other members of the organization. If the ranger's supervisor instructs him to clear the brush from a particular forest trail, he is more likely to accept the instruction than if it came from a visitor in the forest. We will have more to say about this matter of "legitimacy" in later paragraphs, and in Chapter 8.

To the extent that this acceptance develops in the employee, he derives many of the premises of his behavior from his communication with other organization members. This communication may be in the form of orders, information and advice, and training. To a very considerable extent, these various forms of communication can be deliberately designed so as to bring the employee within a planned environment of organizational influence. Examples of such planned influences are formal "lines of authority," report forms and instructions for their preparation and routing, formally established "consultant" positions, and the assignment of employees to partici-

---

of behavior. For an analysis in these terms, see Samuel A. Stouffer, *et. al.*, *The American Soldier: Combat and Its Aftermath* (Princeton: Princeton University Press, 1949), p. 101.

pate in formal training programs. For this reason, the definition and enforcement of these channels of influence has always been a central concern of organization planning.

Expectations. The employee tends to form stable expectations about his relations with other people, and how they will behave under particular circumstances. When the ranger receives from his lookout a report of a fire in the adjoining district, he does not take direct action, but phones his fellow ranger with full confidence that the latter will take charge of the situation. He likewise has confidence that if a lookout in the adjoining district detects a fire in his district, he will be informed about it promptly.

Organizational Morale. The employee tends to assume not just a passive but an active attitude toward the furtherance of the organization's objectives. He does not merely accept the organization goals in deciding those questions that come to him, or accept the instructions he receives, but he exercises more or less initiative in finding ways of furthering those goals. In most cases the ranger would see that the brush was cleared from an overgrown trail long before anyone gave him instructions to do so—often long before anyone besides himself knew that the problem existed.

Active rather than merely passive participation and cooperation is almost essential if an organization is to attain even moderate efficiency. If the organization must drive its employees every step of the way, if they stop and await new instructions each time a specific task is completed, if they contribute little of their own thought and spontaneous effort, then the largest part of the organization's energies will be swallowed up and consumed in overcoming their inertia. The power that operates an automobile comes from the motor, not from the driver. So in an organization the energy that accomplishes its tasks must be secured from the spontaneous contributions of employees who are actively working toward the organization goal. For those who are directing the organization to attempt to supply it with energy would be as effective as for the driver of a car to get out and push instead of starting the motor.

The willingness of employees to participate in a truly active way and to devote their full energies to the organization's task is what is usually meant by high *morale*.[19] If the playground director has high morale—if he is sold on the recreation department's goals

---

[19] The term "morale" is defined in many ways in books on administration. The definition given here will prove most useful for our purposes.

and willingly and enthusiastically contributes his mind and energies toward realizing them—then the organization's influences upon him will serve to channel and direct these energies toward effective activity. Lacking such morale, the organization will be burdened with the almost hopeless task of supplying initiative as well as direction.

Other Characteristics. The science of economics makes great use of a mythical individual known as "economic man"—an individual who goes about his business singlemindedly maximizing his profits. The behavior tendencies we have been describing of individuals in organization might be combined into a picture of an equally mythical individual whom we could call "administrative man." Administrative man accepts the organization goals as the value premises of his decisions, is particularly sensitive and reactive to the influences upon him of the other members of his organization, forms stable expectations regarding his own role in relation to others and the roles of others in relation to him, and has high morale in regard to the organization's goals. What is perhaps most remarkable and unique about administrative man is that the organizational influences do not merely cause him to do certain specific things (e.g., putting out a forest fire, if that is his job), but induce in him a habit pattern of doing *whatever* things are appropriate to carry out in cooperation with others the organization goals. He develops habits of cooperative behavior.

It should not be thought, however, that all the influences operating upon the employees of an organization further cooperation. There may be, for example, conflicting interpretations of the organization goals, or various units of the organization may have inconsistent goals. Incompatibility among members of the organization may lead to friction and may increase, rather than reduce, resistance to organizational influence. Certain methods of supervision may curb rather than stimulate initiative. Nevertheless, the first set of influences—those encouraging cooperation—predominate most of the time in most organizations. If they did not, organized behavior would not be an effective way of carrying out tasks, members would receive no inducement toward continued participation, and the organization itself would disappear. Hence only those organizations survive for any length of time whose net influence upon their members is to preserve and develop habits of cooperation.

CHARACTER OF ORGANIZATIONAL INFLUENCES

We may next inquire into the nature of the influences that impinge upon a person who becomes a member of an organization. All of them derive from the fact that his participation in the organization brings him into frequent communication with other members. He talks to them and observes them, and they talk to him. In the course of this communication, they induce him to behave in particular ways by convincing or persuading him, by attaching pleasant consequences for him to desired behaviors and unpleasant consequences to undesired ones (rewards and punishments), and by providing him with social satisfactions and dissatisfactions from his association with them. Social satisfactions and dissatisfactions may, of course, be regarded as particular kinds of rewards and punishments, but they are of such central importance that they deserve special treatment.

Influencing people by convincing and persuading them are processes that are obviously not peculiar to organization. Organization, by multiplying the occasions for communication, does however greatly reinforce these processes. They are further reinforced by the habits of cooperation that the individual gradually acquires.

Rewards and punishments are important and obvious means of influence. The threat of dismissal, the promise of higher wages or promotion, praise and reprimand are examples of commonly used rewards and punishments. Less obvious, but at least as important, are social satisfactions and dissatisfactions derived from association with other organization members. In particular, most persons are sensitive to the approval or disapproval of those persons with whom they are in close association.

The division of the organization's work and the assignment of particular duties to individuals and groups of individuals bring certain employees into close contact and association with certain others. These associations provide the fertile soil upon which social relations and group loyalties can grow. Organizational loyalties are of particular importance because many of the values that motivate any individual are values that derive from the face-to-face work group with which he identifies and to which he is loyal.[20] The attitudes of an employee toward the organization goals and toward

[20] See the discussion of sociability as a personal attribute earlier in this chapter.

the authority exercised over him are very closely related to the attitudes of the persons who work with him. If his fellow-employees are dissatisfied with their jobs, or think the supervisors are unfair, or evidence low morale in other ways, the typical employee, whatever his original disposition, is likely to develop similar dissatisfactions.

The structure of loyalties in a typical organization is highly complex, embracing loyalties to *groups* as well as loyalties to *goals*. Because of the individual's sensitivity to the social group in which he finds himself, influences upon these loyalties must be primarily influences upon the employee as a member of a face-to-face group rather than as an individual "atom." The whole subject of loyalties will be examined in detail in the next chapter.

REINFORCEMENT OF THE INFLUENCES

The ability of organizations to develop in their members habits of cooperation is greatly increased by the attitudes and habits that these members bring to organizations. The most important of these reinforcing attitudes have already been discussed earlier in the chapter. The mores of the society in which the new member has lived have predisposed him to accept authority, to recognize differences in status, to consider efficiency and group loyalty as positive values. He has acquired certain desires—for example, the desire for a higher income—that give the organization a means of rewarding or punishing him. Moreover, he may have had specific training for the kinds of tasks he will be asked to perform in the organization.

To be sure, not all the habits he has acquired before joining the organization will reinforce the influences that are imposed upon him. In many cases his prior habits will conflict with the new influences. He may have habits of tardiness, of carelessness, of rudeness, or training in methods different from those employed by the organization. Nevertheless, the patterns of cooperation in an organization will generally reflect to a very considerable degree the patterns of cooperation that are incorporated in the mores and training procedures of the larger society. The organization will receive further reinforcement from pre-existing attitudes by selecting those persons as employees who appear most susceptible to its influence.

FORMAL ORGANIZATION

By *formal organization* is meant the pattern of behaviors and relationships that is deliberately and legitimately planned for the members of an organization. Two words in the definition of formal organization need explanation: "deliberately" and "legitimately." In some simple situations an organization may be wholly unplanned. When a car gets stuck in the mud of a country road, the passengers may get out and push without anyone "deliberately" planning their behavior. On the other hand, in most organizations, and certainly in all governmental organizations, there are some employees who spend part or all of their time planning the system of organization behavior—the division of work and allocation of duties, authority relationships, lines of communication, and so forth.

Now of course anyone in an organization (or outside it, for that matter) may make such a plan. Several plans may be made, and these may conflict. Formal organization comes into existence when there is an agreed-upon and accepted procedure for giving "legitimacy" to one of these plans. In the case of governmental organizations, this legitimacy flows ultimately from the action of the legislature in creating the organization (or the larger structure of which it is part) by statute, and providing a procedure by which an executive or board is appointed to direct it. The legally constituted executive, in turn, authorizes more detailed plans for the structure of his organization, and appoints principal subordinates to positions of formal authority in it. This process may be several times repeated down through the structure of the organization. As a result of a series of steps of this kind, we may find that Mr. A has been "legitimately" appointed to a position of section chief, and that he in turn has "legitimately" (i.e., in accordance with the terms of the formal plan of the larger organization) made assignments of duties to the members of his section.

How plans of formal organization are established and made legitimate may be illustrated from the history of the Economic Cooperation Administration. On April 3, 1948, the Economic Cooperation Act of 1948 was adopted by the Congress. This Act established (i.e., promulgated a legitimate plan for) an Economic Cooperation Administration, and provided for the appointment of an Administrator to direct it. Within a few days, Paul Hoffman had been appointed Administrator by the President. From this point on, the administrative orders and regulations of Mr. Hoffman, his appointments of subordinates and his plans for the allocation of duties were legitimate plans—plans for formal organization —in that they were included in, and contemplated by, the formal organization plan laid down by Congress in the Act itself, and by the President in his appointment of Mr. Hoffman.

But still this does not give us a basis for distinguishing formal organization plans from plans that have not been legitimatized. We have merely found the source of one set of formal plans—those of Mr. Hoffman—in another set of underlying formal plans—those of the Congress. Why do we consider the statute "legitimate"? The answer lies in the attitudes of those persons to whom the plans are directed (e.g., the employees of ECA). The only reason why it is important that Congress places its blessing upon a plan by enacting it into law, is that people in this country behave differently toward plans that have been so blessed than toward plans that have not. Acceptance of the legitimacy of Congress and its actions is an acceptance of the legitimacy of the American governmental system. It is an essential and important part of mores of the society in which the employee lives, and which he has accepted long before he becomes a member of the organization. It defines for him the conditions under which the general mores of authority come into play —the situations in which, according to his mores, he feels that he *ought* to accept authority.

We cannot pursue further at this point the subject of legitimacy and the acceptance of authority except to warn against certain misconceptions. First, legitimacy is at root not a legal but a psychological matter. A legal or any other system of authority is legitimate only to the extent that those persons to whom it is directed feel that they ought or must accept it. Second, the legitimacy of an organizational plan is seldom accepted as absolute by those whom it seeks to govern. There are always limits—often fairly narrow limits—which, if exceeded, will cause refusal to accept the plan or even to admit its legitimacy. Third, legitimacy need not be hierarchical in its structure, resulting from successive acts of delegation. Although the examples we have cited were of a hierarchical character, we shall see that legitimacy can arise in many other ways.

Legitimacy and the acceptance of authority will form the major topic of Chapter 8. What is chiefly important for our present purposes is that formal organization plans have an effect upon behavior different from informal plans because they fit within a broader structure of legitimacy and authority that is accepted by the employees.

INFORMAL ORGANIZATION

Almost always the actual pattern of behaviors and relationships of the members of an organization will depart slightly or widely from the formal plan of organization. The actual pattern may differ from the formal plan in two ways: (1) the formal plan may be incomplete—it may not include the whole pattern of behavior as it actually develops; and (2) some portions of the actual pattern of behavior may be in contradiction to the plan. By *informal organization* is meant the whole pattern of actual behaviors—the way members of the organization really do behave—insofar as these actual behaviors do not coincide with the formal plan.

Incompleteness of Formal Organization. There are wide differences in the degrees to which various organizations attempt to plan formally the behavior of their employees. In some organizations the plan is very sketchy. It consists of little more than a few verbal or written instructions that assign tasks to employees, and perhaps specify the principal lines of legitimate authority. The formal plans of small organization units, with a dozen employees, say, seldom amount to more than this. In other organizations the plan is very elaborate—for example, the regulations in an army or navy specify the manner in which an enlisted man shall address an officer, the occasions on which he is permitted to initiate a contact with an officer, and the exact occasions and manner of saluting.

The incompleteness of the formal plan provides a vacuum which, like other vacuums, proves abhorrent to nature. The members of an organization gradually develop patterns of behavior and relationships with each other, and the unplanned aspects of their behavior may come to be as structured, as stable, and as predictable as the planned aspects. Well defined "habits" will almost inevitably develop defining how the boss is to be greeted when he enters the office in the morning (which we have seen is an element of formal organization in a military unit), who is to lunch with whom, and who is to be consulted when a decision of a particular kind is to be reached.

Conflicts Between Formal and Informal. Not only is the formal plan always supplemented by informally-developed patterns, but it is almost always contradicted in some respects by the actual pattern of behavior. These failures to carry out the formal plan may be deliberate or non-deliberate. Refusal to obey legitimate orders—either outright refusal or refusal through "misunderstanding" of intent—is a common phenomenon in almost every organization. Attempts to exercise authority beyond that legitimately assigned are equally common. In extreme instances we may find cliques within the organization attempting to wrest control of it from those to whom control has been formally assigned, and to use this control either to change the goals of the organization, or to benefit the clique members, or both. Such "illegal" activities, which are of the same kind as revolutionary behaviors, are of considerable importance, and will receive a good deal of attention in this book.

Non-deliberate departures from the formal organization plan are probably of even more frequent occurrence, and of equal significance. Organization members who possess strong qualities of leadership will almost inevitably find themselves, even without deliberate purpose, exercising far more influence than is contemplated in the organization plan. Where the plan conflicts with deep-seated habits or attitudes it may be forgotten or ignored, even without deliberate intent, and often at the expense of considerable guilt-feelings of those who ignore it. This occurs very frequently when the formal plans are overelaborate—for example, where elaborate paper-work processes are established whose meaning and usefulness is not apparent to the employees. When employees find that it is too complicated to do things "through channels," new and often explicity forbidden informal channels are employed to supplement and by-pass the formal ones.

MUTUAL INFLUENCE OF THE FORMAL AND INFORMAL

From our discussion of informal organization we can draw two generalizations: (1) when human beings are brought together into frequent contact they will develop more or less definite patterns of relationship even in the absence of a formal plan, and certainly in supplementation to any formal plan that is promulgated; (2) the influence of legitimacy, and the other influences that those who authorize formal plans can bring to bear upon behavior are only a few among the numerous influences, organizational and non-organizational, that determine the behavior of organization members. To the degree that these other influences work at cross purposes to the plan of organization, the actual pattern of behavior is likely to depart from the planned pattern.

It is not easy to distinguish those instances where the behavior of an employee reflects the influence of the formal organization from those instances where it reflects the influence of the informal organization—in most cases these influences parallel and reinforce each other. A forest ranger may take great care to maintain the fire trails in his forest because he has been formally assigned this job. On the other hand, he may do this because he wants his fellow rangers to regard him as a good forest manager. Most likely both these motives, and perhaps others as well, enter into his behavior, and it would be almost impossible to determine the separate importance of each.

Nor is it easy to distinguish between the formal or informal influences of the organization and the responses of the employee to influences that have been internalized and have become part of his own personality. The efficiency criterion is one example. Most people accept employment in an agency with a full expectation that they will attempt to carry out their responsibilities in an efficient manner. The typist knows, even before she receives specific orders, that she is expected to type as rapidly and accurately as possible, not as slowly and carelessly as possible.

We see, then, that the environment in which an employee finds himself in an organization is usually a closely intertwined composition of formal and informal influences. In the first place, many of the informal relationships grow directly out of the formal structure. The planned arrangement of offices, for example, may throw two employees into frequent contact with each other, and as a result they may often converse, have lunch together, and develop social contacts outside office hours. Similarly, the hierarchical relationships tend to bring together employees who are at about the same status level and to create a great social distance between those at high levels and those at low levels. In civilian organizations, where the contacts between subordinates and superiors are not usually formally regulated, this social distance may be almost as great as in an army, where it is embodied in formal instructions.[21]

In the second place, formal and informal are intertwined because relationships that initially grow up on an informal basis may be "ratified" and incorporated in the formal structure by subsequent regulations. For example, most public personnel systems provide for a formal position classification—a detailed statement of the duties and responsibilities of each position. When an employee "works out of classification"—i.e., performs duties not listed in his job description—the procedures usually provide that his job may be redescribed and re-classified to bring about consistency between the formal description and what he is actually doing.

The early months of the Economic Cooperation Administration provide a striking example of the ratification of informal relations. Between April, 1948, when the agency was established, and about July 15, when it already had some six hundred employees, it operated without any formal plan for its internal structure even so elaborate as an organization chart showing its principal divisions. To be sure, certain formal organization decisions had been made by appointing and giving titles to key employees, and by specifying certain procedures for paper flow (which were frequently informally violated), and by settling certain disputes about self-assumed jurisdiction. But the real core of this organization, which was in full operation before May 1, lay in a complex set of behaviors and understandings that had grown up almost spontaneously. The formal plans that were finally issued in July and subsequently were in very large part ratifications of this informal scheme.

Summary: The Individual and the Organization

In this chapter we have examined the tangled scheme of relationships that ties an individual to an organization and makes his behavior a part of the system of organization behavior. Being an employee of an organization alters an individual's behavior by

[21] Observation of a group of executives sitting down at a conference or at lunch where the seats are not assigned ahead of time almost always reveals something of the status system of the group. At a long table, the persons of high status will usually tend to cluster at the middle or one end, with the persons of lowest status occupying the seats farthest from them.

altering the factual premises and the value premises that underlie his choices and decisions. As a result of his employment he works toward different goals, and he has different conceptions as to how to achieve these goals, than if he were in some other environment.

But the individual employee is by no means putty in the organization's hands. His behavior is controlled and controllable only within rather narrow limits. A wide range of influences, past and present, lying outside the organization, and especially outside its formal plans, all have their part in accounting for his actual behavior.

The organization encounters not only individual resistance, but also group resistance to its influences. To the degree that employees are sociable, they are highly responsive to their immediate work groups, which thus become important channels of organization influence. Only in recent years has adequate attention been paid to the role of such face-to-face groups and their importance for administration. It is to the subject of group loyalties and their role in administration that we turn next.

CHAPTER FOUR

⚑

Building Blocks of Organization: Formation of Groups

IN THE previous chapter we focussed attention on the employee as an individual. We tried to find out how he made his decisions in his daily work; how the organization influenced his behavior; and how other influences beyond the organization affected him. In this chapter and the following one we will focus attention on the employee as a member of social groups within the organization.

Both in society at large and in organizations the socially isolated individual is extremely rare. When a person enters government employment he immediately begins to make acquaintances and friends, usually from among the persons with whom he works a great deal, and soon finds himself absorbed in one or more social groups. As has already been indicated in Chapter 3, the behavior of individuals in such groups is greatly modified by the group influences. Large organizations contain considerable numbers of such groups, and most of the important things that happen in organizations can be described as interactions among the social groups of which the organization is composed. In most cases the various members of a close-knit group will share values, will want the same things, and will oppose the same threats to the group values. It is these groups—how they affect the individual employee's behavior, and what the organization does about it—that we will investigate in this chapter and in Chapter 5.

Organization Units

One of the difficulties in discussing this subject is the lack of universally accepted names to designate the various parts of organizations. We will use here the terminology recommended by the U. S. Senate Committee on Expenditures in the Executive Departments.[1] The largest subdivision of a government (Federal, state, or city) will be called a *department* or *agency;* subdivisions of departments and agencies will be called *bureaus;* subdivisions of bureaus, *divisions;* subdivisions of divisions, *branches;* and subdivisions of branches, *sections.* The term *unit* will be used generically to refer to any of these subdivisions, and will also be applied to the smallest subdivision that is recognized in the division of work and in the supervisory structure. The context will usually make clear in which sense "unit" is being used.

In citing specific governmental examples, the actual title of the organization will be used, of course, even when it does not correspond to the recommended usage. Among the Federal departments, for example, are the Veterans' *Administration* and the Railroad Retirement *Board.* In some cities, the detective bureau of the police department is called a *bureau;* in other cities it is the criminal investigation *division.* The *Office* of European Affairs is a bureau of the State Department; and the Forest *Service* is a bureau in the Department of Agriculture.

The smallest units in organizations each consist of a limited number of employees under a single supervisor (whom we will call the *unit chief*), all doing the same or similar work or all working for the accomplishment of the same purpose or objective. A number of units placed together under a common supervisor (the section chief) form a section. In like manner, sections are grouped to form a branch; branches are grouped to form a division; divisions to form a bureau; bureaus to form a department or an agency. All of the departments or agencies together make up the executive part of the Federal, state, county, or municipal government under consideration.

The unit leaders play an important role in such a system of organization. A large part of the communication between widely separated organization units and between executives at the "top" levels and executives or employees at the "lower" levels takes place indirectly, with the heads of various units of organization serving as links in the chain. A great deal of communication takes place

---

[1] See the reports of this committee published as *Senate Committee Prints,* with accompanying charts of the organization of federal executive departments and agencies.

between (1) the head of an organization unit and the heads of the principal subdivisions of that unit (e.g., a bureau chief and his division chiefs, or a branch chief and his section chiefs), and (2) among the various heads of the subdivisions of a given unit of organization (e.g., the heads of sections in the same branch, or heads of branches in the same division).[2]

Because of this close relationship between an executive and the heads of the units reporting directly to him, it is convenient to have a term to refer specifically to such a group of persons. We will call the group an *executive unit organization*. Thus, a city manager together with the heads of the city departments make up an executive unit organization, as do also the chief of the Weather Bureau and the heads of the divisions into which that bureau is divided.

In some cases, it is convenient to speak of the "internal" management of a unit of organization as distinguished from its "external" relations. These terms are entirely relative, depending upon the organizational viewpoint. Thus, from the viewpoint of the Chief of the Weather Bureau, all relationships within the Bureau are internal; while relationships with other bureaus in the Department of Commerce (with the Civil Aeronautics Administration, for example), are external. On the other hand, from the viewpoint of the Secretary of Commerce, relationships between the Weather Bureau and the Civil Aeronautics Administration are internal.

The Formation of Social Groups

When an individual enters an organization he finds that he works with certain people much more than he works with others. If he were to chart his contacts with other employees in the organization he would find that there was a fairly small and definite group of them with whom he had a great number of contacts every day; another larger group with whom he had occasional contacts—perhaps once a day or once a week; and finally, a very large number of people whom he never contacted but only heard about in various ways.

The small number of people who work together day in and day

---

[2] The reader should not make the mistake of supposing that all, or even most, of the communication in organizations follows these particular channels. Other important channels will be discussed at length in later chapters on communication.

out becomes a real social group. The members usually call one another by their first names. They get to know one another in an immediate personal way. They meet not as partial persons—as *officials*—but as whole, complete persons with hopes and fears, ambitions, likes and dislikes, family and social problems, and so forth. Among the members of these small, face-to-face, social groups, enduring friendships are often formed which extend beyond the confines of the organization into social life.

LOYALTY TO THE WORKING GROUP

Members of these working, social groups generally develop a "we" feeling. Persons outside of the group are thought of as "they." The individual members tend to *identify* with the group so that they interpret the values accepted by the group as their own values. The group becomes an extension of the individual's self.

The group develops sentiments as to the proper conduct of its members. Usually officious displays of authority within the groups are frowned upon or met with a "be yourself." [3] If the head of a unit that forms a group does not act according to the group's standards he may not be accepted as a member of the group. For example, a new head of a group of procedure analysts found that he had to be careful in expressing his skepticism about organization charts because the members of the group attached great importance to these devices and interpreted his skepticism as an attack on the value of their work.

Two important rules of conduct within social groups are that the individual members should "go along" with the group; and that they should be discreet—should avoid doing anything that would endanger the values of the group. (The nature of group values will be discussed in the next chapter.)

When an individual enters an organization, if he does not identify with the working group in which he finds himself, if he does not accept the discipline of the group, he will remain an outsider in an atmosphere of hostility or at least indifference. His working relations will not be pleasant; he may be criticized and shunned. Few people can long tolerate such an unpleasant situa-

---

[3] This feeling is probably a matter of the mores of a given society. In places and times other than twentieth-century America, group resentment of the arbitrary authority of the head of the group might be much less.

tion, and so nearly always the individual is either absorbed into the group or finds another job. It is not unusual for the group to take steps to have an unassimilated individual removed—for example, by bringing criticism of his work to the supervisors, or even by deliberately spoiling his work and passing the blame to him. Similar treatment may be accorded a member of a working social group who has violated its code of conduct. His future conduct must be found trustworthy before he can regain the goodwill and confidence of his fellow workers.

THE HIERARCHY OF LOYALTIES

Almost all employees will identify, to a greater or lesser degree, not only with their immediate working groups, but with the larger organization units of which the working groups are parts. For example, within the Economic Cooperation Administration an employee of the Management Engineering Branch (small enough to be a genuine working group) will also identify with the Organization and Management Division, with the Washington office of ECA, with ECA as a whole, and with the Federal government. If these larger organization entities are under attack from critics outside them, the individual will usually rise to their defense. Most people unconsciously feel that criticism by an "outsider" of an organization with which they are associated is in some way a criticism of themselves. There may be many things that a group of city firemen gripe about when they are by themselves, but when someone not in the department criticizes them—possibly for the very things they privately grumble about—most of them will rise to the department's defense.

Employees often find themselves in situations where there are conflicting claims on their loyalties by their immediate working groups and by the larger organizational units of which these groups are parts. For most persons, the loyalty to the working group is stronger than the loyalty to the larger units, and they will usually resist strongly the admission, even to themselves, that what is good for the working group is not always good for the organization as a whole.[4] The merger of the Navy, for example, with the other

[4] Compare the vigorous and often sincere efforts of political special interest groups to convince themselves and others that the group interest is identical with the national interest: "What helps business helps you"; "Agriculture is the mainstay of the economy"; "Strong labor unions mean a strong America."

services into the National Military Establishment has been almost unanimously resisted by the administrators and officers' corps of the Navy. Whatever the merits of the controversy, it is clear that their identifications are primarily with the Navy and secondarily with the Federal government as a whole. In opposing the change, however, their main argument has been that "a strong national defense requires a strong independent navy."

Often, the organization outside the working group appears to the group members as a critic of the group or an obstacle to be overcome. Only when the larger unit is itself subject to attack from outside does it become a strong focus of loyalty or identification. Thus, a regional office of the Forest Service may struggle with the Washington office to increase the region's allotment of budget funds, but when the appropriation of the entire Forest Service is at stake, the regional office will quickly forget these differences and rise to the defense of the Service. Each individual possesses, therefore, a whole hierarchy or pyramid of loyalties, with the loyalties to the smaller, more intimate groups toward the base of the pyramid usually taking precedence over loyalties to the larger groups in case of conflict.

Although most persons behave in this way most of the time, there are some persons who exhibit greater loyalty to the larger than to the smaller groups. First of all, there are those who may be described as "reformers"—persons strongly attached to some broad goal or program for which they are prepared to sacrifice friendships or even their families. Second, among the persons described in Chapter 3 as relatively "unsociable"—i.e., insensitive to the attitudes of the working group—are some who believe their own personal advancement and personal goals will be best served by loyalty to a larger unit at the expense of the immediate group they are in.[5]

Still a third group of persons whose loyalty may lie with larger, rather than smaller, organization units are persons in executive positions. The executive unit organization to which the executive belongs may be the primary focus of his loyalties rather than the working group composed of his subordinates. Or, his loyalties may

[5] The "rate-busters," mentioned in Chapter 3, fall in this category. Their acceptance of management's goals of high productivity is motivated by the fortunate coincidence between these goals and their personal desires for high earnings, rather than by emotional loyalty to the organization as a whole. Dalton's evidence is rather clear on this point. "The Industrial 'Rate-Buster,' " op. cit.

be rather evenly balanced between these two groups. That is, the branch chief will usually be a member of one working group based upon the employees of his branch and another composed of the division chief and the other branch chiefs in his division. As we shall see later in the chapter, this dual membership in face-to-face social groups plays a very important role in executive behavior.

IDENTIFICATION AND MORALE

Several further observations will be useful in understanding identifications and the role they play in organization behavior. Thus far, we have not distinguished between loyalty to *groups* and loyalty to *goals*. Loyalty to groups is based to a considerable extent upon the quality of sociability mentioned in Chapter 3. A person who wants to be liked and thought well of by his associates will accept the standards of conduct the group seeks to impose on him and will work for the protection and preservation of the group and its values. Like a good soldier, if the group objectives are changed and the group accepts the change, he will go along with the new objectives. He is loyal to those goals that his group accepts. His loyalty to goals—for example, to the particular organizational objectives accepted by his group—is largely secondary and will shift if the loyalty of the group shifts.

A typist, for example, very often exhibits high loyalty to her section—frequently working overtime and refusing to divulge information that might injure the group—but she may be perfectly satisfied if important changes are made in the section's work program or policies, provided these changes are acceptable to the section and provided they do not seriously disturb the social structure of the group.

When the attachment of employees to goals is stronger than their attachment to working groups, the organization may encounter great difficulty in securing their acceptance of changes in objectives. This problem is seen frequently in voluntary political organizations where members who participate only a few hours a month do not form strong personal ties and are likely to resign if the organization embarks on a program with which they do not entirely agree.

In organizations with paid employees, however, resistance to organization policies is more often a resistance, not of individuals, but of whole working groups to policies of the larger organization units that conflict with the group goals. At one point during World War II, for example, a large number of the professional employees in the Division of Publication of the Office of War Information resigned rather than accept an OWI reversal of certain publication policies developed in the division. Granted that these individuals were sincerely attached to the policies—thought they were important to the agency's work of maintaining civilian morale—their goal loyalty was strongly reinforced by personal loyalties to the group. We may conclude, then, that a large part of the loyalty to goals which individuals exhibit is derived from their loyalty to the groups that have adopted these goals.

From this discussion, it appears also that there is a close relationship between identification and morale. In Chapter 3 we defined high morale as the psychological condition within an individual that makes him willing to participate actively in the work of the organization and devote his full energies to its tasks. In order to have high morale, either the employee must identify with the goals of the organization or he must identify with a group whose goals are consistent with those of the organization. Conversely, among the important causes of low morale (from the standpoint of the organization) are lack of group loyalty or conflict between the group and the organization as a whole.

Of course, other conditions besides group identification are necessary to secure high morale. Although group loyalty will strengthen the confidence of group members, the obstacles faced by the group may seem so insuperable that it will lose confidence, become frustrated, and behave ineffectively. The French army was demoralized by pessimism during the disastrous campaign of 1940 long before most of the soldiers lost their loyalty to France or to their own fighting units. Over any great period of time, however, group identification as well as morale will disappear in the face of severe frustration.

Hence, the relationship of identification to morale is many-sided. On the one hand, group identification is usually one of the conditions essential to high morale. On the other hand, low morale produced by frustration of the group in its effort to attain its goals will usually destroy or greatly weaken the group identification. Further, strong group identification will strengthen the group resistance to frustration—will enable it to face greater obstacles and disappointments without dissolving than if identification were weak.

An example of these interrelationships may be cited. After a bitter political struggle in 1941, the California Legislature abolished the State Relief Administration (SRA) and turned its functions back to the counties. Observation of several of the district offices of the SRA during its last weeks showed: (1) that during the struggle, workers in a district where group loyalty was very strong showed much less discouragement than workers in a nearby district where loyalties were weak (strong identifications induced resistance to frustration); (2) employees worked much harder in the district where loyalty was strong (loyalty induced high morale); and (3) discouragement and indifference eventually developed in both districts, and with them a lowering of group interest and loyalty (continued discouragement led to frustration, lower morale, and the destruction of group loyalties).[6]

SOCIAL GROUPS AND ORGANIZATION UNITS

It must not be thought that what we have called the daily, face-to-face, working group is necessarily the same as the organization unit. In some organization units—a small typists' pool, for example—such will be the case. However, the formal designation of units, sections, branches, etc., does not always, or even usually, correspond to the working realities of group identification. Often the clerical personnel of a unit—say, the file clerks and typists working in a section or branch—make up one working group, while the professional personnel—for example, those in the same section or branch engaged in program planning or economic analysis—form one or more distinct working groups. A working group may be composed of all planning or technical personnel within a branch; or the branch chief, his sections chiefs, and a few other persons with particular competence within the branch may constitute such a group.

Again, in other cases, a few persons within one section may, because of the nature of their duties, work constantly with the mem-

[6] This illustration is based upon personal observation by one of the authors. Psychological research has accumulated a considerable body of evidence bearing out these propositions as to the relationships between identification and morale. For a review of the evidence, see Maier, *Psychology in Industry*, particularly pp. 75–107.

bers of a working group in another section and become absorbed
into that group. For example, an employee engaged in writing instructions for publication in an administrative manual may be
formally attached to a Procedures Branch in a Division of Administration. If he is definitely engaged over a period of time in
writing instructions for a particular program division of the agency
his daily contact with members of that division may lead him to
identify with one of its working groups and to be accepted by that
group. On the other hand, if he has a variety of assignments that
bring him into contact, now with one program division, now with
another, his primary identification will probably remain with a
group in the Procedures Branch. Under the latter circumstances,
the various instruction writers will probably help one another out
on assignments, talk over their common problems of getting along
with the program divisions, and work out tactics for increasing the
influence of the Procedures Branch in planning procedures for the
program divisions.

OTHER FACTORS IN IDENTIFICATION

To explain further why the working group sometimes coincides
with the organization unit and why it sometimes does not, and to
understand what other possible bases there are for group identification, we must examine briefly some of the psychological bases for
identification. We have seen that, in general, the important conditions for the formation of social groups are that the individuals
work together in daily face-to-face relationships and that they
work for the solution of common problems or the accomplishment
of common goals. Although these two conditions are probably the
most important elements in development of group identifications,
there are other factors that reinforce the tendency for social groups
to form. The most important of these appear to be: (1) common
extra-organizational identifications, (2) like-mindedness, (3) symbols and insignia, and (4) leadership. The first three of these will be
examined briefly, and the next section of this chapter will be devoted to a more detailed consideration of the fourth—leadership.

Extra-Organizational Identifications. People generally belong
to many groups besides their working group—family groups,
churches, schools, political parties, professions, business associations, or labor unions. To any one of these groups, an individual

will feel some loyalty, strong or weak, and will defend the group against outside critics or "dangers."

Now if most or all of the members of a working group are attorneys, or doctors, or economists, or Democrats, or Methodists, or unionists, or businessmen, the group will start with an identification that will provide a strong basis for the development of solidarity. Conversely, many of the social groups in organization that cut across the structure of organization units—for example, a group of economists employed in a number of divisions of a large agency who frequently lunch together—are based on these extra-organizational identifications.

Like-Mindedness. If all the members of a working group share the same social values or the same intellectual habits, it will also be easier for social cohesiveness and group identification to develop. For example, if all the members of a working group have a liberal (or if all have a conservative) social philosophy, a strong group solidarity can easily develop. Of course, this factor is closely allied with the previous one, since persons with common extra-organizational identifications are apt to be like-minded—at least on certain subjects.

Symbols and Insignia. Identification with abstract entities or ideas is greatly aided by concrete symbols that can be seen or heard. Thus the flag is a constant reminder that one is a member of a certain nation (or a certain regiment) and should always take its part, right or wrong. In organizations, the important symbols of identification are usually titles or names. A case study of a forest ranger in the Washington National Forest showed, for example, that "Forest Service" and "Washington National Forest" were the two organizational symbols with which he strongly identified.[7] Possession of a common organization name helps persons to achieve a common identification even when they are not in face-to-face relations.

The Role of the Leader

The work situation, extra-organizational affiliations, like-mindedness, and symbols and insignia provide some of the materials out of

[7] This information is from an unpublished study of the Forest Service by Herbert Kaufman of the Institute of Public Administration.

which identifications develop or can be created. Very often individuals who take a role of leadership play an important part in crystallizing these potential identifications into strong, cohesive working groups. A leader—even one with strong natural capabilities—cannot force a social group into being where there is no basis for it in common tasks, beliefs, affiliations, or symbols; but he can often act as catalyst, and he can sometimes decide the issue between two alternative closely-balanced group structures. A strong leader can sometimes forge his unit into a working group where diverse professional loyalties of its members might otherwise disrupt it.

Leaders are important in other ways than in the formation of new groups. They perform important tasks in holding together groups already in existence. In most organizations, by virtue of their dual membership in the working group composed of their subordinates and the executive group composed of their colleagues and their superior, they also perform the function of tying the numerous working groups to the goals and programs of the organization as a whole. They provide part of the connective tissue that makes of the organization something more than a collection of small, independent, self-centered groups

MEANING OF LEADERSHIP

A *leader* may be defined as a person who is able to unite people in pursuit of a goal. Leadership is always a matter of degree, the strength of influence depending upon the personal qualities of the leader as related to the qualities of those he attempts to influence and the situation surrounding the group.

The acceptability of a person as leader will depend, first, upon the recognition in him by his followers of qualities of excellence—qualities that give them confidence in him and make them willing to accept his influence. Superior intelligence, training, or experience may provide a partial basis for leadership. The quality of ascendance mentioned in Chapter 3—the tendency to take the initiative in interpersonal relations, to direct attention, to suggest solutions —is usually important. Proper professional status is often essential —engineers will be inclined to accept the leadership of another engineer—as is the sharing of beliefs and attitudes by leader and led and his ability to "talk their language."

To the extent that the group accepts the organization's formal status system, leadership can be earned by gaining formal position —placing a man in the position of branch chief may by itself give him influence over the members of the branch. Formal position gains additional influence from the sanctions at its disposal. The branch chief can block promotions and raises; he can make his subordinates' work more or less pleasant or easy. On this basis, we can distinguish "formal" leadership—influence derived from formal organization position—from "natural" leadership—influence derived from the recognition of personal excellence. In most situations, of course, these two kinds of influence are combined to a greater or lesser degree.

The important thing is not that the leader *possess* superior qualities, but that his followers *believe* that he possesses these qualities. Leadership is almost always surrounded by a halo. The followers are seldom in a position to judge accurately all the personal qualities of the leader. If he can maintain a high level of group loyalty, they will be quite prepared to believe that he is intelligent or well-informed. The influence of the accepted leader is greatly enhanced by this quite common tendency of followers to idealize him. Figures like Gifford Pinchot in the U. S. Forest Service, or Daniel Hoan, former mayor of Milwaukee, have come to serve as symbols of the organizations they led, and the accomplishments of their organizations are attributed—probably to a considerably exaggerated extent—to their personal qualities.

The leader's influence is always dependent upon the situation. That is why great crises make great Presidents (although not all Presidents in great crises are great). Seldom, if ever, does the leader have power to alter the more basic attitudes, values, and beliefs of his followers. Rather, as suggested above, his role is to resolve these attitudes and beliefs into an agreed-upon program of action. He is a broker of ideas and values who, by compromise and persuasion, secures assent to policies and proposals. Successful leadership is difficult unless the leader shares most of the values of the group, for if he does not, the burden of compromise on him will be too great. A chief of the Bureau of Agricultural Economics who did not believe in the general principle of "parity"—or who exhibited his disbelief—would not long retain any considerable influence in the Department of Agriculture. A person who thought all unemployed workers were ne'er-do-wells could exert only a negative influence on a group of social workers.

Leadership is also difficult unless the leader is highly sensitive to the attitudes of his followers—whether consciously or because he shares these attitudes. Lacking such sensitivity, he will not know at what point compromise is necessary in order to retain his influence and the cohesion of the group. He will not be able to avoid issues on which the group is badly split, and which would have a disruptive effect. This sensitiveness is a quality that both the friends and most of the enemies of Franklin D. Roosevelt agree that he possessed to a very high degree.

In summary, leadership is a two-way, rather than a one-way, process. How far the "great man" can actually change the course of history is a matter of debate. It is certain, however, that to a very large extent the leader must lead in a direction his followers want to follow.

THE LEADER'S IDENTIFICATIONS

Within a working group there is nearly always a recognized leader, whether he be the unit chief, the section chief, the branch chief, or a natural leader without position in the formal hierarchy. This leader is the recognized representative of the working group in its relations with the rest of the organization or with persons outside the organization. He becomes a rallying point, a symbol of the group's oneness.

The formally designated head of the unit is in favorable position to assume leadership of the group, and more often than not he is the recognized leader. However, his position in the organization, and the fact that he is designated from "outside," place him in a position somewhat different from that of informal natural leaders. In the first place, his desires for further advancement urge him to identify with larger organization units rather than with the group of his subordinates. In the second place, his membership in other working groups of executives may create competing pulls on his loyalties. Each of these points deserves attention.

Personal Ambition. Whether the leader identifies with the working group or with "the administration" will often depend upon how ambitious for personal advancement he is. Since promotion in an organization is an accepted symbol of personal success, an individual with very strong personal ambitions will usually try to rise in the hierarchy as fast as he can. He may feel that he cannot afford to be stopped on the way by emotional attachments to a working group and may therefore identify with the administration, the source of his personal satisfactions.[8]

The extent to which ambition will conflict with group loyalty depends to a large degree upon how completely the leader's personal ambitions have already been satisfied. Often, in units performing clerical jobs an old and faithful employee without the education needed for professional positions is promoted to the position of supervisor. Since he knows he cannot advance any further and does not particularly want to, such a supervisor often identifies very strongly with his subordinates and does all he can to protect their interests.

On the other hand, a young ambitious college man placed in the same supervisory position has only begun to satisfy his ambitions and will very likely identify with the administration. By the time this same ambitious young man has become a division chief in a government agency and finds himself in charge of some important governmental program he may decide, however, that the social values of his program mean more to him than climbing another step in the hierarchy. Thus he may fight for his program and staff against the interference of the bureau or agency, or even the chief executive or the legislative body. In a crisis, he may decide to resign rather than compromise his program and "double cross" his staff.

Personal ambition is a factor in most human situations. Virtually all leaders will at some time make decisions that reflect more their own ambition than the welfare of the group, the goals of its program, the goals of the agency, or even the best interests of the nation. Often they will so successfully rationalize their decision in terms of group values that they will be entirely unconscious of their own motivation. Subordinates not infrequently find that their proposals are blocked because acceptance of them would have damaging effects on the careers of their bosses.

[8] For an excellent case study of the relation between the leader's loyalty to his group and his advancement, see William F. Whyte, *Street Corner Society* (Chicago: University of Chicago Press, 1943), especially chap. 3.

Dual Loyalty. Apart from a possible conflict with personal ambition, a unit head's loyalty to his group may also conflict with his loyalty to an executive unit organization. Indeed, such conflicts, minor and major, are of everyday occurrence in organizations. A police sergeant, for example, may be instructed that his patrolmen on the night shift are spending too much time eating pie in an all-night restaurant and too little time patrolling. He may recognize the force of the complaint and yet feel that some allowance should be made for the men, who are generally doing (he believes) a good job. The sergeant's reaction to the competing demands of his superiors and his working group will depend on the relative strengths of his loyalties. In such situations it is hardly possible to generalize about the result, except to say that in some cases one loyalty, in some cases the other, wins out.

Confronted with such a conflict, the leader will probably do his best to persuade the one group or the other (or both) to change its position so that conflict will be avoided or resolved. To the extent that he is genuinely identified with both groups, he will feel a strong need to retain the confidence, respect, and friendship of the members of both, and the organizational conflict will become a conflict within his own personality. Out of such conflicts arises one of the most important functions of an executive—the function of reconciling the values and goals of the group he leads with the objectives of the larger organization units.

On the one hand, if the leader identifies with the working group, he may fail to bring that group into the larger cooperative system. (The patrolmen continue to eat their accustomed portions of pie.) His section or branch may no longer make its expected contribution to the goals set by the administrators at the higher levels of the hierarchy. If this condition persists, the entire organization may be endangered, or the administration may take steps to depose the leader and appoint another.

On the other hand, if the group leader identifies with the administration—if he does not fully accept the group's values or protect them when they conflict with the goals of the bureau or agency —the morale of the working group may be destroyed. If some group identification remains, the group will begin to reject the unit head, to take steps to protect itself against him, and to develop its own natural leaders. (The patrolmen may seek to conceal their activities from the sergeant.) The basic test whereby the group judges its leader is how he performs in such conflict situations. The leader is expected by them to be on their side and to use his prestige and ability—and that of his superiors, if possible—to protect the group.

THE LEADER AS MEDIATOR

When conflict arises between the goals of bureaus or divisions and the goals of their component branches or sections—and at least some conflict will certainly arise—the ability of the larger organization units to achieve their goals becomes heavily dependent on the success of the heads of their component units, pulled by their competing identifications, in mediating the conflict. In governmental organizations, the typical conflict situations fall roughly into two categories. First, there are employee-employer conflicts—conflicts between persons at the lower levels of the organization who think of themselves as "workers" and other persons in the organization thought of as "management." Second, there are conflicts between groups identified with particular, definite programs and the larger organization structures in which these groups are located. The types of group values that lead to these two kinds of conflicts will be discussed more fully in the next chapter, but for the moment we may concentrate on the role of unit heads in resolving such conflicts.

The first kind of conflict arises frequently when an organization attempts to increase the efficiency of one of its sections by introducing new work methods (as in the example of the patrolmen). The employees, jarred out of their accustomed routines, may interpret the change as an attempted speed-up. Their resistance may take the form of grumbling and complaints about matters that never gave rise to complaint before. Much of the burden of their dissatisfaction will fall on the first-line supervisors—those who are in direct contact with the operative employees.

If the supervisors are strongly identified with the employees' work groups, they may join in the general dissatisfaction and fail to try conscientiously to make the new procedure work. If the supervisors are strongly identified with the executive unit organizations, they may be sold on the new procedure but may encounter strong resistance in trying to put it across and may sense an increased difficulty in getting cooperation.

In either of these two cases, the new procedure may very well fail to bring about the expected improvement in operations. A gap has been created in the chain of identifications linking the working groups to the top executive group—a gap either just above or just below the level of the first-line supervisor—which weakens the influence of the larger organization over the working groups and makes it difficult to secure cooperation toward the organization's objectives. A failure to anticipate and take preventive measures against such gaps has in the past been a common failing of "efficiency experts," whose concentration on the mechanics of work procedures has sometimes blinded them to the problems of securing cooperation.

In some cases, the first-line supervisor may be identified both with the working group and the executive unit organization. In this case, he will find himself in an uncomfortable personal situation with conflicting demands made upon him from above and below. Even if he is not fully aware of the reasons for his discomfort, he will very likely try to allay it by placating one or both groups. He may try to convince the working group that the new procedure is intended to make their work easier, rather than harder. He may try to persuade them of the importance of the organization's program and the need for handling it efficiency. Or he may try to persuade his superiors that the new procedure is unworkable or that it needs to be modified in one way or another. If he is successful, he reestablishes some degree of harmony between the working group's values and goals and the demands made upon it in the interest of the organization's objectives.

The kind of situation just described, and the varying reactions of the supervisors toward it, prevails widely at those levels of the organization where employees are engaged in relatively routine and unskilled tasks and where they are not strongly interested in the goals of the larger organization unit.

A similar gap in the chain of identifications may occur between a section or branch and the division or bureau in which it is located —a gap at a much higher level than that of first-line supervision. Here, the most frequent cause is that the section or branch has a well-defined program with which its professional staff is strongly identified and which they feel is only loosely related to the work of the rest of the organization. Thus, the Fuel Oil Rationing Branch of the Office of Price Administration was responsible for conducting a complete rationing program. In establishing and administering this program, the Branch had few relationships with the rest of the organization. The top executive group in the Branch was strongly identified with its program, but was not so strongly identified with the Rationing Department or the agency as a whole. As a result, executives at the higher levels encountered considerable resistance to attempts to make policies for the Branch or to influence its program.

Comparable gaps in identification can be found between many Federal bureaus and their departments—for example, the Weather Bureau, in the Department of Commerce, or the Rural Electrification Administration in the Department of Agriculture—between regional and central offices of Federal and state agencies, and between city departments and the city government as a whole. It is difficult to bridge such gaps unless the top executives in the smaller units can be brought into an executive group at the higher level and induced to give some of their loyalty to it.

Summary

In this chapter we have examined the smallest structural units of organization, the working groups. We have seen how these groups come into being, the loyalties they create, and the effects of these loyalties upon individual behavior. Of great significance is the fact that individuals may belong to more than one working group and that they may have identifications with groups other than the immediate working group to which they belong. In fact, we have seen that the organizational role of supervisors and executives depends heavily on the identification of such persons both with the working group of their subordinates and with the executive group of their colleagues and superior. This dual identification is of major significance in securing some degree of integration in large organizations.

Our further analysis of organizations will rest heavily upon these concepts of identification and the working group. As the discussion proceeds we will see how they provide the foundation for a realistic and truly dynamic theory of administration.

CHAPTER FIVE

🙰

Building Blocks of Organization:
Group Values

IN CHAPTER 4 we examined how individuals are absorbed into social groups and how they come to adopt the group values. We did not, however, except by way of example, investigate the nature of the values that groups develop and the reactions of groups when their values are endangered.

An organization lives on the contributions of its members (and certain other persons such as appropriating bodies, customers, or clientele, etc.). The members make their contributions because of satisfactions they receive in return. We have seen that these satisfactions may be of many kinds of which money in the form of wages or salaries is only one.

A change in the satisfactions that an organization provides its members is important to the organization in several ways. First, if there is a great decrease in satisfactions a member may refuse to contribute any longer—he may leave his job. Even a small decrease in satisfactions may cause certain "marginal" members to leave—members who had previously found only a slight advantage in this organization as compared with other organizations where they might obtain employment. Often the most able members are the marginal ones, since they have greater opportunities for alternative employment than do the others.

Second, a decrease in satisfactions may lower morale, and consequently lower the contribution the individual is willing to make to the organization. If an employee gets many satisfactions from his work, he may work very hard; but if his pay check is the only

111

satisfaction he receives, he probably will not work any harder than he has to in order to get his pay.

Third, the satisfactions an organization offers an employee may be more or less specifically conditioned on his contribution. The simplest example—although not a common one in governmental agencies—is the piece-work wage. Promotional opportunities and salary increases are quite generally used as rewards for high employee contributions, and the creation or elimination of such rewards is certain to have an effect on contributions.

We see, then, that changes in satisfactions may affect the contributions of employees to the official organization goal (1) by increasing or decreasing turnover, (2) by improving or injuring morale, and (3) by altering the quality and tempo of performance through rewards. But there is no reason why we should look at employee satisfactions solely from the standpoint of organization goals. The typical adult spends almost half his waking hours at his place of work, and the pleasure—or lack of it—that he finds in his work experiences may be of quite as much importance, from a social standpoint, as the product of his work. It is only because our particular society pays a great deal of attention to the output of goods and services, and values work primarily as a means for producing these goods and services, that we tend to neglect the values of working-time experiences in themselves. Hence, there is good reason to concern ourselves with the values that employees seek in their work, quite apart from the effect that the satisfaction of these values has upon their productivity. We may expect that any change that threatens to decrease the net satisfactions of an organization member—regardless of the reasons for the change—will be resisted by him.

These comments on individual behavior also apply to the behavior of groups within organizations. A working group develops what we may call sensitive zones, which are areas of activity involving its values. The group will be relatively indifferent to outside influence that does not touch upon these sensitive zones but impinges only on its "zones of indifference." An attempt to influence the group's behavior within sensitive zones, however, is entirely another matter. If the demand from outside conflicts with values that are important to the group, it will be resisted. In resisting such a demand, the group is resisting a lessening of its satisfactions.

Typical Group Values

Let us now examine some typical group values that define the areas in which a working group is strongly resistant to organization authority. In the first place we must point out that we cannot say anything that applies equally to all groups. The values that any specific group will protect against organization demands can only be known with certainty by observing that group over some period of time. However, there are certain group responses that one is likely to find in almost all working groups.

SOCIABILITY

One source of considerable satisfaction to the members of a working group is the value of sociability or social communication within the group. Simply to be a member of a real social group is a source of satisfaction. Very few of us can endure long periods of physical isolation from our fellows. Almost equally unsatisfactory is social isolation—not having anyone to communicate with. The communication we desire is not simply discussion of common problems—that is, technical communication—but communication about ourselves. People like to tell others about their hopes and fears, about their personal feelings, about their experiences. They like to elicit sympathy from others. To work in a friendly and congenial group is extremely satisfying, and many people will turn down better-paying jobs in order to remain with such a group.

The problem of resistance to a decrease in these satisfactions arises chiefly in activities that involve repetitive mechanical tasks —tasks that have little intrinsic interest for the workers. In these situations the supervisors or "the management" sometimes come to the conclusion that talking and horseplay must be stopped in order to increase production. Although there is some contradictory evidence, the preponderance of evidence indicates that production is actually increased when social conversation is allowed. Of course, if the workers talked all the time, little work would be done. Restrictions of conversation that are accepted as reasonable by the workers will not conflict with the group's values. However, restrictions that have the effect of diminishing the pleasantness of the work situation rob the workers of a significant source of satisfaction and can be expected, therefore, to reduce their efforts. The working group will develop its own rules with regard to talking, the purpose of which will be to restrain its individual members below the point where management might interfere and take away some of the group's privileges.

RESTRICTIONS ON OUTPUT

A group of unskilled or semi-skilled employees will usually develop a notion of a *fair day's work* and resist efforts to increase its output above this point.[1] The employees will argue that trying to maintain a greater output over any period of time would injure them physically and leave no slack for illness or other emergencies. Furthermore, the employees will usually believe that if they show they can do more work the administration will expect them to produce it without additional compensation. Even on piecework jobs in industry, workers generally believe that if they turn out a large amount of work, and hence make large earnings, management will eventually cut the piece rate.

Because of these attitudes, groups doing routine work develop rules of conduct restricting output. Individuals who produce more than the informally accepted standard are criticized, ostracized, or otherwise disciplined by their fellow-workers as "rate-busters." If individual production records are kept, the employees will often keep these fairly level by slowing down when the day's quota is approached, by "lending" excess output to another employee who is falling below the quota because of illness or the like, or by saving excess production for the next day's quota. Any dramatic peaks or valleys in output may, so the group fears, call attention to itself and lead the supervisors to demand a greater work output.

It should be pointed out that the concept of a fair day's work includes a minimum or floor as well as a ceiling. The group will be critical of a "chiseler" who consistently goes far below the rest. The minimum or floor is not only a matter of group protection against management interference but also a socially derived notion of fair play.

Restriction of output is not due to laziness, for in a strongly cohesive working group the individual workers may pitch in and help a fellow in trouble. Nor is it immoral in the sense that it is

[1] See B. Gardner, *Human Relations in Industry*, chap. 7.

contrary to the workers' consciences. Restriction of output is the result of a real or fancied conflict between the goals or values of a work group and the goals or values of the larger organization outside.

Types of government units where group restriction of output can be expected are filing units, tabulating units, typing units, mailing units, mail sorting and routing units, mechanical reproduction units, building maintenance units, messenger units, and, of course, units doing manual labor in government factories such as the mint, the bureau of engraving, and ordnance plants.

STATUS SYSTEMS

Another area of values that can be found to some extent in any working group is the group's status system.[2] Within the group, each person has a certain position, more or less well-defined, to which are attached certain privileges and certain duties. The position of a group member is defined by the attitudes of the others toward him, which attitudes in turn are a reflection of the group's values. The group may attach great value to seniority, and, if so, the members who have been there longest will be accorded certain privileges by the rest. Value may be attached to nationality, to religion, to education, to "pull" with the boss. Among a group of women workers, value may be attached to beauty, to clothes, to ability to get dates. Usually, skill or knowledge about the job will be valued.

Persons possessing the qualities valued will be rewarded by the group in various ways. One way is the deference paid them by the group. Some one individual who possesses the valued qualities to a greater extent than any of the others may become a natural leader of the group. Certain jobs or tasks will be accorded high status and hence regarded as rightfully belonging to those group members who possess the valued qualities to the greatest extent. Associated with the proper distribution of the jobs is the notion that some persons have a right to make more money than others.[3]

[2] On the subject of the social organization of small work groups in industry, see Roethlisberger and Dickson, *Management and the Worker*, Part IV.

[3] Kaufman (in his unpublished study of the Forest Service) cites a case where forest rangers were opposed to an increase in their travel allowances even though their allowance did not cover actual expenses. The increase would have equalized their allowances with those of their superiors who were receiving the maximum allowed by law. Hence, the proposed increase violated the rangers' sense of proper status relations with their superiors.

Over a period of time, certain working locations, for example, a position by a window, may become valued, and the group will then feel that its highest status members have a right to those locations. In like manner, special value may come to be attributed to items of equipment, like desks, typewriters, phones, etc. The group will then feel that its highest status members should have those particular pieces of equipment as a matter of right.

The distribution of perquisites and symbols of status is a sensitive zone in which the acceptance of organization demands is not automatic. Thus, reallocations of equipment, changes in spatial relations, reshuffling of tasks among the group, a new job classification and wage scale plan, the promotion of one of the group's members, all of these may be subjects of more or less strong feelings among the group members. For example, a new pay scale that does not correspond to the group's conception of which jobs are worth the most money may seriously upset the group's morale and hence reduce its contributions; some employees may even start looking for new jobs.

STANDARDS OF WORK

In some working groups, standards of work comprise a sensitive zone. Probably any working group has some minimum standards of work performance or product quality, but work standards as group values are more significant in skilled and professional groups than in most others. Professions develop work standards apart from and outside of any particular organization and indoctrinate all of their members in them. Many professions go further and provide continuing disciplinary machinery to enforce the standards on the members of the profession wherever they may be or whomever they are working for. Disbarment by a bar association is an example.

For many professional working groups, and even for crafts, the area of work standards is one in which the organization's authority is almost completely ineffective.[4] Thus, an agency that attempted to induce its statisticians to doctor figures in order to prepare a report favorable to the organization would very likely either fail or

[4] For a concrete example of the difficulties encountered in persuading professional social workers to lower the quality of their case work see Herbert A. Simon and William R. Divine, "Human Factors in an Administrative Experiment," *Public Administration Review*, 1:485–92 (Autumn, 1941).

many of its statisticians would resign. Of course, many counter examples could be found where the attraction of a high salary or the need of a job induces a professional man to relax his standards, but this is more likely to happen when he is isolated than when he is associated with a strong professional working group.

It is frequently difficult to instill an organizational loyalty into professional groups. For example, attorneys in government agencies frequently regard themselves as protectors of the rights of individual citizens and are often reluctant to accept organization decisions that do not coincide with their notions of the proper protection of these rights. Likewise, many personnel technicians feel that their first loyalty is to the "standards of the personnel profession" and cheerfully disregard what their organization regards its interest to be. To cite another example, a draftsman will often balk at doing a hurry-up job because it would not come up to his standards of good drafting—even if the administrator assures him that the time deadline is more important than artistry.

Work standards as a source of group value are not entirely peculiar to professional and craft groups. Any group planning or operating a government program will come in time to be, or feel, expert in that program—to feel that it knows what makes sense with regard to that program and what does not. Thus, it will resent and resist attempts by the organization or by others (Congress, for example) to make changes in the program. Furthermore, it is very easy for the group to acquire such self-confidence with regard to the program that it thinks any suggestion that does not originate within itself is unwise. In this way, expertness often breeds inflexibility and resistance to change.

SOCIAL GOALS

A source of tremendous value to some groups are the social values that they believe they are promoting through their work— for example, relief, full employment, protection of consumers, or promotion of trade. Consequently, any attempt to change the orientation of the program so as to compromise the social values involved or to achieve a different set of values may be vehemently resisted. For example, the rationing branches of OPA, having identified with the consumer interest, stoutly resisted suggestions from the OPA hierarchy or elsewhere to sacrifice the consumer interest at various points for the benefit of industry or agriculture. Likewise, the Rural Electrification Administration has fought long and hard against opponents of public power both within and without the Department of Agriculture. There has long been a bitter struggle between the Home Loan Bank Board and the Federal Housing Administration about their differing conceptions of a desirable home mortgage financing program.

When a planning or operating group identifies with the social values of its program, organization authority is limited in an unusual way. A government organization exists to carry out public programs; not simply to manage employees. When its ability to determine the content of its programs is limited because program objectives and values comprise a sensitive zone for its planning groups, this limitation on authority goes right to the heart of the organization's purpose. Working groups in which program values are group values may accept readily organization commands or decisions involving working conditions, work output, and even salaries. However, organization decisions involving program content may be the signal for mass resignations—and resignations of persons whose program knowledge cannot be replaced easily.

On the other hand, if unpopular program decisions are imposed, the working group will often reach a low level of morale. In some government units where the group has been unable to prevent undesired policy changes, one finds that the principal interest left is interest in maintaining a job, and that no one will make a decision about anything until all organization clearances have been obtained, all organization procedures followed.

Groups with a strong interest in program values frequently form at high levels in an organization. Thus, in a bureau administering an integrated program, top planners may form a strong identification group around the bureau chief based on common interest in program values. In fact, a whole bureau may feel the contagion of program excitement. In such cases, the organization outside the bureau—other bureaus or the departmental office—may find it very difficult to influence the bureau on program matters. Bureau members dealing with budget or personnel may feel it to be their duty to outwit the departmental budget office or personnel office whenever those offices appear to interfere with the bureau's program.

VALUES RELATING TO ORGANIZATION STRUCTURE

In addition to the group values already described, people acquire by social training notions of the way they or others should be treated in organizations. These socially acquired notions also limit the organization's authority. Socially acquired notions about personnel matters will be described in the chapters on personnel. Social training with regard to subordination, to the roles of superior and inferior, will be described in the chapters on authority. Here we wish to discuss briefly just one such organization stereotype which will be treated at greater length later—the common acceptance of the idea of "unity of command."

It is a common belief in our society—transmitted by everyday conversation, from old employees to new employees, and even in college courses in administration—that in a properly run organization each employee should take orders from only one immediate boss. In spite of the fact that the daily experience of almost everyone is contrary to this principle—people do in fact accept orders from many bosses—the idea of unity of command provides a convenient reason, or rationalization, for refusing to accept unwelcome orders or orders from persons who are disliked. By arguing that the order does not come from *his* boss, the employee legitimatizes his refusal to obey. We are not at this point arguing whether a strict observance of unity of command would or would not make an organization more effective in achieving its goal. We are simply pointing out that the lines of authority and other aspects of organization structure or procedure may constitute a sensitive zone for a working group. For example, a particular branch of an agency may refuse to abide by an order governing working hours if it is sent out over the signature of the personnel director of the agency since "he is not their boss." The same order drafted by the same personnel director but stamped with the signature of the head of the agency may be entirely acceptable.

How Values are Protected

The reactions of groups when their values are endangered or destroyed have been touched upon at various points in the preceding discussion. Here it will be well to restate those reactions briefly and to introduce a particular kind of reaction which we shall call clique behavior.

COMMUNICATIONS

Much group protective activity is of a spontaneous and un-planned kind. Examples are restriction of output and the falsification of output records. Falsification of output records is simply one example of a more general kind of spontaneous protective behavior within organizations: falsification of communications in general. Both groups and individuals tend to communicate only that information which will improve their standing and not cause them trouble. The tendency is to communicate what they want to be heard rather than what "ought" to be heard. For example, the reports of government agencies to Congress or the public uniformly "prove" that the reporting agencies are doing a splendid job. Any failures that must be mentioned are accompanied by good explanations "proving" that the failures were due to causes beyond the agency's control, such as insufficient budget or lack of personnel. (The subject of organization communications is fully discussed in Chapters 10 and 11.)

LOWERED MORALE

In a sense, the lowered morale that generally accompanies an interference with group values serves as protection against such interference. Those outside the group who know they must respect and pay deference to the group values will not interfere lightly with those values; and where they feel it is necessary to make changes that are opposed, they will seek to sell the group on the desirability of the changes or to provide compensating satisfactions elsewhere.

CLIQUES

Occasionally, a group whose values have been impaired or are in danger will consciously plot to remove the source of the danger. When the protective reaction takes the form of conscious plotting, it is called clique behavior. A *clique* is an "illegal" group within an organization the purpose of which is so to change the established organization that the satisfactions of the clique members will be restored, preserved, or increased. The clique will attempt, by means not officially recognized, to change the organization's goals or philosophy or to get the person or persons who constitute the obstacle removed or transferred to a harmless position. The similarity between clique behavior and politics in the society at large is very marked. Cliques have many points in common with the political parties and pressure groups of the broader political scene. However, in terms of the mores of our society, while parties and (to a lesser extent) pressure groups are considered legitimate, cliques in formal organizations are nearly always viewed as "illegal."

Even though clique behavior is contrary to official organization policies, it is very common. An important part of it involves the personal struggle for the distribution of the jobs, status, and other satisfactions the organization has to offer. Where cliques are strong, individuals find that cooperation with the clique will greatly facilitate their personal advancement. Many executive positions, in and out of government, are normally filled by clique methods. Personal contacts, family relationships, the recommendations of friends, outright deals and exchanges, are still important means whereby men reach success or improved status in organization hierarchies.

DISSOLUTION OF GROUPS

If all protective activities fail and the individual's satisfactions are reduced below the point where he is willing to contribute any more, he resigns. The point of resignation will vary from individual to individual and from time to time. If many other attractive opportunities are available, the resignation point will be quite low. But some people have so much personal pride or integrity that they will resign even if no other opportunities are in sight or even likely —the act of resignation, particularly if publicly announced, may be an important source of satisfaction.

Efforts to Keep the Organization Integrated

Usually, the satisfactions of those persons at the top of an organization—"the administration"—can only be obtained by the continuance of the organization as a whole. They are interested in the organization's survival from the standpoint of their jobs and salaries, their prestige as important executives, and their identification with the general organization goals. "Middle management" attempts to reconcile the demands of the working groups and smaller organization units with the demands of the executive unit organizations above them. Similarly, the top administrators of a governmental agency must maintain a sufficiently high level of satisfactions within the organizations at the same time that they secure the support of the budget committee of the legislative body and of outside pressure groups whose friendship is needed for the organization's continuance. If a budget cut is threatened, for example, the administration may attempt to bring about those internal changes required to obtain a more sympathetic response from the appropriations committee. We have already cited the example of the OWI where Congressional pressures caused the administrators to force policy changes on the Publications Branch.

Even if certain organization values must be sacrificed, the loss of these—unless they are of vital importance—will generally be preferred to destruction of the entire agency. Hence, the tactics of the administration will come to be characterized by a certain amount of opportunism. Flexibility to demands from within and without will be recognized as the price of survival. The tactics of opportunism, particularly in relation to the pressures of outside groups, will be examined at length in Chapter 19. In the remaining pages of this chapter we will discuss how administrators seek the support of groups *within* their organizations.

CONSULTATION WITH GROUPS

Both individuals and groups generally respond more favorably to decisions that affect them if they are consulted in advance. This is particularly true in our society because of the wide belief in democratic mores. Consultation of the group, rather than the attempted imposition of arbitrary authority upon it, shows respect for the dignity of the group and of the individual.

Group consultation enhances cooperation in other ways, too. First, it permits the group and its members to share the credit for the decision—an intangible value that may be of considerable importance. Second, it satisfies the desires of the group and its leaders for status. In many government organizations, elaborate procedures for the clearance of instructions before issuance are jealously guarded by the organization units, who feel that their importance is evidenced by the fact that they must be consulted on major decisions. In the early days of the Economic Cooperation Administration, a simple instruction listing the major organization units had to be cleared by the heads of some twenty divisions and offices and was actually refused clearance by several of them because their units were named too far down the list!

Third, consultation often improves understanding between the working group and the executive group at a higher level. When decisions are handed down from above, all sorts of motives and hidden intentions may be read into the instructions, and they may be seriously misunderstood. Through consultation, the executive and working groups have an opportunity to convince each other of their mutual good intentions, and this may help to break down the idea that there is an inevitable conflict of interests between them. Of course, where there is a real conflict of interests—on a salary question, for example—consultation may do nothing to eliminate it. Even here, the opportunity provided the working group to put itself in the executive's place and to understand how the problem looks from the standpoint of his responsibilities may increase willingness to accept an unpleasant decision.

Consultation is an important device for protecting group values because it permits the group to present its objections in advance and to prevent decisions which could only be withdrawn, if they were once made, with a loss of face by the initiating groups. Likewise, by permitting assessment in advance of the reactions of the group consulted, it aids in avoiding unpopular decisions where the loss in morale would outweigh any benefits to be gained.

There has been a considerable growth in the popularity of methods of consultation in recent years since the psychological factors involved have become more generally appreciated.[5] However, in many organizations consultation is still avoided by execu-

[5] The Tennessee Valley Authority, for example, has assiduously cultivated the policy of consultation, both of employees and of clientele groups in the valley area. In some organizations with a core of strongly identified professional personnel—the Forest Service, for example—consultation has been practiced as a matter of course for some time and only recently has it become self-conscious. The practice of consultation is often both highly developed and self-conscious in agencies staffed by social workers, partly by transfer of ideas derived from the theory of case work practice and training in human relations.

tives and supervisors who feel that it involves a lowering of their status by limiting their "right" to exercise authority.

TRAINING AND INDOCTRINATION

Organizations frequently attempt to create an organization loyalty by training or propaganda. An attempt is made to "sell" the organization goal to all of its members either through indoctrination courses and meetings or through other means. The organization attempts to convince its members that what helps the organization helps the individual most, even though in particular cases this may not be apparent. By means of parties, clubs, and athletic contests, the organization may attempt to create the feeling of being part of "one big family." Some governmental organizations attempt to keep everyone informed of all important decisions and the reasons behind them and of how the agency is faring in Congress or in the press. This technique tends to make the individual feel that he is part of the organization and that its fortunes are his fortunes. On a lower level this technique amounts to explaining to individuals the reasons for assignments or how their humble jobs relate to the important goals of the organization. The use of this technique unquestionably affects the attitudes of many people, and hence it is an important management device.

SECURING THE LOYALTY OF EXECUTIVES

Top management usually tries to capture the loyalties or identifications of the executive staff—the unit, section, branch, division, and bureau chiefs. It does this by encouraging a "management" identification by means of executive clubs, dining rooms, luncheons, and conferences. The effort here is to create an executive primary group to win the loyalty of the individual executive away from the group he supervises.

When the administration has secured the loyalties of its executives, they become salesmen of the organization point of view to the working groups. This process and the personal problems it creates for the executives have already been described in Chapter 4.

To capture executive loyalties, and thereby to create a management identification, is seldom simple in governmental organizations. On any administrator there are always downward tugs. He cannot be completely impervious to the attitudes and demands of those below him. His human tendency to seek satisfactions in identification with those below him can be disciplined only by the promise of stronger satisfactions as a reward for identification with those above him. Government agencies, lacking the inducements of high salaries that private business organizations offer, must rely more heavily upon the values of status attaching to responsible administrative positions and upon identification with the social values of organization goals. In general, the concept of "the management" probably has more significance and represents a more homogeneous point of view in private business organizations than it does in most government agencies. As another possible result, governmental administration may generally have a more humanitarian tone in its handling of employees than does business management.

REPLACEMENT OF THE EXECUTIVE

If the loyalty of a unit head cannot be captured, the agency can, and sometimes does, replace him with one who is loyal to it. This technique has its limits, however. In the first place, if the working group was able to hold the loyalty of the previous executive, it may also very well be able to capture the loyalty of the new one. Cabinet members in this country and in England have testified almost unanimously to the great power of the department to secure their loyalty and to mold them to the departmental point of view. New to the work of the department, the executive is forced to rely heavily upon the technical advice of his subordinates. He is subjected to the same pressures from the organization and from outside groups as was his predecessor. He is confronted with the same facts. He is in daily contact with subordinates whom he comes to like and respect. This multitude of influences can hardly fail to produce a profound effect upon him.

In the second place, in those instances where the new executive resists identification with the unit and retains his loyalty with the agency, a new difficulty arises. The previous gap in the chain of identifications between the unit and the agency may be replaced by a new gap between the executive and his unit. The new executive may not be able to secure the cooperation and contributions of his staff, and the situation from the agency's standpoint may be no

better than before. Hence, the replacement of executives is a device
of limited utility for securing a greater loyalty from an organization
unit to the agency in which it is located.

PERSONNEL TRANSFERS

A device of considerable promise for enlarging the identifications and loyalties of organization members is the practice of making frequent transfers of personnel from group to group, or from
unit to unit. Such a practice, if vigorously and intelligently followed, would probably produce a sizeable number of people in the
organization who had had sufficiently varied experience to form
identifications with the larger units—although there is no reason
to believe that it would completely eliminate loyalties to the working groups in which they found themselves from time to time.
These individuals with a broad organization identification would
constitute a sort of corps of organization missionaries and would
counterbalance the dispersive forces of narrow group identification.

The device of constant horizontal transfer is used extensively in
the Army and Navy. At one time in the history of the United States
Army, the permanent assignment of officers to the headquarters
bureaus—ordnance, cavalry, adjutant general, and so forth—led
to very strong and troublesome identifications with these units on
the part of the bureau chiefs. An important part of the reform associated with the establishment of the General Staff consisted in
the weakening of bureau loyalties by the establishment of a policy
of rotation.[6]

In American civilian governmental organizations, the device of
transfers has been less extensively and systematically used, although the Forest Service is a notable exception. Almost all the
professional positions in the Forest Service are filled by men who
have had experience as Forest Rangers. Although in the later
stages of their careers these men may specialize in such areas as
timber management or personnel administration, this specialization does not usually begin until they have had a variety of positions in the district, regional, and Washington offices. The practice
is facilitated by the common professional background of the men

---

[6] For an account of the struggle surrounding this issue see Otto L. Nelson, Jr.,
National Security and the General Staff (Washington: Infantry Journal Press, 1946),
chap. 3.

and the integrated character of the program. It has undoubtedly contributed to the strong agency-wide loyalty encountered throughout the Service.

American civil service procedures, involving narrow, specialized job descriptions and narrow class descriptions, have seriously hampered the use of the transfer device in many Federal, state, and local agencies. Under American civil service notions, a person fitted for a job in one unit is unlikely to be fitted for jobs in many others because the jobs and the qualifications required for them are so tightly and concretely defined. An agricultural economist, for example, would probably have difficulty moving into a position for a professional economist in the Treasury Department or the Bureau of Labor Statistics.

In particular, there have grown up rather impassable barriers between "operating" and "administrative" positions—for example, between the position of a case worker in an unemployment relief agency and the position of a budget analyst in the same agency. Hence, what transfer takes place is largely a transfer within a fairly narrow professional specialization from one agency to another. A personnel specialist, for example, may serve as a classification technician in a city civil service commission, later get a classification job in a Federal agency, and move from that to the position of director of classification for a state personnel agency. The likelihood that he will be transferred from personnel work to some other work in the same agency is slight. Hence, the identifications that develop transcending the immediate working group are likely to be identifications with a professional group rather than with a bureau or department. This problem and related problems of personnel transfers will receive further discussion in Chapter 16.

OFFICE LOCATIONS

Another management device for changing identifications is the appropriate arrangement of office locations. It has already been noted that employees meet and form informal relations with those who work close to them more often than with those who work at a distance. Hence, the formation of a genuine executive group for a bureau or agency may be encouraged by locating the executives in one place or on one floor. The terms "top floor" or "front office," frequently applied to the top administrative group, probably have their origin in such office arrangements.

RECOGNITION OF NATURAL LEADERS

A final management device for controlling group behavior is to discover and control natural leaders. If the natural leader is outside the scheme of formal organization, he is often regarded as a "trouble-maker." He may serve as the nucleus of group resistance to organization influence, and if his qualities of ascendance are strong—if he actively desires leadership—he may consciously or unconsciously develop issues that permit him to lead the group in its resistance to the administration. A capable person in a position much below his capacity may, out of sheer frustration, make use of his energies to stimulate dissatisfactions in his work group. Such persons frequently become the organizers of cliques which they lead into conspiracies to achieve the official organization leadership they feel rightfully belongs to them. An alert management can frequently control and use these disruptive tendencies by absorbing natural leaders and giving them official recognition. The leaders having been stolen, an incipient revolution will often collapse.

Since positions in the organization hierarchy are limited in number, the problem of the natural leader cannot always be solved by promotion. Sometimes horizontal transfers provide an alternative solution. The offending individual (offending from the standpoint of the larger organization) can be moved to a position where he can do little harm, or he can be transferred often enough so that he has no time to do harm. It is not uncommon for captains in a large city police department who are felt to constitute threats to the chief through headquarters politics to be transferred to outlying stations. Conversely, the head of a field office who has built up strong local resistance to an agency's policies may be brought into the central headquarters where he can be more closely watched and where he can be encouraged to develop new identifications with the headquarters organization.

LIMITS OF MANAGEMENT INFLUENCE

No matter what device is used, be it increased pay and promised promotion or the threat of court martial and dismissal, no organization is ever completely effective in securing unswerving loyalty to the top executive group, or even comes close to such a result. This fact—and the corresponding limits upon influence over the individual that we noted in Chapter 3—is of profound importance for a realistic study of behavior in organizations. It means that mechanistic analogies picturing the chief executive as a pilot who directs the organization by manipulating instruments on a panel before him are grossly misleading. It means also that the legalistic analogies (such as the traditional theory of authority to be examined in Chapter 8) which describe authority as a "right" to control an organization are equally wrong.

These analogies are wrong, not because it would be *bad* for executives to have this unlimited power (although it would probably be condemned by the mores of our pluralistic, democratic, liberty-loving society). They are wrong for the very fundamental reason that they do not correspond to the realities of human behavior in organizations. Here will be found the greatest weaknesses in the traditional theories of organization. The science of administration has begun to make some progress in the correction of these weaknesses in the past two decades.

CHAPTER SIX

🔖

Dividing the Work: Assigning Jobs to Individuals

IN CHAPTER 3 we viewed the individual in the organization as a separate person subjected to certain influences upon his decisions and behavior. In Chapters 4 and 5 we viewed him as a member of a group or groups within the organization. We saw that the organization was composed of a large number of working groups; that these groups or units were combined, by means of interlocking executive groups, into a smaller number of sections, the sections into branches, divisions, bureaus, and finally into a single department or agency.

If we try to represent this structure visually, we arrive at the familiar organization chart in the form of a pyramid. In this chapter and the following one, our chief objective is to discover why particular activities are assigned to particular individuals and groups in this pyramid. First, however, we must determine why the structure of an organization has this pyramidal form—why there are a great number of "operatives" who supervise no one, a smaller number of unit chiefs who supervise the operatives, a still smaller number of section chiefs, and so on until finally we find a single person (or board or commission) who supervises the entire organization.

Reasons for a Pyramidal Structure

The sum total of the activities of the members of an organization must be coordinated or meshed together if the organization is to accomplish its purposes. To achieve this coordination, each member will often need to know what the others are doing so that he may dovetail his actions with theirs. A time-honored and tested method for achieving coordination is to have one person responsible for knowing what all the others in a group are doing so that he can relate the activities of each person to the activity of the others in the group. In this way, coordination is sought through the nervous system of a single individual—probably the most effective coordinating mechanism of all. Although the group supervisor is not the only coordinating device, he is one of the most important in nearly all organizations.

The use of a supervisor to coordinate the activities of a group would not in itself explain the need for a whole pyramid of such supervisors. Such a pyramid is needed because no single man can coordinate the activities of a large number of other persons—any individual's *span of control* has limits.

There have been many attempts to specify exactly how many persons one man can supervise effectively—the number stated by various writers ranging from three to around fifteen. Because of widely varying conditions and problems of coordination, no single number can be the right answer in all circumstances. The number of typists in a stenographic pool who can be supervised by a single office manager is almost certainly not the same as the number of commodity analysts who can be supervised by a single section chief.

Certain broad generalizations can be stated about the effective span of control. The maximum size of an effective unit is limited basically by the ability of that unit to solve its problems of internal communication. A unit scattered over a wide geographical area may be limited in size, if frequent communication is necessary, by the difficulty of carrying on communication. A unit requiring frequent internal communication, or communication involving difficult and intangible matters, will have to be correspondingly limited in size. A supervisor with unusual capacity for understanding matters placed before him and communicating with others will be able to supervise a larger group than a person less talented in these respects. All these factors, and many others, cause substantial variations in the effective span of control from one situation to another.

No matter how the limit upon the effective span of control may vary from one organization situation to another, in any one organization unit a limit will ultimately be reached. As any group grows larger, the adequacy of the communication between supervisor and worker diminishes, the supervisor is overloaded, coordination deteriorates; and these effects become noticeable long before any ultimate "breaking-point" is reached.

Consequently, when an organization has a large number of members (because of the size of its task), they must be divided into groups sufficiently small that each can be coordinated by a single supervisor. Again, one of the principal devices used to coordinate the activities of these separate groups is to designate a second-level supervisor to supervise a number of them. And if there are more first-level supervisors than can be coordinated by one man, there must be several second-level supervisors, to be coordinated in turn by the establishment of a third supervisory level. In an organization with one thousand employees, for example, if the effective span of control averaged about ten persons to one supervisor, we would expect to find about one hundred first-level supervisors, ten second-level supervisors, and one third-level supervisor (the head of the organization). If the effective span of control in the same organization averaged only five, it would require two hundred first-level, forty second-level, eight third-level, and perhaps two fourth-level supervisors in addition to the head.

The pyramidal form typical of organizations is therefore a consequence of: (1) the need for coordination of individual activities, (2) the effectiveness of the individual nervous system as a coordinating mechanism, and (3) the limits upon the effective span of this mechanism.[1]

Each supervisor and all those "below" him in the pyramid form a group of people that is doing something—that has some objective or goal related to the ultimate objective of the whole organization. One of our principal tasks in this chapter and the next will be to describe the considerations that govern the allocation of activities to the various groups—to the departments, bureaus, divisions, branches, sections, units—and to the individual employees. In order to do this, we will have to examine carefully the consequences

---

[1] This explanation should not be understood as a description of the time-sequence of steps leading to the development of an organization structure, but rather of the way in which such a structure functions once it is established. Most new organizations develop from the top down—by successive subdivisions of tasks—rather than from the bottom up. This point is discussed more fully at a later point in this chapter and has already been suggested in Chapter 2.

that flow from dividing work one way rather than another. Since it is somewhat easier to see the effects of dividing work among individual employees than it is to see the effects of dividing work among groups of employees, in this chapter we will be concerned primarily with specialization among individuals. In the next chapter, the division of work among organization units will be discussed.

Meaning of Division of Work

The terms "division of work" and "specialization" will be used here interchangeably. If we have a task to be done and a number of employees to do it, we divide the task and assign its parts to the several employees. Each of these employees then specializes in performing that portion of the total task which has been assigned to him.

To understand what is involved in the division of work, we shall have to consider the following points:

(1) To what extent, with a given set of tasks and a given group of employees, can different schemes be devised for the division of the work among the employees?;

(2) What consequences may follow from dividing work in one way rather than another?; and

(3) How can we account for and predict these consequences, as a basis for comparing alternative schemes of specialization?

ALTERNATIVE METHODS OF DIVIDING WORK

Let us suppose that we have a group of stenographers handling three hundred letters a week. The tasks to be performed are to take dictation from the persons drafting the letters, type the letters, carry them to their authors for signature, seal them in envelopes, stamp the envelopes, mail the letters, and file the carbons. (We could, of course, analyze the task in even finer detail, but this will not be necessary for present purposes.)

There are several possible divisions of work for our hypothetical stenographic group. If the group consists of three stenographers handling the dictation of three men, we might assign each stenographer all the tasks incidental to the correspondence of one of these men. Alternatively, we might give one of the stenographers the tasks of taking shorthand and typing the letters, one the task of mailing the letters, and one the task of filing the carbons. There are other possible arrangements. Each represents a particular "division of work" or "specialization." Although in everyday speech we would ordinarily say that the second arrangement represented a greater *degree* of specialization than the first, this way of speaking is inaccurate and misleading. In both cases the stenographers are equally specialized in the sense that each one is assigned a specified one-third of the total task. The total range of her tasks is narrowed correspondingly. But the narrowing is achieved in a different way in the second case than in the first. In the first arrangement, each stenographer narrows her task to the correspondence of a single man; in the second arrangement, each stenographer restricts herself to a specified part of the total process of handling a piece of correspondence.

What we have said about this simple example applies to every case of the division of work among individuals and among organization units. A division of work consists of a subdivision of a given bundle of tasks into smaller one-man (or "one-unit") bundles, and an assignment of one of these smaller bundles to each employee. There are as many possible divisions of work as there are ways of subdividing the total task.

It is just as possible to divide the work of making decisions as it is to divide manual work like typing and filing. Virtually all organization decisions are composite—involving a large number of distinct elements. During World War II, for example, there was in the Federal government an organizational unit which we may call the "Special Export License Branch." It was the task of this unit to decide whether applications for licenses to export certain commodities to allied and neutral countries should be granted or denied. Each decision on a license involved, in turn, decisions on these points: (a) how badly does the country of destination need the commodity, (b) is there a quantity of the commodity available for export, and (c) are the exporter and the consignee reliable—are we sure that they are not attempting to send the commodity indirectly to enemy nations? If we take these specific decisions as the elementary tasks of the agency, we again see various possibilities for the division of work. One possibility would be to divide work on the basis of the application—make one man responsible for all the decisions on a specific group of applications. Another possibility would be to divide work on the basis of the type of decision—to have one man or group responsible for the decisions on country needs, another for the decisions on commodity availabilities, and another for the decisions on the reliability of the exporter and the consignee.[2]

There is a further complication in the division of work of an organization when mechanical equipment is used extensively. In this case, not only must the work be divided among the individual employees, but it must also be divided among the individual machines. They, too, must be kept busy. Moreover, the division of work among employees will depend to some extent on how the work is divided among the machines. For example, in a governmental statistical unit operating punched-card equipment, certain tasks are allocated to the key-punch machines, other tasks to the card-sort machines, others to the tabulators, and so forth. The division of work among the employees of the unit must accord somewhat with this specialization of machines. Nevertheless, there are alternative ways of dividing the work. One employee can follow a particular set of punched cards through all stages—first punching them, then sorting them, and so on. Or, alternatively, certain employees can operate the punches, other the sorters, and so on. Since machinery plays a less important role in most governmental operations than in industrial operations, we can sometimes disregard the complications introduced by machinery.

In this section we have seen: (1) that any bundle of tasks can be divided for assignment in many different ways, (2) that this is as true of a bundle of decision-making tasks as it is of a bundle of manual tasks, and (3) that the use of specialized equipment controls to some extent the division of work among persons.

CONSEQUENCES OF THE DIVISION OF WORK

The consequences that may ensue from dividing work in one way rather than another fall into two classes: (1) the number and types of persons (and machines) required to perform the tasks in a normal working day may vary with the method of division; (2) if we change the division of work we may actually change the values that are attained. Stated differently, the division of work may have

[2] This example is adapted from U. S. Bureau of the Budget, *Production Planning and Control in Office Operations* (Washington, The Bureau, 1949), p. 13ff.

an effect both upon the *efficiency* with which a given set of tasks is carried out, and upon the nature of the *goals* that are actually achieved.

The effect of specialization upon efficiency is quite obvious and has long been emphasized by writers on organization and by economists. Adam Smith, for example, in the *Wealth of Nations*, pointed out that if work in a pin factory were divided by assigning one man the task of making a particular set of pins and another man another set, each man might produce a few dozen pins a day. On the other hand, if one man cut the wire into proper lengths for all the pins, another man formed the heads, and a third man pointed the pins, the factory could produce thousands of pins per man each day. The same sets of tasks would be performed under both arrangements, but under the second arrangement a given group of men could perform these tasks much more quickly than under the first.

The fact that the particular division of work selected may partially determine what goals will actually be achieved has received much less attention than the effect of specialization upon efficiency. Nevertheless, it is quite as easily illustrated. In our example of the statistical unit, the number of errors made in punching will quite probably vary with the method of specialization of the employees. In this case the *quality* of work as well as the *quantity per employee* is affected by the division. In the stenographic example, the average number of days or hours between the time a letter is dictated and the time it is mailed may (and very likely will) depend upon the mode of specialization. In this case the promptness with which a letter is answered, as well as the quantity per employee, is affected.

In our illustration of war-time export license control, the effect on the goal of the method of dividing the work may be even more pronounced. Export license control in war-time involves the weighing of the relative importance of several objectives that will often conflict. One objective is to conserve scarce commodities; another is to meet the needs of the importing countries; a third is to prevent commodities from reaching enemy countries. Changing the division of work may very well change the relative importance that employees attach to these objectives. Certain licenses that are granted under one mode of specialization might very well have been rejected had there been a different mode of specialization.

Finally, the specialization selected may have consequences for the satisfactions of the employees themselves. For example, if one girl in the stenographic group is assigned all the file work, the repetitive nature of her work may produce boredom and fatigue. If each of the stenographers spent a part of her time filing and the rest of her time performing various other tasks, her work might be much more enjoyable to her.

Why Specialization Affects Efficiency and Goals

Why should the method of assigning tasks alter the manpower needed to accomplish them or change the goals achieved? There are a large number of reasons for this, but they are all related to one central point—that each employee, machine, and group of employees in an organization performs a large number of tasks. If each elementary task in an organization were performed by a separate employee operating a separate machine, if each employee and each machine were used once and never again, and if there were no need for communication among employees, there would be no problem of specialization.

The fact that each employee performs many tasks has two consequences. First, the task he performs at one moment affects his ability to perform another task at a later moment. For example, before the stenographer who has been typing can file a letter, she must move from her typewriter to the file. Further, the fact that she remembers the name of the man to whom the letter was written means that she can place it in the proper place in the file without looking at the name again. In one respect, the performance of the first task impedes the performance of the second; in another respect, it aids the performance of the second.

Second, the way in which a person performs a task depends on what he himself brings to the task—which is, in turn, a function of his whole previous conditioning. Habits that the stenographer has developed through her previous experience determine how rapidly and accurately she can type a letter. There may be very large costs in bringing a human being (or a machine) to the point where he can perform a particular task rapidly or well.

Similar interconnections can be observed in a working group. As we have seen in Chapters 4 and 5, a group is much more than a collection of individuals that have suddenly been thrown together.

Group membership produces in the individual possibilities and tendencies of behavior that were not present before he joined the group. In assigning tasks to a group, we must consider both how the group structure aids or interferes with the performance of the task, and how this performance is aided or impeded by the fact that the group has other tasks as well.

Hence, in searching for possible consequences of particular modes of specialization, we must look to the fact that the performance of an individual, a working group, or a machine at any moment in time depends on what has happened to that individual, group, or machine in the past (including what we have "built in" to it); and we must consider what performance we will expect of it in the future. In this chapter we shall see what conclusions we can draw from this notion in regard to specialization of individuals in organizations; we will examine the relationships between specialization of persons and specialization of machines; and we will examine the relationships between specialization among individuals and specialization among groups. In Chapter 7 we will study the consequences of specialization among working groups and large organization units.

We have seen that the way in which work is divided among individual employees will usually affect the volume of production and the character or quality of the product. We can now examine the specific reasons why quantity and quality of product are affected by the manner of specialization. Among these reasons are the acquisition of skills, knowledge, and information; the amount of change-over time required; the complete or incomplete utilization of employees' time; and boredom and fatigue—all possible results of the manner of specialization, which in turn affect quantity and quality of product.

DEVELOPMENT OF SKILLS AND KNOWLEDGE

If we give an employee the task of preparing a legal brief and find that he does it very well, we have reason to believe that he will also do well when given the task of preparing another brief. If we find that a second employee types a particular letter rapidly and accurately, we would expect rapid and accurate performance on another letter. We would have no reason to expect the first employee to perform well if given the task of typing letters, or the second employee to perform well if given the task of preparing a brief. The good performance of each employee is a stable characteristic acquired through considerable time and effort—in short, a skill.

From the examples of the previous paragraph we see that if a person is exposed to a certain kind of experience (e.g., attending law school or taking a typing course), he acquires certain *skills*, which improve his subsequent performance of a particular class of tasks (e.g., writing briefs or typing letters). But any given skill or group of skills only improves the performance of a limited range of tasks. Legal skills probably do not noticeably increase a man's ability to make economic analyses. In fact, a skill in performing one kind of task may actually interfere with the performance of others—a person who acquires the touch needed for rapid typing may in the process lose the touch needed for playing the piano well.

Moreover, it takes time to acquire a skill. If an organization wants an employee to have a particular skill, it must either be willing to pay him while he is acquiring it, or offer a high enough salary to attract a person who has previously paid the cost in time and money of acquiring that skill. Furthermore, most skills decline unless they are practiced with some frequency. Hence, the employee must be given opportunity for frequent practice of his skills if he is to retain them at a high level. For these reasons there are advantages from the standpoint of efficiency in dividing the tasks of an organization in such a way that each employee will be required to employ as few skills as possible, and to employ them frequently enough to retain them.

But most jobs (except possibly some of the most routine jobs in an industrial assembly line) actually involve a considerable range of skills. The volume of work involving any single skill will not usually be enough to keep even a single employee busy. So far as our analysis has gone, it would not matter, in combining tasks involving two or more skills, which skills we combined. In fact, however, it does matter. An organization is usually able, by hiring or training, to acquire an employee with any *specific* skill it may want to use. It is not always—or even usually—able to acquire an employee with any *combination* of specific skills it may want to use. It will usually be easy to employ or train a typist who can also take dictation. It will usually be impossible to find an economist who is trained, or willing to be trained, in stenography, or an accountant who is trained, or willing to be trained, in the skills of fighting fires.

We will have more to say about this rather obvious fact later on. The important point for our present purposes is that, while it may be possible to divide up the work of an organization so that each job requires only a limited range of skills, there may be severe limits as to which groups of skills can, and which cannot, be juxtaposed in the same job. This limitation may often reduce productivity—we might often be able to increase efficiency, for example, if we *could* employ lawyers who were also skilled in stenography.

We must also keep in mind that the possible increase in productivity from the narrowing of the skills required on a job may be more than balanced by other factors. All we can say for the present is that, all other things being equal (which they usually are not), the productivity of individuals may be increased by grouping tasks so that the range of skills applicable to any one job will be relatively small.

CHANGE-OVER TIME

Closely related to the effect of skill upon productivity is the effect of change-over time. By change-over time is meant the unproductive time spent in proceeding from one task to another and "warming up" in the new task. This unproductive time may be the result of either physical or mental operations. The former has been illustrated by the example of a stenographer shifting from typing to filing. The latter is illustrated by the time taken by a patent examiner in shifting his "frame of reference" from one patent application to another and in recapturing from his memory the things he needs to know about the second (so-called "recomprehension time").

Change-over time is also involved when a sequence of tasks is to be performed, each step dependent on the previous ones in the sequence. In the statistical unit previously mentioned, the person who sorts a set of punched cards must know what codes were used by the person who punched them; and the person who tabulates data from the sorted cards must know both how they were coded and how they were sorted. If different persons perform these separate steps, provision must be made for their coordination—

each must know what went on before. Whether the coordination is secured by communicating among the operators themselves, or by the preparation of a set of instructions for the performance of the whole sequence, time and effort is required.

Here we see an example of a situation where gains achieved by skill specialization (separate operators for each step) and one kind of change-over (avoiding movement from one machine to another) may be partially or wholly balanced by other costs of change-over (communication of the instructions). In a routine statistical procedure, where standard instructions can be used again and again, the former specialization might give the higher production, while in a special and complicated statistical tabulation that was not to be repeated it might be preferable to reduce the costs of communication by the latter specialization.

FULL UTILIZATION OF TIME

An employee is generally hired and paid for a day's work whether there is a day's work to be performed or not. Therefore, when the volume of work requiring some narrow range of skills is not sufficient to keep at least one employee busy, the division of work will have to require a broader range of skills if employees are to be fully occupied. Hence, the division of work among the employees of an organization unit will depend upon the range of the unit's tasks and the volume of tasks requiring particular skills.

Where there are fluctuations in work load, the problem of avoiding "dead time" is even more complicated. The usual solution to this problem is to give employees more diverse tasks so as to balance peaks in one type of work against valleys in another. In general, the smaller and more fluctuating the volume of work involving any given set of skills, the wider the range of skills that will be required of any one employee—to avoid the alternative of having him completely unproductive part of the time.

BOREDOM AND FATIGUE

The method of dividing work may have a variety of consequences for the satisfactions of employees. The types of satisfactions that individuals obtain or expect from work situations have already been surveyed in Chapter 3. In this section we will comment on only one aspect of the whole situation—the problem of fatigue and boredom.

On the basis of the numerous studies that have been made in industry and government, there can be no doubt that excessive subdivision and routinization of tasks is one of the important causes of fatigue.[3] Fatigue or boredom may be reflected in low productivity, excessive absenteeism, or rapid turnover of employees. It should not be supposed, however, that the relation between skill specialization and fatigue is a simple one—that fatigue always increases with a narrowing of the skills employed. The amount of attention required, the distribution of rest pauses, the grouping of the tasks themselves, all enter into the picture. A very routine task that permits the trained worker to daydream may prove less boring than a more varied task that requires intermittent but not concentrated attention. The point we wish to make here is that the method of dividing work is one of the factors that determines the level of fatigue and boredom. It is certainly not the only factor.

BALANCING THE ADVANTAGES OF SKILLS IN VARIED JOBS

We have seen that a limited total volume of work as well as other considerations may lead to a method of specialization that combines a variety of skill and knowledge requirements in a single job or position. In such cases, specialization of jobs with respect to certain of the skills required in them may lead to an actual diversification with respect to other skills. If, in our Special Export License Branch, we assign to each employee a particular country of destination, he needs to become skilled with respect to the problems of only that one country, but he will have to master knowledge about the supply of a wide range of commodities. On the other hand, if we assign each employee a particular commodity group, it will be easier for him to acquire skill in dealing with questions of the availability of those commodities, but harder to acquire a thorough knowledge of all the individual country needs. Of course if we could split off the aspects of the decision involving commodity knowledge from the aspects involving country knowledge, and assign them to different employees, this particular dilemma would disappear.

[3] An excellent treatment of this subject will be found in Maier, *Psychology in Industry*, chap. 15.

INDIVIDUAL SPECIALIZATION AND MACHINE SPECIALIZATION

Specialization of machines and equipment can be analyzed in almost the same way as the specialization of individual employees. While machines do not acquire skills, particular "skills" can be built into machines. Ordinarily, a machine that possesses a wide variety of skills—can perform many jobs—is either more costly or less skilled (performs less rapidly) than a machine designed to do a specific task repetitively. When the more flexible machine is used, change-over time may also be involved in going from one task to another. On the other hand, if the work volume is insufficient it may not be possible to utilize fully the time of the more rapid but less flexible machine, and many of the costs of the machine continue even when it is idle.

Where machines and equipment are used, there is also the problem of relating the division of work of the machines to the division of work of the employees. Where an employee operates only a single machine, or only machines of a single type, advantages are obtained by the consequent narrowing of the skills required of him. Where single-purpose equipment is used, change-over time may be lost while the employee turns from one piece of equipment to another, while if more flexible equipment is used, time may be required to shift the machine from one task to another. Where a machine requires only intermittent attention from an employee, much of the employee's time may be unproductive unless his task of operating the machine can be combined with other tasks. Without pursuing the matter further, we can see that the same considerations are involved—although in more complicated form—when we deal with a situation where there is equipment as when we are concerned only with the specialization of employees.

INDIVIDUAL SPECIALIZATION AND GROUP SPECIALIZATION

Conceivably the problem of dividing the work of an organization could be approached entirely "from the bottom up." That is, we could consider the whole array of tasks the organization needed to perform; determine how these tasks could advantageously be grouped into individual jobs; and then see how the organization pyramid could be constructed by grouping jobs into units, units into sections, sections into branches, branches into divisions, and so forth. The range of tasks performed in any actual organization is so great, and the difficulty of picturing in advance just what all these tasks should be is so overwhelming, that such an analysis from the bottom up could certainly not be carried out in practice. Nor is this the way in which organizations are actually constructed. As we have mentioned before, they most often develop through a series of "splitting" processes. Starting with the over-all organization goal, it is determined what major activities have to be carried on to achieve the goal; these major activities are divided in turn into sub-activities; and so forth. The analysis that precedes the development of organization structure—and particularly the structure of new organizations—is primarily an analysis from the top down, rather than from the bottom up.

This fact has important implications for the division of work among individuals. Let us consider a concrete instance. Suppose that we have divided the Patent Office into sub-units to the point where each of these is concerned with the examination of patent applications in a particular field—electric motors, petroleum chemistry, and so forth. Each of these sub-units will require a certain amount of stenographic work in order to accomplish its goals. But the volume of stenographic work in each sub-unit may partially determine the division of work among stenographers. If, for example, there is only enough work for one stenographer in each sub-unit, we obviously cannot keep specialists in typing and specialists in filing fully occupied. Hence, if the structure of organization units is taken as a given—as unchangeable—certain forms of individual division of work are ruled out as possibilities. Conversely, if we do not wish to rule out the possibility of dividing the typing work from the filing work, we must reconsider the way in which the organization units have been specialized—we must consider the possibility of grouping the stenographic personnel in separate organization units.

If we take account of the limitations of the human mind in grasping complex situations in all their detail, we see that a study of the consequences of the division of work in any sizeable organization must combine the bottom-up and top-down points of view. In our discussion of the specialization of individuals, we have talked largely about grouping elementary tasks—the bottom-up view.

In Chapter 7, where we will be concerned with the division of work among organization units, the top-down view will prevail. These two approaches to specialization should be thought of as complementary. Both are essential in any thorough analysis of organization structure.

Plans for the Division of Work

In almost all organizations of any size, the formal organization plans include plans for the division of work among units, and usually among individual employees. These plans may take the form of specific orders that "John Jones shall do thus and thus," a written description of John Jones' job, or a written procedure for accomplishing certain tasks, indicating who is to do each part of the task. Like other formal plans, plans for the division of work may be carried out, or they may be disregarded and violated in the actual pattern of organization behavior. In this section we will present some of the considerations, in addition to those already discussed, that are involved in planning the division of work.

THE LIMITS OF PLANNING

A planned division of work will not be fully accepted in practice unless it takes account of certain inflexibilities, in addition to those already discussed, that are wholly or largely beyond the control of the formal organization. These inflexibilities include the types of job specialization that already exist in society, the roles that individuals picture for themselves, the social structures of existing work groups, and the existence of other—possibly conflicting— organization plans.

Specialization in Society. To a considerable extent the problem of the division of work is "solved" for the job planner by the specialization already existing in society. The job planner is faced with a whole host of "givens." Many persons—perhaps most of the white collar group—have acquired specific groups of skills and abilities by previous experience or training. If an organization needs a particular skill to achieve its objective, it must call upon a person who has specialized in that skill, together with all the skills that are grouped with it in the social training process. Thus, if an organization needs decisions reflecting some kind of economic knowledge, it usually has to hire an economist.

Once the economist has been hired, his job is almost automatically determined—he does economic work. Likewise, a typist types, a stenographer takes dictation, a lawyer gives legal advice. When these people are brought into an organization they bring their jobs with them. Most of the activities they engage in are pre-defined, at least with respect to the groups of skills involved. They are not consciously or rationally planned by the job planner.

Although very many jobs in any organization are wholly or partly socially defined, many jobs, and parts of most jobs, are organizationally defined. In almost any organization there will be many jobs that consist wholly in working with some procedure peculiar to that organization. Persons in such jobs are valuable to the organization because they know the particular procedure in question. It is on those jobs or aspects of jobs that are organizationally rather than socially defined that the problem of allocating tasks to individuals is focussed. Here the supervisor or job planner has an area of choice and must face the difficult question of *how to specialize.*

In a welfare agency, for example, certain jobs will be socially defined to the extent that persons with social work training are recruited to fill them. But among these jobs, the question of which social worker will be assigned which file of cases, and whether the cases will be assigned on the basis of type or location, are problems to be settled in the course of job planning.

Employee Expectations. Although the supervisor has some choice in defining those jobs that are not completely determined by the existing pattern of specialization in society, his choice is also limited by the expectations of his employees as to what the job "ought" to include. Individuals adopt roles or notions about themselves which to a certain extent govern their reactions to work assignments. Some people think they are too good for certain kinds of tasks; others think they are not good enough for those tasks. A stenographer would generally rebel against helping out on the elevators during rush hours.

Social Structure of Groups. In the last chapter we pointed out that working groups acquire a social structure that is symbolized partly by the distribution of tasks. Reassignments of tasks are very likely to upset that social organization, with serious effects on the morale of the group. Having the elevator operator help with the filing would almost certainly upset such a group social system.

Conflicting Organization Plans. The job planner may find that his freedom to allocate duties is also limited by existing organizational plans that he cannot change. In the Federal government, for example, the classification of most civil service positions must be approved by the U. S. Civil Service Commission (or, in other cases, by the central personnel office of the agency). A division head who wishes to reassign duties in his division has no authority to determine the classification of the new positions. Reassignment of duties may change the classification officer's evaluation of a job so that he assigns it a lower classification. Although it is customary when jobs are reclassified to allow the incumbent employee to continue to draw his old salary, still the lowering of his classification is likely to be a serious blow to his pride and satisfactions. Furthermore, the classification limits the salary, and hence the quality, of persons who can be appointed to a particular position.

CONFLICTING VALUES IN JOB SPECIALIZATION

We come now to the final limitation upon the freedom of the job planner. Assuming that there are a number of different ways in which the tasks might be divided or specialized, his choice of one of these ways will depend on the administrative objective he is trying to obtain. The problem is by no means the simple one of selecting that specialization which will yield the highest productivity. Each plan of specialization will likely have both advantages and disadvantages from the standpoint of any particular set of goals or values. These advantages and disadvantages must be weighed in terms of the goals, and consequently a change in program emphasis may require a change in the division of work. This statement is as true of relatively "routine" activities as it is of complex programs, as the following illustration shows.[4]

One of the important functions of the U. S. Patent Office is to supply to the public printed copies of patents that have been issued. Most orders for copies of patents are received by mail. Copies of the more than two million different patents are kept on shelves that occupy a space of somewhat more than two acres. Each order

[4] In the development of the ideas in this section we are indebted to William R. Divine and his associates in the U. S. Budget Bureau. *Production Planning and Control in Office Operations*, pp. 21–26.

generally calls for a number of patents—averaging about six. How will we divide up the work of a unit filling these orders?

What are the values our procedure is supposed to promote? The goals of processes of this kind can generally be classified as: (1) quality or accuracy, (2) speed, and (3) economy. In this case, accuracy would mean principally that the correct patents be taken from the shelves and mailed to the person ordering them. Speed would mean that the interval from the time when the order is received to the time when the patents are mailed be as brief as possible. Economy would mean that not any more money be spent than necessary to perform the operation. Usually the procedure that would be best from the standpoint of speed would not be the most accurate or the most economical, and vice versa.

One solution that suggests itself is to have a clerk pick up each order, go to the files, pick out the correct patents, assemble them, and mail them. This method was very accurate, but proved extremely expensive because of the time lost going from one part of the file room to another.

A second solution would be to have a clerk copy the patent numbers from the order onto separate slips together with an order number or name. Separate groups of clerks could be assigned to each 100,000 numbers in the files, and each clerk could then pull out the patents for a whole batch of slips falling in that range of numbers assigned to him. When the patents were returned to the order desk, they could be resorted by order number and the patents for each order assembled and mailed. Two extra clerical steps would be involved—making out the slips and assembling the orders, but walking time would be greatly reduced.

A third solution would be to subdivide the files as in the second plan but, instead of making separate slips for each patent, to route the order successively to the various sections of the files where the appropriate patents belonging to the section could be attached to it. This method would eliminate the two additional clerical steps in the second plan but probably would increase considerably the time for filling each order since the order would have to pass through a number of work stations. Also, copies of patents might become detached from the order and lost, decreasing the accuracy of the procedures.

Under any one of these procedures, a final step of checking the assembled patents against the numbers requested might be added.

Adding this step would reduce the number of errors but would involve additional cost and time.

The choice among these procedures involves the question of which values or goal is to be promoted; it cannot be made in the abstract. In selecting its procedures, the Patent Office will probably feel on one side the pressure of an appropriations subcommittee of Congress to keep expenditures down and, on the other side, the pressure of the Patent Bar Association to obtain prompt service for patent lawyers. The selection of the criterion or value and hence method of specialization could have a serious impact on the organization's future. The selection of the method could also have some effect on the morale of the unit.

Summary

In this chapter we have begun the analysis of one of the vital elements in an organization's structure—the division of work. The way in which work is divided may have important consequences both for the productivity of the organization and for the goals toward which this productivity is directed. We have examined in detail how these consequences come about in the specialization of individuals. The actual division of work in any organization is a product both of formal planning and of informal processes. In the final pages of the chapter we have indicated some of the limitations imposed upon the planner in this area, and the way in which he adjusts the division of work to the particular aims and values of the organization.

CHAPTER SEVEN

❦

Dividing the Work: Specialization Among Organization Units

IN THIS chapter we will examine the reasons why specific objectives or activities are assigned to particular organization units—that is, the division of work among groups, rather than among individuals. We shall seek answers to questions such as why all economists in a bureau are sometimes grouped together in an economics division rather than scattered throughout the other divisions of the bureau.

Most of the considerations that applied to the division of work among individuals will also apply here. First, the structure of the various professional and occupational groups in society will have considerable bearing on the structure of organizations. Second, the consequences of any proposed scheme of organization must be evaluated in terms of the specific objectives that are sought, and "efficiency" must always be defined in relation to those objectives. Third, any particular division of work among units will secure certain values at the sacrifice of others that could better be attained through a different specialization. Consequently, disputes about organization structure are very often not disputes about efficiency but basic disagreements as to what values the organization is supposed to promote.[1]

---

[1] It is highly regrettable that the dependence of organization structure upon the goals that are sought was almost entirely overlooked by the Hoover Commission, except in certain minority dissents from the Commission's recommendations. That most of the Commission's proposals for "more efficient" organization do involve such value questions is suggested by the opposition that the proposals have evoked from groups interested in particular programs—for example, opposition of Veterans' organizations to the removal of hospitals from the control of the Veterans'

Traditional Structural Theory

Finding the "one best way" of dividing the work of an organization has been the object of considerable study by administrators and theorists of administration. Out of this study has evolved, first, a classification of the different types of specialization that are available and, second, some suggestions as to the characteristic advantages and disadvantages of these several types of specialization. While we shall have little occasion to use the traditional classification of "types of specialization" in this book, the terms have become so deeply imbedded in the vocabulary of administration that the reader may wish some familiarity with them.

TYPES OF SPECIALIZATION

The classification most widely accepted is that of Gulick,[2] who says that the units of an organization may be constructed by grouping together:

(a) activities having a common *purpose* which is a sub-purpose of the over-all organization objective. For example, if we regard the reduction of fire losses as one of the sub-purposes of municipal government, then the fire department represents a division of work in terms of purpose.

(b) activities employing common *processes* out of the whole range of processes used in the organization. For example, almost all of the municipal activities involving the processes of engineering design and construction are generally grouped in a public works department.

(c) activities serving a particular *clientele* group out of all the groups served by the whole organization. For example, most Federal services to Indians are provided by the Indian Service.

(d) activities performed in a particular *area* within the whole area served by the organization. The regional offices of the Federal Security Agency are an example of units based on the division of work by area.

Administration, and opposition of employers' groups to the transfer of unemployment compensation and employment services to the Department of Labor.

[2] "Notes on the Theory of Organization," *Papers on the Science of Administration*, p. 15.

To divide the work of an organization according to this scheme, we would have to identify the major sub-purposes of the organization and establish an organizational unit for each sub-purpose; or identify the major processes employed and establish a unit for each of these; or identify the various clienteles served and establish a unit for each clientele; or divide the jurisdictional area into regions or districts with an organizational unit for each.

DIFFICULTIES OF THE SCHEME

This classification of bases of specialization is suggestive but should not be taken too seriously. It is often difficult to determine which type of specialization is represented by a particular organization unit; in fact, most organizations could be related to all four classes. For example, is a vice division in a municipal police department a purpose subdivision of the department, a process subdivision, a clientele subdivision, or an area subdivision? It shares some of the characteristics of all four. If "suppression of vice" is a sub-purpose under the general heading of "suppression of crime," it falls in the first category. But the vice detail uses some procedures and methods that are different from those used by the rest of the police department and hence also represents a process subdivision. It also has a special clientele (whether this be interpreted to mean the purveyors of vice or their victims), and it is concerned largely with specific areas in the city.[3]

Even if we could agree that a particular organization falls within only one of these classes, this scheme of classification would not tell us how to organize any particular activity. If we group in

[3] The difficulty of deciding what activities should be grouped together to form a "major purpose" organization is well illustrated by the Report of the Commission on Organization of the Executive Branch of the Government (hereafter cited as the "Hoover Commission"). For example, the Commission urged the unification of all medical activities and hospital services in a United Medical Administration. Three of the commissioners disagreed with this recommendation, saying, "In our opinion the proposal . . . violates two of those basic principles which were approved by the full Commission in that report. They are: (1) Government agencies should be grouped into departments according to major purpose. . . ." To this dissent, one commissioner replied: "The creation of a United Medical Administration does not imply any violation of fundamental principles of organization. Bringing together all the major medical functions of the Federal Government under the administration of one agency provides us with one of the clearest examples of organization by major purpose that it has been possible for our Commission to propose." Hoover Commission, report on *Medical Activities* (Washington: Government Printing Office, 1949), pp. 42, 48.

each organizational unit activities having a common purpose, for example, then we will scatter throughout these units activities having common processes, common clientele, or common areas. If each Federal department is a unit grouped by purpose, then legal processes will be found in many departments and not grouped in one; services to veterans will be scattered among several departments; each region of the United States will be served by many Federal agencies. Hence, to know that four or more ways of grouping activities are available does not give any clue as to which of these criteria of grouping should have precedence when they conflict.[4]

The ambiguity of the classification and the fact that it sets up conflicting criteria for grouping activities seriously limit its usefulness. The principal insight we gain from it is that any organizational task can be divided in a number of different ways and that by dividing it in a particular way certain consequences ensue which are different from the consequences that follow on another division of work.

The Process of Subdivision

The division of work in organization is seldom completely planned in advance, except in the most general terms. The hundreds and thousands of jobs, activities, and interrelations of any government agency were never visualized and designed by organization experts at the time of creation of the agency. In general, organizations begin as a single cell and grow by repeated subdivisions.[5]

In Chapter 2, we followed the process of organization origin up to the point where an organization comes into being. This point is usually signalized by the appointment of a top administrator. He will generally call in a few persons in whom he has confidence to confer with him. As problems present themselves to this small group—a unit organization—a particular person will be designated (from within or without the group) to handle a specific problem. This person, in turn, will call in a few persons in whom he has confidence, and the process repeats itself with the creation of secondary unit organizations that begin to subdivide in the same way.

[4] For a more complete discussion of these difficulties, see Simon, *Administrative Behavior*, chap. 2.

[5] See Barnard, *The Functions of the Executive*, pp. 101ff.

For example, the Economic Cooperation Administration, created by Congressional approval of the "Marshall Plan," grew from a unit organization of less than a dozen members at the beginning of April, 1948, to an organization of 700 (in the Washington office alone), comprising at least thirty or forty unit organizations by the end of June. The subdivision process was dominant throughout this period, although it was somewhat modified and molded by the activities of organization specialists. In other cases—say a typical municipal police department—the process is much more gradual and takes place as the organization grows (by the growth of the city) or acquires new functions (e.g., traffic control).

The whole process is controlled by the problems that present themselves and the way the persons involved react to those problems—their value systems and their skills. Because the concrete problems cannot be anticipated in any detail, and because they would in any event not present themselves in any logical order, it is impossible to guide the process of growth so as to end up with a finished department corresponding to some *a priori* ideal of an organization. As a result, any technology of organization structure is chiefly applicable to *reorganization* of existing structures, although the possibility must not be ruled out of exerting at least some influence upon the growth of new organizations.

At the present time, we find in local, state, or Federal governments an elaborate and complex administrative machinery that came into being as described above. There are many departments, each with its many bureaus, divisions, branches, and sections. The concrete organizational problems are problems as to where particular activities should be allocated in this great structure. In our own inquiry, we will want to know why particular activities are allowed to remain where they are; why activities are taken from one unit and given to another; how new activities are allocated.

Consequences of Specialization Among Units

Decisions about organization structure, like other decisions, are choices between alternatives to achieve some desired result. When people advocate a particular organizational change they expect that change to bring about something they desire or consider good. Those who oppose a change do so for the same reason—because by *not* making the change they will achieve something they desire. We cannot in general say that either group is right or wrong—assuming they correctly estimate the consequences of change. We can only say that they desire conflicting results. The group that wins out is the "stronger" in the sense that it has more political support, is in a more strategic position, is more numerous, or is simply more vocal than the other.

Of course, if an error is made in predicting the consequences of change, and if this error can be clearly demonstrated, the attitude of a group toward the change can be altered. But often it is highly difficult to demonstrate what the consequences of a particular organization structure will be, and consequently on matters of organization everyone is his own cook—or wants to be. Lacking adequate empirical evidence, many organization recommendations are influenced by a kind of verbal logic—the play of words upon the imagination. This point will receive more extended treatment below.

In this chapter we will describe the values that people usually expect to achieve by allocating activities in a particular way—the values that lie back of most reorganization moves. These values are often mutually exclusive, so that to organize in one way will be favored by some, while to organize in another way will be favored by others. Hence, the allocation of activities within an organization may be just as "political" as any other governmental decision. Our approach will be to *describe* the influences that usually govern reorganization rather than to *prescribe* "sound principles of organization." In so doing, we will uncover many value premises that ordinarily lie implicit and undisclosed in proposals for reorganization.

The values sought in reorganization that we shall discuss are the following: control and accountability, expertness and economy, settling conflicts at lower levels, executive influence on policy development, and program emphasis. In addition, we will discuss more briefly a number of miscellaneous influences on organization structure.

Control or Accountability

An important element in any organization is the mechanism employed to see that the policies laid down by the legislative body and the top executives are carried out by the organization's members—to exercise control and enforce accountability. One way in which control is exercised is through the executive hierarchy itself. For example, conformity to forest policies adopted by the Congress is generally enforced by a chain of authority that extends from the President through the Secretary of Agriculture, the Chief of the Forest Service, Regional Directors, and the Forest Supervisor, to the District Ranger and his subordinates.

DIFFICULTIES OF ENFORCEMENT

Some of the rules and policies of the legislature and chief executive cannot easily be enforced this way. They lie outside the main areas of interest and attention of the members of the hierarchy and are likely to be neglected if left to the hierarchy for enforcement. For example, if a city council adopted a system of job classifications for municipal employees and left it to the individual departments and units within departments to determine the classification of each employee, there would probably be wide discrepancies in the classifications from unit to unit—if, indeed, the plan were not neglected entirely. Each department would probably try to give its employees as high classifications as possible in order to increase salaries and attract and retain competent employees. The goal of bringing about equality of pay throughout the municipal government would seem unimportant to the unit heads as compared with their goals of fighting fires, apprehending criminals, or cleaning streets.

ENFORCEMENT BY SPECIALIZED UNITS

One way of meeting control problems of this kind is to assign to specialized administrative units the functions of enforcing policies that lie in their particular area of specialization. A central personnel office enforces the rules relating to the hiring, pay, promotion, and dismissal of personnel throughout the entire organization. A central budget office enforces the general rules relating to the preparation of budget estimates and the use of appropriated funds by the various organization units. A central purchasing office enforces the rules relating to the purchase of supplies.

If the management of an organization wishes to establish standards or general rules relating to the design, content, and need of forms and questionnaires, it may also desire to organize for the enforcement of these standards by creating a central forms review or statistical standards unit (e.g., the Statistical Standards Division in the U. S. Bureau of the Budget). Most of the centralized units in an organization will be assigned some enforcement or control functions.

When an organization organizes for enforcement or control, it is in effect saying that, with regard to certain kinds of decisions, organization members or units will not be given complete freedom. Certain premises of the decisions on these matters are to be supplied in advance in the form of general rules or standards, and compliance with these standards is to be enforced by centralized units. All decisions for which standards have been prescribed are cleared with or reviewed by the appropriate centralized unit to assure compliance.

The establishment of central control units is in effect a specialization of the function of securing accountability. The executive hierarchy itself does not know and cannot be expected to know enough about all the many areas of an organization's activities to make sure that all these activities are being conducted according to the expressed wishes of those higher up in the organization, the chief executive, the legislature, or the public. The chain of accountability is maintained by assigning different parts of the review process to centralized units whose personnel then become specialists in securing accountability in their respective fields.

A police or fire department might be careless in the enforcement of a city-wide position classification plan, both through insufficient familiarity with the regulations and through identification with departmental goals that are impeded by the plan. The central personnel agency, on the other hand, will generally be much more expert in its understanding of the classification plan and will also be identified with the goal of enforcing the plan. The central unit will be successful, in terms of the goals with which it is identified, only to the extent that the classification plan is enforced; whereas the other departments may actually achieve more fully the goals with which they are identified by evading the prescribed standards in particular instances. Thus the division of work among organization units can be so arranged as to help in the development and enforcement of uniform decisional premises—i.e., standards.

Securing Expertness and Economy

The last chapter showed how, in the division of work among individual employees, appropriate specialization may increase efficiency toward a *given* objective. The same may be true of the division of work among organization units. The specialization of organization units affects efficiency in at least three ways:

(1) by partially determining the division of work among individual employees;

(2) by determining the division of work among supervisory employees; and

(3) by increasing or decreasing the amount of time and effort spent by employees in communicating with each other.

EFFECT ON INDIVIDUAL SPECIALIZATION

The relation between individual specialization and the specialization of units has already been indicated briefly in Chapter 6. If employees' time is to be fully utilized, the range of tasks that must be assigned them will depend on the volume of tasks of each particular kind that is to be performed by their organization unit. The volume of each kind of work in a unit depends, in turn, on the way in which work has been divided among the various units.

By way of illustration, let us assume that each branch in an agency has one person spending a quarter of his time purchasing supplies for the branch. These employees must be given tasks in addition to purchasing to utilize their time fully. If all the purchasing activities were centralized in one unit for the whole division or bureau, the personnel of that unit could become more expert in purchasing because they spent all of their time at it, the number of separate purchasing operations could be reduced by placing bulk orders, and some specialized equipment could be used full time for filing and accounting operations.

Similarly, if the purchasing for each division of an agency were done by a special unit of, say, two full-time employees, there might be further gains from consolidating the purchasing activity into a single division of, say, ten employees for the entire agency. This grouping would permit further kinds of specialization within the purchasing function itself that would be impossible with units of only two employees each. The clerical and business aspects of purchasing work, for example, might be more sharply separated, and certain members of the staff could specialize in purchasing particular types of commodities—office supplies, building materials, or the like.

Effect of Level of Centralization. In grouping activities to secure greater efficiency, sooner or later we encounter diminishing returns. Replacing a system of part-time purchasing activities in individual branches by a central purchasing branch in each division may greatly improve the utilization of personnel. But if each division has a sizeable purchasing operation, the economies that might be secured by grouping all the purchasing work of an entire bureau in a single purchasing division would generally be much less significant and might also have counterbalancing disadvantages. Hence, it is not enough to say that economies can be secured by grouping. We must also decide how far the centralization of the activities in question is to be carried—whether the central units are to be located at the division level, the bureau level, or the departmental level, or even in a central departmental unit serving the entire city, state, or Federal government.

This point can be illustrated further by examining the difference in organization of school health activities between a small city and a large city. In a small city, the workload in school health activities may be too small to permit the full-time employment of the nurses, medical specialists, and physicians required, or to justify the expense of adequate laboratory or treatment facilities. Consequently, the school health activities in the small city might more effectively be allocated to the health department along with other health activities. In the larger city, however, since the volume of work in school health alone would be great enough to utilize fully all the needed facilities and staff, no economies, in a financial sense, would be realized simply by allocating the school health activities to the health department.

We conclude that in many cases—and particularly when we are dealing with relatively small units—we can, by consolidating certain kinds of activities, enhance efficiency by making fuller use of personnel and equipment. But this conclusion is not enough to solve the practical problem of the organizational analyst. He must know what we mean by "grouping all activities with similar characteristics."

Alternative Bases for Grouping. When we place school health activities in the education department, we are grouping activities with similar characteristics—that is activities that are concerned with the education, health, and welfare of *children of school age.* When we place school health activities in the health department, we are also grouping similar activities—*medical activities.* The requirement that "similar" activities should be grouped does not tell us in this case which method of organization is more likely to give efficiency.[6]

To illustrate further, we may consider an organization problem in the Patent Examining Division of the U. S. Patent Office—a unit with more than one thousand employees. The two most important occupations represented are patent examiners (persons with college training in engineering and patent law) and clerical employees (stenographers and typists). One method of specialization would group together all the stenographers in a central pool. This would have the advantage of smoothing out and balancing the work loads arising from particular kinds of patents. That is, if during a particular month there were a heavy load in chemical patents but relatively little work in electrical patents, the assignments of the stenographers in the pool could be adjusted to take care of the load.

On the other hand, this arrangement of a central stenographic pool would involve some loss in stenographic expertness. A stenographer who was acquainted with the terminology of the chemical field might have a difficult time taking dictation in the electrical field. Permanent assignment of stenographers to the various subject-matter branches in the division would permit them to become more skilled in a particular kind of dictation. Only a quantitative knowledge of the relative importance of these conflicting advantages —*how much* additional speed a stenographer could acquire if limited to one subject-matter field in her dictation, and *how much* fluctuation there was in the work loads of the various subject-matter branches—would permit a sound judgment as to which arrangement would be the more efficient.

Other Consequences of Grouping. It should be remembered, further, that efficiency is only one of the criteria of specialization; and that grouping activities to secure a more efficient use of personnel or equipment may have other consequences as well. Group-

---

[6] See the section, above, on "Traditional Structural Theory," where this same difficulty appears as soon as one distinguishes the similarities of "purpose," "process," "clientele," and "area."

ing activities in a particular way will often lead to an expansion in the grouped activities. The centralization of statistical activities, for example, is very often followed by the acquisition of expensive card-punching and sorting equipment. Then the "services" of such a centralized unit can expand almost indefinitely. Hence, we see that grouping of activities may lead to a shift in activities and emphasis on new programs. This consequence will be examined in detail in a later section. Grouping will not necessarily lead to lower costs, even if it permits greater efficiency, because it may bring about other consequences, such as the expansion of the program of the newly centralized unit.

Finally, routine clerical or manual tasks are often centralized because of obvious savings in personnel or equipment without proper regard for less tangible but no less important wastes that the change may induce in other parts of the organization. When typing or purchasing services, for example, are all allocated to a single centralized unit, the other parts of the organization have to wait on that unit for service they need to achieve their objectives. Waiting for service may reduce the speed with which the other parts of the organization serve their clientele and waste the time of staff in these other parts. Hence, the result of this kind of economizing may be to lower the cost of low-salaried personnel by fully occupying their time while increasing the cost of high-salaried personnel by preventing them from being fully occupied or by requiring them to spend time "expediting" the service they require from the centralized unit. Since this increase in cost cannot often be demonstrated in dollars and cents, it is frequently shrugged off as unimportant.

Even when efficiency is the primary or sole criterion of reorganization, the advantages of a particular method of grouping as against alternative methods of grouping are seldom obvious. Hence, a choice of the proper method of specialization from the standpoint of efficiency will usually require a quantitative evaluation of the respective advantages and disadvantages of each proposed structure—including proper attention to the advantages and disadvantages that are less tangible and otherwise difficult to evaluate.

SPECIALIZATION OF SUPERVISORS

The way in which work is divided among organization units has a second relationship to the division of work among individuals:

it largely determines the ways in which supervisory and executive employees will be specialized. If the school health program is administered by the school system, the school superintendent will have responsibilities for supervision of the school health unit; while if the health department administers the program, the health director will have these responsibilities.

Virtually the entire discussion in Chapter 6 can therefore be applied to the effects of unit specialization upon the performance of supervisors and executives. The skills and knowledge of the supervisor and the change-over time involved in his range of activities will affect the kind of supervision he gives his unit. As was also pointed out in Chapter 6, institutional factors may limit the choice of specializations for supervisors. It may be unacceptable to physicians, for example, to include them among a group that is supervised by a non-physician.

EFFECT UPON COMMUNICATION

Dividing the work among units in a particular way may involve the organization in a greater or lesser burden of communication than if a different division of work were followed. We have seen, for example, that creation of a typing pool may increase the burden of communications between typists and the persons they are serving. There are at least two reasons for this. First, to a certain extent the members of organizations tend to follow hierarchical channels in communication, and placing two activities in separate units increases the length of this formal channel between them. Second, social groups will often develop around the formal division of work, and it is usually simpler to communicate within a social group than between two such groups. In the next section of this chapter we shall see that the division of work among units has an especially strong effect upon the process of conflict settlement—since conflict settlement, more than any other type of communication, depends heavily upon the formal lines of hierarchy and the social group structure of the organization.

THE PROBLEM OF DUPLICATION

By duplication we mean the performance by an organizational unit of a task that has already been performed by another unit. If, for example, an identical questionnaire were sent to the same group of businessmen, first by the Census Bureau and then by the Federal Reserve Board, we would have genuine duplication.

It is a favorite pastime of many members of Congress to point to the enormous waste through "duplication" in the Federal government—the large number of personnel units, of statistical units, and so forth. But simply to show that there are several units performing work that is describable by the same term—"personnel" or "statistics" as the case may be—by no means proves that these units are performing identical work. A personnel office that is conducting a training program in the Forest Service does not duplicate the work of a personnel office that is conducting a training program in the Department of State, and combining these two units in a single organization would not lead to the elimination of any overlapping functions.

On the other hand, it would be silly to deny that in any large organization it is possible for avoidable duplication of effort to develop. One cause for this is the desire of each unit to be able to carry on its program with as little dependence as possible upon other units. Stuart Rice has said of Federal statistical services:

"Each administrator is properly voracious for information from any source which will help him to reach a correct solution of the particular problem at hand. At the same time, he is resistant to any relinquishment of control over the mechanism for supplying the statistical information upon which he depends." [7]

The second important cause that frequently leads to genuine duplication is the lack of knowledge possessed by any one organizational unit as to exactly what is being done by other units. This cause of duplication is particularly likely to be present in new organizations, where the participants are only beginning to learn their own roles and have had little time or opportunity to find out what is going on in other units. Each unit, particularly in agencies with highly integrated programs, tends to think of itself as bearing the main responsibility for the agency's program and to assume that if it does not perform a particular function the function will not be performed. Thus, a survey of a particular Federal agency

[7] Stuart A. Rice, "The Role and Management of the Federal Statistical System," *American Political Science Review* 34:484 (June, 1940). This article contains a valuable discussion of the duplication problem as it applies to the eighty-eight federal agencies of the magnitude of bureaus or independent offices that collect statistical reports from the public.

which handles claims applications showed that three subdivisions of the agency were each maintaining a file against which applications were checked in order that multiple applications for the same claim would not be approved. No one of these units knew of the check that was applied by the other two.

An exact duplication of activities is very seldom encountered. Much more frequent is the case where there is considerable overlapping of the work of two units, with the possibility of eliminating some of the overlap either by placing the whole activity in a single unit or by making a sharper line of demarcation between the tasks of the two units. Moreover, it is seldom possible completely to eliminate duplication without important effects for the program goals. For example, the Census Bureau and the Federal Reserve Board may send out related, but not quite identical, questionnaires because their information needs are related but not identical. Unification of their data gathering processes may satisfy the needs of neither completely and may lead to delays in getting the data to them. These are leading reasons why departmental or divisional accounting activities tend to spring up in large organizations in "duplication" of the central accounts. The central accounting unit may not be willing to supply exactly the data wanted by the departments or may not supply it promptly enough.

Even where there is genuine duplication, it is not automatically eliminated by placing the duplicating activities in the same organization unit. The duplicating activities might simply continue in separate sub-units. As Stuart Rice points out:

"The consolidation of agencies would not automatically produce coherence where this is lacking. Coherence is to be attained only by an item to item adjustment of each task and process to every other related task and process, whether the relationship be one of sequence in operations or one of conceptual congruity." [8]

Lowering the Level for Conflict Settlement

Closely related to the question of efficiency is the problem of arranging the organization so that conflicts between sub-units can be settled at as low a level in the organization as possible. There are several reasons why a lower level of conflict settlement might be

[8] Ibid., p. 485.

desired. First, it conserves the time of the executives at higher levels by minimizing the number of matters that come to them for decision. Second, it permits conflicts to be settled rapidly because the number of links in the communications chain through which they must pass is reduced. Third, it permits face-to-face relationships to prevail in the settlement of conflicts, thus increasing the likelihood that they will be settled informally and amicably by mutual adjustment. Fourth, it permits conflicts to be settled near the point where they arise and hence makes it more likely that the person who is responsible for settling them is adequately acquainted with the relevant facts. Finally, it enhances the power of the executive at the level where conflict settlement is to be located.

An organization that had to depend very little on any other organization for its needs or in making its decisions—an organization, that is, which is self-contained—would have little chance of coming into conflict with any other organization. Although such a self-contained organization does not exist, the possibilities for conflict between organizations can be minimized. Thus if two departments charged with making decisions over the same subject matter are frequently in conflict, the responsibility of one of them for that subject matter can be eliminated. For example, to avoid conflicts between the U. S. Civil Service Commission and the Federal departments, the Commission could be abolished. Or, if only conflicts about classifications were to be eliminated, the authority of the Commission over classification of positions could be withdrawn and each department allowed to classify its own positions.

Even if we were to eliminate this conflict at the departmental level, there would still be conflicts between the bureaus within a department. If each department established its own personnel bureau, disputes over personnel matters might be just as extensive as before, but they would be settled by the head of the department rather than by the President. If the departmental personnel bureau were eliminated in favor of a personnel division within each of the bureaus, disputes would probably be no less extensive, but they would be settled by the head of the bureau rather than by the head of the department.

On the other hand, two units which are "distant" on the organization chart may be able to work out conflicts without carrying these upward to a common superior. The personnel of two units in different departments, both units dealing with the same subject matter, may be so closely identified that they settle their own conflicts through mutual understanding and sympathy. For example, it may be easier for school health officials in a department of education to get along with medical people in the department of health than it is for them to get along with the educators in their own department. Under these circumstances, little would be gained, so far as lowering the level of conflict settlement is concerned, by moving the school health unit to the health department.

This illustration also shows that the need for coordination or rapid settlement of conflicts between two units may be more apparent than real. For example, most persons who discuss war organization are quite emphatic in their belief that the rationing function must be in the same organization as the price control function because, from the standpoint of economic theory, rationing supports price controls. In the last war, however, rationing and price personnel had in fact almost no operating contacts or relationships whatsoever, although both were in the same organization. The area of conflict—the area in which coordination was needed— was the area of relationship between the rationing agency and the supply agencies—the War Production Board, the Office of the Rubber Director, the War Food Administration, the Solid Fuels Administration for War, the Petroleum Administrator for War, and the Office of Defense Transportation.

Organization planners concerned with lowering the level of conflict settlement frequently imagine that conflict will occur where in fact it does not. They also often assume that conflict is bad, an assumption that is not at all obvious.

Control of Policy Development

A criterion of organization flatly in contradiction to the one discussed immediately above is that conflict should be brought into the open at high levels. Why anyone would want to allocate responsibilities in such a way as to assure conflict may appear inconceivable. However, when organizations conflict with regard to a given matter, the executive immediately above them has an opportunity to decide between the conflicting points of view. This may be almost his only opportunity to guide the development of thinking with regard to the subject. When an organization is operating "smoothly" questions may rarely come to the executive for decision, or, if they do come, only one point of view may be presented to him.

In most administrative situations it will be a foolhardy executive who will substitute his point of view for the recommendation—the crystallization of thinking—of the whole complex organization below him. In a "smooth running" organization the executive may be unaware that there is another way of thinking about the matter at hand. The different points of view will have been submerged, or some overruled, in the complex administrative process below him.

If the consolidation of the Army, the Navy, and the Air Force under a single Secretary of Defense had worked as many people had expected, the result would have been to reduce the President's influence in military matters to a relatively minor one. He would have been presented with unified defense recommendations from the Joint Chiefs of Staff through the Secretary of Defense and would have had no knowledge of conflicting points of view among the various armed services and no opportunity for developing defense policy by deciding between them. In effect, the Secretary of Defense would have been given virtually the function of being President with regard to defense matters. Actually, as we know, this consolidation of the armed services into a National Military Establishment has by no means been complete. Even if the various secretaries (Army, Navy, and Air Force) could not make their conflicting points of view known directly to the President, it has been shown that they can achieve much the same result by making their points of view known to Congress or various friendly civilian groups. (The legislation establishing the National Military Establishment expressly provided that the Secretaries of Army, Navy, and Air Force should have direct access to the President.)

Different points of view are necessary for full consideration of most governmental problems. Some argument or discussion will precede the official acceptance of a solution of any problem. The question is at what level different points of view will be resolved and an official stand taken. From the standpoint of any particular executive, there will be some problems concerning which he wishes this level to be his level. Experts in organization structure may be disturbed because "jurisdictions are not clearly defined," but the executive may not care about this violation of esthetics if he knows that only by such a violation will he be able to influence the development of policy.

"Organization experts" have usually been rather harsh in their treatment of Franklin D. Roosevelt because of his violations or apparent ignorance of "sound canons of organization," but it is at least as good an hypothesis that President Roosevelt kept some control over the development of policy in fields in which he was interested by purposely refusing to define jurisdictions in sharp, clear, and mutually exclusive terms. Whether he did this consciously, it is unnecessary to argue. But certainly the lack of clarity in the assignment of responsibilities during President Roosevelt's leadership of the Federal bureaucracy gave his own personality a greater impact on the development of administrative policy than would have been the case had the Federal bureaucracy been organized in accordance with the dreams of a typical artist of organization charts.

It is not uncommon to find one executive urging a clear definition of his own authority so as to release him from the control or influence of his chief while at the same time being rather careless in defining the responsibilities of those below him so that he can have more influence on their decisions. Conflict *per se* is not bad. It depends on the point of view of the person discussing it. The aim of organization is not to eradicate differences of viewpoint in the formation of policy, for when conflict is eliminated, thought ceases. The bone of contention is at what level the conflicts will be resolved. Perhaps each executive would like all conflicts resolved at his level. Then he would become a free and happy man, untrammeled by any effective superior authority but with effective authority over those below him.

Program Emphasis

One of the most important reasons why activities are grouped in particular ways is to secure proper emphasis on what are conceived to be the most important aspects of a governmental program. This consideration may enter into reorganization proposals in several different ways. First, giving a particular activity organizational independence—by grouping the persons performing it in a separate organization unit—will usually lead to a greater emphasis upon that activity. Second, if a small unit is located in an organization to which it is only distantly related, or where its contribution is generally felt to be unimportant by the rest of the organization, it may become a "stepchild" and may consequently be neglected by the top executives and others in the organization unless moved elsewhere. Third, moving an organizational activity from one location to another may bring about a change in the political and organizational pressures to which it is subjected and a resulting change in the direction of its activities.

Organization units that are parts of larger structures tend to judge issues of reorganization largely in terms of the degree of independence the organizational structure will permit them and the amount of support—particularly in budget matters—they will receive from the organization of which they are a part. Separate departmental status will be considered most desirable because then the drive for increased budget or broadened functions will not be smothered by departmental disinterest or opposition. If departmental status is out of the question, then location is preferred in that department which will probably give most support to the claims of the unit.

Groups in the legislature or in the public that are interested in an activity will assist in establishing it at the highest level possible. The Departments of Commerce, Labor, and Agriculture all started as minor activities within other going organizations. The business, labor, and agricultural communities did not stop until they had secured separate departmental status for each of these. During the war, many functions within the War Production Board became so vital or strategic that in order to stress them or push them they were given separate agency status. Examples are the rubber supply program which was finally organized under a separate Office of the Rubber Director, the oil supply program under a Petroleum Administrator for War, and the food supply program under the War Food Administration.

Sometimes it is felt that a new organization is needed in order to establish firmly a new program that might not be received sympathetically within the existing structure. A city manager, desiring to expand in-service training activities in a city government, may feel it necessary to appoint a training director reporting directly to himself. In so doing, he may fully believe that in the long run a successful training program can be conducted only by the supervisory and executive staffs of the departments and bureaus throughout the city government. Nevertheless, a separate training unit may be indispensable in "selling" the training idea to the departments by giving evidence of the manager's real interest in training, and by training the departments in training methods which they can use themselves.

In an organization with a wide range of activities, one or a few of these activities will usually capture the attention of the departmental management. Others will be regarded as sidelines, or as relatively unimportant, and may receive only a small share of the organization's funds. Should higher executives or the legislature decide that some of these slighted activities should be given heavier emphasis, they can be set up in separate organization units. If it is decided, for example, that a unit established for answering and filing correspondence is devoting too much attention to its filing system and not enough care to the way it answers correspondence, the unit can be divided into two units, one devoted exclusively to answering correspondence. The program emphasis can then be controlled through the allocation of budget funds to the two units.

Sometimes activities are allocated, in order to give them greater emphasis, not to a separate newly created organization but to a going organization in which it is known they will receive more friendly treatment. Frequently such reorganization moves are taken because of the pressure of interested groups in the public who feel that the activities will be conducted more according to their interests in another organization. The packers and farmers secured the removal of packer and stockyard regulation from the Federal Trade Commission and its assignment to the Department of Agriculture because they thought the FTC would regulate them more stringently than would the Department of Agriculture. Friends of conservation secured the removal of the activities that we now call the Forest Service from the Interior Department with its alleged "give-away" philosophy and the assignment of those activities to the Department of Agriculture. In 1948, enemies of the United States Employment Service secured its removal from the Department of Labor and its assignment to the Federal Security Agency. (Of course, there were other reasons for the reassignment besides the pressure of interested groups.) Hundreds of other examples could be cited.

Perhaps a "desire for a friendly environment" is not the most accurate way of describing those reorganizations. We must ask: "Friendly to whom?" The issue need not be one of more or less emphasis upon a program, but instead an issue as to the direction that program should go. Federal Food and Drug Administration was long located in the U. S. Department of Agriculture where it was presumably subject to the influence of agricultural groups. Its transfer to the Federal Security Agency was backed by many people who wanted to shift the emphasis of its policies from the producers' interests to the consumers' interests by putting it in a location where the influence of consumer groups would be more powerful and the influence of producer groups less powerful.

Proposals for the reorganization of government have been notable for their concern with the efficiency criterion to the exclusion of the problem of program emphasis that we have been discussing. This neglect of program emphasis considerations is true of the state reorganization movement, the 1937 report of the President's Committee on Administrative Management, and to an almost unbelievable extent of the Hoover Commission.[9] A practical person interested in a program will want that program allocated to the organization where it will receive the most favorable treatment in spite of the fact that "organization experts"—preoccupied with the criterion of efficiency—tell him that such an allocation of functions violates "all sound principles of organization." The groups that backed the removal of the United States Employment Service from the Department of Labor were not simply amateurs, ignorant of the "principles of organization." They had a plan, and they had a logic, but it was a logic that went beyond the criterion of efficiency. Efficiency is a meaningful criterion only when an organizational choice is to be made in terms of agreed-upon objectives. When the very point at issue is the determination of what the organization objectives are to be, or what relative emphasis is to

[9] Reference has already been made to this deficiency in the Hoover Commission's approach in footnote 1, above. As further evidence, we may quote the following dissent of Commissioners Brown and McClellan to the transfer of the hospitals of the armed forces to the proposed United Medical Administration:

"Instead of transferring all but a very few military and naval doctors and hospitals to a civilian agency *under the control of a medical bureaucracy,* Mr. Brown has suggested that the available beds and services in the hospital system of the armed forces be made available for the use of other Government beneficiaries, under proper supervision and restrictions *which will protect their full interests.*" Op. cit., p. 37. The italics are ours. Presumably "their interests" means the interest of the armed forces.

be placed on different objectives, efficiency cannot be the criterion of choice.

Other Reasons for Assignments of Activities

In the preceding sections we have discussed reasons for dividing the work in various ways that are openly acknowledged or avowed in public discussion of organization and reorganization. There are many other reasons for particular structural arrangements that are much less openly avowed. Sometimes they are never mentioned or mentioned only in the narrow circles of the organization planners; sometimes their presence is not even known to the planners themselves.

Much of the distribution of activities in any organization is best explained by the accidents of origin. At the very beginning some problem presented itself, and a few people were set to work solving it. This group of people expanded, acquired an organization name or title, and continued to exist as the same unit while the rest of the organization grew up around it. Perhaps the need for the function disappeared but because of pressure from the unit was continued nevertheless. Having gotten in "on the ground floor," the members of the unit have an unusually strong influence on the organization planning of the organization. Perhaps one of its original members later becomes a top executive of the organization and continues the old unit and the old functions because he has a soft spot in his heart for them.

Once established, organization units develop a strong drive to continue doing the same old business at the same old stand. They often develop legislative friends so that abolishing or reorganizing them becomes almost impossible. To a large extent organizations grow willy-nilly, and, once having taken on form, the vested interests that appear make reorganization extremely difficult in many cases.[10] The organization structure so derived is then justified or explained by "principles of organization" that are actually rationalizations. These "principles," like so many proverbs, can be used to justify any kind of structure that exists.

Many specific reorganizations or assignments of responsibilities result from motivations or objectives of a rather personal or private sort, regardless of the reasons publicly given for them. Frequently,

[10] For a more extended treatment of this survival drive, see Chapter 18, below.

to get some influential but undesired executive out of the main stream of an organization's decisions he will be assigned some new, harmless, but high-sounding activity. He will be "kicked up stairs." Here the reorganization is motivated entirely by a desire to get a particular person somewhat out of the picture without inviting an unpleasant fight by trying to fire him.

Sometimes functions are created and units established largely to make a place for someone who is wanted around. The unit created makes it possible to put a valuable man on the payroll who could not otherwise be kept around without getting rid of someone else. This hoarding of talent is not uncommon. On the other hand, functions are often allocated away from some unit as a means of inducing the chief or others to resign.

Sometimes activities are assigned to a unit in order to raise its level, say from a section to a branch, and thus to secure higher position classifications (and hence pay) for many of its members. Classification theory to the contrary, there is a strong tendency for all executives at the same level of the hierarchy to receive the same classifications and for the classifications at each level to be higher than those of the preceding level.

Less conscious motivations in organizing are those that result from a kind of estheticism. Organization planners are sometimes strongly influenced in their recommendations by preconceived ideas of how an organization chart ought to look. Although it is impossible to assess the force of this influence, "chartism" undoubtedly plays a role in the assignment of functions within many organizations. The spatial analogy of the typical organization chart simplifies and falsifies organization relationships. To the person who knows little about human behavior in organization and who, consequently, relies on charts, all problems of organizational relationships can be simply solved with a few deft strokes of a drafting pencil. Overlappings can be eliminated; jurisdictions clearly defined; and lines of authority clearly indicated—all by rearranging the boxes on an organization chart. From this artistry there are bound to come organizing recommendations, and so "chartism" is one of the influences determining the division of work.

A similar and sub-conscious influence on the division of work is the power of words. Many activities are allocated to particular units because some of the same words are used in describing the activity and the unit. If an activity is described by a group of words one of which is "agriculture," there is certain to be a strong drive to get that activity allocated to the Department of Agriculture. To most people it is likely that a proposal to take the federal Bureau of Labor Statistics away from the Department of Labor would appear preposterous. Should business pressure groups try to do this (to gain the value of a shift in program emphasis, discussed above), it is certain that many well-meaning people would brand their plans as a selfish attempt to take the Bureau away from "where it belongs."

Reorganizations of sorts are often carried out because a new executive feels that it is expected of him and because it gives him a feeling of influencing the organization. The only felt need or problem to which such reorganizations are directed may be a need or problem within the executive himself.

Planning Organization Structure

Our analysis of the consequences of specialization has raised more questions for the organization planner than it has provided answers. The reasons for this fact are not hard to find. In the first place, the objectives of governmental organizations—the values they are supposed to achieve—are seldom clearly defined. Often an organization and its objective represent a confused conflict between many competing interests. Legislative and hierarchical goal assignments are usually superficial and almost certain to be ambiguous. Is an organization to emphasize *speed* of decision; *accuracy* of decision; or *economy* in carrying on its activities? Is it to push some program for all it is worth? Is it to strive for uniformity in decisions or for decisions fitted to local peculiarities? Is the influence of the Chief Executive to be increased through considerable overlapping at the departmental level, or are the burdens on him to be reduced? Are conflicts and different points of view to be resolved in the lower, less public echelons of organizations or brought out into public view by organizing for high level settlement of conflicts?

PROBLEMS IN ORGANIZATION PLANNING

Who can answer all these questions for the organization planner? Who has a right to answer them? He cannot turn to the legislature or to his superiors because they may not know or be able politically to give a consistent answer. We would probably like to achieve many of these contradictory values. We would like speed, accuracy, *and* economy, but we do not know which we are willing to sacrifice, if necessary. We would like to emphasize the programs that give us advantages and de-emphasize those that do not. We would like conflicts settled at a higher level if that will increase our influence, but at a lower level if settlement at the lower level will increase our influence. We want to control the decisions of the other fellow but do not want our own controlled. Where can the organization planner get a clear-cut mandate, a firm authority, a support behind him in making his organizational recommendations?

Even if these values were clearly defined, knowledge of the means for achieving them is very limited. Administrative science has not progressed very far. We are often not at all sure of the consequences of decisions relating to organization. An activity may be centralized in a single unit in order to reduce costs; but this action may so upset established expectations and ways of doing things that morale throughout the agency drops and total output is reduced in quantity or quality. A review unit established to strengthen an executive's control over the decisions of his subordinates may cause some of his most able people to resign. The transfer of a unit to another agency in order to bring all "like" activities together may result in the virtual cessation of its program because of hostility toward it in the new agency.

Not only is knowledge of consequences very limited, but we are often unable to measure the effectiveness of any particular allocation of activities. Administrative measurement is probably the most backward of all the administrative arts. An administration is reorganized to increase the responsiveness of the bureaucracy to the electorate, but we cannot actually tell whether responsiveness is increased because of the move or how much it is increased. To demonstrate an actual reduction in money cost as a result of any reorganizing move is always difficult, and whether a demonstrated reduction results from decreased service or greater efficiency can nearly always be debated.

As a result of the conditions described above, organization planners have considerable freedom in the selection of the values to be achieved in dividing the work and the methods to be used to achieve them. It is difficult to hold them accountable for their recommendations. A general lack of consciousness of the competing values of organization structure contributes to the same result.

Although these difficulties exist, still the work must be divided. In order to divide the work in the most rational way, the organization planner needs to formulate a precise statement of the values to be promoted and needs to obtain acceptance of those values. The values that must be given up by adopting any particular structure must be clearly understood by all concerned. An attempt must be made to visualize all the significant consequences of any move—such as its affect on the satisfactions of other members of the organization—not just the desired end in view. It may be that a move with a very desirable consequence (such as reduced cost) must be given up because other anticipated consequences of the move are so undesirable (such as the slighting of a politically important program). In order to anticipate all the significant consequences of any move, organization planners need a thorough knowledge of administrative behavior; and they need a complete understanding of the particular situation, including the personalities involved, the identification structure in the organization, and often the political situation surrounding the organization.

AREAS OF AGREEMENT ON STRUCTURE

The reader should not be left with the impression that there is never agreement about questions of organization structure. Just as a legal casebook is likely to give the impression that nothing is settled about the law of contracts—because attention is directed to the controversial borderline cases rather than to the wide areas of agreement within these boundaries—so any discussion of organization structure is bound to emphasize the problem areas and to give relatively little attention to aspects of organization structure that are not matters of controversy.

A city government, for example, is a collection of many and diverse services and programs: controlling traffic, extinguishing fires, conducting recreation programs, maintaining streets, apprehending criminals, operating hospitals—the list could extend for several pages. While there is no one way of dividing up the total program, it does fall fairly neatly into a number of discrete parts—

perhaps forty or fifty in all. Each of these parts is characterized by the facts that (1) a fairly definite and socially meaningful program goal or objective can be stated for it; (2) its specializations satisfy current notions of efficiency; (3) it is relatively self-contained—its program can be carried on without serious conflict with other programs within the city; (4) it raises no serious issues of program emphasis or political control. To the extent that these criteria are satisfied, the parts that have been enumerated provide obvious building-blocks for organization structure.

To put the matter another way, the areas from which controversy about organization structure is absent are areas in which all or most of the criteria of specialization discussed in this chapter point to the same general solution; while the areas of controversy are areas in which some criteria point in one direction and other criteria point in another, or where the same criteria point in one direction for some groups and in another for others. The Federal Food and Drug Administration is accepted as a building block because it satisfies the criteria of a definite and socially meaningful program goal, socially acceptable specialization with respect to processes, and the relative independence of its program from other governmental programs. But the location of this agency in the departmental structure becomes a matter of controversy because it is believed that its transfer from the Department of Agriculture to the Federal Security Agency will lead to a change in program emphasis—a change that is desired by consumer groups but opposed by agricultural interests.

The fire department and the police department are accepted as building blocks in a city government, but there is little agreement as to whether anything is to be gained by grouping these two units in a larger department of public safety. The advantages of such a grouping from the standpoint of efficiency and the lowering of the level of conflict settlement are controversial, at best; and each department feels that it might be subordinated to the other and would have less access to the chief executive and the council if a new level of management were inserted in the structure.

In what sense can these accepted building blocks of organization be considered to be "natural" units? By and large, both the areas of agreement about structure and the areas of controversy are socially defined. If a group of governmental activities is developed in response to a common set of political pressures, for example, it is likely to be regarded as a single program. As another possibility, all or most of the activities involving regulation of a given industry may be regarded as part of *the* program for that industry. The U. S. Maritime Commission is a good example of this type of "natural" unit. Or, the rise of a particular occupational specialization in society may suggest a corresponding specialization in the organization structure of government and industry—personnel administration, for example.

A unit which is "natural" or non-controversial at one moment of history may become controversial with a change in circumstances. So long as foreign policy and domestic policy were conducted as relatively distinct activities, the State Department was a well-defined and noncontroversial entity. The growth of intimate relationships among foreign policy, national security, and domestic policy has made this one of the most controversial areas of organization. Until the automobile created a whole new host of felonies, misdemeanors, and regulatory problems, the jurisdictional boundary between the police department and the city engineer's office gave little trouble. Today there is much discussion of how traffic control functions are to be allocated to these and other units.

Much of the acceptance of state and local organization structure must be attributed to the history or origin of new programs and to imitation of one state or city by another. A sudden focussing of attention on problems of city planning or of urban redevelopment will quickly produce a spate of municipal organization units to deal with these problems.

If we examine the structures of Federal, state, and local government of thirty years ago and today, we will see that many new units have been created to deal with the expanded activities of government. Apart from these new programs, the units that existed in the past have shown a tremendous power of survival. Federal bureaus have been shuffled, combined, and moved about, but most of them have retained their identities as bureaus. The same is true of most city departments, for example, the major subdivisions of fire, police, and public works departments. In view of the very rudimentary state of our theory of organization structure, it is perhaps fortunate that so much of the existing structure lies outside the area of serious controversy.

Conclusion

This chapter has been concerned with the problem of dividing work among organization units. The advantages of various methods of division have been discussed, and it has been pointed out that the notion of the "one best way" to organize can have meaning only among a group with a homogeneous system of values. The organization analyst is concerned with identifying possible alternative methods of specialization and with balancing against each other their respective advantages and disadvantages. The long-run survival of the organization may depend upon the correctness of this evaluation.

It must be emphasized again that the division of work that is set forth in the formal organizational plans—the organization chart, statements of organization function, and the like—may or may not correspond to the realities of the organization as it operates from day to day. As we have pointed out in Chapters 4 and 5, organization plans must be evaluated in terms of the actual behaviors they bring about. This applies as fully to plans for the division of work as to other types of formal plans.

In the final portions of this chapter, it was shown that there are certain areas of agreement about the division of work—certain "natural" building blocks in most organizations. In later chapters we will see how these "natural" units lead to the emergence of certain typical organization structures and typical organizational problems that are common to almost all large-scale organizations. Before it will be possible to begin this analysis, however, we must complete our general discussion of organization structure. Thus far only the building blocks have been considered—the specialized units and the identifications that unite or divide them. It is necessary to look next at the connecting tissue. Central problems of coordination will be treated in the following chapters dealing with authority and communication.

CHAPTER EIGHT

✦

Securing Teamwork: Authority

THE division of work, which has been discussed in the last two chapters, and authority, which is the subject of the present chapter, are probably the two most conspicuous features of any organization. When we draw an organization chart, we show the division of work by placing a separate box on the chart for each organization unit. Then we connect these boxes by certain lines which we refer to as "lines of authority."

Unfortunately, the lines of authority shown on a chart often give a misleading picture of the way that authority actually operates in the organization; for these lines generally show only one kind of authority, that associated with the formal "hierarchy" of the organization. The typical organization chart shows only authority "from the top down." It shows the authority that the division head supposedly exercises over his branch chiefs; but it does not show the equally important authority that the division head may in fact exercise over fellow division heads, over *their* subordinates, or over his own bureau chief and his other superiors. Many experienced administrators are so impressed with the importance of these non-hierarchical lines of authority that they believe the real facts of organizational structure and operation cannot be shown on an organization chart.

The Meaning of "Authority"

Traditionally, the term "authority" has usually been approached as a legal concept, to be defined in terms of "rights" and "duties." He who possesses authority, in this sense, has the *right* to demand obedience; while he who is commanded has the *duty* to obey.

With the help of the concept of legitimacy, which was introduced in Chapter 3, we can give operational meaning to the notion of legal authority. When we say that a man has a legal right to demand obedience, we mean that there is a system of law which we accept as legitimate, and which states that under certain circumstances other individuals shall accept decisions made by this man. The system of law usually also establishes an enforcement mechanism. That is, it lends the assistance of its courts, its police, and the like, to individuals who wish to exercise the rights, including the rights of authority, that it grants them.

Legal authority, then, is always traceable back to some fountainhead of legitimacy. In the United States, what makes an enactment (legally) authoritative is that it can be traced back to a delegation of authority in the Constitution of the United States. If a claims examiner in the Railroad Retirement Board allows a claim for unemployment compensation to a railroad employee, his decision rests (in legal theory, at least) upon the regulations established by the Board. These regulations, in turn, are supposed to stem from the legal authority granted the Board by the Railroad Retirement Act enacted by Congress. Congress, finally, obtained its legal authority to enact this statute from the commerce clause of the Constitution, as that clause is interpreted by the Supreme Court. Hence, legal authority vested by statute in the top executive or executives is delegated to their immediate subordinates, and then to the subordinates of these subordinates, until it cascades by successive acts of delegation to the very bottom of the administrative hierarchy.

A PSYCHOLOGICAL DEFINITION OF AUTHORITY

In this chapter we shall treat authority as a psychological rather than a legal phenomenon. That is, we shall be concerned with the fact that under certain circumstances people *do* accept the commands and decisions of others, rather than the fact that a legal system imposes upon them the *duty* to do so. Of course legal authority also has its psychological aspect. When a person accepts a particular system of law as legitimate—when, for example, he acknowledges the authority of the Congress under the Constitution to enact statutes—this may provide him with a motive for actually accepting the legal authority which it is his duty (under this system of law) to accept. As our discussion develops we shall see that legal authority provides a part, but only a part, of the structure of actual psychological authority in an organization.

From a psychological standpoint the exercise of authority involves a relationship between two or more persons. On the one side we have a person who makes proposals for the action of others. On the other side we have a person who accepts the proposals—who "obeys" them. Now a person may accept another's proposal under three different sets of circumstances:

(1) He may examine the merits of the proposal, and, on the basis of its merits become convinced that he should carry it out. We shall exclude such instances of acceptance from our notion of authority, although some writers on administration have called this the "authority of ideas."

(2) He may carry out the proposal without being fully, or even partially, convinced of its merits. In fact he may not examine the merits of the proposal at all.

(3) He may carry out the proposal even though he is convinced it is wrong—wrong either in terms of personal values or of organizational values or both.

We will treat both the second and third cases as instances of the acceptance of authority. Of course in any actual instance all three of the "pure types" of acceptance listed above may be combined in various proportions. In actual practice authority is almost always liberally admixed with persuasion. We will exclude from our concept of authority only those instances of acceptance of a proposal that fall exclusively in the first category.

Suppose, for example that a branch chief in a government agency wishes to add an economic analyst to his staff. He may want to insist that only persons with a Ph.D. in economics be considered for the job. Discussion of his problem with his division head may completely convince him that he should also consider persons who only have a Master's degree, but who have demonstrated their capacity for professional work at the desired level. Under these circumstances, no authority is involved in his acceptance of the proposal that only the Master's degree be required. Suppose, however, that he is not completely convinced; but that his division head continues to insist that the educational requirement be reduced. In this case if the branch chief accepts the lower educational requirement, he is accepting authority. On the other hand, if the division chief gives in without being completely convinced, this is also an instance of authority—in this case authority of the branch chief over the division chief.

This definition of authority will perhaps sound strange to many ears. In particular, it may seem peculiar to speak of the authority of a "subordinate" over his "superior." In the last analysis this is just a question of definition—of how one wishes to use words —and we will exercise an author's prerogative of defining the word in our own way and then using it as we have defined it. Nevertheless, the usage proposed here has good precedent in the writings of Chester I. Barnard and others.[1] It has been adopted because it seems more useful to us than do other definitions in describing the realities of administration. Without any expectation that the reader will accept the *authority* of this proposal, the material in this chapter may help *convince* him of the convenience of the usage.

NATURE OF PROPOSALS

The proposals that one person in an organization makes for the action of others take many forms. They may be spoken or written or even conveyed by a facial expression. They may be called orders, instructions, procedures, suggestions, or not be named at all. The essential thing about a proposal is that it suggests action to meet a problem. Until the proposal is accepted, however, it is not authoritative.

ACCEPTANCE OF AUTHORITY

The second element in an authority relationship is the willingness of the person receiving a proposal to carry it out without necessarily being convinced of its merit. If an employee behaves in a particular way because he has considered the alternatives and has decided that this behavior is the best, or most effective, under the circumstances, he is not accepting authority—even if the action in question was first suggested to him by another person. In a later section of this chapter we will examine the various motives that cause persons to accept the proposals of others. For the moment, the point to be emphasized is that persons in organizations often do things at the direction of others, and even at times in opposition to their own best judgment.

[1] See *The Functions of the Executive*, chap. 12.

When we exclude instances of *conviction* from the authority relationship, we mean instances where the person accepting a proposal is convinced that the proposal is right, not instances where the person accepting the proposal is convinced that he ought to, or had better, accept it. Of course a proposal would never be accepted at all if there were not conviction in this second sense. Where the division head fails to convince the branch chief that he should not require more than a Master's degree in recruiting an economic analyst, the branch chief may still be convinced that he ought to yield to the division head's insistence. He may not want to incur his boss's displeasure; he may feel that this is a question which his boss, rather than himself, has a legitimate "right" to decide; he may anticipate that even if he succeeds in convincing his boss, they will later be over-ruled by the departmental personnel officer. Whatever his reasons, in accepting the proposal without being convinced of its merits he is accepting authority.

THE LIMITS OF AUTHORITY

There are always limits to the acceptance of authority. Within a certain area, an employee will obey orders and accept other proposals. Outside this area—which we will call his area of acceptance —the employee will "forget" to carry out the order, will carry it out in such a way as actually to sabotage it, will refuse to obey it, or will resign rather than carry it out.

The person accepting authority must be able to understand what is demanded of him. One of the most severe limitations on organizational authority is the difficulty of properly communicating proposals. This is true whether information is flowing downward, upward, or across organizational lines. Communication problems will be treated at length in Chapters 10 and 11.

Authoritative communications that conflict with the basic ideas of the recipient as to organization purpose are likely to be watered down or nullified as they are interpreted. This process has already been examined in Chapters 4 and 5.

Authoritative proposals that conflict with the personal interests or the personal value system of the recipient will meet with considerable resistance, and there may be great difficulty in getting such commands accepted as stimuli to action. This difficulty has also been explored in some detail in Chapters 3, 4, and 5.

Proposals are often made which cannot be complied with because the recipient lacks the mental or physical resources necessary to carry them out. Congress may, for example, pass a law commanding a certain action on the part of an administrative agency and then fail to provide sufficient funds for its accomplishment. Such commands are issued more frequently than is generally realized.

In a later section of this chapter we will explore the motives that lead employees in organizations to accept authority. These motives constitute just one part of the total scheme of influences that determines an employee's behavior. Only by appraising the total situation can we predict when, and to what extent, he will accept proposals as authoritative. Hence, in this chapter we will not be concerned with authority as an isolated phenomenon, but with the role that authority plays in the over-all pattern of organizational behavior.

Authority and the Division of Work

Of what use is authority? In what ways does it facilitate cooperative behavior in organizations? Its chief function is to permit a very great flexibility in the division of the work of making decisions. Each employee in an organization makes innumerable behavior choices. Each such choice represents, in part, his own conviction that a certain course of action should be followed, and in part, his acceptance of the conviction of other organization members that this course should be followed (i.e., his acceptance of authority). By parcelling out among many employees the various considerations that are relevant to the choice, we can make sure that these are more carefully and more expertly analysed than if the employee himself did the whole job. If there were no acceptance of authority, each element of each decision would have to be reexamined each time it was communicated from one person to another; and the recipient of the communication would have to convince himself of the correctness of the proposal. If authority were never accepted then either each employee's decisions would have to be self-contained—he would have to make them without the help of other members of the organization—or the task of convincing at each step in communication would become tremendous.

AUTHORITY IN EVERYDAY LIFE

The use of authority to gain advantages from specialization is not peculiar to organizations. It is a common occurrence of our everyday life when we accept the proposal of our doctor that we take a certain kind of medicine, or when we accept the advice of our attorney that a proposed contract should have a certain clause in it. Since we have not had medical training or legal education, we are predisposed to accept the proposals of persons who have had such training and experience, and we do not expect to understand fully the underlying reasons or to be able to judge their correctness. The phenomenon of authority is the same in these situations as it is in organizations. There will be limits to the area of acceptance here as there are in organizational situations; and we shall see that even the underlying psychological motives for acceptance are of the same nature in both cases.

The only important difference between non-organizational and organizational acceptance of authority is that authority is probably used more frequently and more systematically as a method of specializing the decision-making process inside organizations than it is outside. A large part of the work performed by members of organizations—particularly those we call "supervisors," "executives," or "administrators"—lies in making proposals for the behavior of others. Furthermore, most decision-making in organizations is a composite process—decisions are not made by any one person, but are the product of a whole process of planning, discussion, and communication often involving a large group of persons.

COMPOSITE DECISIONS AND AUTHORITY

Let us examine a specific example of this process of composite decision. The principal task of the Economic Cooperation Administration is to grant or loan American dollars to European governments in order to assist them in importing commodities necessary to their economic recovery. First, a quarterly program is laid out to determine how much of each type of commodity each country is to import and what part of these imports are to be financed with ECA funds. Subsequently, the country submits requests for the financing of specific shipments of commodities within the established quarterly allotments.[2]

Let us suppose that an employee of the Economic Corporation Administration with the title of "Economic Analyst" has in front of him a request from the British government for purchase of 10,000 tons of coal to be shipped to Britain. Before approving this request, our economic analyst will check—among other things—Britain's quarterly coal allotment under the European Recovery Program and the volume of coal shipments already financed in the current quarter. If his examination shows that the new shipment would be in accord with the "policy" of ECA, he will decide to approve it.

But what is the "policy" against which he checks the request? It consists of a whole battery of decisions (including the allocation decision) that have been made elsewhere in the agency (in accordance with the accepted division of work), and which have been communicated to the analyst. Hence, the analyst is accepting the authority of these decisions made elsewhere as a basis for his own decision. Except in unusual instances, he does not himself re-decide these questions of policy each time a specific request for assistance is before him.[3]

Nor should it be supposed that the policies accepted by the economic analyst as governing his decisions necessarily or even usually originate with his superiors in the hierarchy. At one time in the ECA, for example, one major organization unit in that agency had the task of establishing the quarterly allotments (the so-called "Programming Division" under an Assistant Deputy Administrator). A separate unit (called "Procurement Transactions") on the same organizational level as the Programming Division and not subordinate in the hierarchy to the Assistant Deputy Administrator was applying these allotments to specific requests for assistance. The official hierarchy of the agency—in the person of the Administrator—entered into this pattern of authority only in

[2] To avoid unnecessary detail, the actual facts of the process have been greatly simplified in this description and only the main outline set forth.

[3] Of course the policies may have been inadequately communicated to the analyst, or he may apply them incorrectly to the decision in question, or circumstances surrounding the decision may lead him to question whether the policy ought not be modified. In extreme instances, he may even think that he can refuse to accept the policy as authoritative and may apply policies derived from other sources to his decision. All of these limitations upon his area of acceptance will receive attention in this chapter.

establishing the accepted division of work, that is, in instructing the procurement transactions unit that it was to accept the policies embodied in the allotments established by the programming unit.

To make the case even stronger, it may be pointed out that this division of work between the programming unit and the procurement transactions unit developed by common understanding among the employees several months before a formal statement of functions was issued by the Administrator making "official" this division of work and this pattern of authority. Unplanned informal authority of this kind is a very common phenomenon in organizations. In many cases, non-hierarchical channels of authority (i.e., a division in the work of decision-making) spring up quite informally when employees in one part of the organization realize that another unit is in a better position than are they to supply certain premises of decision. The department heads in a city, for example, will often accept the decision of the personnel department that there should be rest periods for employees—without questioning the source of authority for the decision—because they have confidence that the personnel department is in a better position than they to judge the merits of this device.

Composite decision—the participation in decision by large numbers of employees and organizational units—is the normal process of decision-making in organizations. Many decisions that are accepted as authoritative are never embodied in formal orders, and even in the case of a formal order, the signature of a particular person who is in a position of hierarchical authority reveals little of the complex process of decision that in almost every case preceded the approval, and even the drafting, of the order. To study authority solely through the formal documents is to obtain a quite misleading notion of the importance of the formal hierarchy in the whole structure of authority in an administrative agency.

So much for a general discussion of authority and its relation to the division of work. A deeper understanding of the workings of authority in organization rests on an analysis of the motives that lead employees to accept authority. It is to this analysis that we turn next.

Why People Obey

Late in the evening we stand at the roadside by an intersection with a stop sign and watch the few straggling cars as they come up to the sign at long intervals. Each carefully pulls to a halt, although it is obvious to the driver that there is not another car (nor a policeman) within many miles. Why do they stop? A clerk processes a great many applications as he has been told to process them and does so without questioning either the techniques used—although they may appear silly to him—or the end sought. Why does he obey?

In another situation, an employee is given clear and specific instructions to do something, and yet he "forgets" to do it or even refuses to do it. Why the variance? Why is it easy to get some persons to obey almost any order, while others will belligerently refuse to obey even the simplest sort of command? Why is the order given by someone who is recognized as a "boss" accepted, but the same order resented and sabotaged if it is given by another person? This is the sort of question we must answer in the following pages. Already, in Chapters 3 and 4, we have brought forward some of the factors that condition obedience. It remains to round out systematically the reasons for obedience and the limitations upon it.

Because the person who accepts proposals may do so for a variety of motives, there will be seen in any organization a number of different types of authority relationship, corresponding to these different motives for acceptance. In the following sections these various kinds of authority will be described as: authority of confidence, authority of identification, authority of sanctions, and authority of legitimacy.

THE AUTHORITY OF CONFIDENCE

People accept the proposals of persons in whom they have great confidence. In any organization there are some individuals who, because of past performance, general reputation, or other factors, have great influence or authority. Their proposals will often be accepted without analysis as to their wisdom. Even when the suggestions of such a person are not accepted, they will be rejected reluctantly and only because a stronger authority contradicts them.

The authority of confidence may be limited to a special area of competence in which a person has acquired a reputation. Thus an executive may sign a requisition for office equipment prepared by his secretary without analyzing it or even reading it because he has confidence in his secretary's ability to make a good decision in that field. In such a case, the secretary is exercising authority over her employer. In any complex organization, an upper level executive, by the very nature of his position, must either accept suggestions from below on the basis of confidence, accept them blindly on no basis whatsoever, or refuse to accept them on the basis of his own prejudices and feeling. The idea that the President of the United States or the mayor of a great city can evaluate intelligently the combined suggestions of a whole complex organization is ridiculous.

In many situations, confidence in the decisions of persons who are not even members of the organization gives authority to these decisions. To take a recent and world-shaking example, the late President Roosevelt is supposed to have based his decision to spend two billion dollars for development of the atomic bomb on the recommendation of Albert Einstein. The President had no basis for independently checking that recommendation. True, he could have, and probably did, get the opinion of other physicists. But if so he was still making the decision upon the basis of his confidence in the physicists he counsulted. He could not even have understood their arguments for this course of action without himself undergoing the rigorous training of mathematical physics.

We have already noted that authority based upon confidence is a familiar phenomenon of everyday life, quite apart from organizations. In society in general, it is probably the principal type of authority that operates. In general, people have confidence that physicians can cure their ills; that carpenters can build their houses; that mechanics can fix their cars; that lawyers can give them sound legal advice. These specialists are usually obeyed within their supposed fields of competence. People who seek and accept their advice do so almost entirely on the basis of confidence in the ability and intention of the specialists to suggest the correct behavior.[4]

Functional Status. The willingness to accept authority on the basis of confidence, both within and outside organizations, goes even one step further. Not only is the layman generally unable to judge the quality of the advice he is getting from the specialist, but he often is in no position to judge the competence of the

[4] For further development of this point see Talcott Parsons, "The Professions and Social Structure," in his *Essays in Sociological Theory Pure and Applied* (Glencoe, Illinois: The Free Press, 1949), especially p. 189.

specialist, except on the basis of certain superficial and formal criteria that give the specialist his *status*.

As we shall see in the course of this chapter, there are at least two kinds of status, which may be called *functional status* and *hierarchical status*. It is with functional status that we are concerned at the moment. A person has functional status in a particular area of knowledge when his decisions and recommendations in that area are accepted as more or less authoritative.

In the established professions, status is generally conferred on the basis of standards developed by the profession itself. The M.D. degree is conferred on the young doctor by the medical profession (acting through an "accredited" medical school). Law and engineering degrees and the certificate of the public accountant are awarded in much the same way. In other cases, job experience in a particular field confers functional status in that field. A person with long experience in a professional position in the Interstate Commerce Commission may acquire status as a transportation economist.

The reader can undoubtedly supply other examples of the acquisition of functional status. It is noteworthy that in most cases the specialists themselves, as a more or less organized professional group, play an important role in determining who has status in their field of specialization. Since there are formal "legitimate" ways of acquiring status, the authority derived therefrom is a composite of authority of confidence and authority of legitimacy.

Relation of the Authority of Confidence to Hierarchy. It should not be supposed that the authority of confidence always operates *across* hierarchical lines. Confidence can be a powerful support for hierarchical as well as for nonhierarchical authority. A subordinate will much more readily obey a command of a superior if he has confidence in the intelligence and judgment of that superior or if he believes that the superior has knowledge of the situation not available to himself.

In particular, where a problem requiring decision affects the work of several units in an organization, the superior who has hierarchical authority in the formal organization plan over all the units involved is often accepted as the person best located—because he has the "whole picture"—to make the decision. Hence, the coordinating functions that are commonly performed by those in hierarchical authority are based, in part at least, upon the authority of confidence—upon the belief of subordinates that the superior is the best informed about the situation as a whole.[5]

Persons at the higher levels of the administrative hierarchy often devote more time than do their subordinates to the organization's external relations—to its relations with other organizations, with the legislative body, with pressure groups, and the like. In the case of decisions having "political" or "public relations" implications, the authority of the hierarchical superior may be accepted by his subordinates because of their confidence that he is more expert or better informed than they regarding the political "angles" of the decision.

One of the techniques of superiors in building morale is that of instilling confidence so that employees will go along with orders willingly, rather than simply because they feel they ought to or because they are afraid not to. The annals of military history are full of the exploits of troops who pushed forward into extremely difficult situations because they had confidence in the ability and wisdom of their commanding officer. General Patton is an example of an officer who instilled a high degree of confidence and whose authority was accepted with enthusiasm, even though he inspired little affection and made unusually frequent use of formal sanctions.

Charismatic Leadership. There are numerous examples in history of leaders—sometimes, but not always, in the formal hierarchy—who inspire such a high level of confidence in their followers that they "can do no wrong." In such cases, the leader usually also becomes a symbol of group identification, and the authority of confidence is reinforced by the authority of identification. In fact, the process is circular, because a group that identifies with a leader becomes less critical of his judgment and more and more confident in the wisdom of his leadership.

Such individuals have been labelled by the German sociologist Max Weber, "charismatic leaders," and the authority they exercise

[5] Of course, in many instances the subordinates prefer to negotiate directly with each other—pooling the specialized knowledge of the various units involved. In such cases, the hierarchical superior may or may not participate in the decision; or he may be asked merely to ratify a decision his subordinates have agreed upon among themselves. In this case, the authority may be exercised by the subordinates as a group over their superior, who places confidence in the decision they have worked out together.

over their followers "charisma." Unfortunately, the discussion of charismatic leadership by Weber and others has had vague mystical overtones, and a satisfactory social-psychological theory of charisma has nowhere been fully developed. As suggested above, charisma is perhaps best understood as some combination of the authority of confidence with the authority of identification.[6]

THE AUTHORITY OF IDENTIFICATION

The role of group loyalties in influencing behavior was discussed in some detail in Chapter 4. It is not necessary to repeat that discussion at this point. Here we will show the relation between identification and the acceptance of authority.

This relation is twofold. In the first place—and this was the central theme of Chapter 4—most individuals have a very wide area of acceptance for decisions agreed upon by a group with which they are strongly identified. It is often more realistic to speak of acceptance of authority *by an identification group* than acceptance *by an individual*. Since the existence of such a group creates new values for its members—in particular, the survival of the group itself—in addition to the values to which they are attached as individuals, the area of acceptance of group members is quite different from the area of acceptance of unattached individuals.

In the second place, proposals advanced by members of the group will often be more acceptable than the same proposals when advanced by "outsiders." This fact is a basic one in pressure techniques. To get an "insider" to sponsor your proposal is to enhance considerably the chance that it will be accepted. Professional people are often far more susceptible to suggestions from their own profession than those from other people, even though the suggestions concern matters entirely outside their professional competence. A fraternity brother is likely to accept the suggestion of a fellow fraternity brother; an attorney may be disposed to look

[6] H. H. Gerth and C. Wright Mills, *From Max Weber: Essays in Sociology* (New York: Oxford University Press, 1946), pp. 245–52. The "founder" of a movement or an organization is often a charismatic leader—for example, George Washington, Gifford Pinchot (the U. S. Forest Service). The feeling of a group that it is surrounded by external dangers undoubtedly encourages group identification and confidence in leaders (as a means of reducing fear). Hence charismatic leadership is characteristic of crisis situations—as evidence, F. D. Roosevelt, John L. Lewis, Abraham Lincoln, and so forth.

favorably on recommendations of other attorneys; a Foreign Service Officer to respect the judgment of other Foreign Service Officers. In addition, common identification makes access to the persons making a decision easier. A person going to Washington may well find it difficult to locate a person who can make or influence a decision. Access is much easier if he can find a friend who "knows the ropes."

For this reason, a person who belongs to two identification groups often becomes an important channel of communications and influence between these groups. The importance of this dual identification has already been shown in Chapter 4 with regard to the dual identification of executives with the work group of their subordinates on the one hand and with their co-equals and their common superior, on the other.

THE AUTHORITY OF SANCTIONS

The most generally recognized weapon of the superior is the sanction—the ability of the superior to attach pleasant or unpleasant consequences to the actions of the subordinate. What is not so often recognized is that this aspect of authority, like those mentioned above, is not a sole prerogative of the hierarchical superior. It is possessed by subordinates and by persons outside the organization as well.[7]

Non-Hierarchical Sanctions. One of the most obvious sanctions possessed by hierarchical inferiors is the strike. Most often the technique of the strike is forbidden or not utilized by government employees, but mass sanctions along the same lines exist nonetheless. Widespread resentment against an order from above can lead to organized or even unorganized slowdowns. It can lead to widespread "misinterpretation" of orders and the like. In Chapter 5, the techniques of obstruction available to a disgruntled work group

---

[7] The term "sanctions" is used broadly here to include both rewards (positive sanctions) and punishments (negative sanctions). The distinction between reward and punishment is a difficult one to make. The failure to receive an anticipated reward is an undesirable experience. For example, is promotion a reward or a punishment? Failure to promote is a typical sanction and is an undesirable experience. If a person expects or hopes for a reward, the power to withhold the reward is the power to apply negative sanctions. Whether a person is motivated by desire for the reward or desire to avoid the negative sanction (i.e., to not receive the reward) is partly a verbal conundrum.

against fellow employers and superiors alike were reviewed in some detail. The point we want to make here is that workers do have sanctions against superiors as well as vice versa.

Similarly, groups outside the work unit or even agency very often have the powers of sanction. For example, a personnel office may refuse to "clear" a desired promotion. To get the promotion may necessitate an appeal to the over-burdened agency head, or even negotiations with some outside agency like the Civil Service Commission. Accomplishing the task might require getting superiors lined up in support; argument, perhaps heated, before the common superior; a decision which is really a division; ruffled feelings and perhaps strained working relations in the future; a test of strength or influence with a common superior which, if lost, may involve a change in the organization power situation; frustration for the losers and their superiors; and so forth. Hence, to the extent that an appeal from the personnel office's ruling is burdensome and unpleasant that office possesses a powerful sanction.

In one sense, any suggestion carries a sanction. People generally dislike to say "no," to turn someone down, their reactions varying all the way from a pathological inability to say "no" to an almost inhuman disregard of other people's feelings. Thus to say "no" to a proposal involves at least the unpleasantness of disappointing someone. Capitalizing on this sentiment, anyone can acquire more authority by learning to make his proposals in such a way as to secure the maximum benefit from this "sanction."

Sanctions and Hierarchy. The relationship of the authority of sanctions with the organizational hierarchy can be viewed from a more general standpoint. When a person joins an organization he is accepting a system of relationships that restricts his individuality or his freedom of action. He is willing to do so because he feels that, in spite of the organizational restraints, being a member of the organization is preferable to other alternatives available to him.[8] To continue as a member of the organization, he must continue, to some extent, to abide by the complex of procedures which constitutes the organization. Although, increasingly, the power to discharge an employee is not lodged in any specific superior (because of merit systems, central personnel offices, labor unions, etc.), nevertheless, this power resides somewhere in the organization,

[8] On this point, see Simon, *Administrative Behavior*, chap. 6; and Barnard, op. cit., chap. 11.

being, in fact, one of its working procedures. The sanctions discussed in this section are increasingly *organization* sanctions, brought into play through the working procedures of the organization, and not the special prerogatives or powers of *individual superiors*. However, at this stage of our development, individual superiors usually have a greater influence on the process than recalcitrant inferiors, and thus hierarchical authority is somewhat strengthened by organizational sanctions.

The Rule of Anticipated Reactions. In essence, a sanction is a whip on the wall—its mere existence tends to induce compliance, although its actual use may be infrequent. For the most part the authority of sanction rests on the behavior responses that are induced by *the possibility* that a sanction may be applied. An organization member is seldom presented with an ultimatum "to do so and so or suffer the consequences." Rather, he anticipates the consequences of continual insubordination or failure to please the person or persons who have the ability to apply sanctions to him, and this anticipation acts as a constant motivation without expressed threats from any person. If actual punishment is necessary, the sanction has failed—anticipation of possible punishment has not prevented the undesired behavior.

Reaction to Sanctions. As a device of authority, negative sanctions (punishments) are of limited usefulness. People, even government servants, resent being "pushed around," and a threat to impose a sanction often imperils a proposal rather than the contrary. A proposal backed by the overt threat of punishment often has many consequences other than the desired one of acceptance. It can be destructive of organization because it is divisive—it divides the organization into hostile camps. It also tends to lower morale, which means that it lessens the unsolicited contributions of organization members.

Such positive rewards as raises in pay, or promotion are likely to be of only moderate effectiveness except for the highly mobile employee (see Chapter 3) for whom these types of rewards correspond to strong internalized values. In many situations, positive inducements based upon the internalized values of the employee—acceptance of the organization goals as his own, desire for approval of the work group, a desire to participate in the planning process—can secure an enthusiasm in the contributors that will make the need for negative sanctions fade into the background.

Other Limits on Sanctions. The power of sanction is restricted even beyond the desire of those who possess sanctions to limit its use. Most executives in government operate within the framework of a civil service system that severely limits the traditional executive sanction—namely, the right to hire and fire. In one of the nation's largest cities, for example, the Police Commissioner has the right to fire police captains only after a trial before the Civil Service Commission and then an appeal to the courts. For all practical purposes, and except in the most extreme situations, he does not really possess this sanction. The same general limitation exists at the national and at many state levels.

But the right to hire and fire may be restricted in many other ways. In a period of a tight labor market, the use of this sanction is quite limited because of the inability of the employer to get workers to take the place of those whom he discharges. Nor does this apply only to discharges. The power of reprimand is also more limited, since the worker can more freely exercise his right to resign.

Very often, organizational peculiarities may prevent the use of particular sanctions. A person may be obligated to carry out a set of tasks but be forced to depend for the execution of those tasks on persons in other units to whom he can apply no effective sanctions. In such a case, dependence must be on other sources of authority than sanction. As organizations grow more complex this problem becomes greater, and probably reaches its peak in the Federal government.

In public administration, sanctions may be limited by the political connections of the employee. This kind of limitation is probably less important in jurisdictions having civil service systems than in others, but it is a factor at all levels of government. Many supervisors will put up with behavior from a cousin of a powerful Congressman which they would not tolerate in other circumstances.

Because the notion of authority is in the minds of most people so closely tied in with the idea of negative sanctions—the fearsome things the boss can do—it is important to emphasize: (1) sanctions do not operate strictly on hierarchical lines: subordinates and "coordinates" have sanctions as well as do superiors; (2) agencies can, and often do, accomplish their tasks when the superiors do not possess all the usual formal sanctions; (3) sanctions are very often not the most effective means of enforcing authority.

THE AUTHORITY OF LEGITIMACY

There is another reason why employees accept the proposals of other organization members—a reason less rationalistic but probably more important than the desire to avoid the organization sanctions discussed above. People accept "legitimate" authority because they feel that they *ought* to go along with the "rules of the game."

Legitimacy.   As we have seen in Chapter 3, throughout their development to maturity and after, people are educated in the beliefs, values, or mores of society. They learn what they ought to do and what they ought not to do. One of the values with which they are indoctrinated is that a person should play according to the rules of the game. This ethic is acquired very early. When a child enters a ball game in the sand lot he does not expect the game to be altered at various points to suit his convenience. Rather he expects to adjust his behavior to the rules of the game. Although there may be disputes as to what the rule is on some point, once this is established, the proposition that he should abide by the rule is unquestioned.

Likewise, when people enter organizations most of them feel that they ought to abide by the rules of the game—the working procedures of the organization. These working procedures define how the work will be done; how working problems will be solved when they arise; how conflicts will be settled. They prescribe that on such and such matters the individual will accept the suggestions of this or that person or organization; secure the advice of such and such unit; clear his work with so and so; work on matters that come to him in such and such a way; etc.

The working procedures of an organization prescribe that the individual member will accept the proposals of other members in matters assigned to them. This acceptance is one of the rules of the game which he feels he should abide by. Thus, individuals in organizations also accept the authority of other persons because they think they *ought* to accept it.

Let us consider, a concrete though hypothetical example. After graduation from college a student decides to embark on a career as a personnel officer in the Federal civil service. As a condition of entry to the service he takes a civil service examination. He passes the examination and is admitted to the service and given a position as Junior Classification Officer in the central personnel office of the United States Department of Agriculture. Upon entering he is assigned a desk, and the procedures and methods of classification followed in that office are explained to him. He is given a manual of instructions which tells him how he is to behave in certain circumstances. His relationships with other persons in the organization are explained to him—who is his "boss," the section of the agency that falls under his purview for classification, and so forth. He would be expected, and he would expect, to govern his behavior along the general lines of the instructions given him. He wouldn't normally decide that the classification methods used were unsatisfactory; or that he should report to someone who was not his boss. He would follow the rules of the game; the established procedures of the organization to which he is attached.

Legitimacy and Hierarchy. The working relationships in an organization designated by the term "hierarchy" constitute a particular organization procedure for handling the authority of legitimacy. Acceptance of the working procedures of an organization by a member includes acceptance of the obligation to go along with the proposals of an hierarchical superior, at least within a limit of toleration—the "area of acceptance." Thus, whether the other reasons for obedience are operating or not (confidence, identification, or sanctions), organization members will feel that they ought to obey their superiors. Legitimacy is one of the most important sources of the authority of the hierarchical superior.

The feeling that hierarchical authority is legitimate is immensely strengthened by previous social conditioning. Hierarchical behavior is an institutionalized behavior that all organization members bring to the organization with them. Like the players in the Oberammergau Passion Play who begin to learn their roles in early childhood, "inferiors" obey "superiors" because they have been taught to do so from infancy, beginning with the parent-child relationship and running through almost constant experience with social and organizational hierarchies until death brings graduation from this particular social schooling. Hierarchical behavior involves an inferior-superior role-taking of persons well versed in their roles. "Inferiors" feel that they ought to obey "superiors"; "superiors" feel that they ought to be obeyed.

Our society is extremely hierarchical. Success is generally interpreted in terms of hierarchical preferment. Social position and financial rewards are closely related to hierarchical preferment, as also are education and even perhaps romantic attainment. Advancement up a hierarchy is generally considered a sign of moral worth, of good character, of good stewardship, of social responsibility, and of the possession of superior intellectual qualities.

Hierarchy receives a tremendous emphasis in nearly all organizations. This is so because hierarchy is a procedure that requires no training, no indoctrination, no special inducements. It rests almost entirely on "pre-entry" training—a training so thorough that few other organization procedures can ever compete with it. Furthermore, hierarchy is a great simplification. It is much simpler to say to a new organization member, "X is your boss," than to say, "in this situation, do this; in that situation, do that."

LIMITS ON HIERARCHY AS SOURCE OF LEGITIMATE AUTHORITY

Although our society does a good "pre-entry" job of training for the procedure of hierarchy, it probably does not do so good a job as other societies or other times. Since the behaviors involved in the phenomenon of hierarchy are behaviors that reflect prevailing social mores, as those mores change so do the behaviors. Western man of the nineteenth century probably received a far better training for this organizational procedure than does modern Western man. It is clear that the days when an executive could do almost anything he wanted to do with his organization are past. As the individual, through education and a wide variety of extra-organizational experiences, acquires an increasing sense of personal dignity, he probably becomes less and less amenable to the particular type of authority associated with the hierarchical procedure.

Furthermore, it seems probable that certain aspects of our modern civilization are changing people's expectations with regard to organizational behavior and treatment generally. Especially is the hierarchical procedure weakened as the social division of labor turns more and more people into indispensable and recondite specialists. With the growing importance of the professional and technical specialist, there is a corresponding tendency for the working rules of organization—the rules that define the authority of legitimacy—to place more and more emphasis upon functional status, and less and less upon hierarchy. Employees are becoming more and more accustomed to accepting the proposals of functional specialists—and to feeling that they ought to accept these proposals. As a consequence the authority of legitimacy is much less an exclusive possession of the formal hierarchy than it was even a generation ago.

CHAPTER NINE

✠

Securing Teamwork: The Structure of Authority and Status

IN CHAPTER 8, we described the psychological motivations that underlie the authority relationship. To complete our picture, we need to explore the ways in which the various forms of authority actually operate in organizations, and some of the interrelationships among them. In this chapter we will discuss the use of status systems to symbolize authority relationships, and will conclude our analysis of the role of the hierarchy in the total pattern of authority.

Status in Organizations [1]

In discussing the authority of confidence, it was pointed out that persons acquire functional status—a recognition by others of their competence to form judgments about matters in their field of specialization. In the same way, persons acquire *hierarchical status* (by some authors called "scalar" status and in military administration, "rank") by virtue of their positions in the formal hierarchy of the organization.

The distinction between functional and hierarchical status (although these two cannot be completely separated) derives from the fact that the former refers to some area of professional or technical specialization, while the latter refers to some idea or

[1] This section is based largely on Chester I. Barnard, "Functions and Pathology of Status Systems in Formal Organizations," in William Foote Whyte (ed.), *Industry and Society* (New York: McGraw-Hill Book Co., Inc. 1946), chap. 4.

system of social "rank" applying to all the persons in an organization and also of the society in which it operates. A soil agronomist in the Department of Agriculture may have functional status by virtue of important research in this field, known to other agronomists. If he holds a modest research position in the Department, his hierarchical status in that organization or in society may be quite low. On the other hand, the hierarchical status of a Secretary of Agriculture by virtue of his position in the Federal government will be substantial. He will be treated with deference by persons outside the Department and even outside the Federal government.

The importance of hierarchical status for organization lies in the fact that the behavior of individuals, and the behavior of others toward them, is greatly influenced by relative status. During the recent war, a story was told in the War Department which, true or not, serves to illustrate the point. A representative from the milling concern, General Mills, had been trying to see General Brehon Somerville, head of the Services of Supply, for a long time without success. One day, in calling, he mentioned his firm's name. Somerville's secretary, mistaking the firm name for a title of rank, immediately connected "General Mills" with General Somerville.

SYMBOLS OF STATUS

If the behavior of persons toward each other is to hinge upon status, means must be available for a person to evaluate quickly the status of another with whom he is dealing. Hence, readily recognizable *symbols of status* are necessary to the operation of a status system. This need applies to functional as well as hierarchical status.

Barnard distinguishes five kinds of status symbols: "(1) ceremonies of induction and appointment; (2) insignia and other public indicia of status; (3) titles and appellations of office and calling; (4) emoluments and perquisites of position and office; (5) limitations and restrictions of calling and office." [2]

Induction. Throughout our society, we follow the practice of ceremony for induction into new status positions. The baccalaureate degree, with its caps and gowns, inducts a person into the company of learned men (and is used to confer that status on men who have been successful without being learned). The elabo-

[2] Ibid., p. 50.

rate ritual used by lodges who elect a new high potentate; the oath of office solemnly administered to an incoming President by a Supreme Court Justice; these are examples of the ceremony which accompanies induction into many positions in the social order. The object of the induction ceremony is to dramatize publicly the possession of status.

Induction ceremonies in the government service, except for top positions, are held to a minimum in this country. Normally there is the routine oath to support the Constitution and nothing more. For the top positions, however, there are induction ceremonies which are meant to dramatize the position and the authority of the executive. A new cabinet member is often inducted amid a fanfare of exploding flash bulbs and inquiring newsmen.

Insignia. Modern America, except for the military services, does not go in as heavily for insignia as do some other societies. Strolling on a Sunday it is difficult to tell the difference between persons of high and low status. The "boss" may wear rumpled clothes, while his clerk may be the office dandy. Insignia are used much more often, however, to indicate the status of employees while they are on the job. Certain government employees—policemen, firemen, and judges—wear distinctive uniforms when at work to induce certain behaviors toward them. Differences in dress clearly distinguish the "white collar" worker—male or female— from other classes of employees.

Titles. Titles and other forms of address are often used to connote status. Often these refer to function—Jones is a lawyer; Smith is a street sweeper—but because our attitude toward these functions varies, scalar status quickly attaches to functional title. Government organizations all use descriptive titles of function. Every major in the Army is probably referred to as "Major So-and-so," and a letter to a bureau chief will usually include his title in the heading (although in a face-to-face contact we would not usually address him as Bureau Chief Adams).[3]

Perquisites of Office. Salaries and privileges of office are perhaps the most important status symbols in civilian government agencies. But, as Barnard points out, "Care should be taken . . . to dis-

---

[3] In Germany, it is customary to refer to persons in terms of their organization position. "Lawyer Schmidt" is the customary form of address. This functions to carry the notion of status outside the particular organization and to the society at large. See Talcott Parsons, "Democracy and Social Structure in Pre-Nazi Germany," *Journal of Legal and Political Sociology,* 1:96–114 (November, 1942).

tinguish between the valuation of them as material rewards and as evidences and elements of status." [4] Wages, as such, are not as important as status symbols in government agencies, perhaps, as they are in private economic organizations where the differences in economic reward are much greater. The most dramatic evidences of status hover around other privileges. As example we may cite some of the status symbols that were characteristic in the Office of Price Administration.[5]

The prestige sentiment is supported and maintained by an extensive drama of distinction. Although the spirit in OPA was much more democratic than in most organizations, this drama played itself out in the rationing hierarchy as it does in all other hierarchies of our society. For example, it expressed itself in the distribution of working facilities. Roughly speaking, working facilities were distributed in inverse ratio to need. At the bottom were the workers crowded together in open halls, their desks placed back to back and side to side. At this level, where the writing took place, there were very few stenographers or typists. Many of the workers spent a fair portion of their time looking or waiting for typists. Most of them wrote their material out in long hand or typed their own first rough drafts. Phones were difficult to get at this level, and usually several people shared one phone. A very few of the lucky ones got a rotary floor fan to put by their desks to help them get through the almost unbearable Washington summer day.

As one went up the hierarchy, conditions improved. Branch chiefs nearly all had offices built around their space in the wing. The offices were equipped with one or more fans. These offices frequently took up about half a bay (a bay usually contained from five to ten workers.) Branch chiefs had their own secretaries and phones with two extensions. The secretaries took dictation and did typing only for their boss. Efforts to get secretaries (of branch chiefs and higher) to help out the workers were usually not successful. Stenographers all looked for the day when they would work for only one man. This desire was not based on laziness, but on the distinction of such a position. The branch chief's secretary took his phone calls, and most of them learned to make the caller state his name and business before he was connected with the branch chief. This practice distinguished the branch chief as an important person. When he wished to make a phone call he asked his secretary to dial the number for him and call him when she got the number (he had an extension on his desk). This practice carried the impression to the party waiting on the other end of the line that the

[4] Op. cit., p. 51.
[5] Victor A. Thompson, *The Regulatory Process in OPA Rationing* (New York: King's Crown Press, 1950), chap. 10.

branch chief was a very busy person who could not waste time waiting for the other party.

At the division director level, the facilities were much more lavish. He had a large office (usually a corner office) which took up a whole bay. Some of these offices had air-conditioners. He had a secretary, and sometimes a clerk-typist as well, who often occupied a little outer office of their own. The division director had two phone lines with one extension on his desk, one outside on his secretary's desk, and a little switch board to enable him to talk only to his secretary outside, or to parties on either of the lines. When he wanted to call someone, he buzzed his secretary and talked to her over the phone asking her to place the call. When she got the connection, she buzzed him, told him over the phone that she had his connection, and he then switched his extension to the line on which the party was waiting. This procedure probably took more time than calling the party in the first place. Persons suddenly elevated to division director's status had some difficulty learning how to operate the phone system.

The Deputy Administrator had about the same facilities as the division director, but in addition he had an administrative assistant (CAF-7 or 9).

In addition to working facilities there were purely irrational evidences of distinction claimed by superiors. Thus, at the division director's level, one could have an executive desk, somewhat larger and more ornate than ordinary desks. Also at this level, one got a leather upholstered desk chair and frequently a red or green rug for the floor. The rugs were particularly prized evidences of distinction. One person suddenly raised to the rank of division director was so anxious to get the rug distinction that he took the first one he saw lying in the hall and put it in his office. It was too large, and so he cut it in half, later to discover that he had cut in half the rug being saved for the OPA Assistant Administrator. Another purely irrational evidence of distinction was the executive dining room where, until 12:15 persons at the grade of CAF-13 and above could eat, and after 12:15 only persons CAF-14 and above could eat.

Many hierarchical superiors had, or acquired, personal habits or traits or tricks which emphasized their lofty positions. Many of them would call subordinates into their office to talk to them rather than go to the subordinate's office or desk. Frequently, they kept their subordinates and others waiting for some time in the outer office with the secretary. (This was sometimes necessary because someone else was in the office.) When the subordinate or other person was admitted, many superiors adopted the trick of placing several phone calls during the course of the conversation and interrupting the conversation to answer them as they came in. This practice often extended the conversation for periods two or three times as long as they needed to have been. There were meetings called by the Deputy Administrator with from five to ten persons present where he spent about half his time placing phone calls and taking them when they came in. Thus, he wasted much time of several people, all CAF-13 and above. This practice is often a consciously adopted trick of the superior, as unnecessary as it is discourteous.

Enough has been said to show that in OPA as elsewhere the drama by which superior status is maintained went on and on. The distinctions sought symbolize and create authority—the ability to influence people. Through these distinctions, the element of social fear is enlisted as a sanction for obedience. These distinctions are an integral part of the institutional pattern of hierarchy.

The symbols around which status revolves are legion: the use of company cars; the privilege of not working by time clocks; physical location of one's desk with reference to windows—in fact anything which can conceivably become a status symbol. Such privileges are regarded as extremely important—often more important than the material inducements for participation. Very often office workers, because of their superior status, accept wages lower than factory workers in order to maintain the privilege of white-collar status.[6]

Limitations and Restrictions on Behavior. Behavior patterns in the sense of restrictions and limitations are also imposed by status. There are certain things that higher status persons are not supposed to do. The branch chief who gets into a dice game with the custodial staff is jeopardizing status. The superior who uses violent language in the presence of inferiors is likely to lose status. Army officers are forbidden to develop social intercourse with enlisted men lest their status be jeopardized.[7] Conversely, high status confers privileges denied to those who are lower in the scale. More adequate income, special services, clubs, etc. may be reserved to those who are high in the rank order of an organization.

STATUS AND THE ENFORCEMENT OF AUTHORITY

One of the chief functions of status is to facilitate the enforcement of the authority of legitimacy. The relation of status to authority is threefold: (1) it relieves the person accepting authority from the task of evaluating the personal qualities of the individual

---

[6] Gardner, *Human Relations in Industry*, chap. 1, has some interesting insights into this problem.

[7] During World War II, at least one Service Command forbade commissioned officers to carry parcels on the street or to patronize ten-cent stores.

exercising authority; (2) it defines patterns of "correct" behavior for employees when they are dealing with each other; and (3) it enables employees to recognize the authoritativeness or "reliability" of the communications that come to them.

With respect to the first point, the person who exercises authority is frequently not better qualified to make a decision than the person who accepts his authority. Very often the hierarchical superior is not, if viewed objectively, superior to the persons whom he must direct, and sometimes the functional specialist is not more expert. Accident, inheritance, bluster, elections, office politics, and the like very often place persons in positions of hierarchical or functional authority who could not, by any stretch of the imagination, be called "natural leaders" or "experts." For such persons, an important part of their authority is derived from the acceptance of their status at face value. The army furnishes a good example. The uniform and the insignia, enforced by rigid status patterns, enable the officer to be treated with deference by the enlisted men regardless of personal qualities.

Status also provides quick indices that enable a person to behave correctly in a given situation. Informed that someone wishing to see him is a "Division Chief," an employee will behave differently than he would if the caller held lower or higher rank in the hierarchy. The status system provides a mental set that enables the employee to respond as he is expected to respond.

Finally, the status system helps to establish the "authoritativeness" of communications. When it is desired to attach the authority of legitimacy to a communication, it need only be signed by a person of appropriate hierarchical or functional status, and transmitted through the "legitimate" channels of the formal organization. This relieves the person receiving the communication from the task of evaluating its legitimacy. For example, a clerk in the personnel office may prepare a statement about Christmas holidays for employees. This statement, signed by the agency head and transmitted through hierarchical channels, becomes an authoritative communication.

THE PATHOLOGY OF STATUS

While the status system does serve useful organizational functions, it also has pathological aspects. Among these are: (1) the tendency to exaggerate the notion that authority always flows from the top down; (2) insulation of the top executives from criticism of those who have lower status, but who may have more adequate judgments on particular decisions; (3) the danger that persons of high status will use their status to influence decisions that lie outside their area of competence; and (4) the difficulty of adjusting status to natural abilities. We will discuss these points in relation to hierarchical status, but functional status raises analogous problems.

Overemphasis of Hierarchical Authority. Undue regard for the status system nurtures the idea that authority comes from the top down and that the functioning or malfunctioning of particular organizations depends upon the genius or lack of genius of the top executive. A great deal of organizational history (including much of the purportedly scientific writing in this field) is written more or less as the biography of an individual. While this may add drama to the story, it generally exaggerates the influence that a single person has over an organization. Ample evidence has already been presented that the ability of any single individual to influence the activities of a complex organization is severely limited. Even in the case of the charismatic leader, a large part of his influence lies not with his traits or behavior as a person, but with the set of ideas that he symbolizes for his followers.

Insulation from Criticism. The adage that "power corrupts, and absolute power corrupts absolutely" sums up this particular weakness deriving from status systems. A person who, because of high status, receives continual and abject deference from his subordinates can scarcely be blamed if he comes to attribute to himself abilities far and above those of the average run of men. If he begins to make decisions on the basis of his snap judgments, he can cause havoc within the organization. The corruption and eventual destruction of the despot through his insulation from truth and criticism is a favorite theme of history and fiction.

Status Without Competence. Closely related to the point just discussed is the tendency for status to be accepted outside the areas where it has any reason to denote competence. The opinions of a highly successful businessman or a famous scientist upon almost any subject will be received with deference. Often, such a person is regarded as competent to hold important organizational positions entirely outside his area of expertness. This would be harmless enough if (1) persons of high status were always extremely able and (2) if ability were always transferable from one field of activity to entirely unrelated fields. Trouble begins in those numerous instances where one or the other of these two assumptions fails to hold.

Imperfect Adjustment of Status to Ability. Exaggeration of the status system also tends to restrict unduly the development of talent from below. Status tends to be frozen, and it is difficult to remove persons whose talents are not commensurate with the tasks of their positions. To remove a person from high office for incompetence or for other reasons calls attention to the imperfections of the organization's allocations of status, tends to be derogatory to the office, and may jeopardize the whole system. Therefore, incompetent persons holding positions of high status often have to be retained, or at best, "kicked upstairs" into honorific but inconsequential posts in order to get rid of them.

Since the stability of status is important and only one person is *allowed* to fill an executive position although many may be *able* to fill it, a strong sense of injustice may be felt by those who do not have high status. The opportunity to rise in status is a very important incentive to many employees, and the frequency with which this opportunity arises is a vital aspect of organization. It will receive careful attention in Chapter 16.

In spite of these imperfections, status systems are a fixed part of life in organizations. Their operations must be understood if they are to be prevented from causing pathological conditions.

Functions of the Hierarchy

In the preceding pages we have insisted on a concept of authority that treats hierarchy as only one part—albeit an important one— in the total pattern of authority relations in an organization. Within this total pattern what are the particular uses that are made of hierarchical authority, as distinguished from the other types of authority that have been mentioned?

We have seen that the arrangement of authority on hierarchical lines is often convenient because it takes over into the organization the mores, already firmly established, of the society in which the organization operates. Beyond this general advantage, hierarchical arrangements have additional conveniences in particular uses. The most important of these uses are in: (1) setting goals and allocating work; and (2) coordinating and settling disputes.

SETTING GOALS AND ALLOCATING WORK

In Chapter 6 we saw that a hierarchical arrangement arises quite naturally out of the usual procedure for dividing the work when a large group task is to be accomplished. The whole task of the group is divided into major segments, each with its sub-goals, and each segment is assigned to a major organizational unit. Each segment is then further subdivided into components, each of which is assigned to a sub-unit, so that the resulting structure is hierarchical. It is quite natural, then, to vest with each level of the hierarchy the task of orienting the work of subdivisions at that level to the goals to which the activity of that subdivision is supposed to contribute. Thus, in a city government, the department heads would normally exercise the principal responsibility for validating the tasks and goals of the major bureaus of their departments, and for seeing that the activities of these bureaus were oriented to their goals.

But there are additional reasons why those in the higher hierarchical positions play a prominent part in the control of goals. First, in terms of the mores surrounding authority relationships, these higher executives are accepted as having the "right" to interest themselves in problems occurring over a wider area than the area of concern to their subordinates. A person who concerns himself with the goals of organization units broader than the one for which he is responsible may encounter resistance from others who challenge the "legitimacy" of his concern.

A second reason why goal validation is related to hierarchy is that the persons at higher levels of the hierarchy may be expected, by reason of their responsibilities, to identify with the broader goals of the organization, while those at lower levels will more often identify with the sub-goals of the smaller organization units. Securing conformity of the goals of these smaller units to the goals of the larger then becomes an important concern of the executives at higher levels.

Another factor that gives hierarchical superiors a particularly close relation to goal-setting is their role in the maintenance of the organization against external demands and pressures. It is in this process—of guarding the organization against "external dangers" —that changes or potential changes in goals and activities are most frequently brought to the attention of the organization. Because of the nature of his activities, the executive near the top is often the first to be aware of the menaces that threaten his program.

CONFLICTING IMPLEMENTATIONS: SETTLING DISPUTES

Even if a common goal is accepted by the members of an organization unit, there are "many roads to Rome." One of the most important jobs of the hierarchical superior is to settle disputes and disagreements that arise among his subordinates. In any complex task there are numerous opportunities for difference of opinion as to the precise objective to be accomplished, and—even more important—as to the best method for accomplishing it. Often there are several courses of action open, each of which would be reasonably effective, but the needs of coordination may require that the *same* course be adopted by the entire organization. In such circumstances, the organization members may be perfectly satisfied to have the issue in dispute settled before a common court of appeal— the hierarchical superior.

The need for a well-understood method of umpiring disputes is recognized wherever the activities of several organization units are so related that coordination is necessary for the successful attainment of goals. The Army, the Navy, the Air Force all want to organize in the way that will win wars. But because of the identifications of personnel with the special viewpoints of the three units, and because of the tendency to overemphasize one's own part in the total program and to over-evaluate the superiority of one's own proposals, there has been a constant struggle for power and position among the several services. Prior to their grouping in a Department of National Defense, the only "impartial umpire" available for the settlement of these disputes was the President. One of the aims of the recent merger of the forces was to get an integrated program —that is, to provide in the Secretary of Defense a person below the level of the President who could make final decisions in such disputes. The success of the new arrangement in achieving this aim will depend, of course, on the willingness of the services to accept the umpire's decisions and of the President and Congress to back him up. This willingness, if it develops at all, will only grow over a long period of time. There have already been several attempts of the services (and particularly the Navy and Air Force) to appeal over the head of the umpire, and even over the head of the President, to the Congress.

It is difficult to overemphasize this coordinating role of the hierarchy. Without a common hierarchical superior, or with a common superior at levels too distant to be appealed to except in acute emergency, administrative units may engage in fratricidal strife that can halt effective work. As we shall see in Chapter 14, the absence of a common hierarchical superior between a budget estimates officer or a personnel classification officer, on the one hand, and a branch or section chief in a "line" agency on the other, often impedes the amicable settlement of disputes between them, and leads to protracted, and sometimes ill-tempered, bargaining and power tactics.

The Structure of Authority Relationships

We have seen that in any organization there may be an extremely complex system of authority relationships. Functional specialists, and others, may exercise authority derived from confidence in their expertness or from their functional status. Group identification may provide a source of authority to members of the group. Some individuals may gain authority by virtue of their power to reward or punish. There may, and usually will, be a broad acceptance of the authority of the formal hierarchy.

Within limits, these authority relationships can be deliberately planned, and created. Certainly the hierarchy can be formally established, and the power to apply formal sanctions allocated. Areas of functional specialization and competence can be created. To a lesser degree, particular group identifications can be nurtured or discouraged.

Interwoven with these planned relationships will be the numerous authority relationships growing out of the informal social organization, and only partially controllable by formal means. Bill Jones has authority in the organization because he gains the respect of many friends. Joe Smith has wide influence over the legal staff because, although not a part of that staff, he has had legal training and experience. Hence, we must steer a careful middle course between exaggerating the extent to which authority relations can be controlled or planned, and discounting too much the importance of the formally established authority relationships. With this caution in mind, we may discuss some of the consequences of structuring the system of formal authority in different ways.

Perhaps the central issue here is how far the formal plan should emphasize hierarchical authority, or how far, on the other hand it should recognize areas of functional authority.

UNITY OF COMMAND

Stated very simply, "unity of command" means that every man has but one boss to whom he reports and from whom he takes orders and instructions. Unity of command would exist if employees only accepted as authoritative those channels that are commonly shown on an organization chart.

The great attraction of the idea of unity of command is its simplicity. It carries the "umpiring" concept of the executive to its ultimate conclusion. Some writers on administration have argued that the authority of legitimacy should attach only to hierarchical authority in order to preserve unity of command.[8]

But unity of command must be regarded as an illusion. Unity of command does not actually exist and cannot be established in real organizations. Indeed, the authors have never encountered any government agency or unit where it was successfully imposed. To impose unity of command, we would have to prevent employees from accepting the proposals of specialists in whom they had confidence or whose authority seemed legitimate to them by reason of their functional status. If in a branch, for example, the accountants were subordinate to the branch chief, we would have to prevent these accountants from accepting the proposals of a central finance bureau for common accounting techniques.

Second, even if it could be imposed, organizations would be unwilling to accept the consequences of observing unity of command. A tremendous time-consuming burden of communication would be imposed by insisting that all proposals follow the channels of the

---

[8] See Gulick, "Notes on the Theory of Organization," *Papers on the Science of Administration*, p. 9.

formal hierarchy. The power of functional specialists to influence behavior in the organization would be greatly weakened.

Unity of command is in fact violated in all organizations. Bowing to this fact, most organizations give explicit recognition in their formal plans to the legitimacy of authority exercised through "functional" channels as well as to that exercised through hierarchical channels. Sometimes, functional authority is "reconciled" with unity of command by some statement to the effect that "functional specialists do not give orders, but their advice is not to be lightly disregarded." We shall have more to say about the significance of such organizational double-talk in Chapter 13.

What most often happens in organizations is that each employee takes orders on technical matters from various sources, but in cases where there is a conflict, he takes his problem to his hierarchical superior. In Federal field offices, for example, the district director is usually the hierarchical superior of the field office employees, but the information on which the individual employee is supposed to operate comes from his technical counterpart in the central office. Under this procedure the loyalty of the employee is somewhat divided, but he has—at least nominally—an avenue of appeal in case of contradictory demands.

AUTHORITY COMMENSURATE WITH RESPONSIBILITY

Along with the doctrine of unity of command, a second characteristic of the authority system that is often asserted to be indispensable is that "authority be commensurate with responsibility." By this is meant that when an individual or organization unit is to be held accountable for carrying out a particular task, it be given sufficient authority to do so. But what is sufficient authority? This is sometimes defined in terms of unity of command: the unit head must have authority to direct his personnel toward a task without "interference" from other units.

A literal interpretation of the idea of authority commensurate with responsibility leads to absurdity. A public administrator is not simply given a task and told: "Do anything that is necessary to accomplish your job." At the very least he is limited by:

(1) judicial review of his actions for the protection of private citizens whose behaviors he may seek to regulate;

(2) budgetary limits on the amount he may spend to accomplish the job.

In addition, in almost every actual government agency, he would also be limited as to his procedures in hiring staff, salary he may pay them, accounting procedures, and a host of other administrative regulations. Finally, unless his task were completely self-contained, which is never the case, he could be defeated by the non-cooperation or insufficient cooperation of other administrative units (each exercising "authority commensurate with *its own* responsibility").

Realistically, then, our criterion boils down to this notion: when an administrative unit is given a job, it is a good idea to allocate it budgetary resources, personnel, formal authority, and other resources of sufficient quantity so that, if its resources are used with a reasonable degree of efficiency, and if its staff are reasonably capable in securing cooperation from others, it will be able to carry out the task assigned to it. In this form, hardly anyone would disagree with the notion that authority should be commensurate with responsibility, and any administrator who had been given authority of this scope would probably be willing to be held accountable for the results of his work. In this form, however, the principle does not settle many questions. A unit head given a difficult assignment will usually feel that he needs greater resources and broader authority than his superiors are willing to give him.

Conclusion

In this and the preceding chapters we have tried to answer several questions about authority in organizations. First, we have given a definition of authority in behavioral terms—a definition that permits one to actually observe when there is an authority relationship and when there is not. Second, we have explored the psychological motives that lead employees to accept authority, and some of the influences that limit that authority. Third, we have assessed the role of formal, hierarchical authority in the total organizational pattern.

In the course of our analysis we have seen that the exercise of authority requires communication between the person who makes a proposal and the person who accepts it. We have seen also that one of the important limitations upon authority is the limit of the communication system in transmitting proposals. This suggests that, in our survey of the anatomy of organizations, we should turn next to the communication system. The next two chapters will be devoted to the study of organization communications.

☙

CHAPTER TEN

Securing Teamwork: The Communication Process

THE American disaster at Pearl Harbor is one of the dramatic examples in modern times of the possible consequences of failure of an organization communication system. Quite apart from the question of who or what was to "blame" for Pearl Harbor, a large part of the military damage inflicted by the Japanese undoubtedly could have been avoided if two serious breaks in the military communication system had not occurred. The first was the failure to secure proper top-level attention to the intercepted "Winds" message that gave warning an attack was impending. The second was the failure to communicate to the military commander in Hawaii information accidentally obtained from the radar system by an enlisted man that unidentified planes were approaching Pearl Harbor.

Less dramatic, but of equal importance, is the role that communication plays in the day-to-day work of every organization. Without communication, not even the first steps can be taken toward human cooperation, and it is impossible to speak about organizational problems without speaking about communication, or at least taking it for granted. In fact, there is hardly any topic in the preceding chapters that does not relate to communication. In particular, we have seen that communication is central to the exercise of authority. The present chapter will be devoted to a systematic study of the nature of communication and the barriers to effective communication. Chapter 11 will indicate the ways in which organization units specialize in communication work.

Role of Communication in Organization

The viewpoint has been taken in earlier chapters that the behavior choices made by organization members in the course of their daily activities can be viewed as conclusions derived from certain premises—value premises and factual premises. The sources of these premises have been referred to as the "influences" upon the employee's behaviors. When the task of making a particular decision is given to a member of an organization, we must be concerned with the ways in which the organization influences that decision by transmitting premises to him and the way in which that decision, transmitted elsewhere in the organization, provides the premises for the decisions of others.

This process, which is central to all organizational behavior, can be illustrated with the example of a policeman operating a patrol car. He is told to patrol in a particular patrol area; he is provided with a manual of regulations and approved procedures; when he reports for duty in the morning, he may receive specific instructions of things to watch for during the day. He may be given a list of license numbers of recently stolen automobiles and perhaps a description of a fugitive. As he patrols his beat, a call may come to him from the police radio informing him of a store burglary to investigate.

The patrolman, in turn, becomes a source of communications that influence other organization members. His report on the burglary investigation is turned over to the investigations division where it becomes the basis of further activity by a detective. Certain data from this report are recorded by a clerk and are later summarized for the weekly report that goes to the chief of police. Information contained in this weekly report may lead to a redistribution of patrol areas to equalize work loads. Meanwhile, other data from the report have gone into the pawnshop file where they are used by other detectives who systematically survey local pawnshops for stolen goods.

COMMUNICATION AND ORGANIZATION STRUCTURE

By tracing these and other communications from source to destination, we discover a rich and complex network of channels through which orders and information flow. Viewing the communication process from a point in an organization where a decision is to be made, the process has a twofold aspect: communications must flow to the decision center to provide the basis for decision, and the decision must be communicated from the decision center in order to influence other members of the organization whose cooperation must be secured to carry out the decision.

The question of where in the organization a particular decision can best be made will depend in considerable part upon how effectively and easily information can be transmitted from its source to a decision center, and how effectively and easily the decision can be transmitted to the point where action will take place. The decision of a social worker in a public welfare agency in granting or refusing an application for assistance illustrates how these factors enter into the picture. The principal facts and values that have to be brought to bear on this decision are: (1) the economic and social facts of the applicant's situation; (2) accepted principles of casework; and (3) the eligibility regulations and casework policies of the agency. The first set of facts is obtained by interviewing the applicant, by correspondence, and by field investigation. The second set of considerations is derived from the education and training of the social worker and his supervisors. Policies governing the third set of considerations are largely established by the legislative body and the top administrative levels of the agency and communicated downward.

If the decision on the application is to be made by the social worker himself, these three sets of considerations must be communicated to him. The costs of communication here are the time cost of his own investigational activities, the costs of training him adequately in the accepted principles of casework, and the costs of indoctrinating him in agency policies by formal training, instructions, discussion with his supervisor, or otherwise. Once he has made the decision, it must be communicated to the applicant—a relatively simple step—and certain reports on his action must be transmitted to his superiors for supervisory and control purposes.

On the other hand, the decision on the application might be placed in the hands of the casework supervisor, rather than the social worker. This might shorten the communication chain required to bring agency policy to bear on the decision and the chain that reports on the action would have to travel. Further, if the social workers were relieved of this decision, they would probably not need to be as thoroughly trained in casework as if they made the decisions themselves—training efforts could be concentrated on the supervisors. However, in other respects new costs of communication would be incurred. It would be necessary to communicate from social worker to supervisor all the circumstances of the applicant's situation—a very voluminous reporting job and an almost impossible one if intangible impressions received by the social worker in the interview are to be communicated. Moreover, there would be an extra step in communicating the decision on the application to the applicant via the social worker.

Ease or difficulty of communication may sometimes be a central consideration in determining how far down the administrative line the function of making a particular decision should be located (or, as it is usually put, "how far authority should be delegated"). Delegation increases the difficulty of communicating organization policies that are decided at the top and reports from the decision center to the top that are required to determine compliance with policy. Delegation may also involve greater training costs by multiplying the number of persons who have to be competent to make a particular decision. Delegation usually reduces the difficulty of communicating to the decision center information about the particular situation in question, and usually reduces the difficulty of communicating the decision to the point where it is placed into operation. All these factors were illustrated in the previous example.

STEPS IN THE COMMUNICATION PROCESS

In the study of communication processes it is convenient to distinguish three steps:

1. Someone must initiate the communication. If the communication is a monthly report, someone must be assigned the task of preparing the report. Many of the most important communications originate outside the organization, or in special "intelligence" units of the organization. Examples of the first would be a fire alarm, a phone call to the police department, or the filing of a patent application or a workman's compensation claim. Examples of the second would be the reports of military reconnaisance aircraft, an information report by an embassy to the State Department on de-

velopments abroad, or a compilation of employment statistics by the U. S. Department of Labor.

2. The communication must be transmitted from its source to its destination.

3. The communication must make its impact upon the recipient. The communication has not really been "communicated" when it reaches the desk of the recipient, but only when it reaches his mind. There is a potential gap here 'twixt cup and lip. It will receive attention in later portions of this chapter.

We shall see that costs and difficulties of communication may be encountered at each of these three stages of the process. Before we proceed to a detailed analysis of these costs and difficulties, however, it is necessary to describe in somewhat greater detail the elements that go to make up an organization communication system.

Elements of the Communication System

Roughly, organizational communications fall in two categories: planned or "formal" communications and unplanned or "informal" communications. Every organization has some formal arrangements whereby knowledge can be transmitted to those who need it. But this formal transmission of information is supplemented by a great deal of communication that springs from the willingness, indeed, the eagerness, of employees to share information with one another even when such transmission is not formally authorized, and even when it is forbidden.

FORMAL COMMUNICATION

The administrative manual of a large organization often specifies who may write officially to whom; who must report to whom and on what occasions; who shall see memoranda on particular subjects; who shall give out information on specified subjects. This attempt to plan and to channel communications can be seen in perhaps its most elaborate form in the armed services, where extremely intricate patterns of communication are incorporated into formal rules and where channels are rigidly enforced.

Where the work of an organization consists of processing applications or claims, the written procedures will usually specify in considerable detail just how the application is to be routed, what information is to be entered on it at each step, and what work is to be performed. Similarly, the form, content, and responsibility for preparation of accounting records is almost always formally determined.

Standard Forms. One important way of formalizing communication is by the use of standardized forms on which information is entered and transmitted. In addition to accounting forms, most organizations have purchase requisitions, certain types of personnel forms, application forms, and form letters. The chief advantage of any form is that it does not leave to the memory or imagination of the person using it the questions of when, how, or what he should communicate. Either instructions printed on the form itself or manual instructions would specify (1) the occasions on which the form is to be used, (2) the number of copies to be prepared, (3) the distribution of these copies, (4) the person responsible for filling in the various items, and (5) definitions and other information to help the person using the form interpret it correctly.

These instructions are themselves a kind of communication and must be skillfully written if they are to lead to a proper use of the forms. Moreover, the instructions will not be effective unless they are adequately communicated to and known by the users of the form. When changes in income tax laws greatly increased the number of returns, the Bureau of Internal Revenue had to devise improved forms and instructions that would be intelligible to income tax payers and that would communicate to the Bureau the information needed to enforce the tax law.

Forms may be used because they have advantages for the initiator of communications. If a person finds that he repeatedly writes letters or memos that say the same thing or many of the same things, the adoption of a form with the constantly repeated material printed on it will save him considerable time. Forms are also used because they are advantageous to the receiver of communications. By using a form, he can specify just what information he needs to do his job. Thus a purchasing officer who uses form requisitions can reduce the communication often needed to get a complete meeting of the minds between himself and the requisitioning officer; and a tax collector can likewise avoid an impossible burden of communication between himself and a great number of taxpayers. Furthermore, by the use of forms, the information needed for a decision can be determined in advance by highly trained persons, and persons with less training can then make the decisions.

A major disadvantage of any form is its inflexibility. Since it determines exactly what is to be communicated, and in what way, it will convey misinformation if the material to be communicated does not readily fit the form. Anyone who has ever filled out a questionnaire has been puzzled by "unanswerable" questions— which, because they do not fit his particular situation, would mislead rather than inform no matter what answer was put down. Hence, the use and design of forms, while it is important in constructing communication systems, does not by any means solve all the problems of communication within an organization or with its clientele.

Other Formal Requirements. The standard form may be considered to represent the utmost limits in the formalization of communication because it leaves virtually nothing to the discretion of the initiator. At the other extreme is gossip—the unplanned and unintended communication that takes place as an incident of the social contacts of organization members and the innate curiosity of human beings. Between these two extremes lie a host of possibilities for the deliberate design and planning of interpersonal communication. Among the rules that organizations apply to internal communication the following are of particular importance:

1. Requirement of periodic reports. An employee may be required to give daily, weekly, monthly, or annual reports of his activities, without complete specification of the form or content of the report. Many supervisors make it a point to contact each subordinate at least daily and to ask "what's new?" Sometimes, the periodic staff meeting is the occasion for such reports.

2. Partial specification of the form or content of communications. Even where the communication is not reduced to a form, certain rules may be imposed as to its general arrangement or contents. The Army has elaborate rules regarding the paragraphing of communications, affixing of signatures, "indorsements," and the like.

3. Specification of channels, distribution, clearances. Organizations often impose rules as to who may communicate with whom or who is to be informed of particular communications. Rules may

determine who is privileged to prepare or approve various types of communications and by whom they must be reviewed before they are communicated.

4. Screening of incoming communications. Rules may establish certain organization units whose task it is to read incoming communications and route them to the proper persons in the organization.

The formal communication plan, and particularly the specification of communication channels, is generally closely related to the organization's formal system of authority. Hierarchical authority may be reinforced, for example by rules that restrict the issuance of legitimate orders to hierarchical channels. Likewise, control by hierarchical superiors may be facilitated by requirements of reports from their subordinates to be channeled upward through the hierarchy. The authority of functional specialists may be similarly enhanced by formally granting them the right to communicate ("inform," "instruct," or "advise") on the subject of their specialties with the other members of the organization. Conversely, authority derived from functional status may be partially curbed by restricting the formal right of the specialist to communicate outside hierarchical channels.

A formal communication plan, like any other organization plan, becomes effective to the extent that it is accepted as authoritative by the members of the organization. This acceptance, or its lack, is based on the same psychological factors as the acceptance of other instances of authority. Sanctions reveal the same strengths and the same weaknesses here as in the enforcement of other types of rules.

A formal communication system has limitations. It is not the complete answer to an organization's communication needs. Every happening in the organization cannot be foreseen so that it can be formalized. The "channels" cannot be expressive of the wide variety of human need for communication. Nor can communication through channels always give "the sense" of what is intended to be conveyed. Formal communication tends to be stiff, slow, inflexible. Often it cannot express the real needs and demands of the organization.

The inadequacies of the formal communication system are always felt strongly by the executive who is newly appointed to the organization and has few contacts that permit him to communicate, or receive communications, outside formal channels. A large part of his activity during the first months in his new position may be spent in making the social contacts that will permit him to find out what is going on, and that will give him direct access to the other organization units with which his own unit must cooperate.

To be effective, communication must be broader than the formal scheme of the rule book. It demands a general "understanding" on the part of participants—an ability to interpret based upon a memory of past communication. It also requires a whole host of communications quite outside the formal pattern of organization.

INFORMAL COMMUNICATION

These difficulties lead to the growth of an informal communication system that supplements the formal, prescribed system. For example, the unit chief who wants advance information as to whether it is going to be easy or difficult to secure a budget increase for the coming year may find that a friend who is assistant to the bureau chief can give him the desired information long before any formal bulletin flows down through the established channels.

Method of Informal Communication. The ways in which information is disseminated informally are many. Jones, Smith, and Goldberg who work in different sections lunch together. Each has connections with various parts of the organization, and they swap information. Mrs. Johnson belongs to the same lodge auxiliary as the wife of Mr. Alexander who is administrative assistant to the bureau chief. Mrs. Johnson gets some information which she transmits to her husband who, in turn, passes it on to his section.

But informal communication is not only the inevitable, if somewhat illicit, shop talk and gossip. It includes any kind of information outside the specified channels. Nor is it always easy to define what is meant by "channels"—normally these include communications along the lines of formal authority, or along lines that have been explicitly authorized by the formal hierarchy. In most organizations, the greater part of the information that is used in decision-making is informally transmitted.

Informal communication derives its principal channels from the social groups that define the social structure of the organization. Frequent contact and common identification—which we have seen are both causes and consequences of the social group structure—provide the means for effective communication. Hence, informal communication stands in about the same relation to the authority of identification as formal communication stands in relation to hierarchical authority. The authority of the functional specialist may depend primarily upon either the formal or the informal communication system, depending on how strictly formal communications are confined to the hierarchical channels.

Consequences of Informal Communication. The informal communication system is at the same time indispensable, inevitable, and sometimes annoying. While it often enables the organization to adapt itself to changing conditions more quickly than the formal procedures allow (by short-circuiting the formal patterns), it also tends to disrupt formal authority relationships and make coordination more difficult. Quite frequently, because it is not subject to formal supervision, it conveys information that is distorted and wrong.

One of the most important techniques employed both consciously and unconsciously by persons who wish to exercise influence in an organization beyond that derivable from their formal positions is to develop effective channels of informal communication. They may acquire social relations with employees in various strategic parts of the organization so as to be able to tap the grapevine and its numerous intertwined trunks. They may also cultivate relations with persons higher up in the organization in whom they can "plant" ideas and proposals.

That real power can be acquired in this way there can be no doubt. For what purposes such power will be employed depends on the motives of the person who acquires it. Persons who build up informal channels of communication of this kind become particularly influential when the formal communications system is inadequate. In such cases other members of the organization turn to them for the information they need in their own operations.

Organizations with a highly developed system of informal communication to supplement the formal often are able to carry out their tasks with considerable speed and dispatch. "Red tape" can be cut; employees can reach a completeness of understanding which would be impossible if the formal system were more extensively relied upon.

To a great extent, the degree to which an organization can rely on the informal communication system will depend upon its size and the relatedness of its goals. Large organizations must depend upon formal communications far more than small ones. It is not so easy to "call up John and find out what he really meant." They cannot depend upon the understanding which comes from a face-to-face relationship. Also in most large organizations, the complexity of the goals and the many diverse primary groups with different interests demand more emphasis on formal communication than in smaller organizations.

INTERNAL AND EXTERNAL COMMUNICATION

Not only must government agencies maintain a constant flow of communication among the members of their own staffs, but at least periodically they find it necessary to communicate with other agencies, with the Congress and with clientele groups, or with the general public. While internal and external communication sometimes overlap, the general administrative problems raised by them may be quite different.

The differing requirements of internal and external communication can be illustrated by an hypothetical case of a drive against traffic violators by a metropolitan police department. Once it has been decided to initiate such a drive various means can be used to inform the policemen of the nature of the drive and where each of them fits into the picture. Meetings can be held; orders and assignments made; traffic maps can be hung in each station house showing danger areas; and so forth. The process of communication is facilitated by the fact that these are trained persons engaged in a common task. It is also facilitated by the authority relationship. If the captain at the local station asks his men to be present at a meeting to hear about the new traffic drive, they will probably get there.

However, since a traffic drive is much more effective if the police secure the cooperation of the public, it is necessary to inform the automobile-driving public that the drive is in progress and what is expected of them in the way of cooperation. The task of so informing them becomes a specialized task within the department. A public relations office, perhaps, will see that the agencies of mass communication—newspapers, radios, and television stations are given information; perhaps posters will be put up at strategic places, or billboards employed. Other organizations like the National Safety Council and certain insurance companies will be asked to aid in spreading the word. This task of communication will be more difficult and uncertain than the internal communication task, and it will require the use of different administrative techniques.

In the balance of this chapter we will be concerned chiefly with communication inside organizations. The task of communication with the external world will be dealt with rather extensively in later chapters.

Barriers to Effective Communication

The amount of misunderstanding in the world caused by failure of people to communicate effectively with each other can hardly be exaggerated. Words are tenuous. The failure of human plans and aspirations are all too often bitterly recalled in terms like "if it could have been gotten across," or "if I had said it this way rather than that, he might have understood."

Blockages in the communication system constitute one of the most serious problems in public administration. They may occur in any one of three steps in the communications process: initiation, transmission, or reception. Those who have information may fail to tell those who need the information as a basis of action; those who should transmit the information may fail to do so; those who receive the information may be unwilling or unable to assimilate it.

THE BARRIER OF LANGUAGE

Among the barriers to effective communication one of the most serious is the use of language that is not understandable to the recipient. In a society as specialized as ours there are literally hundreds of different languages which cluster around the various specialties. Many words quite understandable to a physician are "Greek" to the layman. Many words quite understandable to the skilled machinist are incomprehensible to the doctor. The vocabulary shared by all Americans is meager indeed.

Not only is the shared vocabulary meager, but the words that are shared often mean different things to different people. Philosophers like Ogden and Richards and Carnap have shown how many traps in philosophy have at their base a faulty use of language. At a more popular level, students of semantics have also shown us that many so-called problems are really pseudo-problems which, when correctly formulated, disappear.

Within administration, the written communication is likely to be even more plagued by language difficulties than the oral communication. Most persons in face-to-face contacts try to speak in terms that will be understood by the listener—and if they do not, they will soon be aware of the fact. They can repeat the communication in different terms. They can explain what they "really mean." The author of a written communication has no such an opportunity to assess his audience or to gauge the degree to which his words are being understood.

Measuring Difficulty of Language. There are now available techniques for measuring the level of difficulty of a written communication and for judging whether it can be understood by its intended audience. For example, a printed statement in regard to employment opportunities prepared for persons applying for work in a manufacturing concern contained the following paragraph:

"HOW LONG DOES IT TAKE TO BECOME A GOOD OPERATOR? A power sewing machine, like a typewriter, comptometer, or calculator, is an intricate piece of equipment. A student entering business college spends six months acquiring the fundamentals of typing. Speed and proficiency are acquired only with practice and experience in a business office. The average person with an aptitude for sewing can learn to operate a machine in from 2 to 3 months and become an experienced and skilled operator in from 4 to 6 months. We are required to make an expenditure of more than $300 for the training for each operator."

Analysis of this paragraph showed that the material would probably not be understood by persons without high school or even some college training. The paragraph was then rewritten to read as follows:

"HOW SOON CAN YOU BECOME A GOOD WORKER? People in business school spend six months learning to type or run an electric calculator. Speed and good work come only with practice in school and on the job. Most people we hire can learn to sew well on our electric machines in 2 or 3 months. Some can learn in less time. It usually takes 4 to 6 months to become highly skilled. It costs us more than $300 to train you. This is why we have to be careful about hiring the right kind of worker."

It is obvious that the revised paragraph is much simpler. Measured on the same scale of difficulty as the original version, its score showed that it should be understandable to a sixth-grader.[1]

Gobbledegook. Many "official" communications have a curiously legalistic ring and are punctuated with "herewiths," "aforementioneds," and similar legal ornaments. These may be calculated to produce awe in the recipient but hardly understanding. During World War II, a vigorous attack was made upon such writing by Maury Maverick, then director of the Smaller War Plants Corporation. He issued to his staff a famous memorandum ordering them to: "Stay off the gobbledegook language. It only fouls people up." Although the fight against gobbledegook has not been won—indeed it has only begun—Maverick's blast, coupled with the techniques for measuring reading difficulty developed by Rudolf Flesch and others, is gradually having effect. On this problem, Flesch writes: "By being overexact, overabstract, and overimpersonal, plain English is transformed into . . . the humble, polite, curt, and disagreeable official style. Take a simple sentence like 'I love you' and it becomes 'complete assurance of maximum affection is hereby implied.' "[2]

Gobbledegook is produced partly by the transplanting of outmoded legal forms and partly by a misdirected interest in accuracy. In drafting a law which is later to be interpreted by the courts and which may impose penalties for its violation, painstaking accuracy of statement is necessary. In drafting an administrative order, substantial accuracy that sacrifices exactness to readability may get better results than literal accuracy that is incomprehensible. But the procedures writer is likely to try to visualize every possible

[1] The experiment described here is reported in Donald G. Paterson and James J. Jenkins, "Communications Between Management and Workers," *Journal of Applied Psychology*, 32:71–80 (February, 1948). A specific technique for measuring the difficulty of written material is described in Rudolf Flesch, *The Art of Plain Talk* (New York: Harper & Bros. 1946), p. 210. See also, E. Horn, *A Basic Writing Vocabulary, 10,000 Words Most Commonly Used in Writing* (Iowa City: University of Iowa, College of Education, 1926).

[2] Rudolf Flesch, "More About Gobbledegook," *Public Administration Review* 5:240–5 (Summer, 1945).

qualification, exception, and variation and incorporate them all into his instructions.[3]

Private Languages. Consciously or unconsciously most organizations develop their own peculiar modes of speech. Further than that, specialized units within organizations also develop new words and new meanings from old words. Very often this movement goes so far that official interpreters have to be employed in order to communicate effectively with outsiders.

One of the most difficult, time-encrusted, and respected of such private languages is that of the lawyer. In many organizations lawyers are employed at nearly every level in order to interpret the language of even the internal communications for the non-lawyers. This constant interpretation and re-interpretation not only slows down communication but in many cases impedes its effectiveness.

But lawyers are not the only ones with specialized vocabularies. Personnel officers, accountants, social workers, and nearly all specialists develop a technical jargon of their own. This shorthand speech, understandable to the specialist but often incomprehensible to those outside, may actually speed up and render more effective communication with the initiated. Its great difficulty lies in the fact that continued use and an easy familiarity with such a vocabulary often leads the participants to assume that their speech and the analogies and illustrations used in it are understandable by everyone.

FRAME OF REFERENCE

Very often the communication process is impeded because those giving, transmitting, or receiving the communication have a "mental set" that prevents accurate perception of the problem. The stimuli that fall on a person's eyes and ears are screened, filtered, and modified by the nervous system before they even reach consciousness—and memory makes further selections of the things it will retain and the things it will forget. This selecting process is an important reason why our judgments of people are so often wrong. If we have a favorable impression of a man, we are likely to remember the good things about him that come to our attention

---

[3] Of course college professors writing textbooks are plagued by this same problem of when to leave out minor qualifications in the interest of readability. Whichever way they lean, they are sure not to satisfy some of their colleagues, much less the students.

and to forget, discount, or explain away the bad things. Only a series of several vivid, undesirable impressions is likely to change our initial estimate of him.

Preconceptions. Where an individual or an agency has already made an "appraisal of the situation," isolated facts that run counter to the appraisal are apt to be discounted, however well validated the facts themselves may be. This accounts for many failures of military intelligence; it evidently was one of the main factors in the success of the German surprise attack that led to the almost disasterous Battle of the Bulge in December, 1944. According to Pettee, "Intelligence up to the level of G-2 of the particular Army concerned predicted the attack several days in advance. Intelligence at higher levels reversed this judgment, and reported that the Germans were most probably only strengthening their defensive positions." [4]

Refusal to pay attention to facts is particularly likely when the facts are unpleasant—thus adding an optimistic bias to the executive's judgment. One of the common symptoms of the frustration that develops when people are confronted with a dilemma is this refusal to face facts—an insistence on living in a dream world unrelated to reality. During the Great Depression of the 1930's, the national administration up until 1933 probably believed its own reassurances that "prosperity is just around the corner" and used these reassurances to reduce its own insecurity and to justify a policy of inaction.

The problem is organizational as well as personal. Organizations develop doctrines and commit themselves to positions. Once committed, it is extremely difficult for them to pay attention to communications that challenge the position taken. The first reaction of some Naval officers to the announcement of the Atom Bomb was to give the press reasons why the new weapon did not challenge the supremacy of battleships and aircraft carriers, just as at an earlier date Billy Mitchell's claims for air power were discounted and ignored by the military strategists.

Selective responsiveness to communications applies to instructions and orders as well as to factual information. When Congress restricted the powers of the General Staff of the Army by the terms of the National Defense Act of 1916, Secretary of War Baker

[4] George Pettee, *The Future of American Secret Intelligence* (Washington: Infantry Journal Press, 1946), p. 8.

worked out and accepted an interpretation of the act that practically nullified these provisions. He did so because he was firmly convinced of the usefulness and necessity of the General Staff as it had previously operated and could not bring himself to believe that Congress "really" intended to impair its functioning.[5]

Effect of Specialization. The specialized activities that a person is engaged in and the particular organizational goals with which he is identified help to determine the frame of reference in which he interprets communications. Differing conceptions of functions often lead to distortions in perspective—in a failure to visualize accurately the many facets of any particular problem. Such distortions also prevent specialized personnel from correctly envisaging what needs to be communicated and why.

If a city is troubled by a series of juvenile burglaries, a police chief is likely to interpret these events as indicating a need for a larger patrol force; the recreation department may base on these same facts an appeal for an enlarged program of teen-age athletics; while the welfare department may reach the conclusion that more attention should be given to the care of children from broken homes. Furthermore, unless the police department is relatively enlightened it may not even see the desirability of communicating the facts of juvenile delinquency to the other departments concerned.

Likewise, each group of functional specialists is likely to apply a sort of "principle of least action" to the communications it receives—to interpret them so as to involve the least possible disturbance to the status quo or to their notions as to the best course of action. During World War II orders were issued by the Army Chief of Staff that the Services of Supply should purchase for the Air Force all articles that were used generally throughout the Army, while the Air Force was to purchase articles "peculiar" to it (e.g., airplanes). Far from settling the jurisdictional dispute between the two units, the term "peculiar" was interpreted as narrowly as possible by the Services of Supply and as broadly as possible by the Air Force so that the conflict between them went on very much as before.[6]

In these examples there is present not only the struggle among units identifying with conflicting goals, but also the tendency of

---

[5] Nelson, *National Security and the General Staff,* pp 187–210.
[6] Ibid., p. 448.

each group of specialists to see mainly those aspects of a problem that touch on its specialty, and to deal with the problem in terms of the tools of that specialty.

Cumulative Effect of Communication on Frames of Reference. The frame of reference of a recipient will color his interpretation of any particular communication. Conversely, the communications he receives over a period of time will alter his frame of reference. In particular, the frame of reference can often be broadened by communicating many things that are not immediately essential to the action of the recipients. If the police chief has had opportunities to learn what the recreation department and the welfare department are doing, and how their programs might relate to the delinquency problem, he is more likely to keep them aware of important developments in this area, and to relate the action of his department to their programs.

Those who are effectively informed as to the overall goal of the organization and the way in which their contribution fits into that pattern are less likely to be subject to the paralyzing parochialism induced by a narrow conception of function. As long as we have work specialization, however, the barrier of the frame of reference will be a plaguing and ever-present problem. In many ways those engaged in organizational communications are in the positions of the three blind men in the Aesop fable who defined an elephant in terms of the particular part of his anatomy they happened to touch. Most persons will never be able to see, or even envisage, the whole elephant.

STATUS DISTANCE

In Chapter 9 it was pointed out that most organization contacts take place between persons who are not far apart in status. Communication between persons distant in scalar status most often takes place through a chain of intermediaries. When there is contact between individuals of different status, communication from the superior to the subordinate generally takes place more easily than communication from the subordinate to the superior. If communication were not difficult between persons of widely different status, organizations would not feel the need, as they so often do, to install suggestion boxes that permit low-level employees to bring their ideas to the attention of top executives. And experience with formal suggestion systems shows that even this device is often inadequate to lower the barrier of status difference.

Status differences exert a considerable filtering and distorting influence upon communication—both upward and downward. Upward communication is hampered by the need of pleasing those in authority. Good news gets told. Bad news often does not. The story of Haround al Raschid, the caliph who put on beggar's clothes and went out among his people to hear what they really thought, is the story of the isolation of every high status executive. Most executives are very effectively insulated from the operating levels of the organization. For a number of reasons, pleasant matters are more apt to get communicated upwards than information about mistakes. Subordinates do not want to call attention to their mistakes, nor do they want the executive to think that they can't handle their own difficulties without turning to him. They want to tell him the things he would like to hear. Hence, things usually look rosier at the top than they really are.

In particular, top executives often have a completely unreal picture of the state of morale and of the true attitudes of employees. Because almost all employees will be pleasant, polite, and deferential in their face-to-face dealings with him, the executive easily forgets that these behaviors reflect the status situation and not necessarily the real feelings of employees toward him or toward the organization. Behind his back, they may call him "the stuffed shirt up front."

Even when it is communicated upward, a suggestion coming from a person of low status will not usually be treated with the same respect and seriousness as one coming from a person of high status. If General Short, instead of a non-commissioned trainee, had detected the approach of the Japanese planes to Pearl Harbor, we may be sure that the communication of this fact would not have been delayed for hours. A major reason for discounting the communications of low-status persons is the psychological immaturity of high-status persons. Executives who derive pleasure from their status (and this is probably true to a greater or lesser degree of most executives) find in their right to refuse to listen to others a considerable source of satisfaction. A suggestion stemming from a humble source may be regarded, consciously or subconsciously, as an affront to their position and a challenge to their unfailing wisdom.

Such reactions are often rationalized by pointing out that the low-status person is not in a position to "see the whole situation." He is not able to make useful suggestions because the decision with which he is concerned involves facts known only to higher executives. Of course there may be considerable truth in this. Experience with suggestion systems usually shows that a large proportion of the ideas proposed have previously been considered and rejected at higher levels. Nevertheless, the argument presupposes that decisions are generally made in the organization at those points where the necessary information is readily available; and that if an employee has enough information about a situation to make a useful suggestion, he also has been granted enough discretion to carry it out. In most organizations this is demonstrably false—and the presumption that a suggestion emanating from a low level will be useless is correspondingly weakened.

Apart from the psychological reasons underlying the status barrier to communication, or the rationalizations of this barrier, one consequence follows that may have considerable usefulness. The time of the executive is protected from persons who might occupy it pointlessly. By virtue of his status, the executive retains, in part, the initiative in deciding with whom he will communicate before he makes a decision. Most organization decision-making processes involve the participation of many persons, each of whom contributes certain decisional premises in areas where he is presumed to be expert. The executive of high status has considerable freedom in deciding who his experts will be, but his decisions will still depend as much, or more, on his confidence in persons and their advice as upon his own analysis and reasoning.

Information going downward in the hierarchy is often distorted, also. The way in which casual remarks of someone like the President are interpreted, re-interpreted, and squeezed of every possible and impossible meaning illustrates the point. In the struggle for position on the status ladder, the suggestions and other statements of those higher up are often given more weight as guides to decisions than those who made the statement actually intended.

GEOGRAPHICAL DISTANCE

One of the most striking and far-reaching phenomena of our era has been the tremendous extension of the mechanical techniques of communication. Changes in the technology of communication have changed both the structure and the problems of administrative organizations. Probably more than any other single factor, the improvement of the means of communication has had a centralizing effect upon administration—centralizing in the sense that a field officer can now be supervised in much greater detail than was previously possible.

Far-flung organizations can now be within hour-to-hour communication with their headquarters. This has enabled central offices to keep a far tighter check rein upon the activities of their agents in the field. Ambassadors who formerly had broad discretion to act in their negotiations with other nations, now can and must constantly check their views with a central office. The operations of widely dispersed field offices can come under the constant scrutiny of central headquarters.

Even where geographical dispersion is not wide, such as in modern police and fire departments, the effect of instantaneous communication has changed the whole pattern of their operations. It has made possible a greater efficiency and greater specialization. The radio police car can be summoned rapidly to an area of trouble. The work of the fire department can be directed rapidly and efficiently.

Inadequacy of Techniques. But modern communication techniques have not completely overcome the problems of communicating at a distance, and, in addition, they have added new problems of their own. Communication by letter, wire, or telephone, although it may be rapid, is no effective substitute for the face-to-face interchange. As Latham has pointed out:

. . . impediments to the free exchange of thought are difficult enough to overcome in the same city, building, or even room. They become even more difficult with the increase of distance between the central office and the field. In the same environment, geographical, social, and professional, the common milieu sometimes gives many clues to understanding which precise words could not have spelled out. This element is missing in communications at a distance.[7]

The difficulties of communication at a distance, even with modern means, are several. Oral communication by telephone,

[7] Earl Latham, *The Federal Field Service* (Chicago: Public Administration Service, 1947), pp. 8–9.

while the closest counterpart to face-to-face conference, is by no means a perfect substitute. It is costly, and mechanically imperfect over great distances, and the important overtones of oral communication that are ordinarily conveyed by facial expression and gesture are missing.

Written communication is an even less adequate substitute for the conference. Even in verbal content, a two-page single-spaced letter is the equivalent of only ten minutes' conversation. A division head, with offices adjacent to those of his bureau chief, might confer with his superior individually and in conferences a half hour or an hour daily. To communicate the same material in writing would require an interchange of six to twelve single-spaced pages a day. Even then, the letter is much less likely to convey exact ideas than is a conversation, where misunderstanding can be detected and corrected immediately, questions raised, and so forth.

Insufficient Communication. Moreover, daily personal contact stimulates communication. A man may think to pass on to his superior or subordinate over a luncheon table a piece of information that it would not occur to him to put down in a letter. Where there is geographical separation, the person at each end of the communication line finds it difficult to visualize and keep constantly in mind the needs for information at the other end of the line. A constant complaint of field offices is that they learn from the daily newspapers or from clients things that should have been communicated to them from the central office.

Consider, for example, the problem of communicating a change in rent control regulations. Such a change will probably be publicly announced by the central office at a press conference and instantly transmitted in more or less complete form by newspaper wire services throughout the country. Washington representatives of real estate groups will also advise their local clients of the new regulations, often by telegraph or telephone. To prevent premature disclosure of the regulations, the central office may be reluctant to send them in advance to local field offices, with the result that these field offices may be bombarded by questions from tenants and landlords before they have had any detailed information on the new regulations from the central office. This pattern repeated itself again and again in wartime regulatory programs and was a continual source of friction between central and field offices.

Excessive Communication. Paradoxically, field offices often complain that they receive too many communications at the same time that they complain that they are insufficiently informed on new developments. The attempt of the central office to supervise closely the operations in the field often results in a steady flow of procedural regulations, instructions, bulletins, and what not to the field offices. If too much of this material is trivial, detailed, or un-adapted to local problems—and the field office will often feel that it is—it may remain unread, undigested, and ineffective. This problem is not one of geographical separation alone, but applies generally to organization communications.

SELF-PROTECTION OF THE INITIATOR

We have already pointed out that most persons find it difficult to tell about actions that they believe would put them in a bad light. It is much easier to secure reports about overtime than it is to get reports on the number of times the workers reported late or took extra time for lunch. Furthermore, the ordinary work code demanding loyalty to work groups also prevents the communication of information that would seem to reflect upon one's friends or upon the organization of which one is a part. In consequence, reports flowing upward in the organization, such as reports to Congress, the President, or the public, tend to be "sugar-coated." Information that will evoke a favorable reaction will be played up; the mistakes and the fumbles tend to be glossed over. Information going downward is equally suspect. A casual reading of any house organ will reveal how carefully the higher executives and their actions are "explained" to employees in a way that will show the wisdom of their decisions and their benevolence toward those who occupy the lower levels. In part, this deception is conscious. In part, it is unconscious. These upward and downward distortions make an actual and objective view of the organization difficult to obtain.

PRESSURE OF OTHER WORK

A person in an ordinary work situation is normally pressed for time. He must establish a system of priorities as to the various demands made upon him. In such circumstances he is likely to respond to the pressures of the immediate work situation while giving lower priority to the more abstract demands of communicating with others. Furthermore, the constant demand for information concerning the details of his work often meets with unspoken resentment because it seems to reflect upon his integrity. If he does not know why he is asked for specific types of information, he is likely to conjure up ideas that the "head office" will use the information against him or that the request has no purpose—that it is mere make-work.

Similarly, the central office is likely to take an authoritarian view of the communication process and resent the constant inquiries from those lower in the hierarchy or the field. It, too, is likely to slough off the job of communication and to regard it as less important than the task of setting policy. Thus, in many agencies the task of communication is thought of as something basically clerical—a mere stenographic transmittal of decisions. Communication is likely to be shunted into the background.

DELIBERATE RESTRICTIONS UPON COMMUNICATION

One problem of much government communication is to see that it reaches those who should have the information and yet to prevent it from reaching those who would use it in an undesirable way. There is always disagreement between those individuals who believe that the public should have information concerning every aspect of government policy and policy formulation—particularly those in the press whose business is the dissemination of information—and those in government service who would argue that the compromises which are essential in the formation of public policy would not be possible if every move had to be carried on in the relentless glare of publicity.

Whether or not to have publicity is not a new problem. The founding fathers determined that the only possible way in which agreement could be reached on a new constitution was to conduct the deliberations without continuous publicity. To prevent the publication of the deliberations they even went so far as to establish a guard for the aged, brilliant, but garrulous Benjamin Franklin to see that his disclosures in the neighborhood taverns would not jeopardize the goals of the convention.

Quite often it is believed necessary for the successful handling of government programs that a certain amount of secrecy should surround them, at least at the initial stages. Prior to World War I, the United States Army General Staff had great difficulty with its planning for mobilization because hostile groups in Congress used information that such planning was going on as evidence that the General Staff was seeking to force the country into war. During World War II, a running battle was fought between those who thought that the American people should be given a maximum of information concerning the war effort and those who thought that the American people should be "sold" on the necessity of all-out participation.[8]

The atomic energy program is probably the best modern example of this dilemma. The demands for security require that strict regulations concerning the dissemination of information about atomic energy be imposed. But these same restrictions seriously impede communication among scientists engaged in research in nuclear physics. Such restrictions also hamper Congress in its endeavor to determine defense requirements, for, until Congress knows what the potentialities of atomic warfare are, it is in no position to pass intelligent judgment upon the size and character of the armed forces. As Senator McMahon has pointed out, it must legislate blindfolded without such information.

One result of the fact that most government agencies operate constantly in a goldfish bowl is that they are often unable to correct the mistakes they make, or even investigate those mistakes, without providing material for their opponents in the press or in Congress. One reaction to this is to pull down a curtain of secrecy even within the ranks of the organization.

Clearly, unrestricted communication in government agencies and between the agencies and the public may create administrative difficulties, permit "insiders" to derive personal profit from advance information of future policies, and, in many areas, endanger the national security. On the other hand, the imposition of restrictions may seriously threaten the effectiveness of democratic controls. One of the unforeseen consequences of World War II and postwar international problems was to extend the notion of "security restrictions" in an unprecedented fashion, and to place in the hands of the administrators of these restrictions an extremely

---

[8] See Bruce Catton, *War Lords of Washington* (New York: Harcourt, Brace and Company, 1948).

dangerous weapon. The implications of these developments for the democratic process will be discussed further in Chapters 24 and 25.

Conclusion

In this chapter we have surveyed the role of communication in organization, the nature of formal and informal communication and their respective places in the communication process, and the serious barriers that exist to adequate and effective communication. The communications system in an organization appears, in the light of this discussion, no less vital than the nervous system in a human body—and the consequences of its imperfections no less disorganizing.

We may carry the analogy a step further. The human nervous system is more than a set of communication channels among the cells. It also contains a number of elements that carry on highly specialized functions: in particular the sensory organs, and the various parts of the brain. The communication system of an organization likewise may have important specialized elements, which have a great deal to do with the effectiveness of the communication process. In the next chapter we will turn to an examination of the organization of the communication system and its specialized parts.

CHAPTER ELEVEN

Securing Teamwork: The Organization of Communication

THE emphasis in the preceding chapter upon the failures of communication should not obscure the fact that great volumes of communications are transmitted effectively in any organization. Part of this flow is formally planned and its channels deliberately selected. Another part of the flow is informal, arising out of the social relationships in the organization.

The ease and effectiveness with which communication takes place are strongly affected by the structure of the communication system. Many of the difficulties in initiation, transmission, and reception that have been noted are difficulties that can be reduced by attention to the organization of the communication system. In this chapter, we shall discuss several aspects of this topic, in particular: securing proper distribution of decisions; securing proper clearance prior to decisions; organizing records of past experience; and organizing the intelligence (information-gathering) function.

Securing Distribution of Communications

The distribution of communications can be regulated at the initiating end, in the transmission process, or even at the receiving end. Those who initiate or transmit a communication may decide that it should be distributed broadcast to all the employees of an organization, or to specified classes of employees; that it should be channeled downward or upward through the hierarchy; or that it should be transmitted through specified non-hierarchical channels.

In transmission or at the receiving end, "screening" processes may be set up to protect executives from an excessive volume of communications and to direct their attention to the relevant parts of the flow.

BROADCASTING

One way of making sure that all instructions are adequately communicated throughout an organization is simply to distribute them to everyone. Two obvious reasons have already been given as to why this simple method is not generally used. First, there may be a "security problem"—it may be considered desirable to restrict the distribution of certain information. Second, any system that attempts to broadcast all information throughout the organization deluges its members with a mass of communications most of which are of no concern to them. The result may be a tendency to disregard all communications—to file them in the wastebasket.

Hence, "broadcasting" is used only for distributing information of the most general character—for example, announcement of a special holiday. Information of general news interest to employees can be broadcast through a weekly house organ, by posting on bulletin boards, or by occasional memoranda for general distribution.

HIERARCHICAL CHANNELS

The extreme opposite of broadcasting is to restrict communication to the channels of the hierarchy. Superiors can communicate to their immediate subordinates, and vice versa. Where the hierarchy is used for communication, each step in the communication chain acts as a screening point to decide how much of the information needs to be communicated further down or up the line, as the case may be. The bureau chief may inform the division head, for example, that the agency is going to ask for a smaller budget as a means of increasing its political support in Congress. The division head, after considering how this smaller budget will affect his organization, may then relay to certain branch chiefs a warning that they may soon have to operate under lower personnel ceilings. A branch chief, in turn, may then inform his section chiefs to start transferring certain less valuable employees.

The hierarchy provides the most-used channel of communication for formal orders and for the upward and downward flow of information. Hierarchical channels are usually very slow, however, for the indispensable crosswise flow of information. For example, if branch chief Jones in Bureau A wishes to communicate through the hierarchy with branch chief Martin in Bureau B, the communication would first have to go to Jones' division head, then to the head of Bureau A, then to the department head who has direction over both bureaus A and B, then to the head of Bureau B, then to Martin's division head, and finally to Martin—a total of six steps.

If the hierarchy were used as the exclusive channel, communication between organization units would become extremely slow and cumbersome, and the top executives in the organization pyramid would become bottlenecks in the communication flow. Hence, in actual organizations information flows through many channels, formal and informal, other than the hierarchy.

OTHER CHANNELS

We saw in Chapter 10 that channels other than those just discussed are very frequently used on an informal basis. It is quite possible, however, for the formal communication system to be constructed so as to include some of these other channels. Perhaps their most common formal use is in connection with reporting requirements—requirements that absence reports, for example, be prepared and transmitted to a central personnel unit, or that inventory reports be prepared on specified forms and transmitted to a central property unit.

Non-hierarchical channels may also be of high importance in securing proper communication of plans and proposals before decision is actually reached upon them. For example, if a city planning body proposes to widen a particular street, it may be important that the proposal be reviewed by the department of public works, the city finance department, and other units before a definite recommendation is made to the city council. Either the initiator (the city planning body in this case) must be given the responsibility for determining who should participate in the review of the decision or some sort of formal clearance process must be established to control the review process. Clearance processes will be discussed at length later in this chapter.

SCREENING DEVICES

Where there is too great a volume of communications, the communication system may fail at the receiving end. This point has already been mentioned as a problem that frequently confronts field offices, but it may arise in any large organization regardless of whether there is geographical decentralization. Macmahon, Millett, and Ogden cite a striking, but by no means atypical, case of this kind.

Few administrative agencies have had as strong a determination as the Resettlement Administration to rationalize organization structure and operating procedures. The Resettlement Administration early set up the Procedures Division responsible for the issuance of all orders and instructions. From this division came a veritable flood of administrative orders, notices, instructions, forms and organization charts.

First one and then two large binders were required to hold all the instructions with their subsequent revisions. Before eighteen months had elapsed the Manual of Procedures had expanded to eighteen binders and even this number did not include all the material that had been issued.

Daily, special messengers from the Procedures Division made the rounds of some twenty-five buildings in Washington that housed the Resettlement Administration distributing the latest additions to or revisions of the manual. The different kinds of instructions had many labels: administrative orders, administrative instructions, administrative notices, organization charts, field instructions, Washington instructions, flow charts, W.P.A. orders affecting the Resettlement Administration, rulings of the Comptroller General, rulings of the Attorney General, administration data, regulations, layout plans, handbooks, administration letters, field letters, Washington memoranda.

The material was so elaborate and the headings so numerous that the Procedures Division had to employ two or three full-time persons to go from one office to another making sure that all the material was in the right place. A classification index was prepared as a guide to locating information in the Manual; later a digest of the *Manual of Procedures* was issued. In the summer of 1936 the digest was replaced by yet a second attempt at indexing. One regional director wearily confessed that he tried to get the sense of the instructions sent out from Washington, but that there were not enough hours in the weekend for the task.[1]

While a problem of this kind can sometimes be alleviated by more care at the initiating end with regard to the kinds of com-

[1] Arthur W. Macmahon, John D. Millett, and Gladys Ogden, *The Administration of Federal Work Relief* (Chicago: Public Administration Service, 1941), p. 218.

munications that are sent and the distribution they are given, remedial measures can also be taken at the receiving end. One such measure is to assign to some person or unit the task of screening all incoming communications and routing them to the proper recipients. In the War Department, such screening is an important function of the Adjutant General's office. In many organizations, all incoming mail, however addressed, is opened at the central point, read, and its disposition indicated.

To reduce the burden upon top executives, communications can be reviewed by an administrative assistant before they come to the executive's desk. Out of the whole flow of items coming in, those can be selected that require the executive's personal attention. In some cases, the material can be digested and transmitted to the executive in brief form.

Screening is of equal importance for executives of large units in reducing the number of persons they have to see. An administrative assistant in an outer office can refuse some callers access to the executive, can handle the requests of others himself, and can direct still others to the proper organization unit—keeping from the executive all except those who are important enough and insistent enough to see him.

Review and Clearance Devices

Many communications have the effect of committing the organization, an organization unit, or an executive to a particular policy or line of action. For example, a personnel office may wish to send instructions on payroll procedures to the several divisions of the organization; or a claims examiner may draft a letter accepting or rejecting a claim for unemployment compensation. If the proper points of view are to be brought to bear upon such decisions before they are communicated, the communication system must provide adequate procedures for referral and clearance.

Proposals may be reviewed prior to decision for a variety of reasons—to bring to bear upon them the expert judgment of various specialists; to insure conformity to legislative and executive policies; to secure coordination with the activities of other units; or in part to inform the reviewer about the proposal. When a person is given an opportunity to review a proposal it is very difficult to prevent him, whatever the particular point of view he is supposed to bring to bear upon it, from raising any questions of its adequacy or competence that may occur to him. Hence, although the purposes of each review may be specialized, it is likely that each reviewer will repeat in part what each other reviewer is doing.

SIGNATURE RULES

One way of insuring a review prior to final decision is to maintain rules as to who may sign communications of various kinds before they are issued. The Forest Service, for example, defines several general classes of correspondence and specifies who may sign letters of each class. The classes are: departmental, Service-divisional, regional forester-director, field-divisional, forest, and ranger district. Divisional correspondence, for instance, is defined as: "Communications to Regional Foresters, Directors to Experiment Stations, Forest Products Laboratory, or other field units; other Divisions of the Chief's Office, or other agencies or individuals, on matters which do not involve policy beyond the Division of origin, and which are not included in the Departmental (1) or Service (2) classifications."

Departmental correspondence must be signed by the Secretary of Agriculture, Service correspondence by the Chief of the Forest Service, divisional correspondence by the head of the appropriate division, and so forth. Enforcement of the rules is left with the person originating the communication—it being presumed in this case that he has both knowledge of the rules and willingness to abide by them.[2]

ISSUANCE CONTROL UNITS

Another procedure, designed to make sure that all appropriate points of view are brought to bear on a decision before it becomes official is to require that a proposal be "cleared" by the relevant specialists before it comes to the executive for approval. Since different proposals will presumably need to be cleared by different individuals, it is now common practice in the larger Federal agen-

[2] This example is described more fully in Comstock Glaser, *Administrative Procedure* (Washington, D. C.: American Council on Public Affairs, 1941), pp. 124–7.

cies to set up a clearance control center (often called an issuances control unit) through which communications needing clearance are required to flow. The clearance center then determines what review will be required before the communication is transmitted to the appropriate executive for final approval.

PROBLEMS OF SECURING CLEARANCE

The more persons who review a proposal before it is approved, the more probable that at least one of the reviewers will disagree with some part of its content. Where clearance procedures are established it becomes important for the speed and quality of the communication process to specify how disagreements will be settled.

One method is to permit each reviewer to suggest amendments to the document until a version is reached upon which all can agree. This, in effect, gives each reviewer a free veto over the proposal and can be productive of interminable delays. Those who are anxious to get action may accept compromises without conviction, and often with mental reservations. The prolonged negotiations that are sometimes required often produce a watered-down communication that satisfies everyone only because it means nothing and changes nothing. The compromise on purchasing arrangements between the Services of Supply and the Air Force that was cited in the last chapter is an example of a typical product of such negotiations.

The final step in the clearance process is usually to submit the proposal to an executive superior to the various reviewers for approval. The speed of the clearance process will depend on how far the reviewers are expected to go in settling differences among themselves before the proposal is presented to the executive. Where promptness in reaching a decision is important, this may be secured by (1) submitting the proposal simultaneously to all the reviewers rather than passing it from one to another, (2) setting deadlines for the submission of criticisms and proposed changes, and (3) suggesting or insisting that the reviewers submit their comments to the executive rather than trying to settle differences among themselves. This is the essence of the "endorsement" system used by the armed forces, which gives each reviewer the right to comment on a proposed communication and to transmit the comments to the executive having the final decision—but not to veto the communication, delay it, or prevent it from reaching the executive's desk in its original form.

Where the clearance procedure is considered too cumbersome by persons initiating communications, they may informally by-pass it. The authors are familiar with numerous instances where communications have been "smuggled" past the clearance unit and issued "illegally"—i. e., without proper clearance—because of the virtual impossibility of satisfying and protecting all the units involved in the clearance procedure.

ALTERNATIVES TO USUAL CLEARANCE METHODS

Clearance procedures are a major constituent in government "red tape"—sometimes very necessary and justifiable red tape. Clearance imposes a dilemma: either documents will be approved and communicated without adequate review, or the apparently ir-resistible urge of the reviewer to edit any document that comes over his desk will impose heavy personnel costs and undesirable delays.

In some cases, however, there are ways out of this dilemma. One way is to review only a sample of the decisions rather than all of them. Another way is to post-audit the decisions rather than pre-audit them. Both of these techniques are applicable when the con-sequences of a single mistaken decision are not too serious, and where the primary aim of the review process is to prevent the re-currence of mistakes, if any are made.

Both the use of samples and the substitution of a post-audit for a pre-audit are illustrated by personnel procedures in the Farm Credit Administration. That agency delegated to its regional per-sonnel offices wide discretion over such personnel operations as position-classification. In order to make certain that agency policies were being followed by the regional offices, teams of auditors were sent periodically to those offices and a randomly selected sample of the decisions made by the local employees was examined. This device permitted a great deal of decentralization of decision-making to the local offices, while at the same time securing for the central office a sufficient flow of information to assure it that its policies were being followed.[3]

[3] The procedure described here is essentially identical with the notions of quality control and sampling inspection that have made such important contribu-

USE OF CONFERENCES AND COMMITTEES IN
   COMMUNICATION

Where decisions are complex, requiring the reconciliation of a wide range of points of view, effective communication often requires that all the persons involved in the decision be brought together for face-to-face discussion in a conference or series of conferences. Where it is desired to formalize the conference procedure, and where the same group of persons is involved in a series of conferences, a definite committee can be established.

An important advantage of the conference and the committee over step-by-step clearance as a means of reaching a joint decision is that each participant is exposed directly and simultaneously to the views of all the others. There is a maximum of opportunity for the free interchange of information and ideas.

One of the most dramatic and effective uses of committees in recent times in the Federal government occurred in the drafting of the legislation and analyses of the Marshall Plan proposal for aid to Europe. Staff was loaned by the State, Commerce, Agriculture, Interior, Treasury, and other Federal departments for the work of some dozen committees that explored in detail the proposals that had been drafted by the committee for European Economic Cooperation in Paris. Among the products of this extensive committee work were the draft of the Economic Cooperation Act, reports analysing the status of each major segment of the European economy, and a tentative budget for the new agency. So effective was the planning work that, although there were many later changes in detail, the ECA was actually in operation and granting aid within less than thirty days after the legislation had been adopted by Congress and the Administrator appointed.

There were a number of reasons for the success of the committee process in this case. Two of these cast light on the conditions under which conferences and committees can be expected to facilitate communication. First, the War had developed in Washington a considerable nucleus of high-ranking young administrators who

---

tions in the past few years to the control of industrial operations. The possibilities of applying the theory and techniques of statistical quality control to government operations are only beginning to be explored. It can be predicted with some confidence that these techniques will have increasing application in government during the next decade. See William R. Divine and Harvey Sherman, "A Technique for Controlling Quality," *Public Administration Review*, 8:110–13 (Spring, 1948).

were in frequent informal communication with each other, and who were accustomed to conferring and cooperating on international economic problems. Hence, the committees served to formalize an informal communication system that was already largely in existence.

Second, the problems involved in planning the program cut completely across departmental lines. Almost every major aspect of the plan was of considerable interest to at least a half dozen departments. Where each problem confronting a committee is of interest to only a few of the participants, the committee is likely to be much less successful. For example, many city managers report a lack of interest in weekly staff meetings of their department heads because the relative self-containment of municipal departments is so great as to create few problems of interest to more than one or two departments. Only on such overall matters as the municipal building program, the budget, personnel problems, and the like is there much basis for participation of the entire group. Most city managers who have tried periodic staff meetings have either discontinued them entirely or reserved them for major problems in these areas of common interest.

Apart from their effectiveness in securing a free interchange of views, and hence in securing sounder decisions, conferences and committees serve other important communication functions. First, they communicate a thorough understanding to the participants of the decisions reached. Moreover, by providing a feeling of participation in the decision-making process and a feeling of responsibility for the decisions reached, they greatly improve the motivations of the participants in later carrying out the decisions. There is a considerable and growing body of evidence that group participation in decision-making is an important means for securing acceptance of new programs and organization changes.

In the Federal government alone, there are in existence several hundred committees of inter-departmental scope. The growth of this committee structure is a reflection of the growing inter-relationship of the programs of the several Federal departments—particularly in the impacts of their programs upon foreign policy and upon the domestic economy. Probably an almost equal number of committees knitting together the separate bureaus or divisions can be found within any one of the major Federal departments.

It should not be concluded that committees are an unmitigated blessing—one would certainly not reach this conclusion after hearing the many complaints by Federal administrators about the burden of committee work. Much of this complaint, of course, is really a complaint about the complexity of Federal administration —a complexity that is rather a cause than an effect of the numerous committees. Nevertheless, committees can prove an extremely costly and time-wasting device if they are brought together without a real reason for their existence, if they suffer from ineffective chairmanship or inadequate preliminary spadework by a properly staffed secretariat, or if they continue in existence (as they often do) after their work has been completed. Frequently they are used for inappropriate tasks. For example, a committee can review a document that has been drafted previously, but almost no group of more than two or three persons can efficiently do the work of drafting. Likewise, committees are often bogged down in debate about questions of fact that could be more accurately and quickly decided by a little research outside the committee chambers.

Since our discussion here is concerned with committees as a communication device, it has not included the committee (more often called a board or commission) that is formally established as a part of the administrative hierarchy and that has formal responsibility for administering an agency or other administrative unit. Examples of such boards are the U. S. Maritime Commission, the Federal Trade Commission, state liquor boards, city school boards, and the like. Such boards and commissions are best thought of as plural executives, rather than as devices for inter-unit coordination in a complex administrative structure.

Organization "Memory"

Retaining information so that it will be accessible when needed is a major problem in any large organization. In a small operation, it may be sufficient to rely on the memories of individual employees or upon the files that employees set up for their own use. But even in an office of three or four persons, it will usually be necessary to use systematic filing methods so that records will be available to all the members of the organization.

The two factors to be considered in setting up any system of files are (1) to arrange the system so that the material will be found when needed, and (2) to arrange the system so that the material can be filed and drawn from the files at a minimum of cost. When a suspect is arrested by the police department, the first question that the files must answer is: "Has this man been arrested before?" It is the task of the arrest and fingerprint files to answer this question. Since it would be much too costly to compare the new fingerprints with all those already in the file, a system of classification has been devised that permits the fingerprint, upon examination, to be placed in its proper class. By arranging the files according to this same classification, it can be determined at once whether any fingerprints are on file that are identical with the new ones. For this purpose, almost any classification system will do, provided it clearly separates the fingerprints into classes and provided there are only a few in each class.

A difficult filing problem was solved by the Social Security Board in order to bring together all the wage records referring to a particular person covered by the act. One way of doing this would be to give each worker a number (his social security number), having this number reported with his earnings, and filing the records according to number. The disadvantages of this method would be, first, that it would be easy to make an error in reporting numbers or transferring them to the records, and the mistake might not be discovered until years later, if at all. Second, a worker, by establishing two numbers, might become eligible for larger benefits than if all his earnings had been reported under a single number.

For these reasons, a numerical file was rejected in favor of an alphabetical name file. This kind of file created difficulties of a different sort, both because names might be misspelled or spelled in several ways and because a number of persons would have the same name. The second problem could be solved by subclassifying persons of the same name by social security number; the first, by developing a phonetic, rather than strictly alphabetic, system of filing by name.

Difficulties of still another sort are encountered when it is not known in advance exactly when or for what purpose the file information is to be used. A public employment agency must maintain files of persons seeking jobs. When notice is received of a job opening, the files must disclose the names of those persons who would be competent to fill the job. Filing the names according to a classification of occupations will meet the need in part, but in many

cases neither the qualifications of the job seeker nor the specifica-
tions of the job will fit neatly into the classification no matter how
ingenious it is. Hence, it may be necessary to put the information
about applicants on punched cards that can be sorted mechanically
and rapidly in order to discover persons with any desired combination of qualifications. In other cases, cross-filing or cross-indexing
may improve the flexibility of a filing system.

A library provides a good example of a complex filing problem.
Access to the library materials is secured by: filing books nu-
merically so that any specific one can be located immediately;
basing the numerical classification on a subject classification so that
books will be grouped at least roughly by subject; and maintaining card indexes of books by subject, title, and author with the
location number of each book indicated on the card.

Intelligence Units

A final element in organization communication systems that deserves mention is the intelligence unit—by which we mean a unit
set up with the primary purpose of gathering information for
organizational use either from sources outside the organization or
from sources within the organization. A weather observation station would be an example of an external intelligence unit in the
U. S. Weather Bureau; scouting aircraft would be a military example. An accounting division would be an example of an internal
intelligence unit.

Of course the task of gathering all the information that is
needed in organization decisions is far too vast to be performed
solely, or even mainly, by specialized intelligence units. Almost
every member of an organization has some responsibility for
gathering information that is needed by others. Those members of
the organization in frequent contact with the legislative body, with
interest groups, or with the organization's clients may be especially
important sources of needed information.

The intelligence function of the top executive group consists
largely of gathering and interpreting the reactions of outside
groups of political importance to the organization's program. A city
manager, for example, has frequent contact with local businessmen,
civic groups, labor groups, and city councilmen. The Secretary of

Agriculture and his principal assistants have contacts with the Farm Bureau Federation and other farm organizations, with party leaders in Congress, with the President, and with the top executives of other Federal departments.

The intelligence function of organization members having frequent contact with clients is primarily to funnel upward information regarding the impact of the program upon clients and the reactions of clients to the program. The field offices of the Veteran's Administration have daily contacts with thousands of veterans; the county agents with farms; the field offices of the Bureau of Foreign and Domestic Commerce with businessmen; and so forth.

EXTERNAL INTELLIGENCE UNITS

When specialized external intelligence units are established in an organization, it is not usually with the intention of replacing the intelligence work performed in the regular course of organization operations but of securing additional information not secured through day-to-day contacts or assisting in organizing, analyzing and distributing the information that is already being gathered.

When the Treasury Department, for example, needed detailed information on present and prospective consumer buying habits in order to plan bond drives and other fiscal policies during the War, special surveys utilizing the interview techniques developed by market research specialists were used for this purpose. Using similar techniques, the Office of War Information made civilian morale surveys.

The intelligence function is closely related to the records or "memory" function previously described. In the municipal police department, for example, the central communications room to which information flows from citizens, patrolmen, pawnshop details, other police departments, and other sources is usually a part of the records unit where this information is organized and filed for later use.

INTERNAL INTELLIGENCE UNITS

In Chapter 10, the important barriers to organization communications were listed and discussed. One way of overcoming certain of these barriers is to establish specialized intelligence units whose function it is to gather and transmit information within the organization itself. Such units may be useful in over-coming the barrier of language. A statistical division in a welfare agency, for example, establishes common definitions and common units for reporting activities throughout the agency and hence helps to develop a common language for communication.

A second function of internal intelligence units is to gather information that is needed for control purposes by the top executives. We have seen that executives may not be properly informed as to what is going on because their subordinates do not take time out to report adequately, want to conceal certain information from their superiors, or fail to report for other reasons. In most cases, central units specializing in control functions will take on themselves the task of securing the information they need for control. The central accounting unit is a control unit as well as an intelligence unit for accounting information. The central personnel unit is a control unit as well as an intelligence unit for data on salaries, absences, turnover, and other personnel matters.

It is of some interest to note that many of the *external* intelligence units of government also perform their information gathering functions as an incident to the exercise of controls. To enforce tax laws or regulations over business, an organization must be given power to obtain data from the persons or groups regulated, and the data thus obtained—the income statistics compiled by the Bureau of Internal Revenue, for instance—then prove of wider usefulness for administrative purposes.

Conclusion

In this chapter we have examined some of the formal arrangements that are used to facilitate the communication process and to make certain that the decisions reached in the organization are informed decisions. The formal organization plan can specify what channels are to be used to meet particular communication needs. Formal procedures can be set up for the review of proposals before they are approved and communicated or for the post-audit of decisions. Special units can be given the task of gathering information from outside or inside the organization and transmitting it to those who need it.

The subject of communication is the focus of a considerable amount of research now being conducted, particularly by sociologists and psychologists. A great deal has already been learned about the dynamics of conferences and about the influences that assist or impede communication. In another direction, promising experiments are being made with the use of sampling techniques for control purposes. We may expect considerable progress in the field of communication within the next few years.

In the preceding chapters—beginning with Chapter 4—we have surveyed the main elements in the structure of organizations: the social groups, the division of work, the system of authority, and the communication system. We are now ready to put these elements together and to see how they help us to understand the operation of large and complex organizations.

CHAPTER TWELVE

Large-Scale Organization: The Trend Toward Centralization

IN PREVIOUS chapters we have seen that an organization is composed of individuals who make decisions and perform acts that are somehow related to the organization goal or objective. We have also seen that it is a continuing problem to get the proper premises of decision to the individual members at the right time. This result is sought by various means, some of the most common of which are hierarchical authority; selection of those individuals for membership who are already trained or disposed to make decisions in terms of the organization's goals; training of present members in decisional premises most likely to advance the organization's goals; the provision of a pattern of working relationships, including prescribed lines or procedures for communication among the members; the provision of all possible specialized information and advice needed to make the best decisions; and other more subtle and less consciously planned methods, such as modifying the system of social relationships.

Whereas in each of the previous chapters we have emphasized one factor or element in organization, in this chapter and the two following we will present a picture of the result when all of these elements are combined—a picture of human behavior in complex organizations. Of course, words alone are hardly sufficient; one must live in such an environment for a time before he begins to see or sense the "whole." However, verbal descriptions of the most general patterns of behavior in complex organizations will speed up the learning process after one actually becomes a member of such an organization.

Organization Decisions as Composite Decisions

The reasons for specialization have already been stated. When several people work together toward the same goal, they must all be doing different things, and each generally becomes proficient or "expert" in some one thing. Thus, every organization, no matter how simple, is composed of specialists, each of whom contributes a part to the whole, but no one of whom accounts for the whole. Most organizational decisions are group, or composite, decisions; they are not the decisions of any one individual. Even in a very small organization of, say, five or six members, most decisions will require the participation of several members, each contributing his special knowledge or skill.

THE ROLE OF SPECIALISTS

In large organizations we find many specialized groups each of which contributes premises in some sphere of knowledge to the decisions of the organization. There are economic analysis units, statistical units, legal units, public relations units, field relations units, procedures units, personnel units, drafting units, liaision units, medical units, and an almost infinite variety of other kinds. The economic analysis unit will attempt to see that organization decisions are sound economically; the legal unit, that they are sound legally; the personnel unit, that they do not violate accepted or prescribed personnel standards; and so forth. No one of these units itself accounts for a complete decision. Each decision is an amalgamation of the specialized premises or points of view of many units.

Often the nature of an organization's goals indicates the types of specialized premises that will be needed. In the Department of Agriculture, for example, specialized knowledge about farming methods, plant and animal diseases, and agricultural marketing will be needed. Thus we find in that department, among many other units, a Bureau of Animal Industry, a Bureau of Plant Industry, a Bureau of Entomology and Plant Quarantine, and a Production and Marketing Administration. Likewise, in the Federal Power Commission specialized knowledge about power technology, utility rate structures, and law will be needed. Therefore we are not surprised to find within the Commission a Bureau of Power; a Bureau of Accounts, Finance, and Rates; and a Bureau of Law.

Some specializations, including most of those mentioned above, represent traditional breakdowns of the general field of knowledge and are accepted by almost everyone without dispute. Other specializations within organizations are not to the same extent based upon generally accepted bodies of knowledge. Most of the specializations relating to administrative skills fall in this latter category—for example, personnel management, budget review, accounting, purchasing, public relations, questionnaire review, procedures review, congressional relations, liaison, forms review, and so forth. The distinction between specializations that are accepted as scientific and reliable and those that are not is, of course, a distinction in degree, and one that shifts as new bodies of knowledge gain respectability. As we shall see later in this chapter, the distinction is important in explaining intergroup relations within organizations.

THE INTERDEPENDENCE OF ORGANIZATION UNITS

Since organizational decisions are composite decisions, all units (the smallest groupings of operatives under unit chiefs) are auxiliary to at least some other units; no one unit stands alone. Many writings on administration try to pick out certain types of administrative units, such as personnel and purchasing units, as "auxiliary" and to distinguish these units from the other, or "line," units. That is, it is asserted that units dealing with personnel, purchasing, and so forth, help the other organizational units to "get the job done"; they are auxiliary to something which is "the real thing."

We will take the view here that *all* units in an organization can be considered to be "auxiliary" units; each helps others make organizational decisions. An economics unit helps a legal unit to avoid economic errors in organizational decisions; a legal unit helps an economics unit to avoid legal errors. An information unit helps both to avoid public relations errors.

Furthermore, each unit establishes standards that are supposed to be accepted by other units. If a specialized unit has any justification at all, it is expected to influence the decisions of the organization—not just once or by accident but whenever its special competence is relevant. A medical unit makes sure that sound medical premises inform the decisions of the organization; a statistical unit does the same for statistical premises; a personnel unit, for personnel premises. Each unit is anxious to make sure that accepted decisional premises in its field have been followed in all organizational decisions. Thus, each unit, whether concerned with budgeting or chemistry, is engaged in supplying and enforcing standards or acceptable decisional premises within its field of specialization.

If the term "auxiliary" is used in its everyday sense, we must conclude that there are no special administrative units that are more "auxiliary" than any others. The term "auxiliary" must either be discarded or employed in some more restrictive sense. In a later section of this chapter we will identify the distinguishing characteristics of the so-called auxiliary units and see what bearing these characteristics have upon intergroup relations in organizations.

DIVISION OF WORK IN COMPLEX ORGANIZATIONS

As we have seen in Chapter 6, there is no one best way of grouping the various kinds of specialists who are represented in a complex organization. Any particular method of grouping is likely to gain certain advantages, but to lose others. We illustrated this point with the example of a Special Export License Branch, whose task it was during the war to control the export of scarce commodities to our allies and to neutral countries. That branch was part of a wartime agency known as the Foreign Economic Administration, and we will now use that agency's problems to show some of the organizational consequences of the division of work in large-scale organizations.

We recall that the agency needed two types of expertness: (1) specialized knowledge of the commodity needs of each geographical area, and (2) specialized knowledge of the availability of each commodity. In a large agency like FEA, the volume of work would be sufficiently large so that any particular employee, or small group of employees, could specialize with respect *both* to the areas and to the commodities with which he was concerned. That is, the FEA could consist of a number of groups of employees each concerned with determining the amount of a particular commodity (or narrow range of commodities) that should be shipped to a particular country (or small group of countries). This arrangement might solve satisfactorily the problem of narrowing the range of skills required of each employee or of each small organizational unit. It would leave open the question of how these units were to be grouped into sections, branches, and bureaus.

To understand the administrative problems that arose from the FEA structure (and identical problems arise in other similarly-organized agencies), it is necessary to understand clearly the end-product of the decisional process in the agency. Considering only the establishment of export quotas, the end product can be pictured as a numerical table showing the quantities of each commodity that would be licensed for export to each country for a given period. That is, each column of this table would refer to a particular country and each row to a particular commodity.

We will examine, first, two possible plans of organization for the agency, one emphasizing the importance of integrating area decisions; the other, the importance of integrating commodity decisions.

Plan I. The basic working units would be combined into a number of bureaus corresponding to major geographical areas. Each bureau would consist of divisions each dealing with a major commodity group in the geographical area assigned to the bureau. Thus, we would have a bread grains division, and an iron and steel division, among others, in the Latin American bureau. We would also have a bread grains division and an iron and steel division in the Far Eastern bureau. The Latin American bureau would be responsible for commodity quotas for that area, and similarly the Far Eastern bureau for its area. The obvious difficulty with this plan is that total commodity quotas for all areas taken together could be related to total available quantities only at the agency level—or by informal cooperation "across" organizational lines among specialists dealing with a particular commodity group.

Plan II. The basic working units would be combined into a number of bureaus corresponding to major commodity groups. Each bureau would consist of divisions corresponding to major areas. Thus, we would have a Latin American division and a Far Eastern division in the bread grains bureau. The bread grains bureau would be responsible for the allocation of that commodity among areas, and similarly the other commodity bureaus. The obvious difficulty with this plan is that the total needs of a particular area could be related to each other only at the agency level—or by informal cooperation across organizational lines among specialists concerned with a particular area.

Recognizing the difficulties of each of these plans, the agency sought an alternative plan that would permit it to eat its cake and have it too—to enjoy simultaneously the advantages of over-all commodity and over-all area allocation. This actual plan (much simplified, of course) we will call Plan III.

Plan III. Two principal administrative units were established: a Bureau of Areas and a Bureau of Supplies. The Bureau of Areas consisted of a number of divisions, each division covering a particular country or group of countries to which commodities were being exported. The Bureau of Supplies consisted of a number of divisions, each division covering a particular commodity or group of commodities subject to export controls.

Referring to our hypothetical table of export quotas, we see that the Spanish Division of the Bureau of Areas was responsible for the quotas of all commodities in the column headed "Spain," while the Bread Grains Division in the Bureau of Supplies was responsible for the quotas to all areas in the row labelled "Bread Grains." This procedure involved a dual responsibility. A commodity quota for a particular country was scrutinized by the appropriate area division, running its eyes up and down the column referring to that country, and by the appropriate commodity division, running its eyes across the row referring to that commodity. The Bureau of Areas specialized in vertical head-nodding, while the Bureau of Supplies specialized in horizontal head-shaking.

It is easy to see the seeds of inter-group conflict in such a situation. The viewpoints of the two Bureaus concerned with the allocation decisions were found to differ in many cases. In this particular organization, the area divisions tended to identify with, and become claimants for, a particular country, and hence to advocate larger quotas for that country; while the commodity divisions tended to be concerned with limited availabilities, hence to advocate smaller commodity quotas. As a consequence, a vigorous power struggle developed between the two Bureaus to determine which would have greater weight in the decisional process. For reasons that are not relevant here, the Bureau of Supplies generally, but by no means completely, gained the upper hand.

It is not our purpose to argue that Plans I or II would have been more satisfactory than III. The difficulties that arose were difficulties inherent in the agency program rather than difficulties resulting from a particular organizational structure. The fact was that quotas had to be scrutinized from both an area-need and a commodity-availability standpoint, and this need of dual scrutiny was the basic cause for complexity. Plan I would have complicated the commodity scrutiny, Plan II the area scrutiny. Plan III facilitated both reviews, but at the expense of inter-bureau differences that had to be resolved at the agency level. The fact that the agency gradually migrated in the direction of Plan II perhaps indicated that under the conditions of extreme scarcity in which it was operating, maintaining strict commodity quotas was considered the more important administrative task than adjusting allocations exactly to area needs.

Those points in an organization where different specialties located in separate organization units are brought to bear upon the same decisional problem are the points where the most frequent inter-group contacts occur and where the important problems of inter-group relations arise. The creation of parallel organizational units—like the FEA Bureaus of Areas and Supplies—upon different bases of specialization is a frequent occurrence in large organizations. It is the common root of at least two problems of organization that are usually treated as separate issues. These problems, which will be considered at length in the next two chapters, are the problems of group relations between "line" and "staff," and between "headquarters" and "field." In order to understand the nature of these problems, we must first analyze the notion introduced briefly in Chapter 7 of a self-contained organization.

SELF-CONTAINED ORGANIZATIONS

We can conceive of a self-contained organization—an organization that depended upon no other organization for aid of any kind —an organization that had within it all resources needed to do its work. Actually, of course, no such organization exists. At the very least, government agencies are dependent upon others for funds and are subjected to externally imposed standards in fields of personnel, budgeting, accounting, and usually purchasing.

Although there is no completely self-contained organization, there are organizations that are relatively so. Whereas they will be subjected to standards imposed by other organizations in the fields mentioned above, they will have within them most of the technical specialists needed for making the decisions they have to make. For example, the Forest Service in the Department of Agriculture must occasionally appeal to the departmental personnel and budget offices, but beyond these and a few others it has all the necessary knowledge and skills within it for managing and conserving the forests of the United States. The Forest Service is a relatively self-contained organization.

The level at which relative self-containment is achieved may be the departmental level, the bureau level, the divisional level, or even lower. In city governments the fire and police departments can be regarded as relatively self-contained. They have an independence from other organizations or units not enjoyed by any one of their parts. Many of the bureaus of the U. S. Department of the Interior are relatively self-contained—for example, the Bureau of Indian Affairs, and the Bureau of Reclamation. Although these Bureaus have numerous relations with other departmental offices in the fields of law, public relations, budget, administrative services, and personnel, they have within themselves most of the other means needed to do their jobs.

The Department of the Interior also exhibits examples of relative self-containment at the level below the bureau. For instance, the Geological Survey (a bureau) divides its survey work among four branches: Geologic Branch (mineral surveys); Topographic Branch (preparation of standard topographical maps of the United States and its territories); Water Resources Branch (surveys and evaluation of our water resources); and the Conservation Branch (enforcement of Federal conservation laws for mineral and water resources on public lands). Each of these branches brings together or integrates most of the technical skills needed to create its product. On the other hand, they are not *completely* self-contained. They are all dependent to some extent upon other branches or offices in the bureau (Geological Survey) for advice and instructions with regard to text, illustrations, reproduction, and distribution of reports; personnel; budget; law; central files; accounts; and library. Hence, the branches are relatively much less self-contained than the bureau. Self-containment is always a matter of degree.

UNITARY ORGANIZATIONS: THE LEVEL OF INTEGRATION

The degree of self-containment of an organization unit is an objective fact—it can be observed by noting to what extent decisions can be reached and executed within the unit without contact with other units. Very often we find that units with a high degree of self-containment possess another characteristic—these units often have an organization goal that is thought of by many people as a worthwhile activity in its own right—not just as a means to some more general goal. Organizations possessing such a socially meaningful goal we will call *unitary organizations*.[1]

The level in an organization structure where unitary components are found is the *lowest* level at which the combined efforts of specialized persons or groups can be integrated by relating them to a common, socially meaningful goal. For example, the activities of all the specialists who go to make up a municipal fire department can be integrated by reference to the goal of minimizing fire losses—which would generally be regarded as a desirable social end. On the other hand, the training division in the fire department, or the fourth battalion, are below the level of integration and are not unitary organizations because their activities are regarded simply as means to the departmental goal. As we shall see, however, when unitary organizations are not self-contained, the level at which integration actually takes place will generally be *higher* than the level at which the unitary organizations are found.

In the case of the Geological Survey, some people with good powers of abstraction may think of its activities as having a single socially meaningful goal—the discovery, evaluation, and development of our mineral and water resources. For such persons the Survey is a unitary organization, and the bureau level can be the level of integration. For many people, however, surveys of petroleum reserves in various areas have real meaning regardless of what else the bureau does. These people would want to see such surveys continued even if all the rest of the activities of the Geological Survey were discontinued. They would not regard the surveys as an activity that had meaning only in relation to some other

---

[1] It should be emphasized that the characteristics that define a unitary organization are quite distinct from the characteristics that define a self-contained organization. A unitary organization need not be self-contained, nor a self-contained organization unitary. It is an empirical fact, however, that an organization that is unitary to a high degree is often relatively self-contained.

governmental activity. To them it is a socially valuable objective in itself; the results of the surveys should be published regardless of any other activities of the bureau. For people who feel this way about petroleum surveys, the Geologic Branch of the Geological Survey is a meaningful level of governmental activity. Since the other branches listed are comparable, we can argue that, for many people at least, relative integration in this bureau could take place at the branch level.

For some people with broader interests and greater powers of abstraction, the Geological Survey itself is only a part of a much broader governmental program—natural resources development and conservation. At present this program achieves what integration it has at the Presidential (and Congressional) level since several departments are involved in it. Concern with this broader goal tends to evolve into a suggestion for creating a Department of Natural Resources, with integration thereby achieved at the departmental level. This is illustrated by the dissent of three members of the Hoover Commission from the official report of that Commission.

> Our own view is that the conservation, development, and use of our public resources is a single indivisible problem. It can be solved wisely only by the leadership of one governmental agency which would relate each part of that problem—forests, water, public lands, minerals, wildlife, fisheries, recreation, power—to the others and develop all of our natural resources together.
>
> We therefore recommend a Department of Natural Resources.[2]

FEDERAL AND UNITARY ORGANIZATIONS

We see, then, that whether we consider an organization to be unitary or not depends upon our definition of the organization purpose. To the extent that we can give tangible, concrete significance to broad social goals like "conservation of natural resources," we can regard a Department of Natural Resources as a unitary organization. We may find, however, that such a goal is too abstract—that it fails to give us any criterion for weighing mineral needs against forest conservation. Then the broad abstract goal of

---

[2] Hoover Commission, report on *The Department of Interior*, p. 54. The dissenting opinion is that of Vice Chairman Acheson and Commissioners Pollock and Rowe.

the department ceases to achieve any meaningful unification of the parts, and these parts become socially significant unitary activities in their own right.

Definition of Federal Organization. The Federal Security Agency provides a good illustration of this point. The FSA was established in 1939 to bring together in one department the welfare activities of the Federal government. From time to time other activities have been transferred to it from other departments. In 1948 it consisted of the following major components: Bureau of Employees' Compensation, Employees' Compensation Appeals Board, Food and Drug Administration, Office of Education, Office of Vocational Rehabilitation, Public Health Service, Saint Elizabeth's Hospital, Social Security Administration (with the former Children's Bureau of the Department of Labor added), American Printing House for the Blind, Columbia Institution for the Deaf, Howard University.

In the case of the FSA, it is clear that the general purpose of "welfare" is too vague to provide meaningful integration of the various component parts listed above. Each of the major units has its own socially defined goal, which is independent of the goals of the others. Employees of the Food and Drug Administration, for example, need not be concerned about the decisions of the Social Security Administration; these organizations do not supply specialized premises to be integrated at the departmental or agency level into an FSA welfare decision. The activities of the component parts of FSA are not means to a common end except in the vague sense that all government activities are a means to a common end of happiness or the good life. Each of the several FSA activities is a social end—not a means. In FSA relative integration could be achieved below the agency level and in most cases below the bureau level.

The larger government organizations—departments, and sometimes bureaus or even divisions—that are collections of unitary organizations, without any tangible single over-all goal, we will call organizations of the *federal* or *holding-company* type. FSA is clearly a federal organization made up of such unitary organizations as the Bureau of Employees' Compensation and the Public Health Service.

Coordination Within Federal Organizations. The components of a unitary organization (e.g. divisions in the Bureau of Employees'

Compensation) cannot be self-contained, because the activities of all components are directed toward a common over-all goal. An entire unitary organization can be relatively self-contained, because it can be assigned all the activities that are needed to achieve its socially meaningful goal. In practice, however, a unitary organization may contain only a part of the means needed to achieve its ends. As a matter of fact, the most common consequence of grouping together a number of unitary organizations into a larger federal organization is to reduce the self-containment of the unitary organizations. Almost always, when a holding-company type of agency is created, many activities are centralized at the agency level, and consequently some integration of these centralized activities with the activities of the component parts must be secured by the agency. For example, FSA must secure some integration between any of its component unitary parts listed above and all of the following "Offices" at the agency level: Office of Administration, Office of General Counsel, Office of Research, Office of Publications and Reports, Office of Federal-State Relations, Office of Inter-Agency and International Relations.

Although the distinction between unitary and federal organizations is only a matter of degree, yet it is an important one to make, for the problem of coordination of the component parts is somewhat different in the two types of organization. In the unitary organization, the various activities of the parts can be kept in harmony by reference to the organization's goal. Each activity is a means to that goal, and if all the activities advance the goal then they cannot be in direct conflict with one another. When it is time to determine the budget allocations, the limited resources of the unitary organization can be divided among its component activities by a rational process. An activity that contributes little to the goal gets little; one that contributes more gets more. Of course, in actual practice it is often difficult to determine how much some activity contributes to the goal, but nevertheless each component part of a unitary organization must defend itself by reference to its contribution to the organization's goal.

In the holding-company or federal kind of organization, integration at the top level is much less a matter of logic applied to a goal; for no common denominator exists for the component activities. If the Food and Drug Administration and the Office of Education conflict over the division of the FSA budget, there is no

FSA goal by reference to which the conflict can be settled rationally. It is not possible to follow the principle that the activity contributing most to a common goal gets most because FSA has no single measurable goal. It is a holding company—a federal organization.

The hypothetical conflict between the Food and Drug Administration and the Office of Education mentioned above would almost certainly be settled by a political process. The unit with the strongest political support—in Congress and in the country at large—would most likely win out. We conclude that coordination between specialized units within a unitary organization can be secured by a more rational process than can coordination in a federal organization.

Tendency Toward Centralization

In the preceding section we mentioned that no organization, even of the unitary type, is completely self-contained. In this section we will discuss one of the most characteristic administrative trends of our age—the tendency to lessen organizational self-containment. Since this result is coming about through increasing centralization, it will be well to stop for a moment at this point to indicate precisely how we are using the term "centralization" throughout the rest of this section.[3]

MEANING OF CENTRALIZATION

In a broad sense, any specialization in terms of a particular activity represents a centralization of that activity. Let us imagine a time when all of the smallest work units of an organization handled all of their own personnel functions. Then, let us imagine that for one reason or another all personnel functions were removed from the units and a new personnel unit established in each section. In the former situation conflicts over personnel matters would be settled by the unit chief; he would provide the point at which personnel thinking would be integrated with the other kinds of thinking going on in the unit. In the second situation (after a

[3] For a survey and analysis of the centralization movement, see Waldo, *The Administrative State*, chap. 8.

personnel unit had been established) conflicts over personnel matters would be settled by the section chief; he would provide the integration of personnel premises into the section's decisions whenever that was needed (for example, when a unit chief disagreed with the head of the personnel unit over a promotion). In this case we say that personnel functions have been centralized at the section level.

If personnel sections were established in the branches of our hypothetical organization, we would say that personnel functions had been centralized at the branch level. In like fashion, if the department established a bureau of personnel, personnel functions would be centralized at the departmental level. With the establishment of the U. S. Civil Service Commission in 1883, certain personnel functions in the Federal government were centralized at the Presidential level. Likewise, with the establishment of the Bureau of Federal Supply in the Treasury Department in 1933, many purchasing activities of federal administrative agencies were centralized at the Presidential level.

Since the topic of specialization has already been discussed at length in Chapter 7, we shall be concerned here only with a particular kind of centralization—centralization of activities above the level at which unitary organizations are found. That is, we shall be interested in the tendency to take out of unitary organizations certain of the activities that would be required for self-containment and to place these activities in separate units at the level of a broader federal organization or at the level of the chief executive. Examples of the former are the FSA Offices of Administration, General Counsel, Research, Publications and Reports, Federal-State Relations, and Inter-Agency and International Relations, mentioned earlier. Comparable collections of overhead units will be found in the other departments of a holding-company type: Interior, Commerce, and so forth.

Familiar examples of activities centralized at the level of the chief executive—President, governor, mayor, or city manager— include budget, provision of office space, questionnaire review, printing, enforcement of personnel regulations, management planning, and research.

The 1949 report of the Hoover Commission furnishes a remarkable illustration of the strong tendency toward increasing centralization at the Presidential level in the national government today.

That Commission recommended centralization to the national or Presidential level of the following activities: (a) medical activities (by establishing a new United Medical Administration); (b) organization and methods analysis activities (by increasing the power of the Administrative Management Division of the Budget Bureau); (c) publication activities (by giving the Budget Bureau power to review all publications); (d) statistical activities (by greatly increasing the power of the Statistical Standards Division of the Budget Bureau); (e) the administration of grants-in-aid to states and cities (by establishing a separate agency on Federal-State Relations); (f) the administration of all overseas activities except the diplomatic and consular services (by establishing a new Administration of Overseas Affairs); (g) accounting methods (by establishing an Accountant General in the Treasury Department); (h) review of public works projects (by establishing under the President a Board of Impartial Analysis for Engineering and Architectural Projects "for making certain that only projects which are economically and socially justifiable are recommended for approval." [4]); (i) certain aspects of Federal domestic credit activities (by establishing under an Assistant Secretary of the Treasury a National Monetary and Credit Council to "promote coordination of purpose and avoid overlapping activities and inconsistent credit policies." [5]); (j) all wage and consumers' price research (by transferring these activities from all other agencies to a new Bureau of "Prevailing Wage" Research in the Labor Department); (k) basic science research (by creating a National Research Foundation "to coordinate the various science research programs of the Government." [6]); (l) some unspecified aspects of central-field relations (through "some official in the Government responsible for constant study and simplification and coordination of departmental work in the field." [7]).

To the lower units of organizations, each movement toward centralization means that some area of decision has been taken from them and put in a central unit. The unitary organizations become less self-contained, and their capacity to integrate all activities having a bearing upon their goals is correspondingly impaired. Let us suppose that a municipal fire department, for ex-

[4] Hoover Commission Report on the *Department of the Interior*, p. 5.

[5] Report on the *Treasury Department*, p. 20.

[6] *Concluding Report*, p. 72.

[7] Report on *General Management of the Executive Branch*, p. 42.

ample, must depend upon a central personnel agency for recruiting personnel, a central purchasing agency for buying equipment, and so forth. Then the integration of all activities directed toward municipal fire protection can no longer take place entirely within the fire department but must be correspondingly centralized at the level of the mayor or city manager.

Hence, as the process of centralization goes on, the level at which integration takes place tends to be raised to the level at which activities are centralized. Prior to this centralization a municipal government consisted typically of a number of relatively self-contained unitary organizations each concerned with its own socially significant goals. With increasing centralization we get a federal structure in which the activities directed toward any particular set of goals are distributed between one of the old unitary organizations and a number of new overhead units. Hence, integration of these activities must now take place at the level of the chief executive.

It is likely that if all the recommendations of the Hoover Commission for centralization in the national government were followed, the task of the President would become impossible of performance.[8] At any rate, the kind of integration achieved would be of the holding-company type.

CAUSES OF CENTRALIZATION

As to the forces behind this movement toward centralization we are highly ignorant. It is apparent that improvement in communication has made centralization possible. When national governments can communicate by telephone at any time with their representatives throughout the world, it is unnecessary to allow those representatives much discretion in the choice of decisional premises. However, why particular activities are being pushed up

---

[8] Of course, what would actually happen is that many of the new centralized units would acquire a practical veto power over other government agencies. Conflicts between these agencies and many centralized units would not actually or usually be carried to the President for resolution. For example, a Budget Bureau veto on a publication plan would probably be final in most cases. However, whether this result would occur or whether conflicts with centralized agencies would actually be carried to the President would depend to a large extent on the political situation, especially the relation of agency heads to the President and congressional committees. The type of integration achieved would become dependent, to a large extent, on the ability of agency heads to curry Presidential favor.

to higher and higher levels of government is often very obscure. Here we will present only some very speculative hypotheses as to the nature of these centralizing forces.

Magnitude of Expenditures. One rather obvious consideration comes immediately to mind. As total governmental expenditures have increased until they represent a large percentage of the national income, decisions concerning the division of the nation's resources are pushed to higher levels. Centralized executive budget processes have appeared with the growth of governmental expenditures. This trend is accentuated when government undertakes to adapt its expenditure policy to the business cycle.

Belief in the Efficacy of Law. It is also likely that the almost universal belief in the efficacy of law and regulation in enforcing desired modes of conduct contributes to centralization. If it is desired that all officials accept certain standards or decisional premises in some area, the almost immediate suggestion of many people is to pass laws or regulations prescribing those standards and to establish an agency to enforce them on all other officials. Thus widespread acceptance of "more ethical" personnel standards resulted in the creation of the U. S. Civil Service Commission to develop and enforce personnel standards for the Federal bureaucracy.

Direction of Attention to Particular Activities. The general belief in the efficacy of enforced behavior does not by itself explain why particular activities are singled out for centralization—why attention is suddenly focussed on certain areas out of the whole flux of behavior in administrative organizations.[9] If many people have become aware of the existence of a particular administrative activity, there is a good chance that it will become the subject of centralizing recommendations. In Chapter 7 we pointed out that growing interest in an activity or program is often, perhaps usually, followed by the raising of that program to a higher administrative status, say from a branch to a division. The question to be answered, then, is why certain activities gain attention.

Even if an activity is not regarded as an important social objective in its own right, even if it is only a means toward an important goal, it may yet acquire a good deal of attention. This is so

[9] The reader should understand that here we are talking about the centralization of activities already going on. We are not discussing the process by which new governmental programs come into being. That process was described in Chapter 2.

because the means organizations adopt to achieve their goals are never neutral. They always have consequences in addition to the sought-for goals, and these consequences will be regarded as good or bad by various people. Thus the means to administrative ends— the techniques and methods of administration—may at any time become the objects of hostile attack by members of the public. For example, to accomplish wartime regulation, all administrative agencies used questionnaires. So onerous did the burden of filling out government forms become to small businessmen that the Senate Committee on Small Business introduced and secured the passage of the Federal Reports Act of 1942. This act centralized in the Bureau of the Budget the function of deciding whether or not a particular questionnaire would be released to the public. No one could be required to fill out any form unless the Budget Bureau had approved it. Thus a particular administrative means—use of questionnaires—because it stimulated a growing restiveness among small businessmen, acquired political attention and finally was centralized so that its use could be governed by centrally enforced standards.[10]

Another force that has helped to publicize certain administrative activities has been the modern systematized study of public administration. Students of administration, seeking to identify a specialized field of inquiry for themselves from out of the general field of government, have focussed upon those activities which were not the province of existing scientific and technical specializations. Hence, they have concentrated on such activities as central-field relations, grants-in-aid to states and cities, personnel, budgeting, accounting, purchasing, organization and methods, public relations, and congressional relations.

A startling increase in the cost of an activity may also serve to bring it to the attention of influential people. This is partly an accidental result of the methods of classification used in governmental budgeting. Nevertheless, when an increase in costs comes in whatever manner to the attention of congressmen or reorganization commissioners, a recommendation of centralization often follows. It seems likely that the great increase in costs of Federal medical

[10] As a matter of fact, this process had really begun a decade earlier with the establishment of an inter-departmental committee on Statistical Standards—later transferred to the Budget Bureau—by executive order. The same general pressures were involved at this stage, and the Division of Statistical Standards undoubtedly contributed to the "education" of Congress as to the need for the Reports Act.

services was partly responsible for the Hoover Commission's recommendation that a United Medical Administration be established. On page 4 of its report on *Medical Activities* the Commission points out: "Over 40 Government agencies render Federal medical service. In this fiscal year (1948) they plan to spend nearly $2 billion, about 10 times the amount spent in 1940."

Power Drives of Overhead Units. When particular activities or areas of decision are centralized out of the mass of activities of a relatively self-contained organizational unit, the new overhead units so created often develop a desire for still more power and jurisdiction. They often urge that further areas of decision be turned over to them.

The history of the FSA illustrates this process. FSA was created by the President's Reorganization Plan I in 1939 as a holding company for several different government agencies including the U. S. Office of Education, the Social Security Board, and the U. S. Public Health Service. Over a period of time overhead units were established centralizing decision (or the review of decisions) in the fields of organization and methods; personnel; budget; supply; law; research; public information; certain aspects of federal-state relations; and inter-agency or international relations. It is clear that by now (1949) the component agencies of which FSA was originally formed can make very few, if any, decisions without involvement with one or more of FSA's overhead organization units.

The Drive for Uniformity. Another important reason for centralization is the insistence of overhead personnel on uniformity. In order to achieve uniform performance of activities, it may be suggested either (1) that all those activities be centralized in a new organizational unit at the highest level, or (2) that uniform standards be laid down and enforced by a new, centralized, overhead unit (e.g., the Statistical Standards Division of the U. S. Budget Bureau). The drive for uniformity may stem from esthetic considerations, or it may provide the overhead unit with a plausible substitute for a real goal. The drive for uniformity, in either case, is a powerful force in raising the level of administrative integration. Of course, uniformity may sometimes serve administrative ends as well as esthetic or power ends. For example, the desire of persons doing similar work to receive the same pay may be sufficient reason for uniform classification and pay scales. One can point to many uniformities, however, that cannot be so justified.

Imitation. It is likely that an unconscious mimicry is also involved in some centralizations. When an activity has been singled out for centralization at a certain level in a few organizations, there frequently follows a suggestion either that all agencies so centralize it or that it be centralized at a higher level. Although it would be difficult to prove, it is possible that the centralization of certain aspects of federal-state relations in an Office of Federal-State Relations in FSA may have had something to do with the Hoover Commission's recommendation that a federal Agency of Federal-State Relations be established. In rationing, the existence of "planning sections" and "control and audit sections" in the rationing branches led to the establishment of a "planning division" at the departmental (bureau) level and a constant agitation on the part of some overhead personnel for establishing a departmental control and audit division.[11]

Let us now sum up our speculations concerning the forces lying behind the centralization process. First, improved methods of communication have made a much greater degree of centralization possible. Second, the motive power for centralization may come partly from (1) the desire for emphasis of a particular activity, (2) the belief in the efficacy of enforced behavior, (3) the drive for uniformity, (4) the desire for more power on the part of overhead groups, and (5) the fact that administrative techniques are never valuationally neutral. Third, the singling out of particular activities from all those possible may be the result of conscious or unconscious mimicry or of growing consciousness of a particular activity on the part of important groups. Finally, growing awareness of an activity may be the result of (1) a dramatic increase in money spent on it, (2) the publicity given it by students of administration, or (3) the impact of the activity on the interests and values of important sectors of the community. In the two following chapters, we will see what implications can be drawn from this analysis for the problems that arise in complex organizations.

[11] See Thompson, *The Regulatory Process in OPA Rationing*, chap. 10.

CHAPTER THIRTEEN

Large-Scale Organizations: The Consequences of Centralization

WE HAVE seen that there is a continuing tendency toward the centralization of activities above the level where unitary organizations are found in modern large-scale governmental administration. In this chapter we will be concerned with two main problems:

(1) How our distinction between "unitary organizations" and "overhead units" is related to the distinction commonly made in writings on administration between "line" and "staff."

(2) How centralization gives rise to still another kind of unit—the "counterpart unit."

"*Line*," "*Auxiliary*," *and* "*Staff*" *Units*

Current writings on administration generally distinguish three principal types of administrative units: line units, auxiliary units, and staff units. Because this terminology is rather widely used, the reader has reason to be familiar with it, although the traditional explanations of the relationships among these three types of units do not hold up very well under critical analysis.

We quote (with minor changes in terminology to conform to the present discussion) a statement as to how the distinctions are applied in municipal organization.

> City governments are established and maintained to provide certain public services, such as police protection, the construction and maintenance of public works, or the preservation of public health. Agencies that have as their primary objective or function the provision of such

public services are known as operating or line departments. But all of these line departments have certain common needs that must be provided for if these agencies are to perform their primary functions. Thus, every line department needs men, money, and equipment and supplies. In a decentralized administrative organization each line agency may administer these services itself, but it has been generally found most expedient to centralize these services to some degree in central auxiliary agencies.

In addition to line and auxiliary functions, an integrated organization requires the performance of "staff" functions—over-all planning, direction, control, coordination, and so forth. These staff functions are the responsibility of the chief administrator, but in larger organizations he may require the assistance of one or more aides or agencies to assist him in the exercise of these staff functions. For example the authority and responsibility for budgeting belong to the chief administrator and cannot be delegated by him without producing a harmful division of management; but he can employ a budget officer or a budget bureau to assist him in the exercise of this staff function.

. . . Although it may be convenient to refer broadly to a particular agency as a line or auxiliary or staff agency, it should not be inferred that all of the activities of the agency belong within this category. Most agencies, in fact, engage in more than one class of function or activity, and the general classification refers only to the predominant character of any agency's activities.[1]

DISTINCTION BETWEEN AUXILIARY AND STAFF

From this quotation we see that what are usually called line units are those that we have previously designated unitary organizations—those organized around a socially meaningful program. Both auxiliary and staff units fall under our category of centralized or "overhead" units. The usual distinction made between auxiliary and staff units is that the auxiliary units are supposed to assist the line organizations by performing certain common tasks for them, while the staff units are supposed to assist the chief executive by performing certain tasks for him that he could not otherwise delegate to the line units.

The relations of auxiliary and staff units to the line organizations and to the chief executive are sometimes pictured as follows. Suppose we think of an organization that consists only of a number of self-contained unitary organizations under a single chief executive (e.g., city departments under a city manager). Suppose we now add to this structure: (a) overhead units (auxiliary units) that centralize certain activities previously handled by the unitary organizations for themselves; and (b) overhead units (staff units) that perform certain tasks previously handled by the chief executive. These two types of overhead units will then form a new element in the organization structure located "between" the chief executive and the unitary organizations.

Even if we could account for the separate origins of auxiliary and staff units by such a crude organization-chart picture (a proposition the authors cannot accept), it does not follow that, once established, the auxiliary and staff units would be distinguishable from each other in any important respect. If an overhead unit is responsible, for example, for establishing rules regarding vacations and sick leaves, is it performing an auxiliary or a staff function? If the organization had previously been operating in a relatively decentralized fashion, with personnel questions of this kind decided by the departments, we might consider it to be an auxiliary function. If the chief executive had previously made such rules himself, we might say that the new overhead unit was operating in a staff relationship to him. The position we shall take here is that in most cases it is impossible to draw any line between auxiliary and staff functions, much less between auxiliary and staff *units*. The only real distinction lies in the different justifications commonly given for setting up particular overhead units, rather than in the nature of the activities of such units once they are established.

ATTITUDES TOWARD OVERHEAD UNITS

The commonly accepted distinction between line and overhead is more than a convenient way to classify governmental organization units. It has a psychological meaning to the members of an organization and to others. A line activity is regarded as somehow "more important" than an overhead activity. Both the members of an organization and its clientele *feel* that the line unit is responsible for the success or failure of a program, despite the fact that many very important areas of decision necessary for the fulfillment of the program may be centralized in overhead units.[2]

[2] For an attempt to determine the focus of responsibility in terms of "who gets blamed," see Thompson, *The Regulatory Process in OPA Rationing*, chap. 10.

Since completely self-contained organizational units do not exist, this assignment of responsibility to line units is spurious, but it persists none the less. One reason for this is that the old self-contained unit still retains its old name—a name that is usually descriptive of the socially meaningful activity or objective. Thus, the fire department is still regarded as "responsible" for fire losses, even though it may have lost some of its control over personnel and purchasing functions to centralized overhead units.

Furthermore, clientele and member loyalty to the line unit may continue strongly even though it is now an entirely different unit. Some of the important old-timers may demand that attitudes within the parent holding-company organization toward the decimated unit continue to reflect its old status. And these old-timers may have the prestige to enforce their demand. Members of the public—the clientele of the activity involved—may still look to the unit for help and hold it to blame for any deficiencies in the program. When this occurs, the old unit has a strong moral claim for unusual influence on the activity.

Although many areas of decision have been centralized out of the Children's Bureau (and other FSA units) since its transfer to FSA in 1946, it is likely that the loyalty and attitude structure surrounding the Bureau remain practically unchanged. Although the Social Security Agency has lost many areas of decision to overhead units since its transfer to FSA in 1939, it is still regarded as responsible for the social security program.

In addition to this general feeling that line units are somehow "more important," there are some very interesting generally held beliefs about the nature of auxiliary and staff units. These beliefs are interesting because, although widely held, analysis shows them to be false. A phenomenon of this kind needs to be explained, and so we will now turn our attention to a brief discussion of the myth aspect of the concepts of auxiliary and staff units.

Myths Surrounding the "Auxiliary"
and "Staff" Concepts

The principal beliefs in question here are two. The first is common to both auxiliary and staff concepts—that overhead units do not exercise authority over line units. It is alleged that auxiliary units "serve" line units, but do not "control" them; and that staff units "advise" line units, but do not "command." The second belief is that staff units are closer to the executive than are the line units; that they are "in his office"; that they are "an extension of his personality." [3]

ARE OVERHEAD UNITS ADVISORY?

Defining authority as the ability to elicit obedience (as we have done in previous chapters), it is clear that overhead units do exercise authority; they do control and command. When the central personnel unit refuses to approve a personnel action, or when the Statistical Standards Division of the Budget Bureau refuses to clear a form unless certain changes are made, what alternative is left to the line unit involved except to bow to these commands?

In the form review case, the alternative is to appeal to the Director of the Budget Bureau and, if that does not work, to the President. However, the head of a unit below the departmental level cannot generally go directly to the Budget Director or the President. (Some Bureau Chiefs may be able to.) A branch chief, for example, would have to persuade his division chief to persuade his bureau chief to persuade the Secretary (or agency head) to appeal the matter.

High level superiors, however, resent being asked to take up such matters unless they are very important. Issues of this kind make ruffled feelings all along the line. Eventually a common superior may have to make a decision between the two sides, and this he hates to do because he alienates the losing side. Consequently, superiors have a limited fund of good will for use in appeals of this kind and use it sparingly.

As a practical matter, when an overhead unit gives its "advice" to a line unit the advice is almost always taken. Overhead units can command up to that point where superiors are willing to make a high level issue of a matter. Overhead units exercise as much authority in organizations as do any other units.

[3] An extensive discussion of the staff concept will be found in L. Urwick, "Organization as a Technical Problem" in Gulick and Urwick, *Papers on the Science of Administration*. While Urwick accepts in part the reality of the second belief, his description of staff-line relationships is generally realistic.

ARE STAFF UNITS "PART OF THE EXECUTIVE"?

Let us now examine the second common belief about staff units —that they are somehow more closely identified with the executive than are line units; that they take his point of view and "speak for" him. At the outset let us admit that an executive may surround himself with a few persons in whom he has great confidence and depend upon these people for advice of all kinds. We might term such confidants the executive's staff. They could also be called his "kitchen cabinet" or "brain trust." We cannot tell in advance whether an executive will actually have such a group and who they will be. They might be the heads of some of the line units. Some executives depend upon close personal support and loyalty much more than do others. In short, whether this situation actually exists in any organization, and if so what its nature will be, can only be discovered by actual observation; it cannot be deduced from a concept such as "staff."

The case is quite different when we are dealing not with a handful of advisors or personal assistants to an executive, but with a large-scale organization which is itself subdivided into specialized units. Under these circumstances there is no inherent reason why staff personnel should identify more closely with the top executive than do the line personnel. Furthermore, there is no inherent reason why a top executive should pay closer attention to the staff units than to the line units. In fact, he is likely to be more interested in the socially meaningful activities associated with the line units than, for example, in matters of personnel, organization and management, or accounting.

As they grow in size, overhead units themselves become complex organizations. To get their jobs done, they specialize, or parcel out the component parts of the job to specialized units. The U. S. Bureau of the Budget—regarded as one of the President's principal staff arms—employs more than five hundred persons. These are allocated to Divisions of Estimates, Administrative Management, Legislative Reference, Fiscal Analysis, and Statistical Standards, and to a field service and a personnel office—in addition to almost a hundred who form the "Director's Office." The various divisions are divided, in turn, into branches, and the branches into sections.

Personnel of these specialized units are much more likely to identify with a particular unit, its members and its function, than with the executive for whom they are presumably staff. There is no inherent reason why a budget examiner in the Estimates Division of the U. S. Budget Bureau working constantly and exclusively with the hospital activities of the Veterans Administration should identify with the President more closely than does the head of the Veterans Administration. And even if he did, there is no inherent reason why he should know what the President wanted with regard to hospitals any better than does the head of the Veterans Administration—if indeed the President had ever given the matter a thought at all.

WHY THE MYTHS ARE ACCEPTED

Since these notions about overhead units dissolve so easily upon analysis, we must ask ourselves why people so generally believe in them. They must perform some function for administration. And indeed, if we scrutinize the myths closely, we see that they do perform a function—they perform a myth function, like fictions in law. They help to bridge a gap between the way people feel they should be treated in organizations and the way they are actually treated.

In society people acquire many notions as to how they should be treated in organizations. These notions form an integral part of the mores. The myths discussed above are important in reconciling these notions with reality. The most important of these accepted beliefs, which have already received some attention in Chapter 9, are: (1) that a person who is given responsibility for a task should be given authority commensurate with his responsibility; (2) that a person should have only one immediate superior; and (3) that a person should not be required to take orders from a person of lower status.

Authority and Responsibility. It is generally felt that if an organization unit is to be held responsible for achieving certain objectives, it must be given authority to control all the means employed in reaching these objectives. If a police department is to be responsible for apprehending criminals, and if patrol cars are an important means to this end, then the police department should have authority to maintain the motor equipment and presumably to purchase such equipment.

But, the argument continues, if we were to give a purchasing department, or any other auxiliary unit, power to control the police department, the authority of the latter would be abridged and would no longer be adequate to the responsibilities assigned. Hence, if we establish a centralized purchasing department, we must deny that this department exercises any control over the police department. We must insist that its only function is to provide service. The fact must be rationalized away that the purchasing department can reverse the judgment of the police department as to what kind of patrol cars the department should buy. The principal function of the myth is to conceal the fact that centralization of auxiliary activities does reduce the self-containment and the authority of line departments.

Unity of Command. Although people generally feel that they should only take orders from one person (that there should be "unity of command"), we have seen that in the reality of organization experience members of organizations take orders from many people. If this were not so, specialization would be impossible. Of what advantage would a central personnel office be if no one followed its decrees regarding personnel? If no one did what the lawyers said, why have a central law division? The fact is that a member of an organization, in addition to the orders of his superior, accepts the orders of personnel officers, attorneys, and a whole host of others.

How does the concept of staff help bridge the gap between the notion of "unity of command" and the actual facts of organizational experience? It does so by denying that the commands of these specialized staff units are really *their* commands. They are the commands of the executive. The staff units "speak in his name"; they are "part of the executive"; their authority is "really" his authority.

Command and Status. This same kind of realistic analysis will show that the commands issuing from centralized staff units are often, or even usually, the commands of specialized junior members of these units. One of the advantages of specialization is to simplify tasks so that less highly accomplished (and expensive) persons can perform them. Thus it often happens, for example, that a GS-7 classification officer in central personnel has a practical veto over the plans of a GS-14 branch chief to raise some of his employees' salaries by reclassifying their jobs or his plans to set certain salary levels for new jobs he is creating. Here again the myths of

staff do service—this time in explaining away a gross violation of
our ethics of status. The junior member is not "really" giving
commands to the senior member. Actually it is the high status
executive giving the command "through the staff officer" who is
only speaking "for" the executive.

Often the myth is given additional symbolic recognition by
having orders that are actually decisions of junior personnel
signed by the executive—either personally or by proxy. When the
signature is not accompanied by an actual review of the decision—
as it often is not—its function is a ritualistic one of giving appropriate status to the command.

INCOMPLETE ACCEPTANCE OF THE MYTHS

In general, the myths of staff conceal violations of common expectations by denying that they occur. But as overhead organizations become larger and more specialized and complex, the myths
become less readily believable by members of the line units. These
persons can hardly fail to notice that actual authority is exercised
by the classification technician and the budget examiner, and that
the overhead personnel cannot really know what is in the mind of
the chief executive—that they are as far removed from communication with him as are subordinates in the line units. Perhaps that
is why we commonly find personnel in these larger overhead organizations tenaciously holding on to the myths, for these myths are
the means by which their authority is legitimatized.

We cannot expect the myths to disappear so long as there is
general belief that authority should be commensurate with responsibility, that unity of command should be maintained, and
that authority should always be exercised from persons of higher
to persons of lower status. Some writers on organization, perceiving
the dilemma, have attacked these latter beliefs, but their heretical
positions have not yet gained wide acceptance.[4]

Because it is sometimes difficult to get line officials to accept the
myths of staff, we should not conclude that as yet these myths have
seriously lost power over men's imagination. For example, the
official report of the Hoover Commission appears to be based upon

[4] Frederick W. Taylor (functional foremanship), Chester I. Barnard, Schuyler
Wallace, and Macmahon, Millett, and Ogden are among the heretics who have
challenged one or another of these "principles of administration."

a complete acceptance of them as true descriptions of what goes on in organizations.

One of the Commission's chief organizational principles, constantly reiterated throughout its report, is that there must be a clear line of authority from the top to the bottom and a clear line of responsibility from the bottom to the top. "The line of command and supervision from the President down through his department heads to every employee, and the line of responsibility from each employee up to the President has been weakened, or actually broken in many places and in many ways. . . . On some occasions the responsibility of an official to his superior is obscured by laws which require him, before acting, to clear his proposals with others. This breaks the line of responsibility, and encourages indecision, lack of initiative, and irresponsibility," says the Commission disapprovingly.[5]

Under the President, the heads of departments must hold full responsibility for the conduct of their departments. There must be a clear line of authority reaching down through every step of the organization and no subordinate should have authority independent from that of his superior.[6]

How well does this often and strongly stated principle agree with the Commission's other recommendations? It does not agree very well. In the last chapter we pointed out that the Commission made more than a dozen recommendations for further centralizing activities at the Presidential level (that is, the President would be the first common superior for settling disputes concerning these activities). All these centralized activities, and others already centralized, are areas where specialized decisional premises are supplied for other departments and agencies of the government. When it is realized that all of these centralized staff organizations are further subdivided into many more specialized units and levels of staff organization paralleling the levels of the line organizations, it is clear that any Federal employee may find himself subject to orders from literally dozens of other persons besides his immediate superior.

A few examples drawn from the Commission's report will illustrate this inconsistency between the "clear lines of authority" concept mentioned above and the Commission's other recom-

[5] Report on *General Management of the Executive Branch*, pp. 3–4.
[6] Ibid., p. 34.

mendations. With regard to the functions of the Civil Service Commission the Commission says:

> The Commission's responsibility should be to furnish leadership for personnel administration in the Government by (i) setting standards for the handling of personnel programs by the agencies, (ii) post-auditing personnel programs to determine that there has been adherence to standards, (iii) applying appropriate sanctions wherever there has not been adherence to standards. . . .[7]

The Commission recommended that supply, records management, and the operation and maintenance of public buildings, among other functions, be consolidated in a new Office of General Services. With regard to supply activities, the new organization is to be "clothed with adequate authority to provide the leadership necessary to achieve in the executive branch an efficient supply organization. . . ."[8] The nature of this authority is apparently to be quite substantial. Some examples will illustrate this point. The Office of General Services is, among other things, to "assign responsibility for the purchase or storage of commodities peculiar to the use of an agency to the agency best suited to make such purchases or to store commodities; designate certain agencies to purchase specified supplies for all agencies; determine what products should be inspected; make inspection assignments to specific agencies; make testing assignments; make rules and regulations on inspection policy and methods; develop property use, maintenance, and replacement standards and rules and regulations, and determine the extent to which property disposal functions should be delegated to civilian agencies."[9]

Examination of the rest of the Commission's centralizing recommendations reveals the same pattern of giving to many centralized organizational entities the power to "prescribe and enforce" standards and rules and regulations upon the rest of the departments and agencies. How can these recommendations be reconciled with the Commission's emphatic insistence upon unity of command? The answer is that the Commission accepts without question the myths of staff. To the Commission all these new centralized units, along with the old ones, are part of the President's staff. As such, they do not command. Their standards and

---

[7] Report on *Personnel Management*, p. 9.
[8] Ibid., p. 42.
[9] Ibid., p. 47. A General Services Agency has since been established.

rules and regulations are "really" those of the President. When they enforce standards it is "really" the President enforcing them. If these staff offices appear to be exercising authority, that is just an illusion, for all their authority "actually" belongs to the President, to be exercised "in his name."

Responsibility and accountability are impossible without authority —the power to direct. The exercise of authority is impossible without a clear line of command from top to the bottom, and a return line of responsibility and accountability from the bottom to the top.

The wise exercise of authority is impossible without the aids which staff institutions can provide to assemble facts and recommendations upon which judgment may be made and to supervise and report upon the exercise of decisions.

Definite authority at the top, a clear line of authority from top to bottom, and adequate staff aids to the exercise of authority do not exist. Authority is diffused, lines of authority are confused, staff services are insufficient. Consequently, responsibility and accountability are impaired.[10]

Such complete acceptance of the myths of staff by a commission composed of such important and well-known public figures testifies to the strength of these myths, to the strength of the notions about organization which these myths harmonize with the contradictory facts of organization, and to the utility of the myths in harmonizing these contradictions.

Creation of Counterpart Units

We have seen how the process of centralization adds to the structure of simple organizations (consisting of a number of unitary organizations and one or more layers of top executives) another set of elements, the overhead units. But there is yet another chapter to this story of growing complexity. The numerous contacts between line and overhead units almost always lead to the growth of a third set of elements *within* the unitary organizations themselves. We will call these additional elements of the unitary organizations *counterpart units*, because they represent the same specializations as the overhead units, but at a lower organizational level.

[10] Report on the *General Management of the Executive Branch*, p. 1.

Thus, in the U. S. Department of Agriculture we find a personnel office, an overhead unit. But within the Forest Service, one of the unitary components of the Department, we also find a personnel office. From the standpoint of the internal structure of the Forest Service, this specialized personnel office is no different from any other specialized unit—say the Division of Timber Management. As we pointed out earlier in the chapter, within a unitary organization all units are auxiliary to all others, and it is meaningless to pick out particular specializations and call them "auxiliary." The only fact that distinguishes the personnel office of the Forest Service from other Forest Service units is that the former is a *counterpart* of overhead units at the departmental and Presidential (U. S. Civil Service Commission) level.

Virtually every Federal department or agency has a departmental personnel office, as do many bureaus. All departments and bureaus have budget offices; all have administrative services units; most have some central printing activity. Many of these counterparts to centralized activities are reproduced, in turn, at lower organizational levels, until we often find an administrative assistant to a branch or section chief specializing in personnel, budget, purchasing, and other "auxiliary" and "staff" activities.

There are at least three reasons why one finds many of these centralized activities reappearing as specializations at many levels within the unitary organizations: sometimes they represent a carry-over from a previously decentralized structure; sometimes they are established at the instance of the overhead unit; and sometimes they represent a defensive reaction of the line units to the pressure of overhead controls.

RESIDUES OF DECENTRALIZED STRUCTURE

As activities are centralized at higher and higher levels, residues are left behind. Personnel recruitment and classification may be centralized in a civil service agency, but the establishment of rules governing hours and working conditions may be left to the departments, while bureaus or divisions may continue to conduct training activities. Sometimes there is outright duplication of activity—a new overhead unit is created, but the old units doing the same thing at the lower level are left intact and continue to perform as before, but with additional problems of relationships with the new overhead unit.

INDEPENDENT CHANNELS OF COMMUNICATION

Centralized overhead groups often seek to establish independent channels of communication with the organizational entities they must deal with—that is, with units on the level below. By securing these direct channels, the overhead units can exercise authority over their counterparts more effectively than if communication is indirect. The establishment of departmental personnel offices throughout the Federal government is to a considerable extent the result of efforts of the U. S. Civil Service Commission.

Many other examples can be cited of the same tendency. When the Statistical Standards Division of the U. S. Budget Bureau was charged with execution of the Federal Reports Act of 1942, it immediately sought the creation of statistical standards offices in all agencies affected by the Act. The Administrative Management Division of the U. S. Budget Bureau has constantly urged the creation of its counterparts ("O and M" units) in all departmental budget offices.

Although this pressure from overhead groups for the creation of counterparts at the lower levels is very common, we should also point out that sometimes the creation of counterparts raises the question of the usefulness of the overhead unit. This situation occurs when the overhead organization is justified chiefly as a means for providing better *service* for the line groups. Then, the creation of service units at the lower levels raises the question of the usefulness of the centralized overhead service entity. For example, if a department established a central graphics and art unit for the whole organization, the appearance of graphics units at lower levels might deprive the centralized unit of its function and thus jeopardize its existence. Consequently, the centralized graphics unit would probably resist the creation of its counterpart at lower levels.

NEED FOR LIAISON

Third, lower level units often feel a need to duplicate the overhead specialization either because they do not feel that they are being adequately served by the overhead units, or because they want an officer or a unit to deal with the centralized overhead units at higher levels. The bureau chief may find that the departmental accounting unit fails to supply him with all the accounting data he thinks he needs, or does not transmit accounting reports to him promptly enough. Furthermore, because of the frequent conflict between the overhead unit and the line units, the latter often feel the need for a person "on their side" who is expert in dealing with the overhead units. Overhead units often develop their activity into a real or make-believe technology with a jargon only the initiated can understand—position-classification is a good example. Then, unless the line units can obtain the services of people who have mastered that jargon, they are sorely at a disadvantage in all encounters. After a branch chief has lost some decisions in his dealing with the departmental personnel office because he did not know that an employee who "works under the direction of . . ." can only be classified P-2, while one who "works under the *general* direction of . . ." might rate P-3, he is likely to feel his need for an assistant who knows the difference between such phrases.

Where there is not enough work to justify a counterpart to each of the overhead units, relations with those units may be assigned to an "administrative officer" who then hires specialists, and parcels out the various problems of liaison and negotiation to them. One person may work on clerical personnel actions; another on professional personnel actions; another on supplies and travel. The administrative officer may himself handle budget, and take up personally the knottier negotiations with overhead units.

Conclusion

In this chapter and the proceeding one we have attempted to isolate and describe the principal types of organizational units that are almost always found in large-scale organizations. There are unitary organizations, each of which has its own socially meaningful goal. Unitary organizations are subdivided into components, each of which is usually highly dependent upon the others for carrying out its work, that is, each of which has a low degree of self-containment. On the other hand, unitary organizations are often grouped into larger "federal" aggregates that do not have single well-defined goals. There is a tendency to reduce the self-containment of the unitary components of the federal organizations by establishing overhead units that provide common "services" and apply common "controls" to the unitary organizations. Finally, counterparts to the overhead units spring up at various levels in the structure, serving as "contact points" between the line units to which they are attached and the overhead units.

With this picture of the anatomy of large-scale organizations, we are ready to proceed to a study of the relationships that develop among administrative units in such organizations.

CHAPTER FOURTEEN

✠

Large-Scale Organizations: Intergroup Relations

OUR analysis of the roles of overhead units reveals that, apart from the peculiar beliefs surrounding them, these units create many of the same problems of intergroup relations that exist within complex unitary organizations. In many respects, the problems of relationship between a centralized personnel office and a line organization are the same as the problems of relationship between a Bureau of Areas and a Bureau of Supplies in the Foreign Economic Administration. In both cases, the complex specialization of decision-making functions, and the distribution of responsibility for decisional premises among numerous organizational units create the necessity for cooperation among these units in order that decisions may be taken and the work of the organization accomplished.

The chief distinction between overhead-line relations and relations between components of unitary organizations is that the latter are tempered by the common objective of the unitary organization, and by the common identifications that frequently exist among the personnel of its various parts.

In the present section, we describe the typical relations that exist among organizational units, and include in our discussion both types of relations mentioned above. The discussion will be general, except where it is specifically stated to apply only to overhead-line relations.

Conflict and Cooperation

In our discussion, we will perhaps pay more attention to the causes of disharmony in intergroup relations than to the conditions of harmony. We do not intend to imply by this that disharmony is the rule, and harmony the exception. Certainly there is much harmony between some administrative groups and some harmony among all. Especially when an external danger threatens a whole organization does one find all groups within it pulling together to ward off the danger, even as conflict within a nation diminishes during time of war.

In fact, of course, harmony and disharmony are merely opposite sides of the same coin. To understand the conditions of war is to understand the conditions of peace. If we know under what circumstances conflict is likely to emerge, we will know also what conditions must be satisfied to produce cooperation. Our main justification for focussing attention on conflict situations is that these are easier to observe and document than situations where harmony prevails.

CAUSES OF CONFLICT: EMPIRE BUILDING

By empire building we mean the efforts of organizational entities to enhance their jurisdiction and authority. Usually this also results in increased size—in more positions and consequently better chances of promotion. Members of organizational units usually identify with their unit and its activities. They usually think in terms of maximum achievement of their unit's goals rather than in terms of what other goals could be achieved if they used less of the scarce resources of the organization. Thus, at budget time, each unit of an organization usually tries to get all of the funds it can.

For unitary organizations, interest in achieving a goal is likely to be especially strong. The unit will usually try to acquire what it considers to be a full complement of means for achieving its important goal, including more funds and authority. Conversely, these units are especially touchy about any reduction in funds or authority. They resist any centralizing of their activities in overhead units and keep a very suspicious eye on the activities of such units. They are often resentful of their dependence on overhead units. Feeling that they are responsible for a socially important activity while overhead staff units are not, personnel of these unitary organizations often look down somewhat on members of the overhead units.

The overhead units, on the other hand, also try to increase their authority and prestige, necessarily at the expense of the line units. Overhead personnel feel that their activities take on social meaning through their influence over the line activities possessing socially important goals. As a result, overhead units sometimes acquire activities or controls that are not generally accepted as necessary throughout the organization. This produces resentment on the part of the line groups and further widens the breach between the two.

Empire building is by no means peculiar to the relations between line and overhead units. Power struggles also take place between component parts of unitary organizations, and between unitary organizations whose paths cross. An example of a struggle between the parts of a unitary organization was cited in Chapter 12 —the relationship between the Bureau of Areas and the Bureau of Commodities in the Foreign Economic Administration.

It sometimes happens that two unitary organizations deal with somewhat the same subject matter—or that the accomplishment of the one unitary organization's goals affects the ability of another unitary organization to achieve its goals. Often the two are charged with somewhat incompatible goals by Congress—a reflection of conflicting group values in our society. One such conflicting situation in the national bureaucracy is the conflict between the Army Corps of Engineers and the Bureau of Reclamation in the Interior Department. Both groups, in the course of their respective histories, have staked out claims to jurisdiction over river development activities. When a comprehensive program of development of the Missouri River was proposed to the Congress, a mighty battle marked by attacks, counterattacks, armistices, and treaties ensued between these agencies, each seeking an exclusive or at least a preponderant role in the proposed river development program.

CAUSES OF CONFLICT: DIFFERENCES IN BACKGROUND

Two groups that come in contact may conflict simply because of the different backgrounds of the members of the groups. These conflicts may involve actual conflicts in values or only communication difficulties because of different training and consequently different outlook and terminology. Within a unitary organization, an economics section may have difficulty dealing with a legal section because neither understands the other very well and because the economists have been trained in a scientific outlook while the lawyer's training has emphasized moral and traditional elements. Likewise, line officials may find it difficult to communicate with classification technicians or budget analysts.

Furthermore, it is possible that the preponderant outlook in one group is conservative while that in another is liberal. Thus, if our legal section were conservative and our economic section liberal, conflicts between them in the course of their work would be almost inevitable and certainly keen.

Differences in viewpoint are an important element in the conflict, already mentioned, between the Bureau of Reclamation and the Army Engineers. The Bureau of Reclamation, both by Congressional charge and bureau philosophy, is oriented toward broad, social conservation objectives. The Corps of Engineers is a much more opportunistic organization, which has built its strong political position from its activity in river and harbor improvement, and its consequent relationship to the "pork barrel," local-benefit aspects of Federal appropriations. Although the Bureau of Reclamation has usually had Administration support in its conflicts with the Corps of Engineers, the latter has an almost impregnable political position by virtue of its direct relations with members of the Congress.[1]

CAUSES OF CONFLICT: DIFFERING GROUP IDENTIFICATIONS

Even without differences in background, intergroup conflict would develop simply because of differing group identifications. There is a strong tendency for each group to think that its function is more important to the organization than that of other groups— that is to say, members of an organizational unit tend to identify with that unit. Thus, specialized units within a unitary organization may conflict bitterly because each feels that its point of view is more in harmony with the parent organization's goal than that of the other. Conflicts arising out of differing identifications are often observable in social welfare agencies. Units staffed by social

[1] The situation is very well illustrated by an unpublished case record, prepared for the Committee on Public Administration Cases, which reviews the history of the King's River Project. The Hoover Commission has recommended the transfer of the civilian functions of the Army Engineers to the Interior Department.

workers and having direct contacts with clients tend to be client-oriented; while units responsible for the accounting and auditing functions tend to be taxpayer-oriented.

Since overhead groups work with a number of different line units, there is much less chance that they will identify with any one program. Thus they may advocate moves which, from the standpoint of line personnel who strongly identify with their program, are actually harmful to the program. From the standpoint of line personnel, staff people appear to emphasize administrative means rather than ends—they appear to act, for example, as though the organization were created to further personnel administration, rather than the personnel office created to further the organization's goals. Members of overhead units not identifying with any particular program are likely to give their loyalty to some such concept as "good administration," "efficiency," "personnel science." On the other hand, overhead personnel are likely to accuse line personnel of being provincial, exclusive, stubborn, and unduly possessive of their programs. These differing attitudes are bound to result in a good deal of conflict and mutual suspicion between the two types of units.

Relations of Counterpart Units

The intergroup relations of counterpart units—being in the middle, so to speak, between the tugs and pulls of overhead and line units—are particularly complex. First, there are competing claims to their identifications and loyalties. On the one hand, these units represent specializations for achieving the unitary organization's goals just as do other units of the unitary organization. On the other hand, they are engaged in the same kind of work as the corresponding overhead units and the career lines of their employees generally tie them to those units. The employees of a personnel office in a unitary bureau, for example, are likely to look to the departmental personnel office for their promotional opportunities. Thus, although there are forces that tend to make employees of the counterpart units identify with the unitary organization of which they are a part, there are also forces which tend to make them identify with the corresponding centralized overhead units.

Consequently, personnel in the counterpart units often manifest a divided loyalty that makes them suspect to other members of the unitary organization. These other members expect their budget officer to get the organization what it wants in spite of the central budget office; their personnel officer to get the desired classifications in spite of the classification technicians in the central personnel office. The budget officer in a unitary bureau is faced with the dilemma of either "fighting" for the bureau's budget and encountering the displeasure of budget officers at higher levels, or of seeking to temper the budget demands of his line unit, and encountering the displeasure of his superiors in that unit.

The struggle for the loyalties of counterpart personnel often centers on the issue of "who is to be permitted to communicate with whom." The personnel office in a department, for example, will insist on direct lines of communication with the personnel officers of the unitary bureaus. The bureau chiefs, on the other hand, may insist that all such contacts should channel through themselves—or at least that their personnel officers should communicate with the departmental personnel office only by permission or delegation of the bureau chief.

. The struggle for control of the channels of communications becomes even more complicated when there are several layers of overhead units above the level of the unitary organization. The resulting complications are well illustrated by the experience of the rationing branches of the Office of Price Administration. In general, these branches were the unitary organizations within OPA, and the units above the branch level were considered by the branches to be overhead.

Direct contact between the rationing branches and the OPA Printing Branch (which actually placed printing contracts) were opposed by the Printing Coordination Branch, an overhead unit in the Rationing Department, which claimed the right to "exclusive contact" with the Printing Branch. Another rationing overhead unit, the Administrative Services Division, tried to be the exclusive contact with the OPA Personnel, Budget, and Administrative Services Divisions (overhead units at the agency level). The rationing Statistical Division (earlier a branch, still earlier a section) insisted upon exclusive contact with the OPA Statistical Standards Office; and that Office insisted upon exclusive contact with the Statistical Standards Division in the Bureau of the Budget.

The result of the "exclusive contact" system was that the rationing product was "sold" by less and less experienced salesmen, or else that branch personnel had to educate several different reviewing levels concerning the same subject. The branch person responsible for obtaining clearance knew all about the material being cleared. He had helped develop it. But the person involved at the first reviewing point explained it to the one above, and so on. The explanation became less expert and more garbled at each step. Frequently, the final reviewing point had questions that would come down through the same channels to the branch expert and answers that would go back up the same way, with tremendous loss of time. Sometimes, the branch expert would get permission to go along with the "exclusive contacter" and explain the material personally. Sometimes, one of the higher clearance points would call the branch expert directly to get an answer. This was generally frowned upon by the intermediate "exclusive contact" points— as was a call by the branch expert directly to the higher clearance point, unless prior permission was obtained from the intermediate points.

Because of the necessity of the situation, because it was actually impossible to prevent direct contacts skipping the intermediate levels, and because neither the clearance officers in the Budget Bureau and other central clearance points nor the branch personnel were impressed by the need for "exclusive contact," the procedure was frequently ignored in practice. Near the end of the rationing program, both the rationing Statistical Division and the OPA Office of Statistical Standards were abolished.[2]

Special Aspects of Overhead Review

Although we have seen that there are conflicts between all kinds of organizational units, there are special aspects in overhead-line relationships that make these relationships frequently productive of conflict.

OVERHEAD SPECIALIZATIONS NOT FULLY ACCEPTED

In the first place, the specializations represented in overhead units are frequently of a kind that is not fully accepted as valid and

---

[2] This example is taken, with some abridgement, from Thompson, *The Regulatory Process in OPA Rationing*, chap. 10.

scientific. Few of these specializations correspond to established bodies of scientific knowledge. Consequently, standards and controls imposed by overhead units are not as acceptable to most persons as are the standards on controls of a generally accepted scientific discipline. Personnel management and budgeting are less well established sciences—if, indeed, they are sciences at all—than engineering or medicine.

It is often hard to make a line officer believe that the personnel expert actually has a fund of real knowledge that the line officer does not possess; or that an overhead unit can construct forms better than his own subordinates; or that he and his subordinates do not know as much about publicity as the central information office; or that some person in the central congressional liaison office can sell his program to congressmen better than he can. With the correctness of these doubts we are not concerned. The important fact is that they exist, and that they induce resistance to overhead controls.

REVIEW FOR COMPETENCE

In the second place, it is often hard for the overhead specialist, reviewing a decision made in a line unit, to distinguish between the correctness of the decision from the point of view of his technical specialty, and the general competence of the decision.

Whenever an overhead unit is given the function of reviewing the work of line units to see that it is good work, or whenever its specialized review strays over into the area of general competence, there is bound to be a strong reaction. The line group is bound to question the ability of the overhead group to improve its work. The line group is apt to feel that if the overhead group actually has more skilled personnel, these should be reassigned to the units where the work is done in the first place. If the overhead groups are *not* more skilled, how is the review justified?

A good example of review for competence in the Federal government is the review of all public reporting forms by the Statistical Standards Division of the Budget Bureau. This division not only reviews forms to see whether the information requested is already available in the files of some other agency; it also reviews the forms from the standpoint of their "technical adequacy." In the words of the Budget Bureau:

Careful attention is also given to the content and technical adequacy of a form. The instructions and questions must be concise and clear. The format must be simple and easy for the respondent to follow. The data must be presented in such a manner that the tabulation process is made easy. They must also conform to customary business practice in record-keeping.[3]

This review is quite irritating to the line organizations of the Federal bureaucracy. When a form leaves one of the agencies, it has been reviewed by all the relevant specialized units within the agency. It is a group product. On the other hand, as is the usual practice in overhead reviewing organizations, review in the Statistical Standards Division is by one person to whom review of all the forms of that agency has been assigned as his particular function. It is rather obvious that he will not know more than the combined specialists of the agency about such things as those listed in the quotation above.[4] The Hoover Commission has recommended that the Statistical Standards Division's authority be increased and that it intensify its reviewing efforts both in coordinating federal statistical activities and in improving their technical adequacy.[5]

Often the creation of a new overhead unit or the centralizing of some activity results more from empire building than from a widespread feeling throughout the organization that the new overhead unit or new centralization meets an actual, felt organizational need. If such is the case, as it often is, many units within the organization never accept the new overhead unit.

ENFORCEMENT OF OVERHEAD CONTROLS

A third aspect of the conflict between line and overhead relates to the fact that overhead units nearly always have some police

[3] *Two Years of Progress under the Federal Reports Act, Report of the U. S. Budget Bureau to the Senate Committee to Study Problems of American Small Business,* 79th Cong., 1st Sess., Report No. 47, Part 2, p. 5. For a more extended treatment of forms review by the Statistical Standards Division, see Thompson, op. cit., chap. 9.

[4] We should emphasize that here we are discussing only review for competence ("technical adequacy"). Central forms review may also be for the purpose of avoiding duplicating or contradictory statistical activities, and if standards or uniform methods are desired, they can be developed and enforced by a central overhead organization such as the Budget Bureau.

[5] *Report on Budgeting and Accounting,* pp. 30–1, and pp. 91–7.

functions. Regardless of the merits of the standards enforced by overhead units, it is quite natural that organizations resent having them imposed. Most people resent being ordered around, investigated, and punished. Although a counterpart group in a line organization, such as a personnel section, also enforces its specialized decisional premises upon the other specialized groups in the organization, this group is thought of as "one of the family," whereas the overhead unit is an "outsider."

Relations Between Central Offices and Field Units

Central-field relations are often discussed as a very distinct and separate set of administrative problems. When we examine these relations in the light of our previous discussion, we see that they are really exceptional in only one respect—the fact of actual geographical separation. The lack of face-to-face relationships does pose special problems. The telephone and the memorandum are not substitutes for the conference in ironing out differences and securing group decisions.

Beyond the special problems of spatial separation, which we have already treated in Chapter 10, central-field relations are strikingly simular to overhead-line relations. In this section we will examine this parallelism between the two phenomena.

Field offices distributed over the geographical area in which service is provided are an essential feature of many governmental activities. Examples in large cities are fire companies and district police stations. In state government, field offices are often established for welfare activities, state institutions are distributed widely throughout the state, and large cities are often serviced by branch offices of the major departments. In the Federal government, the vast bulk of civilian employees—more than four fifths of them, in fact—are located outside Washington. The largest field service here is the Post Office, numbering almost a half million employees, but the majority of Federal departments or bureaus have one or more sets of field offices covering some or all of their activities.

THE CENTRAL OFFICE AS "OVERHEAD"

There is a considerable tendency for each field office, or for each unit within a field office dealing with a single socially meaningful program, to regard itself as a unitary organization. Each region may have its own peculiar problems and the personnel of the regional office will be much more sensitive than will the central office personnel to the demands of regional client groups and interests. If these pulls are strong enough—and particularly if the problems differ significantly from region to region—the personnel of the field office may acquire a much stronger identification with the regional than with the national program.

When the field offices develop strong local identifications, the whole central office may be regarded by them more as a group of overhead units than as line units. The regional director will feel responsible to the head of the central office, but not to the various specialized units in the central office. The field office will look upon itself as a major subdivision of the organization, on a par with, and not subordinate to, the subdivisions located at headquarters. Moreover, the field office is apt to consider itself the most important subdivision—it does the actual work of the agency.

Just as myths have developed to explain the authority exercised by overhead over line units, so myths have developed to explain the authority of specialized headquarters units over field offices and to reconcile that authority with the doctrine of unity of command. It is said that these various units in the central office provide "technical supervision" to field offices, while "administrative direction" comes directly from the head of the central office to the regional directors and hence on down to his subordinates. Realistically speaking, of course, "technical supervision" involves just as much real authority as does the "advice" provided by staff units, or the "serice" given by auxiliary units. The very fact that conflict frequently arises between "technical" instructions and "administrative" instructions demonstrates the authoritative character of both. The plain fact of the matter is that field personnel receive commands from many sources besides their immediate "administrative" superiors—unity of command is actually not observed.

TENDENCIES TOWARD CENTRALIZATION

To the extent that each field office behaves like a separate unitary organization, we can regard the central office staff in the same light as any other set of overhead units. As in the relations between overhead and line units in federal organizations, central office units usually try to restrict the discretion of field offices. There are constant efforts on the part of these central units to impose more and more standards of decision upon field offices in the form of voluminous instructions. The results are that fewer and fewer areas of decision are left to the final discretion of field offices, and administrative discretion is increasingly centralized in the central office.

As in the case of centralization within the central office, so centralization as between field and central offices usually reaches an equilibrium. Field offices usually get enough local political support to keep the process from going all the way (in fact, increased local interest may occasionally reverse the process), and the results of attempting complete central office government sometimes become so glaringly unsatisfactory as to stop the process.

Central office units urge that further controls over field offices are necessary to secure "uniform application of the law." Here our legal institutions come to the aid of further centralization with the notion of "a government of laws, and not of men." This notion, and its corollary centralization of controls in the central office, is quite inconsistent with one of the principal reasons for establishing field offices in the first place. This reason is to achieve expertness in the local factors affecting decisions. Field officers are, among other things, specialists in local conditions. Thus, as soon as a principal purpose of field offices begins to bear fruit—that is, as soon as administrative decisions start to reflect local peculiarities and hence cease to be nationally uniform—this desired result becomes the occasion for urging a reduction of field office discretion. We are torn between two desires. We want government to recognize individual differences and peculiarities; but we also want "evenhanded justice."

INDEPENDENT CHANNELS OF COMMUNICATION

When specialized units in the central office come to be regarded as overhead units, this leads in turn to the almost inevitable growth within the field offices of counterparts to these specialized overhead units. Overhead units try to get an officer or unit corresponding to them established in each field office. Then each major central office unit has some person or group in the field office working on its program exclusively, and it can write instructions or plan programs for that group and increase its influence upon operations by its direct line of communication.

As a counterweight to this centrifugal tendency, there is sometimes established in the central office a "bureau of field operations" claiming the right to exclusive contact with the field offices, and attempting to weaken or destroy the independent line of communications established by other central office units with the field. Naturally, resistance to a bureau of field operations is strong among the other specialists in the central office—it being a troublesome restriction upon their authority. The regional director is likely to look upon the establishment of such a bureau with mixed feelings. On the one hand, it strengthens his own position by limiting the right of his subordinates to communicate with the central office. On the other hand, it limits his own right to communicate directly with the head of the agency, or with specialized units in the central office.

FIELD OFFICES IN HOLDING-COMPANY DEPARTMENTS

The pattern of central-field relationships will also be affected to a considerable degree by the relationship between the field organization and the level of integration. The most common scheme is for each unitary organization to have its own field service—the Forest Service, for example, has a number of regional offices, each, in turn, having jurisdiction over a number of National Forests; and each of the National Forests being divided into a number of forest districts.[6]

Sometimes, however, a single field service is established for a holding company department that is made up of a number of unitary components. There is a single field service, for example, for the Federal Security Administration, covering among other things public health, old age assistance, aid to dependent children, aid to the blind, retirement insurance, and unemployment compensation. Even before this centralized field service was established, the Social

---

[6] It is instructive to note that recent proposals for unification of bureau-field services in the Department of the Interior are hinged on the assumption that the department is shifting from a holding-company to a unitary status through the emergence of the socially meaningful goal of "resource development." See Alfred C. Wolf, "The Blending of Area and Function," *Public Administration Review* 9:282–9 (Autumn 1949).

Security Board had always had a single field service covering the various unitary organizations under its jurisdiction.

In this case—when the field service is attached to a federal organization—the field offices themselves will take on the character of federal or holding-company units. Thus each regional office of the Social Security Board was a miniature replica of the Washington office, and the regional units dealing with the several programs under the Board's jurisdiction showed the same centrifugal tendencies as did the program units in the Washington office.

Under these circumstances there is a strong tendency for the field office to fall into fragments, each fragment attaching itself to its corresponding unitary organization in the central office. The Old Age and Survivor's Insurance units, for example, in Social Security field offices always showed a strong tendency to consider themselves as field units for the Old Age and Survivor's Bureau in the Washington office, and to resist attempts at regional "coordination." Personnel, budgeting, and administrative services units in the regional offices were treated by the program units more like overhead than like counterpart units. Even the regional director was often regarded by the regional program units as an overhead "coordinator" rather than a link in the chain of communications and authority leading upward to the central office.

The actual experience with Federal field organization verifies the expectations we would derive from our general theory that conflict and complexity in administrative relationships arise when field offices are attached to federal rather than to unitary organizations. All the informal forces in such organizations conspire to break down the solidarity of the field office and to reestablish direct relationships between the program units in the field and the unitary organizations in the central office. The program units in the field experience the same conflicting pulls upon their loyalties as are experienced by counterpart units.

COMPETITION FOR LOYALTIES OF FIELD PERSONNEL

We have now seen that where the central office contains a number of unitary organizations or a number of overhead units, each of these will seek to gain control over its particular aspect of field operations. Part of the struggle is centered upon the formal organizational structure. As a first choice, each sizeable unit in the central office will seek to establish its own separate field service, responsible only to it. If it cannot get separate field offices established, it tries at least to get a unit in each field office that works exclusively on its program and to establish direct channels of communication with these units.

When the specialized headquarters units are unsuccessful in obtaining satisfactory formal structural arrangements, they may use other means to increase their influence upon operations. If they are required to deal with the field through a bureau of field operations, they will constantly badger this overhead office to see that their instructions are vigorously enforced on the field office.

Beyond and in addition to all these various attempts to secure and increase influence over field offices, headquarters units engage in a constant process of trying to capture the loyalty of their counterparts in the field. These field personnel are periodically called in to the central office, partly for instruction on new matters, but even more to be subjected to propaganda designed to win their loyalty. Dinners and parties are arranged for them when they come to headquarters, and they are addressed by high central office executives, the administrator if possible.

Headquarters units with field counterparts usually either maintain a corps of travelling ambassadors called "field men" who constantly travel in the field, or else their regular staff makes periodic visits to counterparts in field offices.[7] The ostensible purpose of this travelling is to instruct, but there can be little doubt that the chief purpose is to capture the loyalty of field counterparts. When the method of the professional travelling ambassador or field man is employed, little instruction can take place, because these men usually know little if any more about central office thinking than field office personnel themselves. However, the travelling field man can do tremendous service in creating and maintaining loyalty to the central office unit. If strong loyalty of this kind can be manufactured and maintained, other formal arrangements are relatively unimportant—the central office unit will enjoy a preponderance of influence in field office affairs.

In summary let us say that when one understands the relations between line and overhead units, he also understands the problem of central-field relations. Solutions for these problems are essen-

---

[7] See William D. Carey, "Control and Supervision of Field Offices," *Public Administration Review* 6:20-4 (Winter, 1946).

tially the same. The same kinds of hopes and expectations, the same kinds of indignations and frustrations, are involved.

Conclusion

It may be well at this point to repeat our opening remark: we do not mean to assert, simply because we have focussed attention on conflict situations, that administration is nothing more than a continuous battle among contending groups. But if conflict has occupied a disproportionate amount of our attention, it also occupies a disproportionate amount of the attention of administrators. The matters that flow smoothly and without conflict require much less of the effort of administrators, and particularly of top administrators, than do the disagreements and failures of cooperation.

Anyone who has participated in large-scale organizations is aware that conflict and the resolution of conflict are major facts of everyday experience. The frustration of unitary organizations lacking unchecked authority to carry out the programs for which they feel responsible; and the frustration of overhead units, separated by the line units from the socially important goals of government which they seek to influence—these frustrations have as their common product the activity known as empire building. Each unit seeks, by reaching out and absorbing functions and controls, to grasp within its own hands the powers it feels necessary to accomplish a socially useful task.

We should also warn the reader not to regard conflict as necessarily or inherently bad. Conflict may be the means for bringing to bear on individual decisions a wide range of specialized competences. It may also be the means for bringing into the view of high level administrators, of legislators, and the public basic issues of public policy that need resolution. It may prevent these issues from being decided anonymously at obscure levels of the bureaucracy, and hence may be an important means of securing democratic control.

CHAPTER FIFTEEN

✺

Selection of the Team: Civil Service and Recruitment

THERE are a number of important aspects of organization that are usually discussed under the heading of "personnel administration." In a broad sense, since all administration is concerned with people and their behavior, all administration might properly be described as personnel administration—and some specialists in personnel work would like to use this broad definition of their specialty. In actual practice the personnel specialist is concerned with a more limited range of matters—with matters, however, that are of the greatest long range importance to the organization. Personnel administration in this narrower sense deals principally with the recruitment of employees for organization positions (including promotions and transfers from one position to another), with the separation of employees from the organization by retirement, dismissal, or resignation, with the training of employees, with their salaries and wages, and with their health, safety, and welfare.

In this book no attempt will be made to treat in detail the techniques of personnel administration. A whole separate profession has developed around these techniques, and even an elementary treatment of them would require an entire volume. What is important for our purposes is to understand what part personnel administration plays in the overall picture of organization and what guides can be derived for basic personnel policies from a study of general administrative theory. Thus, we will want to know what role testing methods play in the selection of personnel, and what the purposes of testing procedures are, but we will not need to concern ourselves with the technical aspects of the construction and use of tests—matters that are best left to the personnel technician.

The narrower the "area of acceptance" within which employees can be ordered, directed, and controlled—and the previous chapters have shown that the limits of acceptance of direct organizational influences may be narrow indeed—the more important become the long-term influences that are exercised through selection and training processes. In the short run, the organization must work with the personnel it has. It can do only those things that its employees can be ordered, persuaded, or motivated to do and that they have the understanding and skill to do. In the long run, the organization can change its whole character by its control over the admission of new employees and over the processes that gradually condition them during the period they are in it.

These long-term influences are of particular importance in relation to those employees who hold positions of administrative responsibility. Direct organizational influences are at their weakest at these higher organizational levels. There is the constant danger that too close and too direct supervision will destroy initiative and swallow up the energies of administrators. To the greatest extent possible, it is necessary that administrators be "self-starters," possessing within themselves the knowledge and organizational identification that will make them active rather than passive participants. Hence, particular attention will be paid in this chapter to the effect of personnel processes upon employees who occupy administrative posts.

Problems of Recruitment

For reasons that will become clear as the discussion proceeds, the recruitment of new employees from outside an agency cannot be discussed without considering also the promotion of employees within the agency. Hence, the term "recruitment" will be used here, somewhat more broadly than usual, to refer to both of these processes.

Because recruitment for the government service must be related to its political setting, it is a far more complicated matter than recruitment for positions in private business. In the first place, government agencies in the United States are only now emerging from a period when political patronage or "spoils" dominated government employment. In some areas—including the portion of Federal employment that is covered by civil service—political recruitment has been virtually eliminated. In some city and state governments—and in most county agencies—the spoils system is still firmly entrenched.

In the second place, government employment methods must take into account the demand for "equality of employment opportunity" that derives from our democratic institutions. "Equality" means many things to many groups. In general, it means that selection should be on the basis of merit, and hence the demand for equality is inimical to the spoils principle.

A third special problem of public recruitment is the existence of conflicting demands that particular groups be given preference when they seek government employment. It is argued that veterans have a specific claim on their country for their services, or that local jobs should be reserved for local boys, or that positions in the Federal service should be allocated geographically, or that particular racial or religious groups should be employed in proportion to their numbers in the population.

To argue that if public agencies must adapt themselves to these political conditions they cannot be expected to operate as efficiently as business organizations is probably true—at least to an extent. But true or not, it is irrelevant. The fact remains that public administration is a part of the political process. To be sure, there has been growing acceptance of the idea that the responsibilities of government today can be properly discharged only if jobs are filled on the basis of merit. Tremendous progress has been made during the past fifty years toward the elimination of spoils. Whether the demand for other types of limitations—veterans' preference, for example—will similarly yield to the requirements of efficiency is much more doubtful. In any event, the issue involves questions of basic political values, and the decision is not likely to be entrusted to the administrator.[1]

[1] It should be pointed out that private business is not by any means completely devoted to appointment on the basis of efficiency. The relatives of executives, and even of other employees, are often favored for employment and promotion. Many business concerns deprive themselves of the services of able persons through racial and religious discrimination, and bitterly oppose attempts to impose upon them legal requirements of "equality of opportunity."

The Merit Principle

The primary goal of civil service reform in this country has been office-holding according to merit—the appointment to each public position of the candidate best qualified to fill it. This goal is a reflection, in turn, of certain widely held values in our society: (1) that in the administrative branch, employees should be concerned with the efficiency of government service, and that the competence of employees is a major determinant of the level of efficiency that will be attained; (2) that employees of the administrative branch are not concerned with matters of "policy"—i.e., basic value questions—and hence, that the civil service can and should be politically neutral; and (3) that the economic opportunities of government employment should be accessible to all citizens without favor.

A merit system is designed to secure these qualities in the civil service:

competence—so that government will be served with trained skill and intelligence;

neutrality—so that the administrative branch will carry out the political will of the legislative body, and not impose its own;

equality of opportunity—so that governmental institutions will contribute toward economic democracy.

COMPETENCE

The objective of securing for government competent, competitively selected civil servants is a corollary, of course, of the criterion of efficiency. If governmental services are to be provided without waste, then it is important that government employ the most skillful people available. Implicit in this objective is the assumption that the goals of government are given—that the task of the administrative branch is to take given value premises (the declarations of legislative policy) and use the resources of government to reach them. If administrative employees decide only questions of fact (questions of how to realize values), then we will want to have employees qualified to deal correctly with factual issues (we will seek expertness and skill).

If, on the contrary, we admit that the civil servant has discretion over many value questions as well as factual questions, the concept of "competence" becomes hazy. In this case, we have to take account not only of differences among candidates in skill or intelligence, but also differences in their attitudes toward the policy questions that lie within their discretion. Hence, the proposition that civil servants should be selected on the basis of competence rests on the prior assumption that civil servants can and should be "neutral" on questions of value. The assumption of neutrality will be examined further in the next section.

Even if we admit that civil servants can and should be neutral, we still have the problem of testing for competence. Do we possess the technical means for determining which of several candidates will actually be the most competent employee? Without valid testing methods, the merit principle is simply a statement of good intentions, lacking any means of attainment.

On its positive side, the merit principle requires that methods be discovered for selecting employees on the basis of competence. On its negative side, the principle requires methods for preventing considerations *other than competence* from entering into the selection process. One important part of eliminating these other considerations in selection is the elimination of party spoils. But spoils are not the whole story. Whenever a subjective element of whatever sort enters into the selection process, there is a danger that other factors than competence will be considered. Objective methods for testing administrative ability are so inadequate at the present time that no sensible person would rely entirely upon them in filling an important executive position. Often, personal acquaintance or recommendation from a reliable professional source are better indications of competence than any test. But if personal judgment of this kind is to be admitted, what is to prevent its abuse? Will not loyalty to friends or the "school tie" spirit inevitably warp judgement? If so, we cannot be sure that the most competent will be selected or that there will be real equality of opportunity. This problem, too, must be kept in mind as we examine the selection process.

NEUTRALITY

The goal of neutrality stems from the traditional distinction between "politics" and "administration"—from the assumption that the civil servant does not make value judgements but only carries out the politically formulated "will of the state." The assumption that neutrality is either desirable or attainable in the civil service has been challenged on several grounds.

The Argument for Program Loyalty. Defenders of the spoils system, as well as many proponents of the merit principle, have argued that those who carry out policy should be sympathetic supporters of the legislative program. This argument is often used in opposition to the extension of civil service coverage to the top positions in the administrative hierarchy. Even if it is admitted— and we will see that the proposition is debatable—that employees in the lower ranks of the civil service exercise little discretion over "policy," the heads of major organizational units one or two steps below the chief executive certainly have important policy-making functions. For this reason, the secretaries, undersecretaries, assistant secretaries, and many of the bureau chiefs have always been exempted from the provisions of the Federal civil service law.

The real question is: at what point shall we draw the line? Is the element of discretion over policy sufficiently important in the job of a city department head to justify excluding him from civil service procedures? What about a Federal bureau chief or the heads of the principal divisions in a bureau? Should distinctions be made on the basis of the controversial or noncontroversial nature of the work of the organization unit? Since there is no simple answer to these questions, there is room for much debate as to what positions should be included in the civil service.

Few voices are heard today openly advocating that all governmental positions should be awarded on the basis of party loyalty, although in fact, of course, many government jurisdictions are still operated largely on the spoils principle. An interesting suggestion— arising out of the early experience of New Deal agencies that were not at first subject to civil service—has been that positions might be filled on the basis of both party loyalty *and* competence. That is, employees could be appointed on the basis of competence from among those who obtained clearance from the party organization. This plan was actually used in some New Deal agencies where the Democratic Party set up its own informal examining system for choosing among candidates who were politically acceptable.

How, under favorable conditions, a mixed patronage-merit

system might operate is well described by Paul Appleby in reporting the experience of the Civilian Conservation Corps:

It was his (the Chief of the Forest Service) duty to make sure the CCC was
staffed with the same kind of personnel as the Forest Service and managed
in the same way. He immediately proposed to the Secretary a departmental order providing for this, voluntarily extending Civil Service coverage to the new agency. This made it possible to get a skeletal structure
and personnel for which the Chief could accept responsibility. After the
beginning had been well made, I called in Major Stuart, the Chief of the
Forest Service, and proposed that he now help us out of our political
trouble. To persuade him I had to make it easy. I asked him to locate in
the new set-up one hundred jobs which could be filled just as well as not
from lists of politically endorsed persons, provided the lists were long
enough. "You set up the requirements," I told him; "you determine what
jobs are to be so filled; you fix the required qualifications. You can be assured that you and not the politicians will actually select the individuals—
the politicians will make the lists but you will choose the particular men.
You can require lists as long as you want. If you don't find a satisfactory
man in a given list, we'll call for more lists, with as many names as you
want." It took two or three weeks to persuade him and to work out the
arrangement. But it proved to be so satisfactory that the Forest Service
voluntarily extended the system to cover several thousand CCC jobs.
With some variations, this became the departmental system for obtaining
personnel for new, non-Civil Service agencies. In order to persuade Major
Stuart, I had stumbled upon principles that now seem to me to be of basic
importance in handling patronage where patronage has to be handled.
The responsible administrators should determine what jobs are of the
type that require only simple qualifications and where, consequently, controlled patronage will not result in deterioration of personnel.
The responsible administrators—not the politicians—must select the
specific people who are employed.[2]

The Problem of Job Security. One problem that would have to
be faced in abandoning the principle of neutrality would be the
security of employees already in office at the time of a change in
party control. A vital argument against political clearance has
been that persons of ability will avoid the public service if their job
security depends on the fate of a political party. On the other hand,
if political clearance is required only for appointments to vacancies,

---

[2] Paul Appleby, *Big Democracy*. (New York: Alfred A. Knopf, Inc., 1945),
pp. 151–2.

how will the sympathy of the public employees whom a party "inherits" when it comes into power be assured for the program of that party?

We are caught, therefore, on the horns of a dilemma. If neutrality is undesirable, then political clearance should be required of all employees—old as well as new. But if this is done, government employment will become highly insecure, and the competence of the public service will suffer.

This difficulty does not arise when a change in administration brings into existence new government programs with new agencies to administer them, as was the case in the national government after 1932. As a matter of fact, it has been argued—although there is little tangible evidence on the point—that the desire for civil servants sympathetic to the New Deal was one of the principal reasons why the Democratic administration preferred not to entrust the old-line agencies with the administration of the new legislation. When a new administration establishes new programs and new agencies, the preferability of a strict merit system over a system requiring political clearance is far from clear.

Still another view is taken by some observers (Harold Laski was a well-known example), who argue that while neutrality is possible and even desirable so long as the party issues involve only minor changes in government policy, a corps of civil servants could probably not be trusted by a new administration committed to a program basically different from that which had prevailed previously. Thus, Laski questioned whether the British civil service could or would serve loyally a Labor government. This proposition is being tested at the present time.[3]

Party Affiliation and Program Loyalty. This distinction leads to yet another line of thought. The argument in favor of party clearance and against neutrality assumes that a person's sympathies with a governmental program can be tested by his party affiliation. This assumption is hardly tenable under the conditions of the American two-party system. Since each of the major parties is a collection of diverse, and often hostile, political groups, there is very little assurance that the persons put in office through a system of patronage will be sympathetic with all or most parts of the pro-

---

[3] See Friedrich, *Constitutional Government and Democracy* (Boston: Ginn & Co., 1946), chap. 19; also, Herman Finer, *Theory and Practice of Modern Government* (Rev. ed., New York: Henry Holt & Co., 1949), pp. 871–85.

gram of the party in power, or even that they will have any particular political philosophy at all.

Under these circumstances, if patronage is to be a reward for loyalty to a party organization, it cannot always be at the same time a reward for loyalty to a particular political program. The "organization stalwarts" whose loyalty is most often rewarded by office are usually persons for whom the goal of party success takes precedence over loyalty to any particular governmental program. Under these conditions, it is not surprising that Jesse Jones, violently opposed to most of the New Deal philosophy, could be placed and maintained in the directorship of the Reconstruction Finance Corporation—an organization that was expected to operate as an essential part of the New Deal administrative mechanism. Nor is it unexpected that patronage positions should be reserved in agencies like the Post Office, whose activities have no discernable relation to party issues, quite as often as they are reserved in politically oriented agencies.[4]

Allegiance to party is not the only source of an employee's value premises. In the American public service, professional allegiances have probably been far more important than party affiliation in determining attitudes toward policy. Agriculture, the labor movement, the personnel movement—these and many others have had their particular ideologies and have indoctrinated their respective professional groups with these ideologies. To the extent that American government agencies have been oriented toward interest groups or groups of "clients," and to the extent that they have been staffed by the members of particular professions, these group and professional allegiances have supplied many important value premises to administrative decisions. In this respect, the American civil service has been far from neutral, and civil service

[4] In 1938, of 25 Federal bureau chiefs whose selection was not subject to a formal merit system, six had been selected on a political basis. These were in the Bureau of Internal Revenue, the Bureau of Customs, the Treasurer, the Bureau of the Mint, the General Land Office, and the Bureau of Fisheries. Of these, only the last two are in agencies where the policy views of the bureau chief might conceivably affect the agency's program to any significant extent. On the other hand, the chiefs of such agencies as the Bureau of Reclamation, Bureau of Foreign and Domestic Commerce, the Children's Bureau, the Women's Bureau, the Conciliation Service, the Office of Education, the Wage and Hour Division, the Bureau of Immigration and Naturalization, the Bureau of Indian Affairs, and the Division of Grazing had all apparently been selected on a non-political basis. Arthur W. Macmahon and John D. Millett, *Federal Administrators* (New York: Columbia University Press, 1939), chaps. 21–4.

procedures, insofar as they have reinforced professional standards, have actually been opposed to neutrality.[5]

Summary. In conclusion, the traditional argument for neutrality assumes that the civil servant is a mere agent who carries out a policy formulated by the legislature. Even if this assumption is false—as it certainly is if interpreted strictly—an attempt to secure the sympathy of civil servants to the program of the dominant party would make difficult the creation of careers in the public service. Moreover, patronage as it operates in the American party system would not necessarily guarantee loyalty to a program.

EQUALITY OF OPPORTUNITY

Since about one-tenth of the employed population in the United States works for government, the opportunity to compete for public employment is an important economic right. The development of a government career service based upon the merit principle has been generally considered a valuable guarantee of this right.

The Jacksonian Theory. But this is not the only way of viewing the matter. The first thorough-going Federal spoils system—that of Andrew Jackson—was instituted partly on equalitarian grounds. In arguing in his first annual message, for a principle of rotation in office, he said:

> Office is considered as a species of property, and government rather as a means of promoting individual interests than as an instrument created solely for the service of the people. Corruption in some and in others a perversion of correct feelings and principles divert government from its legitimate ends and make it an engine for the support of the few at the expense of the many. The duties of all public officers are, or at least admit

[5] Macmahon and Millett's data show the importance of clientele and professional allegiances in the selection of Federal bureau chiefs. The Department of Agriculture yields numerous examples of professional, as opposed to "organizational," careers—many of the bureau chiefs had had extensive experience outside the department in state agencies and universities. The head of the Women's Bureau had had extensive early experience as a labor organizer; the Commissioner of Education had been a city school superintendent; the head of the U. S. Employment Service had had social work experience; the chief of the Bureau of Indian Affairs had been executive secretary of the Indian Defense Association; the Commissioner of Patents had long been in private patent practice; the head of the Bureau of Marine Inspection and Navigation had held responsible executive positions in the shipbuilding industry. Ibid.

of being made, so plain and simple that men of intelligence may readily qualify themselves for their performance; and I can not but believe that more is lost by the long continuance of men in office than is generally to be gained by their experience. . . .

In a country where offices are created solely for the benefit of the people no one man has any more intrinsic right to official station than another. Offices were not established to give support to particular men at the public expense.[6]

The Jacksonian theory was hostile to any great separation of the civil service from the general body of citizens, either by long-term careers in government or by the selection of public employees from a special segment of the population. Jackson relied on rotation in office to prevent the rise of an anti-democratic professional bureaucracy.

Today, there is little inclination to accept Jackson's thesis that rotation in office protects equality of opportunity. The need for competence in the public service, already discussed, has convinced most people that rotation in office would be incredibly wasteful, if not entirely impossible. Instead, it is argued that the merit principle itself is the most democratic basis for a civil service.

Possibilities of Favoritism. Nevertheless, all doubts have not been quieted. It has already been noted that it is very difficult to apply an objective, competitive principle to the higher administrative, scientific, and technical positions in the public service because of the lack of valid testing methods. As a result, there cannot be any doubt that even in the Federal service "amicism"—the reliance on personal friendship and recommendation—plays a highly important part in appointments to these higher positions. This does not result primarily from the desire of administrators to establish personal patronage systems but from their very understandable reluctance to rely on imperfect testing methods for selecting subordinates who will be charged with the execution of large and complex programs.[7]

[6] James D. Richardson, ed., *A Compilation of the Messages and Papers of the Presidents* (2nd ed., Washington: Bureau of National Literature, 1913), vol. 2, p. 1012.

[7] The following two examples cited by Macmahon and Millett are typical of this process, which occurs at both high and low levels:

a. "(William H. McReynolds) was taken into the new established Farm Credit Administration as director of personnel.

"When the Governor of the Farm Credit Administration, Henry Morgenthau, Jr., was appointed Under-Secretary of the Treasury in December, 1933, he took

Equality of Opportunity. A second type of doubt arises from the fact that, in a society where opportunities for education are far from equal, appointment by examination gives every advantage to those who have had such opportunities. Partly for this reason, Congress has insisted that, in general, positions in the Federal service should be apportioned on the basis of the populations of the several states; while a number of state legislatures have forbidden the requirement of formal education for eligibility to state and local civil service positions. To be sure, some of this opposition to the merit principle has stemmed from ideas of patronage —geographical if not partisan. But it also reflects a genuine suspicion as to whether a civil service whose higher officials are drawn largely from the college-educated population will be truly democratic.

The British civil service provides a case in point. Traditionally, the top administrative positions have been filled on the basis of competitive examinations designed to select the best products of the English universities—students who came almost exclusively from the "public" (actually private) secondary schools. As a result, these positions have in the past been almost entirely closed to the "lower classes" and the British civil service has been a faithful reproduction of the class structure of the society in which it operates.[8]

The "Reward" Philosophy. A somewhat different objection to the strict application of the merit system is reflected in demands that positions in the public service be used as "rewards" for particular groups in the population. During the depression of the 1930's there was widespread feeling, often enacted into state and local laws, that "local jobs should go to local boys." Of a similar character is the demand that veterans be given special preference in appointments to the public service. Veterans' preference laws of

McReynolds with him as his assistant. A month later Morgenthau became the Secretary of the Treasury and McReynolds was formally attached to the office of the Secretary as Administrative Assistant." Op. cit., pp. 27–8.

b. "Burlew became a confidential clerk to the new Postmaster General, Will H. Hays. He was retained in a similar capacity by Dr. Hubert Work, and when Dr. Work was appointed Secretary of the Interior in 1923, he took Burlew to his new assignment with him." Op. cit., p. 30.

[8] Correspondingly, the weakening of the British class structure, hastened by World War II and the accession of a Labor government, is bringing about fundamental changes in the structure of the civil service. It is too early to forecast the ultimate scope and exact nature of these changes.

one kind or another are virtually a universal feature of civil service in all jurisdictions today.

The demand for preference laws is strongest at a time when there is much unemployment and jobs of all kinds are at a premium. It is also during such periods that laws of this kind are most difficult to reconcile with the demands of an efficient public service. Since unemployment is apt to eliminate a greater portion of the less able employees from private industry than those of high ability, preference laws—particularly if they contain provisions waiving age limitations for appointment—encourage the dumping of mediocre persons on the public service.

The experience of the Federal Government with veterans' preference between the two World Wars is of interest in this connection. Veterans were eligible for 5 points addition to their civil service grades; disabled veterans for 10 additional points. Of the total appointments to the classified service, the percentage going to veterans ranged from a low of 21.6 in 1925–6 to a high of 32.4 in 1932–3, although veterans constituted only 12 per cent of the male population. Of the 10-point preference eligibles who were appointed, about one-sixth had earned less than the passing grade of 70, and of the 5-point eligibles about one-eighth.[9] Data gathered by Sims shows that the scholastic ratings of veterans appointed to junior professional positions in the period 1935–39 averaged substantially lower than those of non-veterans; and veterans averaged 37 years of age as against 26½ years for the entire group.[10]

On the other hand, the case against preference laws should not be exaggerated. If government is able to compete effectively for the services of able men, if salaries and other incentives are not unfavorable in comparison with those offered by private industry, it should not be impossible to recruit an able corps of civil servants largely from the great reservoir of talent to be found among veterans or any other sufficiently broad group. If the provisions of a preference law are moderate, its desirability or undesirability would seem to hinge as much on the question of its fairness or unfairness to various groups in the community, as upon its possible effect upon the competence of government employees.

[9] Mosher and Kingsley, *Public Personnel Administration*, pp. 240–2.
[10] Lewis B. Sims, *The Scholarship of Junior Professional Appointees in the Government Service* (Washington: President's Committee on Civil Service Improvement, 1940), pp. 25–30.

Elimination of Patronage and Spoils

The principal arguments for and against a spoils system have been discussed in connection with the topics of competence and neutrality. The whole growth of modern personnel practices has been closely related to the movement to replace spoils by the merit principle. Systematic attention to personnel matters and organizational units specializing in personnel work had their origin in this movement. The whole structure and procedure of government personnel agencies has been strongly conditioned by this fact. Their primary function (and, in the early period, almost their sole function) has been to guard the public service against political appointments, political removal and political coercion of civil servants.

EFFECTS OF A SPOILS SYSTEM

A spoils system generally has two important effects upon a government agency subject to it. First, it places in public positions employees who are incompetent—or at least not the most competent—to do the work. Second, it weakens the formal organization established by law and responsible to the legislative body and encourages the growth of informal controls exercised by political machines. The party organizations that have operated spoils systems have usually been more devoted to their own growth and survival and the enrichment—legal and illegal—of their "professional" adherents than to the advancement of political policies endorsed by the voters.

Under a spoils system, the political appointee owes his loyalty to, and depends for his job upon, the party or machine leaders instead of the administrators who appear as his superiors on the organization chart. Because of this dependence, a corrupt party organization can force subordinate employees to cooperate with its schemes of graft. The police captain who raids the wrong gambling house finds himself transferred to an outlying district; the building inspector who overlooks the illegal practices of contributing contractors is rewarded by his "cut" of the protection payments. A civil service system, consequently, is intended not merely to insure competence, but also to weaken or destroy the influence of the political machine over public employees.

CHARACTERISTICS OF CIVIL SERVICE SYSTEMS

The typical American civil service law has several principal ingredients: (1) it illegalizes the practices of appointing or removing employees for political reasons, or of forcing employees to contribute money or services to a party organization; (2) it creates a civil service agency, usually headed by a board appointed but not removable by the chief executive, to exercise the controls provided in the law; (3) it establishes a system of procedures, usually involving examinations, for filling civil service positions; and (4) it usually establishes a system of procedures for protecting employees from removal for political reasons.

Legal Penalties. Civil service laws provide legal penalties for forbidden acts of political interference with the public service, but legal penalties would in most cases be largely ineffective without machinery for the enforcement of the rules. Hence, the real backbone of a civil service system lies in procedures for appointment and removal of civil service employees—these procedures to be administered by a specially constituted civil service agency.

The Civil Service Agency. The typical civil service agency is headed by a commission made up of three members appointed by the chief executive for fixed, overlapping terms and not removable by him.[11] It is usually required that not more than two of the commission members be members of the same political party. The terms of office are often so arranged that a chief executive will not have an opportunity to appoint more than one member during a single term of office.

The obvious purpose of these provisions is to preserve the civil service agency from political domination, but like all organizational schemes—which must ultimately be operated by flesh-and-blood human-beings—the device is not infallible. Civil service commissions can be, and not infrequently have been, captured by corrupt political machines that have been in power long enough to appoint a majority of the commission members. Even the position reserved on the commission for a representative of the minority party has sometimes been filled by the appointment of a "friendly"

[11] The Federal law is rather atypical in this respect, since the commissioners, who are appointed by the President with the advice and consent of the Senate, are removable by the President.

opponent who has been bought off through some kind of bipartisan deal.

On the other hand, that great progress has been made toward the elimination of spoils cannot be doubted. Whether this progress is to be attributed largely to the independent civil service agencies is a more debatable question. Of equal or greater importance have been changing public attitudes toward government, resulting in a more effective public demand for efficient administration. At the same time there has been a growing professionalism in the public service itself, particularly in the administrative ranks, with the result that those who are in the higher levels of the civil service are themselves frequently prepared to resist political encroachment. None of these developments has proceeded in independence of the others, and it would be difficult to say to just what extent each is responsible for the improvement that has undoubtedly taken place in the public service.

Persons who are inclined to deny the importance of formal legal and organizational structure and to emphasize the importance of the social attitudes and beliefs that lie behind the structure would argue that patronage can be eliminated without formal civil service controls. As evidence for their position, they can point to many cities with city manager government operating in a non-political manner without an independent civil service commission (although the examples usually cited are small suburban communities with a long tradition of non-political administration).[12]

Opponents of the independent commission argue that its statutory independence from the chief executive invariably leads it to identify too strongly with the function of preventing spoils, and to underemphasize the "positive" personnel goals of selecting and retaining the most effective employees. A statutory shift to a

---

[12] Commissioner James K. Pollock, in an addendum to the Hoover Commission report on personnel administration states his conviction that "a statute outlawing political favoritism in the appointment of Federal employees, coupled with enlightened agency management is sufficient to provide adequate protection. This combination has proved to be effective in the case of the Tennessee Valley Authority. In the opinion of many, including former members of the Civil Service Commission, the usefulness of the commission form of organization to preserve the merit principle is grossly exaggerated." *Personnel Management*, p. 55. The majority of the Hoover Commission, however, recommended the retention of a three-man civil service commission reorganized "to vest in its chairman the responsibility for the administrative direction of its work." Ibid., p. 9.

personnel agency responsible to the chief executive would give a strong psychological impetus, it is argued, to a shift toward identification with the latter goals. Experience with central personnel units responsible to the executive (e.g., departmental personnel offices in the Federal government) indicates that while some shift in identification may take place, it probably will not be by any means complete. The departmental unit, in attempting to prevent removal of employees for political reasons or to prevent political favoritism in appointment, may impose controls on the other units of the organization almost as strict as those imposed by the independent agency. There is probably some difference in degree and emphasis between the departmental personnel office and the independent commission, but the evidence on this point is by no means conclusive.

Examinations. The civil service law usually provides that positions in the service shall be filled by open competitive examinations. Here again difficulties arise in reconciling the prevention of spoils with the function of selecting the most able candidates. In the examining procedure, the personnel agency possesses a powerful tool for determining the whole character of the civil service. But the type of examination that is most satisfactory for protecting the service against spoils is not necessarily the type that is best for developing a competent and alert corps of civil servants.

If the elimination of spoils and favoritism is the main objective, then the examining process should eliminate as far as possible the element of subjective human judgment. Oral examinations are particularly suspect because of the opportunities they provide for political bias to enter into the scoring. On the other hand, the technique of testing is still very imperfect, particularly when it comes to measuring traits of personality and character or the quality of previous experience. In order to protect against the dangers of spoils, civil service agencies have sometimes been led to use excessively mechanical and quantitative methods of comparing candidates. They have sometimes ignored personal qualities or have counted prior experience in terms of years without regard to its quality.

Not all the observable defects in examining methods can be attributed to this matter of goals, however. In many cases civil service agencies have not been supported with the appropriations they would need to do a thorough job of preparing, administering, and rating examinations. In other cases the agencies have been limited by laws which require that the examinations be "practical" in character and apply to the specific job for which the candidates are being considered. Such limitations prevent the agency from testing capacity for development as distinguished from immediate ability to perform. In New York and several other jurisdictions, the courts have seriously handicapped personnel agencies by restrictive interpretation of civil service laws. Other statutory limitations, such as those forbidding the establishment of minimum educational qualifications or restricting examining techniques, have been equally bothersome.

There is great variation among civil service systems in the extent to which positions are filled by open competitive examinations. The Federal system has been relatively flexible in this respect. Entrance positions in the Federal classified service are normally filled by open competitive examinations. For positions of a professional, scientific, or administrative character above the junior level, the examination ordinarily consists of a review of the applicants' training, experience, and ability as determined from written evidence. For other entrance positions, assembled written examinations are used. Partly because of the travel that would be involved, the Federal service has not made nearly so much use of oral examinations as have some state and local personnel agencies.[13]

Open competition for positions that might be filled by promotion has not been common in the Federal service, except in the lower grades. More often, promotions are made on the basis of competition restricted to civil service employees, or employees of a particular agency; or are made by the agency concerned on the basis of non-competitive selection. The U. S. Civil Service Commission has authority to control the method of promotion but has generally given the appointing agencies a great deal of latitude.

Removal of Employees. There is considerable variation, also, in the extent to which the independent civil service agency controls or supervises the dismissal of employees. The Federal civil service has an "open back door"—the power of removal rests with

---

[13] In California, for example, oral examinations conducted by a board that includes unpaid experts from outside the state service have been frequently employed.

department heads, and the employee who is dismissed has no right of appeal to the Civil Service Commission.[14] The department head is required, however, to submit a written statement of the reason for dismissal.

In many state and local systems, the "closed back door" prevails—the employee may appeal his dismissal, and in some cases other disciplinary actions as well, to the civil service agency. The commission then proceeds to hold a hearing on the charges, usually with a considerable degree of court-room formality. In some jurisdictions the commission's decision is only advisory, and the final power of dismissal rests with the department head or the chief executive. More frequently where an appeal is provided, the commission may actually reinstate the employee if it decides that the charges are unfounded. In addition, the employee sometimes has a right of appeal to the courts from the decision of the commission.

While the objective of protecting employees from dismissal for political reasons is laudable, a supervisor who wishes to remove incompetent employees is seldom enthusiastic about the "closed back door." The competence or incompetence of an employee is a matter of judgment that is not easily reduced to formal proof under rules of evidence. Overzealous civil service commissions have often placed a very heavy burden of proof on the department, and even where this has not happened, administrators often prefer to put up with an unsatisfactory employee rather than to go through the unpleasantness and inconvenience of a hearing.

In large organizations like the Federal government, the presence or absence of an independent civil service agency enforcing a closed back door may not be of very great significance. From the viewpoint of a section chief or branch chief who wishes to remove an incompetent employee, formal procedures established by the departmental personnel unit, responsible to the department head, may be obstacles as formidable, or nearly so, as the review processes of a civil service commission.

It is an increasingly common practice to deprive the first-line or second-line supervisor of the power of dismissal, by giving the dismissed employee a right of appeal at least at the departmental level. If the reviewing authority is zealous in requiring tangible

[14] At the present time (1950), employees who are veterans may appeal a dismissal to the Commission.

evidence of incompetence and placing a heavy burden of proof on the supervisor, the effect may be as powerful as if there were a review by an independent commission or a court. Hence, although the "open back door" in the Federal service has produced few scandals over political removals, this may simply be because the departmental review boards have behaved very much like independent civil service agencies.

Conclusion

There has been a steady trend for half a century toward the merit system of selecting employees for the American public service and toward the elimination of party patronage. Typically, the personnel agency has been organized as an "independent" commission insulated from the chief executive in order to insulate it from politics. In the past few years, certain disadvantages of this arrangement have been felt—particularly the excessive concern with the patronage problem exhibited by civil service commissions and their general lack of vigorous leadership toward modern personnel practices. As a result, there has been some demand for agencies more fully subject to executive influence, which would take a more positive view toward the development of a career civil service based on the merit principle.

The evidence is inconclusive as to whether spoils can be kept out of the public service without an independent civil service agency acting as watchdog. The initial progress toward a nonpolitical civil service was certainly made in most jurisdictions at the time when civil service agencies were established. The municipal governments that provide the most important counter-examples are to be found principally in relatively small, well-to-do communities where political machines have never been entrenched. The spoils tradition has continued strong in the filling of many classes of Federal positions outside the classified service (e.g., administrative positions in the Federal courts). Finally, the spoils system still prevails in a sufficiently large part of the public service in the United States so that it cannot be asserted with any confidence that public attitudes, unsupported by legal mechanisms, as yet provide a sufficient support for the merit system.

Of course, civil service law provides no automatic guarantee against spoils. All depends upon whether the civil service commission can itself be insulated from the political machine, whether prosecuting officials are sufficiently non-political (or politically opposed to the machine in power) to bring infractions of the law into the courts, and whether the courts themselves are free from political domination. The Federal civil service system has a remarkably fine record so far as the elimination of spoils is concerned, and the open back door has rarely been abused. As a result, control by a civil service commission over removals, a procedure that has led to serious abuses in many jurisdictions, has greatly fallen in favor.

CHAPTER SIXTEEN

Selection of the Team: Careers in Government

THE long-term influences of personnel processes upon the whole character of an organization have gained some recognition in personnel administration through the concept of a "government career service"—an idea first set forth at length by the Commission of Inquiry on Public Service Personnel.[1] The Commission defined a career as "an honorable occupation which one normally takes up in youth with the expectation of advancement, and pursues until retirement," and a career service in government as a "public service which is so organized and conducted as to encourage careers." [2]

Philosophy of the Career Principle

The basic aim of a career service is to attract to, and retain in, government employment men and women of talent and ambition. A number of serious difficulties have confronted government agencies seeking to attain this objective. First, local residence requirements and civil service rules restricting promotions to single departments and bureaus have unduly limited the promotional opportunities of able employees. Second, inadequate education and age requirements and the "charity concept" of public employment have hampered the recruitment of the most promising candidates. Third, knowledge of these unsatisfactory practices, to-

[1] *Better Government Personnel* (New York: McGraw-Hill Book Co., 1935).
[2] Ibid., p. 25.

gether with low salaries and the low prestige of governmental employment among the general public, have discouraged many talented persons from seeking public service careers.[3]

A career service might take a number of different forms depending upon such factors as the following:

(1) Which positions will be selected as the normal points for initial recruitment? Will virtually all new employees come in at the bottom (as is the case in most police and fire departments), or will there be separate points of normal entry for persons with college or professional education (as in the Department of State)? How many separate "career ladders" will there be in the organization, what will be the relation among them, and how hard or easy will it be for outstanding individuals to cross the barriers between different career groups? To what extent will outside personnel be considered for appointment to positions above the bottom of each ladder?

(2) How specialized, or how generalized, will the separate careers ladders be? How many organization units will be included in a single career ladder? Where careers are specialized, what will be the basis of specialization?

(3) What will be the advancement opportunities? What portion of the employees at any level can expect to advance to the next level, and what will be the normal ages at which advancement will take place? What will be the bases of selection for promotion?

(4) Will the system have at its apex a group of careerists in "general administration," or will top positions be divided among a number of career groups? How will employees be prepared for advancement to top administrative positions?

Each of these problems needs careful consideration and will form the subject of one of the ensuing sections of this chapter.

Initial Recruitment for the Career System

The characteristic structure of the job pyramid in a government agency (and in a private business organization, for that matter) reveals a broad base of manual workers—skilled and unskilled— or clerical workers. In the middle portions of the pyramid are found

[3] See, for example, *A Career Service in Local Government* (Chicago: International City Managers' Association, 1937).

technicians, employees with substantial supervisory responsibilities, and the junior scientific, professional, and administrative employees. At the higher levels are the employees who carry heavy scientific, professional, or administrative responsibilities. In most organizations, a very large percentage of the employees are found in the lowest group, a smaller but substantial percentage in the middle group, and a very small minority in the upper group. A city planning agency, or the U. S. State Department will have as many, or more, employees in the middle as in the lower ranks; but in a police department, a state highway department, or the U. S. Post Office, the pyramid will have a very broad base, and will narrow rapidly toward the top.

STRUCTURE OF CAREER LADDERS

An organization may be made up of one, or of several, career groups—in the latter case, each with its own career pyramid. Typical examples of the single or "linear" career agencies are police and fire departments and the U. S. Post Office Department. Here, new employees are normally recruited at a very low level, and the higher positions are generally filled by promotion from below. This pattern, which prevailed quite generally in the past, is being increasingly replaced by schemes that provide relatively distinct careers for groups of employees brought in with different educational and training qualifications. In particular, it is increasingly common to find the higher levels of the organization almost closed to persons without college education, although lower supervisory positions still often provide a bridge that can be crossed by the able non-college man who proves his administrative ability. The trend toward educational requirements is an example of the influence that the educational system has upon the structure of the career ladder.

CAREERS AND THE EDUCATIONAL SYSTEM

Although less in the United States than in others, there has been a close relationship in almost all countries between civil service careers, particularly in the administrative ranks, and the national educational systems. In the Chinese Empire, entrance to the administrative service was formalized in a system of literary and philosophical training. Skill in the writing of the Chinese language and a thorough knowledge of the Chinese cultural tradition, tested by competitive examination, were the requirements imposed on the civil servant. Except for the important ethical emphasis in Chinese philosophy, there was nothing in this training that was specifically "vocational," and the system was largely destroyed by the impact of the Western technology and economy.

The English system up to the present time has been remarkably similar in its general philosophy to the Chinese. Its function has been to select for the higher civil service brilliant representatives of the upper classes who have graduated from a broadly cultural educational curriculum. On the continent, on the other hand, starting in the early nineteenth century a relatively specific curriculum with public law at its core prepared young men for the civil service. In France, the emphasis was on legal and literary studies while in Germany the legal training was somewhat tempered with instruction in the social sciences.[4]

In more recent years, with the growing need for scientists and technicians in the public service, the tradition of classical or legal education as preparation for public service has been challenged in all these countries. The man with scientific, medical, or engineering training has been less and less willing to concede the top administrative posts to the lawyer or the classically educated gentleman. Even more recently the social scientist has been putting in his claim for recognition. These trends have been reinforced by the progressive democratization of society, particularly in England.

In the United States, a close relation between the civil service and the system of higher education has existed only in the case of a few professions in which government is virtually a monopolistic employer. Thus, the land grant colleges have created a definite professional group of agricultural specialists who have staffed the agricultural teaching posts in the rural schools, the agricultural experiment stations, the state departments of agriculture, and the United States Department of Agriculture. Until very recently, almost the entire product of the state schools of forestry was absorbed by the U. S. Forest Service and state forestry departments. The training of public school teachers has long been an important

---

[4] See Friedrich, *Constitutional Government and Democracy*, pp. 50–1, 386–92.

function of the universities and the state teachers colleges. More recently, public health, librarianship, social welfare, and public administration have been added to the list of public service occupations for which specific college training is available.

In the cases mentioned above, definite career opportunities within particular professions have developed in government, open largely to persons who have undergone prescribed types of training in the colleges. Other professions offer a choice between public or private careers. The training programs for these professions have not usually been specifically adapted to the needs of the public service. There are many opportunities for lawyers in government—apart from the important role they play in elective and other political offices—but until recently virtually no law school has provided special instruction for government (as distinguished from private) attorneys.[5] In the engineering profession, too, there has been no sharp line between the government engineer and the privately employed engineer, although there have been some "municipal engineering" curricula in civil engineering departments. Most of the physicians employed by government agencies have probably had no specific training in the public health field. With the growth of accounting and other business subjects in the colleges, many college trained accountants are employed by government—again usually without much specific training in governmental accounting methods. In all these occupations there is a considerable amount of movement, backward and forward, between governmental and non-governmental employment. Probably only a small proportion of the persons in these occupations employed by government consider themselves "career civil servants." Instead, they most often identify themselves with their particular professions and often hold the same low opinion of the public service that is held by much of the general population.

In the case of most governmental programs, there is even less opportunity for formal educational preparation than in the two categories just discussed. Police and fire departments at the local level and the Post Office Department in the Federal government are examples. These agencies have in the past made little use of university-trained employees. The traditional pattern has been to

[5] Esther Lucile Brown. *Lawyers, Law Schools and the Public Service* (New York: Russell Sage Foundation, 1948).

recruit personnel with grammar or high school educations at the lower levels and to fill the higher positions by promotion from below.

As a matter of fact, the career pattern in American government has not been very different from the pattern in private industry. There too, it is only in the last generation that college training has become at all an important factor in advancement to high positions, and even today the door is not usually closed for the high school graduate—although it is gradually closing.[6] With the rapid increase in the number of college graduates there has been an insistent trend in both government and industry toward the segregation of two groups of employees—those without college degrees and those with them. Perhaps the growth of the junior college movement will create a third, intermediate group of employees with some college training but without degrees.

In summary, in one group of public agencies we find no separate corps of college graduates. These agencies tend to have "linear" promotional structures, with the higher positions filled by promotion from the ranks below. In a second group of agencies we find a large proportion of college graduates whose training was not specifically adapted to the public service employed in the professional and administrative positions. In a third group of agencies we find college graduates in the more responsible positions trained specifically for these particular public service occupations. In the latter two types of agencies, personnel without college training in the appropriate field generally find that there is a ceiling on their promotional opportunities when they reach the levels commonly occupied by college-trained men. In the third group, the professional personnel tend to make their whole careers in government although not necessarily in a single governmental agency. In the second group there is generally a considerable flow between public and private employment.

RECENT CHANGES IN RECRUITMENT PRACTICES

The system just described has grown to its present form with little overall planning. Government has drawn upon the estab-

[6] See F. W. Taussig and C. S. Joslyn, *American Business Leaders* (New York: Macmillan Co., 1932), pp. 247–50; "The 30,000 Managers," *Fortune* 21:61 (February, 1940).

lished professions—engineering, law, medicine—wherever the need for technically trained personnel became sufficiently evident. The schools have instituted professional curricula for the public service when opportunities have appeared for the placement of graduates. Only in the past few years has there been much conscious attempt on the part of civil service agencies to adapt their recruiting procedures to the structure of the American educational system or to relate recruitment to career opportunities. Some of these recent developments will be commented upon in the course of this chapter.

Until the depression of the 1930's, college trained men found employment in government chiefly in positions in the natural sciences or in the established professions. Even in private business, college training in accounting was just beginning to make itself felt. A few agencies employed economists and statisticians in relatively small numbers, but few college-trained specialists in public administration were employed. The past fifteen years have seen a great expansion of opportunity for university-trained social scientists and graduates in public administration, particularly in the Federal government and some states. At the municipal level, the percentage of city managers with college degrees increased from 41% to 48% in the eleven-year interval, 1935–46, although few of these had been specifically trained in public administration.[7]

These developments have led some to propose that American civil service systems should make greater provision for careers in "general administration" not based upon any of the traditional professional subject-matter specializations. The proposal has met with no universal approval. Its pros and cons will be discussed later in this chapter.

Specialization in the Career Structure

Of course, there is no such thing as *a* career system for technicians, *a* career system for high school graduates, or *a* career system for college graduates. Each of these groups is further subdivided in terms of special training, and a large number of separate career ladders can be identified within each group. In the Federal professional service, for example, a college graduate may enter as a junior civil engineer, a junior electrical engineer, a junior attorney, a junior physicist, a junior economist, a junior statistician, a junior

[7] *The Municipal Year Book,* 1936, p. 218; 1947, p. 481.

agricultural economist—just to mention a few of the large number of sub-groups. Each of these special fields has its own promotional opportunities—which are usually further subdivided at higher levels—although there are some possibilities for the man of broad training and experience to cross over, particularly when he reaches positions of administrative responsibility.

DISADVANTAGES OF NARROW SPECIALIZATION

The question of how broad or narrow the areas of specialization are to be is vitally important. In general, it can be said that government career lines in this country have been excessively specialized and that in many peoples' opinion the advantages of securing personnel with extensive training and experience in particular fields has been outweighed by serious disadvantages. Among these disadvantages are: (a) an unequal supply of qualified personnel in particular specialized groups; (b) unequal promotional opportunities in the several fragmented career ladders; and (c) experience that is too narrow to prepare employees effectively for higher administrative responsibilities.

Inequalities in Supply. Excessive fragmentation of specialized groups in original recruitment frequently leads to a situation where there is an insufficient number of positions for all the qualified persons in one group, while it is necessary to appoint mediocre candidates in order to fill the quotas in other groups. In recruiting patent examiners, for example, the Patent Office sometimes has an excessive number of applicants in electrical engineering, while it cannot find enough mechanical engineers—or *vice versa*. In such cases, it may be better to combine the two groups and seek individuals of greater general ability, even if this means some initial sacrifice in specialized training. This is the more feasible to the extent that the training of applicants has been broad and fundamental rather than highly specialized.

Local residence requirements, preventing the recruitment of out-of-town persons, are a rather curious form of "specialized" recruitment—since in this case the restriction upon the source of recruitment adds nothing to the competence of the candidates. Residence restrictions have been a major barrier to the recruitment of able young employees to state and municipal government.

Inequalities in Promotion. Narrowly specialized career ladders also lead to serious inequalities in promotional opportunities. One career group may grow more rapidly than others, permitting its members to advance at earlier ages and with more modest abilities than employees in the other groups. Or the advancement opportunities of a particular employee may be blocked because the only job to which he might be promoted is held by a young and healthy incumbent. Inequalities of these kinds tend to be averaged out if the career group is sufficiently large.

Effects of Specialization on Competence. Finally, it is doubtful whether the highly specialized experience that an employee acquires when career lines are narrowly limited is as valuable to him and to the organization as a broader and more varied experience would be. The doctrine of the Navy that any line officer can fill any position may be an exaggeration to the opposite extreme, but it provides the service with higher officers who have had a bird's eye view of virtually the entire organization. This breadth of experience has two advantages. First, employees who have had varied assignments are more apt to have broad identifications with the whole organization than employees whose careers have been restricted to a particular specialized field or a particular segment of the organization. Second, such employees are better prepared to coordinate their own activities with those of other units because they understand the work and responsibilities of the units with which they are cooperating.

Like most administrative problems, this question is one of degree and emphasis. Since few people can qualify as universal geniuses, it is necessary to permit employees to become expert in particular specialized areas of work. But in seeking the real advantages of specialization, it is necessary to keep in mind some equally real disadvantages: that most persons are capable, without too much difficulty, of acquiring several specializations during a long career—and the more able the man, the greater his capacity for transfering to new responsibilities; that there comes a point of diminishing returns when the mere cumulation of specialized experience diminishes rather than increases the competence of an employee.

ALTERNATIVE TYPES OF SPECIALIZATION

Parallel with the question of *how much* specialization is the question of *what kind* of specialization will be introduced. Specialization in terms of educational level has already been discussed, but even within a particular educational level—e.g., college graduates—career groups can be organized in many different ways. Three examples will serve to illustrate different possibilities:

The Forest Service. The Forest Service recruits its professional employees from schools of forestry. During their first few years they serve in a variety of junior positions under forest rangers and in district and regional offices. Upon completion of this "apprenticeship" they receive appointments as forest rangers with management responsibilities for particular forest areas. The higher administrative personnel of the Forest Service—including district and regional foresters, division heads in Washington, regional office specialists in timber management, fire protection, personnel, financial administration, and so forth—are recruited by promotion from the group of forest rangers. There is some tendency for a man, once he has become a specialist in some phase of the Service's activities, to remain within that specialty during his subsequent career, but there is considerable interchange of personnel throughout the organization.

Some of the consequences of this structure are: (1) most of the professional personnel identify strongly with the Forest Service as a whole, even though they may have specialized interests; (2) there is no wide psychological gap, such as exists in many organizations, between line administrators like the forest ranger and overhead specialists in the regional offices; and (3) there exists a problem of training personnel in specialties other than those acquired in college—e.g., personnel and budgeting.

Federal Personnel Units. The Forest Service is not typical in its method of recruiting personnel specialists. Most Federal departments and bureaus have personnel units whose professional employees are selected for their training and experience in personnel work. At the junior levels, personnel specialists are increasingly drawn from college graduates in public administration or psychology. They may pursue their careers within a single department or agency but more often move rather freely among personnel positions in the various Federal departments.

An important consequence of this kind of specialization is the strong identification that the personnel specialist generally develops with his profession and its standards and techniques. This strengthens the channels of communication and authority between the central personnel agency (the Civil Service Commission) and the departmental personnel offices. It tends to produce a corresponding gap in the relationship between personnel specialists and the rest of the organization and often creates a feeling of divided loyalty in the counterpart personnel units.

City Health Officers. The peculiarities of the career system in municipal health work derive from three factors: the sharp professional dividing line separating physicians from persons who do not possess the M.D. degree, the small size of the professional staff in most health agencies, and the lack of a sharp dividing line—particularly in smaller cities—between public health work and the practice of medicine. As a consequence of the first factor, certain positions in a municipal health department are traditionally held by physicians and others are not, although the allocation of positions may shift from time to time. Hence, side by side with the medical staffs, other responsible administrative positions, particularly of an overhead character, may be held by non-medical personnel. Because of the small size of health agencies, individuals who make a career in this field generally must look to other cities and to state agencies for promotional opportunities, and there is considerable movement of personnel between agencies. Partly for the same reason, doctors are often brought into public health positions at fairly high levels without previous public health experience, and therefore public health administrators do not form a completely closed career group. Nevertheless, on the whole, public health administration has created a distinct professional identification for most members of the profession—as evidenced, for example, by a distinctly different attitude toward "socialized" medicine from that held by the bulk of the medical profession.

These examples illustrate the relationship between career lines and organizational structure. Where the career group and the organizational unit (or at least its professional corps) correspond closely, organizational unity and communication within the organization are facilitated. Where career lines cut across the structure of formal organization, professionalism may create strong psychological ties that compete with the influences of the formal organization. Where a particular career group occupies the top positions within an organization (as do the medical personnel in public health agencies), a "caste" structure may develop in the organization, creating a gulf between the members of the career group and others

—very like the gulf between officers and enlisted men in military organizations.

ALTERING CAREER LINES

Modifications in recruitment practices that alter career lines may have fundamental effects upon the organization and may be strongly promoted or opposed by particular career groups. When President Roosevelt appointed Archibald MacLeish, a prominent literary figure, as Librarian of Congress, strong protest was made by the American Library Association, whose members considered this position a rightful pinnacle to the profession of library administration.

Another example is provided by the Foreign Service. Prior to 1939 the Departments of Agriculture, Commerce, and the Treasury appointed attachés to serve in technical capacities in the principal U. S. foreign missions. These attachés were much more closely identified with the departments from which they were drawn than with the State Department. After 1939 the attachés were incorporated in the foreign service, and a unified career system was devised which was to provide the technical as well as the general diplomatic staffs of the missions. This change was endorsed by the State Department, but has never been fully accepted by the other departments concerned because of the loss of direct influence it entailed over the loyalties and activities of technical personnel abroad.

Promotional Opportunities

The structure of the career system will have an important bearing upon the number and kinds of promotional opportunities available to various types of employees in the organization. The important variables that determine the number of promotional opportunities are: (1) the rate of growth (or decline) of the organization, (2) the shape of the career pyramid (in particular, how rapidly the number of jobs at each level decreases toward the top), (3) the number of appointments that are made from outside, rather than by promotion from within, and (4) the average length of time that employees serve in positions at any given level. The fourth variable depends, in turn, on (a) the average age at which appointments are made to each level and (b) the average age at which employees at and above a given level are separated from the organization by retirement, resignation (including promotions to better jobs in other organizations), death, or dismissal. When these facts are known for any organization, it is possible to estimate what percentage of the employees appointed at the lowest level in a career ladder will reach any given higher level before they are separated from the organizations.[8]

RATE OF GROWTH

Even a moderate rate of growth in an organization may produce as many (or more) promotional opportunities as are provided by normal replacement—at least in the short run. Even a five per cent annual growth may double the annual number of promotions that can be made at each level. This will probably have the effect of (a) increasing each employee's chances of reaching the higher positions, and (b) reducing the average age at which promotions are made. As a result of the growth, larger numbers of employees will also have to be brought in at the lower levels, hence increasing the competition for promotion after the initial impetus has been spent —but still retaining promotional opportunities at a higher level than in a static organization.

A cessation of growth after a period of rapid increase will generally find the top levels of the organization staffed with relatively young men. This will seriously interfere with the continued promotional opportunities of those further down the line. As a result, the organization may exhibit cycles in promotion—periods

[8] In an organization that is not changing in size, the actual calculations can be carried out as follows. Suppose it is desired to estimate what percentage of the incoming employees will sooner or later reach the fourth level. Assume that: (1) for each 100 positions in the whole organization, 12 are at the fourth level and above; (2) the average length of service of employees in the organization as a whole is 22 years (obtained by subtracting average age at appointment from average age at separation). Then $100/22 = 4.5$ replacements must be appointed each year per 100 employees. Assume further that: (3) employees who reach the fourth level serve, on the average, 14 years at that level or above (obtained by subtracting average age at promotion from average age at separation for these employees). Then, for each 12 positions at these levels (or each 100 in the whole organization), $12/14 = .9$ replacements must be promoted each year. It follows that of all employees appointed to the agency, .9/4.5 or one-fifth, will receive promotion to the fourth level before separation.

in which the top group is relatively youthful and promotional opportunities are few, followed by periods when considerable numbers of the top men are retiring each year, permitting rapid advancement below. The length of such cycles is likely to correspond roughly to organization "generations" of twenty to thirty years—the length of time that top personnel normally spend in the organiation from original appointment to separation.

SHAPE OF THE CAREER PYRAMID

It has already been pointed out that the typical organization is divided into a number of relatively isolated career groups. The promotional opportunity of an employee belonging to one of these groups depends not on the number of high level jobs in the organization as a whole but on the number of high level jobs attainable to one in his particular group. Even when the organization as a whole has a pyramid-like shape, a particular career group may have a relatively few jobs at the entrance level, a larger number of jobs at middle levels, tapering off to a smaller number of jobs at the higher levels. Several typical career pyramids are illustrated in Table I.

TABLE I

Factors Determining Opportunity for Promotion

	NUMBER OF POSITIONS		
Level	*(1)*	*(2)*	*(3)*
V	3	32	14
IV	12	64	80
III	47	129	240
II	188	257	480
I	750	518	186
Total	1000	1000	1000
Level III, and above	62	225	334
Per cent			
Promoted A	9.3	33.9	50.0
to Level B	12.5	45.3	66.7
III C	10.3	37.5	56.0

Columns (1), (2), and (3) show the distribution of positions by level in three hypothetical career pyramids. Out of a total of 1,000

positions in each pyramid, 62, 225 and 334, respectively, are at the
third level, or above. On the last three lines are shown the percent-
ages of the employees in each pyramid who could expect to reach
the third level or above before separation, under three different sets
of assumptions.

Assumption A: age at initial appointment, 25; age at promotion to
Level III, 35, age at separation, 55.

Assumption B: appointment age 25; promotion age 40; separation
age 55.

Assumption C: appointment age 25; promotion age 35; separation
age 50.

Ordinarily, all employees in a group will have an excellent
chance of reaching those levels where the pyramid is widest—
where there are a larger number of jobs, (e.g., level II of the third
column in Table I)—but the percentage reaching the levels that
taper up to the peak will drop off rapidly. In the pyramid shown in
the first column of Table I, probably not more than ten per cent
of the persons recruited at the lowest level would ever reach the
third level; while in the pyramid of the third column, probably half
or more of those recruited at the bottom would sooner or later
reach the third level. The higher the age of promotion, the larger
the percentage of original employees reaching these levels, since the
percentage of top personnel replaced each year would be greater.

AVERAGE LENGTH OF SERVICE AT A GIVEN LEVEL

As already pointed out, the time an employee is likely to remain at any level depends on the normal age of promotion to the
level in question and the normal age of separation of those who
reach this level. Long length of service at high levels—due either
to young appointments or a high retirement age—obviously reduces the annual turnover in such positions and correspondingly
reduces the promotional opportunities of those below.

Increasing from 35 to 40 the average age at promotion to top
levels may increase by as much as a third the number of individuals
in the lower ranks who will eventually receive such promotions. A
similar result may be produced by lowering the retirement age by
five years. The effects at lower levels, with a younger normal promotion age, would be considerably less striking. Two conclusions
can be drawn from this:

(a) the organization may find it advantageous to strike a balance between restricting promotions to a small and highly selected group of employees (and promoting these at relatively early ages) and providing promotional opportunities to more employees, but raising the average age at promotion.

(b) a compulsory retirement plan has values in increasing promotional opportunities, as well as in separating, in a relatively unembarrassing fashion, those employees who are no longer capable of the best performance. The U. S. Navy has for some time pursued the policy of retiring officers who are passed over for promotion to the highest ranks in order to keep open the promotional opportunities of junior officers.

APPOINTMENTS FROM OUTSIDE

Quite obviously, appointments to higher-level positions from outside the organization decrease correspondingly the promotional opportunities of those within the organization. Hence, outside appointments may be strongly resisted by employees, and a large number of such appointments may have serious effects upon morale. The effects will be most serious if there are few promotional opportunities within the organization itself (through lack of growth, or for other reasons) and if employees do not have corresponding opportunities for promotion to higher positions in other organizations.

In this respect, restrictions on appointments from outside—local residence requirements, for example—produce somewhat the same effects as restrictive tariffs. They work to the short-run advantage of the employee within the organization, but they encourage reprisals by other organizations and thus restrict the opportunity of the employee to move outside—by reducing "imports" they produce the long-run effect of reducing "exports." During the depression, when residence requirements for local public employment became increasingly popular, employees in organizations without such restrictions could argue convincingly that their lack of "protection" placed them at a disadvantage.

Like all coins, this one has two sides. Some very able administrators have developed organizations of national reputation by the process of attracting able young men and keeping advancement lines open by "promoting" them to positions outside the organization and then replenishing the supply. The Berkeley, California, police department under Chief August Vollmer and the Wichita, Kansas, department under his protege, Chief O. W. Wilson, supplied a dozen or more police departments in the United States with able, college-trained young chiefs.

The constant raiding by patent law firms of the staff of examiners of the U. S. Patent Office has had similar effects. On the positive side, in such a situation the agency may be able to attract —and retain for a period—more able employees by offering them opportunities for rapid advancement. Further, the agency does not suffer from excessive aging of its staff in the lower and middle ranks. On the negative side, the agency must constantly replenish and re-train its junior staff and continually loses the benefit of the experience of those who leave. It also continually loses men who would be valuable in the higher administrative posts. Only by study of the individual situation can the point be found where the advantages balance the disadvantages.

Career Service in General Administration

The proposal has been put forth from time to time that a more or less separate career group should be developed to staff the top administrative positions in the Federal government. The basic assumption underlying this proposal is that competence in high administrative posts derives from generalized skill in administration —highly transferable from one organization to another—rather than from knowledge of any specific subject matter.

It is quite true that the director of a public works department has less need for technical engineering knowledge than do many of his subordinates. It is also true that a number of eminent men have been successful in transfering administrative skills from one kind of organization to a totally different one. From these facts the conclusion is drawn that the special skills of administration can be sought and nurtured quite independently of the skills required of the subject-matter specialist.

SKILLS REQUIRED IN HIGH-LEVEL ADMINISTRATION

If the administrator is not a subject-matter specialist, then what are his particular skills? A partial answer is that they are the skills of organizing and managing complex groups of men and skills of negotiating and of representing these groups in their relations with other groups. Such skills are obviously required in any organization, and a person who has successfully exercised them in one should be able to do the same in another.

But the executives of a large organization are not engaged wholly in administration in this narrow sense. They also participate in policy formation. Granting that the problems of managing men are the same in a Department of Agriculture, a Commerce Department, a Health Department, or a Police Department, the program problems are certainly not the same. Problems will come to the executive of an agricultural agency that require for their solution a special knowledge of agriculture, and to the public health officer that require knowledge of medicine.

In the relatively small organization, technical problems will frequently rise to the top, and the chief executive must be prepared to cope with them. In a large, complex organization, however, the problems that are faced at the top levels are seldom narrow problems of technology. More often they are concerned with economic, political, and social implications of technical facts or of a technically sound plan that has been formulated at lower levels. The Secretary of Agriculture does not need to decide what are good farming practices for increasing the nitrogen content of the soil. He may need to decide—or to participate in deciding—what the implications of a soil conservation program are for American agriculture.

The top administrator's decisions are not without content. But their content is much more likely to involve economics, sociology, or politics than biology or physics. The large programs of government for which his agency is responsible must be fitted into the society they are designed to serve. It follows that if a class of "general administrators" were to be recruited, they would need to be recruited for their sound understanding of the social sciences as well as skill in administration.

SOME CONSEQUENCES OF A CAREER SYSTEM IN GENERAL ADMINISTRATION

It is probably not technically impossible, then, to develop a corps of "general administrators" who could be used flexibly to fill the top positions in the administrative hierarchy without regard to organizational lines. But even if possible, is it desirable? Such a scheme would offer unusually attractive career opportunities to a small and highly selected group of men. Hence, it might attract to the Federal service first-class men who would otherwise not go into government service.

Critics of the proposal have raised a number of objections to it. Are our selective mechanisms good enough to pick out superior administrators at an early age, or can administrative ability only be discovered by a gradual weeding out during the course of progressive careers? Should the subject-matter specialists who show capacity for administration be virtually barred from the top positions in the hierarchy? Cannot the same result be attained within the framework of the present career system by encouraging more interagency transfers in the higher levels of the service?

Since the idea of a separate administrative career group has little basis in the traditions of the American public service, it does not seem likely that such a development will take place in the near future. The discussion of the proposal during the past decade has already had the effect, however, of calling attention to the excessive specialization of career lines in the higher levels of the hierarchy. This discussion may well lead to a greater recognition of administrative ability and to greater opportunities for men of proved administrative competence to broaden their experience and advance with less regard than in the past to organizational or professional lines.

Conclusion

The United States has lagged far behind England and many of the countries on the continent in creating careers in government employment. There are a number of interrelated causes for this, including the low esteem in which government service is generally held in this country, the prevalence of the spoils system until relatively recent times, the relative absence of a class structure on which an "administrative class" could be built, and the lack of relationship between recruitment channels and the educational system.

In recent years, and particularly during the past two decades, there has been a rapid movement toward the development of career opportunities, which has manifested itself in diverse forms. In some instances specific public service professions (e.g., forestry) have grown up. In other instances, greater efforts have been made to draw upon the established professions by recruitment of college-trained personnel. Although the low prestige of government service and the limits upon salary advancement still handicap public agencies in recruiting and retaining able men, the situation is undoubtedly better than it was at the outset of the Great Depression.

There is still no clear pattern of recruitment for the higher administrative positions in government, and the idea of separate careers in general administration has not met with unqualified approval. It seems unlikely that the English pattern will be copied to any great extent.

We have seen in this chapter that the operation of a career service depends not only upon recruitment practices, but also upon what happens to the government employee after he has entered the service. These "internal" aspects of personnel administration—the effect of personnel processes upon the going organization and its employees—will provide the subject matter of the next chapter.

CHAPTER SEVENTEEN

✠

Selection of the Team: Personnel Processes

IN CHAPTERS 15 and 16, we dealt with two aspects of personnel management: recruitment and personnel movement. In the present chapter we will consider a number of other personnel activities: position-classification, compensation, service ratings, and training. In line with our general aim, they will be discussed not from the standpoint of the personnel technician, but in a way that will reveal their connection with over-all organizational problems.

Position-Classification

The position-classification plan is a device widely used in public civil service jurisdictions to simplify and standardize personnel procedures. The *position*, the fundamental building block in such a classification, is a group of duties and responsibilities that are to be assigned to a single employee. The basic idea in a position-classification is that all those positions in an organization which involve closely similar duties and responsibilities should be grouped together for purposes of recruitment, compensation, and other personnel matters.

Examples of position classes in the Federal classification system are: junior clerk-stenographer, assistant agricultural economist, and principal budget examiner. In the Federal Service, position classes are further grouped into grades and series. The General Schedule, which includes professional, scientific, administrative, subprofessional, fiscal, and clerical employees is divided into eighteen grades, designated GS-1 through GS-18.

POSITIONS AND PEOPLE

It is a fundamental tenet of the philosophy of position-classification that the *position* is to be classified, and not the *person* who is currently holding it. One junior clerkship may be held by a highly efficient employee, a second by an incompetent employee, a third may be vacant; but if all three positions involve the same duties and responsibilities they should fall in the same class. This rule may create problems when an unusually able employee, having been appointed to a position, begins to accumulate additional duties and responsibilities; or when a relatively poor employee is relieved of some of the more difficult work pertaining to his position. Administrators and supervisors, desiring to make the best use of the abilities of their employees, may dislike the idea that they should not assign to able employees work that is "out of class."

This difficulty is not inherent in the position-classification. It may result from particular personnel procedures that surround it. In the Federal service, for example, if a junior stenographer is doing work of a senior stenographer grade, it is usually possible for her supervisor to obtain a desk audit of her work [1] and to secure a reclassification at the higher grade. In some civil service jurisdictions that are stricter in requiring competitive examinations for promotion, such a reclassification would not be possible, and the employee would either have to continue with senior stenographer's work at junior stenographer's pay or be relieved of her additional duties.

MEASURING DUTIES AND RESPONSIBILITIES

One of the most severe practical problems in position-classification is actually to determine what the duties of a position are, and particularly the degree of difficulty and the level of responsibility of these duties. For some types of positions—junior clerk, for example—this determination can be made on a fairly objective basis; but in positions where the amount of discretion, amount of super-

[1] By a "desk audit" is meant observation by a personnel technician of the employee's work to determine the duties and responsibilities of the position. The information needed for assigning jobs to classes is generally obtained from questionnaires prepared by the employees and their supervisors, usually supplemented by a desk audit.

visory responsibility, or level of difficulty of scientific work are in question, the process becomes highly subjective. Note, for example, the descriptions of certain positions in the Federal professional service:

Assistant Economist (GS-7): "work requiring . . . previous experience, and, to a limited extent, the exercise of independent judgment."

Associate Economist (GS-9): "*responsible* work requiring *extended* professional, scientific, or technical training and *considerable* previous experience."

Economist (GS-11): "*difficult and responsible* work requiring *considerable* . . . training and experience and the exercise of independent judgment."

Senior Economist (GS-13): "important specialized work requiring *extended* . . . training and experience, the exercise of independent judgment, and the assumption of responsibility for results, or for the administration of a *small* scientific or technical organization."

By what mystical process the personnel technician distinguishes between "work," "responsible work," "difficult and responsible work," and "important specialized work" has never been revealed to the layman. The technician also has occasion to distinguish, in his classification work, between an employee who works under "close supervision," one who works under "general supervision," one who works under "direction," and one who works under "general direction."

Under these circumstances, it is not surprising that the personnel technician is sometimes forced to use various rather arbitrary rules of thumb in classification work. If an employee is head of a unit with a large number of employees, his chances of securing a high classification are better than if the number of employees in his unit is small. If his boss has a GS-13 classification, he has a good chance for a "12"; but if his boss is only a "12," probably the best he can hope for is an "11." The latter consideration was very clearly apparent in the Economic Cooperation Administration. The statute creating this agency permitted the appointment of a limited number of employees at grade 16, above the then top civil service salary of $10,000. As a result, one or more of these "16" positions was created for almost every principal division in the agency, and there was ample room for a large number of 15's,

14's, and 13's below them. Many persons believe that ECA positions received classifications one, or even two, grades higher than comparable positions in other Federal agencies.

Other inconsistencies of like nature can undoubtedly be found in the Federal and other classified services. The rapidly expanding war agencies were generally able to secure higher classifications for positions than were the "old line" agencies. It is also commonly believed that positions in Washington receive somewhat higher classifications than comparable positions in the field.

POSITION-CLASSIFICATION AND RECRUITMENT

Since all positions in the same class are supposed to involve comparable duties and responsibilities, it would appear reasonable that an examining procedure that was satisfactory for filling one position in a class would also be satisfactory for filling all other positions in that class. This principle is generally accepted so far as initial recruitment is concerned. In a typical civil service jurisdiction, the civil service commission will give an examination for junior clerk-stenographer, and establish an eligible list of persons who are successful in passing the examination. When positions in this class are to be filled in the various departments, appointments are made from this common eligible list.[2]

The use of a common eligible list for each position class requires that the classification be sufficiently refined that a person qualified to fill one position in the class will be equally qualified to fill the others. To the extent that the governmental jurisdiction in question is searching for, and examining for, basic aptitudes and abilities rather than narrowly specific job knowledge, this requirement creates no great difficulty.

Difficulty is more likely to arise in the use of general eligible lists for promotion within the service. Here, the issue arises as to the relative merits of intra-departmental versus inter-departmental circulation of personnel—an issue that has already been discussed in the last chapter. If the position classification is to be used as a basis for promotional examinations, then broad classes of positions will encourage inter-departmental promotions while narrow classes

---

[2] In many jurisdictions, the department is not required to take the person at the top of the eligible list, but may choose any one of the first three. Practice on this point is by no means uniform, and the "rule of three" is sometimes restricted by veterans' preference laws.

will discourage movement between units. If specific job knowledge and experience in a particular agency or unit of an agency is important for successful performance in the higher position, the position classification would have to be so detailed—in order to be used as a basis for promotional examination—as to be almost unworkable. Certain intermediate procedures can be devised (and are used in some jurisdictions) which preserve the broader position-classification, but which give weight in promotion to experience in particular agencies.

POSITION-CLASSIFICATION AND COMPENSATION

Salary schemes will be discussed in the next section of this chapter, but some comments are in order here on the relation between the position-classification scheme and the compensation scheme. In general, the position-classification plan provides a satisfactory base for assigning salary rates. No serious difficulties arise in assigning the same minimum and maximum salaries to positions in the same class. As a matter of fact, the desire for greater standardization of salaries—equal pay for equal work— was a prime motive for the spread of the position-classification idea.

Of course, any inequities or inaccuracies in assigning particular positions to classes will carry over to the salaries paid employees in these positions. We have already seen that the classification of positions is a very approximate process at best. But if we admit its deficiencies, we must also recognize the evils it was designed to correct. Prior to the establishment of position-classification, legislative control over personnel budgets was exercised either by the *line-item* method or the *lump-sum* method. Under the *line-item* method, the legislative body specifies to the dollar what salary is to be paid to each employee. Without any definite meaning attached to job titles, there is no basis for legislative comparison of the salaries paid different employees. Hence, inequities of the grossest sort are bound to—and in fact do—arise. Moreover, the line-item budget encourages the individual employee to try to secure a salary increase by direct political influence. A considerable number of states and cities still use the line-item budget for personal services, and any number of examples of the two abuses just mentioned can be found.

Under the *lump-sum* method, each administrative unit is given a definite appropriation for personal services to be allocated at the discretion of the head of the unit. It is clear that under this method, while some measure of equality is likely to be attained in the salaries paid within any one appropriation, salary levels in one department or division may bear no resemblance whatever to those in another.

The weight of evidence indicates that classification systems have on the whole been instrumental in bringing about much more consistent compensation rates than those that prevailed under other methods of fixing salaries. Lewis Meriam has noted that although there is considerable criticism of position-classification in the Federal service, administrators who were in the service prior to the adoption of the present classification system express few doubts as to the improvement it represents.[3]

POSITION-CLASSIFICATION AND ORGANIZATIONAL STRUCTURE

An important proposition insisted upon by specialists in classification work is that a position-classification *reflects* but does not *determine* the structure of an organization. That is, the position-classification does not, according to this view, prevent the administrator from organizing his unit in any way that appears to him proper and efficient.

Administrators in charge of organization units are not always willing to accept at its face value this assertion that position-classification does not limit their freedom to organize as they see fit. The reasons why they are skeptical are several:

(1) In those jurisdictions where promotion is by examination, a supervisor cannot gradually adapt his organization to the abilities of his employees by adjusting the allocation of duties as old employees leave, new employees enter, and employees become capable of assuming new responsibilities. Under such a system, the supervisor is under obligation not to require or permit his employees to work "out of class." Any change in the division of work in the unit might require a complete reclassification of positions—and worse, a series of promotional examinations—before employees could be

[3] Lewis Meriam, *Public Personnel Problems from the Standpoint of the Operating Officer* (Washington: Brookings Institution, 1938), p. 34.

permitted to assume their new duties. In jurisdictions—like the Federal service—where promotion is handled less formally, and where it may be accomplished after a desk audit upon a reassignment of duties, this objection is less important.

(2) Where a classification plan is established for an existing organization, it may fairly be said that the position-classification merely reflects the existing division of work and does not establish a new plan of organization. But once a position-classification scheme has been adopted in a governmental jurisdiction, it must be extended to the positions in new units and agencies as these are created. The classification of new positions that are not yet filled, in an agency that has not fully come into existence and whose future pattern of activities can be anticipated in only a very vague and indefinite way, is an almost impossible task. No desk audit can be made of the duties of a particular position. The classification technician must accept (or refuse to accept) the administrator's prediction of what the duties of the position will be once the organization is in full operation.

Now, if the technician is generous in the grade allowed for a particular position, the position will probably be filled with a person of higher caliber than if the position is assigned a low grade. Once the position is classified and filled, there can be no doubt that, in a new agency, the caliber of the employee will have a tremendous influence upon the actual duties and responsibilities of the position. Hence the decision of the personnel technician will, in fact, have a considerable bearing upon the organizational structure of the new unit or agency.

Much of the friction that develops between the overhead unit responsible for position-classification and the operating unit can be traced back to these considerations. The operating administrator knows from his experience that the position-classification plan restricts his ability to make gradual adjustments in his organization structure and often restricts his discretion with respect to promotions. He knows further that if a position is classified too low, the employees he will be able to recruit for it will not be able to discharge the duties and responsibilities he visualizes for it and that the classification will have a consequent effect on the actual division of work in his organization.

Added to these factors will be the identification of the operating administrator with the employees of his unit and his desire, by raising their classifications, to secure for them increases in salary. Recognition of this identification by the classification technician leads the latter to be suspicious of the job descriptions prepared by the line units and to assume (sometimes correctly) that the job descriptions are inflated.

Compensation

Without falling into the economist's traditional fallacy of viewing employees as completely rational "economic men," we must still recognize that questions of salary are of great importance to them. Salary is important in enabling the employee to satisfy his own and his family's economic wants and equally important to him as a symbol of his place in the scale of status. An employee's satisfaction or dissatisfaction with his salary may be a function of several sorts of comparisons. He may compare it with the salary he might be earning if he were working in another organization; and he may compare it with the salary of others in his own organization.[4]

The comparison of salaries with those outside the organization is of primary importance in discovering the prospects for recruiting employees or retaining employees already in the organization. The comparison of salaries within the organization is of primary importance in the maintenance of morale—which may be seriously affected by the feelings of employees that the salary or status system is not fair and equitable. Particularly in government, where factors other than economic may lead a person to prefer public to private employment, an equitable allocation of salaries within the organization (or, more precisely, one that is considered by the employees to be equitable) may be more important than the comparison of salaries with those in private employment—especially for professional and administrative positions. A government executive may be much less disturbed by the fact that he could increase his income by $5,000 if he entered private employment than by the fact that a fellow-employee to whom he does not concede a higher status or higher abilities is earning $500 more than he.

[4] He may even compare it with the salary his father earned when the employee was a boy—or at least with the standard of living his father's salary maintained. In our society the desire of an individual to reach or exceed the economic and status position of his parents probably plays an important part in determining the level of his aspirations.

EQUAL PAY FOR EQUAL WORK

As mentioned in the previous section, the drive for equity in salaries *within* government—equal pay for equal work—provided a prime motive for the introduction of position-classification plans. Where there is a position-classification plan established, salary rates are almost always tied to this plan. That is, for each class of positions there is established a minimum and a maximum salary. At the time of first appointment to the position, the employee generally receives the minimum rate. While he remains in the position, his salary may be increased by gradual steps until it reaches the maximum, but it may never exceed the maximum unless he is promoted to a position in a higher class. Sometimes the maximum of the lower class will overlap somewhat the minimum of the higher class, although this is not usually the case.

Salary increases "within grade"—that is, within the maximum fixed for the position—are sometimes given automatically at stated intervals. It is more customary, however, for the increase to be conditional upon a satisfactory service rating by the employee's superiors. Under such a plan, an unusually able employee can be advanced in salary more rapidly and a less-than-average employee less rapidly than the usual rule. The effectiveness of a tie-up between salary increases and service ratings depends, of course, on the effectiveness of the service rating system. As we shall see in the next section, the construction of a foolproof service rating scheme is still one of the unsolved problems of personnel administration.

RELATING SALARIES TO RATES FOR PRIVATE EMPLOYMENT

There is no consistent pattern in the relationship between salaries paid for government employment and salaries paid for comparable positions in private business. The comparison involves difficulties at the outset for there are many governmental positions for which no really comparable private positions can be found: policemen, firemen, teachers, military officers, and so forth. In these cases, it is only possible to compare the positions with those in private business requiring roughly the same levels of educational preparation and experience. Moreover, in such a comparison, there is a danger of confusing cause with effect. The employment of teachers in the primary grades with only junior college preparation may be a consequence of the low salaries paid such teachers. If the salaries were raised, it might be possible to attract sufficient teachers with higher qualifications. In this case, and in other similar cases, the "level" of the job may be determined by the salary rather than vice versa.

In those areas where some comparison between salaries in governmental and private employment is possible, certain general observations can be made—although there are undoubtedly many exceptions to these in particular government agencies. In the lower positions of the hierarchy, salaries paid by government tend to be higher, and in the higher positions, lower, than those in comparable private employment. This was probably less true of the War period than of the period before World War II, but the generalization still holds to a certain extent today. The mechanic and the stenographer are likely to earn more in governmental than in private employment; the top-level administrator, scientist or professional man, much less.

In the case of the trades, governmental wages are generally equal to prevailing union rates, but the government employee is assured of steadier employment, and hence a higher annual wage when he is paid on a day-rate basis, than the employee of a private contractor. During a time of full employment the advantage of the government employee is obviously less than during a depression. With regard to clerical positions, governmental salaries are less subject to fluctuations with prosperity and depression and higher in the long run than those in business—at least, up to the $3,000 or $4,000 level at present prices.

At the higher salary levels—scientific, professional, and administrative positions—there is no doubt that governmental salaries are lower than those that prevail in business and industry. The chief problem here is in the low ceilings that mark the limits of advancement of the government employee. A few city managers have salaries in the $15,000 to $25,000 range—comparable to the salaries paid executives of substantial business. Some college presidents, school superintendents, and a few state department heads have salaries in excess of $10,000. For the rest, the ceiling is generally $11,000 for federal employees [5] and $6,000 to $8,000 for department heads in cities and states.

[5] Under the Classification Act of 1949, positions not to exceed 400 in number may be classified in grades with salaries of $11,000 to $14,000, and salaries of top administrators, from bureau chiefs to department heads, range from $14,000 to $22,500.

Under these circumstances, if government is to compete with industry for men of professional and administrative ability, it can only do so on the basis of the "psychic income" that government employment provides to supplement the relatively low money income. For many individuals, of course, the feeling of working for a public purpose rather than private gain, and the desire to further important social objectives, undoubtedly provide an added incentive to compensate for their financial sacrifice. There is a general belief, too, that under civil service, government employment provides a greater degree of security than does private employment.

Nevertheless, there has been continual criticism of the niggardliness of government in providing adequate financial incentive for its top employees. The failure of salary scales in these top brackets to rise during the inflationary period in pace with the rise in prices or even with the rise of professional and executive salaries in industry has intensified this criticism. The evidence is fairly convincing that government agencies are failing today to retain an appropriate share of persons capable of filling the higher professional and administrative positions with distinction.[6]

Although the prevailing salary pattern cannot be said to stem from any deliberate or consistent principles or policies that have been followed by legislative bodies, it does reflect fairly accurately certain underlying social and political forces. The general "levelling" tendency in governmental salary scales can be attributed in part to the numerical supremacy of lower income groups in the voting population. A constituency whose median family income, even in 1947, was as low as $3,000 can hardly be expected to consider salaries above $5,000 as anything but high, and will probably consider salaries above $10,000 astronomical. Moreover, the public employees in the lower brackets, both because of their greater number and because of their alliances with the trade unions, are in a much better position to exert pressure upon legislative bodies than are the professional and administrative groups. Members of the skilled trades, policemen, firemen, and teachers in urban school systems

[6] This failure is of course not entirely a question of salaries. The low esteem in which government service—and particular state and local service—is generally held by the public is undoubtedly an important contributing factor. See Leonard D. White, *The Prestige Value of Public Employment* (Chicago: University of Chicago Press, 1929). The linear promotion systems of some departments must also share the blame for this condition.

have been particularly active—and relatively successful—in using political influence to secure higher salaries.

One consequence of the lag in salary adjustment for professional and administrative positions during World War II and the postwar period has been the "up-grading" of positions. Under the tremendous pressure of securing adequate staffs to administer the great wartime agencies, personnel technicians tended to relax the standards of classification in order to permit higher salaries. This is a major reason for the present inconsistencies in position-classification among the various Federal agencies. With the growth of wartime agencies, there were many opportunities for young administrators in these agencies to rise rapidly and far. For those whose training and experience would place them in the bracket of "middle management," the salaries they were receiving at the end of the war were often as high or higher than they could obtain in private employment. There was a noticeable "bulge" in the pyramid of positions in the $5,000 to $10,000 salary bracket. With the end of the expansion period, the prospects of further salary advancement for many of these younger employees were dim, and with the decline of the war agencies, many were forced to seek private employment. There was a considerable danger, undoubtedly partly realized, that through this process there would be left behind an undue proportion of the less able men who had been promoted too rapidly and too far.

These comments will serve to illustrate some of the problems of setting governmental salary scales and to show the relation of salaries to the flow of personnel, discussed at length in the last chapter.

Service Ratings

A service rating plan is a procedure for answering the questions: "How well is the employee performing on the job?" and "What are his strengths and weaknesses?" [7] Service ratings are sometimes called "efficiency ratings." In many governmental jurisdictions, and particularly in the Federal government, a formal system for the

[7] For a brief, judicious, summary of the practices, problems, and practical results of service rating schemes, see Leonard D. White, *Introduction to the Study of Public Administration* (3rd ed., New York: Macmillan Co., 1948), pp. 408–20. See also Mosher and Kingsley, *Public Personnel Administration*.

evaluation of all employees by supervisors at periodic intervals has been in operation for a number of years. In the Federal civil service, some form of service rating has been used since 1923.

A discussion of the role of service ratings in the general administrative process may well start with the following premises:

1. There is no way of avoiding the rating of employees. Many personnel decisions—in particular, those concerned with promotions, lay-offs, transfers, and salary increases—require the evaluation of employees and the comparison of the abilities of several employees. The absence of a formal rating system simply means that when these decisions are made they are based on the informal ratings of employees by supervisors. The practical questions, then, are whether the rating of employees should be formalized or left an informal process; and, if ratings are to be formalized, what rating method is likely to be most satisfactory.

2. Except for the most routine positions, it is an extremely difficult matter to find objective criteria for rating an employee and his work. At the present stage of our knowledge of the qualities required of employees, and methods for measuring these qualities, a service rating scheme must be considered a procedure for systematizing and formalizing the subjective judgments of supervisors about their employees rather than a procedure for eliminating this subjective element from the judgment.

3. If a service rating scheme is used in any formal way as a basis for promotions and changes in salaries, then the supervisors responsible for the ratings will shortly discover what effects the ratings will have and make their ratings in terms of these effects. That is, if a service rating procedure says that a score of 90 is superior performance, and if "superior performance" is required in particular circumstances to justify a salary increase, a supervisor who wants to get such an increase for a particular employee will learn how to score that employee so that he will receive 90.[8] Through such manipulation, the term "superior performance" comes to mean "that level of performance which the supervisor thinks justifies a pay increase." But this brings us back to exactly

[8] Professor White suggests that in order to keep such manipulation within reasonable bounds, the service rating scheme probably has to be changed every few years. Op. cit., p. 414. It is likely, however, that with the increased experience of supervisors and employees in dealing with various types of service ratings, even this device will be ineffective because they will probably learn to manipulate any new system in a relatively short time.

the sort of subjective evaluation that the service rating is supposed
to eliminate.

The history of efficiency ratings in the federal government has
been the history of a continual struggle between the Congress, the
old Bureau of Efficiency, and the Civil Service Commission, on
one side, and the Departments on the other, to outwit each other.
Congress and the central personnel and budget agencies have
sought to prevent excessive rates of salary increases and the "piling
up" of salaries in the top rates for each class, while the departments
have sought (with a considerable measure of success) to give salary
increases whenever they considered these justified or necessary in
order to retain employees.

It should not be concluded from these comments that service
ratings are worthless. Once it is admitted that they do not provide
an "automatic" and completely objective basis for making personnel decisions, certain advantages of formal ratings over completely
unsystematized supervisory judgment become apparent. First, a
well-designed service-rating system forces the supervisor to consider just *why* he believes a particular employee to be particularly
good or bad. In this way, it probably diminishes the "halo" effect
whereby a man comes to be considered outstanding because one or
two instances of outstanding performance have blinded the supervisor to the employee's specific weaknesses. Second, the service-
rating system requires the supervisor to place himself on record
and to place on record also the specific reasons why he thinks an
employee superior or deficient. Undoubtedly, this has the effect of
tempering the enthusiasm of a prejudiced supervisor out to "get"
an employee who has incurred his displeasure. Third, the system
may be the basis for counselling with employees and training them
to eliminate the weak points in their performance.[9]

Training

Because, as we have seen in previous chapters, the direct influences
which an organization may bring to bear on its members are very

[9] The reader may find it interesting and useful to compare the characteristic
problems of devising and administering a workable employee service rating scheme
with the corresponding problems of devising and administering a university course-
grade system.

limited, selection and training of personnel become important controls in organizations. If employees cannot always be "ordered" to do what is considered best for the organization, at least organizations may be able to select people who will act to its advantage or gradually train them to do so. In a previous chapter we discussed the method of selection. Here we will discuss the method of training.

Although some people distinguish between training and education, we will not make this distinction. By training we simply refer to conscious efforts directed toward the improvement or increase of a person's powers, skills, or understanding, and the development of his beliefs or values.

TRAINING AND ORGANIZATION THEORY

Training "internalizes" the organization's influence. It changes the person in such a way that he will act as desired by his own motivation rather than by the stimulus of moment-by-moment instructions. No organization could exist if its members did not have a considerable ability of self-direction and the desire to take independent action of the right kind—the kind that promotes the cooperative effort of the organization. However, this ability and desire to take independent action in harmony with the efforts of other members of the organization can be increased by training.

No individual in an organization is allowed always to act entirely on his own discretion. Many of the premises of individual decisions are supplied elsewhere in the organization. Premises relating to legal effects of a decision come to the deciding point from the law department; those relating to economic effects from the economic section; those relating to political effects usually come from the hierarchy; and so forth.

Although individuals in organizations are not allowed complete discretion, organizations differ in the extent to which individuals or units within them may select their own premises of decision. When this is permitted to a relatively large extent, we say the organization is decentralized. When the opposite is true, we say that the organization is centralized. When each division in a bureau has its own lawyer, economist, statistician, etc., and hence does not have to "clear" legal, economic, or statistical matters with another legal, economic, or statistical unit, the organization is decentralized as to these matters down to the level of the division. If, however, the bureau has *central* legal, economic, and statistical units, it is centralized with regard to legal, economic and statistical matters.

The relation between training and decentralization is clear. If individuals have been trained in the premises required for their decisions, they can be allowed more discretion—that is, more decentralization is feasible. For example, if all the employees were thoroughly trained in law, no central legal review would be necessary. In some organizations it might be practicable to train one person in each section in the law (through pre-entry training in law school) and thus decentralize the supplying of legal premises of decision to the section level but centralize it within the section (one person in each section would supply the legal premises for all the others).

There is an economics of selection and training. Depending upon the circumstances of each individual organization, it might be cheaper to hire highly trained people at a higher personnel cost and thereby reduce the cost of supervision or centralization; hire semitrained people at a lower cost and pay the cost of training them within the organization; or hire more untrained or unskilled people at a low cost and pay the cost of increased supervision or centralization.

TRAINING AND SPECIALIZATION

The organizations, public and private, within a society are interdependent. The product of one organization makes possible the operation of others. The development of textile factories, for example, could take place only as factories came into existence for the manufacture of textile machinery. In like fashion, organizations cannot exist until other organizations turn out prospective employees with the skills and knowledge that are needed. The development of the U. S. Forest Service and the development of colleges of forestry are inseparable.

When there is a large and continuing demand for particular skills or bodies of knowledge that take some time to acquire, it becomes economically feasible for organizations to specialize in training people in this skill or knowledge prior to their employment. Thus, with increased specialization and standardization of occupations, training increasingly becomes pre-entry training. Today, we have all manner of schools to prepare people for standardized jobs—metal-working schools, radio schools, business schools, schools for medical technicians, and scores of others. The universities and colleges, too, are increasingly adapting their curricula to the vocational needs of organizations in our society. In the previous chapter we saw that many college course offerings are designed solely to supply governmental training needs, while many more train in skills required for either private or public employment. Increasingly, the idea is prevailing that formal education should prepare a person for some gainful occupation.[10]

This specialization of training in pre-entry training organizations is possible because of increasing standardization of the skills needed by organizations. Specialized training organizations, in turn (since they turn out people uniformly trained to fill standardized types of positions) contribute to the standardization of organizational activities. Employees find that their training is applicable in many organizations and that they can go from one to another. In the personnel field, for example, where specialized training has expanded rapidly in the past generation, large personnel units have been established in government and business, drawing upon this specialized training.

One consequence of a system that trains most persons for rather specific jobs is that it may produce over-specialization and a consequent inability of the employees so trained to advance up a career ladder from narrower to broader responsibilities. With special career lines for the engineer, the personnel technician, the accountant, and others, recruitment for positions requiring skill in general management may prove difficult. This problem has already received attention in the previous chapter.

THE OBJECTIVES OF TRAINING

We have defined an organization as a group of people cooperating to achieve some common goal. The function of training, both pre-entry and post-entry, is to make organization members more effective in promoting the organization's goal. To promote the

---

[10] It would take us too far afield to inquire into other factors that are accelerating this development in American society—for example, compulsory school attendance laws. The trend toward vocationalization of education also raises broad social problems that lie outside the scope of this book.

goal, organization members need certain personal "tools" or abilities which training provides.

1. They need the particular manual or physical skills required to promote the goal.
2. They need to understand and accept the values that the organization is promoting—such as its goal and the value of efficiency.
3. They need the knowledge, the factual premises of decision, to select those means or actions that will best accomplish the goal within the value framework supplied them by the organization.

We will discuss each of these points in turn. With regard to training in each of these elements, there is a possibility for conflict between pre-entry and post-entry training. We point this out to emphasize again that the organization exists within the larger society. It comes into being, is judged, and is allowed to exist by virtue of its ability to satisfy criteria developed in that larger society.

Skill Training. Often it is more economical for an organization to depend upon specialized pre-entry training organizations for skill development than to hire untrained employees and train them within the organization. However, this economy may be non-existent in very large organizations with a continuous and large demand for some specific skill. Here the organization can sometimes more economically establish its own permanent training activity to supply this continuous demand—as is typically the case in fire and police departments. Furthermore, if the skill is acquired very quickly—say, in a few hours—it will not be economical to provide specialized pre-entry training; the organization will have to provide its own training.

Skill training that must be handled by the organization itself is done in various ways. Sometimes a "vestibule" program is established where the employee is allowed to practice for a while under competent supervision until he acquires the necessary skill. More often, the training of the new employee is left to other workers or the supervisor—the employee is trained "on the job." Where on-the-job training is used, the emphasis shifts to training supervisors in how to train their workers.[11]

[11] For a useful, but somewhat uncritical, account of the war-time training program for industrial supervisors, developed by the War Manpower Commission,

Training in Values: Indoctrination. The organization's objective is the central value that members must accept if the organization is to succeed. Consequently, an important part of any post-entry training will be to get employees to accept the organization's goal and to see the relation between what they are to do and that goal—i.e., to get each employee to accept the sub-goal which is his immediate objective. Although some of this training or indoctrination will be done on a post-entry basis, much of it will be done before the employee joins the organization. The organization can select people who already accept its goal. Furthermore, self-selection may bring about the same result. Persons who go into welfare work usually believe in the values of that kind of work. Many of the people who flocked to the New Deal agencies were already strongly predisposed toward New Deal values.

There are many more value elements in decision than just the agency's goals. Many different means may contribute to the same end, and the selection between them must be on the basis of some ethical principles. The accountant, the personnel specialist, the physician, all learn certain methods that they are taught to regard as "workmanlike."

Particularly important in the indoctrination of values is the school system. The importance attached by the Army to West Point training or by the Navy to Annapolis training refers more to the attitudes and values that are supposed to be inculcated by these institutions than to the training they provide in military skills. Experience has shown, too, that whatever the pronouncements of legislative policy, a public welfare agency staffed predominately with persons having social welfare training will emphasize quite different values than a welfare agency staffed predominantly with accountants. In general, the kind of pre-entry value training an organization's members have received is probably more influential in determining what values the organization will implement than are the legislative acts that define its objectives.

It is quite possible for the pre-entry value training to conflict with attempts at post-entry indoctrination. Many conflicts, for example, within the National Labor Relations Board can be traced to the divergence between the attitudes toward labor in which em-

see its, *The Training Within Industry Report 1940–1945* (Washington: Government Printing Office, 1945). The general role of supervisors in training will be discussed in the last section of this chapter.

ployees of that agency had previously been indoctrinated and the goals that the prevailing majority of the Board were, at any given time, trying to implement. Selection of pro-labor employees may be the only effective way of staffing an agency that is supposed to serve labor, pro-agriculture employees, an agency that is supposed to serve agriculture. As we have seen in the previous chapter, however, the principle of selection by merit limits severely the recruitment of employees in terms of their attitudes and values; that is, limits the use of pre-entry value training.

Training in Factual Premises of Decision. The factual premises that employees need in carrying out the organization's objectives are of at least three kinds: (1) general knowledge of a scientific character (natural or social) and generally approved or successful solutions to the kinds of problems frequently encountered (known methods and processes); (2) local information about particular positions and procedures in the organization; and (3) current data on changing conditions (e.g., information about the political situation, forecasts of crops or of business conditions, and so forth).

General knowledge is acquired chiefly by pre-entry training in the schools. Organizations hire people already trained in economics, engineering, medicine, law, or biology; they do not create them by post-entry training. One of the principal problems with regard to general knowledge, largely because of this reliance on pre-entry training, is how to keep it up to date. There are many professional men in positions of high responsibility in government today whose pre-entry training was completed before World War I. Hence, we may expect a lag between the development of general knowledge and its use in organizations. The pipelines of communication are slow. Recommendations of economists who learned their economics thirty years ago may not be very reliable in the light of advances in economic science.

Fortunately, professional and scientific training need not terminate with the completion of formal pre-entry education—although it often does. Professional journals and associations try to keep their memberships informed of latest developments, but many people do not take the trouble, or do not believe they have the time, to keep up. To counter this difficulty, some organizations, in conjunction with near-by educational institutions, encourage their employees to take refresher courses, usually in the evenings; other organizations grant leaves to promising employees to take additional schooling. Among the more ambitious programs of the first sort in the government service are the Graduate School of the U. S. Department of Agriculture, a semiofficial adjunct of that department, and the programs for government employees sponsored by universities in Los Angeles, New York, and other large urban centers.

The Littauer School at Harvard University has as its principal objective the training of persons who have already had responsible experience as social scientists or administrators in government. A program that combines both aspects is the U. S. Naval Post-Graduate School, which conducts for naval officers full-time educational programs of one to three years' duration, some under the auspices of the Navy itself, others by arrangement with cooperating universities. In civilian agencies, legislative bodies have been less willing to appropriate large funds for in-service educational purposes of this sort.

The improvement of general knowledge is not merely a matter of keeping employees up to date. It also involves training them in knowledge they will need for new and more responsible positions as they progress up the promotional ladder. This need is growing as increasing specialization renders more and more people unprepared for the responsibilities of administrative work.

The constant replenishment of the organizational ranks by new recruits from the colleges assists in bringing newer discoveries to bear on organizational decisions. It also creates possibilities of conflict between the new ideas and the outmoded knowledge of the organization's managerial and technical staff. Since the new recruits generally enter the organization with relatively low status, they may encounter serious obstacles to introducing new ideas until they reach positions of responsibility—by which time their training, too, may be badly outmoded.

To state the matter more positively, new general knowledge is fed into organizations through two major channels: the continuing professional training and activity of those already in the organization, and the continual introduction at the lower levels of new professional staff with recent training. While these channels of communication cannot be depended upon to eliminate completely the lag between new discoveries and their actual use in organizations, they serve to keep this lag within limits.

General knowledge is not enough. An organization member

must also know things about his specific organization, his job or position, and its relation to the organization. He has to know the kinds of problems he will meet; who to talk to about them; who to "clear" his work with; etc. He has to be "wised up" before he can be effective. It will be some time before he has an effective list of telephone numbers in his list finder. This kind of local information, so necessary for coordination and communication, must be acquired by post-entry training. Here again, as in the case of much skill training, various methods are used, by far the most common being on-the-job training by fellow workers or supervisors. Much less common is a "vestibule" program wherein the new recruit is carefully trained in his job before he starts to work.

The final category of necessary factual premises, to which we referred before, is information about current changing conditions— the weather, the stock market, the progress of a bill in the legislature. Here, training merges into communication. This kind of information is gathered by special investigative processes and is made available to organization members through the channels of communication.

TRAINING METHODS: TRAINING AS COMMUNICATION

We will confine ourselves chiefly to a discussion of the problems likely to be encountered in developing an in-service training program and give relatively little attention to specific training methods as such. We do this because the selection of appropriate methods is not difficult once the underlying problems are understood.

The actual process of training within an organization is simply a part of the larger process of communication—a subject to which several chapters have already been devoted. We can understand the problems of training most easily by referring back to the typical problems of communication discussed in those earlier chapters.

Understanding. As in all communication, the task is not merely one of bringing ideas *to* the trainee, but of getting these ideas *into* him—so affecting him that he will react to each new situation in the way we want him to.

Level of Ability. The ability of the trainee to learn or do may place an absolute limitation on any training process. An in-service training program that attempts to teach people to do things that they are physically unable to do or to learn things that they have not mental ability to learn is obviously futile.

Acceptance. Perhaps the most common problems encountered in in-service training are those that relate to the trainee's acceptance of the training. In discussing communications, we have noted that acceptance depends upon status relationships, manner of presentation, the authenticity of communication, and the authoritative nature of the communication.

In training, as in other communication, most people do not like to be told what to do by persons of lower status. The problem of status is least severe in the case of vestibule training. Here the trainees are usually low-status employees and are sufficiently new to the situation to admit the propriety of training. In-service training of low-level employees who have been in the organization for some time need not create serious status problems, particularly if the training is handled so as not to challenge the employee's functional status—i.e., his know-how in the particular specialized sphere of organization tasks with which he is concerned. The status problem is far more severe in the training of supervisors or higher levels of management. It would usually be inadvisable, for example, for a GS-12 training officer to attempt to conduct a management training course for GS-14 and 15 executives.

Many of the training techniques used in organizations are actually attempts to overcome the problem of status in training. One technique used in the training of higher status people is the training conference. The persons to be trained are all brought together for discussion purposes under a discussion leader who adopts the role of a moderator. The various trainees then compare notes and exchange experiences or discuss problems that the moderator introduces. By this process these persons of higher status appear to be training one another and developing the new learning themselves rather than receiving instruction from a person who, being lower in the status scale, could certainly not know as much as they. Although the conference method has helped to overcome this status problem in training, it has serious limitations which have been graphically described by Coyle in her discussion of the process of collective thinking:

> Personal habits of participation further affect the process as it continues. The constant talkers, the orators, the silent members, all serve to determine the course of discussion. The speed of response is a further

factor. Individuals react some slowly, some promptly to the flow of suggestion. In the course of a discussion there will often occur belated responses to ideas farther upstream which have just come through to articulation. Individuals with stock panaceas can be counted on to trot out their hobbies, no matter how remote they may seem from the subject in hand. Many discussions will contain also participants with diffuse minds who contribute large masses of unrelated and unorganized material; leading citizens and authorities with selected quotations from their own speeches always at hand to be unleashed; women who rise to express their husband's opinions; impatient extraverts who feel that there has been too much talk; parliamentarians who will allow no deviation from Roberts' Rules of Order; constitutional objectors to whatever is being said; and an infinite variety of others.[12]

More direct teaching methods may be used if the person doing the instructing is recognized as having a sufficiently high status. An outstanding or famous person may be brought in to lecture to the group. Evening courses in a local university may be acceptable because of the high status of the professor. Some universities acquire such status that the most prestigious individuals feel no hesitancy about studying there. An example is the Littauer School at Harvard, a graduate school in administration, catering chiefly to established governmental administrators. Management training by the organization itself can avoid the status problem if the instructor has higher status within the organization than the trainees.

In the chapter on communication it was pointed out that acceptance is usually facilitated by a *non-authoritarian* method of communicating ideas. One of the strengths of training as a means of communication is that it is well adapted to a non-authoritarian approach. A person placed in the role of teacher usually feels obligated to state not only his conclusions, but also the reasoning and evidence upon which he bases these. He seeks to convince rather than to intimidate.

However, when the training task is a responsibility of the supervisor, there may be a greater problem in securing such a non-authoritarian approach. The supervisor, who is very often accustomed to authoritarian methods of dealing with his subordinates, does not easily alter these habits unless he himself is given explicit training in training methods. Hence, a program for

[12] Grace Longwell Coyle, *Social Process in Organized Groups* (New York: Richard R. Smith, 1930), pp. 187–8.

training supervisors in methods of job instruction may be a very essential part of the total in-service training program. Where on-the-job training by the supervisor is a large part of the training job, as it often is, the training problem may resolve itself into training supervisors in non-authoritarian methods of supervision.

Training is also not accepted if there are doubts as to its reliability. As we have seen in the general discussion of communication, attention must be given not only to the hierarchical status of the trainer, but also to his credentials in the functional area of specialization in which he is to train. If the training objective is one of indoctrination, or the inculcation of values, perhaps no better instructor can be selected from the standpoint of reliability than the head of the organization. Consequently, when the training officer detects a flagging of zeal in the organization's membership he will often ask the head of the organization to address the group.

A final characteristic of an effective communication is that it be authoritive—the person to whom it is directed must feel that he ought to comply with it. Applying this criterion to an in-service training program, we can say that enthusiastic support for the program on the part of the training officer or the personnel branch is not enough. The trainees will need to feel that the organization's management is strongly supporting the program and really wants the employees to cooperate with it. Hence, the training officer will usually try to sell the top administrative group on the need and importance of the program before he expects to make much headway with the rank and file. One of his principal jobs will be to secure this authoritative backing for training from the management.

DEVELOPMENT OF THE TRAINING PROGRAM

In many ways the most difficult problem in training is determining what to train. This involves, first, locating the deficiencies of employees that can be corrected by training—in itself, a difficult task. It is first necessary to decide what the organization or its top management expects from each employee or group of employees in order to see whether and how far they fall short of this expectation. Finding out what management expects will usually not be easy because management itself may not know. Consequently, a training officer will often find himself in the position of determining what management *ought* to expect from its staff.

Hence, the process of determining training needs, often called the training audit, frequently requires a management audit as its first step.

The Training Audit. Once the expectations of management with regard to its employees have been determined or created, the next step is to find out what groups of employees fall below these expectations and why. If deficiencies are due to lack of skill, knowledge, or acceptance of the organization's programs, training may be able to erase them. If the deficiencies are due to mental or physical limitations or firmly imbedded personality characteristics, personnel actions other than training are indicated. Although a series of tests or examinations to determine the employees' training needs might be constructed, in actual practice such a method would probably be too elaborate and expensive and create too much employee hostility to be used successfully. Furthermore, the technique of measurement through tests has probably not progressed to the point where it could be used widely for determining training needs. What the training officer is more likely to do in determining the existence and nature of deficiencies is to question supervisors about their subordinates, to ask the employees themselves what they feel they need in the way of training, and to examine service records. In this way a rough idea of training needs may be gained.

Although such a training audit is easy to describe, it will not be easy to conduct. In the first place, the training officer will usually have difficulty in getting management to state or develop its expectations with regard to the employees. Management may be too busy with its own immediate and pressing problems to give much time to such an endeavor. The management may not feel the need for the audit and may regard the demand that it think through its own problems as a kind of impertinence.

In the second place the training audit may encounter resistances from the rank and file. People do not like to have their deficiencies exposed. In fact they will often feel that they do not have any deficiencies. Furthermore, a training audit, since it takes on many of the characteristics of a management audit, may create feelings of insecurity among members of the organization. Therefore it is not likely to receive the whole-hearted cooperation of the rank and file and the supervisory staff. The training officer may run into a blank wall of opposition and hostility.

Participation in Planning. Because of these difficulties training officers often begin their audits with a selling campaign directed at the higher executive staff. Sometimes training officers get the higher executives organized into a training committee. By discussing the problems of training with such a committee, the training officer may finally induce it to recommend ways and means of determining training needs and supplying them. Having to some extent developed the training program themselves, the various members of the committee are likely to support it among their own subordinates. If any restatement of goals and expectations is required, it is essential that such a restatement be shared by the top management staff and not simply come from the training officer himself.

The technique of the training committee (which is the technique of overcoming opposition to plans by participation in planning) may be extended to lower levels embracing a greater proportion of the organization's members. Sub-committees of the major training committee can be formed to plan for training in specific areas. Ideally, the whole organization could be brought into the planning of its own training, thereby enlisting a maximum of cooperation and support for the training program. However, much as the training officer may wish it, it is unlikely that any organization will give up its normal activities for any extended period of time and devote itself exclusively to its own improvement.

It must be faced frankly that the participation-in-planning method of obtaining cooperation for a training audit and the training programs which follow involve an element of manipulation. If the training officer has some ideas of what he wants to accomplish, he must get the training committees to accept those ideas as their own. He must try so to direct and control the committee discussions that the committee conclusions are in line with his training goals and his general knowledge of training methods.

Frequently, however, training officers stimulate a vast training activity with no pre-formed ideas or goals, and training becomes training for training's sake. Having been appointed to positions as training officers, some individuals cast about wildly to promote training at any cost. They are likely to feel that training *per se* is good, and the more training the better. Even as many budget officers, identifying too strongly with their own activities, act as though the budget procedures are the end of the organization rather than means to the end, so many training officers behave as though the organization was established in order to train its members.

This kind of behavior is perfectly understandable—it is identical with all the other situations in which a specialist, by reason of his identifications, exaggerates the importance of his specialty. It is accentuated in the case of the training officer because he is in a much weaker position to impose his wishes, even if given formal authority by the top administrator, than is the budget officer or the classification specialist. Because of the close relationship of training to the other means of organization influence, the training program will be effective largely to the extent that the training officer is able to convince administrators and supervisors that training is a normal and highly useful part of the supervisory process.

Here again we reach the conclusion, already suggested earlier, that the chief task of the training specialist is not to train (although he may be very useful as a technical advisor on training techniques), but to secure the acceptance of training as an essential element in the communication system. Although formal training courses have their place in an in-service training program, by far the greatest part of the training that takes place in organizations occurs in the normal course of supervisory activity.

CHAPTER EIGHTEEN

The Struggle for Existence: Organizational Equilibrium

IN THE last few chapters we have been examining how governmental organizations secure the cooperation of their employees. The focus of attention has been upon the *internal* relations of the organization members with each other. It is now necessary to see how organizations adjust themselves to the world about them; their relations with other and competing organizations, with Congress and with the general public. These adjustments and relations are essentially of a political character, and indeed, the topics we are about to discuss are sometimes referred to as "the politics of administration."

Which organizational relations are "internal" and which "external" depends on the standpoint. From the standpoint of the Chief of the Forest Service, his relations with the Secretary of Agriculture are external; from the standpoint of the Secretary, these same relations are internal. In this chapter we will be concerned largely with relations that are external to major organizational units—departments and bureaus.

Organizational Equilibrium

In earlier chapters, organizations and organizational units have been treated as social systems that maintain themselves in some sort of dynamic equilibrium. We must now examine more closely the nature of this equilibrium. We may describe it thus:

1. An organization is a system of interrelated social behaviors of a number of persons whom we call the *participants* in the organi-

zation. The participants in a governmental organization include not only its employees, but also the executive hierarchy to which the unit head is responsible, employees of other organizational units (overhead units, for example) with which it cooperates, legislators, members of interest groups and lobbies that are concerned with its program, citizens who are regulated by it and those who receive its services, and so forth.

2. Each participant and each group of participants receives *from* the organization *inducements* in return for which he makes *to* the organization *contributions*. For example, the inducements that a mail carrier receives from the Post Office Department are his salary, conditions of work, associates, and so forth. The contributions the mail carrier provides are his time and effort, utilized by the organization for the delivery of mail.

3. Each participant will continue his participation in an organization only so long as the inducements offered him are as great or greater (measured in terms of *his* values and in terms of the alternatives open to him) than the contributions he is asked to make. The mail carrier will quit if his salary is reduced while other work opportunities are available; and he may refuse to perform overtime work unless he is paid for it at a high hourly rate.

4. The contributions provided by the various groups of participants are the source from which the organization manufactures the inducements offered to participants. The funds provided by the legislative body (its contribution) provide an inducement in the form of salaries to the employees; the services performed by employees (their contribution) induce the legislative body to appropriate funds.

5. Hence, an organization is "solvent"—and will continue in existence—only so long as the contributions are sufficient to provide inducements in large enough measure to draw forth these contributions. If the legislative body does not believe that the public is receiving its "money's worth" in service from an organization, it may reduce or even eliminate its appropriation, hence cutting off from it the means to induce the employees to contribute further services.

In previous chapters we have already paid a great deal of attention to the equilibrium berween the inducements offered to employees and the contributions demanded of them; and in Chapter 2 we examined the inducements offered to outside groups to assist in the promotion of new organizations. In the present chapter, taking up the story where we left off in Chapter 2, we shall study in detail the relationships between the equilibrium of inducements and contributions of employees *inside* the organization and the equilibrium of individuals and groups *outside* the organization who contribute to its support.

Kinds of External Support Needed

Among the participants, other than employees, with whom we shall be concerned are the legislature, the chief executive, other governmental organizations, groups regulated or served by the organization ("clientele" groups), and the general public.

LEGISLATIVE SUPPORT

No administrative organization in this country can come into being or long exist without the support of the legislature and usually the chief executive. The legislature provides the legal authority and the funds for the organization. The legal basis of the organization includes not only the definition of its goal or objective, but very often also a rather detailed description of the organizational structure. The legislative body also passes many laws that stipulate how the organization may carry out its objective—laws relating to the management of personnel, accounting for funds, expenditures, procurement, the rights of the citizen as against the organization, and many others. In most cases these laws or statutes, which provide the legal basis for administration, must be approved by the chief executive before they go into effect.

In addition to laws of this kind, the legislature and the executive pass appropriation bills which allow the organization to spend money for personnel and for other purposes and without which it could spend no money. In some cases the chief executive has various kinds of legal authority, either in his own right under the Constitution or by delegation from the legislature, that he may redelegate to an administrative organization. Given this legal framework, it is clear that an administrative organization must have the support of the legislature or the executive—and usually both—if it is to come into existence and continue to exist.

SUPPORT OF OTHER ORGANIZATIONS

From this ultimate dependence of administrative organizations on the legislature and the chief executive there develops in a democracy a dependence upon many other persons and groups in the society. In the first place, other governmental organizations, such as a central budget agency or a civil service commission, will have considerable power to hinder or aid any administrative organization in the accomplishment of its goals. Thus the support of these other governmental organizations also becomes necessary.

CLIENTELE SUPPORT

In the second place, the backing of groups or individuals that can influence the behavior of the legislature and the executive must also be sought. For some administrative organizations there are groups within society whose support, working through their representatives in the legislature, can guarantee the survival of the organization against almost any odds and whose opposition, in like fashion, is tantamount to the death of the organization or at least considerable modification of its objective and methods. Thus farmer organizations working through the farm bloc in the Federal Congress can often make or unmake agricultural programs and the agencies that administer them.

The group within society that is most immediately interested in an organization's program may be called its *clientele*. Thus, organized labor is more directly concerned with the activities of the Department of Labor than is any other segment of the community. American business is more directly concerned with the activities of the Department of Commerce than is any other segment of the community. The railroads and the shippers are directly concerned with the activities of the Interstate Commerce Commission, and so forth. If the clientele group is large, united in interest, and well organized, it can have an impact on the legislature that makes its support or at least acquiescence important, if not necessary, to the existence of the administrative agency in question.

There is another reason why the support of outside groups must be sought. The administrative organization plans and carries out programs that require the cooperation of segments of the public or even the whole public. If the required amount of cooperation is not forthcoming, the organization will fail to accomplish its objectives and hence to satisfy its supporters. Those who are regulated must generally approve of, or at least accede to, these programs. Administrative regulations can not be enforced against a generally hostile public. The reader can appreciate this point if he will try to imagine an attempt to enforce a draft law toward which most of the people were actively hostile. Even in dictatorships administrative organizations must cultivate some general feeling of support or acquiescence in their programs or they will not be able to carry them out.

THE GENERAL PUBLIC

Finally, the general public through its vote may become a source of support or opposition to an administrative organization. The party in power may come to feel that the activities of a particular agency are so affecting general public opinion that it must interfere with the operations or objectives (or even the existence) of that agency.

Since public opinion concerning any particular governmental agency is generally rather vague, groups with specific interests in an agency's activities will usually have more effect than an incoherent general public. Thus it sometimes happens that opinion polls will show a majority of the people in favor of some activity which nevertheless is abolished or greatly modified by the legislature or the executive or both. A good example is the ill-fated Veteran's Emergency Housing Program of 1946 which got almost nowhere against solid blocks of opposition both within and without the government.

Although public opinion is usually not as influential as are pressure groups in affecting an agency's programs, still an enthusiastic general public support could probably not be negated by any pressure group. Likewise a general public hostility would probably result in abolition or substantial modification of any governmental program.

IMPORTANCE OF NON-LEGISLATIVE SUPPORT

Traditional political theory, confining its attention principally to the legal structure, has tended to overemphasize the dependence of administrative agencies upon the formal legislative and hierarchical controls, and to underemphasize correspondingly their dependence upon outside groups. Realistic study of the political process has begun to correct this emphasis. In the words of Norton Long:

> It may be urged that for all but the top hierarchy of the administrative structure the question of power is irrelevant. Legislative authority and administrative orders suffice. . . . Neither statute nor executive order, however, confers more than legal authority to act. Whether Congress or President can impart the substance of power as well as the form depends upon the line-up of forces in the particular case. A price control law wrung from a reluctant Congress by an amorphous and unstable combination of consumer and labor groups is formally the same as a law enacting a support price program for agriculture backed by the disciplined organizations of farmers and their congressmen. The differences for the scope and effectiveness of administration are obvious. . . .
>
> A similar criticism applies to any like claim for an agency head in his agency. Only in varying degrees can the powers of subordinate officials be explained as resulting from the chain of command. . . .
>
> To deny that power is derived exclusively from superiors in the hierarchy is to assert that subordinates stand in a feudal relation in which to a degree they fend for themselves and acquire support peculiarly their own. A structure of interests friendly or hostile, vague and general or compact and well-defined, encloses each significant center of administrative discretion. This structure is an important determinant of the scope of possible action. As a source of power and authority it is a competitor of the formal hierarchy.[1]

The Motives for External Support

In general, the inducements to external supporters come from the goals and objectives of governmental organizations or the values created by them. Even as the customer of a commercial organization is interested in its product, so the "customers" of governmental organizations are interested in the products of governmental action. They give their support, their contribution to the organization, in return for the satisfactions they derive from the values created by the organization, whether these be increased educational opportunity or national defense.

[1] "Power and Administration," *Public Administration Review* 9:257-264 (Autumn 1949), pp. 257-8.

When a group of people in a society becomes aware of an opportunity to achieve certain of the values that it holds either by supporting or opposing a governmental program, we call this set of values an *interest*, and the group that is organized around the promotion of the values an *interest group*. The activities of any particular governmental organization promote certain interests that have developed in society, are irrelevant to many interests, and are antagonistic to still others. Thus, for every administrative organization there are groups whose interests are promoted by the organization's activities, and who give in return their political support (e.g., the support of the American Legion for the Veterans' Administration). Other people and groups will be indifferent to the organization because it does not affect their interests (e.g., the Bureau of Foreign and Domestic Commerce has generally received neither support nor opposition from farm groups). Still others may develop an interest in its abolition or the modification of its activities because these activities challenge or destroy some of the values of the groups in question (e.g., a rent control agency becomes a target for landlord groups; pacifist groups oppose appropriations to the military departments).

THE CHANGING ENVIRONMENT

Since the structure of interests in society is dependent upon the physical and social environment, when these environmental conditions change, the pattern of interests in society changes with them. A change in environment may create a new group of interests; it may intensify or diminish old ones; it may cause an interest to disappear. An environmental change may greatly increase or decrease the number of persons sharing an interest; or it may shift the interest to an entirely new group of people.

As fire hazards increase, the fire department receives more support. As good land runs out, an interest in public irrigation appears. As floods become worse, an interest in flood control intensifies. When depressions occur, interest in relief becomes much stronger. As employment rises, the support of relief agencies and unemployment insurance agencies wanes. As the dependence of business upon technical knowledge increases, an interest in cheap technical education appears. As war becomes total and more terrible and imminent, an interest in the health of young men and the development of skills in the labor force begins to appear. As the economic situation of the railroad industry deteriorates, hostility toward the Interstate Commerce Commission decreases.

CONFLICTS OF INTERESTS

For most goals in society there are antithetical or conflicting interests. Hence programs that satisfy one group of people often reduce satisfactions of other groups. Regulating prices in the interest of consumers decreases profits of producers and sellers. Protecting and strengthening the collective bargaining interest of unions destroys the advantages many employers derive from weak unions or from power over working conditions. Protecting the interests of shippers in fair and uniform rates reduces earnings of railroad companies derived from the ability to impose high and discriminatory rates. Protecting the broadcasting industry (and the listening public) by licensing broadcasters interferes with people who would like to enter the industry but are not allowed to by the Federal Communications Commission.

Which interest will be protected and which sacrificed is determined by the political process. In fact, many political scientists would take this as the very definition of politics—in the words of Harold Lasswell, politics determines "who gets what, when, how."

When one interest is politically strong and well organized and its opponents are weak and unorganized, the answer is simple—as witness the defeat of the public housing program in the 80th Congress. Sometimes, however, the conflicting interests are of roughly the same strength, and the conflict resolves itself in some sort of compromise. Subsequent shifts in the relative strengths of conflicting groups then are reflected, from time to time, in program changes. Thus, successive changes in labor legislation over the past generation have reflected changes in the strength and degree of organization of labor and employer groups.

Few, indeed, are the administrative agencies that have all friends and no enemies. There is almost certain to be some hostility towards any administrative organization and its program. To survive with any given program of activities, an agency must find friendly groups whose political support is strong enough to overcome the opposition of hostile groups. To preserve its friends, it must to some degree adapt its program to their interests. To neutralize its enemies, it must sometimes sacrifice elements in its program that attract the most effective political opposition. Hence, organizations are in a continual process of adjustment to the political environment that surrounds them—an adjustment that seeks to keep a favorable balance of political support over political opposition.

The Psychology of Adjustment

We have described briefly the nature of the environment to which administrative organizations must adjust. It is clear from the discussion that unless adjustment takes place organizations will cease to exist for they will lose the support necessary for their continuance. But we must be careful not to attribute to organizations any mythical "will to survive." If organizations do commonly adjust to their environments in order to survive, the explanation for the adjustment process must lie in the aims and motivations of their executives and other employees. What we have already learned about the motivations of executives and employees helps to explain their attempts to adapt organizations to their environments.

In Chapters 3, 4, and 5 we have seen that individuals and social groups in organizations may be identified with the goals of the organization, with the organization as a social group, or with their own personal advancement and aggrandizement. Usually, they are partially identified with all three. Any of these motivations—goal identification, group identification, or desire for personal advancement—may permit those adaptations of the organization to its environment that will assure its survival. To the extent that members are sincerely attached to the organizational goals, they will seek to preserve the organization as a vehicle for achieving those goals, or coming as close to this achievement as possible. To the extent they identify with the group, survival of the organization takes on direct value. In so far as they wish their own advancement, they will work for the survival and especially the growth of the organization. All three motivations will prepare the members for compromise and opportunism when these are essential to survival.

INTEREST IN GOALS

It may appear paradoxical that the strong attachment which an executive may feel for the goals of his organization unit should make him adaptive to the demands made by external groups upon the organization for changes in these goals. For many people working in relief agencies, helping needy people is a tremendous source of satisfaction. Employees of a park department may get positive enjoyment and a sense of accomplishment out of creating and maintaining beautiful parks. Why, then, will such individuals not resist external forces that attempt to change the organization's goals?

The answer is that goal-attached individuals *will* resist, but that in many cases their resistance will be tempered by tactical opportunism—the willingness to accept half a loaf rather than none. If the external opposition is too strong, compromise may be the price of the agency's survival. Even the individual with a strong goal attachment may prefer compromise to the complete destruction of the agency's program, although the willingness to compromise is undoubtedly in inverse relation to the importance of the goals to the individual and the extent of sacrifice required for survival.

For most people, aspirations are always tempered by the possibilities of achievement. Hence, attachment to goals has two aspects. On the one hand, it involves a striving toward the desired goal, and consequent satisfaction or dissatisfaction to the degree that it is secured or lost. On the other hand, it involves an estimation of what is possible, and a choice among possible alternatives of that which seems to come closest to the desired goal (even though every achievable alternative may fall far short of it).[2] To the extent that the first aspect prevails in behavior, compromise will be rejected. Under these circumstances, failure to reach the desired goals produces frustration, rather than a modification of aspirations.

To the extent that an individual tempers his aspirations by realistic expectations of what is possible, attachment to goals is

[2] The distinction we are making here is very close to Max Weber's distinction between *Wertrationalität* (uncompromising attachment to goals) and *Zweckrationalität* (attachment to preferred attainable alternatives). See *The Theory of Social and Economic Organization*, trans. by A. M. Henderson and Talcott Parsons (New York: Oxford University Press, 1947), pp. 115–17.

entirely consistent with compromise and adaptation. Under these circumstances, the adjustment of the organization to its political environment will not be rejected, but instead that mode of adjustment will be sought which will assure survival with the least sacrifice of the desired goals.

The reaction of an individual who derives strong satisfactions from his organization's goals when these goals are threatened by outside forces will depend, then, not only on the strength of his attachment, but also on his optimism as to their achievability, and upon the strength of his "utopianism" (by which we mean his resistance to tactical opportunism). If an appropriate attitude scale could be devised, individuals would undoubtedly exhibit a wide range of reactions to a utopianism-opportunism scale. For some individuals (the utopian ones), strong interest in a goal renders them unwilling to compromise, and such individuals may resign rather than accept a change in goals. Other individuals (the opportunistic ones) may be willing to compromise when the outcome of an uncompromising fight seems dim and when the compromise does not appear to damage too greatly the goals they are seeking to achieve. When an individual is faced with such a choice, his reactions will depend upon his assessment of the chances of a successful fight, upon the depth of his attachment to the goals, and upon his ethical attitudes toward the morality or immorality of compromise.

GROUP IDENTIFICATION

The "we" feelings that attach individuals to groups are by no means exclusively or even primarily derived from acceptance of specific goals. When an army officer develops a deep attachment to the First Division, and resists a transfer to another unit, this need not be because the objectives of the two units are different. Rather, the attachment represents a feeling of "belongingness" quite akin to the identification a person forms with his family or his country.

Pride in membership leads an individual to attach direct value to the prestige, importance, and survival of the organization—a value very similar to that which he attaches to his own personal prestige and status. Under these circumstances he may value the organization's goals just because they are the values of his group, rather than, in converse order, identifying himself with the organization because he values its goals.

To the extent that the members of an organization have this kind of identification with it, their identification suffices to explain their interest in organizational survival. They will seek to find for the organization program goals that will assure its survival and enhance its prestige, and, in so doing, they will seek to adapt the group to the political and other conditions of survival. They will resist specific changes in program goals only when such changes would endanger the existence of the organization or damage its prestige.

INTEREST IN PERSONAL ADVANCEMENT

Even as most persons become more or less strongly attached to goals and to organizations, so most persons are also interested in personal success or advancement. People range from the highly selfish or mobile individual discussed in Chapter 3 to the martyr who gives up his life in the promotion of some organization or goal. Organizations may satisfy the interest in personal aggrandizement by providing good salaries, prestige, power, and promotional opportunities.

To the extent that a person's satisfactions depend upon personal advancement rather than goal achievement, modification of the organization's goal will, by itself, cause no decline in satisfactions. A mobile person will be willing to compromise or sacrifice goals if necessary to preserve or increase these personal satisfactions. This willingness to sacrifice goals in the interest of personal aggrandizement represents another kind of opportunism, to be distinguished from the kinds previously discussed. The survival drive, to the extent that it is dominated by self-advancement, expresses itself as a drive to maintain personal positions of power and importance regardless of organizational objectives and to maintain the organization as such regardless of its programs.

RESISTANCE TO ADJUSTMENT

We find among organizational members, then, three sets of motives that tend to make the organization adapt to the demands of external forces, if these demands are sufficiently strong. The first is a tactical opportunism which arises out of a desire to preserve the organization as an effective means of goal accomplishment, even at the cost of a partial modification of goals and program. The second is an opportunism that seeks to preserve the organization as an object of the pride of membership. The third is a self-protective opportunism which arises out of a desire of the individual to protect his position, power, prestige, and salary.

On the other side of the picture, we find two forces within organizations that resist adjustment to external pressures. The first of these—goal attachment—may countenance adjustment, but only grudgingly and with minimum sacrifice of goals, as we have just seen. The second may be described as "inertia"—resistance due to the painfulness of altering habitual and accustomed ways of doing things. This inertia is derived from a number of psychological forces, including the disinclination to admit that the old ways are not the best ways and the personal cost of thinking out and trying new ways.

A good illustration of the inertia factor is the appeal made to the Congress in 1903 by General Miles, Commanding General of the Army, in opposition to the establishment of the General Staff.

> More than 100 years ago our Army was organized by the genius of Washington, Steuben, Hamilton, and others. In all the wars in which we have been engaged it has in the end been victorious. It has withstood intrigue and contaminating influence from without and has absorbed the injurious elements that have been forced upon it, sustaining the honor of the Nation, and the glory of American arms in every campaign and in its present organization is best adapted to our great Republic. In my judgement a system that is the fruit of the best thought of the most eminent patriots and ablest military men that this country has produced should not be destroyed by substituting one that is more adapted to the monarchies of the Old World.[3]

ORGANIZATION DANGER

Since members of organizations seek to maintain an equilibrium between satisfactions and contributions, anything likely to reduce these satisfactions and thereby destroy or disturb the adjustment is a danger, to be warded off if possible.

Danger to Tradition. In a tradition-bound agency almost any suggestion for change may constitute a danger. Organization mem-

---

[3] Quoted in Nelson, *National Security and the General Staff*, pp. 53–4.

bers often become very adept at proving that all suggestions for new methods, especially those from outside the organization, are founded in ignorance. Past decisions tend to become rationalized in a developing philosophy which shows that they were consistent with one another and which tends to control new decisions. Any break in this façade of consistency, such as the acceptance of a new suggestion not easily harmonized with past decisions, not only casts doubts on the past decisions but requires the development of new harmonizing principles.

Danger to Organizational Goals. Anything likely to result in a redefinition of an agency's goal is a danger. Reduction or limitation of legal authority, reduced appropriations, personnel ceilings, increased judicial oversight of an agency's operations—all will constitute dangers to the goal and hence to organization members who depend heavily on goal accomplishment for satisfactions. It must be remembered that the crippling actions listed above are a final result. Before them come an increase in the agency's enemies or a decrease in its friends. Hence, the growing hostility of a pressure group; or a growing public indifference; or the increasing unpopularity of a program, an office, or an official may also constitute dangers.

Danger to Personal Goals and Pride of Membership. The satisfactions that come from personal advancement or success and from the sense of "belonging" to a prestigeful group are threatened when the agency loses prestige or other opportunities for personal satisfactions. Thus, reduced funds or personnel ceilings will also constitute dangers for this type of equilibrium. Furthermore, since a reduction in legal authority or a change in goal may affect the prestige of an agency, these actions may also constitute dangers to the group-identified and mobile individuals.

Thus we see that many kinds of situations may be interpreted as dangers by all members of an organization; the whole organization may be united in opposition to these threats to survival. However, as far as the satisfactions of personal aggrandizement alone are concerned, these may survive many changes in goal. That is, changes in goal that do not affect opportunities for personal success will not destroy the satisfactions that come from personal aggrandizement and will not, therefore, be regarded as serious dangers by highly mobile persons.

The Executive and Organizational Adjustment

The principal organ of adjustment within an organization is the executive hierarchy. There are several reasons why the executives (increasingly so as we mount the hierarchy) are normally more adjustive, more compromising, than the bulk of the organization's members.

"NATURAL SELECTION"

In the first place, a sort of natural selection brings about this phenomenon. The executive hierarchy has a much greater influence on the organization than the bulk of its members, and so, if that hierarchy were incapable of adjustment, the organization would cease to exist. In other words, if an organization continues to exist it is a safe conclusion that its hierarchy is adjustable.

MOBILITY OF EXECUTIVES

Highly mobile individuals—individuals with very strong personal ambitions—gravitate into positions of power. In order to mount the ladder of hierarchical success it is often necessary to take actions or make decisions of a somewhat cold-blooded kind. One must "go to lunch with the right people." Sometimes friends must be by-passed. Occasionally someone must be fired who badly needs his job. Yearnings and aspirations of incapable people must sometimes be disregarded. Most persons, except those who have strong personal ambitions or unusually strong attachments to a goal, find such behavior difficult. Consequently, many highly mobile people climb upward in organizational hierarchies by a kind of self-selection.

IDENTIFICATIONS OF EXECUTIVES

There is yet another reason why the executive hierarchy is usually increasingly adjustable or compromising as we go up toward the highest levels. The head of an agency, if he identifies with anything, is likely to identify with the whole agency, with its total program rather than with any of its parts. If it is necessary to sacrifice one branch or the program it administers to obtain the necessary support for the whole agency, that sacrifice may appear to the top executive merely a means to an end—and not the sacrifice of the end itself, as it may appear to the branch personnel. This difference in the breadth of identification between the executive and the people below him will usually be evident from the lowest supervisory level to the highest.

EXTERNAL CONTACTS OF EXECUTIVES

A final reason for executive adaptability is that the executive is less insulated from the rest of the world than those below him. He must answer questions and justify the operations of his staff to his superiors. Higher level executives must often justify the operations of their agencies or bureaus to legislative committees. Interested groups and individuals and other administrative agencies will usually make their demands known through the executives; and it is the executives who are often singled out for criticism by the press. This wide range of interests and influences that play upon the executives sharpens their awareness of other points of view, and the political consequences of the agency's decisions will have a special impact on them. It is easy to be firm and uncompromising only when one is remote from the political consequences of his own actions.

The executive hierarchy has a particularly important role to play both in adjustment and in resistance to adjustment. Both because of the expectations of their staffs and because of their own desires, executives will play a leading part in warding off external dangers. Because of position and prestige they will have influence with external groups and individuals, be they the Civil Service Commission, the chief executive, or a legislative committee. A good deal of their attention will usually be given to preventing actions within the organization that might stimulate the antagonism of external individuals and groups. Frequently the very top executive of an administrative organization, whether he is elected or appointed, is a representative of an important political constituency.

The importance of the opportunistic or compromising element in the satisfactions of the executive hierarchy is that it renders the executive more flexible and adjustable; it enables him to see the importance of, and to act on the principle of, "doing a little wrong to do a great right." Through his efforts persons interested in the organization's goals, both within and without the organization, may accomplish part of their desires whereas otherwise they might accomplish nothing.

AN ILLUSTRATION OF THE EXECUTIVE ROLE IN SURVIVAL

In April of 1943 a situation arose in the Office of War Information that illustrates many of the problems of survival, especially the role of the executives in it. The OWI was established in June, 1942, to consolidate several government information agencies then existing. The Domestic Branch took over the Office of Facts and Figures (OFF). The Division of Publication of OFF continued in OWI with little change. Its function was to write pamphlets on various war subjects. The members of the division understood their function to be the "honest presentation of war information" on the assumption that "the better the American people understand what this war is about, the harder they will work and fight to win it." The division of publications was allowed to select its own subjects and make its own interpretations, and little provision was made for reviewing or clearing its work before release.

Some of its pamphlets caused a great storm of criticism and controversy, especially from the Congress. "Negroes and the War," aimed at improving Negro morale, caused bitter criticism from southern Congressman.[4] The Army decided the pamphlet should not be generally distributed to the troops. "Battle Stations for All," a pamphlet published in March, 1943, dealt with inflation. This pamphlet excited extreme criticism of OWI both in the press and in Congress. For example, David Lawrence wrote in the Washington *Evening Star*, April 19, 1943, under the title of "New Dealism Colors New O.W.I. Booklet," that "no more flagrant case of abuse of power and misuse of public funds could be found." He said, "the book is a splendid piece of propaganda for the renomination and reelection of President Roosevelt for a fourth term. Some parts of it read like a campaign textbook for stump speeches." Many others echoed this criticism.

Top OWI officials began to fear for the existence of OWI be-

[4] See *Congressional Record*, House, Feb. 10, 1943.

cause of this growing hostility of outside groups towards it. Consequently, they made some reorganizing moves and reassignments so
that the work of the division of publications would be reviewed before release by a more extensive top staff dominated by people
with much practical experience in publishing, radio, and advertising. In April of 1943, this strengthened top staff suppressed a report
on the food situation from the division of publications on the
ground that the figures had been challenged as inaccurate by Secretary of Agriculture Wickard and James F. Byrnes, Director of the
Office of Economic Stabilization. Furthermore, OWI top officials
stated that the report would have a depressing effect on the public.[5]
This effort on the part of the top OWI management to protect the
relations and support of the agency did not come off without a
hitch. The head of the division of publications and a large part of
his staff believed the report was correct and that the real issue was
between the presentation of "honest facts" and the artifices of
"slick salesmanship." They resigned, making a public statement,
part of which is reprinted below.

> We are leaving because of our conviction that it is impossible for
> us, under those who now control our output, to tell the full truth. No one
> denies that promotional techniques have a proper and powerful function
> in telling the story of a war. But as we see it, the activities of the Office of
> War Information on the home front are now dominated by high-pressure
> promoters who prefer slick salesmanship to honest information. These
> promoters would treat as stupid and reluctant customers the men and
> women of the United States. They delude themselves that the only effec-
> tive appeal to the American public in wartime is the selfish one of "What's
> in it for me?"
> We know that Americans have an intelligence, a will to win, and a
> dignity which deserves the facts as well as the slogans.
> We believe, as Elmer Davis has said, "That the better the American
> people understand what this war is about, the harder they will work and
> fight to win it."

While it is not possible to know the exact motives of the participants in this drama, several of the propositions stated earlier
in this discussion are well illustrated here. The publications division employees who resigned exhibited a strong attachment to
organizational goals and a refusal to compromise (even for tactical
reasons). The subjection of their division to review by top OWI

[5] *New York Times*, April 14, 1943, p. 25, col. 4.

officials probably represented also a reduction in their personal prestige and power and the satisfactions derivable from these. The top OWI officials were less strongly attached to the goals as defined by the publications division (and probably shared some of the critical attitudes of the Congress) and were sensitive to the danger to which the agency was exposed by an uncompromising adherence to these goals. Further, their success in gaining a power of review over the work of the publications division enhanced their status and prestige in the agency. These essential features in the OWI struggle could be duplicated in numerous internal crises in governmental agencies, federal, state and local.

The Conditions of Survival

We have seen that various groups and individuals, both within and outside of administrative organizations, make contributions to them in return for satisfactions derived from them. Groups and individuals outside contribute political support in return for satisfactions derived from the accomplishment of the organization's goal. Members of the organization contribute time, skills and knowledge in return for the satisfaction of personal and organizational goals to which they are attached.

SURVIVAL FOR WHOM?

However, as we have also seen, the satisfaction-contribution equilibria of various organizational members may not all be the same, so that a readjustment to the external world which is desired by some may not be acceptable to others. Even as some individuals and groups outside the organization gain at the expense of others, so within an organization the survival of one set of satisfactions may be at the expense of another. Prestige and power may not survive unless goals are modified; but goal modifications may be impossible unless some accustomed ways of doing and thinking are sacrificed. For organizations to survive there must be a continuous and delicate adjustment of several different sets of satisfactions and contributions to the conditions that determine the shifting interests within society.

ADJUSTMENT TO WHAT?

The problems of survival are not the same for all administrative organizations. Some promote or protect newly recognized interests that have struggled long for recognition, such as the interest of labor unions in worker organization and collective bargaining. Here the external support is enthusiastic and the external opposition bitterly hostile. Here also strong goal attachments within the organization are likely. Such organizations are quite insecure because a shift in the political tide may bring the organization's enemies into political power. In the 1946 elections, the enemies of the National Labor Relations Board secured political power and vastly modified its program (through the Taft-Hartley Act), turning it to some extent into an enemy of organized labor. Many employees of the Board found it difficult to accept the new orientation and resigned or were shunted into positions of relative unimportance.

Other organizations promote interests so thoroughly accepted that no one questions the organization's goals any longer. Such is the case with fire and police departments, the Post Office Department, and many others. Here, strong goal attachments are more difficult, though not impossible, to maintain. External "dangers" are more likely to consist in demands for better, more courteous, or more efficient service.

Some interests are obviously and admittedly short-lived, and it is expected that the organizations established to promote them will disappear when their objectives are completed. Here, although organizational members may wistfully wish that their agency could be continued, the fact that it cannot is so absolute as to be acceptable. Organizations in this class include emergency agencies dealing with floods, wars, and the like. Even in this kind of agency there may sometimes be a struggle for continuance. An example is the difficulty of disarming after a war—a difficulty not ascribable solely to the "dangers of the international situation."

Whereas some organizational goals represent a clear triumph of one interest over conflicting ones, many represent compromises among conflicting interests. In this category we would include much governmental regulatory activity. For example, railroad regulation is always a shifting compromise among the interests of the road managements, the shippers, the passengers, railroad labor, the small stockholders, railroad suppliers, and railroad financial control groups.[6] In this kind of organization, the attempts of the conflicting external interests to get complete control are constant, and the organizational members are, for this reason, constantly embroiled in the politics of survival.

Whether or not there are external conflicts of interest in an organization's goals, the problem of survival is continuous. A new high executive may have ideas about reorganizing or "improving operations"; or a citizen's group may demand a "shakeup"; or some executive, agency, or bureau may begin to acquire more power within the whole government or the whole organization. Any of these may threaten the survival of satisfactions derived from accustomed methods, from prestige and other personal opportunities, and even from the values reflected by the organization's operations.

Conclusion

The material set forth in this chapter gives considerable credence to the charge often made by critics of government that government agencies are exceedingly hardy and long-lived. But our analysis does not lend support to the doctrine that this longevity is due to some bureaucratic "will to survive." To be sure, there are many strong motivations at work within organizations that lead these organizations to adapt their activities to the requirements of survival. But government agencies cannot exist without appropriations or enabling statutes. They can survive only so long as they can continue to secure the support of politically effective groups in the community and continue through these groups to secure legislative and executive support. "Bureaucrats" can wish to survive, but they do not determine the conditions of survival.

[6] See Merle Fainsod and Lincoln Gordon, *Government and the American Economy*, (New York: W. W. Norton & Co., 1941), chap. 9.

CHAPTER NINETEEN

❧

The Struggle for Existence: The Tactics of Survival

IN THE foregoing chapter we have described the social, psychological, and political factors underlying the survival drive; the need for adjustment to a changing environment; and the principal organs of adjustment within administrative organizations. Next we will describe some of the tactics of survival adopted by administrative organizations in order to illustrate the generalizations of the previous chapter. The material will be presented under five general headings: (1) seeking legislative support; (2) seeking the support of superiors and other persons of prestige; (3) executive compromise and survival; (4) seeking the support of important extra-governmental groups; and (5) seeking public support.

Seeking Legislative Support

Special treatment of legislators and legislative committees is automatic and axiomatic within the bureaucracy. Requests of legislators are handled swiftly and with special care. Most federal governmental organizations have special "congressional correspondence" units whose function is to see that congressional inquiries receive prompt attention and are answered with the proper tone. Some Federal agencies maintain special congressional liaison officers who work constantly with congressmen, anticipating their needs and seeing that these are fulfilled.

TECHNIQUES FOR SECURING SUPPORT

Both the need of good congressional relations and techniques of seeking it can be illustrated from the experiences and practices of the fuel rationing officials during World War II. Fuel oil rationing got off to a bad start in the autumn of 1942. The program was somewhat complicated, and not everyone concerned had been properly instructed in his part. Many instances of error and injustice occurred, and the general confusion surrounding installation of the program received a good deal of publicity. The Truman Committee held hearings and published a very critical report on December 11, 1942.[1] The Senate Special Committee to Investigate Gasoline and Fuel Oil Shortages reported in February, 1943, that "whatever one's view of the theory underlying the system of calculating the ration, in practice it has collapsed." [2]

Forced by these experiences to become conscious of the need for better relations, the fuel rationing officials set out to win the support of congressmen for their program. Some of the things they did, and their results, are described in the following excerpts from an inter-office memorandum.

The need for aggressively fostering good relations with Congress was brought home somewhat painfully by the hostile and unfounded attacks on the fuel oil program by the Truman Committee and the Maloney Committee and also by the unsympathetic and critical letters from Congressmen. In attempting to solve this problem we have taken several steps:

1. To each member of Congress from the rationed area we wrote a letter on February 24 requesting their criticisms and suggestions in the development of next year's fuel oil rationing program. The response to this letter was extremely favorable. It was read into the Congressional Record. Over 70 percent of the senators and a large majority of the representatives replied. Some congressmen requested suggestions from their constituents and passed them on to us. Many of these were very helpful. . . .

2. When the new program was crystallized we sent an advance copy of a tentative draft outlining the changes in next year's plan. The response to this was almost unanimously favorable; of approximately 150 replies, only two or three were critical or unfavorable. . . .

3. Mr. B. and I discussed the fuel oil rationing program personally with many members of Congress who requested an interview. We saw most of the senators from the affected area and a fairly large proportion of the representatives. We observed that their reaction to this approach was quite favorable. They appreciated being consulted and they welcomed the opportunity to make a direct contribution. . . .

[1] Senate Report No. 480, Part 13, 77th Cong., 2nd Sess.
[2] Senate Report No. 59, 78th Cong., 1st Sess., Feb. 22, 1943.

LEGISLATIVE PROTECTION AGAINST EXECUTIVE CONTROL

Legislative support is sought not simply as protection against extra-governmental groups but also as a protection against higher reaches of the executive hierarchy, including the chief executive and overhead agencies. Conversely, simply being in an executive hierarchy does not mean that one can direct freely those below him. Often the executive must seek legislative support to overcome or overbalance the legislative support that his subordinates have built up for themselves. This situation is well illustrated by the following summary of General Otto L. Nelson's description of the establishment of the General Staff.[3]

Elihu Root, a lawyer, was made Secretary of the War by President McKinley after the conduct of the Spanish-American War had shown a deplorable lack of coordination between the various branches of the Army. He accepted as his task a major reorganization of the War Department, especially with regard to the creation of a General Staff. He soon found that he would be unable to accomplish this until he had built up support for his idea in the public, in Congress, and within the War Department. As his biographer says, "Officers long entrenched in sinecures in Washington had been successful in . . . firmly establishing their political position with congressional and senatorial backers." [4] At that time, positions in the staff services in Washington were filled by permanent appointment (rather than by the rotation system now used).

In this situation Root moved very slowly. Some of his young officers, who favored the General Staff idea, urged that it be included in the 1901 Act relating to the Army, but Root and McKinley thought that sufficient support had not yet been obtained.[5] Root made speeches on the subject, wrote about it in his annual report, sent material on it to magazine and newspaper editors, had a book recommending it published at government expense and widely circulated, won as many high ranking officers to the idea as he could, and did many other things before he finally introduced a bill into Congress, which became law on February 14, 1903.

---

[3] Nelson, *National Security and the General Staff.*
[4] Phillip C. Jessup, *Elihu Root* (New York: Dodd, Mead, and Co., 1938). Vol. 1, 1845–1909, p. 220. Quoted in Nelson, op. cit., p. 40.
[5] Ibid., p. 48.

Even Root's skillful, careful management, however, had not overcome all the legislative support for survival of the old system. Nelson reports:

The original War Department draft had suffered several major alterations at the hands of Congress. Most important was the refusal of Congress to eliminate the Inspector General's Department and transfer its functions. This was due to the political adeptness of the then Inspector General, Brigadier General Joseph Breckinridge. Root realized that an organization for thought must have facilities which would enable it to perceive what it must think about. Congress, however, decreed that an inspecting service was not necessary to the operation of a General Staff.

Another subtle change, destined to bring future trouble, was what might appear to be a harmless enough modification of the original War Department draft. In the War Department draft it was proposed "the Chief of Staff under the direction of the President and Secretary of War shall have supervision of all the troops of the line and of the several administrative staff and supply departments. A bureau chief, without public hearing, evidently influenced a modification. . . . The change was adroitly accomplished by specifying in detail the bureaus subject to the supervision of the Chief of Staff and omitting the one of which he was head. Another adroit change was one limiting the Chief of Staff to supervision of military duties not otherwise assigned by law . . . [which] opened the door of opportunity for any bureau chief with influence enough to secure legislation assigning matters definitely to his control." [6]

Even legal limitations on the machinations for survival may have little significance if an administrative organization has strong legislative support. For example, the Budget and Accounting Act of 1921 prohibits Federal departments from seeking appropriations larger than those recommended by the President in the annual budget or supplements thereto. How the bureaucracy can get around such executive controls and present its case to its congressional friends is illustrated by the following interchange between Congressman Tarver of the House Appropriations Committee and Marvin Jones, Head of the War Food Administration.

Mr. Tarver: . . . I have noted with a great deal of misgiving this proposal of the Budget to cut down A. A. A. funds to $290,000,000 and to provide for a further cut in the next fiscal year to $200,000,000. . . . Do you feel that that is a wise course of procedure? If not, what are the reasons which cause you to arrive at your conclusion?

[6] Ibid., pp. 58–9. The quotes within the quotation are from General Carter in *Senate Document* 119, 68th Cong., 1st Sess., p. 45.

Mr. Jones: I can only give you my personal opinion on those matters because we submit our requests to the Bureau of the Budget, and, of course, the official Budget then comes up to Congress by way of an estimate. I do not hesitate to give you my personal opinion on these matters if you wish me to do so. . . .

Mr. Tarver: I would be very glad to have you do so.

Mr. Jones: I think it would be very unfortunate if through a reduction in funds, especially at this critical period of the war, the A. A. A. is handicapped.

I would like to see, if it were left to me personally, full provision made by direct appropriation for soil-conservation payments. They have paid great dividends. There is no question about it.

Mr. Tarver: You mean for $300,000,000?

Mr. Jones: Yes. That is what I personally would prefer. I am giving you just my personal viewpoint.[7]

In addition to the kind of "lobbying" mentioned above, many federal agencies engage in active lobbying before state legislatures to remove obstacles to the accomplishment of their objectives. Thus, the Federal Housing Administration, in order to promote its program of mortgage insurance and thereby advance its housing objectives, has secured the passage of many state laws allowing state-chartered banks to participate in the program. "The Public Works Administration, during the period of its activities, was instrumental in bringing about the passage of over 300 state legislative acts affecting its relationships with political subdivisions of states." [8] State administrative agencies are an extremely important source of pressure on state legislatures.[9] In addition, national associations of state and local officials, in a good position to bring pressure to bear on their national Representatives and Senators, have become active and influential lobbyists before the national Congress, especially with regard to federal grants-in-aid. "The American Association of State Highway Officials and the American Vocational Association, for example, have succeeded in pushing through Congress bills upsetting presidential budget estimates." [10]

[7] House Committee on Appropriations, 79th Cong., 1st Sess., *Hearings* on Agriculture Department Appropriation Bill for 1946, Pt. 2, p. 10, 1945; quoted in V. O. Key, "Legislative Control," in Fritz Morstein Marx, ed., *Elements of Public Administration*, (New York: Prentice-Hall, Inc., 1946), p. 350.

[8] V. O. Key, *Politics, Parties, and Pressure Groups*, (2nd ed., New York: Thomas Y. Crowell Co., 1947), p. 709.

[9] See Elisabeth Mck. Scott and Belle Zeller, "State Agencies and Lawmaking," *Public Administration Review*, 2:205–20 (Summer, 1942).

[10] Key, op. cit., p. 709.

DEFENSE AGAINST LEGISLATIVE OPPOSITION

Not only do, and must, administrative organizations seek legislative support; they also try to minimize legislative hostility. They often operate with very inferior statutes in order to avoid opening up legislative debate by asking for needed amendments. This practice is an instance of a more general protective practice— the withholding of "dangerous" information or, even, the falsifying of reports. The falsification of administrative reports, either to the public, to the legislature, to the clientele, or to executive superiors, is a widespread organizational phenomenon. A good illustration of falsification of information requested by a Congressman, in order to forestall an administrative "danger," occurred in the Rural Electrification Administration in the Department of Agriculture in 1940.

The REA was established in 1935 to finance electric service to farmers who had not before had it. REA encouraged farmers' cooperative electric companies and came constantly in conflict with the foes of public power. Able and ambitious young men who believed in public power came into the agency, and their promotion was rapid.

When the REA was incorporated in the Department of Agriculture on July 1, 1939, Congress provided that there should be no promotions for one year. In anticipation of this law, the REA Administrator made many promotions just before July 1. Later, Representative Dirksen, an enemy of public power, requested a report as to the number of persons receiving three or more steps of in-grade promotions during the year. This request came to REA, and the report was prepared under the direction of Mr. Foss. Mr. Foss and his associates "knew of [Mr. Dirksen] as one who does not favor public power," and concluded that the request was a "fishing expedition." [11] Consequently, they decided to "use every legitimate means available to keep this report from appearing unnecessarily top-heavy." [12] Specifically, they omitted fifty-six names on the ground that the promotions had been made on the "eve of reclassification." [13]

[11] Hearings before a Subcommittee of the Committee on Agriculture and Forestry, Senate, 78th Cong., 2nd Sess., May 1940, pt. 5, p. 2037.

[12] Op. cit., p. 2036.

[13] Op. cit., p. 1980.

Mr. Dirksen found out about this falsification by checking it with the REA budget estimates submitted to Congress by the Bureau of the Budget. He then asked for independent reports from the Department of Agriculture and the General Accounting Office. These reports agreed with one another and showed that the REA report was false. In the hearings on the 1942 Agriculture appropriations, the REA report and REA promotions during 1939 were again brought up. Some of the questions and answers afford a good insight into the survival drive and false reporting as a survival tactic.

Question: This whole matter of the R.E.A. report, the way it was prepared, the request which was made, and instructions which were given, is all under consideration now. There must have been some reason for not telling Mr. Hendrickson (then Chief of Personnel in the Department of Agriculture) that "Here is the report, but we have omitted all promotions which were given pending reclassification," when he had actually asked for all promotions in all positions held by such employees.

Answer: If those matters are under discussion, there were, I believe, already at that time numerous intangible, but to my mind unmistakable, evidences that Mr. Hendrickson was more concerned with pleasing an anti-public-power Congressman than with defending a new member of the Department of Agriculture. I therefore probably felt that in the larger problem of the Administration's public power program I could not count on Mr. Hendrickson as an ally, and accordingly would have to take steps which I felt I could defend, but go no further than I had to in taking other people into my confidence. . . .

Question: Did the power fight enter into this inquiry?

Answer: It certainly did in my mind, because I knew that Mr. Dirksen was anti-public-power and I had no doubt of the correctness of my deductions that he was on a fishing expedition.[14]

Mr. Foss' motivations were ably set forth in his closing testimony.

Question: Before we close the record, Mr. Foss, do you have any other comments or remarks that you would like to have inserted?

Answer: I do. From the tenor of the questioning this morning I feel that my integrity and loyalty to the Government is not established. I want to call attention to the fact that the agency with which I was associated had at that time been experiencing some rough weather, the program was under attack, the future was far from clear. I accept responsibility for the execution of this whole incident, but I point out that there was absolutely nothing for me to gain personally, that my motives

[14] Op. cit., pp. 2049–50.

here that appear to have led me into action at variance with specific requests, were wholly and entirely dictated by a desire to protect R.E.A. against any and all comers from whatever side. . . . Any public relations man recognizes automatically that R.E.A.'s record of salary increases throughout 1938 looks extraordinary. As I see it, I had my choice between saying, "Well, the record is Mr. Carmody's record. It is nothing to me. I will shoot the works and put it all down without any regard to what is made of it," or saying, "Whether it is Mr. Carmody's or not, it is the record of the R.E.A. with which I am associated. I detect the hand of an enemy of public power behind this simple administrative request and I will be damned if I will give him anything I don't have to. I will try to be sufficiently prudent so that I can defend my actions and I will hope for the best." But the motive in all of that is absolutely simple; it is to endeavor to ward off what appeared to me to be a disguised utility attack. That is all.[15]

Using the Prestige of Superiors and Others

Because of the prestige attached to hierarchical status, administrative officials look to high level superiors to carry a good deal of the load in warding off dangers. Their prestige makes their requests harder to turn down. They can deal with other high level people, especially their own superiors, and thereby elicit still more prestigious support. If an administrative officer is prestigious enough, he can even awe some Congressmen. One of the important functions of superiors is warding off dangers, be they difficult clearance problems with other agencies or talking to unfriendly "big shots" among the clientele. The way superiors perform this function is one of the principal criteria by which their subordinates judge them.

The appeal to the superior for aid is illustrated by Frances Perkins's comments about General Hugh Johnson's (the NRA administrator) appeals to President Roosevelt to help him out of some of his difficulties. After having failed for some time to get the coal operators to accept a code, and with the miners pressing him for action, he finally appealed to the President. As Miss Perkins says, "At this point General Johnson asked the President to invite some individual coal operators to the White House and to try personally to persuade them to agree to a code. This was an illustration of General Johnson's almost touching but naive feeling

[15] Op. cit., pp. 2057–8.

that the President was all-wise and all-persuasive and that anybody would do anything the President asked him to do." [16]

To increase the prestige, hence protective power, of a superior, it is common practice to build up his personality in the public imagination. Almost any agency or bureau or division independent enough to handle its own public relations will have procedures for securing a popular build-up of its top executive, and often other high-level officers. This technique may be so effective that the agency becomes almost completely immune from either legislative or executive attack. The best illustration of this technique in American government, and the resulting security of the agency, is furnished by the FBI. As Key says,

> The Federal Bureau of Investigation furnishes an excellent example of this technique. Its chief, J. Edgar Hoover, has diligently cultivated public favor with after-dinner speeches, dramatic news releases, and books and articles extolling the fearless work of the "G-Men." So effective has been his continuing campaign that when Mr. Hoover makes a request of Congress newspaper editors all over the land editorialize in support of his position.[17]

The prestige used need not be that of an executive. Any high status or politically influential person may be a great aid to an administrative organization. For some years Bernard Baruch has served the public function of helping to get support for administrative proposals. For example, OPA was ready to install nationwide gasoline rationing as a tire-saving device in July of 1942 when a storm of congressional and public opposition from the West made it politically necessary, apparently, to have Baruch present the proposal to the nation. Using OPA data compiled by the OPA staff he endorsed OPA's recommendation, after which much of the opposition subsided.

Executive Compromise and Survival

It often happens that individuals or programs within an agency will become so unpopular that the higher executives decide to sacrifice them in order to continue the necessary support for the

[16] Frances Perkins, *The Roosevelt I Knew*, (New York: Viking Press, 1946), p. 232.
[17] Op. cit., p. 711.

rest of the agency and its programs. The American chief executives' practice of sacrificing unpopular officials is well established. Both Leon Henderson and Chester Bowles were asked to give up their positions as head of OPA because of strong congressional antipathy towards them.

SACRIFICE OF UNPOPULAR PERSONNEL AND PROGRAMS

A more serious deluge of this kind of executive opportunism is the current administrative loyalty program. During 1948, many governmental executives were so afraid of offending a hostile Congress, and especially a hostile House un-American Activities Committee, that they suspended employees as soon as any question of loyalty was raised and regardless of any proof. Thus there developed a kind of competition between the administrative organizations and the Congress to see which could detect a faint suspiciousness first.

The sacrifice of the program of a part of an agency as a measure of protection for the rest of the agency can be illustrated by the fate of the Federal Theatre Project in WPA. This unit was not allowed to campaign actively in its own behalf and was eventually sacrificed to mollify its enemies and maintain support for WPA. "Miss Flanagan complained that the requirement of central clearance prevented the theater project from getting out effective information to counteract the unfavorable attention being given its work. By 1939 the WPA evidently decided to sacrifice the theater activities to the public clamor rather than make a last-ditch stand that might have threatened all work relief efforts." [18]

ENFORCEMENT POLICY

Another field in which executive opportunism plays an important protective role is in the development of enforcement policy. Such executive activity is particularly important in organizations concerned chiefly with prosecuting functions, like the Department of Justice, but development of enforcement policy is of interest to governmental executives everywhere. Whether to proceed against particular people or groups is a question which oc-

[18] Macmahon, Millett, and Ogden, *The Administration of Federal Work Relief*, p. 298. Hallie Flanagan was director of the Project.

cupies much of the time of the very top executives of an enforcement agency. Anti-trust prosecutions follow the pattern of political
support of the administration. At some periods, the support of the
administration is such that almost no prosecutions are feasible. At
other times, some prosecutions are a political necessity.

Seeking the Support of Important Groups

As we indicated in the last chapter, simply having good congressional and executive relations is not enough. If some politically
powerful group or groups in the public become hostile to an agency
or bureau, its congressional and executive support may wane.
Therefore, government agencies must identify the groups that are
important to their existence and attempt to gain their support, or
at least keep their hostility to a minimum.

IDENTIFYING SIGNIFICANT INTEREST GROUPS

Identifying these groups is not difficult. People who are directly
affected by an agency's activities will soon make themselves
known, and will insist on having something to say about its activities, either in the administrative process or by bringing pressure to bear on the legislature. This insistence of clientele groups on
representation in the administrative process is well illustrated by
the following statement of the National Cooperative Milk Producers' Federation in 1943:

> Eleven months from now the people will go to the polls. They will
> decide many important issues. One of the greatest issues which farmers
> will help decide will be on the question of who controls the Department of
> Agriculture. We believe that the organized farmers of America will de-
> mand of both political parties that they will provide a reconstituted De-
> partment of Agriculture. Other departments of Government serve the
> groups for which they are named. The Department of Agriculture today
> is not being permitted to function for the farmers. We call for definite
> pledges on this great and fundamental issue.[19]

The fact that administrative agencies must give careful consideration to the demands of powerful clientele groups is well illustrated by an early experience in the history of the Federal Trade

[19] *A Dairy Polity for 1944*, p. 7, quoted in Key, op. cit., p. 705.

Commission (FTC). Soon after the FTC was established, President Wilson initiated an investigation by it into the food industry. One phase of this undertaking was an investigation into the meat-packing industry. This industry fought bitterly against the investigation and the publication of the resulting report. As one Senator said, "The packers have tried to employ men (lobbyists) who had influence with members of Congress or the Government agencies. They have stopped at nothing in their propaganda." [20]

In spite of this powerfully organized hostility, the FTC finished its investigation and made its report available to Congress at its request. The report showed illegal operations by the five largest packers and made some bold recommendations about remedying the situation. A political storm thereupon broke loose. A resolution was introduced in the Senate demanding an investigation of "socialism" in the FTC, and the employees suspected of socialism, though exonerated by a private investigation, were later dismissed. The packers' lobby kept on until the regulation of the meat-packing industry was taken from FTC and given to the Department of Agriculture in the Packers and Stockyards Act of 1921. As Herring says, "what happened to the trade commission when it interfered with the meat packers provides a concrete illustration of the administrative and political problems involved in attempting to regulate a powerful industry." [21]

RESPONSIVENESS TO GROUPS

As is the case with legislators and legislative requests, important clientele groups or members of them get special attention from governmental agencies. Although an inquiry from an ordinary citizen may be kicked about for some time and eventually answered by a form paragraph, inquiries from important members or representatives of clientele groups receive careful and usually high level consideration. When plain ordinary Mrs. Jones comes to an agency to make a complaint, she is almost certain to be turned over to a

[20] *Congressional Record*, Oct. 22, 1919, p. 7310. Quoted in E. Pendleton Herring, *Public Administration and the Public Interest*. (New York: McGraw-Hill Book Co., 1936), p. 118.

[21] Ibid., p. 118. To help the reader gain a further insight into the relative strengths of the two contenders in this battle, we should mention that in 1919 the advertising expenditures of Swift and Co. alone were about six times the Commission's appropriation. Ibid., p. 119.

lesser official. When John L. Lewis comes to Washington he can probably see anyone he wants, including the President.

In recent years it has become fairly common administrative practice for administrators to call in advisory committees made up of representatives of important clientele groups and to ask their opinion before making important governmental decisions. This practice will be examined further in Chapter 21.

GROUP PRESSURES AND AGENCY PERSONNEL

The appointment of officials acceptable to important external groups is common practice. OPA's attempt to staff top positions with academic rather than business persons caused so much hostility that Congress finally legislated on the subject, forbidding OPA to appoint any person to a "policy-making" position who had not had five years or more of business experience. Frances Perkins's reports that labor's fears that the Civilian Conservation Corps idea was a plan for "dollar a day regimentation" were met by the appointment of Robert Fechner, Vice-President of the Machinists Union, to head up the CCC. "Characteristically, he [Roosevelt] had decided to appoint a labor leader as director on the theory that that would make organized labor well disposed to the project." [22] Fechner headed up a committee in charge of CCC on which the Labor Department, Army, and Forest Service each had a representative. When it was pointed out to Roosevelt that Fechner's appointment as director of such a set-up might not conduce to smooth operations he said, according to Miss Perkins, "Oh, that doesn't matter. The Army and the Forestry Service will really run the show. The Secretary of Labor will select the men and make the rules and Fechner will 'go along' and give everybody satisfaction and confidence." [23]

If an agency cannot or will not mollify an important group by selecting many of the group's representatives for key positions, it *can* build up those characteristics of its personnel that appeal to such groups. For example, previous business experience, such as running a service station, may become the basis for a claim to the business community that the agency's chief officials are highly "practical" and cognizant of the "needs of business," and that they

[22] Perkins, op. cit., p. 180.
[23] Ibid., p. 181.

have had that most sobering of all experiences—"meeting a pay-roll." [24] Photographs and the proper background stories of the agency's chief officials are often kept in readiness for dissemination to the trade press and association circulars. Top agency or bureau officials usually cultivate a wide acquaintance among members of important clientele groups (who also, of course, cultivate the ac-quaintance of important top officials). For some regulatory agencies, the most potent organized groups to whom they can turn for support are the group or groups which they regulate. This rather common situation raises the interesting and disturbing ques-tion of "who is regulating whom?" This problem for democratic government will receive special treatment in later chapters.

Seeking Public Support

As we have mentioned before, administrative agencies must secure public understanding of their programs, whether they are providing services to the public or regulating it. If no one knows of their services, officials will be frustrated in their attempt to supply them, and they will not long receive legislative support. If the people to be regulated do not know what they are supposed to do, they *cannot* do it; and if they do not agree with what they are supposed to do, many of them *will not* do it. Consequently, administrative agencies must engage in a great amount of public educational ac-tivities. They disseminate great volumes of information gathered by research; they constantly inform the public of various services available to it; and they constantly inform the public (or parts of it) of its duties under their regulations.

PUBLIC INFORMATION AND PROPAGANDA

This kind of activity, admittedly a necessary part of ad-ministration, creates support for administrative organizations as well as understanding of their programs; it makes them less sub-ject to the influence or control of conflicting interests expressed through legislative or executive action. For example, community satisfaction with the services of the Forest Service, and community

[24] Concerning the use of this protective device in OPA rationing, see Thomp-son, *The Regulatory Process in OPA Rationing*, chap. 5.

understanding of those services, brought about partly by the public relations activities of the district forest ranger, have created sufficient support to keep the Forest Service in the Department of Agriculture in spite of constant pressure from the conflicting interests of stock grazers and lumbermen to transfer it to the Department of Interior where those interests have considerably more influence.

The public relations activities of administrative agencies almost inevitably veer over beyond what is necessary to create mere public understanding. Agencies usually paint their activities in glowing terms in order to "sell" people on them. This selling activity produces strong reactions from hostile groups and the legislators who represent them. It tends to weaken the power of the legislators to do anything about the activities and thereby help out political groups hostile to the program. Therefore, unfriendly legislators bitterly resent the use of too many adjectives in administrative public relations, and even friendly legislators are vaguely uneasy about it (they may be on the other side some day if the winds of politics change). And yet, the best way to get the admittedly necessary public cooperation with administrative programs is to create an enthusiastic public support for them.

LEGISLATIVE REACTIONS TO PUBLIC RELATIONS ACTIVITIES

Legislative attitudes toward administrative publicity are illustrated by the reaction of Congressman Disney of Oklahoma to the Interior Department radio dramas on oil conservation. He said they were "hysteria" which might lead to a "bloodless revolution, with the transfer of authority over our industrial life from free enterprise to government dictatorship." [25] The hostility of Congress to administrative publicity resulted in an Act in 1913 to prohibit the payment of money to any employee called a "publicity expert" unless specific appropriations authorized such payment.[26] The result of this legislation is that the title "publicity expert" is no longer used by federal agencies.

In 1919 Congress passed an Act prohibiting the administrative

[25] *Congressional Record*, March 1, 1940, p. 3465. Quoted in Key, op. cit., p. 718.
[26] 38 Stat. L. 212.

use of money, unless expressly authorized, to influence legislation in Congress.[27] This Act was aimed chiefly at the practice followed by many officials of getting their agency's friends to put pressure on Congress by telegrams, letters, and so forth. It has forced administrative officials to use more subtle methods. To handicap the New Deal agencies in their prodigious transmittal of publicity through the mails, Congress in 1939 prohibited federal agencies from sending informational material through the mails free of charge unless it was expressly asked for.

Because of the obvious difficulty of distinguishing between "legitimate" and "illegitimate" publicity, the enforcement of these laws has been left largely to congressional criticism—a method not completely without effectiveness. However, as Key says, "The chief effect of the regulatory legislation seems to be to discourage administrative agencies in openly organizing support throughout the country for or against specific bills." [28] It has not, that is, prevented them from building up a bank of popular support for times when "the going gets rough" in Congress.

PUBLICITY TECHNIQUES

Most administrative agencies have "information officers" and units whose function is to prepare handouts to the press describing what the agency is doing and generally attempting to secure sympathetic treatment for the agency in the press and other channels of mass communication. It is the function of these officers and units to find acceptable reasons for the agency's decisions, be they blunders or strokes of genius. Generally speaking, administrative organizations do not publicly admit mistakes, not because they are filled with liars but because any such admission would be pounced upon and exploited by their enemies. While their many successes will receive little attention from hostile groups, no one is allowed to forget their mistakes. Consequently, to maintain support, they toot their own horns.

Many administrative organizations have taken to the radio and the movies to sell their wares. The radio was one of the principal methods of administrative propaganda used during World War II, although it had been used very little prior to that time. In

[27] 41 Stat. L. 68.
[28] Key, op. cit., p. 716.

general agencies do not actually make their own movies (though some of this is done), but they maintain a friendly cooperative relation with Hollywood so that regular commercial movies will appear romanticizing and glorifying their activities. The Marine Corps has for many years been very successful in this type of public relations with such films as *Guadalcanal Diary*, *Sands of Iwo Jima*, *Marine Raiders*, and others. The Air Force has now come in for such good publicity through movies and in other ways that its appropriations are almost beyond executive control: note such recent films as *Winged Victory*, with "scenes from guarded Air Force vaults." The FBI, always alert to the survival value of good public relations, has many glorifying movies to its credit, one being the "semidocumentary" film *Street With No Name*. Not to be outdone, the Bureau of Narcotics in the Treasury Department has "made its files available" to Hollywood to portray the unrelenting attack of its narcotics agents on the international dope racket, while the Secret Service has been similarly accommodating in order to display to the world the activities of its agents in tracking down counterfeiters in the "semidocumentary" film *T-Men* (not to be confused with G-Men).

CONTROL OF PUBLIC STATEMENTS OF ADMINISTRATORS

In the quest for survival by way of public relations, the public utterances of administrative officials present a special problem. A complete gag rule seems to run counter to democratic values. Yet, uncontrolled speeches and articles by employees can be embarrassing. Always there are controls on such employee activities, but sometimes they are rather subtle. To "endanger" the agency is not a likely road to success within the agency.

Very often there is an understanding that public appearances or articles are to be cleared with the information officer. (More recently it is sometimes required that they be cleared with the security officer.) Information offices sometimes maintain a speakers' bureau, encourage external groups that want speakers to contact it, and in this way control to some extent what is publicly said by the employees. The practice of ghost writing is generally accepted now, and higher officials almost always have their speeches and articles written for them by someone who has the time and ability to study the possible public reactions.

The importance that administrative organizations attribute to

these informational activities in survival can be illustrated from
the reactions of the WPA headquarters to increasing employment
(which would change the external interest structure and hence
WPA's political support):

> Perhaps the WPA's biggest problem in its public relations arose
> from the question of the permanence of its activities. The continued need
> for work relief was a delicate subject that the WPA nonetheless felt con-
> strained to stress from time to time. But it had to recognize the rather
> general hostility to the idea that the WPA was a relatively permanent
> attack upon unemployment. Any suggestion that the federal government
> was promising job security to workers was apt to alienate private business
> elements. Yet if an increase in private employment was emphasized,
> doubts were raised about the justification for the WPA's continuance.
> WPA headquarters required that state administrators submit all proposed
> local radio broadcasts for prior approval as one means of guarding against
> the utterance of untimely remarks.[29]

"UNAUTHORIZED" PUBLICITY

Although gag rules, formal or informal, are applied to public
remarks of employees, there are methods by which lower officials
can protect their satisfactions from the controls of higher officials.
By these methods a subordinate unit or subordinate official can
take part in the never-ending struggle for survival. Friendly relations with the staff of a Congressional Committee can be used to
release a report or a memorandum that a superior refuses or is
afraid to release. An example was the release by Captain Crom-
melin and other Navy officers to Congressmen and newspapermen
of documents bearing on the "super-carrier" fight in 1949.

Another method by which survival is pursued in the lower administrative echelons is well described by Key:

> A different type of publicity—a sort of administrative guerilla
> warfare—flows from the informal and almost surreptitious relations of
> administrators, often at subordinate levels, with columnists and other
> journalists. Information is often fed to these persons who report it on
> "high authority" or as from "informed sources." By this means Congress
> may be needled, the President nudged, a fire lighted under a superior,
> and, on occasion, officials in another department may be stirred to action
> or to anger.[30]

[29] Macmahon, Millett, and Ogden, *op. cit.*, p. 297.
[30] Op. cit., p. 712.

CONTACTS WITH CLIENTELE

Any agency has some employees contacting the public, either personally or by correspondence. If these employees make a good impression, the public support for the agency may be greatly strengthened. If the "counter clerks" are polite, informative, and anxious to help, the public that meets them is more likely to "go to bat" for the agency. Consequently, many governmental agencies spend considerable time in training those of their employees who meet the public to make a good impression. Some go further and try to influence the after-hours behavior of their employees by understandings usually unwritten, of how the successful employee of the ABC agency conducts himself out of office hours, in public or in private. The present federal administrative loyalty program has expanded this intrusion into private lives to a considerable extent. (A person so unstable as to imbibe or to get involved in a divorce may be regarded as a "poor security risk.")

PROPAGANDA OF THE DEED

There is one device of public relations that is completely unassailable by an organization's enemies or any one else. If the agency's plans are popular—if they are easy to understand, reasonable, obviously adapted to the end in view, and presented in a friendly, humble fashion—that agency will get a good deal of support regardless of hostile legislators.

The relationship of popular planning to popular support is just beginning to be understood. It involves a change in the attitudes of many people—certainly those who find themselves in governmental positions. The "high and mighty" attitude, the attitude of "be it enacted," so prevalent among people in positions of power, is not conducive to public acceptance. More will be said about this point in later chapters on planning and executing plans. Here we only want to emphasize that popular plans and programs will build up a bank of popular support as well if not better than the devices of propaganda. It is important not only to use selling technique but also to have something to sell.

In this connection the administrative official has a new and powerful tool of survival—the public opinion poll. By use of polls, he can find out who likes his program and who does not like it and why.[31] With this information he can plan popularly and thus increase his power *vis a vis* hostile legislators and interest groups.

Conclusion

In the picture that has been drawn of the tactics used by administrative agencies to assure their survival we see a confirmation of the general propositions set forth in the preceding chapter. In the struggle for existence, administrators are by no means neutral implements of a public policy that has been fashioned by the legislative process. Public administrators, and particularly those responsible for the direction of unitary organizations, are themselves initiators and transformers of policy—brokers, if you like, who seek to bring about agreement between the program goals of government agencies and the goals and values of groups that possess political power.

We see, moreover, that the formal process that links the administrative agency with the statutory acts of the legislative body is by no means the whole, or even the chief, process for transmitting political influence over administration. The true structure is indeed "feudal." Legislative bodies become complex clusters of committees, each one concerned with a subject matter area, and each mediating between political groups and administrative agencies that are interested in that area. Each administrative agency seeks in its relationships with groups in the legislature, with its own clientele, and with other interested groups to find sources from which it can draw the power it needs to carry on its program and survive.

We do not mean to imply by this that there is no distinction between the activities of legislative bodies and the activities of administrative agencies. We shall have more to say about this distinction later. The evidence is clear, however, that the political process

[31] See Henry A. Wallace and J. L. McCamy, "Straw Polls and Public Administration," *Public Opinion Quarterly*, 4:221–3 (June 1940), and David B. Truman, "Public Opinion Research as a Tool of Public Administration," *Public Administration Review* 5:62–72 (Winter 1945).

does not end when the work of administrators begins. As Paul Appleby has said: "The great distinction between government and other organized undertakings is to be found in the wholly political character of government. The great distinction between public administration and other administration is likewise to be found in the political character of public administration." [32]

[32] *Policy and Administration* (University, Alabama: University of Alabama Press, 1949), p. 12.

CHAPTER TWENTY

The Strategy of Planning

THE word "planning" is more often used today as a political slogan or a political cuss-word than as a precise label for some definite kind of administrative activity. In the eyes of its friends, planning is synonymous with "coordination," "foresight," and "concern with the future"—almost with the whole of rationality. In the eyes of its enemies, planning is sometimes described as though it were identical with "regimentation" and even "collectivism." [1] Most of the current emotion that centers around the term planning concerns itself with a particular kind of planning: governmental planning and intervention in economic affairs. The strong enemies of planning have been those who believe that, to the greatest possible extent, economic activity should be regulated by the decisions of individual business firms operating through the price mechanism, rather than by governmental decisions and central controls. Hence, "planning" has become a central symbol (and, in the minds of many, a central stereotype) in the great individualism-collectivism controversy of our time.

In the present chapter, we shall use the term planning in both a broader and a more neutral sense. We shall attempt—and ask our readers to attempt—to avoid the emotional implications of the term, and to use it to refer to a broadly defined type of administrative activity. Planning, in our sense, is that activity that concerns itself with proposals for the future, with the evaluation of alternative proposals, and with the methods by which these proposals may be achieved. Planning is rational, adaptive thought

[1] "Friendly" definitions of planning will be found in George B. Galloway and associates, *Planning for America* (New York: Holt, 1941); Barbara Wootton, *Plan or No Plan* (London: Gollancz, 1934). The term is used in a "hostile" sense in von Hayek, *The Road to Serfdom*.

applied to the future and to matters over which the planners, or the administrative organizations with which they are associated, have some degree of control.

An individual plans when he decides to buy a ticket for next Saturday's ball game, or when he decides to undertake a university program leading to a law degree. A business firm plans when it decides to open a branch sales office in new territory, or when it enters on a policy of reducing inventories over the next six-month period. A municipal fire department plans when it decides to purchase a new ladder truck; the U. S. Bureau of the Census, when it draws up a questionnaire to be used in the Census of Population; the Social Security Board, when it drafts legislation extending social security coverage to employees not now included in the program; a city charter revision committee, when it proposes the establishment of a city planning commission. (In this last case we have an example of planning to plan—of proposing a plan which, if carried out, will result in new planning activity.)

Nature of the Planning Process

Governmental planning takes the most diverse forms. A very partial list of large-scale governmental planning activities in recent years would have to include at least the following:

1. Planning for the conservation and use of natural resources— the activities of the National Resources Planning Board; forest use planning by the U. S. Forest Service; irrigation planning by the Bureau of Reclamation; planning for the use of regional resources by the Tennessee Valley Authority; and many others.

2. City planning—including the planning of streets, utilities, and public buildings; planning of park systems; and land-use planning to be implemented through zoning, subdivision control, slum clearance, and urban redevelopment.

3. Planning for full employment—public works scheduling by the Federal Works Agency; reports of the Council of Economic Advisers; plans for monetary and bank policy by the Treasury Department and the Federal Reserve Board; and, during periods of unemployment, the program planning of relief agencies like the Works Progress Administration, and the Public Works Administration.

4. Planning for personal and family security—unemployment compensation, old age benefits, health and medical care.

5. Planning for agriculture—soil conservation, and agricultural price and marketing problems.

6. Planning for the improvement of governmental organization. At the Federal level, the two most significant recent efforts were made by the President's Committee on Administrative Management (1937) and the Hoover Commission (1948).

7. Planning for total war—allocation of raw materials, commodities, and consumers' goods; price planning; manpower planning; as well as the planning of military procurement and operations.

From this highly incomplete list, it is clear that underlying virtually every program of government will be found an extensive planning effort. Planning is involved in the development of program goals, in the formulation of legislation, and at every step in the path of executing continuing programs. But there are certain elements common to this wide range of planning activities. In virtually every plan will be found (1) proposals for the behavior of human beings (organization members or clientele) other than the planners, (2) an explicit or implicit statement of goals or of criteria for preferring one set of plans to another, and (3) proposals for implementing the planning goals. The next sections of this chapter will be devoted to an explanation of these elements of planning activity.

Concern of Plans with Future Behaviors

Plans are always concerned with the future behaviors of human beings, but they are not always set forth in this form. A city plan, for example, may be embodied in a map showing streets, location of public buildings, distribution of land uses by type, and so forth. In what sense is this a plan for human behavior?

ULTIMATE AND INTERMEDIATE BEHAVIORS

In spite of appearances, future human behaviors are envisaged in a city plan—and human behaviors of two sorts. First, there are the *ultimate* behaviors that may be anticipated if the plan is carried out. If the city achieves the land-use pattern anticipated in its master plan, this will have many effects on the behaviors of the people of that city. The street plan may shorten (or lengthen) the time that will be required by individuals to commute from their homes to their offices; it may decrease (or increase) the number of traffic accidents they have; it may lead them to decide to purchase groceries in one location rather than another; it may affect their decisions to build homes in one place or another. The list could be extended *ad infinitum*. In fact, the only basis on which a city plan can be evaluated is by determining what it will do, if carried out, to the behaviors of the people who live in the city.

The plan is concerned not only with these ultimate behaviors that form the goals of planning. It is also concerned with the *intermediate* behaviors that will be required in order to carry out the plan. City planning involves not only the construction of some pattern of desired future behaviors, but also a series of proposals that will carry the city from its present situation to the future envisaged in the plan. In this case, the intermediate behaviors may include the behaviors of city councilmen (in authorizing an appropriation for a street widening), of government employees (the public works officials and employees who actually construct the new street), of regulatory officials (the employees of the city planning agency who enforce zoning regulations), and of courts (in granting an injunction against a use of property not permitted by the zoning ordinance).

The sequence of behaviors—intermediate behaviors, leading to the ultimate behaviors that are the planning goal—that arises out of the planning process may be likened to the ever-widening circle of ripples that is produced when a stone is dropped in a pond. These ripples bring about "ultimate behaviors" when they move the pebbles on the beach. If something obstructs them, or if the original impulse is too weak, they do not reach the shore—the plan is ineffective. So, a Washington agency entrusted with sugar rationing must plan and influence the behaviors of many intermediate persons before it can achieve its desired effects upon the ultimate behaviors of the sugar-consuming public (equitable distribution of a limited supply). The "top management" of the agency must direct the behaviors of the staff of the Washington office into the necessary channels. The Washington office must direct the behaviors of the field offices into the desired channels, and these, in turn, must influence the behavior of the public. Perhaps, in order to inform or convince those who are to be regulated, certain behaviors of newspapers, radio stations, and moving picture houses must be elicited—to distribute stories and information as to the need for the program, and as to what the public should do to comply with it.

PLANNING AND SUNK COSTS

We have said that plans are always concerned with the future behaviors of human beings. The longer the time span over which we attempt to plan, the more difficult the process becomes. If we make decisions only for today or tomorrow, we can suit our choices to known conditions and existing situations. Why, then, do organizations attempt to project their decisions into a hazardous and uncertain future? Why not adapt the proverb to read: "Sufficient unto the day are the decisions thereof?" Why undertake guesses as to next year's farm prices, or as to what the city's population will be twenty years hence?

Organizations are forced to plan primarily because the decisions made today and the activities carried out today limit the choices that are available tomorrow. When a city constructs a new sewerage system, it constructs it not simply to discharge tomorrow's sewage, or next year's sewage, but to take care of sewage disposal needs over several decades. An incorrect decision about the capacity of the sewerage system may, indeed, result in short-run savings, but only at the cost of expensive replacements when the capacity is exceeded. Whenever the execution of a decision involves *sunk costs*—expenditures that will produce services over a considerable period of time—a decision that disregards the future over which these services will be provided may turn out to be expensive in the long run—either expensive through an excessive investment in plant, or expensive because of an inadequate investment requiring a more costly expansion later.

Sunk costs are usually involved, of course, even where a decision has nothing to do with the construction of physical structures. A government regulation limiting petroleum production next year directly affects future petroleum supplies. The decision to appropriate funds to the military establishment has an important bearing not only upon immediate military preparedness, but also upon the pool of equipment and trained manpower that will be available some years hence.

That personnel decisions may involve important sunk costs has already been shown in Chapter 16. Rapid increases or decreases in the size of an organization are by no means painless or costless operations; hence, decisions to recruit or to reduce in force must be based on long-term as well as short-term needs if they are to avoid excessive sunk costs. New recruitment must also take into account the long-run promotional needs and possibilities in the organization.

If the term "sunk cost" is interpreted in the broad sense suggested here, it is clear that only rarely will today's decisions not impose sunk costs upon the future. The importance that organizations attach to planning is not due to confidence that the future *can* be predicted with any accuracy—most often it cannot—but to the realization that the future *must* be predicted as accurately as possible as the only alternative to guesswork and chance. Not to make a virtue of this necessity, the planner's horizon—the period over which he plans—does not need to be longer than the period over which today's sunk costs will be liquidated. Even this is often subject to uncertainty—in wartime, decisions often hinge on whether we are planning for a long war or a short war.

Goals and Criteria of Planning

A large part of all planning activity lies in determining what goals are to be sought—what pattern of ultimate behavior among the many possible patterns is to be preferred. The traditional distinction that is made between "politics" and "administration" is a distinction between the setting of goals, and the carrying out of activities to reach these goals. This distinction was supposed to provide the basis for a division of functions between legislative bodies and administrative agencies. According to this theory, which was for a long time accepted by democratic political philosophers, the legislature was supposed to declare the "will of the state" (i.e., formulate goals), while the administrative agencies were supposed to execute this will.

PLANNING BODIES SELDOM NEUTRAL

However desirable such a division of functions might be—and this question will be discussed in Chapter 25—it certainly does not conform to the actual state of affairs in modern government. The executive branch of government by no means confines itself to the "neutral" carrying out of whatever well-defined social goals the legislature may desire to lay down. Instead, the executive branch—at both high and low levels—is intimately involved in the very process of goal formulation and goal evaluation. Any realistic analysis of the activities of the policeman walking his beat shows him to be an important policy-making (goal determining) official.[2]

Among administrative agencies, none are more deeply involved in goal formulation than are planning bodies; and particularly those planning bodies that are engaged in long-range planning. Hence, the recommendations and influence of these bodies on the goals of government activities make them peculiarly subject to political attack. The goals of governmental activity are at the very heart of politics. Underlying long-range government planning activity will always be found explicit or implicit assumptions as to what are the desirable goals.[3]

[2] The Kinsey report contains an interesting discussion of the discrepancies between the social goals with respect to sexual behavior that are formulated by legislatures and courts, on the one hand, and the goals that are actually enforced by police officials, on the other. See also, August Vollmer, *The Police and Modern Society*, (Berkeley, University of California Press, 1936).

[3] In the preface to *Planning for America* by George B. Galloway and Associates, we find the following statement of goals:

1. That prolonged depression with continuing large-scale idleness of capital and labor gives rise to economic and social problems that call for intelligent long-range planning rather than a series of crusades or improvisations.

2. That the underlying causes of the Great Depression are to be found in a number of basic changes in the structure of the American economy, e.g., the disappearance of the geographic frontier, the decline in the rate of population growth, the spread of monopoly, etc.

3. That we are passing through a period of transition from a more or less free economy to a controlled economy.

4. That ours is now a hybrid or mixed economy made up of five economies (small enterprise, big business, public utilities, government enterprise, cooperatives) that coexist simultaneously.

5. That a hybrid economy which is half slave, half free, "half steel, half putty," cannot function at anything like full employment of resources.

6. That full use of our human and material resources is a *sine qua non* of adequate national defense, a healthy economy, and a satisfied society.

Since these goals are by no means always accepted by the society at large—and especially by politically powerful groups in society—planning bodies are subject to hostile political attack and funds for such activities are frequently withheld, or very meagerly provided. The National Resources Planning Board, for example, was eliminated by a Congress that was unsympathetic to the Board's proposals with regard to post-war governmental finance and spending policy. Frequently, legislatures or interest groups seek to influence planning and to channel it in desired directions by control over its personnel rather than its appropriations. Thus, the initial appointment in 1946 of a group of relatively conservative economists to the Council of Economic Advisers undoubtedly increased the acceptability of that body to a conservative Congress.

GOALS IN SHORT-RUN PLANNING

Acceptance of a set of broad planning goals (e.g., the approval of a master plan by a city council, or the adoption by Congress of the Social Security Act) provides a framework within which more specific planning takes place in order to implement these goals. This more specific planning is concerned with working out the details of the broad planning goals, and with devising methods of achieving these goals—that is, it is primarily a process of planning for intermediate behaviors which, if carried out, will realize the ultimate behaviors contemplated in the broad plan.

---

7. That the long-run centripetal and collectivist trends in our economic and political life will project themselves into the future and be accelerated by the exigencies of war.

8. That private enterprise must be stimulated and public enterprise must be expanded to take up the slack in employment.

9. That we must streamline our government and put a sustaining economy beneath our political structure if the America of tomorrow is to remain democratic.

10. That in the development of the national defense program, the economic and social gains of recent years should not be sacrificed, but should be preserved and strengthened, for they are an essential part of the sinews of total defense on the home front.

11. That the threat of total war requires total mobilization of our military, economic, and moral resources.

12. That there must be national power to prescribe positive remedies for national problems.

13. That regardless of fluctuations in party politics, the government will steadily extend its control over the machinery of investment and credit, the management of basic industries, the distribution of the labor force, and the direction of foreign trade.

The goals of specific or short-run planning are less subject to attack than the broad planning goals because they are constantly submitted to a well recognized and accepted process of validation. They acquire their respectability, in the first instance, by legislative enactment. The legislature orders the administrative agency to accomplish certain results—consolidation of railroads, regulation of radio stations in terms of "public convenience and necessity," securing fair trade practices, securing healthful conditions in restaurants, and so forth. Although the broad goals may be attacked by hostile groups, the attack must be directed primarily against the legislature that validated them, rather than the planning body that plans behavior to secure them. (Of course, failing to change the goals, interest groups will direct their attentions to the planning bodies and attempt to affect or alter the plans. This subject will be discussed in a later chapter.)

Legislative Changes in Goals. It must not be thought that the broad goal, once validated by a legislature, remains constant. The goals are ever changing and ever revalidated. In planning the behaviors necessary to achieve the goal, the administrative planning body often selects an alternative that proves to be politically unpopular. Then the legislature may amend the basic statute and forbid the use of that particular alternative in achieving the goal. For example, when Congress ordered OPA to control inflation, OPA adopted the device of punishing violators of price ceilings by denying them rationed commodities, such as gasoline. This practice proved so unpopular that the price control extension act of 1944 prohibited it—the OPA goal had been changed to controlling inflation without the use of the undesired sanctions. Likewise, when OPA placed price ceilings on agricultural goods, the powerful congressional farm bloc got the price control act amended to provide that OPA could not place a price ceiling on basic agricultural commodities below 90% of the parity price. Thus, in effect, OPA's goal was changed to controlling inflation without controlling the prices of basic agricultural commodities.

Successive Stages in Planning. The goal validation process in governmental planning is not simply a matter of legislative enactment. The legislative order to plan for the achievement of a certain goal is usually given to an administrative agency or to the chief executive. Before plans for the ultimate behaviors are finally formulated, the agency goal must be broken down into subgoals and these assigned to various parts of the agency. This process is what we mean by planning for planning. If the legislative order is given to the chief executive, he and his advisors must decide what existing agencies should carry out various parts of the project, what new agencies are needed (if any), their nature, who should head them, whether the goal should be broken down into subgoals at all or whether the planning for its accomplishment should be entrusted to a single agency, and so forth.

Thus the Second War Powers Act authorized the President to allocate scarce commodities and services whenever necessary to the effective prosecution of the war. At first the whole allocation goal was entrusted to the War Production Board. The WPB, in turn, asked OPA to ration commodities at the consumer level. Later it was decided to change the organization for allocation planning, and several new agencies were established. The Office of the Rubber Director was created to handle all matters relating to rubber, especially the synthetic rubber program. That office continued the practice of having OPA ration tires. The Petroleum Administration for War was created to plan all matters of petroleum production and distribution above the consumer level. The Solid Fuels Administration for War was created to do the same for solid fuels. The War Food Administration was created to achieve maximum output of food and to control its distribution. This agency also continued the practice of having OPA ration food to consumers. The Office of Defense Transportation was created to plan and control the commercial transportation services of the country. ODT maintained control over gasoline rationing for commercial vehicles (trucks, cabs, busses, etc.), but had OPA perform the mechanical operation of issuing the ration coupons to holders of ODT Certificates of War Necessity for the amount of gasoline stated thereon by ODT officials. Planning for the use of shipping services was entrusted to a War Shipping Administration, and control of exports and imports to a Foreign Economic Administration. The settlement of conflicts between these agencies was entrusted to an Office of War Mobilization and Reconversion. Thus it can be seen that a tremendous amount of planning for planning took place at the presidential level, based upon the war goals entrusted by Congress to the President. These general, presidential plans are frequently embodied in executive orders.

Once a goal has been given to an agency, it must break the goal down into further subgoals and allocate them to various bureaus. The bureaus, in turn, allocate parts of the planning job to their various divisions. Eventually, a specific group of people will plan for the behavior of field personnel and the clientele. But planning for planning has to come before this, and it involves determining the organization structure, making provision of technically competent personnel, devising procedures for coordinating plans, and so forth.

The whole process of planning for planning, from the legislature through the chief executive and the top agency officials down to the concrete program planning group, is also the process by which the concrete goals of actual, immediate planning of clientele behavior are validated. The goals so validated are constantly modified by reference up and influence down, from the specific planners to the legislature itself. This channel of influence on planning goals is the principal tie between government and people that is the basis of democracy. Special interest or "pressure" groups also influence planning goals by direct consultation with and by bringing pressure on officials at any likely point in the channel from the specific planners on up.

CONSISTENCY OF PLANNING GOALS

In any complex society where a great many planning activities are being carried on by different groups, the serious problem arises of preventing or at least minimizing the amount of inconsistent and self-defeating planning that goes on. If the immediate or the long-range goals of various planning activities are contradictory, one plan will tend to undo another. Hydroelectric power planners may seek to build up industry in certain areas through cheap power while defense planners may be seeking to keep industry out of those areas for defense reasons. One group may seek to build up an agricultural area by means of irrigation and land reclamation, while transportation planners are planning transportation development away from that area because of its low productivity. Industry groups may be planning retrenchment while government groups are planning for full employment.

Because of the many possibilities of contradiction, there is much concern with the coordination of planning. Coordination has been sought largely through organizational structure—committees and super-committees. There are planning organizations representing business, agriculture, and labor. There are national, regional, and local planning committees. The organizational structure of long-range planning is bewilderingly complex. The organizational structure of actual, concrete, short-range planning is the American governmental structure, itself. Despite all the activity and good intentions, however, the basic ingredient of coordinated planning for the nation at large—a coherent set of over-all goals—is lacking.

Consistency in Unitary Organizations. Of course if an organization has an over-all goal or dominant value as is the case with unitary organizations, conflicts between plans for that organization (or for its parts) can be resolved by reference to its goal. For example, if the dominant goal of the Department of Agriculture were to increase farm income, any plan with a contrary effect would not have a chance to conflict with other plans. On the other hand, if an agency does not have a dominant goal, conflict can still be avoided by killing administratively one or the other of the conflicting plans. The trouble is that there is no rational basis for deciding which to kill without reference to goals common to both plans—lacking this the decision is no more rational than flipping a coin. Hence, a dominant agency goal or value is indispensable to rational coordination of planning.[4]

When the problem of coordination is moved above the level of the agency to that of the government as a whole—the Administration—the same considerations apply. To coordinate all government planning rationally, there must be a dominant government goal or value. Sensing this fact, many people are interested in a national plan by which all other plans and planning activities could be coordinated. And certainly to coordinate rationally all government activities such a national goal would be needed.

Consistency in War-Time. Looked at in this way, it can be seen that rational government coordination above the agency level (or

---

[4] It would take us too far afield here to discuss the economic market as a rational planning device that permits decentralization of actual planning decisions to the individual economic enterprises, and does not require a central planning body. Even in this case it can be shown that the rationality of this process depends upon the acceptance of market price as a general over-all criterion of social value, of the existing distribution of incomes, and of the right of the consumer to dispose of his income as he pleases. If these, and certain other, assumptions are admitted, it can be shown that the price mechanism, operating through the market and without a central planning body, can bring about rational and consistent planning.

even above the bureau level in many cases) depends upon the development of a dominant national goal—not upon the proliferation of coordinating mechanisms. The goal of winning a war approaches the requirement for coordination, and during a war a much greater coordination of effort is secured than at any other time. In such a period the various special interests of which our nation is composed give up somewhat their special strivings and cooperate for a national objective.

Even a war, however, does not bring a complete coordination of goals and strivings. Thus the farmers, a politically important group, found time during World War II to lobby through the Congress the exemption of the basic agricultural commodities from any meaningful price control. This special interest activity insured some inflation and consequently a more expensive war. Likewise, the farm bloc induced the Congress to pass an act, later vetoed by the President, which provided that only butadiene made from grain alcohol could be used in the synthetic rubber plants that were to be created. (Virtually all government experts favored butadiene from petroleum.)

Consistency in Time of Peace. During normal peacetime there is no common dominant national goal. Instead, there are many special interest groups that seek legislation advantageous to themselves. To the extent that these interest groups have political power, they can induce the Congress to pass laws which reflect their varied and often conflicting goals, and hence the statutes provide conflicting goals for the many administrative planning bodies. While one group of officials is busy raising farm prices, another group is trying to lower prices in general. While one group is trying to control rents, other groups are raising price levels by spending billions for foreign aid and by reducing tax collections. While one group is anxiously trying to import certain strategic materials from Russia and Eastern Europe, another group is forbidding nearly all exports to that area.

The lack of coordination in government planning (and organization) reflects the lack of coordination in the society, upon which government, in a democracy, depends. Rational coordination of government planning by reference to a dominant government goal is not possible without a dominant social goal. Coordination becomes essentially a political process instead of a process of relating plans to a single set of consistent, acceptable, overall goals.

Administrative Machinery for Achieving Consistency. Under these circumstances, coordination of government planning, beyond the point of resolving more or less accidental conflicts, cannot be achieved by administrative organization or reorganization. A central reviewing body, such as the Statistical Standards Division of the Budget Bureau, can point out to a planning unit that a proposed survey is unnecessary because the information has already been collected by another planning unit, but beyond this not much can be done except during war or other crises (e.g., the early days of a depression).

Since the turn of the century there has been a great deal of interest in the executive budget, and the central budget agency, as an administrative mechanism for achieving consistency in governmental programs. A realistic understanding of how the U. S. Budget Bureau—which represents a highly developed mechanism of this kind—goes about reviewing departmental budget requests shows that this mechanism does not solve the problem of providing an integrating over-all goal where none exists.

The Budget Bureau presumably reviews expenditure programs of the Federal departments for conformance with "the working program of the President." But in point of fact, the "working program of the President" is something that is largely created in the minds of the Budget Bureau staff themselves. No directives come to the Bureau from the President with sufficient detail and explicitness to determine whether $30,000 or $3,000,000 should be spent by the Department of Agriculture on corn-borer research; or whether the budget of the Anti-Trust Division should be doubled or halved. The Budget Bureau presumably has from the President certain indications of the desired overall magnitude of Federal expenditures, and perhaps some specific directives with respect to a few issues that are in the focus of attention (whether the Navy should be given funds for the construction of a super-carrier). The Bureau is probably also influenced by its assessment of the broad political philosophy of the President, quite apart from specific directives. Thus a Budget Bureau under a President who emphasized "economy" might act differently from a Bureau under a President whose political pronouncements focussed upon "welfare." Beyond this, the budget examiners are largely "on their own."

Whatever the process that takes place in the Budget Bureau, it is certainly not a process of relating specific activities to a few over-all goals. It is, in fact, a far more complex process in which chance, bargaining skill, actual and anticipated political pressures, and the prejudices of particular budget estimators all play an important role. The resulting estimates are "consistent" only in the sense that they add up, more or less, to a predetermined total—a total that is later upset by Congressional review, and by agency requests for deficiency appropriations when they have not lived within their allotted incomes.

In 1946 an act was passed that purported to establish full employment as a national and continuing goal. A Council of Economic Advisers to the President was established. This Council is required to investigate continually the economy and the effect of various government activities and policies upon full employment, and to prepare a report on the subject for the President, including recommendations as to what should be done to achieve the goal. The President is then required to make a similar report (presumably based on the Council's report), which goes to a congressional Joint Committee on the Economic Report. That Committee is supposed to consider the report and recommend measures for the Congress to pass. Thus far, it is difficult to see that this elaborate coordinative machinery has accomplished much.[5] It can only accomplish something if full employment is really the dominant national goal, which, except in time of actual economic crisis, is very doubtful.

Implementing Planning Goals

From the previous discussion we see that planning is concerned with the future behaviors of human beings, and that it requires the establishment of goals of behavior by which alternative plans may be evaluated and the preferable ones selected. Broad goals, once established, are then subdivided into more specific short-run goals, and plans devised to accomplish these. In this process of subdividing goals we pass over to the third element in the planning process: working out proposals for implementing the planning goals.

---

[5] For some early assessments, generally consistent with the above view, see Fritz Morstein Marx (ed.), "Formulating the Federal Government's Economic Program: A Symposium," *American Political Science Review* 42:272–336 (April 1948), and particularly the papers by Paul H. Appleby, the Hon. Clarence Cannon, and Norton E. Long, therein.

PRACTICAL AND UTOPIAN PLANNING

A plan is concerned with the future, but it is carried out by successive actions that always take place in the present. Our plan may envisage a future city properly provided with sewage disposal facilities; or a future nation with an adequate oil supply. We move towards those goals from day to day by taking action to build sewers or to regulate the rate of production of oil.

A plan that cannot secure the behaviors it envisages is utopian. A practical plan—one that can be effective—is based upon a consideration of what people will do and can be induced to do. How do we arrange a chain of behaviors—starting with immediate organizational activities—that will bring about the desired behaviors?

Since it is behavior that we intend to modify, our plan and the steps taken to implement it must be based upon sound conceptions of human behavior and psychology. We found in the case of prohibition that temperance cannot be achieved by dreaming or wishing that people would not drink. In that instance it could not even be brought about by commanding them not to drink, or by threatening with punishment those who sold alcoholic beverages. The American scene provides such a wealth of examples of unenforced and unenforceable laws (perhaps they should be called "legislative wishes") that the point does not need to be labored.

Persons engaged in planning activities are generally much more realistic in accepting the physical and biological laws to which their plans must conform than they are in accepting limitations imposed by human psychology. The triumphs of modern engineering science illustrate man's power to employ in achieving human goals the fixed and unchangeable rules that nature insists upon. Social planning has generally been much less modest in accepting limitations upon what can be changed and varied, and this has been a major cause of its failures. Brave new cities are laid out (on paper) with careful regard for the law of gravitation, the movements of the sun, and the prevailing winds, but with little regard for the complexes of political, economic, and social forces that must be provided for before the plans can be implemented.

It is perhaps not quite fair to say of utopian planning that it ignores rules of human behavior, but it is certainly fair to say that such planning—if taken seriously—makes implicit assumptions about these rules that are largely incorrect. One such assumption is that most people can be induced to accept a plan if it is shown to them on rational grounds that the plan, if carried out, will reach a socially desirable goal. Another assumption is that the persons who cannot be so convinced are acting from morally bad motives, and that if the majority accepts the plan the dissenters can and ought to be deterred by the threat of punishment.

A major disadvantage of such simple hypotheses about human behavior is that they stifle the imagination of the planner. Modern psychology and sociology have learned much about human behavior, and about the behavior patterns that are shared by most human beings. They have discovered many of the mechanisms and causes whereby these patterns of behavior are acquired. With a knowledge of human psychology, the planner can often predict the human reactions to his plans. He can often know in advance what psychological obstacles must be overcome in order to elicit the behavior he desires. He can counter resistances to his plans not only with moral indignation but also with specific measures to remove those resistances.

The notion that human behavior has discoverable psychological causes releases the imagination of the planner. It encourages him to use these psychological mechanisms as means to the achievement of his goal instead of regarding them as barriers to be levelled by legislative fiat.

Since practical planning must concern itself with the actual characteristics of human behavior, it is important to know what those characteristics are. We cannot, of course, include here a complete discussion of human psychology. We can only indicate certain broad types of human behavior patterns that are particularly important for the planner to understand.[6]

RESISTANCE TO PLANS

When attempts are made to change people's behavior in such a

---

[6] The reader will note that, insofar as the intermediate behaviors we are planning are behaviors of organization members, the psychology of planning has already received extensive discussion in the first half of this book. To avoid a repetition of our discussion of individuals in organization, group values and group resistance, reactions to authority, communication problems, and the other subjects already treated, we will confine our analysis at this point to the general reactions of individuals and groups (whether employees or "clients") to proposed changes.

way as to reduce their satisfactions, they resist. The successful planner must understand the types of changes in behavior that are resisted so that he can avoid them or plan ways for overcoming the resistances. How the resistances to change may be overcome is discussed in the following chapters. Here we will only identify the principal types and describe them briefly: (1) inertia; (2) community or personal mores and beliefs; (3) personal self-interest; (4) the desire to be rational; and (5) the dislike of subordination.

Inertia. People resist new ways of behaving simply because they are habituated to the old ways. To learn new ways—to make new adjustments—is painful. It involves uncertainty. Established expectations and practices no longer guide one. People are not sure what the consequences of the change will be. A single small change in current practice may bring many other unanticipated changes in common practices; no one knows where these disruptions will stop.

Mores and Beliefs. People resist strongly any plan that requires them or others to behave in a way they think is wrong. It is in defense of their moral beliefs that people become martyrs. Government at variance with the deeply held convictions of large numbers of people totters on the verge of revolution. To overcome the resistances it creates, such a government must go to tremendous expense in its police or enforcement activities. It may be that the resistances that spring from the community or personal moral codes are the strongest of all and the most difficult to overcome.

Personal Self-Interest. Behavior in accordance with the folkways and mores of society is unthinking and non-rational. Another kind of resistance to change is associated with rational behavior—behavior that involves a calculated choice of means for the accomplishment of personal gains or values. A change in behavior which thwarts a person's plans for personal gain or enjoyment involves a cost—a dissatisfaction—to that person, and will, consequently, be resisted.

Resistance to Irrational Proposals. Although people are often irrational, they do not like to have their attention called to this fact; they seem to have a strong desire to appear rational to others and to themselves. If the clientele, persons whose behavior is to be affected by the plan, feel that the requirements of a plan are senseless—that it accomplishes nothing worth accomplishing—they will resist those requirements. The resistance expressed in the term "red tape" is a resistance to requirements that either have no worthwhile purpose or whose purpose is not known, understood, or accepted.

Resistance to Subordination. Another human characteristic that the planner must take into account is the desire of people to be treated with dignity and respect. People, in this country at any rate, do not like to be "pushed around"; they tend to push back. Consequently, "do this or else" is often an ineffective approach; it creates resistances that would not appear if the plan or proposal were presented on a different, more dignified, basis. In particular, resistances are created if the order-giving source is a person of lower status than the person or persons to whom the orders are given.

DYNAMIC NATURE OF PRACTICAL PLANNING

A concrete plan for human behavior cannot remain static if it is to be effective. A plan seeks to control, change, or affect only certain factors in the situation. Whether or not the plan will have the desired consequences depends upon what happens to the factors that are not so controlled. If it is predicted that the uncontrolled factors will remain constant, and in fact they change; or if it is predicted that they will change in some particular way, and in fact they follow a different path of change, the plan will not achieve its desired results.

For example, the historical price formula (fixing maximum prices on the basis of prices existing at some previous date) in price control sought to control only one aspect of business behavior—namely, the prices at which merchandise could be sold. It was assumed (or hoped) that other aspects of business behavior, such as decisions by businessmen as to what they would produce, would remain constant. Under OPA, however, these other uncontrolled behaviors began to change—producers began to concentrate on those items which, under price control, gave them the largest profit margins. As a result, there was an increasing scarcity of low-priced clothing, and the plans had to be changed to stop this practice and to bring under some control the decisions of what to produce.

City plans have often been rendered more or less ineffective by failure to predict accurately the reactive behaviors of the city's people to the controls placed on them. This has been particularly true of traffic plans. Street widenings and other measures to alleviate congestion in the central business district have almost always been followed by increases in traffic that reproduced the congestion on a larger scale than before. Only by establishing broader controls (restricting, for example, the height and density of buildings in the central district) can such undesired repercussions be avoided.

Often plans must be changed, not because of failure to achieve the desired results, but because they achieve additional undesired results as well. These unlooked for consequences may be good or bad in the view of the planners. One striking example (which most people would put in the category of "good" results) was the invention of a new architectural form—the modern skyscraper with setbacks—partly as a result of height and bulk restrictions upon buildings. In many cities the zoning of frontage on all major through streets for commercial use had the unanticipated result of leaving a large part of such frontage vacant.

Among the consequences of plans that are often unanticipated are the costs of securing compliance—including the psychological costs to those persons who want to resist the plan. Plans that run counter to self-interest, that appear irrational or immoral, or that involve excessive subordination of the individual all involve great costs to the persons complying.

In rational planning these non-monetary costs must be considered, just as the money costs are. Moreover, there is a direct relation between the two. If the costs of compliance are high, the monetary costs of the intermediate enforcement behaviors will go up accordingly. Many more enforcement officers will be needed. More money will have to be spent on publicity and propaganda, and in analysing and changing the plans themselves. In extreme cases, the monetary costs of enforcement may become prohibitive.

Organization for Planning

Planning, as the term has been defined here, is a major part of the activity of virtually all members of organizations. Every act of choice and decision that precedes actual behavior is a plan. Moreover, most governmental employees never perform any ultimate behaviors whatsoever—behaviors that are intended as final steps in executing plans. The principal exceptions to this are some of the "operative employees" of so-called "service agencies." A postman delivering a letter, a fireman climbing a ladder, a forest ranger's assistant gravelling a road are in a certain sense engaging in ultimate behaviors—that is, their behaviors are directed at altering physical conditions, rather than at influencing the behaviors of other persons.

However, most of the behaviors of "operative" employees of regulatory agencies are intermediate—they form one link of a chain whose object it is to secure the desired ultimate behaviors of the persons regulated. Thus, a traffic policeman is engaged in intermediate behaviors aimed at securing desired ultimate behaviors from motorists. Moreover, all the supervisory employees in an organization are engaged almost exclusively in intermediate behaviors—the object of their behavior is to influence the behaviors of their subordinates and other associates.

It follows from this that planning is an activity that cannot be separated to any considerable degree from the whole complex pattern of organizational behavior. Even when we establish special organizational units that are designated as "planning units," these specialized parts of the organization will account for only a very small part of the planning and intermediate behavior that takes place.

SPECIALIZED PLANNING UNITS

In spite of the all-pervasive character of planning, this is one of the activities—along with personnel, purchasing, and accounting— that has increasingly been an object of administrative centralization. At the municipal level, city planning bodies have become almost universal in cities of any size. The Federal government established its National Resources Planning Board, later supplanted by the National Security Resources Board, the Council of Economic Advisers, and several other interdepartmental committees. Numerous state planning bodies were established during the 1930's. The General Staff of the Army and the Bureau of Agricultural Economics in the Department of Agriculture have set a pattern, increasingly popular, of departmental specialization in planning.

There are several explanations for the seeming paradox that is involved in the specialization of planning. First, many of these so-called planning bodies are really not only planning specialists for other administrative units, but are also entrusted with their own substantive administrative programs. This is particularly true of city planning agencies, which are responsible for the regulation of urban land uses. A city planning department not only plans—so do the police department, the street department, and the public library—but it plans and enforces zoning regulations, subdivision regulations, and the like.

The second part of the explanation is that specialized planning bodies are generally concerned with long-range aspects of planning while shorter-range planning takes place throughout the administrative structure.[7] Long-range planning usually involves difficult problems of prediction of consequences and of reactions to plans, and specialization permits the research required for such prediction to be assigned to the specialized unit.

The third part of the explanation is that we have always had specialization for long-range planning, but we have not always called it that. When Alexander Hamilton, as Secretary of the Treasury, prepared his *Report on Manufactures* he was engaged in long-range planning very like that carried on by the National Resources Planning Board. As governmental activities have become more complex, and as our economy has become more integrated, the level of integration has tended to rise higher in the administrative structure. When units are established to deal with this higher-level integration, we tend to attach the label "planning" to the new units—at least we did until this label became a politically questionable one.

Thus, the growth of planning units in the U. S. Department of Agriculture marks the transition of that department from an organization of the holding-company type to a unitary organization. The growth of city planning units reflects the increasing interdependence of physical construction projects of the various city departments and the dependence of these on land uses. The National Resources Planning Board and its successor the Council of Economic Advisers are an adaptation to the increasing responsi-

[7] We do not mean that all or most long-range planning is done by special units, but that such units are concerned with long-range planning to a greater degree than other units.

bilities of the national government for resource management and control of the business cycle.

The history of state planning bodies indicates what is likely to happen when a specialized planning unit is established at an inappropriate level—a level where there is no common unitary goal cutting across departments. The state planning boards of the 1930's were mostly a hot-house growth—stimulated by the National Resources Planning Board. Since their establishment did not reflect the development of new unitary goals within state governments, and since most states are not appropriate units for resource planning, these agencies were hard pressed to find programs of activities.

Most state planning bodies became inactive during World War II, and when reactivated after the war, turned their efforts primarily to encouraging the location of new industries in the state. This activity is, of course, no more a "planning" activity than is the operation of a system of state hospitals. It is a substantive governmental program, and involves just as much, or just as little, planning as does any other governmental activity. Hence, very few of these agencies really represent a specialization for planning. They illustrate the point that almost any governmental agency that is entrusted with a goal and with very few and ineffective means for achieving that goal is likely to be called a "planning" agency.

RELATIONSHIPS OF PLANNING UNITS

We have seen that a genuine specialization of some aspects of long-range planning may take place in an organization at a level where there is a unitary socially meaningful goal. Such a specialization may accomplish several things. First, it may secure proper attention to the research that is needed as a basis for realistic plans. The planning unit may become one of the important centers of external intelligence for the organization.

Second, the pressure of day-to-day activities upon the organization may prevent the administrative personnel from giving adequate attention to long-range problems. Immediate short-range problems—"keeping the program going"—fix their own deadlines. Long-range planning is something that can always be done tomorrow, and if problems requiring immediate solution come thick enough and fast enough, that tomorrow never arrives.

A prime reason, then, for specializing long-range planning is to assure proper program emphasis—proper emphasis upon the long-range as well as the short-range consequences of decisions. If, for example, a city school system is crowded, immediate administrative pressures may lead to the construction of a school on a small inappropriate site, in a district where the child population is decreasing. A long-range construction plan may not only anticipate the shortage before it actually occurs, but may also provide for it in an orderly and efficient way. Trends in population movement may be predicted, needed sites may be secured well in advance, rising building costs may be anticipated, Federal aid for construction may be secured by synchronizing it with the business cycle, and so forth.

The problems of the relationship of planning units with the other parts of an organization have already been explored at some length in Chapters 12 through 14. There are no fundamental differences between planning units and the other units regarded as "overhead"—indeed we have seen that most overhead units are in part specialized planning units. A personnel unit, a purchasing unit—all prepare plans in their respective functional fields.

While we should expect to find no differences in kind, there are probably some differences of degree in the problems encountered by those overhead units that are engaged primarily in long-range planning. The first problem is related to the very reason for creating such units—the rest of the organization is preoccupied with day-to-day problems and gives insufficient attention to the long-range problems. For this reason, the planning agency may encounter strong resistances in securing acceptance of and compliance with its plans. Administrators preoccupied with everyday concerns may not wish to be disturbed by the planning unit, and may attach great weight to the short-run inconvenience of making planned changes, even if long-term benefits can be demonstrated.

The very separation of long-range planning from the rest of the administrative program may encourage this resistance by relieving the rest of the organization from any continuing concern with long-range problems. Hence, the immediate gain in attention to planning through the establishment of the specialized unit may not be a net gain, when weighed against the increased cost of securing compliance. A major weakness of city planning agencies has been this separation from the "operating" agencies of the city government and (when the city planning board is an independent body) from the chief executive. To the extent that the planning group separates itself psychologically from the rest of the organization—establishes itself as a separate identification group—it will encounter resistance to its plans.

A second difficulty derives from the essentially political nature of plans—and particularly of long-range plans. As we saw earlier in the chapter, the process of establishing goals cannot be separated from the activity of the legislature and of political interest groups. Any government agency is likely to become the target of political groups that oppose its program. A unit specializing in planning is likely to become a special target of unfriendly groups—as the National Resources Planning Board discovered.

In the American governmental structure, where the legislature and the chief executive are generally both politically important, and usually independently elected, the political problem of planning units is increased accordingly. Unless legislature and chief executive are in almost complete harmony—which has certainly not been characteristic of the national government since 1930—a planning unit that serves one of them will have great difficulty in serving the other. The U. S. Bureau of the Budget, which conceives itself as a Presidential servant, has not always succeeded in convincing the Congress of its political neutrality. On several occasions when Congress has appropriated funds for uses that the President (or his Budget Bureau) has disapproved, the President has placed on the Bureau the duty of impounding the funds and preventing their expenditure. This, in turn, has subjected the Bureau to strong Congressional criticism at subsequent budget hearings.

Recognition of the political character of planning has sometimes led to proposals that budget and other planning units should be appointed by, and should report to, the legislature rather than the President. A legislative budget bureau has actually been established in the state of Virginia. The structural arrangement is really a symptom rather than a cause of the political difficulties involved in planning. In any democratic structure specialized long-range planning units must always remain the most vulnerable units in the administrative organization.

Pathology of Planning

We will leave to others the question of whether too much or too little planning is going on in government today. That debate is not so much one about planning as about the proper scope of governmental activities. Of more relevance to a study on administration is the question of the effectiveness of the planning that is actually going on.

There is little doubt that much planning is ineffective, and that the prime reason for this ineffectiveness is the failure of planners to appreciate the difficulty of the problem they set themselves. The task of planning is not merely one of visualizing brave new worlds. It is a task of constructing sequences of behavior that can be carried out and that will bring these brave new worlds into actual being. Planning is likely to be successful only in proportion as the planner recognizes the magnitude of the problem and starts out with a proper humility as to what can be accomplished through planning.

Most human planning probably results in failure if we measure it by comparing the results achieved with the results originally intended by the planners. As Barnard has pointed out, even in a field where the planners have a maximum control over the variables in the situation, as in planning a building, rarely is the result the same as the one envisaged. What often happens is that the result, although not the one envisaged, is satisfactory to the persons concerned and the planners therefore claim a success when actually they have failed.

Planning is probably successful as it comes close to thought that just precedes action. Man constantly perceives obstacles to his satisfactions and devises ways to overcome them. As soon as he overcomes one obstacle, he perceives another. His attention is controlled and directed by his perception of these obstacles, and he directs his behavior to overcome them as he perceives them. This immediate planning and acting is probably the area of man's greatest planning success.

A particular type of over-confidence in planning is one that results in detailed blueprints for an undefined future event. An example of peculiar importance to us all is mobilization planning. Beginning early in 1930, the Army and Navy Munitions Board developed an industrial mobilization plan for use in event of war. This plan purported to spell out just how industry would be mobilized in event of war, what government organizations would be established, how they would be organized, what they would do, etc. The plan was "kept up to date," the last revision being in 1939. When war finally came upon us, this 1939 plan was not used. The failure to use the plan has sometimes been explained by planners as due to the lack of intelligence and cooperativeness of the people in charge of mobilization in 1942. A much better explanation, however, is that the blueprint did not fit the political, economic, and strategic conditions that actually prevailed in 1942 and which could not possibly have been predicted in 1939.

Mobilization planning of the type done by the Army and Navy Munitions Board before the war, which is still the prevailing concept of mobilization planning, is a confusion between long-range and short-term planning, as those concepts have been defined above. A mobilization planning body, such as the present National Security Resources Board, is of necessity engaged in planning for an indefinite future event. To prepare detailed blueprints of actual behavior to accomplish goals or overcome obstacles is meaningless on its face, because we do not now have those concrete goals, know what the obstacles are, or know the nature of the conditions within which that future behavior will take place.

Mobilization planning during peacetime must follow the long-range planning pattern. It must consist of two parts. First, it must develop technologies—knowledge—that future concrete mobilization planners will use in developing their actual plans for immediate human behavior. And, second, it must suggest goals for present, immediate planning of behavior by the relevant administrative planning groups, both governmental and non-governmental (such as the steel industry). These goals will be discovered by observing what our war-making deficiencies and weak spots are as fast as they develop. To do this, the mobilization planning body needs current information on total resources requirements and total resources supply. With this information, our weaknesses will become apparent as fast as they develop, and suggestions for correcting them can be made continually. These suggestions, when regularly validated, become the goals for immediate, concrete plans for human behavior. Both of these functions—preparing technologies for the actual future mobilization administrators, and suggesting current planning goals—will be discharged through the activity of research. In the final analysis the only sensible activity of a peace-time mobilization planning body is research. The preparation of concrete blueprints for human behavior not only fails to provide the nation with any real security but may also lull it with a false sense of security and become an intellectual Maginot line.

Conclusion

We have seen that planning is an activity that pervades every part of the administrative structure. It is an activity that is concerned with goals, but equally and necessarily with the steps required to realize goals. Because it is concerned with goals, planning can never be politically neutral unless the goals themselves are noncontroversial and neutral. Because it is concerned with implementation, planning activity can be separated only to a very moderate extent from the other activity that takes place in organizations.

In the next two chapters of this book we will explore further the ways in which planning goals can be implemented. We will try to develop what might be called a theory of administrative regulation—but we will be concerned not only with the regulation of persons outside the organization, but also with the task of securing intermediate behaviors from those within.

CHAPTER TWENTY-ONE

♯

The Tactics of Execution: Reducing the Costs of Change

IN THE last chapter we discussed planning as the designing of human behavior to achieve goals. We saw that if plans are to be more than wishes, the planners must give consideration to the resistances that are inevitably encountered, and must include in the plans devices for overcoming these resistances.

Discussion of means for securing compliance with plans usually focusses upon *enforcement*—the detection of violators of a law, and their prosecution and punishment. In our analysis we will be concerned with the whole range of *inducements* that can be offered to secure conformity, and not merely with enforcement activities as just defined. There are many forms of inducement other than the application of formal sanctions to individual violators. Educational and propaganda devices (e.g., the advertising of War Bonds), rewards (e.g., soil conservation payments under the AAA), and many other techniques play a much more important overall role than does the machinery of the courts in inducing members of the public to accept the plans of government agencies.

In fact, apart from the work of devising plans, the employees of a regulatory agency are engaged almost exclusively in inducement activities. Employees who process forms, who write letters, who audit, who investigate, who write news releases, who prepare educational programs, who talk to the clientele, who instruct field offices, are all engaged in activities designed ultimately to secure the planned behavior of the clientele.

A plan is directed toward a specific group of people, and the inducements must likewise be so directed. To use the same devices to regulate children's behavior as to regulate adults' behavior would normally lead to failure (although the success Russia is alleged to have had with candy as an adult inducement may require some modification of the statement). Likewise, the problem of securing compliance may vary as between educated and less educated, old and young, foreign born and native, Northerners and Southerners, middle class and lower class, and so forth. Because of these differences, the inducement aspects of plans must be chosen with particular groups in mind as targets and must be aimed at those targets. An appeal to religious sentiment will not move noticeably a society of atheists.

Of course, not all plans encounter resistance. There are situations in which nearly everyone concerned asks only to be told what to do in understandable terms. These are situations in which *doing something* is generally agreed to be much more important than *what is done*. Plans made for such situations might be called "rules of the road." It makes no difference which side of the road we travel on so long as everyone on one side is going the same way. What little success has been achieved in international regulation has been with regard to "rules of the road" (international postal union, ship signals and the like). The number of situations in which noncontroversial "rules of the road" may be imposed are not many, however. Even the synchronization of clocks, where consistency of behavior appears to be the only obviously significant value, finds thousands violently denouncing daylight saving time as contrary to the will of God and the laws of nature. In most cases, the administrative planner finds that human behavior does not respond automatically to his wishes. He must devise ways to overcome the resistances to his plans.

Overcoming Resistances to Plans

In very general terms, the problem of inducement is to make the person to whom the plan is directed feel that conformance is preferable to nonconformance. The individual to whom the plan is directed must be induced to *choose* the new behavior of the plan in preference to the old behavior. He is not "forced" to behave according to the plan in any literal sense. Literally to force a person is to apply physical force to his body as by dragging him. Inducement does not use physical force except occasionally in some aspects of the apprehension and punishment process. Instead, it operates on the individual's motivations so that he directs himself to behave as planned.

THE PSYCHOLOGICAL BASIS OF INDUCEMENT

All of the techniques of inducement involve two basic psychological approaches. A person's behavior can be changed either (1) by changing the criteria or values he applies in choice, or (2) by changing the things available for him to choose from. The first method of inducement is sometimes involved in education or propaganda. The second method is the method involved in rewards and punishments.

A simple illustration may clarify the distinction between these two methods. To induce people to park their cars at a proper distance from fire plugs, a sustained educational campaign may finally convince them that the whole community, which includes themselves, is endangered if free access of fire engines to fire plugs is not maintained. Thereafter they will not *want* to park in front of fire plugs and will *choose* not to do so. On the other hand, this same result may be approached by providing that anyone who parks before a fire plug will be fined $15. In this case, the values of individuals remain the same, but the alternatives available to their choice have been changed. Although there are only two basic psychological inducement techniques, there are many variations in their application. We will now turn to a consideration of these variations.

REASONS FOR RESISTANCE

At the time a plan is installed, the people to whom it is directed are behaving in a certain way. This existing pattern of behavior has qualities of persistence; it is valuable in some way or it would not be maintained. These qualities of persistence are five: habit, moral standards, expediency, rationality, and resistance to subordination. That is to say, the existing behavior pattern exists and persists partly because of habit, partly because the group's moral code decrees it, partly because it is personally advantageous to the individuals involved, partly because they do not understand the reasons for change, and partly because they dislike to accept subordination. Into this situation the plan attempts to bring changes in the existing behavior pattern. The problem of inducement is to overcome persistence in the old behavior by making the values of behaving according to the plan relatively greater, and to do this without incurring large new costs of subordination.

INCORPORATING INDUCEMENTS IN THE PLAN

Inducements can be incorporated in a plan in two ways. One method is to reduce those undesirable features or "costs" of the planned behavior that make people resist the change. Reducing such costs to the minimum enhances the relative attractiveness of the planned behavior as compared with present behavior and thus increases the likelihood that people will behave as planned.

The second way to make compliance relatively more attractive than non-compliance is to attempt to add desired values to the new behavior of the plan—making the new behavior relatively more attractive than the old in a positive sense. The first approach mentioned—reducing the costs of change—will be discussed in this chapter. The second approach—attaching new values to compliance—will be described in Chapter 22.

Inertia Costs

Because it is so difficult to change habits, realistic planners will attempt to achieve their goals with a minimum disturbance of normal practices. A plan that requires extensive changes in normal practices will usually be extensively violated. One that requires few changes may secure a high degree of compliance with a minimum of effort on the part of the intermediate (enforcement) personnel.

MAKING COMPLIANCE EASY

Since behavior tends to find paths of least resistance, a plan that requires people to go to a lot of trouble will secure less compliance, other things being equal, than one that requires little effort on the part of the clientele. It is easier to get people to fill out a simple form than a complex one. It is easier to get people to comply with a requirement by mail than by personal appearance at an office. When other inducements are lacking or very weak, it is essential that compliance be made just as easy as possible if the plan is to be effective.

Although this proposition seems obvious, it is often violated in governmental regulation. For example, when the Federal government wanted labor leaders to file non-Communist affidavits with the National Labor Relations Board, a distasteful duty to many union officials, it gave them a very limited time in which to do so. The penalty for not filing on time was refusal of the services of the NLRB to the unions whose leaders did not file. Actually, the government wanted all unions to use the NLRB as a device for minimizing industrial strife. Thus the government was defeating its own plans by making it difficult for unions to do what the government wanted them to do.

MAKING NON-COMPLIANCE DIFFICULT

Although it is important to make compliance with plans as easy as possible, it is equally important to make non-compliance difficult. If the planners wish to discourage or depress a certain type of behavior, they can put many obstacles or difficulties in its way. This technique of manipulating inertia costs could be called "regulation by impedimenta." An example would be a city zoning ordinance which establishes a complicated review procedure for persons who seek a variance—who want a minor modification of the plan as applied to their property.

SHIFTING THE COSTS OF COMPLIANCE

Inertia costs can be shifted to a certain extent from the clientele to the intermediate persons—the regulatory agency's employees. Such a shift of inertia costs is implied by the phrase "the customer is always right." A shift of the burdens of a plan is possible because the organization usually enjoys more inducement power over its own employees than it does over the clientele.

A good example of the use of this technique to enhance compliance is the present income tax report for persons in the lower income brackets. These people, who comprise the bulk of reporting persons and for whom negative inducements such as detection and prosecution are relatively weak, only have to enter a few simple items on the withholding statement given them by their employers. The rest of the work is done by processors in the Internal Revenue Bureau who compute the lowest possible tax and the amount of refund or additional tax due.

Sometimes planners have strong inducement power over the clientele and can therefore shift a part of the burden to it. For example, the rationing planners had strong inducement power over consumers: consumers could not purchase rationed commodities without ration books. In order to ease the burden on the overworked and largely volunteer ration boards, application forms were often designed for ease in processing rather than ease in filling out. The shifting of the burden of inertia costs to the clientele is a central feature of licensing programs, discussed in the next chapter.

Sometimes the shifting of inertia costs to the clientele because there exists great inducement power over them is abused by government officials, and they adopt an officious attitude of "take it or leave it." This tendency is one of the genuine evils of bureaucracy that must be watched constantly if plans are to be effective without unnecessary damage to the feelings and interests of the individual citizen.

Reducing Moral Costs

In the preceding chapter, moral costs were defined as the resistances produced when plans run counter to, or are not supported by, the mores or beliefs of society. If moral costs are present to any high degree, the costs of the behaviors required to induce conformity will also be very high. In extreme cases, e.g., a draft riot, it may be necessary to employ military forces to break resistance. Such a situation occurs when the plans of the government so violate the sense of right and justice of large numbers of people that a revolution threatens. Today, this situation is the prevailing one in many countries of the world.

ADJUSTING THE PLAN TO PREVAILING VALUES

The most obvious way to reduce moral costs is to make certain that plans are in harmony with the basic values of the community. This proposition is particularly important when plans classify people into groups for special treatment. Within the community there will be widespread and often strongly held notions as to who should be included in each class. If the plans fail to correspond to these community beliefs or values, cries of discrimination will go up and it will be very difficult to secure compliance.

Because of the many conflicts within our society, it is rarely possible to base plans on values challenged by no one. For example, grave difficulties result from the absence of a common moral code with regard to race relations. At the present time it is impossible for the Federal government to devise plans for non-discrimination (or for discrimination) in the armed forces, in voting, in employment, and in federally financed housing that will satisfy Negroes, other minority groups, white Northerners, and white Southerners alike. Any plan that is evolved will almost certainly evoke widespread non-compliance from disapproving groups.

IDENTIFYING THE PLAN WITH VALUE SYMBOLS

Community values are seldom explicit, coherent, and concrete. In the case of most plans it is never entirely clear how far they are consistent with, or inconsistent with, the values of society. Hence, an important technique for influencing attitudes toward any program is to attempt to identify that program with prevailing symbols of value that are widely accepted. Thus, an anti-trust program may attach itself to the symbol of "the American system of competitive private enterprise." This procedure may be viewed either as a means of reducing the moral costs of change or a means of attaching positive values to the plan. It will be discussed more fully in the next chapter.

Reducing Self-Interest Costs

When governmental plans interfere with personal plans for gain or enjoyment, compliance involves a personal sacrifice. Such sacrifices we have called self-interest costs.

MINIMIZING DISTURBANCE

These costs, like inertia costs, are often reduced by attempting to accomplish objectives with a minimum of disturbance of normal practices and relations. Thus plans to ease the housing shortage have depended heavily upon private building and financing. Even these plans have met strenuous resistance from builders because they involved some public housing. Similarly, war production in World War II was promoted almost entirely through regular business channels under general governmental supervision by businessmen employed by the government for the purpose. Actual governmental intervention and management of facilities, such as the operation of the railroads during World War I, occurred only when industrial disputes threatened output.

PROVIDING COMPENSATION

Frequently the self-interest costs of compliance can be measured in dollars and cents. In such cases, the persons affected can be compensated for their losses, a very common method in American government. Examples of the reduction of costs through compensation are cost-plus war production, crop reduction payments under the Agricultural Adjustment Act, and the compensation the petroleum industry received during the second World War to offset the additional costs of bringing petroleum into the Northeast by tank cars rather than by tankers.

Reducing Rationality Costs

We have defined rationality cost as the dislike of doing things that do not appear to accomplish anything worth accomplishing. Although there may be much subconscious behavior that is not rational, when people are asked or required to do something, they want to know why, and often "just because" is not a sufficient answer.

MINIMIZING REQUIREMENTS

The first step in reducing the resistances which stem from the drive toward rationality is to review the plan carefully to determine if there is a good reason for each requirement. Many of the requirements of government plans simply reflect a blind following of other government plans, of ancient governmental ways and procedures. The rapid increase of management consultants in private business and of organization and methods experts in public management bear eloquent witness to the persistence of outworn and useless procedures and requirements. A similar development in the field of governmental regulation of the public would undoubtedly find an equally fertile field for improvement. A simple example is the large amount of time uselessly spent finding notaries to witness signatures. The field of legal administration is so hopelessly encased in ancient and now useless requirements as to be quite inadequate for much modern regulation. Much information requested on governmental (and private) forms is never used; the questions are still asked merely because they always have been, or because some official in the form planning process felt vaguely that the information might be useful.

DEVELOPING ACCEPTABLE JUSTIFICATIONS

Having made certain that all the requirements of the plan are needed, the next step in reducing rationality costs is to develop acceptable reasons for the requirements and to communicate them to the persons affected. If people are convinced that the requirements of the plan make sense, they will not feel that the requirements are arbitrary or bureaucratic. It should be remembered that the kind of reasons required are *acceptable* reasons. People may argue about what the "real" reasons are, but whether a reason is *acceptable* or not depends upon whether people *accept* it.

COMMUNICATING JUSTIFICATIONS

Perhaps more difficult than finding acceptable reasons for requirements is communicating those reasons to the persons affected. If widespread understanding of the reasons behind requirements is required, as it is for mass regulation, every medium of communication may be needed. Increasingly, modern governments are turning to the radio, the movie, and to billboard and poster advertising, as well as to newspapers, in an effort to reach everyone. Where a plan relates to a restricted or limited clientele, direct mail is often used. The communication channels of the clientele's own organizations, such as private trade association bulletins, are also being used increasingly. An extension of this latter device is consultation in planning. If representatives of the groups affected by plans are consulted in the planning process, they learn of the reasons behind requirements by participating in the planning of them. Then they may become, in a sense, salesmen of the plan among the members of their own groups. More will be said about group consultation later in this chapter.

Reducing Subordination Costs

In Chapter 8, it was pointed out that people may obey for various reasons other than fear of punishment or receipt of a command from an authorized person. To reduce the resistances that spring from dislike of threats or sheer displays of authority, plans must seek to harness motivations other than fear and must not be presented in an imperious or haughty manner. Suggestions and appeals to self-interest do not involve subordination costs. When a plan has been thoroughly "sold" so that the people affected by it can see its sense and utility, complying with the requirements of the plan is not demeaning; it does not sacrifice the sense of personal dignity as does compliance under threat of punishment.

Subordination costs stem chiefly from a "be it enacted" attitude on the part of government planners. Our traditional approach to government has been legalistic. It has been assumed that people have an absolute duty to obey the government and that, therefore, all the government planners have to do is issue an order and the desired results are automatically obtained. This attitude about government, with its "light switch" theory of regulation, is not adapted to the mass regulation problems of the modern age. In the long run, perhaps the best way to reduce subordination costs is to educate government planners—to instill in them the attitude that government regulation is not different in kind from any other regulation, such as a club's regulation of its members.

Subordination costs are partly a result of status differences. Many people do not like to be commanded by someone of the same or lower status. This fact helps to explain some of the resistance of the business community to governmental regulation. American businessmen earn much more and have a much higher social status than do American government officials. Because subordination costs are related to status distinctions, they can be reduced somewhat by having plans proclaimed by persons with very high status. A Presidential proclamation is such a technique. The President's 1948 food conservation program was an attempt (not too success-ful) to gain voluntary compliance by using the high status of an American businessman, Mr. Charles Luckman, then president of Lever Bros., who headed the President's Citizens' Food Com-mittee.

As is true of other resistances to plans, subordination costs can be reduced by consulting the persons affected when the plans are being developed. Because group consultation in planning will re-duce all kinds of resistances and because it is increasingly used in government, a more extended discussion of this process is in order.

Group Consultation

Group consultation is the participation in planning by persons to whom the plans are directed or by representatives of these persons. Before launching into a discussion of the process of consultation, we need to review in general terms the nature of the relationship between a regulatory agency and the clientele for whose behavior it plans. We will treat the problem with specific reference to regula-tory agencies.

POLITICAL RELATIONS WITH CLIENTELE

In our discussion of organizational survival, it was pointed out that the clientele of an agency stands in a dual relationship to that agency. On the one hand, the agency wishes to elicit from the clientele certain behaviors—the behaviors contemplated in its plans. On the other hand, the clientele may possess considerable political influence and be able to exert strong pressures on the organization that is seeking to plan for it. If the organization tries to enforce a regulation that is strongly disliked, it must anticipate both great difficulties of enforcement and vigorous political re-actions.

Up to this point we have not distinguished sharply two mean-ings of the word "clientele." In Chapters 18 and 19 we used the term in reference to groups whose interests were strongly affected by an agency's activities—the groups, consequently, who provided the principal sources of political support and opposition. In our chapters on planning, we have used "clientele" to refer to groups whose behaviors are to be modified by planning. In the case of governmental *services* there is generally a large degree of coincidence between the two groups; in the case of *regulation*, there may or may not be such coincidence. In the present discussion we see that regulation may involve groups favorably interested in a plan, but whose behaviors are not a part of the plan; groups favorably interested, and included in the plan; and groups adversely interested, and included in the plan.

Consent of the Governed. In terms of this analysis, it becomes something of a mystery that government can ever regulate anything at all. A careful examination of actual regulatory programs helps to dispel the mystery. The survival of effective regulation, like the survival of any governmental activity, requires a positive balance of political support over political opposition. The necessary political support may be forthcoming from any of three sources (not necessarily mutually exclusive):

1. Support may be provided by large or politically powerful segments of the community that are not included in the agency clientele and whose interests are in some respect opposed to those of the clientele. For example, powerful farm groups succeeded in imposing rate regulations upon railroads because farmers believed that high railroad rates were a major cause of low prices for agricultural products. Labor groups, in periods of political ascendancy, have similarly been able to secure regulations of wages and hours, and the enforcement of certain collective bargaining procedures.

2. Governmental regulations may actually advance, rather than oppose, the interests of politically powerful segments of the clientele group. For example, milk price laws, although these ostensibly control the behaviors of dairy farmers and milk distributors, actually have been administered in such a way as to increase the profits of these groups at the expense of milk consumers. Professional licensing laws have been increasingly used to protect the economic and status positions of established members of the professions by limiting entrance to the professions.

3. A clientele group may accept regulation, even though somewhat adverse to its short-run interests as a means of anticipating and heading-off potential political forces that would otherwise impose more severe and less palatable regulations upon the group. For example, the resistance of public utilities to rate regulation has

been considerably tempered by the realization that in any event consumers would probably sooner or later organize to restrict the power of monopolies to fix their own prices. Too vigorous resistance to rate regulation might even lead to the disaster of public ownership.

From our analysis of survival, we would conclude then that a clientele group or some segment of such a group, can be regulated when its interests clash with those of groups that are even more powerful than it is; when the interests of powerful segments of the clientele group are actually advanced rather than opposed by the regulation; or when the regulation is the only alternative to something even more unpleasant (really a combination of the first two categories). In any case, where regulation exists, interest groups in the clientele will have strong reasons to try to influence or control the regulatory process. To the extent they succeed, regulation becomes a process of "control by the governed"—or by powerful segments of the governed.

Control by the Governed. Let us consider, for example, regulations that exist in every state for the licensing of physicians. The ostensible purpose of such regulations is to protect the public from the ministrations of incompetent medical practitioners. As the medical profession has long since discovered, however, licensing also protects the trained physician from the "unfair" competition of those who wish to practice without the expensive preparation of a medical education, and from "unethical" methods of advertising and practice. The medical profession has also discovered that licensing laws, and the control of entry to approved medical schools, can be used to protect the economic rewards of medical practice from dilution resulting from the entry of too many persons into the profession.

Moreover, the regulatory process is held securely in the hands of the profession itself. This does not mean merely that the group is consulted by the regulatory body. The actual political control of the state regulatory authorities rests in almost every instance with the state and county medical associations, rather than with the state legislatures.[1]

The medical profession is by no means a unique, or even rare,

---

[1] This statement must be somewhat qualified in those states where competing professional groups, like the osteopaths, are able to exert political pressures counter to those of the physicians.

example of the control of regulations by and for the regulatees. Almost equally good examples are provided by the barbers, cosmetologists, plumbers, and stationary engineers. The lawyers and the professional engineers look enviously at the physicians, but have not yet achieved a comparable measure of success in using the regulatory powers of government for their ends.

If we survey the field of governmental regulation of business, the same pattern repeats itself endlessly. In general, the regulations that are best accepted and best enforced are those that have been turned by the business community into means of protecting itself from dangers within. The Securities Exchange Act illustrates the usual course of events. Public losses from speculation in the 1929 stock market crash resulted in almost complete lack of confidence in the whole investment mechanism. The Securities Exchange Act was enacted to protect the public from unscrupulous professional speculators and brokers. While originally opposed by most stockbrokers (and certain of its provisions still are), it was soon realized that the Act placed all of them on an equal plane of competition, and indeed protected the responsible members of the profession from the unethical competition of the less responsible.

More recently, investment brokers have sought to use the regulatory mechanism in a more positive way to advance their goals. The established exchanges, like the New York Stock Exchange, have sought to impose stricter regulations on over-the-counter dealers who are not members of the Exchanges. Encouraged by the Maloney Act of 1938, the over-the-counter dealers formed their own National Association of Securities Dealers to counter the legislative pressures of the exchanges, and to perform self-policing functions in their own group that would head off more severe regulation by the Securities and Exchange Commission.

REASONS FOR CONSULTATION

Consultation may be strongly desired by the clientele of a regulatory program as a means of enhancing its influence over the program and protecting its interests. On the other hand, a sophisticated group may realize that by accepting responsibility through participation in program planning it gives up some of its right and ability to act as critic. For example the War Labor Board was organized in such a way as to give equal representation in board membership to labor, employers, and the public. By participation in the Board's decisions, even when they voted against the decision of the majority, labor leaders or employers, as the case might be, accepted a share of responsibility for the Board's decisions. Consequently, by continued participation on the Board, they were put in the position of publicly supporting its policies—or at least of urging compliance with Board decisions—even when they opposed those policies. At various times a boycott of the Board was threatened, now by labor and now by management. In general, a clientele group will be willing to continue its participation only so long as it feels that it has a real influence upon policy, and that it will be able to secure a program somewhat consistent with its interests.

The administrators of a regulatory program may desire consultation with its clientele either as a means for securing information required for intelligent planning, or as a means for reducing resistance, or both. However, from the standpoint of the regulatory agency, too, consultation has its costs. It provides the regulated group with an additional channel of influence, and usually requires the organization to make considerable concessions from time to time in order to retain the amicability and viability of the relationship.[2]

FORMS OF CONSULTATION

Consultation can be achieved through a number of devices, formal and informal. On the informal side, the staffing of an agency with persons drawn from the clientele group, and still partially or wholly identified with it, is really a form of consultation. The business community certainly regarded the statutory requirement that OPA employ businessmen (however vague that term may be) in policy positions as a means of securing a representation of their views in that agency.

On the formal side, consultation may take the form of official representation in the hierarchy or on official boards, the establishment of advisory committees, or the appointment of consultants from the clientele group. The War Labor Board provides an example of official representation. Another example are medical

---

[2] Phillip Selznick's study, *TVA and the Grass Roots* is a valuable study of the consequences of consultation in an agency that has put great stress on the "grass roots" planning of its program.

licensing boards, which are almost always made up of physicians (this is frequently a statutory requirement). City planning agencies are frequently supplemented by advisory committees, representative of various kinds of local interests—realty interests, racial and national minorities, industries, labor, and the like. Industry advisory groups are frequently used for consultation on programs that concern the particular industry in question. The Federal government, especially, often employs consultants under similar circumstances.

The effectiveness of these alternative arrangements depends in part upon the purpose of consultation. For example, the appointment of consultants is often the most effective method for securing technical information about a specific industry. The consultants can be chosen with a view to their knowledge of the situation, their intelligence, and their ability to express themselves. However, if the information needed is information about the probable reactions to plans, a representative committee, where the planners can meet the group representatives face to face and observe their reactions, is likely to be more fruitful.

Where the primary reason for consultation is to reduce resistances to plans, the advisory committee may prove the more suitable device. The effectiveness of such a committee in securing widespread assent from the clientele group will depend largely upon its representativeness. If important groups or areas are omitted, they will feel slighted, and may react to the program more adversely than if no advisory committee existed.

Advisory committees, by participation in planning, learn the reasons that underlie regulations. If the committee members are convinced of the need for the plan, they will defend it to other members of their groups. They become, in effect, an extension of the government's public relations activities. Because they belong to the clientele group, its members are more likely to listen to them than to outsiders.

While, in general, consultation with representatives of groups affected by governmental plans tends toward the creation of consensus between the governed and the governors, the reader should be reminded again that such consensus is bought only at some cost in compromise. If a man's advice is sought in order to reduce his resistance to a plan, this result is not likely to be achieved unless some heed is paid to that advice. In establishing consultative devices, their value in securing compliance must be balanced against possible disadvantages that result from giving the regulated group additional means of influence.

Conclusion

In this chapter we have been discussing one approach to the problem of inducement, namely, reducing the costs to the clientele group of complying with the plan. The other approach is to add preference value to the planned behavior relative to existing behaviors—to give the clientele positive reasons for compliance. Both approaches lead to the same result—inducing people to choose to behave according to the plan. In the next chapter we will examine the second approach.

CHAPTER TWENTY-TWO

✍

The Tactics of Execution: Securing Compliance

IN THIS chapter we continue our discussion of how people are induced to accept plans, and examine various kinds of inducements, other than the reduction of costs already discussed, that may be incorporated in plans. These inducements fall into two main classes: (1) enlisting the support of existing preferences and values, and (2) making the planned behavior relatively attractive by detracting from the desirability of the behaviors that are to be changed. Rewards for compliance are an example of the first; penalties for failure to comply, an example of the second.

Enlisting the Support of Existing Values

As was pointed out in Chapter 21, an existing behavior pattern often persists because group mores demand it or because it has results that are currently desired (such as making money or acquiring social prestige). If these existing motivations can be lined up behind the planned behavior instead of the existing pattern, they will serve as a strong influence toward compliance. In seeking to harness the community's moral code, propaganda and education or the sanction of legitimacy are the principal devices used. If the appeal is to self interest, either a system of rewards may be established, or the clientele may be educated as to its own self interest.

THE METHOD OF PROPAGANDA

The use of propaganda to enlist community mores in support of plans has already been mentioned. It is well illustrated by war propaganda which seeks to convince everyone that it is his patriotic duty to obey war-time regulations. During World War II such community mores as altruism and patriotism were exploited in governmental propaganda. Newspapers, radio programs, posters, and movies all carried the message that violation of war regulations was chiseling; hoarders were depicted in posters as rats; violators of regulations were called "tools of Hitler" or fifth columnists; critics were "misguided persons who unconsciously aid the enemy"; non-cooperative persons were "slackers." All of these were appeals to the morals of the community; they were attempts to locate the planned behaviors in the area of moral conduct so that 140 million consciences would serve as 140 million policemen.

Propaganda was also used during the war to relate the planned behaviors to highly valued objectives or goals: to make people believe that behaving as desired would accomplish worth-while results. Since it was generally assumed that most people very much wanted to win the war, much war-time propaganda attempted to show the relation between compliance with particular governmental plans (price control, rationing, bond buying, conservation, etc.) and victory. People were told that bond purchases furnished money to buy guns, ammunition, planes and other war materials. In much of the propaganda there was a strong implication that failure to buy a bond would result in the death of an American soldier. Groups of factory, store, or office workers were told that their bond purchases had resulted in a "gift" of a specific plane to the Air Forces. A good example of this approach to inducement is provided by the preamble to Ration Order 13, the plan for processed foods rationing.

Our soldiers and sailors in combat areas must be fed—they must be well fed. The armed forces of our allies must be fed. War is fought, and won, as much be food as by munitions. Food is a weapon which we must forge and send wherever needed—to the millions of our fighting men—to our allies and their fighting men—to their fighters on the home front, in factories, in shipyards, in munition plants.

Processed foods—canned and frozen fruits and vegetables, and dried fruits—have been aptly called "fighting foods."

. . . our supplies are not sufficient to meet normal civilian demands. The supplies of processed foods which are available must therefore be rationed so that everyone can get his fair share.

THE SANCTION OF LEGITIMACY

Throughout our analysis of the execution of plans we have warned against the "be it enacted" attitude—the notion that behaviors desired from a clientele can be secured simply by passage of a law embodying the planned behaviors. We should not neglect the fact, however, that the *legitimacy* of behavior—its sanctification by law—does provide a psychological motive for compliance. The fact that a particular behavior has been approved, and another disapproved, by statutory enactment does operate as an inducement for people to behave in the approved rather than the disapproved way. In Chapter 8, we pointed out that legitimacy is one of the important motivations for the acceptance of an organization's authority by its employees. In exactly the same way, legitimacy is one of the important motivations for the acceptance of a government's rules by its citizens.

Our excuse, if an excuse be needed, for placing so little emphasis upon legitimacy as a motive for compliance is that traditional analysis of administrative regulation has placed entirely too much emphasis upon this particular motivation, to the exclusion of others. There is a considerable body of evidence that, in our society at least, the emphasis has been excessive.

There is a strong tradition in American society of disregard for laws that run contrary to popular opinion. This "frontier" tradition—whether or not it really emanated from the Western frontier—is still strong, and is reinforced by institutions like the lay jury, and by a widespread belief in a natural law that transcends man-made law. Even people who accept the proposition that the sovereign state—like its ancestor, the king—can do no wrong are inclined to believe that the state does not always say what it means, and that, moreover, the agents of the state do not always correctly interpret its will. Hence there are many ways of rationalizing the refusal to obey a law or an administrative regulation without denying the claims of legitimacy.

From time to time, this defiance of law is dramatized by the public refusal of some respectable individual to comply with governmental demands upon him. When the President ordered seizure of the Montgomery Ward offices because of the refusal of that company to comply with orders of the War Labor Board, Sewell Avery, the chairman of the board, had to be carried from the building by soldiers. Mr. Avery undoubtedly believed that he was challenging the legitimacy of the action taken against him (although the Supreme Court later upheld that action), and not that he was challenging the sovereignty of the state.

It is very difficult to weigh the power of legitimacy as a sanction, in comparison with the claims of self-interest, on the forces of public opinion. Perhaps two valid claims can be made for the sanction of legitimacy:

1. When a plan is enacted into law, there is created a psychological "presumption" of obedience. This presumption will prevail unless the costs of compliance are too great, or unless disobedience by some persons undermines the confidence of others in enforcement.

2. Those persons who are formally charged with the enforcement of law will generally give great weight to the claims of legitimacy. Hence, the enactment of a plan into law brings to its support the whole legal enforcement machinery—the courts, the employees of police and regulatory agencies, and when necessary, even the military forces. But even these agents of the state may on many occasions rationalize their refusal to enforce law, and in extreme instances may revolt. A study of the theory of revolutions gives us deep insights into the strength of legitimacy as an inducement to obedience, and into the limits of obedience.[1]

THE METHOD OF REWARDS

The technique of rewards consists in making the desired behavior a means for accomplishing personally valued results. Although signs reading "Fifty dollars reward for information leading to. . . ." are seen less often now than in the past, rewards are still basic inducement devices.

The reward for compliance may take the rather concrete form of cash prizes, citation, certificates signed by the President or mayor, buttons, or what not; or it may take the indirect form of economic betterment (as in bond selling programs). During World War II, increased production was sought by guaranteeing profits to producers through the cost-plus system, by allowing premium prices for scarce items, and in other similar ways. Workers were in-

[1] See Charles E. Merriam "The Poverty of Power" in his *Political Power* (New York: McGraw-Hill, 1934).

duced to go where they were most badly needed by manipulating wage ceilings. Less tangible but no less effective rewards were also used—for example, the Navy's E award to plants for high production.

The system of rewards is usually associated with the actual outlay of money and is, consequently, sometimes rejected as too expensive. However, a treasury of rewards can often be created by legislation without a direct outlay of money. In two of the examples mentioned above, the government, having initiated a prohibition (wage or price ceilings), acquired a power of reward in its power to relax the prohibition.

As we shall see, this procedure is the basis of all licensing programs. A certain activity is prohibited unless licensed. Then, because people want to engage in that activity, they will meet stipulated conditions in return for permission to do so. All of the rationing programs were based on a general prohibition coupled with the relaxation of the prohibition in return for compliance with rationing plans. For example, no one was allowed to buy fuel oil without coupons. To obtain the necessary coupons from a local board, a householder had to fill out a rather complicated form; measure the floor area of his house; get a statement of past consumption of oil from his dealer; in some cases, get an engineer's certification of normal requirements; if he were sick, get a doctor's certification and an engineer's certification as to how well he had maximized the thermal efficiency of his house; and so forth. For doing these things he was rewarded with coupons that allowed him to purchase oil—the issuance of coupons was an individual relaxation of a general prohibition.

It may be argued that the type of situation described above can hardly be termed a technique of reward—that to allow a person to do what he had always done before, after arbitrarily prohibiting it, is not exactly a "reward." However, if the prohibition as a plan of regulations is properly installed, and the cost factors overcome, the resulting situation will be accepted as the normal situation, and a relaxation of the prohibition actually will be regarded as a reward by the persons affected.

These comments point up the ambiguity in the concept of a reward. When a person responds to a reward, he may be regarded either as acting *to secure the reward* or as acting *to avoid losing the reward*. If we interpret his behavior in the latter way, failure to secure the "reward" becomes a "punishment." Thus, whether a particular plan is to be regarded as using rewards or punishments as inducements depends upon the psychology of the persons affected by the plan. What is a reward motivation for one person will be a punishment motivation for another.[2]

Detracting from Desirability of Old Behavior

The second basic method of making the planned behavior relatively attractive is to detract from the desirability of the old behavior. This is the method to which the term "enforcement" generally refers. Penalties are applied by gaining control over strategic factors in the situation and using this control to alter the conditions of the old behavior—the one to be changed. The *power* to enforce is simply the *ability* to change those conditions. After the installation of the plan the individual must choose not between the behavior envisaged in the plan and the old behavior, but between the behavior envisaged in the plan and the old behavior *plus* the penalty. The conditions of the old behavior have been changed.

Informal Penalties

Penalties may be either formal or informal. If an administrative organization or a court applies a definite punishment to a specific person or persons brought before it for judgment, we call the penalty a formal one. However, everyone frequently follows certain paths of conduct in order to avoid some undesirable experience, which does not, however, take the form of a formal penalty. Thus, we may leave a tip for the waiter in order to avoid being embarrassed by him. We do many things to avoid being "bawled out by a cop." These unpleasant experiences which we seek to avoid are what we mean by informal penalties. Informal penalties are discussed first.

COMMUNITY DISAPPROVAL

One of the conditions of choice is the attitude of others towards one's behavior. If a person makes choices that run counter to the

[2] The relativity of rewards and punishments has already been discussed in Chapter 8, as applied to authority within organizations. The same considerations apply to the exercise of authority over the clientele.

community value system, he will be criticized. For most persons such criticism is very unpleasant, and hence its anticipation tends to keep them within the channels of behavior approved by the community.

These social sanctions of the community can be utilized by planners as inducements. If the community in general can be persuaded that non-compliance with the plan is wrong, then a specific non-complying person may be subjected to community disapproval. The sanction of community disapproval was extensively used during World War I. In that war many regulatory programs were "voluntary"—that is, did not use formal legal sanctions. However, fear of the disapproval of a community that was deeply moved by patriotic fervor kept most would-be violators in line. Persons suspected of violating "voluntary" gasoline rationing often found their automobiles painted yellow. The label of "slacker" was widely used to punish persons suspected by their neighbors of being non-cooperative. In many communities, anything less than enthusiastic support for the whole war program was physically dangerous.

During World War II there was less general patriotic fervor, and formal penalties were used a good deal more widely than in World War I. However, constant attempts were made to stigmatize non-compliance with war regulations. A concrete application of the sanction of community disapproval was the windshield sticker device in gasoline rationing. Persons deemed essential to the war were allowed all the gasoline they needed for the performance of their essential functions. Their rations were called "C" rations. A person who received a "C" ration was required to paste a sticker with a large "C" on his windshield, on the theory that if he were not really eligible for a "C" ration his neighbors would treat him as a chiseler, and perhaps report him to OPA. The sticker was also supposed to act as a deterrent to the use of the "C" ration for pleasure—driving to races or ball games.

ECONOMIC PENALTIES IMPOSED BY COMMUNITY

Community reactions to violators of regulations often reinforce disapproval with substantial economic penalties. For example, public knowledge about violators of safety, fire, health or sanitary regulations may lose patronage for the violator. An official public statement that a particular theatre is a fire trap or that a particular restaurant does not follow proper sanitary practices is not very good for business.[3] Although the U. S. Securities and Exchange Commission can initiate legal action to prevent the issuance of securities where a full disclosure of pertinent information has not been made, such a step is rarely necessary. If only a rumor of the Commission's doubts were circulated, a security issue would have little chance of being sold.

Another use of community reactions to punish non-compliance by economic loss is "yardstick" regulation. If a private utility cannot be induced to lower rates as desired by the government, the government can go into competition with it. Then, in order to stay in business, the private utility may have to meet the standards of the public enterprise. In effect, "yardstick" regulation says to the clientele, "reduce your rates and improve your service or suffer economic loss."

A significant example of "yardstick" regulation is the Tennessee Valley Authority. The TVA is a public corporation established in 1933 with a multi-purpose program for development of the drainage basin of the Tennessee River. Its functions include improving navigation on the Tennessee River; preventing floods; preventing soil erosion in the area; reforestation; manufacturing and experimenting with fertilizer; and, in the pursuit of the foregoing, building dams and reservoirs on the Tennessee River and its tributaries. The TVA is also engaged in large scale generation, transmission, and sale of electricity. It is charged with the duty of developing consumption of electricity in the area and fostering municipal and cooperative electricity distributing systems. Much of the property of the private utilities formerly operating in the area has been purchased by TVA or by municipalities. The continual existence of the threat that cities in the area might establish their own electric light and power systems, aided by cheap wholesale power from TVA, has had a very striking effect on private utility rates and on consumption.[4]

---

[3] Restaurant owners in Pittsburgh, well aware of the force of this sanction, sought a court injunction in 1949 to prevent the city health department from making public the scores of restaurants upon sanitary inspection.

[4] Fainsod and Gordon, *Government and the American Economy*, p. 360.

One of the most thoroughgoing applications of informal sanctions in our administrative history was the use of the coupon flowback system in rationing during World War II. Coupon flowback was the heart of rationing inducement. Every exchange of rationed goods had to be accompanied by an exchange of coupons of equivalent value. Thus a dealer, to replenish his stock, had to give up coupons to his supplier; the supplier, to replenish his stock, had to give up coupons to his supplier, and so forth, until the ultimate producer was reached. If the dealer did not collect coupons from his customers when they made purchases from him, he would not be able to replenish his stock, and eventually he would have to go out of business. Hence, his self-interest induced him to collect coupons as desired by OPA. The same inducements operated on the higher levels of the trade until the manufacturer was reached. The manufacturer was subject to monthly reporting requirements, periodic audits, and legal sanctions for non-compliance.

Formal Penalties

Whenever the planners control something much desired by the clientele that can be denied to or withdrawn from it, they have a sanction power. If certain activities can only be carried on with government approval, the possibility that the government may withdraw approval serves as a constant inducement to compliance with the requirements imposed as a condition of approval.

LICENSING

Use of formal sanctions is best illustrated by licensing techniques. The first step in a licensing program is to prohibit anyone from engaging in the activity unless he has a license. This prohibition is easy to enforce because the lack of a license can usually be detected easily and cheaply. Generally the licensee is required to exhibit his license in a conspicuous place. A patrolman can then see at a glance whether or not the required license has been obtained.

Having prohibited an activity to unlicensed persons, the administrative authorities are in a position to determine who will be allowed to engage in the activity—that is, to choose the clientele who are to be subject to the regulatory plans. In choosing the clientele, persons who are not likely to comply with the plan can be eliminated. The process of selection can be made relatively simple because the burden of proof can be shifted to the applicant, and since he wants the license badly, he will assume many of the administrative burdens. Having issued the licenses, the administrators of the plan know exactly who are subject to the plan and where they are located. Reaching the clientele with any changes in the plan is relatively easy.

Under a licensing scheme, non-compliance with regulations, if it is discovered, can be punished with revocation or suspension of the license. If the infraction of the rules is minor, or a first offense, the license may only be suspended for a time. For very serious or continued violations, the license may be permanently revoked. Types of activities most commonly regulated through licenses are the operation of restaurants, saloons, hotels and other public buildings, professions such as medicine, dentistry, and law, radio stations, public carriers, and many others.

PUBLIC CONTRACTS

There are other favors that an administrative body may have to bestow besides approval of activities. Public contracts are an example. Under the Walsh-Healey Act of 1936, persons who contract to supply goods or services to the United States in amounts over $10,000 must comply with regulations covering wages of employees, hours and conditions of work, and child labor. For example, persons employed by the contractor must be paid at least as much as the prevailing minimum wage of the industry, as determined by the Secretary of Labor. The penalty for non-compliance is the withholding of Federal government contracts for a three-year period. That this sanction has been an effective inducement is attested by the following statement from a study of the administration of the Act:

In the something over three years that this statute has been in effect some 16,500 separate contracts have been negotiated subject to its terms. They have involved a total of approximately $1,189,936,000. It is estimated that the working conditions of 2,000,000 employees of 9,000 employers have been directly affected. During this period 30-odd wage determinations were made by the Secretary, relating to industries of such dissimilar character as the commercial fireworks industry, the drug manufacturing industry, and the men's cap and hat industry. Thus, it may be seen, the regulative force of the law may not be inconsiderable.[5]

ALLOCATION CONTROLS

A sanction used to induce compliance with the rules allocating scarce materials under the Second War Powers Act was the denial to violators of materials under allocation control. Orders that accomplished this result, called Suspension Orders, were the basis of rationing enforcement and were important in enforcing priority controls. Like license suspension orders, the war-time Suspension Orders could be modified to make the punishment fit the crime. They could be partial or complete, for a short time or for the duration of the war.

JUDICIAL SANCTIONS

The most familiar formal sanctions are fines and imprisonment (or death for very serious crimes like murder). These sanctions are imposed by the existing judicial or legal machinery of society. Usually the person accused of violation is prosecuted by a public prosecutor before a court, although sometimes a private individual injured by the violator's acts is given legal rights against him. Then the injured person, if he desires and can afford it, may sue the violator for damages. One of the sanctions provided by the anti-trust laws is the private triple-damage suit, whereby a person injured by the illegal practices may sue for three times the amount of damages he incurred.

Legal punishment is ill adapted to many of the problems of modern regulation, especially mass regulation. It is very expensive of time and energy, for the non-compliance of one offender brings into play an elaborate organization of policemen, prosecution, and courts. Unless there is a widespread disposition to obey the law in question, the legal enforcement machinery will break down, as illustrated by the breakdown of prohibition enforcement. Most compliance with a legal requirement results from general acceptance or support of the requirement—from a widespread feeling that it *ought* to be obeyed—not from fear of legal punishment.

[5] See Attorney General's Committee on Administrative Procedure, *The Walsh-Healey Act*, Monograph No. 1 (1939), p. 3.

The chief significance of legal sanctions is in punishing the few deviants from a generally accepted norm of conduct. If compliance involves any considerable trouble or cost, and non-compliance is not punished, the complying person may come to feel that he is being treated unjustly and his belief in, or support for, the law may vanish. Punishment of the few deviants from a legal norm also acts as a deterrent to those persons who do not accept the law.

Legal punishment must always be used in conjunction with other inducement techniques. In some situations it cannot be used at all. Where great numbers of people do not believe that the prohibited behavior is morally wrong or the behavior commanded morally right, it is futile to depend upon legal sanctions as effective inducements, for the intermediate behaviors needed to enforce the laws will be too expensive. The strong predisposition in this country to believe that any behavior can be controlled by threatening punishment has filled American statute books with hundreds of unenforced and unenforceable laws. In the final analysis, the chief inducement force of legal sanctions is social—the desire to avoid the social stigma of being publicly branded a law breaker.

Determining the Degree of Compliance

Once a regulatory plan is installed, there must be some way of determining whether people are complying with it. If they are not, the plan will have to be changed—either its substance or the inducements provided for compliance.

SAMPLING SURVEYS

One approach to this problem is statistical. Surveys can be made which show the extent of non-compliance of various classes of people and in various parts of the country, and perhaps also the reasons for non-compliance. Armed with this information, planners can determine whether anything should be done and, if so, what to do. For example, by means of sample compliance surveys, the OPA kept itself informed of the price areas where non-compliance was heaviest. When this information was related to analyses of the importance of particular items to the whole price structure or to family budgets, OPA could direct its very small enforcement staff into the channels that would be most effective in controlling inflation. Information from compliance surveys also pointed the way for new educational drives and sometimes for changes in price orders.

Information about the reasons for non-compliance can be especially helpful. Thus, if a survey discovered a widespread belief that the regulations were only enforced against the "little" businessman, that would be a signal for some dramatic prosecutions of "big" businessmen. Or, if it were discovered that many people did not think the regulation necessary, that information could provide the basis for an efficient public information program. Knowledge of clientele attitudes is almost essential for intelligent planning. For this reason, public opinion polling is a very important administrative invention.

DETECTING SPECIFIC OFFENDERS

When formal sanctions are to be used, it is necessary to discover specific cases of non-compliance. In the early period of the development of the modern state, the function of complaint, or reporting non-compliance, was left to private individuals, who were supposed to file complaints against law violators. Gradually this function became specialized in a group of functionaries whom we now call police. However, there still remains of the older practice the duty of the individual to report violations of law and to arrest criminals caught in the act of breaking the law. Until modern times, government has relied heavily on injured individuals to bring action against law violators. Thus early railroad regulation relied chiefly upon the complaints of shippers to start the enforcement activities of the Interstate Commerce Commission.

Inspection. As social regulation increased and became more technical, the process of complaint became even more specialized. Today the police are no longer the chief agents of complaint. Policemen work with the settled criminal law and with matters like traffic regulation and have a general function to keep the peace, but increasingly the discovery and reporting of violators of specific regulations is entrusted to specialized groups of inspectors. Thus there are building, health, sanitary, fire inspectors and many others. The regulations which these inspectors are engaged in enforcing are too numerous and too technical for the regular police to enforce at all effectively.

In the Federal government as in local jurisdictions, there are officials who have a *general* function of seeking out violations of law: in particular, FBI investigators and the U. S. Marshals. Their function is more the apprehension of violators than discovery of violations, however. Increasingly, Federal regulatory programs have their own special investigating staffs. Thus, within the Treasury Department, itself, there are five separate groups engaged in the discovery of violators of various Treasury Department and other regulations: the border patrol of the Bureau of Customs; internal revenue agents of the Bureau of Internal Revenue; the Secret Service (detection of counterfeiting and protection of the President); the agents of the Bureau of Narcotics; and the U. S. Coast Guard (detection of smuggling and illegal entry). During the war there were also Treasury agents enforcing the program for the control of foreign funds in this country. All of these enforcement activities are generally coordinated by a Coordinator of Enforcement who reports to an Assistant Secretary of the Treasury.

The Federal regulatory commissions all have their own inspectors and investigators. Writers on administration frequently distinguish administrative regulation from judicial regulation by saying the former is preventive while the latter is corrective or retributive. The chief difference, however, is that the administrative agencies actively seek out violations that would never be reported under judicial regulation with its reliance on the regular police and the public prosecutors. As a consequence, administrative regulation achieves more compliance because it engages in more enforcement—it has a more highly organized complaint system.

Where the clientele or a substantial part of it is known and is not too numerous, administrative inspectors usually make regular rounds of visits or inspections to determine compliance. For example, factory inspectors are assigned definite areas in which they visit all the factories covered by their regulations at definite intervals. Instances of non-compliance are usually corrected on the spot when the inspector points them out and suggests specific changes. If the violations have not been corrected by the time the inspector calls again, he may report them to his agency which then warns the violator in more formal terms. If the violator still persists in his violation, the regulatory agency will then take whatever action it is authorized to take to punish the violator for non-compliance.

Alternatives to Inspection. Often it is impossible to make periodic inspections of the clientele because it is too large, not known in advance, or because the regulatory body does not have sufficient personnel or money. In such a situation, the regulatory agency may encourage others to report suspected violations to it. If this method of discovering non-compliance has to be relied on, the complaint procedure must be made very easy, and usually the self-interest of the complainant must be involved. The regulatory agency does all the investigation of the complaint and finally prosecutes it as its own complaint. Both the Federal Trade Commission and the National Labor Relations Board rely on complaints of interested persons in the enforcement of fair trade practices and fair labor practices.

Another device used when the regulatory body cannot make actual inspections is reporting. The members of the clientele may be asked to make periodic reports covering their activities. These reports may then provide clues as to where actual inspection and investigation is needed. Most regulatory bodies require some kind of reports at some time.

Except for licensing authorities, most regulatory bodies are primarily highly organized complaint systems. After violation is discovered, the formal sanctions available to an administrative body are generally very few. Of course, it can always threaten publicity, which may be an effective enough sanction in many cases. Its primary sanction, however, is to threaten prosecution before the courts. The statutes that establish regulatory agencies usually allow them to issue orders "enforceable in a court of law." Thus, when the FTC issues a "cease and desist" order to a firm engaged in unfair trade practices, it is telling that firm that if it does not change its ways it will be prosecuted in a court by the FTC for violation of law. However, since a public court action may be bad for business, even if the business firm wins, the mere threat to prosecute is often sanction enough.

When detection of violation is unusually difficult, and the plan does not have strong moral support behind it, planners often try to devise schemes to make the plan "self-enforcing." The coupon flowback system used in rationing, mentioned above, was such a device. The display of licenses or of "certificates of public convenience and necessity" (as ICC licenses are called), a central feature of licensing programs, is such a device. The device of "preticketing" used in price control is another example of a "self-enforcing" technique. Producers were required to ticket their goods showing the OPA retail price ceiling for the item. Consumers could then be expected to refuse to pay more than the ceiling price as shown on the ticket. Requirements that automobiles undergo periodic safety inspections are enforced partly by a windshield sticker on approved automobiles, which also shows when the next inspection is due so that automobiles without stickers can be spotted easily by policemen.

None of these devices, nor others like them, actually makes a regulation "self-enforcing." They do make the detection of violation much easier, so that fear of punishment and the probability of being caught contribute to a high degree of compliance. When the costs of compliance are high, fear of punishment may become important in the inducement scheme, and, since detection must precede penalties, devices to facilitate the detection of violation become correspondingly important.

The Ethical Climate of Inducement

In planning the inducement schemes, planners do not have a free hand to adopt any device they like. Within our society there are rather definite beliefs or values about how individuals should be treated by government. Inducement devices that violate these social "rules of enforcement" will be offensive to the clientele and also to the intermediate persons—for example, the courts. Thus, rather than increase compliance, such inducement devices will decrease it.

The formalized study of these social rules of enforcement is administrative law. The rules of administrative law describe what protection the courts will give to individuals against administrative action that violates these social rules of enforcement. However, the ethical climate of inducement is much broader than administrative law, for many administrative actions which are legal will generally be considered unfair. In the following discussion we will indicate briefly some of these rules.

Our discussion will not go much beyond the concept of "due process of law." Under our Constitution, each individual is entitled to due process of law—a term that means, broadly, fair play. A person who feels that he has been denied fair treatment can usually appeal the administrative action to a court of law. Thus, the courts are the principal organized protection of the individual against administrative treatment which violates the social rules of enforcement.

THE PRESUMPTION OF INNOCENCE

An important rule of enforcement is that an individual is innocent until proven guilty. This rule means that a court will withhold punishment until the public agency proves to its satisfaction that the accused person has actually violated the law as alleged. This rule has a broader implication, for in our society the public often sympathizes with the accused rather than the prosecution. Especially is this true when the requirement violated is not strongly supported by public opinion.

The extensive use of the jury in this country allows public sympathy to express itself in the actual conduct of a trial. Thus, confessed violators of a law are often adjudged "not guilty" by a jury that sympathizes with the accused, does not sympathize with the law in question, or is hostile to the prosecution.

A FAIR TRIAL

Another important social rule of enforcement is that an individual accused of violation be given a fair trial before a penalty is imposed. This rule applies whether the penalty is imposed by a court or by an administrative body. The notion of a fair trial includes several things. First the accused person must be notified a reasonable time in advance of the trial as to just what the prosecution intends to try to prove against him. This rule allows the accused to prepare his defense against specific charges. Second, the accused must be allowed to be represented by someone of his own choosing. Third, he must be allowed to cross-examine witnesses against him and be given power to compel the attendance of witnesses in his behalf (subpoena power). Fourth, an impartial person or persons must hear the evidence on both sides and make a finding of the facts. Finally, if, in the accused's opinion, any of the elements of a fair trial has been denied or the law improperly applied to the facts, the accused must be allowed to appeal until he does get a fair trial.

METHODS OF DETECTION

A third social rule of enforcement is that violations of law must be discovered by open and above-board methods. There must be no snooping. Police must wear distinctive uniforms or ride in distinctive vehicles. Houses or persons may only be searched if the searchers have a search warrant that gives an approximate description of what they are looking for.

In Federal courts and many state courts, evidence improperly obtained may not be introduced in a trial. Evidence obtained for one purpose may not generally be used for another. Individuals can refuse to give information to administrative bodies unless assured that the information will not be used in a prosecution against them for violation of law.

In general, the feeling is that a violator of law should get more than an even break. Traps to catch violators are generally frowned upon, except for felonies—in which case the community thoroughly and unitedly condemns violation. Most regulation does not enjoy the thorough community support enjoyed by laws against theft, murder, rape, or kidnapping.

EQUALITY OF TREATMENT

A final social rule of enforcement which we will mention is that the formal sanctions for violation of regulations must be equitably applied. A general feeling that the laws are being enforced in a discriminatory fashion will undermine support for the laws and thus increase violations of them.

DISTINCTION BETWEEN RIGHTS AND PRIVILEGES

The courts have made many distinctions as to the degree of protection to be given individuals in different situations. The chief distinction that is made is between the denial by administrative agencies of things that belong to citizens as a matter of "right" and the denial of things that are only "privileges." Thus, reason the courts, since running a business and owning property are rights, any administrative interference with business or property will be scrutinized carefully. On the other hand, since entrance into this country is regarded not as a right of aliens, but a privilege, somewhat arbitrary treatment of persons seeking entry is not prevented by the courts. Likewise, since no one has a right to a public contract, no great protection will be provided by the courts against arbitrary imposition of the Walsh-Healey Act penalty.

PROTECTION BY PUBLIC OPINION

By far the most important bulwark of the social rules of enforcement is the reaction of the public to high-handed inducement methods. Violation of the accepted rules of enforcement simply leads to less compliance and is therefore self-defeating.

The difficulty of administering an unpopular program makes administrators tend to seek popular ones, and failure to achieve a popular program is probably more often a result of administrative ineptitude than of administrative viciousness. For this reason, probably the greatest hope for individual protection, for liberal administration, lies in the education of administrators rather than the introduction of outworn judicial procedures in administration. [6]

Inducements as Operations

The tendency to think of inducement in traditional legal terms has obscured the fact that all the intermediate behaviors of employees of regulatory agencies, all the activities between planning and clientele compliance, are inducement activities. Legal traditionalism has resulted in a tendency to think of inducement as enforcement. Separate enforcement units or divisions are often established, staffed with attorneys who interpret their function as that of bringing violators to trial. On the contrary, our analysis shows that legal prosecution of violators, while an inducement device that often has its place in the whole program for securing compliance, is only one approach among many.

[6] Disagreement with this point of view was expressed by the Congress in its adoption of the Administrative Procedure Act of 1946, which strengthened formal legal and judicial controls over the Federal regulatory agencies.

All of the activities of the regulatory body that relate to the clientele are a part of inducement. The planning of inducements is an integral part of all planning. Procedures analysts who remove clumsy, difficult, or unnecessary requirements from plans are furthering compliance. Employees who prepare press releases and publicity programs are furthering compliance. All personnel who meet members of the public can further or depress compliance by their treatment of the clientele. Correspondence clerks who reply to inquiries from the clientele can further or depress compliance. Researchers who gather information about the operation of the program are providing the basis for changes in the plan designed to secure more compliance. Supervisory and training personnel can further compliance by encouraging the right attitudes among the agency's personnel. All the members of the agency in their contacts outside the organization can contribute to the same result. In fact, the "enforcement" of the regulatory agency's plans is the business of the whole agency. The persistence of the notion that this function can be delegated in whole or part to a group of attorneys in an enforcement division is a tribute to the force of legal traditionalism. If this belief persists, regulatory administration may be converted into a new set of courts with an old set of priests.

If duplications, contradictions, and inefficient use of resources are to be avoided, inducement policy must be a consistent whole including all the elements previously mentioned, and the sanctions of legal prosecution must be coordinated with all of the other activities of the agency. Enforcement activities cannot be a monopoly of attorneys if excessive legalism is to be avoided. To secure compliance, the public relations or educational activity must be kept coordinated with all other activities and especially with planning. Prosecution drives and public relations must be a part of a single plan, if much energy is not to be wasted; both must be dependent upon current research into the effects of the plan; all three must change as the plan is changed. Effective governmental regulation is a single, total activity. Excessive separation of the "administrative" from the "judicial" powers, as has been urged from several sources,[7] can only mean less effective and successful regulation. One suspects that, in many cases, this is the reason why the fragmentation of the regulatory process is being urged.

[7] See Chapter 24.

CHAPTER TWENTY-THREE

※

Evaluating Administration: Efficiency

IN ALL the foregoing chapters we have been describing administrative organizations and what goes on in them. In this chapter and the two following we will examine what people mean when they say that one organization or procedure is better than another. That is to say, we will examine some of the criteria of *efficiency* and *responsibility*. In this chapter we will discuss efficiency; in the two final chapters we will discuss responsibility.

The Meaning of Efficiency

When we evaluate administration—or any other form of human behavior for that matter—we are evaluating the wisdom of the choices that people make among the alternative actions that are open to them. In expressing judgments about administrative programs we sometimes divide our evaluation into two parts:

(1) the extent of our agreement or disagreement with the values that the plan seeks to attain or maximize; and

(2) our judgment of how efficacious the plan will actually be in attaining these values.[1]

As an example of the first aspect of evaluation, we might approve or disapprove of the goals of the Economic Cooperation Administration—e.g., recovery of the European economy and the reestablishment of relatively free, balanced international trade. As an example of the second aspect, we might form a judgment as to

[1] In logical terms, the first aspect of evaluation concerns our agreement or disagreement with the value premises on which the plan is based; the second, our judgment of the correctness of the factual premises involved in the plan. See Simon, *Administrative Behavior*, chap. 3.

whether the ECA program—the financing of European purchases from America—will in fact accomplish these goals, and to what degree.

RESPONSIBILITY AND RATIONALITY

Instead of asking whether *we* agree with the values underlying an administrative decision or an administrative program, we may ask *whose* values underlie the program. That is, we may ask where an agency got the particular values it seeks to attain, to what groups or influences it is responsive. Why is the ECA seeking to promote European recovery and international trade? Is this because of Congressional direction, a mandate from the Executive, or the influence of pressure groups, or do the program values originate in some other source? When the question is stated in this way, we are dealing with the problem of *responsibility*. To whom or what is the program responsible or responsive? We will postpone further discussion of this question to the next chapter.

The second aspect of evaluation may be termed the evaluation of *rationality*. That is, we call decisions rational which are correctly designed to achieve the values they seek to achieve. Assuming that the ECA program seeks to promote European recovery and international trade, it is rational *if it will in fact* promote European recovery and international trade.

Since our judgment as to whether a decision is rational or not hinges on what values we apply in evaluating it, any statement that an administrative activity is "rational" or "irrational" is ambiguous unless we make clear just what values we have in mind as the goals of the activity. For example, we might believe that the ECA program will in fact succeed in temporarily preventing acute hardship in Europe, but that it will not succeed in promoting permanent recovery or restoring trade. In this case, the program would be considered rational if judged in terms of the prevention of hardship, but irrational if judged in terms of long-term recovery or trade.

There has been much confusion in the literature of public administration arising out of the fact that many writers in this field fail to state explicitly the values in terms of which they are judging the rationality of particular decisions or programs. In many cases confusion is worse confounded because writers insist that they are judging the rationality of administration when in fact they are expressing agreement or disagreement with particular program values.[2]

RATIONALITY AND EFFICIENCY

The term "efficiency" is one of the most-used, and almost certainly one of the most-abused, words in the dictionary of administration. In its broadest sense, it is often used as a virtual synonym for "rationality."[3] And as suggested in the previous paragraph, "efficiency" or "inefficiency" is often *said* when agreement or disagreement with particular values is really *meant*. Certainly this latter confusion was involved when the Hoover Commission, charged with studying the efficiency of the federal government, recommended that "the Congress place restrictions on direct loans [to persons or enterprises] in order to insure that the normal channels of credit are utilized to the maximum extent possible or, alternatively, provide for the guarantee of loans made by private or other established agencies."[4] As three members of the Commission pointed out in dissent: "Here the Commission's recommendations depart, we believe, from organizational questions of efficiency and economy in the executive branch, and venture into substantive legislative programs"[5]—i.e., questions of what values shall be implemented.

The reader needs to be warned, therefore, that when he encounters the word "efficiency" in writings on administration it may mean economy (i.e., reducing expenditures), or it may simply be used as an epithet of approval. The term "efficiency" is also used quite frequently in a different and more special sense than those just mentioned. This fourth usage is the one usually intended by economists when they speak of efficiency, and by most of the writers on

[2] Numerous illustrations have already been cited, particularly in the chapters dealing with large-scale organizations, of the almost complete failure of the Hoover Commission to recognize this vital distinction. For extensive documentation of the fact that the Hoover Commission was no worse in this respect than the mine-run of writers in public administration, see Waldo, *The Administrative State*, particularly chap. 10.

[3] This is the meaning to which "apologists" for efficiency—i.e., those who believe that efficiency is the proper criterion for administrative evaluation—are inevitably driven. See, for example, chap. 9 of Simon, op. cit.

[4] Report on Federal Business Enterprises, p. 24.

[5] Ibid., p. 99.

administration who have tried to construct a relatively precise formal theory of organization. It is a usage that has probably been borrowed from the engineers (e.g., the efficiency of a steam turbine—the ratio of useful energy output to energy input), and its application is still surrounded by some of the implicit assumptions that it acquired from its engineering origins.

In succeeding sections of this chapter we will first set forth this particular definition of efficiency as carefully and explicitly as possible. We will then see to what extent the criterion of efficiency, so' defined, does or does not lead to the same administrative choices as the broader criterion of rationality. This analysis will help us to understand what administrators are really doing when they make choices with a view to maximizing efficiency, and what effects such choices have upon the organization and the satisfactions of its members. It is an observable fact that persons in administrative situations frequently *do* employ the criterion of efficiency in making choices, and it is for this reason that an understanding of the criterion is so important. Whether, or to what degree, administrators *should* employ this criterion is a question of values whose answer lies outside the science of administration.

A NARROWER DEFINITION OF EFFICIENCY

Human beings, confronted with a problem of choice, cannot deal with reality in all its complexity, but must deal with some simplified model of reality. For example, even if the science of economics were much further developed than it is, it would be impossible to trace out all the consequences, long-run and short-run, of the ECA program. To mention just one such untraceable consequence out of an infinite multitude, what effect will the program have upon the European birth-rate, and what effect will the birth-rate have upon the military situation twenty years hence? In any actual situation we cannot judge rationality in any absolute sense, but only within the limits of the foreseeability and predictability of consequences. As we pointed out in our earlier discussion of long-range planning, the unanticipated consequences of large governmental programs are likely, in retrospect, to appear as important or more important than those consequences that were weighed in the decision.

But the simplification of reality for purposes of decision-making generally goes far beyond the omission of unanticipated consequences. One further simplification that is very often made is to divide the consequences of a plan into three parts: (1) those consequences which are to be sought or avoided—the positive and negative values to be weighed in judging the desirability of the outcome; (2) those consequences toward which the decision-makers are relatively neutral—they are relatively indifferent as to whether such consequences occur or not; and (3) the alternative consequences they have to give up by carrying out this plan instead of some other —what economists call the "opportunity costs" of the plan.

We may illustrate these distinctions by the example, in rather over-simplified form, of a decision by a city council to construct a water filtration plant. (1) The consequences in terms of which the council would evaluate the proposal might be the improvement in the quality of drinking water. (2) The council might be indifferent (other consequences being equal) as to whether the sand for the filters is trucked in or brought in by barge. (3) The council might measure the opportunity cost of the project in terms of money costs—the appropriation of funds that could otherwise be used to repair streets, or be left in the pocketbooks of taxpayers.

It must be emphasized that the distinctions just made are not *logical* but *psychological*. The category into which particular consequences fall will depend upon the values of the person making the decision. The city council may consider improved drinking water important, but a person who buys bottled spring water may be indifferent. The council may consider the method for bringing in sand inconsequential, but this may be a matter of great concern to the owner of a barge. The council may treat tax dollars as opportunity costs, but a local resident whose share in the tax burden is slight may put the cost of the project in the "neutral" category.

We see that the distinction we have made among three types of consequences of a plan is a subjective one; it resides in the mind of the person making the decision. Nevertheless it is a distinction that is very often employed in actual decision-making processes in administration. The fact that people in organizations frequently structure their decisions in these terms makes the distinction vital to an understanding of the practice of administration and the ideology of current administrative theory.

Postponing for a moment a further examination of the distinction, let us see to what kind of an efficiency criterion it leads.

Efficiency could be defined to mean the maximization, in some sense, of the ratio of net positive *results* (the balance of desired over undesired consequences) to opportunity costs. Stated more precisely, a choice could be defined as efficient *if it achieved the greatest possible results with given opportunity costs, or if it achieved a given level of results at the lowest possible opportunity cost.*

In terms of this definition, if our hypothetical council were considering three alternative plans for a filtration plant, each costing a million dollars, the efficient choice would be the plant that would produce water of highest quality. Conversely, if they were considering three plans, each providing a plant that would produce water of the same quality, the efficient plant would be the cheapest of the three.

ASSUMPTIONS UNDERLYING THE CRITERION

Another way of expressing this simplified method of choice is to say that a person confronted with a decision focusses on certain desired and undesired results. He regards as his "ends" or "objectives" the attainment of the desired and the avoidance of the undesired results. To achieve these ends, he considers the use of various "means," but as to different means that would achieve the same ends he has no preference, except insofar as one set of means involves greater opportunity costs than another. This way of stating the matter leads to exactly the same definition of efficiency as the one we have just given.

Under what circumstances would a person use efficiency, so defined, as a criterion for choosing between plans? Two conditions are necessary:

(1) The human and material resources that he proposes to employ, and that he designates as his "means," must be *scarce*. (E.g., "if governmental funds are used to carry on a European recovery program, the resources purchased with these funds will not be available for other governmental programs or for consumption in the United States.") This is what is implied by the term "opportunity costs."

(2) Apart from this opportunity cost, he is *neutral* as to how resources are used, provided they are used so as to maximize those consequences he regards as "ends." (E.g., "it is unimportant whether a particular group of ECA employees spend their time

writing letters or examining statistical reports, except insofar as their doing the one thing will contribute more to European recovery than their doing the other.")

If the means of administrative action were not scarce for the person making the decision, then no opportunity cost would be involved in using resources for one objective rather than another. He would be interested only in maximizing net results regardless of cost. He would make his choice between alternatives in terms of adequacy—the level of results attained—rather than *efficiency*— the level of results relative to the costs incurred.

If the means of administrative action were not neutral to him, he would not compare the costs of alternative actions purely in terms of the aggregate quantity of resources used and without regard to the particular way in which these resources were used. If, for example, he believed that government contractors should pay prevailing wages, then he would not be neutral as between two choices that involved the same money cost, but one of which involved a contract with a firm paying substandard wages while the other did not.

Of course if the second assumption fails—if our decision-maker is not neutral as to means—he can always patch up his criterion of efficiency by broadening the concept of "results." He can include in "results," for example, the effect of an administrative plan upon the health and satisfactions of his employees or upon the wages of contractors' employees, if this is something with which he is concerned. But in so doing, he gradually merges the criterion of efficiency with the broader criterion of rationality, and the two terms again become synonymous. The efficiency criterion simplifies the process of decision for him only if there is actually a large area of consequences that he is willing to regard (at least approximately) as neutral, scarce means.

BASIS FOR THE NOTION OF "NEUTRAL MEANS"

Since the classification of particular aspects of a decisional situation as neutral means is a reflection of the values of the person making the decision, we would expect the category of things that are treated as means to vary from one person to another, and from one society to another. An amateur weaver does not regard it as a matter of indifference whether a rug is made on a hand loom or a power loom, even if it is almost impossible to detect from the final product which method was used. For a person who wants an attractive living-room rug and who is not particularly interested in weaving, the type of loom used to make the rug is inconsequential. A department head may want his attorney to draw up a contract to accomplish a certain result, but may not care about the language of the contract so long as it covers the points he is concerned about. His attorney may take great pride in clothing the contract in appropriate traditional legal language, even if this language adds nothing to its enforceability, and even serves to obfuscate the meaning of the contract for laymen.

But there is one particular conception of neutral means that has wide currency in our society, and particularly in the making of administrative decisions. It is the conception that is implied by the definition of public administration as "the management of men and materials in the accomplishment of the purposes of the state." [6] More specifically it is the conception that the behaviors of employees are to be treated as neutral means for accomplishing results beyond the behaviors themselves. It stems from the particular social values widely held in our particular society and much less widely accepted in other societies. It rests upon deep-seated social attitudes toward "work." It is the conception held by the hypothetical rug buyer mentioned above; as distinguished from the conception of the weaver.

One of the most striking features of Western civilization since the Industrial Revolution is the sharp distinction that is made between the activities of production and consumption. Production is regarded as an activity that is carried on during certain specified hours of the day; consumption as an activity to be carried on at other times. Production is not supposed to be enjoyed for its own sake, but for the claims it gives the producer to rights of subsequent

[6] This is the definition employed by Leonard D. White in the first edition of his *Introduction to the Study of Public Administration* (New York: The Macmillan Co., 1926), p. 2. It is followed by the statement that "the objective of public administration is the most efficient utilization of the resources at the disposal of officials and employees." These statements were subordinated in the second edition (1939) and disappeared from the third (1948), partly in recognition of the limiting assumptions implicit in them. This same efficiency criterion is postulated even more explicitly by Gulick in "Science, Values and Public Administration," *Papers on the Science of Administration*, pp. 192-3.

consumption. The postman is not expected to enjoy his daily exercise, but to perform his duties because other members of society want mail service, in return for which they are willing to grant the postman claims upon consumption (his pay check).

If production or work is considered to be intrinsically valueless (except for the negative value of depriving the workman of leisure), then it follows that there is no inherent value in doing one kind of work rather than another. The individual accepting this belief should be willing to choose between one kind of work and another on the basis of the relative claims upon consumption—the "external" consequences of his work—that these two kinds of work give him. Hence, there should be an area of indifference or acceptance within which he should be willing to accept direction as to what he should do in return for these claims.

The statements of the last two paragraphs are of course exaggerated if taken as actual descriptions of the attitudes held by people in our society. They should be viewed not as realistic description, but as "ideal types" to which real attitudes conform only approximately.[7]

While people will frequently be unwilling to regard their own behavior as neutral means for accomplishing results, they will just as frequently regard the behavior of other persons in this way when they are making plans for that behavior. Persons in administrative positions, particularly when they are several layers removed from the employees whose behavior they are planning, are especially likely to treat the men and material in their organizations as neutral means to be used "for accomplishing the purposes of the state" (or the purposes that the administrators consider important and desirable).

Moreover, this attitude in our society has strong ethical overtones. A stenographer may be by no means indifferent as to whether she transcribes dictation or works in a filing unit. Her employer is apt to feel that she *ought* to be indifferent (i.e., that her choice should be dictated by the "requirements of the organization" rather than her personal preference). And, if she accepts the legitimacy of the organization's authority, she also may feel that

---

[7] They are, in fact, part of the "ideal type" that Max Weber has designated as the "Protestant ethic." We have already seen in earlier chapters that the Protestant ethic plays an important role in organizational behavior in our society.

she *ought* to be indifferent (i.e., ought to accept her employer's decision) even when she is not.[8]

The extent to which administrators and employees do, or do not, treat work as a neutral means has important implications for the equilibrium of the organization. We will explore these implications at a later point in the chapter.

THE MEASURE OF OPPORTUNITY COSTS

Thus far we have not explained why opportunity costs are distinguished from the other desired and undesired consequences of an administrative choice. Improvement in the quality of the water supply is a desired consequence of building a filtration plant; the cost of building the plant is an undesired consequence—but only because if the plant were not built, the same resources could be used to accomplish some other desired purpose (e.g., reducing fire losses). A rational decision about a filtration plant would require not only a comparison of Plan *A* for the plant with Plan *B*, but also a comparison of these plans with all the other possible uses of the resources.

The notion of opportunity costs is another device (like the notion of neutrality of means) for simplifying a complex reality in making choices. The administrator (or the city council) does not know exactly what would be done with the dollars saved by not building the filtration plant. He does know that they could be used in *some* other way, and the notion of opportunity costs permits him to take account of this alternative possibility without evaluating it in detail. The opportunity cost is an *index* of the value of foregone alternatives. This index is devised to avoid the necessity of a simultaneous comparison of all possible alternative uses of resources. An individual uses such an index when he decides to forego an activity because it would be "a waste of time," without deciding just how he will use the precious time he has saved.

For some purposes, manpower is taken as a measure of scarce resources, for other purposes money or material. The manpower used to achieve a particular social goal is no longer available for

[8] The whole of wage theory as developed by economists is based on this assumption of neutrality. When the economist encounters a situation where there is obviously *not* indifference among means, he explains it away by assuming a "psychic income" that must be added to or subtracted from the money wage.

achieving other desirable goals. Hence, the use of manpower involves an "opportunity cost"—other possible uses of this manpower must be foregone if it is employed in the particular task at hand.

More often, scarce resources are measured in terms of total money costs. For example, if the question is one of whether to install certain labor-saving equipment, it would not be sufficient to know that the equipment would decrease manpower requirements. This manpower saving would be balanced against the value of the resources used up in constructing and maintaining the equipment. The common denominator generally used in such comparisons is money cost as determined by the prices of the market place.[9]

Efficiency and Organizational Equilibrium

We have mentioned that the application of the efficiency criterion to administrative decisions has an intimate connection with organizational survival. Let us review briefly what has already been said about survival. Each member of an organization decides from time to time whether he will continue his participation in it. If he decides that the satisfactions he derives from participation outweigh the disadvantages of participation, he will continue; if the disadvantages outweigh the satisfactions, he will leave. He weighs these positive and negative outcomes in his own scale of values—a scale that may be quite different from the scales of other members or of the organizational hierarchy. If the organization fails to provide a net balance of satisfactions over dissatisfactions to its members, it must accept the loss of some members until a favorable equilibrium is restored, it must find new members for which it can provide a favorable balance, or it must go out of existence.

THE BALANCE OF INDUCEMENTS AND CONTRIBUTIONS

The storehouse out of which an organization provides satisfactions or inducements to its members is the sum of the contributions that these members make by their continued participation.

[9] In public administration it may not always be agreed to take the market prices of resources as the measure of cost. The reader who wishes to explore this point may consult Simon, op. cit. pp. 174–5.

The postman delivers mail, a source of satisfaction to citizens that makes them willing to pay postage and to support continued legislative appropriations to the Post Office; the postage payments and appropriations pay salaries of postmen who deliver the mail. The amount of mail service that is provided for a dollar must be worth a dollar or more to citizens and legislators (in their scales of values), and the number of dollars the Post Office will pay for a given amount of the postman's work must be regarded by him (in his scale of values) as a sufficient recompense for his work. If the rate of conversion of appropriated dollars into mail delivered is too low, or the rate of conversion of working time into salary dollars and other work satisfactions is too low, one or the other set of participants will withdraw its support.

But these "rates of conversion" are really measures of the organization's efficiency—from the standpoints of citizens and postmen, respectively. From the citizen's standpoint (and perhaps from the standpoint of high-level executives in the Post Office) speedy mail service is the desired result; the work of postmen is the neutral means; and the expenditure for postage and appropriations to the department is the opportunity cost. From the postman's standpoint, his salary and satisfactions derived from his work are the results he desires to maximize; the mail service is a neutral means (with the important qualification that pride in his work and identification with the organization may lead him to attach positive value to this); the use of his time, which might be devoted to other employment instead, is the opportunity cost. The citizen's viewpoint is the one that is almost always taken in traditional discussions of efficiency (and in the occasional use of that term in earlier chapters of this book). But this is simply a reflection of the particular values of our society, as already explained, and not an intrinsic property of the organizational system.

We conclude that each participant, or group of participants, in an organization may be striving to maximize efficiency as judged by his set of values, but that these several efficiencies need not—indeed usually will not—coincide.

DISTRIBUTION OF THE "SURPLUS"

If each participant were receiving an inducement *just* sufficient to retain his contribution to the organization, an increase in efficiency of one group would usually decrease the efficiency of another, and consequently lead to withdrawal. But this is seldom the case. In general, an organization that is meeting the test of survival is providing a *surplus* of satisfactions for most participants. That is, the inducements provided to most participants could be reduced slightly without causing their withdrawal.[10] Under these circumstances, the question arises as to which participants will get the surplus.

The management of the organization cannot reduce the inducements to any particular group of participants beyond a certain point. To do so would endanger survival. But there is still left an area of choice within which the criterion of efficiency would lead to different decisions, depending on *whose* values we put in the numerator of the efficiency ratio, and *whose* opportunity costs we place in the denominator. Postmen desiring higher wages might argue that users of postal service would be willing to pay higher postage rates. Users of the service, on the contrary, might argue that suitable postmen could be retained or secured at lower salaries.

Salary is by no means the only, or even the most important, respect in which employees resist being regarded as mere implements. The numerous aspects of the work situation to which employees and working groups in organization attach positive or negative value have already been explored in Chapter 4 and elsewhere. The degree and kind of sociability permitted by the work, the quantitative level of output, the structure of the status system, the standards of work quality, the social goals of the organization, and the structure of the organization itself are all conditions affecting the amount of satisfaction and dissatisfaction that employees receive. Where a change that would increase efficiency, as viewed from management's standpoint, impinges upon any of these areas, adverse effects upon efficiency as viewed from the standpoint of the employees will be strongly resisted.

INFLUENCE OF MORES ON THE EQUILIBRIUM

The way in which the surplus of satisfactions in an organization gets distributed depends to an important extent upon the bargain-

---

[10] There may, of course, be some marginal participants the cost of whose contributions is just balanced by the inducements given them.

ing power and skill of the various groups that may seek to appropriate it.[11] The distribution of the surplus is also influenced greatly by the mores of our society, and particularly by the attitudes toward work described earlier. Acceptance of work as a neutral means for accomplishing extrinsic goals implies acceptance of the ethical right of the organization to determine the employee's activities during working hours. The organization has purchased the employee's time and has the right to determine the use of that time—within, of course, limits of reason expressed in such terms as "a normal day's work" or "duties appropriate to a particular kind of employment" or "safe and healthful working conditions."

If the area within which the employee will accept authority is wide, then the administrative hierarchy *can* treat his efforts as neutral means to the values they wish to achieve.[12] On the other hand, where the employee does not accept this particular definition of the ethics of his role, he may bargain with the administrators, not only on such questions as salary, but on work pace, conditions of work, and work standards as well. That is, he may insist that decisions be made not only in terms of organizational goals but in terms also of employee satisfactions.

Employees in government, like those in private industry, have two principal means for persuading the managerial group to take account of their values and satisfactions in making decisions. The first—bargaining—has already been mentioned. The second influence derives from the fact that efficiency—even when measured in terms of the values of the managerial group—is heavily dependent upon morale. When employees are deprived of satisfactions by unpleasant decisions, morale may be so lowered, even without any organized or conscious protest, as to more than balance any gains in efficiency resulting from the decision. Hence, the "enlightened self-interest" of the administrative hierarchy requires some allowance to be made for the satisfactions of employees, even when the administrators do not admit the satisfactions or dissatisfactions of employees directly into their measures of results.

[11] Bargaining on the terms of the employment contract, for example, is no less important in government than in industry, and is fundamentally very much the same process, regardless of whether governmental employees are formally organized in unions affiliated with larger labor organizations.

[12] The word "can" is used advisedly here, rather than "should." The ethical question of the proper attitude of administrators towards the demands they make upon employees is quite another issue.

We should not be led by this observation, as some writers on administration have been, to imagine that there is a preordained identity of interests among the various participants in administrative organization, by virtue of which the "enlightened self-interest" of the managerial group corresponds to the long-run self-interest of employees. To say that the managerial group is well advised to take account of the effect of their decisions upon employee morale does not imply that this will thereby eliminate the area of bargaining between the employees and management as to the division of the organization's surplus.

SIGNIFICANCE OF THE MANAGERIAL GROUP

We now can see why the term "efficiency" is most commonly used in connection with the values and opportunity costs of activity as viewed by the managerial group in an organization, rather than the values and opportunity costs as assessed by employees or some other group. The political mores of our society place upon the managerial group the task of maximizing the achievement of democratically defined values with the use of resources that are to be regarded largely as neutral means. In discharging this task they are limited, of course, by the necessity of maintaining the organization in a condition of positive equilibrium, and to do so they must take account of the satisfactions and values of the various participating groups, including employees. Nevertheless, there is usually a surplus of satisfactions over dissatisfactions which the managerial group can dispose of in many ways. If they seek to dispose of it by maximizing "efficiency" in the sense in which they define it, this may be done at the expense of the satisfactions of employees.

The more fully employees accept the legitimacy of the authority that is exercised over them, and the wider the area within which they permit management to determine the values to be weighed, the more likely it is that employees will be treated as "neutral" resources when management evaluates the efficiency of alternative choice.

The degree to which, under actual conditions, employees are "exploited" (i.e., their satisfactions are disregarded) in order to maximize efficiency as defined by the hierarchy should not be exaggerated. Probably the usual situation in government today is that each hierarchical level, including the legislature, has rather liberal standards of performance in mind for those below, and the lower levels can easily attain these standards without strain and with a consequent high surplus of satisfaction.

This looseness in control even permits a considerable measure of independence at the lower levels of organization in determining the social goals at which the program will be directed, and the weights to be given to different goals. The county agent, to cite a somewhat extreme example, has considerable autonomy to define in collaboration with local interest groups the goals and direction of the local farm program. This gets us back again to the question of whose values are to be implemented—that is, to the question of responsibility that will be explored in the next chapters.

According to a narrowly authoritarian and economy-minded point of view adjustment to the values of individuals and groups within the organization would be regarded as highly inefficient, because the surplus is then not allocated to taxpayers (in the form of reduced expenditures) or citizens (in the form of improved services). But although the Protestant ethic plays an important role in our society, it is no longer (if it ever was) taken to imply a literal disregard for the satisfactions of the work situation. With respect to working conditions, for example, governmental jurisdictions (and particularly the Federal government) have taken the point of view that they should be model employers. Thus, the Federal government was the first important employer to introduce the forty-hour week; retirement plans for employees were common in government long before they were found extensively in industry; and the Federal government has sought to put pressure on private employers for good labor conditions by the Walsh-Healey Act and similar legislation.

Hence in the ethical framework that predominates in this country today, the "neutrality" of intermediate behaviors is an acceptable assumption only when at least minimum standards have been reached for the compensation, working conditions, and other satisfactions of employees and their working groups. The administrator who takes too literally the notion that he is supposed to maximize efficiency is likely to find himself or his legislature visited by a grievance committee, or by representatives of a pressure group that disagrees with his measurement of efficiency.

The Measurement of Efficiency [13]

We have seen that the efficiency criterion is a method of ap-
proximating a criterion of rationality in the making of decisions. A
judgment that a choice is efficient, like a judgment that a choice is
rational, is always made *relatively to the particular values that are to
be implemented*. Hence, when we wish to measure or evaluate
efficiency, we must first specify what or whose values we are trying
to maximize. Having defined the values that are to be maximized,
we must next determine how the degree of attainment of these
values is to be measured. Next we are faced with the task of connecting achievement with activity—of predicting what results will
be achieved if a particular administrative alternative is chosen.
Finally, we must balance these results against the opportunity cost
of the alternative.

In the following pages we will discuss how the measurement of
efficiency, viewed in terms of the "citizen's" values, can be approached. If we accept as given the classification of the consequences of an administrative program into values, neutral means,
and opportunity costs, how can we go about determining whether
the program is efficient? The assumption will be implicit throughout this discussion that *if* we want to change our classification of
consequences, our measurement of efficiency will have to be altered
correspondingly.

DEFINING OBJECTIVES

Before we measure results, we must define a set of values or objectives in terms of which the appraisal is to be made. Before we can
evaluate the work of the city fire department, we must decide just
what the function of the fire department is. This task of defining
objectives is perhaps the most difficult step in the evaluation of
efficiency. For one thing, few governmental departments have objectives as clearly defined and generally accepted as those of a fire
department. A recreation department may state as its objectives:
to "improve health," "provide recreation," "develop good citi-

[13] This section is based largely upon Clarence E. Ridley and Herbert A. Simon,
Measuring Municipal Activities (2nd ed., Chicago: International City Managers'
Association, 1943), chap. 1.

zens." These must be stated in far more tangible and objective terms before they become amenable to measurement. When we come to the U. S. State Department, or a public school system, specification of the objectives in meaningful and measurable terms becomes almost impossible.

Further difficulty arises if an activity is regarded as directed simultaneously toward two or more objectives. What is the relative importance of the two objectives? Shall the health department next year redistribute its funds to decrease infant mortality, or shall it increase the facilities of the venereal disease clinic? Measurements can at best tell us what the results of two courses of action will be. Unless both actions are directed toward exactly the same objective, the measurements cannot tell us which course of action is preferable.

Going hand in hand with the task of defining objectives is the task of securing agreement on objectives. Suppose that we are told by one group that the objective of the public school system is to train people to earn a livelihood, and by another group that the purpose of the school system is to prepare people for good citizenship and a well-rounded life. Which (if either) of these is *the* objective of the school system? Here we have returned to the question of responsibility. The appraisal of administration is meaningful only after objectives have been defined through politically responsible processes.

MEASURING RESULTS

The second and third steps in appraisal are to determine what level of results (in terms of the agreed-upon objectives) is being achieved and to predict the effects of various alternative courses of administrative action upon the level of results attained. If we are evaluating the Economic Cooperation Administration, and if we assume its objective to be European economic recovery, we still have to determine what degree of recovery is being achieved, and how recovery would be affected if, say, a half billion dollars were subtracted from or added to the agency's budget. Answers to these questions would require very extensive economic research, and in the present state of economic knowledge the answers would be very approximate at best.

In some cases the measurement of results is relatively easy, but the task of relating results to administrative programs exceedingly difficult. Any city can measure its fire loss with a reasonable degree of accuracy. But how does it determine what the effect will be upon fire losses of appropriating an additional sum to the fire department? The reader who will examine the research literature in this field will readily convince himself that only the crudest, rule-of-thumb estimates are possible even in such a tangible field of activity as municipal fire protection. The situation in most other areas of governmental activity is much worse.

MEASURING EFFICIENCY

The final step in the measurement of efficiency—comparing results in terms of their costs—can be taken only when all the previous steps have been carried out. The measurement of efficiency cannot be more valid than the process by which objectives are defined. It cannot be more accurate than the measurement of results, or the estimation of the effects of administrative actions upon results. Hence, we may be certain that when confident assertions are made about the efficiency or inefficiency of governmental operations, as they often are, these assertions are seldom capable of any very rigorous proof.

While we know very little at the present time as to how to measure the efficiency with which the results—the final goals—of government are attained, it is a far easier task to measure what Waldo calls "the efficiency of various instruments and procedures of mechanical and routine nature . . . that serve ends that are important only in terms of other or higher ends." We can determine, with a reasonable degree of accuracy, whether one method of cleaning streets will do the job more cheaply than another method, whether one type of road surface will hold up better than another, whether it would save money to use punched-card equipment to do a particular statistical job. It is in such areas, where the connections between means and ends can be most easily traced, that the evaluation of efficiency can be objectified most successfully.[14]

In spite of the formidable difficulties involved in the measurement of efficiency, abandonment of the search for improved meth-

[14] Numerous examples of efficiency measurements of these kinds are cited in Ridley and Simon, op. cit. See also the interesting publication by the U. S. Budget Bureau, *Production Planning and Control in Office Operations* (Washington: The Bureau, 1949).

ods of evaluation is tantamount to abandonment of the attempt even to approximate rationality in decision-making. Behavior can be rational only to the extent that it can predict and evaluate the consequences of action. The only fulcrum on which rationality can rest is a set of definable values; the only lever it can use is a knowledge of the relations of administrative choices to the realization of these values.

Moreover, improvement in methods of measuring efficiency is not unrelated to improvement in methods for securing responsibility. Many (but certainly not all) of the disagreements about governmental policy among groups in our society are really not disagreements about final ends but disagreements about how ends can most effectively be attained. Improvements in our techniques for measuring results—for measuring, say, the effects of a pump-priming program upon employment—would focus more sharply the real extent of agreement or disagreement on goals. Such clarification is lacking in much political debate today.

When, for example, a system of postal savings banks was proposed at the beginning of the century, extravagant claims were made by the banking interests that the proposed legislation would lead to a virtual "socialization" of banking and a destruction of the commercial banking system. Equally extravagant claims were made by proponents as to the advantages of postal savings banks for rural inhabitants who did not have easy access to commercial banks. Four decades of hindsight now show us that the consequences of establishing a postal savings system were much less significant than either proponents or opponents predicted.[15] Even had these consequences been known when the measure was proposed, bankers and farmers might still have disagreed as to its desirability. But each group would have been in a much better position than it actually was to evaluate the measure and to decide how vigorous a support or opposition it merited.

Similarly, the middle-of-the-road voter today is confronted with the dual problem of how much laissez faire he is willing to give up for how much economic security, or vice versa; and also how much laissez faire he *will* give up, and how much security he *will* gain if particular measures are placed or retained on the statute

---

[15] For example, the banks were not much used by Southern farmers, as had been predicted, but primarily by immigrant groups, mostly urban, that had had experience with similar banks in their native lands.

books (e.g., minimum wage legislation). Even if he can make up his mind on the first question—the relative importance to him of these and other values—he still cannot choose rationally unless he can predict the consequences of specific measures. The primary aim of research on the subject of administrative measurement is to provide the basis for such prediction.

Efficiency and the Budget

In the past fifty years, efficiency has been a central objective of governmental reform—although the reformers have seldom been agreed as to which meaning of the word they had in mind. It has been understood, however, that efficiency had something to do with the effective allocation and control of governmental expenditures. Hence the reform of governmental budgeting methods has always been an important aspect of the efficiency movement.

The typical budget-making procedure in large governmental jurisdictions today is the following:

(1) Each major organizational unit prepares an "estimate" of expenditures it will "need," for the next fiscal period. Estimates made in divisions are reviewed, combined and revised by the bureau; bureau estimates are reviewed, combined and revised by the departments; departmental estimates are reviewed, combined and revised by the chief executive. In the larger units, of course, the review may be made by specialized overhead budget units—culminating in the Federal government with the over-all review by the Estimates Division of the Budget Bureau.

(2) Estimates of revenues are made, usually by a financial officer, sometimes by the central budget unit. Expenditures and revenues are adjusted to each other, and plans are made for the financing of deficits, if any.

(3) An executive budget, including revenue and expenditure estimates, is submitted to the legislative body, which reviews and revises it and adopts the legislation necessary to give it the force of law.

(4) Accounting mechanisms are established to limit the expenditures of administrative units to the amounts authorized in the budget.

EXPENDITURE ESTIMATES

It should be noted that the estimates that lie at the base of the budget process are in the nature both of predictions and of plans. As a matter of fact, as budgeting is usually done, it is seldom very clear to what extent they are the one and to what extent they are the other. They are predictions in that they say, implicitly:

"If you want to carry on an administrative program of such and such a kind, you will need to appropriate so and so many dollars."

They are plans in that they say, implicitly:

"We propose that you carry on an administrative program of such and such a kind."

We see that there is a very close connection between the rationale underlying the budget process and the theory of efficiency. A rational budget decision could be made if we could agree:

(1) as to the goals we wanted government to attain, and the relative importance of these goals; and

(2) as to the optimal way of allocating our scarce funds in order to maximize the attainment of these goals.

In the actual conduct of the budget process today, these two distinct sets of questions are seldom explicitly separated. The administrative unit that prepares the estimates regards its requests as statements of its "needs." There is an astoundingly universal failure to recognize that the "needs" of an agency are entirely relative—if it undertakes an expanded program it "needs" more money, if its program is curtailed, it "needs" less. To rest the estimating process on the concept of "need"—as is generally done—is to beg the whole question of what goals are important, and to what extent the expenditure of a little less or a little more money will affect the level of goal achievement.

Some professional associations, identified with particular governmental goals, have gone so far as to specify the minimum amounts that should be spent by agencies directed toward these goals. We are told by the American Library Association and the National Recreation Association, for example, that an American city should spend a certain number of dollars per capita for libraries or for recreation, respectively. It is not surprising that such efforts to set minimum expenditure levels are made; we would expect librarians to think public libraries important, and recreation directors to be convinced of the value of recreation. What is surprising is that such expenditure proposals are put forth as *technical* judgments, with apparent unawareness that in each such proposal is imbedded a set of value judgments as to the importance of spending scarce resources to achieve certain goals.

Because of the prevalence of misunderstanding of the sort just described, and because of the difficulties involved in the objective evaluation of the results and efficiency of governmental activities, budgeting, as it is actually carried on, departs very widely from its underlying rationale. In terms of this rationale, budgeting is a procedure for the efficient allocation of scarce resources to achieve an agreed-upon scheme of values. In practice budgeting is a procedure that brings about some relationship between the expenditures and revenues of government, and, through a complicated process of negotiation and bargaining, brings to bear in a somewhat haphazard fashion a wide range of influences, political and other, upon the pattern of expenditures.

To say this is not to assert that budgetary procedures are worthless or should be abandoned. The deficiencies in the procedure are largely inherent in the complexity and incoherence of the value systems that enter into the democratic process, and in the difficulties of measuring efficiency.

Efficiency as a Political Symbol

In the course of this chapter we have seen that the term efficiency is used in a number of ways, and is often used vaguely and ambiguously. In common speech, to say that something is "efficient" is often equivalent to saying that it is "good" or "desirable." The term is ambiguous because what is good depends on the values we apply in judgment, and the values will be almost as numerous as the persons who apply them.

Because of the ethical views that prevail through much of our society, because efficiency is generally regarded as something desirable, the word is a political symbol of considerable potency. It has the power of organizing sentiment behind the proposals to which it is attached. Most people feel that they *ought* to be efficient, and that they ought to want efficient government.

It is not surprising, therefore, that many debates in our political scene about "efficiency" are really debates about what values government should implement. We have already cited several examples of this. Taxpayer groups have wrapped the banner of efficiency about themselves by identifying efficiency with the reduction of governmental expenditures—paying attention to the denominator of the efficiency ratio, governmental costs, and ignoring the numerator, governmental services. On the other side of the fence, groups seeking the expansion of governmental programs have talked about "social efficiency"—presumably meaning that if a governmental program is desirable, it deserves to be called efficient.

It should not be supposed that the slogan of efficiency always evokes favorable reactions. The history of the term is so closely tied up with the idea of production as a neutral, goal-directed activity that it has a harsh ring in the ears of those who view organization from the position of the employee. Labor groups, in particular, are likely to associate with efficiency the ideas of unconcern with employees' welfare, the speedup, and authoritarian methods of management.[16] Hence, efficiency is not a slogan that can be used indiscriminately in political appeals to all groups.

Conclusion

In situations where we are willing to separate means from ends, we can define efficiency as the maximization of the attainment of our ends by the use of scarce, neutral means. It is this meaning of the term that has the greatest relevance to traditional administrative theory. Because of the prevalent ethical attitudes in our society toward work, the behaviors of organizational employees are often regarded in the decision-making process largely as a neutral means.

When we look at organizational decisions from the viewpoints of the various participants, we see that each set of participants has a different set of values that it is seeking, and regards different things as neutral means and as opportunity costs. Hence, each group of participants would measure efficiency in a different way. The survival of the organization requires that it maintain a suffi-

---

[16] This is perhaps best illustrated by local campaigns for adoption of the council-manager plan. Such campaigns are generally conducted in the name of "efficiency" and are quite commonly opposed by local labor groups for this reason.

cient level of all these different efficiencies to provide its members with reasons for continued participation. When the efficiencies exceed this minimum level the several groups of participants may each seek to share in the "surplus" thus created. The traditional management-oriented theory of efficiency seeks to appropriate this surplus for the reduction of expenditures or for advancement of the politically defined goals of the organization.

The term efficiency has also acquired ethical connotations. For many, perhaps most, persons in our society it is a symbol that has positive value. As a result of its use as a political symbol, the term has acquired a wide range of meanings, in addition to those already discussed, and it has become correspondingly difficult to use it in a precise way in scientific discourse. Forewarned of this difficulty, the reader should be prepared to probe into the underlying assumptions of value that are implicit in almost every discussion of governmental efficiency.

CHAPTER TWENTY-FOUR

Administrative Responsibility:
Formal Controls

IN THE last chapter we saw that a central question to be asked in evaluating administrative decisions is: What values or whose values is the decision designed to promote? In the following two chapters we will examine the methods by which the values and goals of administrative choice are determined. We will seek to determine to what or to whom governmental administration is responsible.

The term "responsibility" is used in different senses. It is used almost as a synonym for legal authority in such expressions as "Hiring personnel is his responsibility." It is used to denote the compliance with generally accepted moral obligations in such expressions as "she is an irresponsible mother; she left her child alone for six hours while she went to a party." It is also used in another sense—as responsiveness to other people's values. This is the sense in which the term will be used here. We will want to determine the extent to which administrators are responsive to other persons or groups, in and out of the bureaucracy. This analysis will show us where the values of administrative choice come from.

To discover to whom the administrator is responsible, we must discover to whom he is *accountable*. By accountability we mean those methods, procedures, and forces that determine what values will be reflected in administrative decisions. Accountability is the enforcement of responsibility. The processes of accountability in a democracy will be different from the processes in non-democratic forms of government, and there will be differences even between democracies. Here we will be concerned with administrative accountability in twentieth-century America—with the processes

513

that determine what values and whose values will be reflected in administrative decisions in this country.

The processes of accountability include both planned procedures and unplanned social and political forces. Although the two are intermixed, we will separate them for convenience and discuss the formal procedures first. These procedures include (1) the court system, (2) the legislature, and (3) the executive hierarchy.

As our discussion proceeds we will see that no one of these controls, nor all three jointly, provide the administrator with the totality of value premises that enter into his decisions. On the contrary, we will encounter an incredibly complicated patchwork pattern of formal and informal influences and cross-influences. Our task will be to isolate and highlight the salient features of this pattern. As we examine, in turn, each mechanism of control we will see that it suffers from severe limitations and leaves many areas of discretion untouched. Our procedure will be to examine the various controls in succession, in order to see what part of this discretion each whittles away—somewhat like the chemist's procedure of analysing a compound by precipitating out each of its components in turn. When we are through we hope that not too much of the compound we call "discretion" will remain in the bottom of our test tube as an unanalysed and unknown residue.

Judicial Controls

One of the most hallowed methods of administrative accountability is the recognized right of the individual to appeal to the regular courts against actions of the administration. The system of judicial accountability moves at three basic levels: (1) An action may be challenged because the statute or order on which it was based is claimed to violate the Constitution. For example, in the period from 1933 until 1937, a whole series of state and Federal agencies were wiped out on the grounds that their basic statutes were unconstitutional. (2) The courts have the power to determine whether a given action or class of actions is within the law. Judges, rather than administrators, decide precisely what legal authority has been delegated to administrative agencies by legislation. In many cases, administrative officers cannot be sure of the validity of their actions until these have been tested in a regular court of law. In this connection, it should be noted that no law can authorize what the courts regard as arbitrary action. (3) The courts may impose penalties—financial or penal—on administrators who act outside the scope of the law. In the American legal system the government as such cannot be sued without its own consent, but an officer acting outside the scope of his powers can be held personally accountable for his actions.

ROLE OF ATTORNEYS

Because administrators must make their decisions with one eye constantly on the courts, the position of the attorney within administrative agencies is very strong. His advice must constantly be sought, and he would be less than human if he did not go a little further in his advice than was strictly necessary to protect his agency's actions from reversal by the courts. Since his principal will rarely know how much the term "legal" embraces, much of this extra-legal advice will be reflected in administrative decisions. Since one finds attorneys with every shade of political, social, and economic opinion, this unusual power of attorneys does not necessarily give a preference to the value system of any one economic, political, or social group within society. However, it does give a preference to the values that attorneys hold in common—namely, a deep-seated respect for the procedures and ritual of the court system and the governmental methods embodied in the settled law. As a result, American public administration is highly legalistic.

LIMITATIONS OF JUDICIAL CONTROLS

As a procedure for enforcing responsiveness, judicial controls are seriously deficient. Most administrative decisions are not scrutinized by courts; and most value premises of any specific decision never come under judicial question. There are many reasons why this is so.

Accountability for Failure to Act. In the first place, judicial review relates only to actions taken by administrators; it does not relate to their failure to act:

> . . . Judicial review is rarely available, theoretically or practically, to compel effective enforcement of the law by the administrators. It is

adapted chiefly to curbing excess of power, not toward compelling its exercise. Constitutional limitations may in some cases forbid the use of judicial power to correct underenforcement. But constitutional difficulties aside, the courts cannot, as a practical matter, be effectively used for that purpose without being assimilated into the administrative structure and losing their independent organization. To assure enforcement of the laws by administrative agencies within the bounds of their authority, reliance must be placed on controls other than judicial review.[1]

Infrequent Intervention.   In the second place, the volume of administrative actions is so great that to subject even a small fraction to the detailed and somewhat cumbersome procedures of the courts would bring the whole process of administration to a halt. Designed as it is to protect private rights against encroachment, judicial procedure moves much too slowly and much too expensively to handle the informal kind of adjudication for which the administrative agencies were constructed. Much of the reason for placing particular actions in the hands of administrators rather than the courts is the need for speedy, informal action. It has been pointed out, for example, that "if the local (ration) boards could have cleared their dockets no faster than the courts of law this nation would have starved to death in the first two weeks of food rationing." [2]

Cost to Individual.   More important than the fact that courts can review only an infinitesimal fraction of the totality of administrative decisions is the fact that most people cannot afford the protection of the courts anyway. The judicial process is incredibly expensive, for the courts will only review the effect of an administrative action on a single individual or organization—there must be a "case or controversy." Court and attorney fees are steep, and one cannot predict in advance how long they will continue or what the outcome of the case will be. Consequently, the "little man" suffers the indignities of administrative actions, and the "rule of law" is often to him an empty mockery.

Inadequacy of Remedies.   Another fact that limits the usefulness of judicial control is that it provides no meaningful remedy for many administrative decisions. As the Attorney General's Committee pointed out, "When the Securities and Exchange Commis-

---

[1] Attorney General's Committee on Administrative Procedure, *Administrative Procedure in Government Agencies*, Senate Document No. 8., 77th Cong., p. 76.

[2] Thompson, *The Regulatory Process in OPA Rationing*, p. 235.

sion issues a stop order or delists a security, later reversal by a court may show the Commission to have been in error, but it cannot recapture the transactions which the Commission's action prevented." [3] In many cases mere announcement of a proposed decision by an administrative agency, or even a rumor concerning a proposed action, can work an injury that no later review could possibly repair.

Limited Scope of Review. Another limitation of judicial control is that many kinds of administrative decisions will not be reviewed by the courts, and there are many other kinds where, by judicial self-restraint or legislative enactment, review is strictly limited to a specific aspect of the decision. Administrative decisions conferring what the courts regard as privileges rather than rights are not reviewable or are reviewable only within a very narrow scope. In the recent Federal administrative loyalty check, thousands of decisions were made affecting drastically the futures of thousands of persons, and none was reviewed by a court. Federal employment is not a "right," say the courts. Decisions concerning the letting of government contracts for goods and services are for practical purposes not reviewable by courts. The same is true of decisions concerning the admission of aliens. Millions of decisions granting or denying rations were made during the last war, and, as far as the authors know, none of them was reviewed in a court of law. Many other examples could be cited.

Review of Technical Matters. Another fact that saps the force of judicial review is the highly technical nature of many administrative decisions. Since these decisions are devised to a large extent by experts, lay judges cannot be expected to criticize them intelligently. Consequently, whether a particular decision was guided chiefly by technical knowledge or by the value preferences of its makers often cannot be known by courts. In this situation, all a court can do is call in expert witnesses to inform it. Then we have one set of experts on one side and another on the other side, and the court must decide which expert is more expert.

Enough has been said to show that judicial controls barely scratch the surface of accountability. They still leave the administrator a wide field for selecting the values he will promote in his decisions. Nevertheless, because administrators may have to

[3] Op. cit., p. 77.

face a court review, and because of the strong influence of governmental attorneys arising from this possibility of review, judicial controls do force responsiveness to certain values—those values associated with our system of law. Let us see just what these values are.

JUDICIAL ACCOUNTABILITY AND ADMINISTRATIVE RESPONSIVENESS

Judicial controls give a heavy emphasis in the administrative process to traditional legal forms of procedure. In many cases where administrative action involves the imposition of penalties against specific individuals or groups of individuals (administrative adjudication), the procedures followed are almost identical with those followed by courts. The courts demand a certain amount of this mimicry, and the attorneys inside and outside the administration demand even more. Although there are still many areas of administrative adjudication where speedy, inexpensive, and informal procedures are used, such as the adjudication of workmen's compensation claims, the tendency is for administrative adjudication to become more and more like court adjudication.

The Administrative Procedures Act of 1946. Agitation for administrative procedures that would conform more closely to those of the courts and provide for wider judicial review became very strong early in the Thirties when a plethora of new administrative techniques was introduced by the New Deal Administration to accomplish the reforms of that period. This agitation resulted in the passage of an administrative procedures bill, the Walter-Logan Bill, which was vetoed by President Roosevelt. The President, in turn, directed the Attorney General to set up a Committee on Administrative Procedures to study the problem more closely. This Committee, after a long and detailed study, recommended some mild changes in existing practices, but saw no indication of widespread administrative arbitrariness or tyranny. After the publication of its report in 1940, a number of agencies re-drafted their procedures to correspond more closely to its recommendations.

In the upsurge of conservatism after the war, a revised version of the Walter-Logan Bill, under a new name, passed the Congress without even the formalities of a hearing. It was signed by the

President and became, as the Administrative Procedures Act of 1946, part of the legal framework within which Federal administrative operations now function.

Although it is too early to have anything like complete evidence as to the impact of this Act on Federal administration, students of public administration have expressed two basic fears concerning it. First, the Act attempts to formalize all governmental procedures and to make them conform more closely to traditional legal procedures even though the tasks performed are so enormously varied that any such attempt is likely to cause an enormous amount of confusion and delay.

The publication requirement may be used as an example. Save only for matters of legitimate secrecy and matters of national security, the Act requires that each agency must publish in the Federal Register descriptions of its organization and functions; the way in which it makes its decisions, including its procedures; its "substantive rules" as well as pronouncements of its general policy and interpretations of the law under which it considers itself bound. It must also publish its decisions in cases that come before it for adjudication. Since a single issue of the Federal Register can contain as many as 500,000 words (twice the number in this book), and since an issue is published five days a week, it is obvious that publication gives "due notice" only to organizations with legal staffs sufficiently large to read this array of material. It does not inform either the small business man or the ordinary citizen. The Act also tends further to emphasize the position of the government attorney by freezing agencies within rigid sets of legal rules.

The second fear that has been expressed about this Act is based upon its apparent extension of judicial review of administrative actions. Many students of administration have argued that, far from adding to the liberty or freedom of the great mass of the people, a great extension of judicial review would deprive the many of liberty in the interest of those who can benefit from the law's inevitable procrastination.

The probable effects of the Act have been summarized as follows: "Its most readily visible effects are likely to be increased complexity of administrative organization; augmentation of staffs; considerable multiplication of 'red tape,' delay, and technical opportunities for evasion of controls; enhancement of the role of legal divisions and lawyers within the agencies; and a rabbit-like proliferation of opportunities to litigate at every reluctant step along the path of the regulatory process." [4]

Protection of the Individual. Although judicial controls emphasize traditional legal procedures, it would be unfair to characterize these controls simply as a group of procedures for the sake of procedures. Back of our judicial system are some important values of individual protection. It is very easy for government agencies to lose sight of the individual person. Administrators cannot take into consideration precisely how their actions will affect each person; they must and do seek a general or statistical result. If their actions benefit *most* people, or suppress *most* of the behaviors deemed undesirable, they are likely to feel successful and, in fact, to be generally credited with success.

However, beyond the "most" are many individual persons who may not be benefited—individuals for whom the inevitably general administrative action is not designed, to whom it is oppressive and appears unfair. Administrators may, and perhaps most of them do, try to minimize these cases of individual hardship, but even with the sincerest efforts some individual instances of "injustice" will result from administrative actions.

Judicial control provides at least the possibility that some individuals may receive an independent review of their cases with all their unique aspects. It attempts to provide an impartial and deliberate consideration for the individual's point of view—a point of view sometimes obscured in the administrative process because of carelessness or the pressure of time or infeasibility. The fact that administrative actions as applied to individuals may be overruled through judicial review undoubtedly spurs administrators to greater efforts to discover means for sparing the individual from needless oppression.

However, this judicial protection of the individual against governmental action is restricted to certain conventional notions embodied in our legal institutions—bills of rights and court decisions interpreting them. While it would be foolish to minimize the importance of these conventional protections, they represent

[4] Vincent M. Barnett, Jr., "Judicialization of the Administrative Process," a review of the published proceedings of an Institute on The Federal Administrative Procedures Act and the Administrative Agencies conducted by the New York University School of Law on February 1–8, 1947, *Public Administration Review*, 8:126–33 (Spring, 1948), at p. 133. See also Frederick F. Blachly, "Sabotage of the Administrative Process," *Public Administration Review*, 6:213–27 (Summer, 1946).

only a very small number of the ways in which administrative action may affect individuals oppressively.

Furthermore, because of the slowness, complexity, and expensiveness of our legal procedures, judicial protection of individuals against oppressive administrative action is, by and large, protection of corporations and other large organized interests against restrictive governmental action taken to protect the rest of the community. Utility regulation provides a striking example. Rate cases in our courts run, on the average, for several years.[5] Appraisal fees (to determine "fair value" of the property) are enormous, costing, as some estimate, between one half and one percent of the total reproduction cost of the property.[6] Consequently, appraisal costs in the neighborhood of $1,000,000 are not unusual. It is clear that in this situation, regulatory agencies cannot afford very often to issue rate orders that might be challenged in the courts. The accountability process embodied in our judicial controls forces responsiveness to the values of the industrial giants that the agencies are charged with regulating. "As a result of the difficulties created by protracted and expensive litigation, some commissions virtually abandoned formal proceedings as a method of securing rate reductions. Particularly after the onset of the depression in 1929, many of them turned to negotiation, hoping to

[5] "The *Ohio Bell Telephone* case, 301 U. S. 292, was in process of adjudication about fourteen years. The Missouri Public Service Commission required over eight years to reach a determination in its proceedings against the Union Electric Light and Power Company, 17 P.U.R. (N.S.) 337; and over seven years in its proceedings against the Ozark Utilities Company 18 P.U.R. (N.S.) 408. The North Dakota Board of Railroad Commissioners required almost three years in its proceedings against the Northern States Power Company, 15 P.U.R. (N.S.) 126. The New York Public Service Commission consumed at least five years in determining reasonable rates for the Long Island Lighting Company, 18 P.U.R. (N.S.) 65. . . .

"The proceedings before the Illinois Commerce Commission to determine rates for the Illinois Bell Telephone Company, initiated in September, 1921, did not reach a final conclusion until twelve and a half years later, in 1934. See *Lindheimer v. Illinois Bell Telephone Co.*, 292 U. S. 151. More than ten of these years were consumed in litigation in the Federal courts subsequent to the Illinois Commission's findings in the case. The *New York Telephone Company* case was instituted in 1920 and determined by the New York Public Service Commission in 1924; yet it was not until 1934 that the case was finally settled. See the concurring opinion of Justice Brandeis in *St. Joseph Stockyards Co. v. United States*, 298 U. S. 38, 90." Fainsod and Gordon, *Government and the American Economy*, p. 320, footnote 27.

[6] Harry Booth, General Counsel of the Illinois Commerce Commission, in the government brief in *Driscoll v. Edison Light and Power Co.*, 307 U. S. 104, at p. 54.

secure reductions by mutual agreement. . . . But in most cases, negotiations were not especially successful, since utility companies preferred to stand on their legal rights." [7]

SUMMARY: JUDICIAL CONTROLS

The kind of responsiveness associated with our system of judicial controls may be summarized as follows: (1) American administration tends to adapt itself to traditional legal forms of procedure; (2) judicial controls undoubtedly encourage administrators to seek methods that minimize individual oppression in the eyes of the courts; and (3) our system of judicial controls forces responsiveness primarily to economically strong interests. Beyond this, most value premises of administrative choice are not greatly influenced by judicial controls.

Accountability to the Legislature

In the American system of government, the legislature is recognized to be the principal organization for setting the values by which we are governed. According to our legal theory, there must be some legislative authorization for all administrative actions imposing or enforcing duties upon members of the public; and other kinds of administrative action are similarly controlled by the requirement that no money may be spent unless appropriated by an act of the legislature. In enacting statutes and appropriations the legislature lays down the administrative goals—the basic value premises of administrative decision—and often prescribes means for accomplishing these goals or forbids the use of certain means.

ENFORCING RESPONSIBILITY TO LEGISLATURES

Conformance to the values laid down by the legislature is enforced, in the first place, by the courts. These, as we have seen, are empowered to overrule administrative actions that, in their eyes, are not authorized by legislative enactment. In the second place, the legislature itself enforces compliance with its commands by questioning administrators when new statutes are being debated,

[7] Fainsod and Gordon, op. cit., p. 322.

when new appropriations are being considered, and at other times. Legislatures have legal power to compel people to testify before them on any matters that may become the subject of legislation. If as a result of its investigations or questionings the legislature is not satisfied with the conduct of administration, it has the power to "punish" an administrative agency either by changing its legal authority or by reducing its appropriations. It can prescribe certain value premises of decision either in the enabling legislation or by specifying the purposes for which money is to be spent and how much is to be spent for any one thing.

Thus, American legislatures have a strongly recognized right to prescribe the values of administrative decision and considerable power to enforce these values on administration. Next we must ask how effectively this accountability is employed. Do all or most of the value premises of administrative decisions come from legislatures and the traditional legal system or is there still a large area of free administrative choice beyond these accountability processes?

SCOPE AND LIMIT OF LEGISLATIVE CONTROLS

Legislative accountability is subject to a number of heavy limitations. These stem both from the separation of powers and from the complexity of administration. As a result of the deficiencies in the tools that the legislature may use to hold administration accountable, administrators exercise a much more positive role in policy formation, and legislatures are forced to delegate in much broader terms to administrators than is contemplated in the traditional democratic theory which asserts that legislatures "establish the will of the state" while administrators "execute the will of the state."

Political Independence of Executives. An important limitation on legislative control of administration results from the American governmental system of separation of powers. Chief executives in America—the President, the governor, the mayor—are elected directly by the people, as are also many lesser executives in state, county, and city government. These executives have political programs, and are expected to work for the enactment of these programs into law or their embodiment in administrative action. Subordinates are usually loyal to the elected executive, and in any event, are expected to obey his directives. Thus, many value premises of administrative decisions are supplied by the executive branch itself. The executive branch is not completely, either in theory or in fact, politically dependent on the legislature.

Complexity Leads to Perplexity. A second limitation of legislative control results from the increasing complexity and volume of governmental activity. Legislators, trained chiefly in law or the arts of staying in office, are highly dependent on the very administrative agencies they seek to control for the information necessary for rational choice, for recommended solutions to public problems, and even for the identification and description of the problems themselves.

The highly disadvantageous position of legislators faced with the complexities, technicalities, and vastness of modern government is easily seen in the appropriation process. The Federal executive budget as submitted to Congress in 1949 was a volume the size of two large telephone books. Even working twenty-four hours a day, the Congressmen could not have been able effectively to review the document itself, let alone appraise the expenditures it outlined. Some of their despair over this state of affairs was expressed on the floor of the House of Representatives during the course of debate on the appropriations for the Department of Defense. Recognizing that the Appropriations Committee could not have done an adequate review job, Mr. Scrivner urges more help for the Committee·

> This committee should be given adequate experienced help. I say that for a good reason. Every time any admiral heading one of the Navy bureaus or any general heading one of the departments of the Army or Air Force come before this committee he is always backed by a big staff of experts, never less than five and sometimes as many as 15.
>
> What did this committee have to work with to help them except their own experience, their common sense, and their knowledge of affairs relating to the Army, Navy, and Air Force? They had one committee clerk—and a good one—and one minority clerk—he is a good clerk. There were these seven men pitting their judgment and their knowledge and their skill, their insight, and their vision against this great array that comes up before them one after the other.[8]

Although he was recognized as one of the foremost economists in the country prior to his election to the United States Senate,

[8] *Congressional Record*, 81st Cong., April 12, 1949, p. 4515.

Senator Paul Douglas expressed considerable bafflement over the 1949 budget. "I find myself so overwhelmed by the functions of the agencies concerned," he said, "that I am unable to pass intelligent judgment—I confess it—as to individual items of appropriations." [9]

Administrative Initiative in Legislation. The increasing volume and complexity of government has had two important results from the standpoint of administrative responsibility. It has shifted the initiative in legislation to the administration, and it has vastly increased the amount of actual legislating by the administration itself. Increasingly legislation is drafted by members of the executive departments, and is then introduced by friendly Congressmen. Hence, a good part of the initiative in the formulation of new goals or in the revision of existing goals lies not with the Congress, but within the bureaucracy.

A good example of this was the Veteran's Emergency Housing Program of 1946. After V-E day, some members of the OPA Rent Department's Planning Division began to realize that with the return of millions of veterans rent ceilings would be almost impossible to hold unless a great housing program were launched. They persuaded Chester Bowles, then OPA Administrator, to urge publicly the need for a public housing program. Because the Administration feared that this idea would be very unpopular politically, Mr. Bowles was ordered to desist from his agitation. Nevertheless, officials of the Rent Department's Planning Division drafted a housing bill and persuaded Representative Wright Patman of Texas to introduce it in the House. When the bill came up for committee hearings, Mr. Bowles was of course called upon to testify. In this way the Planning Division officials again got Mr. Bowles before the public with his housing program. Although the idea was very unpopular with private housing interests and hence with many congressmen, millions of veterans were returning to the country. A majority of the Congress, possibly deciding that voting against the bill would be politically dangerous, approved it.

Legislative Delegation. Initiative in proposing legislation gives the administration considerable power to choose the goals and values by which its own decisions are to be guided. However, this power is increased still further by the growing complexity and volume of governmental problems. This complexity has created an

[9] Quoted in the Chicago *Sun-Times*, June 5, 1949.

increasing necessity for legislatures to delegate their powers to administrative agencies on an ever wider scale. General laws, under which the agencies themselves set up specific rules and regulations, are more and more characteristic of our governmental system.

We must recognize, of course, that the reasons for general and even ambiguous laws are sometimes political. The legislature, faced with a hot issue, may prefer to "pass the buck" to an official in the executive branch. An interesting example was the Rent Control law of 1949. Under terrific cross-pressure from landlords and tenants, the Congress provided that landlords should have a "fair net operating return" but resisted all attempts to define that somewhat ambiguous phrase or to substitute more concrete language for it. From a political standpoint, it was easier to saddle the Housing Expeditor with the disagreeable task of definition.[10]

Vagueness of Legislative Intent. Even where the legislature has no political reasons for evading specific definitions and specific legislation, it must still enact many laws that only spell out legislative intent in a general way, leaving the gaps to be filled in by the administrative agencies. In many matters the legislature cannot anticipate the problems that will arise under the law, and therefore must leave the administrator sufficient scope to deal with whatever situations arise.

The extent to which broad general statutes, to be filled in by administrative decision, leave the administration legally free in the choice of values and goals to be promoted or recognized can be strikingly illustrated by the Second War Powers Act (56 Stat. 176). Probably more than half of the civilian wartime regulations were issued under the authority of the following section of that Act: "Whenever the President is satisfied that the fulfillment of requirements for the defense of the United States will result in a shortage in the supply of any material or of any facilities for defense or for private account or for export, the President may allocate such material or facilities in such manner, upon such conditions and to such extent as he shall deem necessary or appropriate for the public interest and to promote the national defense."

The Exceptions Principle. Our preceding discussion may have created the impression that most governmental decisions are made by the administration almost free from legislative control. Such

---

[10] For other instances of this type of legislation, see Herring, *Public Administration and the Public Interest, passim.*

an idea would be far from accurate. While it is true that most of the value premises of administrative decision are not supplied by the legislature, the influence of the legislature is felt constantly through the operation of what is sometimes called the "exceptions principle." While the legislature does not supply *all* values for administrative decisions, it can question *any decision*. For example, the anticipation of legislative investigation, whether by standing or special committees, undoubtedly acts as a powerful control over administrators. To avoid painful investigations, administrative agencies try to make decisions that will not be too displeasing to members of any committee likely to investigate.

Still, many different kinds of choices are possible within the limits imposed by fear of investigation. Moreover, committees are still chiefly dependent for information upon the very agencies they seek to investigate, and suffer from the handicaps, already mentioned, of dealing with highly technical matters in which they do not possess expert competence.

When the chief executive and the majority of the legislature are of the same party, investigating committees will not often embarrass the chief executive by disclosing questionable conditions within his administration, even if they could. And when they are of different parties, legislative investigations are frequently of a sensationalist character designed primarily to embarrass the executive. To be sure, hostile investigating committees have sometimes been effective in turning up situations of a scandalous or venal nature—for example, graft in the letting of government contracts. While this is important, the problem of administrative responsibility is not chiefly one of preventing corruption. Most persons, in or out of administration, are not corrupt.

The "exceptions principle" operates not only through legislative investigations, but also through the revision of statutes when the legislature is dissatisfied with the way in which delegated power has been employed by administrative agencies. Examples have already been cited of the curbing of OPA powers by statutory limitations when the Congress did not approve of specific enforcement practices used by the agency. Similarly, certain provisions of the Taft-Hartley Act can be interpreted as an exercise of legislative control to limit the discretion that had previously been delegated to the NLRB under the Wagner Act.

When the Anti-Trust Division of the Justice Department exercised its discretion under the Sherman Act to start proceedings against insurance companies and railroads, attempts (so far unsuccessful) were immediately made in the Congress to reverse the value premises underlying the prosecutions by amending the Act to exempt these two industries from its provisions. Thus, the delegation to administrative agencies of broad, ill-defined powers may be only a temporary abdication by the legislature, subject to a later resumption of control if legislators do not agree with the values on which the administrative agency is operating. The power to withhold appropriations—e.g., the virtual "starving" of the Anti-Trust Division during the 1920's—also provides an important means for reasserting control when broad discretion has been delegated.

Role of Individual Legislators. Before leaving the topic of the scope and limitations of legislative control, we should discuss briefly the influence of individual legislators over administration. Those legislators particularly who hold influential positions on strategic legislative committees acquire considerable personal influence. This influence is used largely in two types of situations.

In the first place, legislators are expected to secure special favors for "the folks back home" or for important persons in their constituencies. These favors most often take the form of local "pork-barrel" governmental expenditures (e.g., securing or retaining a veterans' hospital in the home city), or securing exceptions from a general program in the interest of some local group (e.g., relaxation of civil service requirements imposed by the Social Security Administration upon local welfare appointments in grant-in-aid programs). If the legislator is powerful enough, and strategically placed on an appropriate committee, he may be able to insist on such favors as a virtual condition for an agency's continued survival. Unless the legislator can endanger survival, his requests for special favors are likely to be rejected.

The second kind of influence of individual legislators over administrative decision relates to the protection of individuals from oppressive administrative action. A letter to one's congressman or alderman is often a much more effective, and certainly less expensive, way of securing relief than an appeal to the courts. When legislators register complaints about individual cases of arbitrariness, agencies will usually take considerable time and trouble to investigate the situation and correct it if this can be done consistently with the rest of the program.

LEGISLATIVE CONTROLS AND ADMINISTRATIVE RESPONSIVENESS

We have seen that, in spite of serious limitations upon their capacity to control administrative discretion, legislatures and individual legislators do provide and enforce many of the values entering into administrative decision. Consequently it is important to ask, as we did in the case of judicial controls, to what or whose values do the legislative controls make administration responsive.

At the present stage of our knowledge of politics, the question is a very difficult one to answer. We will present here some of the beliefs about the legislative process that are held by perceptive men in public affairs and students of politics.

Popular Control and Interest Groups. There is a greatly over-simplified theory about democratic political institutions to the effect that the "people" govern themselves through their popularly elected representatives. The "people" decide what they want, elect men who promise to get it for them, and then keep these men in office as long as they do what the "people" want. The difficulties of this simple theory are so great that we can only indicate some of them briefly; a veritable library of books would be needed to describe the realities of our political life.

Who are (or is) the "people"? Even on a simple numerical basis they are a minority. A bare majority of those voting in any election seldom constitutes more than one-fifth of a total constituency. Yet they elect their candidate. Moreover, the mass of voters has very little influence in the selection of candidates; political party organizations usually decide this for the voters. Furthermore, as a rule, voters know little about the candidates or what they believe in. To the extent that parties select the candidates and determine campaign issues, these important matters are decided by relatively hidden and secret oligarchies—not by the "people."

Does this fact mean, then, that the people have nothing to say about the values by which they are governed? To answer "yes" would certainly be false. Government in any country must be in some sense responsive to public opinion—to general or widespread attitudes of the citizenry toward public matters. However, the notion of government by public opinion is also subject to important qualifications. In the first place, the means by which opinion is formed—the channels of education and propaganda—are themselves subject to the powerful oligarchic pressures of interest groups and organized segments of the community. Public opinion will be strongly influenced by the values of those persons and groups who control the media of public education.

In the second place, voters do not usually have specific ideas about most governmental activities. If they are members of organized groups, they will have definite and even strong ideas about matters that affect the interests of those groups (e.g., veterans about the Veterans' Administration, labor about the NLRB). As to other matters, one usually finds widespread ignorance or indifference. Consequently, when the representative goes to the legislature, he worries little about such a politically vague concept as public opinion; he worries much more about satisfying specific demands of specific, organized, interest groups. And here again, the oligarchic character of the political process shows itself. For the interest groups he must be responsive to, if he is to stay in office, are those that can affect his reelection. A small and weak group can be disregarded, a strong and well-organized interest cannot. Whereas the rank and file of the voters will forget how he has voted on most matters at the legislature, the interest group will not forget how he has voted on matters of interest to it. In case of a conflict of interest between two groups in his constituency, he has strong reasons to vote on the side of the one that can affect his chances of reelection.

Power of Legislative Committees. The problems of modern legislation, discussed above, reinforce these oligarchic tendencies. Because of the mass and complexity of governmental problems, and because of the size of legislatures, legislation in America is reviewed principally by small committees of the legislature. By appointment of each member to one or a few committees, and by referring all proposed legislation of a certain type to the relevant committee, some experience with a limited range of governmental problems can be attained by individual legislators and some intelligent and detailed consideration given to each proposed bill. Except in matters commanding widespread interest the report of a committee is usually accepted by the legislature as a whole when considering a bill for passage. (There are of course many exceptions, and sometimes, on Administration bills, a strict party vote is demanded.)

It is to the committee hearings that the lobbyists swarm. There they serve as "experts" for the committees, supplying them with badly needed technical information and advice, which is, however, rarely if ever disinterested. Representatives of interest groups also perform legal drafting services for the committee members, presenting them with nicely drafted versions of proposed legislation in a form acceptable to their principals. Where the proposal is of interest to a powerful group within a committee member's constituency, his actions within the committee can often be completely controlled by that group. Since the committee's report is so influential with the legislature as a whole, and since a committee can often as a practical matter kill a proposal simply by failure to report it out, control of a few members of a committee is often all an interest group needs to impress its desires on the whole state or nation.

SUMMARY: LEGISLATIVE CONTROL

In summary, legislative controls still leave the administrator with a wide area of ethical choice. However, to the extent that these controls impose values upon administration, the values are to a large extent those of politically powerful group interests within our society. Business groups, farmers, organized labor, veterans—these and similar groups, through their organizations, have acquired a very powerful position in our administrative and political life.

Although the powerful pressure groups are frequently in conflict, such is the nature of our political institutions that conflicting groups are often successful in promoting contradictory values through government. As a result, legislative mandates to the administration are often inconsistent. One administrative agency may busily promote values that another is equally busily resisting. Conflicts in administrative decisions reflect the conflicts within our society.

Occasionally, public interest may be so widespread (for example, interest in rent control) that even though unorganized it makes an impact through legislation on administration. Examples of this kind do occur, but they are rare. Generally speaking, public opinion on most issues reflects the conflicts among the organized interests of society. Political leadership and control is predominately oligarchic. As would be expected, administrative responsiveness through legislative controls merely reflects this fact.

Hierarchical Controls

The nature of administrative hierarchies and the relationships within them have already been much discussed in this book. In this section we will apply our previous analysis to the specific question of administrative responsibility. The traditional theory of hierarchical control of administration is stated succinctly by the Hoover Commission: "Responsibility and accountability are impossible without authority—the power to direct. The exercise of authority is impossible without a clear line of command from the top to the bottom, and a return line of responsibility and accountability from the bottom to the top." [11] If the top executive is elected by the people, if he can hire and fire his first-line lieutenants, if they can hire and fire their immediate subordinates, and so forth, then the values in administrative decisions will come from the people and flow down this line of command, always enforced on those below by threat of the sanction of dismissal. Then administration will be responsible and accountable to each higher hierarchical level in turn and to no one else—ultimately, through the chief executive, to the people. Such is the very common notion of hierarchical control. Let us now see to what extent administrative decisions actually are determined by this particular accountability procedure.

LIMITATIONS OF HIERARCHICAL CONTROLS

The conception of hierarchy just stated is very far from describing the realities of public administration in America. The power of hierarchical superiors to hire and fire is hedged in on all sides. Merit systems restrict it; in many jurisdictions, many of the chief executive's "subordinates" are elected rather than appointed; many heads of Federal administrative agencies are appointed by the President "with the advice and consent" of the Senate and can be removed by the chief executive only for special causes.

Because the traditional theory does not describe actual conditions in America, we must limit our analysis to its basic underlying idea—that the value premises of administrative choice can be controlled through an organization hierarchy. To what extent is

[11] Report on *General Management of the Executive Branch*, p. 1.

the discretion of subordinates in value questions restricted by hierarchical control?

Separation of Powers. In the first place, the separation of powers in this country between legislature and executive somewhat beclouds the right of the chief executive to control administration. The President, for example, sometimes orders the Budget Bureau to impound money appropriated specifically by the Congress for a particular activity. Such orders have not gone unchallenged in the Congress, but the issue has never been clearly resolved.

Likewise, in a case involving the removal by the President of a Federal Trade Commissioner, the Supreme Court took the somewhat remarkable position that the independent regulatory agencies were really accountable only to Congress and the courts and not to the President. Instances are not unknown at state and local levels, too, where legislatures have challenged executive controls over subordinates. The question most often arises when the chief executive instructs his subordinates to execute laws in a manner that the legislators say is contrary to their intent.

Complexity. There is a still more serious question. How can the high-level executive influence more than a very few aspects of the discretion of his subordinates? The same forces that have reduced the potency of legislative controls have reduced the potency of hierarchical controls—the increasing variety, complexity, and number of governmental problems. Increasingly as one goes up the hierarchy, the executive has time for only the most cursory review of his subordinates' decisions. Tremendous volumes of technical staff work will be reduced to a single recommendation by the time a problem reaches an executive only moderately far up the line. Modern organization depends upon specialization. The executive is always to some extent a generalist, and increasingly so as one mounts the hierarchy. Thus, even if he had the time, the executive would not have the knowledge to criticize his specialists' work intelligently.

For the same reasons, the lower echelons initiate most administrative decisions. To a very large extent, especially at the higher hierarchical levels, executive approval of staff recommendations is based almost entirely upon confidence in subordinates. To speak of a "line of confidence" from top to bottom describes administrative behavior more realistically than to speak of a "line of command." Of course, as we have pointed out before, when conflicting recommendations are presented to hierarchical superiors they may influence the outcome by choosing between them. But even in such cases, the particular recommendations that reach the executive, out of all possible ones, are determined by the organization below. A big part of the executive's job is to give official status or legitimacy to the decisions of his subordinates.

We do not want to create the impression that *no* values or goals are handed down from above. The hierarchy, as we have seen before, is a channel by which the values of important external groups make themselves felt in administrative decisions. Later we will want to learn more about the sources of such values. The important point to emphasize here is that most ethical choice in administration must be ascribed to other than hierarchical sources.

Overhead Units. The desire to overcome these limitations on hierarchical control frequently leads to the proliferation of overhead control or "staff" organizations. "The wise exercise of authority is impossible without the aids which staff institutions can provide to assemble facts and recommendations upon which judgments may be made and to supervise and report upon the execution of decisions," says the Hoover Commission.[12] As we saw in our earlier discussion of staff, these aids are conceived to be "part of the executive," not independent and scattered sources of control. Certainly they can impose decisional values upon administration more effectively than can a single executive. By organizing and specializing their staffs they can to some extent overcome the problem of lack of time and expertness that so limits the control exercised by individual executives.

However, overhead units also suffer under the handicaps of lack of time and expertness. Unless the overhead control organizations are just as extensive and specialized as the organizations they seek to control, they will understand only meagerly the administrative decisions they seek to control, and in most cases the power of inititative will not be with them. If they are just as extensively organized, duplication will result and the cost of administration will be enormous. But more important, who will then control the controllers? If overhead units enforce responsibility upon lower echelons of the hierarchy, to whom or what will the overhead units themselves be effectively accountable?

[12] Ibid.

Identifications. A further limitation on hierarchical controls as means of enforcing responsiveness is that the supervisor of an organizational unit usually comes to identify with it. He takes its point of view and generally tries to defend it against outside critics. Once he becomes a member, whether by political or merit appointment, he no longer has the role of outside critic. The unit becomes "his" unit; the personnel, "his" personnel. In fact, hierarchical control involves a serious dilemma. If the superior does not identify with his subordinates, if he maintains a completely independent point of view, he will have little authority over them—little ability to get them to accept different decisional values. If he does identify with them, so that he has authority, he will largely share their administrative or program values and hence will not want to impose other values on them.

Limits on Communications. A final limitation on hierarchical control is the frequent failure of communication. This subject has been extensively treated before. We need only repeat here that if decisional premises are not communicated, or are filtered or distorted in the process, to that extent hierarchical controls are not operating at all. And if the top man knows little about what those at the bottom are thinking, it is also true that those at the bottom know little about what the top man is thinking. As far as we know, no one has investigated systematically the extent to which communication fails of its function in administration, but the evidence of everyday experience suggests that the failure is considerable.

We conclude that although hierarchical controls do affect administrative decisions—although many decisional values can be ascribed to them—still much freedom of ethical choice is left to almost every administrative employee at every level in organization.

HIERARCHICAL CONTROLS AND ADMINISTRATIVE RESPONSIVENESS

We have now reached the third stage in our analysis of the components that go to make up administrative accountability. To the controls, partial and limited, exercised by courts and legislatures, we have added the controls, also partial and limited, exercised by the administrative hierarchy. To understand the significance of this third set of controls we must again ask the question: accountability to what? Whose values or what values does the hierarchy enforce?

We have already examined the traditional theory that the hierarchy is merely an intermediate link in a strong chain between the legislature and the individual governmental employee—that the hierarchy merely sees to the execution of the "will of the state" as defined by the legislature. We have seen that this theory explains very few of the facts. Executive controls impose values that are in many cases additional to, or different from, those imposed by the legislature.

Moreover, the executive hierarchy is itself not a single, monolithic structure. At each step in the administrative pyramid from bottom to top responsibility may be directed outward as well as upward. Many hierarchical controls originate at the level of the chief executive—President, governor, or mayor. Many others originate at the level of departments or smaller unitary organizations, particularly organizations that have close relations with clientele groups. Still others originate in the overhead units. In our examination of hierarchical controls we will consider, first, the nature of the forces operating at the level of the chief executive; next, the forces operating directly upon unitary organizations; and finally, the forces operating upon overhead units.

The Chief Executive. In American government, the chief executive (with almost the sole exception of the city manager in council-manager cities) is an elected party leader. The President must command a majority of the electoral vote; governors and mayors, a majority of the popular votes in their constituencies. The program of the chief executive must appeal, therefore, to many diverse and conflicting group interests.

The range of pressures that impinge on the chief executive is of course much greater than the range impinging upon a single legislator. For this reason the political leadership of the President or of a governor is less likely to be tinged by particularism and sectionalism than the leadership of a legislator or legislative bloc. Nevertheless, when we speak of the chief executive as being responsive to public controls, we must mean primarily controls exercised by those organized groups in the public that possess real political power.

It is sometimes argued that because the chief executive is a single person rather than a group of persons, he can achieve a unified or internally consistent program. While there is some truth in this idea, it should not be taken too literally. The chief executive, if he wishes to remain in office and continue his party in power, must satisfy enough groups to achieve this result, even though it involves many inconsistencies in his program. To be sure, majorities are formed by compromising among diverse interests, but "compromise" does not imply "consistency." A compromise between urban consumers and farmers can sometimes be secured by giving the former an anti-trust law to lower prices by enforcing competition, while giving the latter crop controls to raise agricultural prices.

This is by far the most typical kind of compromise in our political scene. Each major interest, or group of interests, seeks to stake out an area of governmental activity in which it can enforce its values. From the chief executive's standpoint, this kind of compromise implies a delegation of the enforcement of hierarchical responsibility to the individual unitary organizations with which interest groups are concerned.

Accountability of Departments. The appointed subordinates who head the major administrative units in nation, state, or city become, then, important foci for external pressures on administration. The chief executive often must appoint them on the basis of their acceptability to the relevant interest groups. A President who appointed as Secretary of Agriculture a man opposed by the Farm Bureau Federation and the National Grange would take a long step toward political suicide.

Once appointed, the department head has a political obligation to the chief executive to keep the relevant interest groups satisfied so that their political support will be forthcoming. This ties accountability again to these interest groups and to the legislative committees that they use as principal channels of influence.

In a previous chapter we pointed out that the survival of an administrative organization depended upon its ability to change its values in response to the changing interest structure of external groups. We also argued that the opportunistic kind of outlook needed to make this adjustment was chiefly found in the hierarchy. Executives, for many reasons, tend to be opportunistic. We pointed out that one of the principal functions of executives was to watch the external scene, perceive when changes in administrative direction are required for survival, and then try to persuade the rest of the organization to modify its decisions accordingly. The executive hierarchy is frequently a channel by which these new politically inspired goals or values make their impact on administrative decision. Since the basic consideration here is survival, the values imposed on administrative decisions by the hierarchy are the values of groups that can affect survival. Hence, the chief impact of departmental executives on administrative decision is much the same as that of the legislature or the chief executive. Administrative hierarchies are a part of the political process. If that were not so, democratic administration would be impossible to attain or even to approximate.

Accountability of Overhead Units. The control exercised by overhead "staff" groups presents a different problem. Because of the widespread belief that staff units have no power of command over administration, but only advise the executive or help him command, their actual influence on administrative decisions comes under little scrutiny. It is greatly underestimated because of the myths surrounding the staff function. We have seen in earlier chapters that these overhead groups can demand and secure all sorts of changes in administrative decisions. Where do the values they impose come from?

Although there is little systematic evidence about the way in which the discretion of overhead units is exercised, our theory permits us to make some relatively definite predictions on this score. First, overhead units can realistically be considered "a part of the executive" only to the extent that the chief executive has a well defined program, and only to the extent that the balance of forces impinging upon the chief executive is somewhat different from the forces impinging upon individual legislative committees and administrative agencies.

With respect to the first point, we have seen that, in the Federal government at least, "the program of the President" is in considerable part a mythical concept. When a budget analyst in the Estimates Division of the Budget Bureau decides to slash the budget estimate of a unit in the Veterans' Administration, there is usually no overall governmental philosophy, goal, or program of the President to rationalize that action. The decision is just as likely to reflect personal dislike of someone on the staff of the VA as any other value.

On the second point, to the extent that overhead units are able effectively to enforce accountability, they simply provide a new focus for attack of the political interests that can impinge directly upon these units and their associated legislative committees. For example, if the Hoover Commission recommendation were adopted that a continuing agency on federal-state relations be created, it is not hard to predict that the new agency would become a focus for the pressures of local and state governments upon the Federal government.

Beyond these considerations, if the formal controls we have described in this chapter leave wide areas of discretion to the employees of unitary organizations, they will leave equally broad discretion to the employees of overhead organizations. The issue then resolves itself into the question of *whose* discretion is to control. Since the discretion of agricultural experts or construction engineers is likely to be exercised somewhat differently from the discretion of personnel experts or accountants, the question is one of considerable importance.

Formal Controls: Conclusion

Two conclusions emerge rather distinctly from what we have said about the formal controls exercised by courts, legislatures, and administrative hierarchies. The first is that these controls place bounds upon, but do not by any means eliminate, the discretion exercised by governmental employees over the value premises entering into their decisions. Administrators and employees still have considerable freedom to decide matters on the basis of their own ethical promptings.

To be sure, actual acceptance of values expressed in court decisions, statutes, and administrative orders goes considerably beyond the power of the formal mechanism to hold subordinates accountable. "Due process" may be respected even when it is known that there will be no appeal to the courts. The "intent of the legislature" may be diligently searched out and accepted even when there is little prospect of legislative investigation or scrutiny. Executive orders may be carried out respectfully even in a field office where accountability is weakened by a distance of three thousand miles. But responsiveness to values under these circumstances can hardly be regarded as accountability to formal controls. It is best regarded as an aspect of informal control—responsiveness, because of the ethical beliefs of the subordinate, to a system of *legitimate* authority. As such, it will be discussed further in the next chapter.

Our second conclusion is that the values imposed upon administration by formal accountability procedures—especially those of legislature and hierarchy—are primarily those of the politically powerful groups in our society. Hierarchical accountability is accountability to a politically responsive legislative body acting largely through politically responsive committees. Hence, in the American administrative process formal accountability becomes almost synonymous with adaptation in order to survive. The formal accountability procedures establish the rules of a game within which the struggle of administrative units for continuing existence takes place. These procedures do not isolate administration from the process of politics, or even confine the influence of politics upon administration to the traditional channel of elections, legislation, hierarchy and court review.

Further, as a result of the particularistic structure of interest groups, and the corresponding structure of legislative bodies and the administrative branch, the pattern of administration is full of inconsistencies. Contradictory goals must be pursued at the same time—by different agencies or even, sometimes, within a single agency. These administrative inconsistencies are simply reflections of the inconsistencies and conflict of values in our complex pluralistic society.

🚩

CHAPTER TWENTY-FIVE

Administrative Responsibility: Informal Controls

THERE remains the task of analysing informal controls over administration. The sum total of formal controls—judicial, legislative, and hierarchical—still leaves an important area of discretion that we must explore and seek to understand. Even with all these controls on the selection of goals of choice, persons in administrative organizations are not marionettes whose strings are held by others. A counter clerk may smile at you, or he may scowl; he may help you fill out a form, or he may tell you to go home and fill it out properly; he may try to explain the reason for some burdensome requirement, or he may tell you to "take it or leave it."

A traffic policeman makes all kinds of ethical choices as to whom he will warn, and whom he will present with a ticket. A program planner has a considerable area of choice, within the limits of the accountability procedures and forces, as to whether he will shift the burdens of a program to the clientele or to the agency's employees. A forms designer has considerable latitude as to what information he will request and how heavy a reporting burden he will place on respondents.

Types of Informal Controls

In the first half of this chapter we will examine informal controls—that is, we will ask where the administrator's or employee's value premises come from that are not supplied by the formal accountability procedures. In a sense, we will be returning to our starting

541

point in Chapters 3 and 4, where we first posed the question of how individuals behave in organizations. We will not attempt to review in this chapter our whole earlier discussion of the influences upon behavior, but will concentrate our attention on those influences that appear to be the most important in supplying the value premises of decision.

EXTERNAL SUPPORT AND SURVIVAL

We have already, in the last chapter, crossed the line that separates formal from informal controls by showing that the realities of formal administrative accountability are closely related to the struggle for organizational survival. Formal controls are of primary importance as channels through which political power can bear upon administration, and can, by setting the conditions of survival, force adaptation of political programs to the values of the holders of power. Where the formal channels of responsibility correspond to the structure of powerful and important political groups, these channels become significant parts of the mechanism of accountability. Where the formal channels do not correspond to political realities, they are likely to atrophy. Hence, the most important formal channels in our system of accountability are those that link agencies administering particular programs to their respective legislative committees and to interested and organized clientele groups.

But "external" groups—executives, legislatures, courts, and interest groups—are not the only groups that can affect the chances and conditions of survival. Unless the expectations of employees receive some recognition and satisfaction, management plans will be frustrated against a wall of resistance. The notions of employees as to how they ought to be treated are largely derived from the *mores* of the society in which they live. These socially acquired notions of proper treatment within organizations set solid limits to the organization's ability to mold the behavior of its members. This is another important way in which society's institutional patterns—the general beliefs as to what is right and proper—become important values in administrative decisions.

Even the notion of survival, however, does not explain completely what value premises will enter into decisions. An organization that is adjusting itself successfully to the demands of internal and external groups generally is providing an excess of satisfactions over contributions to its participants. As we saw in Chapter 23, the persons making decisions in the organization can, without endangering survival, dispose of the surplus thus created in many different ways. The larger the surplus—the greater the satisfactions the participants are receiving in proportion to the costs of participation—the wider is the area of discretion that remains.

BUREAU PHILOSOPHY

In the area of residual freedom, one important part is blocked out by what we may call "bureau philosophy." By this we mean the sum total of the group values, the accepted ways of doing things, that grow up in an administrative unit, and with which the members of the unit identify. An agency working with a stable program over a long period of time develops a definite philosophy and point of view. It develops strong tendencies to harmonize its present decisions with past ones, and both present and past decisions with future ones. A body of rationalizing principles develops which reconciles past and present.

Strong psychological forces work to secure conformity of decisions to such a "bureau philosophy." Since decisions inconsistent with this philosophy put all the agency's past decisions in doubt, they require difficult and painful explanation. The philosophy tends to grow in the same way as does the common law. Changing conditions require the elaboration and adaptation of the principles so that new decisions can be reconciled with previous ones, and consistency restored.

A bureau philosophy makes group decisions possible where otherwise anarchy would prevail—each participant attempting to impose his own "inarticulate major premises" upon the rest. By relating particular decisions to a coherent set of principles, it facilitates their defense. By providing a rule of *stare decisis*, it fills in most of the gaps of discretion left by the formal controls and provides organizational members with safe ways of exercising discretion and making decisions.

A bureau philosophy tends to be self-maintaining. The agency tends to recruit and retain personnel in terms of their acceptance of the philosophy, and to subject its members to continual indoctrination in its values. So far as civil service procedures allow it, the organization examines new recruits and potential recruits to make sure they are "our kind." Group identification reinforces acceptance of the philosophy, for to be fully accepted as a group member, the individual must in turn identify with the group values. Life is uncomfortable in the organization for persons who do not accept these values, and over a period of time, such persons generally leave. Only under unusual circumstances does a sufficient number of dissident individuals remain in the group for a sufficient length of time to threaten successful "revolution" and alteration of the bureau philosophy.

When an administrative organization's point of view has become institutionalized in this way, the organization may resist strongly demands inconsistent with the bureau philosophy that are pressed through formal accountability procedures. Resistance is limited, of course, by the requirements of survival, but often demands can be qualified or compromised without jeopardizing the organization's existence.

NEEDS OF THE PERSONALITY

The distinction we wish to make between behavior that expresses the "needs of the situation" and behavior that expresses the "needs of the personality" corresponds roughly to the distinction made in everyday speech between "objective" and "emotional" behavior. At various points in this book we have given examples of emotional behavior—the conference participant who "wants his way," the traffic cop who gets satisfaction from bawling out a motorist, and others. The full story of these emotional needs and the ways in which they get expressed in administrative behavior remains to be told by psychologists. Enough is known already, however, to demonstrate that the fulfillment of the needs of the personality has an important influence on administrative behavior.[1] One example will suffice.

Lasswell and Almond studied a group of receptionists in the office of a public social work agency to determine under what circumstances they would make exceptions in the agency's policies

---

[1] See, for example, Harold D. Lasswell, *Psychopathology and Politics* (Chicago: University of Chicago Press, 1930); and Robert K. Merton, "Bureaucratic Structure and Personality" *Social Forces* 18:560-8 (1940).

in favor of a client, and under what circumstances they would deny requests for exceptions or favors. They found very different reaction patterns among the various receptionists. One responded favorably to clients who approached her submissively, but would usually deny the requests of clients who approached her aggressively. In another the pattern was exactly reversed. The investigators were able to relate these reaction patterns to other elements in the personalities and life-histories of the receptionists.[2]

Some observers, and particularly the critics of bureaucracy, have hypothesized that positions in public administration attract individuals whose personal needs produce in them "authoritarian" tendencies. By authoritarianism we mean the love of power over others, whether or not it is accompanied by a philosophy rationalizing it. A love of power may derive from either sadistic or paranoic tendencies. The first possibility is illustrated by persons who seek jobs in jails and mental hospitals so that they can maltreat the inmates. The German Nazi regime made systematic use of persons with sadistic tendencies in the administration of concentration camps and prisons.

Paranoic tendencies may be present in individuals who enjoy the feeling that high governmental position gives them of power over whole industries or a whole nation. Paranoic individuals who are failures in private employment may later seek importance and prestige in government careers. Self-identification with the power of the omnipotent state may provide a deep source of satisfaction to the paranoic personality.

Authoritarian attitudes, whatever their psychological bases, lead to most of the petty tyrannies at the periphery of administration—the insolent counter clerk and the raging traffic cop. In the planning process such attitudes oppose efforts to find ways of accomplishing objectives that will impose least trouble and cost on the clientele. Authoritarianism leads to excessive use of legal punishment as an enforcement sanction, and to indifference to the fates of individuals whom the plan does not quite fit. In internal management it leads to disregard for the feelings of subordinates and excessive insistence on the "neutrality of means." Since it tends to divide people into governed and governors, it is the basis for much of the fear and distrust of bureaucracy.

[2] Harold D. Lasswell, *The Analysis of Political Behavior* (London: Kegan Paul, 1948), Part III chap. 3.

PROFESSIONALISM AND EXPERTNESS

A profession is distinguished from non-professional occupations by its possession of (1) a code of ethics of some kind to guide its members, and (2) methods to enforce this code (e.g., disbarment). A professional code limits the ends or goals to which the skills of the profession may be applied. Thus it frequently happens that professional codes come into conflict with the organizational goals and values. When this happens, hierarchical and even legislative controls may be quite impotent.

In fact, professionalism might well have been included among the formal accountability controls because professional ethics are sometimes enforced by formal means. Many professions have secured legal power to determine who may be licensed to practice the skill, and whose license is to be taken away. Law and medicine are familiar examples.

Apart from professional codes of ethics, there is another way in which all technical expertness affects responsibility—whether we are talking about medicine or plumbing. A person who has mastered a socially recognized technique or skill or trade has mastered a set of standardized solutions to a specific set of common problems. These standardized solutions are regarded as the "right" solutions. The person who has mastered them acquires functional authority in society—that is, he is recognized as a person who has the right answers in his field of specialization, and whose opinions in this field ought to be accepted. But any standardized solution is laden with implicit value assumptions: someone has decided that the solution is the *best* way to solve a particular type of problem. In selecting the solution, he has also decided what particular values are important and what unimportant.

The extent to which experts really make decisions about values is fairly obvious in the case of city planners and architects. Members of these professions are often quite explicit in telling us that we *ought* to have plenty of green spaces among our dwellings, or that we *ought* to build our public structures in a modern style rather than an imitation of Gothic or Renaissance. Other professions and trades are less explicit about their values. Engineering procedures for designing highway bridges contain implicit assumptions about the relative importance of safety, convenience, economy, and so forth, but these assumptions are never actually stated. It is somehow (and quite erroneously) assumed that the engineer is only making "technical" decisions—that he really has no discretion with respect to values.

Thus it happens that great deference is paid to the recommendations of experts, and that these recommendations covertly introduce into administrative decisions values of which even the experts are unaware. Further, because nonexperts hesitate to contradict experts, experts may inject into administrative decisions value preferences of which they definitely *are* conscious. And because experts often learn their standardized solutions with little or no understanding of the basic reasons for them, they are often very inflexible and resistant to new ideas.

All of these difficulties in the relationship between expert and layman are apparent in the debate about compulsory health insurance. Quite apart from the merits of the question, it is quite clear that: (1) medical men treat the issue as though it were a technical medical question which they, by virtue of their training, have peculiar competence to decide; (2) the lay public is never quite sure when it is challenging the medical judgment of medical men, and when it is challenging their judgment of social issues; and (3) most doctors, not having been exposed during their training to an analysis of the problems of the organization of medical practice, simply react to the whole debate with emotional traditionalism.

The extreme specialization of our age and the high status accorded to the expert accentuate the pluralistic character of our society and further the development of independent pluralistic centers of administrative power. If personnel specialists say that "sound personnel practices" require a particular kind of decision, who has competence to challenge them? If experts in air warfare tell us that the defense of the country requires B-36's, who (except a competing expert) will dare substitute his judgment for theirs? Alongside political groups formed to promote particular economic interests or social or religious interests, we have a growing array of political groups formed to preserve the right of experts to make unchallenged decisions in the areas of their special competence (as defined by themselves).[3]

[3] The atomic scientists are an excellent example of a group that, by virtue of expertness in physics, claims a special right to be heard on social and political issues more or less related to the atomic bomb.

POLITICAL AND SOCIAL PHILOSOPHIES

The distinction we are making between value premises stemming from "needs of the personality" and premises arising out of "political and social philosophies" is a rather arbitrary one. The authoritarian person whom we described under the former category may have a systematic and comprehensive rationalization in philosophical terms of his authoritarianism. Conversely, devoted disciples of Freudian psychology would argue that *any* political and social philosophy is simply a rationalization of some need of the personality.

Without taking sides in this dispute, we wish to discuss certain attitudes, whether they be philosophies or rationalizations, that have an important bearing on value judgments. By "philosophies" we mean here the individual's general outlook, his notions of the proper role of government, of its relations to the individual, and of the individual's obligations to his fellow men.

There is a common core of ethical beliefs that almost all of us share. Most of us accept such general mores of our society as belief in honesty, fair play, the dignity of the individual, and so forth. Most of us believe in maintaining our general form of constitutional government. Without such a belief democracy would be impossible, because many people would be unwilling to accept political defeat— winning an election would be more important than maintaining the electoral process.

Around this core of common beliefs, we find other areas where there is some degree of agreement, but by no means unanimity; and still other areas where the widest range of beliefs is held. There are two areas of belief that are of particular importance to the conduct of administration: (1) ethical attitudes toward responsibility, and (2) ethical attitudes toward the role of government in the economy.

Attitudes Toward Responsibility. In the last chapter we defined responsibility as responsiveness to values, and accountability as the enforcement of this responsiveness. But responsiveness may be much broader than accountability. Individuals may accept particular values even if there is no effective way of forcing them to do so. In particular, in a country where democratic values prevail, most persons who are placed in public administrative positions will feel that in their decisions they *ought* to be responsive to democratic values. They may actively seek out such values as bases for their decisions, quite apart from the power of the legislature, the courts, or their hierarchical superiors to enforce particular values upon them. The difficulty is that even if an administrator most sincerely wishes to obey "the people's will," he will have a most troublesome time discovering just what that will is; and where he will find it will depend on his own particular notions of democracy—i.e., his own particular values.

(1) *Legislative Intent.* One administrator may believe strongly in the right of the majority to pass any law it wants. This administrator would seek the "will of the people" in the actions of its representative—the legislature. He might search for the "intent of the legislature" in committee hearings and floor debates, hoping thus to fill the gaps and resolve the ambiguities of the statute he is administering. It is not at all uncommon to see a great deal of time and effort devoted in Federal agencies to the study of committee hearings with the object of discovering the legislative thinking that led to the inclusion of particular clauses in a statute.

The search for the intent of the legislature is likely to prove largely chimerical. In the first place, the hearings are often as ambiguous in intent as the legislation. For example, the Economic Cooperation Act of 1948 provided that the choice between outright grants to Marshall Plan countries and loans to be repaid "shall depend upon the character and purpose of the assistance and upon whether there is reasonable assurance of repayment considering the capacity of such country to make such payments. . . ." Here, in a single sentence, are stated two distinct criteria that might lead to very different decisions as to when repayment should be required. But in the committee hearings and committee reports on the bill, these same two criteria are mentioned without any clear indication of when the one was to apply, and when the other.

A second difficulty in seeking the intent of the legislature from these supplementary sources is that hearings only set forth the statements of particular witnesses or congressmen, and committee reports only set forth the views of the committee. It is highly dangerous to assume that these statements and views also represent, in some sense, the "collective" view of the legislature that enacts the bill. In the last analysis, the statute itself is the only medium through which the intent of the whole legislature, as distinguished from the intentions of individual members or committees, can be expressed.

(2) *The Popular Will.* Another administrator, equally devoted to democracy, may distrust the legislature, suspecting it to be controlled by powerful private interests, and may search for the will of the people in some other direction. In the case of the falsification of REA records, discussed at some length in a previous chapter, the REA officials responsible for the concealment thought they were protecting the public will against the attack of a legislator who, they believed, was opposing that will.

The difficulty here, as in the discovery of legislative intent, lies in the intangibility of the "will of the people." In a democracy there are certain procedures of party activity, elections, legislation, executive action, and sometimes initiative, referendum, and recall. These are the procedures through which the citizenry influence the course of their government. It is hard to see what operational meaning can be given to the phrase "popular will" except to define it as the outcome, whatever it may be, of these political processes.

The development, in the past two decades, of nonofficial public opinion polls like the Gallup poll has led to a resurgence of the idea that there may be a popular will to which administrators should respond, apart from the decisions of the legislature. Some administrators may even feel that when legislative actions conflict with opinion as measured by the polls they have a right to disregard the legislature (if they can safely do so) and follow "public opinion."

Certain notions championed by the TVA were also based on the idea of finding a popular will apart from legislative expression of that will. The TVA idea was that there should be "grass-roots" participation—that is, direct clientele participation—in the formulation of policy. Through this direct channel between clientele and the administrative agency, the former could supply some of its values to the latter. We have already pointed out that the TVA procedures did, in fact, have this result. Whether the clientele views that were thus influential should be regarded as expressions of a popular will is a difficult question of semantics and ethics.

(3) *The Public Interest.* Other administrators may not admit that there is any political process that effectively expresses the popular will, and may search their own consciences for guides to

the "public interest." That is, while granting that the will of the people should determine governmental action, these persons may have confidence mainly in introspection as a means for discovering the public will.

A public librarian making a decision as to what books to order for the library collection; a welfare worker making a recommendation for foster home placement of a child; a rent director considering a request for the lifting of rent ceilings—all are making value judgments within broad bounds set by legislative and administrative instructions that are usually vague and general. To the extent that such persons are identified with particular social values, they will derive from these values a conception of the public interest that they can and do apply to their decisions.

Of course, when one looks in a mirror, one sees one's own image. Responsiveness to public interest, so defined, is responsiveness to one's own values and attitudes toward social problems. Nevertheless, this responsiveness provides a major channel through which values that are commonly or broadly held through our society (or those parts of society from which particular groups of administrators are drawn) enter into administrative decision.

(4) *Natural Law.* A few steps beyond this nonoperational concept of the public will lies the belief that what people say they want, by whatever method, is irrelevant in determining the goals of government. Here we begin to encounter "natural law" concepts of just and right.

Natural law concepts—even stated as limits upon the supremacy of the popular will—are an important component of the political tradition of this country. The most significant of these are beliefs in natural rights of individuals that may not be infringed even by majorities: the right of the individual to the use of his property, and the right of the individual to the freedoms of speech, religion, and assembly.

We see that administrators and governmental employees, like other people in our society, hold certain concepts of democracy, and as a consequence, are prepared to accept as value premises for their decisions those values which they believe have been legitimatized by democratic process. To the extent that democracy means to an administrator the formal processes of courts, legislatures, and hierarchy, his democratic beliefs make him responsive to these processes even beyond their power to hold him formally accountable. To the extent that the administrator has some conception of a popular will, a general interest, or natural rights that goes beyond the formal political processes, his democratic beliefs may actually make him less responsive and more resistive to judicial, legislative, and hierarchical accountability. Each policy that is imposed on the administrator will be interpreted and executed by him in terms of his conceptions of legitimacy. If he regards a statute as the ultimate expression of the popular will, he may go to great lengths to execute statutes faithfully and literally. If he believes he has other means of assessing the popular will, he may sometimes refuse to enforce laws (e.g., Sunday blue-laws). If he believes there is a higher law (e.g., the inviolability of freedom of speech), he may refuse to accept the authority of a statute that he believes encroaches on the higher law.

The Role of Government. As another example of the way in which political and social philosophies enter into decision we may examine beliefs about the proper role of government, and particularly its relations to economic institutions. The principal competing viewpoints here, in the current American scene, are those usually called "conservatism" and "liberalism." By "conservatism" in this context we mean the beliefs: that the broadest possible freedom of private property and contract should be preserved; primary reliance should be placed upon private enterprise for the production and distribution of goods; individuals should stand on their own feet, with a minimum of help from government; and government itself should be run in a "business-like" way, with proper attention to economy and efficient organization. By "liberalism" we mean the beliefs: that considerable governmental intervention in the economic mechanism is needed to prevent the domination of selfish over public interests, and to insure an adequate degree of economic democracy and an equitable distribution of incomes; that governmental assistance and protection should be provided to the weak and the underprivileged; and that government should be operated with humanitarian aims and regard for the welfare of the individual foremost.

Of course there has never been any clearcut opposition, in American politics, between these antithetical views. Both Democratic "New-Dealism" and Republican "Standpatism" have drawn alike upon conservative and liberal values. The practical political question has always been one of emphasis. But the issue of how much emphasis should be given to conservatism at the expense of liberalism, or vice versa, has been a dominant theme in American politics throughout the history of our institutions.

If the issue were fought out entirely at elections and in legislative halls, we would not need to mention it here. In fact, it enters at every stage of the administrative process through the decisions of the persons who execute and interpret law. An administrator operating in a conservative political climate who goes too far in his espousal of liberal values will feel political pressure, as will a conservative administrator when liberalism is politically dominant. But here again we find nooks and crannies of discretion—sometimes very sizeable spaces—into which the administrator can interject his personal values.

We can even identify whole agencies where one or the other viewpoint becomes relatively dominant. The Reconstruction Finance Corporation and the Tennessee Valley Authority provide examples of Federal agencies, established in about the same political climate, whose policies placed quite different emphasis upon conservatism and liberalism. The RFC was generally strongly dominated by a conservative viewpoint and an emphasis upon "business-like" procedures and policies. The TVA, particularly in its early period, reflected a much more liberal viewpoint.

In part this difference between the values dominant in the two agencies was simply a reflection of the differences, in our pluralistic society, in the political pressures to which they were subject. But the values held by dominant administrative personalities in the agencies were also of considerable significance. Political pressure was not needed to force Jesse Jones of the RFC to view matters from a conservative angle—in fact he resisted strong political pressures to view them otherwise. Nor can there be any doubt about the depth of David Lilienthal's attachment to the philosophy of liberalism.

Congressional awareness of the importance of administrative attitudes of this kind is reflected in the significance that Congress attaches to appointments to key administrative positions—the opposition, for example, of a conservative Congress to the appointment of Henry Wallace as Secretary of Commerce; and the insistence of Congress that top OPA positions be staffed by businessmen.

In general, recruitment procedures in American administration (with exceptions at the higher levels) are not designed to select along the lines of these attitude types. According to our merit system theory, no one is to be questioned about his political and social beliefs, let alone selected on the basis of them. Enough is known about attitude testing so that over a period of time the character of the whole bureaucracy could probably be determined. However, no conscious official effort to select one of these types rather than the other would be politically feasible—it would conflict too sharply with our general beliefs (however unrealistic these may be) about the neutrality of the public service.

Nevertheless, individual agencies or organizational units may tend, or even attempt, to get a concentration of employees holding either a conservative or a liberal attitude. What we have called the bureau philosophy generally reflects, to a greater or lesser degree, some viewpoint toward conservatism and liberalism. The particular professions from which agencies select their personnel may be strongly indoctrinated with social attitudes of the one kind or the other. Individuals will find the philosophy in some organizational units more congenial than in others, and there will consequently be a considerable degree of self-selection.

We should not exaggerate the degree to which a uniformity of social outlook is present in governmental agencies. Nevertheless, we must not overlook the importance of social attitudes in determining the value premises of decision, or the degree to which the social attitudes of the individual are modified by the climate of the organization in which he finds himself.

Is Bureaucracy Responsible?

We have now canvassed and attempted to evaluate the accountability procedures and forces in America which enforce responsiveness upon our bureaucracy and thus determine the values and goals reflected in administrative decisions. With regard to these controls we can safely say that a bureaucracy is always to some extent free from them, and the bigger and more complex it is, the more it is free. The administrator is always to some extent an initiator of values, partly as a representative of some interest group or groups, but also independently, in his own right. He can never be completely governed by others, and, as a matter of fact, he has considerable latitude of choice before the consequences of his decisions will bring reactions that threaten survival.

Perhaps because of awareness of this inevitable area of administrative discretion, writers throughout history have warned of the dangers of a large bureaucracy. Increasing recognition of the political role and actual political power of administrators has led to suggestions that managers, public and private, were slowly taking over society in a kind of managerial revolution.

Such may be the case, but it hardly need occasion alarm. "The managers" is rather a misleading phrase. We have seen that administrators do not constitute a class with a uniform outlook: they reflect all the points of view and conflicts of interest in our society. Now one point of view may dominate in a particular governmental organization, now another. Never does a single outlook, a homogeneity of interests, dominate the whole bureaucracy. The "managerial revolution" is a metaphor referring to the fact that much of the initiative in governmental problem-solving is passing to the executive branch of government.[4] But the administrators are not insulated from society like Plato's guardians. They are tied to society by all the formal procedures of accountability, by the need to satisfy politically powerful clientele groups, and by their own social training and identifications.

Strengthening Accountability Procedures

Concern about administrative responsibility or irresponsibility has led to proposals for making our government more responsible. A full discussion of such proposals would take us far beyond the scope of a book on public administration, for we are really concerned here with the whole structure of democratic institutions—political and administrative. We cannot talk of making administration more responsible without considering the organization of political interests, the mechanisms that define and record the public will, the procedures of legislative bodies, and the role of the executive. When

[4] The phrase was coined by James Burnham. See *The Managerial Revolution* (New York: John Day, 1941). Burnham was not considering government only. Indeed, his strongest evidence for the prediction of a managerial revolution was the growing divorcement of ownership and control in business corporations, and the increasing power of organization hierarchies in an increasingly organized society.

we talk of responsibility, we are talking of the imbedding of administration in the entire political and social process.

In this section we will confine ourselves to a brief mention of some of the major proposals that have been offered for improving accountability procedures, and some discussion of those proposals that involve primarily changes in administrative organization, as distinguished from reorganization of the rest of the governmental structure.

PARLIAMENTARY DEMOCRACY

Some persons have suggested that we abandon the separation of powers—and particularly the relative independence of executive and legislative branches—and adopt a parliamentary or cabinet system like that in England and most Continental democracies. Under this system, the chief executive and his cabinet are the leaders of the dominant party in the legislature, and hence, responsibility to the cabinet and responsibility to the legislature are largely merged.

How much effect upon the enforcement of responsibility such a change would bring about depends upon one's assessment of the role of interest groups in the American political process, and on this there is little unanimity of opinion. If the pluralistic structure of interests is primarily a result of the structure of our social and economic institutions, then these interests will operate in much the same way under parliamentary as under presidential democracy—although the formal channels they would employ might be altered. If, as some believe, the fragmentation of interests is in part a result of the separation of powers and the fragmentation of legislative bodies into committees, a change in the structure would have an important effect upon policies of government. Unfortunately, the evidence on this crucial question is highly inconclusive.[5]

STRENGTHENING THE CHIEF EXECUTIVE

Management-minded students of government in our country have for a long time argued that bureaucratic responsibility can

[5] The literature on this subject is voluminous. The reader who wishes to explore the question further may well begin with Don K. Price, "The Parliamentary and Presidential Systems," *Public Administration Review* 3:317–34 (Autumn 1943); and "A Response to Mr. Laski," ibid., 4:360–3 (Autumn 1944); and Harold J. Laski, "The Parliamentary and Presidential Systems," ibid., 4:347–59 (Autumn, 1944).

only be achieved through strengthened executive controls. The Hoover Commission reports illustrate this point of view, as does the entire state reorganization movement and the 1937 report of the President's Committee on Administrative Management. We have already discussed some of the difficulties in this viewpoint in Chapter 24—both the limitations of hierarchical controls, and the degree to which the chief executive is responsive to the same political pressures as the legislature. Other problems are raised when we ask not only whether the chief executive *can* be strengthened, but whether he *should* be—e.g., the implications of the strong independent executive for accountability to the legislature and the courts.[6]

INDEPENDENT REGULATORY COMMISSIONS

Almost diametrically opposed to the foregoing proposal has been the attempt to reduce the responsiveness of some administrative agencies to the chief executive—to "take them out of politics." One method that is often suggested for isolating governmental programs from "politics" is to entrust these programs to independent regulatory commissions.

The independent regulatory commission is an agency with a plural executive—that is, it is headed by a board or commission. The commission membership is often required to represent both major political parties. The terms of office of commissioners are generally longer than that of the chief executive, and are staggered so that the chief executive cannot appoint a majority during any one term. In the Federal government, appointments must receive Senate approval, and removals may only be made for specified causes. Similar provisions govern the appointment and removal of most state and local independent commissions. By these means it is hoped to reduce executive control over the agency, and hence the agency's responsiveness to the values represented by the chief executive. Examples of independent regulatory commissions are the Federal Trade Commission, the National Labor Relations Board, state utility commissions, and city planning boards.

Independent regulatory commissions are often established when regulation of a new area of the economy is undertaken, on the theories: that the new venture should be left alone to feel its way

6 See Waldo, *The Administrative State*, chap. 8.

and develop new standards and methods; it should not be made subject to all the accountability processes of political democracy; and especially, that it should be responsive to the legislative policy declared in its enabling statute, and not to executive directives. As noted previously, the U. S. Supreme Court has on one occasion said that these commissions are agents of the legislature, not the executive, and that they are responsible only to the law as made by Congress and interpreted by the courts.

We have already seen that accountability to Congress and the courts is necessarily very limited. Therefore, if independent commissions need not be responsive to the will of the chief executive, does it follow that they are responsive only to the values held by board members? Experience indicates otherwise. To survive, these organizations, even more than others, must be responsive to their clientele, and particularly to the groups they regulate. The problem of "independence" of regulatory commissions is most often a problem, then, of securing independence from the regulated groups. The only place where support can be sought for such independence is from the legislature and from the executive who appoints commission members, and this brings them back into the same political arena from which their formal independence was supposed to remove them.

Independent commissions are often urged for "service" programs as well as regulatory programs. In particular, many municipal libraries, recreation departments, and even fire and police departments are headed by independent boards. Here, the pressure for an independent plural executive usually comes from groups interested in the agency's program. Thus the American Library Association has been the strongest proponent for library boards, the National Fire Protection Association for boards of fire commissioners, and so on. To these groups, "taking an agency out of politics" means placing it in the hands of the experts who are identified with the program values. In urging this course of action, the professional groups concerned are undoubtedly sincere, and undoubtedly naive about the nature of the political process.

GOVERNMENTAL CORPORATIONS

Another arrangement that is often proposed for removing agencies from "political" control is to give them corporate form.

The arguments for governmental corporations (such as the TVA, the RFC, and the Inland Waterways Corporation) are somewhat different from the arguments for the independent commission— although the corporation is usually headed by a commission or board, rather than a single executive. In the case of the corporation it is argued that if a governmental activity is similar to an activity conducted by private business corporations, it should be organized in a manner resembling as closely as possible a business corporation. Thus, the corporate form has been most often adopted for governmental "business enterprises" like generating and distributing electricity, operating barges, making loans, and the like.

The government corporation is not just a matter of a name, however. To have these business-like activities conducted more like businesses, it is necessary to remove some of the controls usually imposed on regular governmental departments so that the corporation will have more independence and freedom to run its own affairs, like private business corporations. Thus the governmental corporation is usually freed from most or many of the personnel, budget, accounting, and expenditure controls imposed on other government agencies. The corporation is a device for freeing an agency from such controls without attacking the rationale of these controls in general. It would be difficult to decide, for example, that personnel activities in the Agricultural Marketing Administration shall no longer be subject to control by the U. S. Civil Service Commission. It might be possible to decide that this agency will henceforth be a government corporation (and hence automatically free from such control).

Some persons appear to believe that calling a government agency a corporation will change the attitudes of the courts to the agency. Specifically, they appear to believe that courts will treat these agencies like private corporations, allowing them to sue and be sued and, in general, equalizing the legal status of these organizations and competing or associated private firms. The courts have shown a little more sophistication than this, however, and in general have treated them like any other governmental organizations.

Anything a governmental corporation is allowed to do that other agencies are not allowed to do, and any freedom from restriction imposed on other agencies, are the results of legislative enactment. The legislature can legally free any agency from personnel, budget, or any other control by simple enactment. It need not call the agency a corporation to do this. The legislature can allow the Post Office Department to sue and be sued, to spend its receipts without appropriation, or to borrow money on its own securities, without calling it a corporation. However, in the climate of opinion in which we live, all of these things would be more feasible politically if the Post Office Department were called a corporation. It may be that for some kinds of proposed new governmental activities, opposition to undertaking the activity would be much less if the agency charged with it were given corporate status with the usual independence from executive and overhead controls associated with that status. The corporate form connotes sound business methods, and independence from hierarchical controls may enhance clientele influence.

OTHER PROPOSALS

There have been other suggestions for improving responsiveness. One, the more extensive use of interest group consultative arrangements, has already been discussed at some length. Consultative arrangements formalize the influences of clientele groups. They require administrators to give some thought to who *ought* to be represented, and thus rationalize somewhat the representation of interested parties. Many persons feel that formal consultative arrangements are good because they bring interest group influence out into the open. Apart from the fact that the group influences brought to bear on administration by consultative arrangements are not actually "in the open," this point of view seems a little too sanguine because consultative arrangements are *in addition to*, not *in substitution for*, the less formal methods of clientele influence.

Conclusion

Is American public administration responsible? One way of answering the question is to say that if organizations survive in a democracy, they are being responsive to the goals and values promoted by the democratic political processes. Certainly we have presented sufficient evidence to show that the path of survival in this country is not an easy one—that administrative organizations are, indeed, responsive to a multitude of forces.

This is not the same as saying: "What is, is right." The procedures of accountability we have today are not the only possible procedures. We have suggested some of the alternatives in the preceding section, and have raised some of the questions of fact and of value that will have to be settled before we can make an intelligent choice among them. Our analysis has shown, of course, that the problem is much deeper than the simple rearrangement of organizational boxes on the chart, or the revision of formal procedures. Really fundamental changes in responsibility involve equally fundamental changes in the whole political structure.

But even if we accept the present accountability procedures as given, we still have an opportunity as individuals to participate in these procedures. As individuals in a democratic society we can criticize surviving, and even flourishing, administrative organizations. Our criticism, if it becomes widespread enough, enters into the survival picture, becomes a part of the political process, and forces changes in administration.

We have pointed out that the administrator still has many alternative ways of doing things within the limits imposed by the requirements of survival. He still has the power to bring us satisfaction or irritation and frustration. If we do not like what the administrator does within his residual area of freedom—if we do not like the policeman's lack of manners—we can do something about it. We may not be able to do anything alone, but we can try to find others who feel as we do, and with whom we may combine forces. Then, what was previously a matter of discretion to the administrator may be moved into the area of the political process—the administrator may have to change his ways to survive.

If people are lethargic, the administrator may have a wide area of freedom of choice. If they are alert and willing to give some effort to their government, they may bring more of the administrator's decisions within the controls of the political process. If survival is the test of responsibility, an alert citizenry can change the conditions of survival. Today, as always, eternal vigilance is the price of freedom.

Bibliographical Notes

THE footnotes in this book have been limited for the most part to supplementary comment and references on specific points in the text. These bibliographical notes are added for the reader who wishes to pursue further his study of public administration. We include basic materials that we drew upon in building our general framework and approach, important materials not usually considered under the heading of "public administration" that have a direct bearing upon that field, and further reading in important areas that are treated only briefly in the text.

The notes that follow are not intended to be a complete bibliography of the field of public administration. Those interested in systematic coverage of the literature may refer to Cathryn Seckler-Hudson, *Bibliography on Public Administration—Annotated* (Washington, 1949) and Alfred de Grazia, *Human Relations in Public Administration* (Chicago, 1949). Albert Lepawsky's *Administration* (New York, 1949), while not a bibliography but a collection of selections, includes copious references to writings in public administration and related fields.

In our comments we have sought merely to indicate the general slant of the references cited, and not to analyze the content. Where particular areas have been covered adequately in the footnote references of the text, these have not generally been repeated. More extensive references are cited for the earlier chapters than for the later, because many of the basic ideas presented in these earlier chapters are simply carried further and developed in subsequent chapters. Some areas are lacking in references because they have not yet been extensively studied from the general viewpoint taken in this book.

CHAPTER ONE

THE general approach to administration as a system of cooperative behavior has its main origins in sociological writings. Among the most important of these, with a direct bearing on administration, are Max Weber's *The Protestant Ethic and the Spirit of Capitalism* (London, 1930) and *The*

Theory of Social and Economic Organization (ed. by L. J. Henderson and Talcott Parsons, New York, 1947); Emile Durkheim's *The Division of Labor in Society* (Glencoe, 1948); Vilfredo Pareto's *The Mind and Society* (New York, 1935); and Talcott Parsons' *The Structure of Social Action* (Glencoe, 1949).

Works dealing specifically with administrative organizations include Chester I. Barnard, *The Functions of the Executive* (Cambridge, 1938); Fritz J. Roethlisberger and William J. Dickson, *Management and the Worker* (Cambridge, 1939); Herbert A. Simon, *Administrative Behavior* (New York, 1947); and Victor A. Thompson, *The Regulatory Process in OPA Rationing* (New York, 1950). Perhaps the best survey of the more traditional approach is to be found in Luther Gulick and L. Urwick (eds.), *Papers on the Science of Administration* (New York, 1937).

On the relationships between public and private administration see Henri Fayol, *Industrial and General Administration* (London, 1920); Dan Throop Smith, "Education for Administration," *Harvard Business Review*, Spring, 1945; Paul Appleby, *Big Democracy* (New York, 1945); and Robert A. Brady, "Bureaucracy in Business," *Journal of Social Issues*, 1:32–43 (1945). On the attitudes toward the conduct of public and private officials, see Barbara Wootton, "On Public and Private Honesty," *Political Quarterly*, 16:213–23 (1945); and John Vieg, "Growth of Public Administration" in Fritz Morstein Marx (ed.), *Elements of Public Administration* (New York, 1946).

Public administration as a study of the executive branch of the government originated, both in terms and in outlook, from the article by Woodrow Wilson, "The Study of Administration," *Political Science Quarterly*, 2:197–222 (June, 1887). The demarcation of the field was based largely upon a rigid distinction between politics and administration. See Frank Goodnow, *Politics and Administration* (New York, 1900).

On the study of public administration see George A. Graham, *Education for Public Administration* (Chicago, 1941); and Frederick F. Blachly, "Educational Training for Administration in America," *Public Administration*, 3:159–63 (1925). References on the philosophical problems of the relation between fact and value will be cited below in Chapter Three. As to the scientific nature of public administration, see Robert A. Dahl, "The Science of Public Administration: Three Problems," *Public Administration Review* 7:1–11 (1947); also Herbert A. Simon, "A Comment on the 'Science of Public Administration,'" *Public Administration Review*, 7:201–03 (1947); Alexander Leighton, *The Governing of Men* (Princeton, 1945), Appendix; and, Gunnar Myrdal, *An American Dilemma* (2 vols., New York, 1944), Appendix IV; on the nature of the scientific method consult Morris R. Cohen, "Scientific Method," *Encyclopaedia of the Social Sciences*, Vol. V, pp. 389–95 (1937).

CHAPTER TWO

PERHAPS the most original and provocative work on the origin of organizations is Grace Longwell Coyle, *The Social Process in Organized Groups* (New York, 1930). This book is concerned with voluntary, rather than governmental organizations, but the propositions advanced apply equally well to both. Important case studies, upon which we have drawn in the text, include John M. Gaus and Leon O. Wolcott, *Public Administration and the United States Department of Agriculture* (Chicago, 1940); Arthur W. Macmahon, John D. Millett, and Gladys Ogden, *The Administration of Federal Work Relief* (Chicago, 1941); and Otto L. Nelson, Jr., *National Security and the General Staff* (Washington, 1946). Extensive new case materials are now being made available by the Committee on Public Administration Cases.

John W. Forsythe, "The Legislative History of the Fair Labor Standards Act," *Law and Contemporary Problems*, 6:464–90 (1939) presents an interesting if somewhat legalistic analysis of the origin of the Wages and Hours Administration. The war histories, some of which have been published, give some valuable, if not always frank, data on the creation and development of particular agencies—e.g., W. J. Wilson, J. A. Hart, and George R. Taylor, *The Beginnings of OPA*.

The social and cultural environment of governmental administration early attracted the attention of foreign visitors to America, who produced such insightful, pre-scientific analyses as Alexis DeToqueville, *Democracy in America* (2 vols., New York, 1946), and Lord Bryce, *The American Commonwealth* (New York, 1893). More recently, the "American culture" has been examined by Dennis Brogan, *The American Character* (New York, 1944), and Harold Laski, *American Democracy* (New York, 1947). For a comparative view of the social environment of bureaucracy see Carl J. Friedrich, *Constitutional Government and Democracy* (Boston, 1946).

We can cite only one or two of the most relevant examples of the numerous community studies made by sociologists and anthropologists. Some attention is given to the place of government in the social structure by Robert and Helen Lynd, *Middletown* (New York, 1929), and *Middletown in Transition* (New York, 1937); in W. Lloyd Warner and associates, *Yankee City* (6 vols., New York, 1941–5); and John Dollard, *Caste and Class in a Southern Town* (New Haven, 1937).

The sampling of public opinion, attitudes, and behaviors through polls has cast much light on problems of administration, and promises to cast much more. Examples of fruitful studies using these techniques are Samuel Stouffer, *et al.*, *The American Soldier* (Princeton, 1949), which contains valuable data on motivation and the conditions affecting morale and obedience; and Kinsey, Pomeroy, and Martin, *Sexual Behavior of the*

Human Male (Philadelphia, 1947), which contrasts law and mores with actualities in the realm of sexual behavior.

Perhaps the best sources on the character of innovation are biographical. A few examples are William Alanson White, *Autobiography of a Purpose* (New York, 1938); Lord Haldane, *Autobiography* (New York, 1929); Alpheus Mason, *Brandeis: A Free Man's Life* (New York, 1946); and Ralph Korngold, *Two Friends of Man* (Boston, 1950). The political aspects of innovation are even better documented. Examples are Peter Odegard's study of the anti-saloon league, *Pressure Group: The Story of the Anti-Saloon League* (New York, 1928); Frances Perkins, *The Roosevelt I Knew* (New York, 1946); and Robert Sherwood, *Roosevelt and Hopkins* (New York, 1948).

On states' rights see Herbert Hoover, *A Challenge to Liberty* (New York, 1934); Harold Gosnell, *Grass Roots Politics* (Washington, 1942); V. O. Key, *Southern Politics* (New York, 1949). Some of the most critical and interesting analyses of the notion of "a government of laws" have come from the lawyers themselves. In particular see Jerome Frank, *Law and the Modern Mind* (New York, 1930); *If Men Were Angels* (New York, 1942); and *Courts on Trial* (Princeton, 1949); also, Thurman Arnold, *Symbols of Government* (New Haven, 1934). On the question of the independent boards and commissions see The President's Committee on Administrative Management, *Report* (Washington, 1937) for an integrationist view. For the contrary see Harvey Walker, *Public Administration in the United States* (New York, 1937). For an acute analysis of both points of view see Schuyler Wallace, *Federal Departmentalization* (New York, 1941).

CHAPTER THREE

THE problem of factual and value premises—the means-ends problem—is treated here in terms which are largely those of the logical positivists. On the philosophical level this is discussed at length in Charles W. Morris, *Foundation of the Theory of Signs;* Rudolf Carnap, *Foundations of Logic and Mathematics* in the International Encyclopedia of Unified Science, Volume I, Nos. 2 and 3 (Chicago, 1937 and 1938); P. W. Bridgman, *The Logic of Modern Physics* (New York, 1937); and Alfred J. Ayer, *Language Truth and Logic* (London, 1936). A briefer review is contained in Morris Cohen and Ernest Nagel, *An Introduction to Logic and Scientific Method* (New York, 1934).

Attention was turned to the non-rational aspects of human behavior by Sigmund Freud, *Introductory Lectures in Psychoanalysis* (New York, 1938); Vilfredo Pareto, *The Mind and Society;* and Emile Durkheim, *Suicide* (Glencoe, 1950), and *Philosophy and Sociology* (Glencoe, 1950). See also, Charles Cooley, *Human Nature and the Social Order* (New York, 1902) and William Graham Sumner, *Folkways* (Boston, 1906).

On incentives in administration, see Barnard, *The Functions of the Executive;* Talcott Parsons, "The Motivation of Economic Activities," in *Essays in Sociological Theory* (Glencoe, 1949); Robert K. Merton, "Bureaucratic Structure and Personality," in *Social Theory and Social Structure* (Glencoe, 1949); Dollard, Doob, *et al.*, *Frustration and Aggression* (New Haven, 1939); Roethlisberger and Dickson, *Management and the Worker;* Allison Davis, "The Motivation of Underprivileged Workers," in W. F. Whyte (ed.), *Industry and Society* (New York, 1946); Clinton S. Golden and Harold J. Ruttenberg, "Motives for Union Membership," in Schuyler Dean Hoslett (ed.), *Human Factors in Management* (New York, 1946); M. L. Blum and J. Russ, "A Study of Employee Attitudes Towards Various Incentives," *Personnel*, 19:438–44 (1942); Burleigh Gardner, *Human Relations in Industry* (Chicago, 1945). The problem of incentives is directly related to the structure of identification groups, and more information bearing on this question will be cited in the bibliography for Chapters Four and Five.

On the role of personality in informal group meetings, see Kurt Lewin and associates, "An Experimental Study of the Effect of Democratic and Authoritarian Group Atmospheres," in *Studies in Topological and Vector Psychology*, No. 1 (University of Iowa, Iowa City); see also Kurt Lewin, *Resolving Social Conflicts* (New York, 1948).

The influence of childhood experiences upon adult behavior has long been the subject of intensive study. A few examples of important investigations in this area are Kurt Lewin, "Environmental Forces in Child Behavior and Development" in Carl Murchison (ed.), *Handbook of Child Psychology* (Worcester, 1931), pp. 94–127; Jean Piaget, *Moral Judgment of the Child* (Glencoe, 1949); Abram Kardiner, *The Psychological Frontiers of Society* (New York, 1945), a study of child-rearing techniques in various societies and their relation to the adult personality.

The impact of the community upon the individual has been studied extensively by anthropologists and others. B. Malinowski, *Crime and Custom in Savage Society* (London, 1926); and *Coral Gardens and Their Magic* (New York, 1935); Ruth Benedict, *Patterns of Culture* (New York, 1946); Karl Llewellyn and E. A. Hoebel, *Cheyenne Way* (Norman, 1941); M. Fortes and E. E. Evans Pritchard (eds.), *African Political Systems* (London, 1940); Melville Herskovits, *Man and His Works* (New York, 1948) all point up the way in which the society drills patterns of behavior into its members. On modern societies, see Erich Fromm, *Escape from Freedom* (New York, 1941); John Embree, *Suye Mura* (Chicago, 1939); Karen Horney, *The Neurotic Personality of Our Time* (New York, 1937); and A. H. Maslow, "The Authoritarian Character Structure," *The Journal of Social Psychology*, 18:421–44 (1943).

The inculcation of group loyalty into the individual is discussed by

Charles Merriam, *The Making of Citizens* (Chicago, 1931). Supporting monographs by Samuel Harper, John M. Gaus, Oscar Jaszi, Herbert W. Schneider, Paul Kosok, Robert C. Brooks, Carleton J. H. Hayes, Bessie L. Pierce, and Elizabeth Weber trace in detail the methods used in various societies. See also V. O. Key, *Politics, Parties and Pressure Groups* (2nd ed., New York, 1947), Chapter 21; and A. B. Hollingshead, *Elmstown's Youth* (New York, 1948).

On personality and politics, the pioneering study is that of Harold D. Lasswell, *Psychopathology and Politics* (Chicago, 1930) which brings psychoanalytic theory to the analysis of political problems. Although the idea of unconscious motivation is basically Freudian, it is accepted today by most psychologists. On the breakdown of the personality in crisis situations see the excellent study by Roy R. Grinker and John A. Spiegel, *Men Under Stress* (Philadelphia, 1945), dealing with the psychiatric problems of air force personnel. For a good summary of materials on frustration in industry see Norman R. F. Maier, *Psychology in Industry* (New York, 1946). See also Joseph M. Goldsen and Lillian Low, "Manager Meets Union: A Case Study of Personal Immaturity," in Hoslett, *Human Factors in Management*.

The relation of the individual to the work situation—particularly the informal organization—is the main subject matter of the next two chapters, and material relevant to this problem will be cited there. On the problem of loyalties to outside groups, the most extensive literature, as one might expect, relates to the problem of union-management relations. See Fritz Roethlisberger, *Management and Morale* (Cambridge, 1944); Neil W. Chamberlain, *The Union Challenge to Management Control* (New York, 1948); C. S. Golden and H. J. Ruttenberg, *The Dynamics of an Industrial Democracy* (New York, 1942). On the conflict of values of business men temporarily working for the government during wartime, see Bruce Catton, *Warlords of Washington* (New York, 1948).

CHAPTERS FOUR AND FIVE

THE nature of the face-to-face relationship was explored very early by Charles Cooley, who labeled this the "primary group." See Cooley, *Human Nature and the Social Order*. For a review of the sociological data concerning primary groups see Edward Shils, *The Present State of American Sociology* (Glencoe, 1948); for a summary of the materials concerning the psychological process of group formation, see M. Sherif and H. Cantril, *The Psychology of Ego-Involvements* (New York, 1947) which also contains an elaborate bibliography of the data in this field.

Loyalty to the work group and the way in which such loyalty is enforced is examined in Roethlisberger and Dickson, *Management and the Worker;* Stouffer, *et al., The American Soldier;* Maier, *Psychology in Industry;* and, Gardner, *Human Relations in Industry.* On the psychology of identification, see Gordon Allport, "The Psychology of Participation," *Psychological Review* 53:117–32 (1945); M. Sherif, *The Psychology of Social Norms* (New York, 1936); Floyd Allport, *Social Psychology* (Boston, 1924); and J. T. MacCurdy, *The Structure of Morale* (New York, 1943).

On methods for measuring morale, see Conrad M. Arensberg and Douglas MacGregor, "Determination of Morale in an Industrial Company," *Applied Anthropology,* I (January–March, 1942). See also Goodwin Watson (ed.), *Civilian Morale* (New York, 1942). For a broad methodological discussion of the method of studying small groups, see Robert F. Bales, *Interaction Process Analysis* (Cambridge, 1950).

The problem of extra-organizational identifications is considered by Barnard, Coyle, Mayo, Roethlisberger, Gardner, and many others. An interesting study of the breakdown of organizational identifications and the development of loyalty to an outside group is contained in Warner and Low, *The Social System of the Modern Factory* (New Haven, 1945). Neil W. Chamberlain, *The Union Challenge to Management Control* examines the problem as it relates to labor unions.

On the role of the leader, see Chester I. Barnard, "The Nature of Leadership," and "Dilemmas of Leadership in the Democratic Process" in his *Organization and Management* (Cambridge, 1948); Douglas MacGregor, "The Conditions of Effective Leadership," in Hoslett, *Human Factors in Management.* On the relations between leadership and the adjustment of the worker, see J. McV. Hunt, *Personality and Behavior Disorders* (New York, 1944). On re-training supervisory personnel, see J. R. P. French, Jr., "Re-training an Autocratic Leader," *Journal of Abnormal and Social Psychology,* 34:224–37 (1944); also J. L. Moreno (ed.), *Group Psychotherapy* (New York, 1945); H. Meltzer, "Humanizing Relations of Key Persons," in Hoslett, *Human Factors in Management.* Gringer and Spiegel, *Men Under Stress,* present the most exhaustive report.

On the contrary tugs on the loyalty of the leader, see Fritz J. Roethlisberger, "The Foreman: Master and Victim of Double Talk," in Hoslett, *Human Factors in Management.* The same author's *Management and Morale* also considers this problem as does Gardner, *Human Relations in Industry.* Perhaps the most complete empirical study is Stouffer, *et al., The American Solder,* Volume 1, Chapter VIII. A novel based on this theme is William Wister Haines, *Command Decision* (Boston, 1947) which is concerned with decisions of Air Force generals during the war.

On the development and protection of group values, the most complete study is that of Roethlisberger and Dickson. Much of the material already cited contains either an implicit or an explicit examination of this point.

On restriction of output see Orvis Collins, Melville Dalton, and Donald Roy, "Restriction of Output and Social Cleavage in Industry," *Applied Anthropology* 5:1–14 (1946); Robert N. McMurry, "The Problem of Resistance to Change in Industry," *Journal of Applied Anthropology*, 31: 589–93 (1947); S. B. Mathewson, *Restriction of Output among Unorganized Workers* (New York, 1931). Status and its relation to group values is treated in detail in Chapter Nine and material will be cited at that point.

On group consultation and democratic leadership see Elton Mayo, *Social Problems of an Industrial Civilization* (Cambridge, 1945). On specific problems and techniques of group consultation, Thompson, *The Regulatory Process in O.P.A. Rationing* shows the advantages and limitations of the techniques used in wartime rationing. See also Robert L. Hubbell, "Techniques for making Committees Effective," *Public Administration Review* 6:348–53 (1946).

CHAPTERS SIX AND SEVEN

THE division of work has been the subject of increasing interest as organization has become more complex. On the theoretical level see Weber, *Social and Economic Organization*, and Durkheim, *The Division of Labor in Society*.

In the United States, the division of labor has been a central interest of the scientific management movement. See Frederick W. Taylor, *Scientific Management* (New York, 1947); and Frank B. Gilbreth, *Primer of Scientific Management* (New York, 1912). Recognition by the scientific management movement of the "human factor" in work organizations began with the Hawthorne studies, reported by Roethlisberger and Dickson. This growing awareness that human behavior *is* organization is reflected in a set of Harvard Business School cases, John D. Glover and Ralph M. Hower, *The Administrator* (Chicago, 1949). The human relations approach has produced a good deal of raw data from which a theory may be built. See, for example, W. F. Whyte (ed.), *Industry and Society* (New York, 1946).

Perhaps the most complete attempts to construct theories of organized behavior are Barnard, *The Functions of the Executive;* Simon, *Administrative Behavior;* and Phillip Selznick, "Foundation of the Theory of Organization," *American Sociological Review* 13:25–35 (1948).

In public administration, the division of work has largely been dealt with in terms of organization units. Leonard D. White, *Introduction to the Study of Public Administration* (New York, 1925) and W. F. Willoughby, *Principles of Public Administration* (Washington, 1927) pioneered in an effort to find principles of public administration to guide in dividing the work. Although there have been some modifications of their points of view, these works set the tone of public administration. Luther Gulick's "Notes on the Theory of Organization" in Luther Gulick and Lyndall Urwick (eds.), *Papers on the Science of Administration* (New York, 1937) provided students of public administration with a systematic statement of this theory of the division of work.

There has been criticism of these principles. Charles S. Hyneman, "Administrative Reorganization: An Adventure into Science and Theology," *Journal of Politics*, 1:62–75 (February, 1939) contains a biting criticism of the state reorganization movement in particular; Schuyler Wallace, *Federal Departmentalization* (New York, 1941) raises a skeptical eyebrow at the proposals of the President's Committee On Administrative Management and others; Simon, *Administrative Behavior*, Chapter II, attacks the traditional principles as "proverbs" containing logical contradiction; Macmahon, Millett, and Ogden, *Administration of Federal Work Relief* raise serious questions concerning the unity of command; Robert A. Dahl, "Validity of Organization Theory," *Public Administration Review* 7:281–3 (Autumn, 1947), gives a devastating criticism of the "principles" approach.

CHAPTERS EIGHT AND NINE

THE political pluralists were perhaps the first to challenge the monolithic theory of sovereignty. But their concern was with "rights" and "duties" of persons in society rather than the psychology of authority. For examples of the pluralist argument, see Harold J. Laski, *A Grammar of Politics* (New Haven, 1925); *The Problem of Sovereignty* (New Haven, 1917); *Authority in the Modern State* (New Haven, 1919); Leon Duguit, *Law in the Modern State* (tr. by Harold and Freda Laski, New York, 1919); on the application of the pluralistic idea to a specific institution, see J. N. Figgis, *Churches in the Modern State* (London, 1913).

Perhaps first to challenge the traditional notions of authority in administration was Mary Parker Follett. See her *New State* (New York, 1918); *Creative Experience* (New York, 1924); and the collection of her papers, H. C. Metcalf and Lyndall Urwick (eds.), *Dynamic Administration: The Collected Papers of Mary Parker Follett* (New York, 1942).

The idea of legitimacy was systematically examined by Weber and Durkheim in particular. For its development see Parsons, *The Structure of Social Action*. The term, as it is used here, is somewhat similar to that used by Barnard, *The Functions of the Executive* and Simon, *Administrative Behavior*, although it is somewhat further developed in these chapters. See also Selznick, "Foundation of the Theory of Organization." On the limits of authority, see Bruno Bettelheim, "Individual and Mass Behavior in Extreme Situations," *Journal of Abnormal and Social Psychology* 38:417–52 (1943); Alexander Leighton, *The Governing of Men;* and Stouffer, *et al.,*

The American Soldier. On the nature of composite decisions and the decision making process, see Paul Appleby, *Big Democracy;* and *Policy and Administration* (University, Alabama, 1949).

The psychology of obedience is a very important consideration in the relationship of the individual to the organization, and many references have been cited in Chapter Three. The nature and the psychological underpinnings of charisma are examined in a very sophisticated form in Donald W. Calhoun's forthcoming *Psychology of Subordination.* The "rule of anticipated reactions" was introduced by Carl J. Friedrich, "Public Policy and the Nature of Administrative Responsibility," *Public Policy* (Cambridge, 1940) Volume 1.

For a theoretical analysis of the problem of stratification see "An Analytical Approach to a Theory of Social Stratification," in *Essays in Sociological Theory* by Talcott Parsons; Kingsley Davis, "Conceptual Analyses of Stratification" *American Sociological Review* 7:309–21 (1942); and Chester I. Barnard, "Functions and Pathology of Status Systems in Formal Organizations," in Whyte, *Industry and Society.* For a review of the material in this field, see Edward Shils, *Present State of American Sociology.* For an empirical study see Warner and Lunt, *The Status System of a Modern Community;* James West, *Plainville, U.S.A.* (New York, 1945); Harold Kauffman, *Prestige Classes in a New York Rural Community* (Cornell University Agricultural Experiment Station Memoir, 260, 1944); A. B. Hollingshead, *Elmstown's Youth;* for a study of a foreign community see Martin Yang, *Chinese Village* (New York, 1945); on special problems see W. Lloyd Warner and Leo Srole, *The Social Systems of American Ethnic Groups* (New Haven, 1946); Franklin Frazier, *The Negro Family in the United States* (Chicago, 1939).

For general considerations of the problem of status and role, see John W. Bennett and M. M. Tumin, *Social Life* (New York, 1948); Richard Centers, *The Psychology of Social Classes* (Princeton, 1949); on the prestige levels granted various professions, see W. Coutu, "The Relative Prestige of Twenty Professions," *Social Forces* 14:522–9 (1936); Mapheous Smith, "An Empirical Scale of Prestige Status of Occupations," *American Sociological Review*, 8:185–92 (1943).

On status rankings in the industrial situation see the Hawthorne studies and the writings of that group. See also Burleigh Gardner, "The Factory as a Social System," in Whyte, *Industry and Society;* and Norman R. F. Maier, *Psychology in Industry.*

CHAPTERS TEN AND ELEVEN

On a philosophical level, the problem of communication is considered by Suzanne K. Langer, *Philosophy in a New Key* (Cambridge, 1942); Rudolf

Carnap, *The Logical Syntax of Language;* Charles W. Morris, *Sign, Language and Behavior* (New York, 1946); A. N. Whitehead, *Symbolism: Its Meaning and Effects* (New York, 1927); Ernst Cassirer, *Language and Myth* (New York, 1946), and his *Myth of the State* (New Haven, 1946); Ogden and Richards, *On the Meaning of Meaning* (London, 1923); and Frederick Bodmer (Lancelot Hogben, ed.) *The Loom of Language* (New York, 1944).

On a more popular level the most significant studies are those of the students of semantics. Although sometimes oversimplified, these studies do indicate some of the problems arising from the use and misuse of words. See for example, S. I. Hayakawa, *Language in Action* (New York, 1939) and Stuart Chase, *The Tyranny of Words* (New York, 1940). See also the magazine *ETC.* published by the Institute for General Semantics.

Beginning after the First World War, there was a dawning realization, not only of the power of public opinion, but also of the manipulatibility of such opinion. Walter Lippmann, *Public Opinion* (New York, 1922) made what was probably the first systematic analysis of the nature of public opinion. Harold D. Lasswell, *Propaganda Technique in the World War* (New York, 1927) raised the question as to the influence of mass media in directing that opinion. Since that time interest in mass communication has increased. Lasswell, Casey, and Smith, *Propaganda, Communication and Public Opinion* (Princeton, 1946) cites more than 2500 references to relevant books and articles on the subject. Most of the attention, however, has been directed toward a study of the influence and effect of mass media, rather than to organizational communication.

A great deal of effort has been made to set up empirical tests of content. The administrator should be able to use such devices both on incoming and outgoing communications. See, for example, Harold Lasswell, *Analyzing the Content of Mass Communication* (Washington, 1941); N. C. Leites and I. Pool, *On Content Analysis* (Washington, 1942); A. Geller, D. Kaplan, and H. D. Lasswell, *The Differential Use of Flexible and Rigid Procedures of Content Analysis* (Washington, 1942); I. Janis, R. Fadner, and M. Janowitz, *Reliability of Content Analysis Technique* (Washington, 1942); H. D. Lasswell, "Some Provisional Categories for the Analysis of Symbolic Data," *Psychiatry* 1:197–204 (1937); Milton Stewart, "Importance in Content Analysis: A Validity Problem," *Journalism Quarterly* 20:286–93 (December, 1943).

The ability of the administrator to know how the clientele and others are reacting to his program has been made much easier by another branch of communications research—the development of the public opinion poll. Since this concerns mainly the execution of programs, materials will be cited in Chapter Twenty-three.

Available data on organizational communication is extremely scanty.

On a general level, both Barnard, *Functions of the Executive* and Simon, *Administrative Behavior* deal with the problem. There are also some insights on scattered aspects of the problem. For example, J. J. Corson, "Weak Links in the Chain of Command," *Public Opinion Quarterly* 9:346-9 (1945) recognizes that blockages in the communications system can hinder commands. Rudolph Flesch, *The Art of Plain Talk* (New York, 1946) recognizes the problem of barriers due to overly difficult language. Roethlisberger, *Management and Morale*, points up the problem of language difficulties due to status differences as does Gardner, *Human Relations in Industry*. Leighton, *The Governing of Men*, notes the problem as it relates to differing frames of reference. Stouffer, *et al.*, *The American Soldier*, also points this up in connection with the relations between officers and their men. The problem of administrative communication needs not only systematic statement but systematic research.

CHAPTERS TWELVE, THIRTEEN, AND FOURTEEN

On the orthodox concepts of staff, line, and auxiliary functions see Leonard D. White, *An Introduction to the Study of Public Administration* (3rd edition, New York, 1948); John B. Thurston, "Managerial Control Through Industrial Engineering," U. S. Bureau of the Budget, *Conference on Organization and Methods Work, First Series, 1946;* Marshall E. Dimock, *The Executive in Action* (New York, 1945); Fritz Morstein Marx, *The President and his Staff Services* (Chicago, 1947); John Millett, "Working Concepts of Organization," in Fritz Morstein Marx (ed.), *Elements of Public Administration* (New York, 1946); The President's Committee on Administrative Management, "The White House Staff," *Administrative Management in the Government of the United States* (1937); and, finally, of course, the Hoover Commission Report.

On the trend toward centralization as a general social phenomenon, see the monographs of the Temporary National Economic Committee; Robert Brady, *Business as a System of Power* (New York, 1942); Adolf A. Berle and Gardiner C. Means, *Modern Corporations and Private Property* (New York, 1933); James Burnham, *The Managerial Revolution* (New York, 1941); Joseph Schumpeter, *Capitalism, Socialism and Democracy* (New York, 1943); Karl Polanyi, *The Great Transformation* (New York, 1944).

Political scientists have treated centralization largely in terms of area rather than decision-making. See, for example, George C. S. Benson, *The New Centralization* (New York, 1941); also David B. Truman, *Administrative Decentralization* (Chicago, 1940); George C. S. Benson, "A Plea for Administrative Decentralization," *Public Administration Review* 7:170-8

(Summer, 1947); Carle C. Zimmerman, "Centralism versus Localism in the Community," *American Sociological Review* 3:155–66 (1938); James W. Fesler, *Area and Administration* (University, Alabama, 1949); Graduate School, U. S. Department of Agriculture, *Washington-Field Relations in the Federal Service* (Washington, 1942).

For a criticism of the trend toward centralization in decision-making see Williard N. Hogan, "A Dangerous Tendency in Government," *Public Administration Review* 6:235–41 (Summer, 1946). A contrary view is contained in O. Glenn Stahl, "Straight Talk about Label Thinking," *Public Administration Review* 6:362–7 (Autumn, 1946). See also George W. Bergquist, "Coordinating Staffs—are they really Dangerous?" *Public Administration Review* 7:179–83 (Summer, 1947); Felix A. Nigro, "Some Views on the Staff Function," *Personnel Administration* 10:10–13 (November, 1947); Dimock, *The Executive in Action*.

CHAPTERS FIFTEEN, SIXTEEN, AND SEVENTEEN

THE standard text on public personnel administration is Mosher and Kingsley, *Public Personnel Administration* (revised edition, New York, 1941). For the industrial scene up-to-date texts are those of Paul J. Pigors and Charles A. Myers, *Personnel Administration: A Point of View and a Method* (New York, 1947); and Milton L. Blum, *Industrial Psychology and its Social Foundations* (New York, 1949).

On problems of recruitment see Paul W. Boynton, *Selecting the New Employee: Techniques of Employment Procedure* (New York, 1949). OSS Assessment Staff, *Assessment of Men* (New York, 1948) reviews the selection methods employed by this organization during the Second World War; Carl J. Friedrich, William C. Beyer, Sterling D. Spero, John F. Miller and George A. Graham, *Problems of the American Public Service* (New York, 1935) contains recommendations on some problems of recruitment; Lucius Wilmerding, *Government by Merit* (New York, 1935) presents a favorable view of a career service.

For a review of the development of civil service and the fight against spoils, see Dwight Waldo, *The Administrative State* (New York, 1948); United States Civil Service Commission, *History of the Federal Civil Service* (Washington, 1941); Leonard D. White, *Introduction to the Study of Public Administration* (revised edition, New York, 1939); for an account of red tape in the Federal Civil Service see John Fischer, "Let's Go Back To The Spoils System," *Harpers Magazine* 191:356–67 (October, 1945); also Floyd B. Reeves, "Civil Service as Usual," *Public Administration Review* 4:327–40 (Autumn, 1944).

On the problems of constructing a career service in the United States, see Commission of Inquiry on Public Service Personnel, *Better Government Personnel* (New York, 1935); Leonard D. White, *Government Career Service* (Chicago, 1935); International City Managers' Association, *A Career Service in Local Government* (Chicago, 1937); Arthur W. Macmahon and John D. Millett, *Federal Administrators* (New York, 1939). On careers in personnel administration, see D. M. Smythe, *Careers in Personnel Work* (New York, 1946). On a career service in other countries, there are a number of illuminating studies. On Britain, see Herman Finer, *The British Civil Service* (London, 1937); J. Donald Kingsley, *Representative Bureaucracy* (Yellow Springs, 1944); on France, see Walter R. Sharp, *The French Civil Service: Bureaucracy in Transition* (New York, 1931); on Switzerland, see Carl J. Friedrich and Taylor Cole, *Responsible Bureaucracy, a Study of the Swiss Civil Service* (Cambridge, 1932); on Germany, Carl J. Friedrich, *Constitutional Government and Democracy*.

On the relationship between educational levels and public service careers, see Leonard D. White, *Government Careers for College Graduates* (Chicago, 1937); Commission of Inquiry on Public Service Personnel, *Better Government Personnel;* Lewis Meriam, *Public Service and Special Training* (Chicago, 1936); George A. Graham, *Education for Public Administration* (Chicago, 1941); Lloyd M. Short, *Personnel Problems Affecting Social Scientists in the National Civil Service* (New York, 1946); The Interdepartmental Advisory Committee on Scientific Personnel for the President's Scientific Research Board, United States Advisory Committee on Scientific Personnel. *The Scientist as a Government Employee* (Washington, 1947). On the relation between colleges and the career service, see Charles W. Weitz, "Joint College-Federal Service Council," *Public Administration Review*, 8:13–17 (Winter, 1948).

On position classification, see Mosher and Kingsley for a comprehensive review of the methods in use; see also Lewis Meriam, *Public Personnel Problems from the Standpoint of an Operating Officer* (Washington, 1938); Philip M. Mayer, "Facing the Federal Classification Problem," Personnel Administration 1:1–4 (May, 1939). For a history of position classification, see Ismar Baruch, *History of Position Classification and Salary Standardization in the Federal Service, 1789–1938* (Washington, 1939). A standard work on the position classification is Ismar Baruch, *Position Classification in the Public Service* (Chicago, 1941).

On training see Earl Brooks, *In-Service Training of Federal Employees* (Chicago, 1938); George D. Halsey, *Training Employees* (New York, 1949); Morris B. Lambie (ed.), *Training for the Public Service* (Chicago, 1935); Civil Service Assembly of the United States and Canada, *Employee Training in the Public Service* (Chicago, 1941); Earl G. Planty, William S. McCord, and Carlos A. Efferson, *Training Employees and Managers for Production and Teamwork* (New York, 1948); John E. Devine, *Post Entry*

Training in the Federal Service (Chicago, 1935). As far as the authors are aware, there has been no attempt to relate administrative training to the other institutional configurations in society in any systematic fashion.

CHAPTERS EIGHTEEN AND NINETEEN

ON a theoretical level the most comprehensive picture of an organization as a system in equilibrium is unquestionably that of Chester Barnard, *Functions of the Executive.* See also Simon, *Administrative Behavior;* Thompson, *The Regulatory Process in O.P.A. Rationing;* and Selznick, *TVA and the Grass Roots.* See also the cases of the Committee on Public Administration cases. A discussion of the problem of equilibrium in business organizations is contained in Wroe Alderson, "Survival and Adjustment in Behavior Systems," in Reavis Cox and Wroe Alderson, *Theory in Marketing* (Chicago, 1949).

Odegard, *Pressure Group; The Story of the Anti-Saloon League* and Pendleton Herring, *Group Representation before Congress* (Baltimore, 1929) focussed attention on the problem of interest groups and their tactics. The examination was extended to the regulatory agencies by Pendleton Herring, *Public Administration and the Public Interest* (New York, 1936). These studies were all concerned with the pressure of private groups upon government, rather than with the inter-action between the two. Kenneth Crawford, *The Pressure Boys* (New York, 1939) investigates the reaction of both private and public interest groups to the proposals of the President's Committee on Administrative Management. For a discussion of lobbying including that of administrative groups see Dorothy Detzer, *Assignment on the Hill* (New York, 1948); on the problem of farm group pressures, see C. M. Hardin, "The Bureau of Agricultural Economics under Fire: A Study in Valuational Conflicts," *Journal of Farm Economics* 28:635–68 (1946). V. O. Key, *Politics, Parties and Pressure Groups* (revised edition, New York, 1947) presents a very well documented analysis of the survival tactics of administrative organizations.

On the tactics of publicity see James L. McCamy, *Government Publicity* (Chicago, 1939); Harold L. Stokes, "Executive Leadership and the Growth of Propaganda," *American Political Science Review* 35:490–500 (1941).

CHAPTER TWENTY

As stated in the text, much of the discussion of planning in recent years has been concerned with the political question as to the responsibility of the government in planning the economic future of the nation. On this debate representative points of view can be found in Friedrich Hayek, *The Road to Serfdom* (Chicago, 1944) and Barbara Wootton, *Freedom Under Planning* (Chapel Hill, 1945) and *Plan or No Plan* (New York, 1935). Herman Finer, *The Road to Reaction* (Boston, 1945) criticizes Hayek from the standpoint of a political scientist.

On the nature and meaning of planning see George B. Galloway and Associates, *Planning for America* (New York, 1941); on planning in industry, see E. H. Hempel, *Top Management Planning* (New York, 1945); Carl Landauer, *The Theory of National Economic Planning* (revised edition, Berkeley, 1947); Abba P. Lerner and Frank D. Graham (eds.), *Planning and Paying for Full Employment* (Princeton, 1946); Abba Lerner, *The Economics of Control* (New York, 1944). On planning in various countries see National Resources Planning Board, *National Planning in Selected Countries* (Washington, 1941); on governmental planning, see John Millett, *The Process and Organization of Governmental Planning* (New York, 1947). Seymour Harris, *Economic Planning* (New York, 1949) reviews planning in various countries; Arthur Holcombe, *Government in a Planned Democracy* (New York, 1935) considers the planning implications of the early New Deal. Lewis L. Lorwin, *Time for Planning* (New York, 1945) argues for planning the postwar era. On one of the experiments in planning undertaken by this government, see Charles E. Merriam, "The National Resources Planning Board: A Chapter in American Planning Experience," *American Political Science Review* 48:1075–88 (December, 1944). On city planning, see Institute for Training in Municipal Administration, *Local Planning Administration* (revised edition, Chicago, 1948); Robert A. Walker, *The Planning Function in Local Government* (Chicago, 1941).

CHAPTERS TWENTY-ONE AND TWENTY-TWO

THOMPSON, *The Regulatory Process in OPA Rationing*, explores a war time regulatory program. Robert K. Merton, *Mass Persuasion* (New York, 1946), a study of the sociology of a war bond drive, also provides valuable data. Lewis Dexter, *So You Want to Do Something About It* (to be published), analyses the tactics of social reform.

On the problem of overcoming inertia, one of the best studies is John Dewey's classic, *Human Nature and Conduct* (New York, 1922); also his *The Public and its Problems* (New York, 1927). W. F. Ogburn, *Social Change* (New York, 1922) deals with the problem in terms of the concept of "cultural lag." Most of the material relating to overcoming resistances deals with the resistances of employees within the organization rather than with resistances of the clientele. Cox and Alderson (eds.), *Theory in*

Marketing, contains several articles which see the problem as it relates to the marketing of products.

On group consultation, again, the most significant studies have been concerned with getting employee cooperation. Here the work of the Mayo group has been significant.

One of the best accounts of procedure is that of Dwight Waldo, "Government by Procedure" in Marx, *Elements of Public Administration.* See also Comstock Glaser, *Administrative Procedure* (Washington, 1941). On the procedures of various agencies, the following have some insights. Herring, *Public Administration and the Public Interest;* V. O. Key, *The Administration of Federal Grants to States* (Chicago, 1937). Selznick, *TVA and the Grass Roots;* Robert E. Cushman, *The Independent Regulatory Commissions* (New York, 1947); Gaus and Wolcott, *Public Administration and the U. S. Department of Agriculture;* Macmahon, Millett, and Ogden, *The Administration of Federal Work Relief;* all show how the problems of particular departments influence their methods of executing plans.

On the techniques of propaganda, see Leonard Doob, *Propaganda* (New York, 1935); Talcott Parsons, "Propaganda and Social Control," *Psychiatry* 4:551–72 (November, 1942); on the limitations of propaganda see Lazarsfield, Berelson, and Gaudet, *The Peoples' Choice* (2nd edition, New York, 1948); for a bibliography of material in this field see Lasswell, Casey, and Smith, *Propaganda, Communication, and Public Opinion.*

Licensing, although one of the most commonly used techniques of enforcement, has had little attention in the literature. A useful review is contained in W. Brooke Graves, *Public Administration in a Democratic Society* (Boston, 1950); see also, Hugo Wall, "The Use of the License Law in the Regulation of Businesses and Professions," *Southwestern Social Science Quarterly,* September, 1931, pp. 1–13.

Judicial sanctions are the most familiar to everyone. For an analysis, see Jerome Frank's astute *Courts on Trial;* also Arnold, *The Symbols of Government.*

On the use of sampling surveys as a tool of administration, see David B. Truman, "Public Opinion Research as a Tool of Administration," *Public Administration Review* 5:62–72 (Winter, 1945); see also Joel Gordon, "Operating Statistics as a Tool of Management," *Public Administration Review* 6:189–96 (Summer, 1944). On inspection as a device for securing compliance, see Ford P. Hall, *State Control of Business Through Certificates of Convenience and Necessity* (Bloomington, 1948).

CHAPTER TWENTY-THREE

On the concept of efficiency as generally used in American public administration perhaps the best sources are reports of the two most recent investigating committees—The President's Committee on Administrative Management and the Hoover Commission.

Efficiency has ideological as well as logical meanings in our society. Weber, *The Protestant Ethic and the Spirit of Capitalism* and R. H. Tawney, *Religion and the Rise of Capitalism* (New York, 1926) provide historical evidence of the association of efficiency with the Reformation, while Vernon Parrington, *Main Currents of American Thought* (3 vols., New York, 1927, 1930) traces the same pattern in American history. Waldo, *The Administrative State*, examines the role of the efficiency concept in the public administration movement. Waldo also includes copious bibliographical documentation.

Both Leonard D. White and T. V. Smith, *Politics and the Public Service* (New York, 1939) disavow the "penny-pinching" concern with monetary reduction in expenditures which characterized much of the taxpayer economy movement. See A. C. Millspaugh, "Democracy and Administrative Organization," in J. M. Mathews and J. Hart (eds.), *Essays in Political Science* (Baltimore, 1937) who argues that the efficiency movement has slipped from favor. But also see his *Toward Efficient Democracy: The Question of Governmental Organization* (Washington, 1949) which takes a view quite similar to that of the Hoover Commission.

On the concept of "social efficiency" see Marshall E. Dimock, "The Criteria and Objectives of Public Administration," in Gaus, White, and Dimock, *The Frontiers of Public Administration* (Chicago, 1936); also the same author's "Administrative Efficiency within a Democratic Polity," in *New Horizons in Public Administration* (Alabama, 1945).

On the measurement of efficiency, see Clarence E. Ridley and Herbert A. Simon, *Measuring Municipal Activities* (revised edition, Chicago, 1943), which contains an extensive bibliography.

CHAPTERS TWENTY-FOUR AND TWENTY-FIVE

THE literature on formal controls is voluminous, and only a few of the most significant items can be mentioned here. On the role of the courts, the Attorney General's Committee on Administrative Procedure, *Final Report* (Washington, 1940), and the supporting monographs present the most complete analysis; for an earlier, but perceptive review from the standpoint of a distinguished attorney, see John Dickinson, *Administrative Justice and the Supremacy of Law* (Cambridge, 1927); on the relation of administrative law to court procedures, see James M. Landis, *The Administrative Process* (New Haven, 1938); for a rather legalistic review of the problem of the relation of the courts to administration, see Roland Pennock, *Administration and the Rule of Law* (New York, 1941). One of the standard casebooks is Walter Gellhorn, *Administrative Law—Cases and Comments* (2nd edition, Brooklyn, 1947). On the role of lawyers within administration see Esther Lucile Brown, *Lawyers, Law Schools, and the Public Service* (New York, 1948); for a more detailed and specific account of legal problem-solving see Thompson, *op. cit.* One of the most devastating criticisms of judicial review of administrative actions is Jerome Frank, *If Men Were Angels.*

On legislative controls, see the perceptive analysis of V. O. Key, "Legislative Control" in Fritz Morstein Marx, *Elements of Public Administration* (New York, 1946); also, Leonard D. White, "Congressional Control of the Public Service," *American Political Science Review* 39:1–11 (January, 1945); also his "Legislative Responsibility for the Public Service," in *New Horizons in Public Administration;* Marshall E. Dimock, "Forms of Control over Administrative Action," in Charles G. Haines, and Marshall Dimock (eds.), *Essays on the Law and Practice of Governmental Administration* (Baltimore, 1935). See also Roland Young, *This is Congress* (New York, 1943). On Congressional investigations, see George B. Galloway, "The Investigative Function of Congress," *American Political Science Review* 21:47–70 (February, 1927); see also the same author's *Congress at the Crossroads* (New York, 1946); for the history of the investigative power, see M. N. McGreary, *The Development of Congressional Investigative Power* (New York, 1940). On Congressional appropriations as a control over administration see Arthur Macmahon, "Congressional Oversight of Administration: The Power of the Purse," *Political Science Quarterly* 58:161–90, 380–414 (June, September, 1943).

For a more realistic view than most of the nature and limitations of hierarchical controls, see Carl J. Friedrich, "Administrative Responsibility," in Friedrich and Mason, *Public Policy* I (Cambridge, 1940); and Appleby, *Big Democracy.* The problem in general is related to topics treated earlier, especially in Chapters Eight and Nine, and the reader is referred to the references there cited.

As to informal controls, the reader is referred particularly to the references under Chapters Three, Four, and Five, which examine the sources of individual premises, and to Chapters Eighteen and Nineteen dealing with the problem of survival. On the institutionalization of points of view, see Max Weber, (Gerth and Mills, tr.) *Essays in Sociology,* particularly the essay on bureaucracy. Frank, *Law and the Modern Mind* examines the psychology of precedent in the light of Freudian psychology; Thompson examines its operations in the war-time gasoline rationing eligibility committee.

On the political and social theories that tend to be predominant in American Life, see Peter Odegard, *The American Public Mind* (New York, 1930); Parrington, *Main Currents in American Thought;* Herbert Goldhammer, "Public Opinion and Personality," *American Journal of Sociology* 55:346–54 (January, 1950); Arthur Kornhauser, "Public Opinion and Social Class," *American Journal of Sociology* 55:333–45 (January, 1950); Gardner Murphy and Rensis Likert, *Public Opinion and the Individual* (New York, 1938) and, Stouffer, *et al.*, *The American Soldier*.

INDEX

Absenteeism, and fatigue, 142
Acceptance of organizational influence, 80–1; *see also* Authority
Accountability, 215–16, 513–61; to chief executive, 47–8, 125, 404–06, 532–7; to courts, 50–3, 514–22, *see also* Judicial review; effect of specialization upon, 155–8; and external support, 386; and group values, 118; to hierarchy, 532–9; to interest groups, *see* Interest groups; to legislature, 49–50, 402–09, 431–3, 522–31; limits of, 515–18, 523–8, 532–5; and organizational equilibrium, 540, 542–3, 554–5, 560–1; of organization planners, 175–6; and security regulations, 242–3; strengthening procedures of, 555–60; and surplus of inducements, 503
Accounting: creation of counterpart units for, 294; and expenditure control, 508; as intelligence function, 256; *see also* Overhead units
Accuracy, as administrative goal, 148
Adequacy, 494
Adjudication, administrative, *see* Regulatory administration
Adjustment for survival, *see* Equilibrium of organization, Opportunism, Survival
Administration: definition of, 3–4; growth of, *see* Growth of government; study of, 16–19; universality of, 6; *see also* Organization, Public administration
Administrative law, 483; *see also* Judicial review, Regulatory administration
Administrative man, 82
Administrative manual, 222–3
Administrative Procedures Act of 1946, 486, 518–20
Administrator, personality of, 73–6; *see also* Executive, Supervisor

Advisory committees, *see* Group consultation
Agency, definition of, 93
Aggression, 74
Agricultural Adjustment Administration, 37
Agricultural bloc, 60
Agriculture, Department of: adjustment to new conditions, 38, 41; careers in, 336; equilibrium, 412; and forestry, 32; group values in, 104; and new programs, 33; origins, 26; planning in, 444; and REA, 118, 407; specialists in, 261; training program, 373
Allocation controls, 478
Allocation of duties, *see* Division of work, Specialization
Almond, Gabriel, 544
Ambition: and leadership, 105–06; as personality trait, 75; *see also* Mobile individual
American governmental system, 28, 86, 351
American Library Association, 344, 509, 558
Amorality of science, 22–4
Anticipated reactions, rule of, 196, 441
Anti-governmentalism, 28, 44, 51; *see also* Individualism
Anti-Trust Division, 527–8
Appleby, Paul, 318, 422, 437*n*
Appointment, *see* Recruitment
Appropriations, and accountability, 522; *see also* Budget
Area: specialization by, 151, 264–5, 305–11; of acceptance, 187
Army, U. S., 126
Ascendance, as personality trait, 75
Aspiration level, 360*n*, 390–1
Assignment of duties, *see* Authority, Division of work
Atomic bomb, 190
Atomic energy, 242
Attention and fatigue, 142

i

Date Due